BEST ACTRESS

BEST ACTRESS

The History of Oscar-Winning Women

Stephen Tapert

RUTGERS UNIVERSITY PRESS

New Brunswick, Camden, and Newark, New Jersey, and London

A British Cataloging-in-Publication record for this book is available from the British Library.

Library of Congress Cataloging-in-Publication Data
Names: Tapert, Stephen, 1974- author.
Title: Best actress : the history of Oscar-winning women / Stephen Tapert.
Description: New Brunswick : Rutgers University Press, [2019] | Includes bibliographical references and index.
Identifiers: LCCN 2019006604 | ISBN 9781978808058 (hc-plc : alk. paper) | ISBN 9781978809598 (web pdf)
Subjects: LCSH: Academy Awards (Motion pictures) | Motion picture actors and actresses—Biography.
Classification: LCC PN1993.5.U6 T278 2019 | DDC 791.4302/80922 [B] —dc23 LC record available at https://catalog.loc.gov/vwebv /search?searchCode=LCCN&searchArg=2019006604&searchType =1&permalink=y

♾ The paper used in this publication meets the requirements of the American National Standard for Information Sciences—Permanence of Paper for Printed Library Materials, ANSI z39.48-1992.
www.rutgersuniversitypress.org
Manufactured in the United States of America

To my mother, Carol Tapert, and my sister, Susan Tapert

CONTENTS

FOREWORD

I love movies—the good, the bad, and everything in between. I can get down with the stylized action of the *John Wick* franchise as much as I enjoy a taut and intense drama like *Room*, for which Brie Larson won the Best Actress Oscar. I'll laugh at the implausibility of romantic comedies and sit, holding my breath, as I watch Natalie Portman take on the role of a prima ballerina in *Black Swan.*

As a feminist cultural critic, I am particularly interested in women's stories, whatever those stories may be. Each year, I see as many movies as I can—to be entertained, for sure, but also to understand how movies reflect what we value as a culture, and what we imagine to be possible for women. People are often surprised to learn that one of my favorite movies is *Pretty Woman* (1990), for which Julia Roberts was nominated for Best Actress, playing Vivian, a prostitute who shows a brooding billionaire how to love and be loved. Roberts was incredibly charming—sexy but just innocent enough to be appealing instead of intimidating. She was smart but human. She was bad but good. Despite her charismatic performance, Roberts did not win that year. Kathy Bates did, for her turn in *Misery* as Annie Wilkes, a lonely, obsessed fan, who held her favorite writer captive in icy Colorado until he re-wrote one of his stories to her satisfaction. Bates's win was particularly gratifying because she did not fit the typical mold of women who win acting Oscars.

Clearly, some years, cinematic offerings are more encouraging than others. Some years, the film industry offers us the distinct impression that we cannot imagine anything for women that doesn't revolve around derivative stereotypes and the expectation that women are merely decorative and involved in any given story only insofar as she will help a man learn something significant about himself or achieve some grand ambition. But then, there are the years when women get to be fully inhabited, fascinating characters. Take, for example *The Piano,* where Holly Hunter plays a mute woman and evokes so much with her remarkable performance, much of which is rendered in silence.

There are exceptions yes, but they are exactly that—exceptions. The film industry has, historically, offered women so little in the way of depth, nuance or intelligence that the Bechdel Test exists. For a movie to pass the Bechdel Test, it needs to feature at least two women, who talk to one another, about something other than a man. This test is so desperately simple. The bar is so very low and yet here we are. Alison Bechdel gave rise to this test in 1985 and to this day not nearly enough movies actually pass her test.

Throughout cinematic history certain, persistent and limiting tropes have dominated women's roles. The Manic Pixie Dream Girl is a woman who is quirky and offbeat and helps a disaffected young man find happiness and fulfillment.

The Mary Sue is a woman who is seemingly perfect—beautiful, intelligent, always saying and doing the right thing at the exact right time. When a woman is an Ice Queen, she is cold and ambitious until, of course, the right man melts her heart. The Psycho is the woman who wants and needs too much and dares to let those wants and needs be known. Women of color deal with even more restrictive tropes, when they are given a rare opportunity for representation. There is the sassy black friend or the sassy Latina friend or the Magical Negro, full of wisdom for everyone but themselves. They do not have inner lives. They neither want nor need for anything but to serve the white characters around them.

This, however, is not always the case. Though the roles available to women in film are often quite lacking, though these roles often treat women as caricatures rather than characters, the best actresses make the most of the material they are given. That is what makes their performances so extraordinary—how these actresses soar past the limitations of their work. These actresses transcend narrow tropes and infuse their roles with heart and courage, grace and intelligence. In *The Accused*, Jodie Foster plays a woman who has been brutalized by a gang of men but is determined, with the help of a committed lawyer, to finding justice for herself. Charlize Theron brings unexpected nuance and grit to her portrayal of serial killer Aileen Wuornos and manages to inspire empathy rather than disgust. In *La Vie en Rose*, Marion Cotillard embodies the spirit of Édith Piaf bringing an icon vibrantly to life once more.

Best Actress: The History of Oscar®-Winning Women focuses on the first seventy-five women who won the Oscar for Best Actress between 1929 and 2018. It is a testament of just how talented the best actresses are despite the constraints of misogyny. These women are remarkable but in looking at the list, what is striking is who has won this award year after year. From Janet Gaynor in 1929 up until today, only one black woman, Halle Berry, has ever received this recognition. She did so in 2002 for *Monster's Ball*. No other woman of color has ever received this award. No out lesbian has ever won the award. The women who have won this award are generally conventionally attractive, thin, and gender conforming. They represent what we, as a culture value in women. The best actresses should be lauded for their work, certainly, but this is also a valuable opportunity to consider who has been left out of the conversation, to consider the best of the women who have been overlooked on and off the screen.

ROXANE GAY
June 2019

BEST ACTRESS

Introduction

It has been said that if you want to learn the history of a culture, then you must learn the history of its women, for it tells you an intimate story of what is truly the full picture. Unfortunately, more often than not, when we look back in history and at "women's contributions to any kind of advancement," we find that stories have been "discounted, dismissed, . . . overlooked, erased, [or not even] acknowledged."[1]

This book attempts to correct that imbalance by exploring a segment of film history by way of the first 75 women to have won the "world's most distinctive and prestigious award for achievement" in acting—the Academy Award for Best Actress.[2] Among these individuals, there is a princess (**Grace Kelly**), a wife to a future U.S. president (**Jane Wyman**), a member of British Parliament (**Glenda Jackson**), a pioneering AIDS activist (**Elizabeth Taylor**), a lifestyle maven (**Gwyneth Paltrow**), an industry whistleblower (**Olivia de Havilland**), an exercise guru/revolutionary (**Jane Fonda**), and a founder (**Mary Pickford**) and president (**Bette Davis**) of the Academy of Motion Pictures Arts and Sciences. Behind their success, there is often a history of hard work, strong risks, tough fights, and deep sacrifice.

Much more so than the Academy Award for Best Picture, the Oscar for Best Actress always seemed to come closest to capturing the cultural zeitgeist. Without exception, the women who received this award won it for tackling a certain form of prejudice and discrimination in their work. To have that annually acknowledged by way of such a coveted, internationally recognized honor seemed to provide a certain blueprint as to where we were, and where we are, on this long and complicated road toward gender equality.

During my eight years (2003–2011) at the Academy of Motion Pictures Arts and Sciences, I worked at the Margaret Herrick Library (which holds the largest collection of film material in the world) and as a researcher for the Academy's then-forthcoming film museum, the Academy Museum of Motion Pictures. By going through the Academy's world-renowned repository of photographic stills, scripts, books, clippings, posters, and special collection materials while attending the numerous Academy screenings, tributes, and public events presented throughout the year, my career as a film scholar could not have started in a more mesmerizing, movie-history-centered environment. In the midst of my research at the Academy, I discovered that no author had ever connected the Best Actress Oscar to the larger scope of film history, world history, and feminist studies. In addition, no book had ever retraced the history of the Academy Awards through the particular point of view of the women working in the industry, who are often neglected and considered less important than their male colleagues. Without a doubt, a great deal has been written on the Academy Awards, but no book had ever pulled together the individual stories, gender-specific struggles, and courageous ventures of these women into one single narrative. No book had examined their images as global stars and the social and political issues connected to the role(s) for which they won. Moreover, no book had provided historical context while interweaving the trends and threads that link these extraordinary women together.

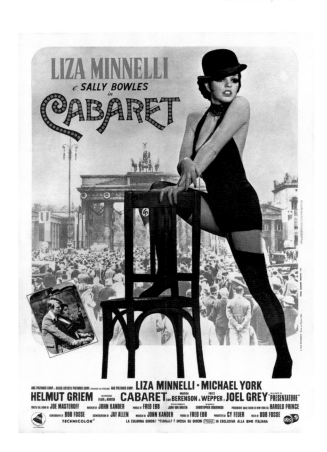

While not necessarily taken for granted, the Academy Award for Best Actress has certainly been overlooked with regard to its relevance to a world that is still dealing with gender stereotypes, gender-based violence, laws that omit rape as a crime, modern slavery (via forced labor, debt bondage, trafficking, forced prostitution, and/or forced marriage), and the denial of providing women with fairer "access to education, health, employment, and influence within their own communities."[3] Existing in a sexist and ageist industry that is "notoriously bereft of strong female characters," that tends to prioritize the female body over talent and intellect, and where female protagonists are only accounted for in approximately 16 percent of the general movie output, the Best Actress Oscar has become "essential to maintaining even a tenuous presence for talented women in Hollywood."[4]

Advantageously, the Best Actress Oscar has additionally elevated its recipients to a unique stature of leadership and respectability for the world to envy, emulate, and admire. Fearlessly driven, these women — both in life and in their movies — have often shaped public opinion by tackling issues they believe are important. Both modestly and stridently, they have contributed to the unfolding of social, political, and/or sexual revolutions that, in one way or another, have had an enormous impact in relation to issues of equality, opportunity, inclusivity, diversity, democracy, visibility, empowerment, social policy, humanitarian intervention, freedom of expression, and so forth.

In my work and as someone who, by way of my employment, frequented the Academy Awards and experienced the ins and outs of orchestrating such a gigantic global event, I began to come across stories and materials that made me feel that such a book would not only be fascinating, entertaining, and highly informative but also vital to a world lacking in enough stirring anecdotes of female

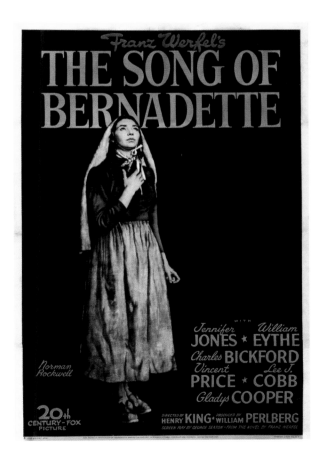

self-empowerment. Naturally drawn to issues surrounding prejudice and discrimination, I began to dive deeper into researching the history of the Academy's Best Actress category.

Despite the often inexplicable, subjective, and politicized results of the Academy Award, it uniquely represents the longest-standing, non-sports-related honor annually guaranteed to a woman. Nonetheless, it has remained a comparatively elusive honor, with the majority of gold-plated statuettes handed out to men. Only in 2010 was a woman finally awarded the Oscar for Best Director (Kathryn Bigelow for *The Hurt Locker*), and from the time the awards first commenced in 1929, only approximately 200 competitive Oscars (of the approximately 3,000 awarded overall) have gone out to women in nonacting categories. Since acting awards for supporting roles were not introduced to the Academy Awards schedule until 1936, the only honor guaranteed to women from the very outset—and the one that remains the most coveted and internationally esteemed for female performers—is the Academy Award for Best Actress. As of early 2019, 75 women have won this award. Thirteen have won it twice, and one—**Katharine Hepburn**—has won it a record four separate times.

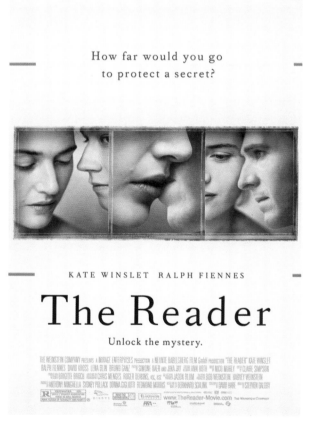

Taking into consideration that rules once precluded women from performing at all (as exemplified by **Gwyneth Paltrow**'s Oscar-winning turn in *Shakespeare in Love* [1998]), it is extraordinary how far women's freedoms have evolved, and how cinema—as a vehicle of mass communication capable of altering perception and eradicating prejudice—has helped to propel this evolution. Whereas before, women could only find fulfillment through child rearing or homemaking or under a masculine pseudonym, the movies—a synergy of art, commerce, and technology that first went public in 1895—helped to give women a new perception of themselves and, ultimately, a new, important, and effective voice. Quickly replacing theater and literature as the most dominant art form of the 20th century, the movies, both visually and narratively, presented women with a wide variety of behavioral paradigms. Through the guise of fashion, politics, and social mores, they helped to make things that were once considered immoral, illegal, and inconceivable become possible, acceptable, and standard. "The media creates a worldview that becomes deeply ingrained into people's perception of the way things are," explained Nanette Braun, chief of communications and advocacy at UN Women.[5]

Indeed, countless films have contributed to this ideological thrust forward, while others have negatively branded women as objects "to be desired, investigated, pursued, controlled, and ultimately possessed by a subject who is masculine," perpetuating "'discriminatory attitudes and sexist behavior' and the notion that girls and women 'don't count.'"[6] Among these films, only a small number have been formally awarded and thereby elevated to a more global realm of collective consciousness. Currently watched by estimates of up to half a billion viewers worldwide, the annual Academy Awards, the most glamorous and anticipated event in Hollywood, has served as a supreme catalyst for furthering women's empowerment and equality. By honoring performances from such bold, socially challenging, and often-groundbreaking benchmarks in women's cinema as *Gone with the Wind* (1939), *Mildred Pierce* (1945), *I Want to Live!* (1958), *The Prime of Miss Jean Brodie* (1969), *Network* (1976), *The Accused* (1988), *The Piano* (1993), *Monster's Ball* (2001), and *The Iron Lady* (2011), the Academy has cast its inimitable spotlight on work by women that—spanning 90 years of filmmaking—has educated, compelled, provoked, and inspired.

In the revealing autobiography of the Best Actress Oscar winner **Joan Fontaine**, *No Bed of Roses*, she characterized those who were lucky enough to actually win

the Oscar as "minor members of royalty suddenly elevated to the throne. One suddenly has international recognition, the best table in restaurants, preferential treatment whenever one travels. It is a fishbowl existence until the next year's awards, when a new winner will occupy the throne."[7] To be sure, the award has often been used successfully as leverage to command higher fees and has been known to add millions to a film's gross, to inspire lucrative endorsement deals, to preserve careers beyond their typical sell-by date, and to generate interest in future projects just by attaching the winner's name.

For the recipients of the Best Actress Oscar, that spotlight has earned them not only the genuine respect and recognition of their peers but also the prompt ascension to a pantheon of actress-deities by which all other actresses are inherently measured. As **Helen Mirren** warmly acknowledged upon receiving her Academy Award for *The Queen* (2006), the Oscar is "the biggest and the best gold star,"[8] a paragon of excellence, and an honor so great, so thrilling, and so overwhelming that it seemingly dwarfs all other honors. "[It] sanctifies you," **Simone Signoret** once admitted.[9] "[People] think you have some special wisdom or magic touch," **Louise Fletcher** observed.[10] "I'm terrified of the Award," **Shirley Booth** conversely acknowledged. "I've watched some wonderful performers get it, and it seems to do something to them. Everything they say afterward is spoken in solid capital letters."[11] But for many actresses, the award represents the ultimate dream and carries with it an exceptional stature, appellation, and sisterhood that only few will ever know.

If we pull back the curtain, however, the process of obtaining an Oscar surely involves more than merely acting in front of a camera. Operating within a cutthroat, male-dominated industry and a star-system construct that still echoes the objectifying, image-creating tactics of classical Hollywood, many actresses have had to face a never-ending barrage of double standards. In order to succeed, many have jumped a high bar and submitted to "whatever was necessary" (from accepting lower pay to cosmetic and dental surgeries, trendy diets, arranged marriages, abortions, and exceedingly sexualized appearances on screen).[12]

Campaigning for the Oscar has become another type of necessity. At first, the Academy sent telegrams three months prior to its May 16, 1929, inaugural ceremony to those who were selected to receive its brand-new "award of merit for distinctive achievement"—an ergonomic, Art Deco statuette of a naked swordsman cast in gold-plated bronze and known today as "the Oscar." From the very beginning, the Academy Award—at 13.5 inches in height and 8.5 pounds in weight—felt important. While it soon took its place alongside the Olympic medal and the Nobel Prize with regard to the reverence and international recognition accorded to it, at the time of its inception it was only preceded in motion picture award-giving history by the fan magazine *Photoplay*, whose Medal of Honor was annually conferred to a single film beginning in 1920. But unlike **Janet Gaynor**, the first recipient of the Best Actress Oscar, today's winners—with the assistance and pressures of their talent agents, managers, publicists, and stylists—actively (and at times outlandishly) campaign for the honor. In the process, studio backers have spent exorbitant amounts of money on promotional events, movie trailers, and print and media advertisements, not to mention the arrangement of interview and press junket

appearances (seen by many actors as "a kind of live performance").[13] When the Greek actress Melina Mercouri was told she would not win the Best Actress Oscar for her nominated role in *Never on Sunday* (1960) unless she actively campaigned for it, she jokingly inquired as to what kind of campaign she should forge. "I'm not a Kennedy," she stated. "I'm an actress, not a politician. What do they want me to do—ring doorbells in Beverly Hills?"[14]

More now than ever before, public interest in the Academy Awards operates at a fever pitch, with swarms of reporters, photographers, and screaming fans lining the famous red carpet—gazing briefly at their idols of the moment—as the film world's finest converge for Hollywood's most extravagant coronation. Evolving over time from a small black-tie dinner banquet to the epic display of fashion, beauty, and commercialism that it is today, the Academy Awards is undoubtedly a tradition like no other. As **Emma Thompson** described, "Being nominated for an Oscar is a cross between having a very severe virus and getting married. . . . It's very nerve-racking. I brought a lot of tranquilizers with me."[15]

In 2011, I off-handedly mentioned my Best Actress Oscar book project to Alberto Barbera, the artistic director of the Venice Film Festival and the world's

largest film museum—the Museo Nazionale del Cinema in Turin, Italy. I had met Barbera in Turin the year before when visiting his beautiful museum. To my surprise, Barbera proposed the idea of utilizing the source material of my book project for a large-scale museum exhibition that I would curate alongside his in-house curators, Nicoletta Pacini and Tamara Sillo. The exhibition, which was presented in Turin as a world premiere in April 2014, retraced the history of the women who won the Oscar for Best Actress from 1929 to 2014. Gathering over 370 works from collectors and lenders ranging from the **Audrey Hepburn** Children's Fund to **Jodie Foster**, **Susan Sarandon**, Giorgio Armani, Valentino, Bob Mackie, and beyond, the exhibition presented rare portraits and photographic stills, posters, props, screenplays, design sketches, film sequences from each Best Actress Oscar–winning movie, numerous documents, set costumes, and formal gowns worn by the actresses on Oscar night. Because of the show's warm reception by critics and popularity with the public, the exhibition traveled in December 2015 to Berlin, Germany, where it was presented and expanded at the Deutsche Kinemathek.

Through stories of glamour, sacrifice, self-empowerment, prejudice, and social change, this book—like the exhibition that came before it—contextualizes these actresses in their time while exploring their creative, risk-taking, and often struggle-filled journeys on the road to career success, Oscar glory, and beyond. Complete with rare and predominantly unpublished photographs spanning each Best Actress Oscar winner from **Janet Gaynor** to **Frances McDormand**'s performance in *Three Billboards Outside Ebbing, Missouri* (2017), this book additionally serves to promote an appreciation for their achievements and their tremendous, transformative influence on both the Hollywood landscape and the world at large.

Culturally, it is thought that women (who constitute 52 percent of all filmgoers) "will watch stories about men, but [that] men won't watch stories about women."[16] As the Best Actress Oscar nominee and activist Geena Davis (*Thelma & Louise*, 1991) once stated, "It is a horrible indictment of our society if we assume that one half of our population is just not interested in the other half."[17] This book ultimately aims to reverse that assumption.

Janet Gaynor

W hen 22-year-old **Janet Gaynor** received a telegram indicating that she had won the Academy Award for Best Actress three months prior to the inaugural, May 1929 Academy Awards, she was elated. "We obviously didn't know just how important the awards would become," she later admitted. "Still, it was very exciting . . . because I was so young, and there were actresses who had been stars for a much longer time, people like **Mary Pickford** and Gloria Swanson,"[1] as well as Clara Bow, Marion Davies, Lillian Gish, Colleen Moore, and Norma Talmadge.

Born Laura Augusta Gainor on October 6, 1906, in the Philadelphia neighborhood of Germantown, Gaynor was encouraged to pursue acting by her stepfather (a benevolent mining engineer). Joining the cavalcade of "movie-struck girls" eager to break into the film industry, Gaynor descended on Hollywood during the youth-mad, flapper-crazy boom years of the early 1920s. She initially worked at a shoe store before gaining assignments as a movie extra.

Around this time, American women—liberated from the legal shackles of Victorian repression—enjoyed a new taste of freedom. Marking what "many enlightened people considered [to be] the beginning of the breakdown in traditional family values,"[2] the Nineteenth Amendment to the United States Constitution "barred states [in 1920] from denying voting rights based on gender" (a major milestone for white women even as countless women of color—"particularly African-Americans in the Jim Crow South—remained shut out of the polls for decades").[3] While still beset by the contraception-prohibiting Comstock Act of 1873, women began to gain better access to birth-control methods such as diaphragms, condoms, and spermicide, resulting "in real changes in sexual behavior."[4] Thanks to the influence

7th Heaven (1927)

Sunrise: A Song of Two Humans (1927)

Street Angel (1928)

Janet Gaynor—the inaugural recipient of the Best Actress Oscar and the first woman to win an Academy Award—poses with the statuette that she won for *three* performances: *7th Heaven* (1927), *Sunrise* (1927), and *Street Angel* (1928). (© A.M.P.A.S.®/ Photofest)

of such designers as Coco Chanel and Jean Patou, women abandoned corsets for open-necked shirts, sleeveless and knee-length dresses, tailored suits, flesh-colored silk stockings, and the newly invented brassiere. On account of the cosmetic-industry rivals Helena Rubinstein and Elizabeth Arden, more women began to apply lipstick and makeup (something previously "associated with bohemians and prostitutes").[5] As long hair signified "having to tend it, comb it, and tie it up in a severe bun," many women began to bob their hair in a more "loose and liberating" style.[6] Women also began to drive cars, smoke cigarettes, drink prohibited liquor, engage in sports and jazz-age dance styles, and, like **Katharine Hepburn**, attend colleges and universities like never before.

Given the confluence of these factors, coupled with the power of movies to shape and spread the image of the New Woman, a range of career opportunities opened up, offering for many women, including Gaynor, a means to financial independence and an outlet for creative expression.

At the same time, Hollywood swiftly transitioned from an isolated backcountry surrounded by citrus groves to the thriving movie capital of the world. Initially "built by women, immigrants, and Jews," Hollywood became a "magnate" for "people who would not be accepted in any other profession."[7] By 1926, it developed into the fifth-largest industry in the United States and helped to create America's "first army of prominent career women."[8] From acting to directing, producing, editing, scenario writing, and beyond, women across the board—such as the pioneering filmmakers Grace Cunard, Cleo Madison, Jeanie MacPherson, and Lois Weber—seized on the challenge. But with so many newcomers arriving, the local government had to intervene, attaching "on all mail leaving Hollywood" a disclaimer not "to break into the movies" until hopefuls had "obtained full, frank, and dependable information from the Hollywood Chamber of Commerce." "It may save disappointments," the message underlined.[9]

The same year, the Western Associated Motion Picture Advertisers (WAMPAS)—a "body comprised of leading professional Hollywood publicists"[10]—selected Gaynor as one of its "WAMPAS Baby Stars." Between 1922 and 1934, 13 promising starlets annually received the coveted honor. Recipients included **Joan Crawford**, **Loretta Young**, and Gaynor's close friend **Ginger Rogers** (who regularly attended movie screenings with the actress in the opulent theaters of downtown Los Angeles). With this honor, Gaynor, at 18, clinched her first lead role in *The Johnstown Flood* (1926) and went on to sign a long-term contract with the Fox Film Corporation.

The late silent era proved to be an aesthetic apex in cinema history, and the films featuring Gaynor's trio of Academy Award–winning performances—*Sunrise: A Song of Two Humans* (1927), *7th Heaven* (1927), and *Street Angel* (1928)—ranked among the best. Among these films, the allegorical *Sunrise* is considered a masterpiece. At its inaugural ceremony at the Hollywood Roosevelt Hotel—a presentation that garnered little press coverage and offers few photographic illustrations to convey what the night was like, the Academy honored *Sunrise* as the most "Unique and

Sensing peril, a dog comes to Janet Gaynor's rescue right before her husband attempts to drown her in *Sunrise* (1927). (Twentieth Century Fox Film Corporation/Photofest)

Artistic Picture" (the only movie ever to receive such a distinction). Decades later, the French film journal *Cahiers du cinéma* hailed it as the greatest film ever made.

Sunrise was helmed by the German director F. W. Murnau, and it became famous for its atmospheric lighting, false-perspective sets, dynamic tracking shots, and synchronized Movietone score. Taking cues from the Theodore Dreiser novel *An American Tragedy* (1925; which was later adapted in 1951 as the **Elizabeth Taylor**–starring movie *A Place in the Sun*), the story centers on a farmer (played by George O'Brien) who is plotting to kill his plain and nurturing wife (Gaynor) so he can run away with a sophisticated temptress. In one of several films to depict a woman's mortal fear of her own husband (alongside *Suspicion* [1941] with **Joan Fontaine**; *Come Back, Little Sheba* [1952] with **Shirley Booth**; *Coming Home* [1978] with **Jane Fonda**; and *The Piano* [1993] with **Holly Hunter**), Gaynor's character pleads for mercy as her husband attempts to throw her from a rowboat. Just as he is about to carry out his fiendish act, however, he succumbs to guilt and spends the remainder of the film regaining his wife's trust.

Similarly, in inaugural Best Director Oscar recipient Frank Borzage's "tender, luminous, and achingly poetic" tearjerkers *7th Heaven* (1927) and *Street Angel* (1928),[11] Gaynor, at 5-foot-0, sparkled alongside her 6-foot-2 costar Charles Farrell. While completing *Sunrise* during the day, the actress, with the assistance of a four-piece mood-music ensemble (cello, organ, trumpet, and violin), worked on *7th Heaven* at night. Exploring the "inner life of [young] lovers,"[12] both *7th Heaven* and *Street Angel* placed Gaynor in the roles of vulnerable, submissive, and delinquent waifs transformed by the redemptive power of self-sacrificial love. In *7th Heaven*, Gaynor's character of Diane is on the verge of suicide before she encounters Farrell's big-hearted Parisian street cleaner. The devoted pair ultimately "form their own private world . . . [as] World War I rages outside their door." In *Street Angel*, Gaynor's Angela, a character forced into prostitution by desperate circumstances, again finds "refuge in the arms of Farrell," a "vagabond painter . . . who perceives her as an incorruptible Madonna."[13]

Gaynor and Farrell appeared in 12 pictures together (including the 1932 remake of the **Mary Pickford** melodrama *Tess of the Storm Country*) and became one of cinema's most beloved on-screen couples. Before **Marie Dressler** teamed up with Wallace Beery, **Ginger Rogers** with Fred Astaire, **Olivia de Havilland** with Errol Flynn, **Loretta Young** with Tyrone Power, **Greer Garson** with Walter Pidgeon, **Katharine Hepburn** with Spencer Tracy, **Jennifer Jones** with Joseph Cotten, **Simone Signoret** with Yves Montand, **Joanne Woodward** with Paul Newman, **Elizabeth Taylor** with Richard Burton, **Sophia Loren** with Marcelo Mastroianni, **Diane Keaton** with Woody Allen, **Sally Field** with Burt Reynolds, **Nicole Kidman** with Tom Cruise, **Jennifer Lawrence** with Bradley Cooper, and **Emma Stone** with Ryan Gosling, Gaynor and Farrell made a fortune for Fox with stories brimming with optimism. Together, they transitioned from silent films to sound and accompanied audiences on the journey from jazz-age decadence to Depression-era gloom.

As early Academy rules allowed for an actor's entire year's work to be honored, Gaynor became the first and only actress in Academy history to win a single Oscar representing multiple roles. Also nominated in the Best Actress category were Louise Dresser (*A Ship Comes In*) and one of Hollywood's reigning silent queens, Gloria Swanson (*Sadie Thompson*), whose cosmopolitan style could not have contrasted more with Gaynor's modest, gamine-like appearance. At the inaugural ceremony, Gaynor plainly "wore a store-bought Peter Pan–collared dress."[14] Her image, however, matured throughout her 20-year marriage to Adrian—the discreet but largely understood-to-be-homosexual costume designer.

Emboldened with the film industry's top acting prize, Gaynor became Fox's highest-paid star and was groomed to be the next **Mary Pickford** (whose acting style had "laid the groundwork for a new relation between films and viewers").[15] While early film productions featured actors incorporating histrionics carried over from the stage (e.g., fiery stares, overdeliberate postures, and so forth), Gaynor—a film

actor with no previous stage experience—devised a more restrained approach that was better suited to the camera. In addition to underplaying in complex situations (with the slight tilt of an eyebrow or the sinking of a shoulder, best exemplified in close-ups), she embodied a warmth, sincerity, and earthy spirituality that "audiences of the 1920s and '30s appreciated and understood."[16]

Moreover, like **Pickford**, **Norma Shearer**, **Marie Dressler**, and **Joan Crawford**, Gaynor became one of the few actresses who were equally successful in both the silent and sound eras. After receiving a final Best Actress Oscar nomination for her role in the Technicolor box-office hit *A Star Is Born* (1937; in which she plays, similar to herself, an ingénue who becomes an Academy Award–winning star), Gaynor largely retired from acting.

Following the birth of her son in 1940, she split her time between California and her remote 200-acre Brazilian farm. In 1980, she took on the role of Maude in the Broadway stage adaptation of *Harold and Maude* before playing Ethel Thayer in a 1982 touring production of *On Golden Pond* (for which **Katharine Hepburn** had won the Oscar). Two years after being critically injured in a San Francisco traffic accident that left her in the hospital for four months, the actress died in 1984 at the age of 77. As the inaugural recipient of the Best Actress Oscar and the first woman to ever win an Academy Award, Gaynor has a place in movie history that is uniquely ensured.

Janet Gaynor and costar Charles Farrell playfully interact with their mannequin doubles on the set of *7th Heaven* (1927). (Twentieth Century Fox Film Corporation/Photofest)

P.1656

Mary Pickford

At a time when worldwide celebrity had no precedent, **Mary Pickford** was a first. Compared to our current 24/7 media-obsessed culture in which 15 minutes of stardom is extended to anyone, Pickford emerged from a simpler time when movie stars did not exist and when idolized images of kings, queens, and religious leaders were still seen as the only celebrity-type representations to circle the earth.

Pickford, at the age of 17, appeared in her first film in 1909 (14 years after the first public movie screening). Before long, she began to attract the attention of early filmgoers. Featured in expressive close-up shots intended to reveal psychological traits that were only intensified through the human eyes, her illuminated face began to communicate "thought." This simple but revolutionary concept operated in direct opposition to both the earliest years of cinematic performance and the distant "arm's-length relationship" that audiences experienced while watching live actors on stage.[1] At the center of this invention was the pioneering film director D. W. Griffith, who turned Pickford into a recognizable "picture personality."[2]

Gradually, fan cultures demanded the disclosure of Pickford's name and any biographical information they could gather pertaining to the anonymous girl with the long golden curls. Much to the chagrin of early film producers who feared that the promotion of actors as "stars" might have "relevance to the success of a film and thus be worthy of a higher salary," Pickford, following in the footsteps of "Biograph Girl" Florence Lawrence—the "first name credited" in cinema—was formally publicized.[3] Indeed, her promotion initiated what became known as the Hollywood star system—a method of creating, promoting, and exploiting Hollywood film stars for economic profit. By 1911, the year the fan magazines *Photoplay* and the *Motion Picture*

Coquette (1929)

In this off-camera shot, Mary Pickford is seated next to director Sam Taylor and surrounded by members of the crew for *Coquette* (1929). In addition to being the most popular actress of her era, Pickford was also the first truly powerful businesswoman in Hollywood. (United Artists/Photofest)

Story Magazine first appeared, Pickford's star image circulated rapidly. Four years later, her "wordless stories" were being projected "in every country where films were shown" to a reported "12,500,000 people every 24 hours."[4]

Long before the frenzy of movie fandom circled the likes of **Elizabeth Taylor**, **Julia Roberts**, and **Jennifer Lawrence**, Pickford, in one city after another, was forced to put up with an unprecedented and seemingly never-ending bombardment of mob scenes, where fans showed "grim determination to pet and fondle [her] or die in the attempt." At one event, Pickford "was swarmed and almost trampled by fans who tried to pull her from an open car." During a visit to Paris, "a riot erupted in an open market when Pickford was besieged by fans," forcing the actress—at the insistence of "a quick-witted butcher"—to hide inside a "meat cage for her own protection."[5]

While girls working in factory sweatshops at the time earned a salary of $9 per week, Pickford, by 1916, demanded an astronomical weekly salary of $10,000 in addition to "a $300,000 bonus" and a percentage of her film's total earnings.[6] Undoubtedly, her demand raised "the level of star salaries."[7] Before long, she became the first female star (and second only to Charlie Chaplin) to earn an annual salary of more than $1 million. After setting up her own production studio (the Mary Pickford Co.), the actress cofounded her beloved independent distribution and marketing company, United Artists, alongside Griffith, Chaplin, and her soon-to-be-husband, the actor Douglas Fairbanks. As the "business brains" behind the company,[8] she went on to sign the best directors, cinematographers, and scriptwriters and even took an uncredited part in the direction of many of her own scenes.

First arriving in Hollywood in 1910, when "movie companies popped up as gypsy encampments" and when "the lowest state of the movie business . . . sheltered a variegated collection of former carnival men, gamblers, [and] ex-saloon keepers,"[9] Pickford witnessed the area transform into a bustling kingdom of make-believe. In less than ten years, she would be driven between her studio and Pickfair—the Beverly Hills estate that she inhabited with her famous husband. Long before **Vivien Leigh** and Laurence Olivier, **Joanne Woodward** and Paul Newman, **Elizabeth Taylor** and Richard Burton, and **Nicole Kidman** and Tom Cruise, Pickford and Fairbanks operated as the first celebrity "super couple." Together, they hosted a multitude of visitors to their "royal" court. The list included titled European dignitaries, U.S. President Calvin Coolidge, Albert Einstein, Amelia Earhart, the queen of Siam, and the crème de la crème of Hollywood. With movie stardom producing the equivalent of European royalty, Pickford fell into the role of Hollywood's queen. When she entered the room, guests would reportedly stand.

Considering Pickford's poor, uneducated background, her ascent to such power is astonishing. The future actress was born Gladys Marie Smith in Toronto, Ontario, Canada, on April 8, 1892. She grew up as the eldest of three children to an actress/seamstress mother and an alcoholic father who abandoned his family when Pickford was three years old before dying two years later. As her widowed mother rented out rooms to actors, Pickford, at age five, was introduced to the stage

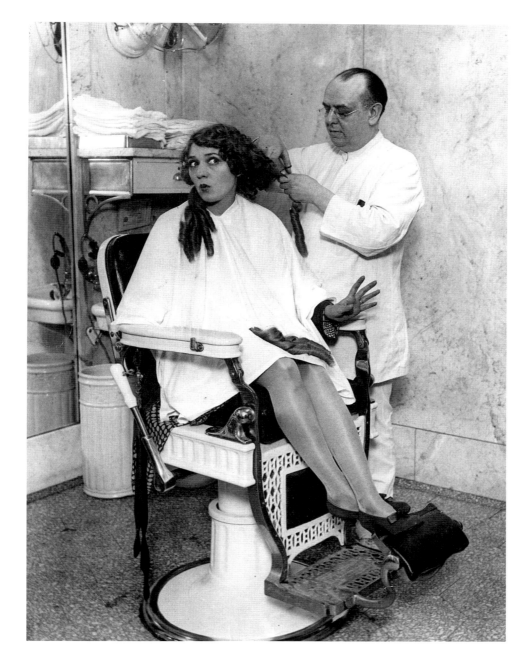

Prior to her performance in *Coquette* (1929), Mary Pickford daringly cut her world-famous curls (something her managerial mother, who had recently passed away, would have disapproved of). (Photofest)

and found success under the auspices of the American theatrical producer David Belasco, who gave the child actress the new stage name "Mary Pickford." At an age "when most children are still learning to read," Pickford, like **Julie Andrews** and **Jodie Foster** several decades later, fell into "the role of breadwinner" and continued to support her younger actor siblings (Jack and Lottie) throughout their short but fun-filled lives.[10]

Although Pickford portrayed little girls in "only seven of her fifty-two feature films" while venturing into mature parts such as Cho-Cho-San in *Madame Butterfly* (1915),[11] her youthful image in waifish/ragamuffin-like roles somehow precluded her from being taken more seriously. Consequently, Pickford was dubbed "America's

Sweetheart" and "Our little Mary." Indeed, the world seemed to prefer the 20-some-thing-year-old actress in candy-coated, Victorian-indebted idealizations of youthful innocence that **Janet Gaynor** and the child superstar Shirley Temple later repli-cated in the 1930s. In films such as *Cinderella* (1914), *Rebecca of Sunnybrook Farm* (1917), *The Poor Little Rich Girl* (1917), *Daddy-Long-Legs* (1919), and *Pollyanna* (1920), Pickford dutifully played the part. "Forever photographed in outfits far too youth-ful for her age,"[12] she unwittingly promulgated a confusing, eroticized model of female sexuality to male audiences in darkened theater auditoriums. According to many scholars, this model inadvertently lent itself to a "pedophilic gaze."[13]

In a final attempt to break free from the public's misconstrued perception of her image, Pickford, who had competed throughout her career with vamp-like depictions of female sexuality (via Theda Bara, Pola Negri, Greta Garbo, and so forth), daringly cut her world-famous curls. With her trendy new flapper bob, she shocked audiences as a wealthy southern temptress named Norma Besant in her first talking picture, *Coquette* (1929). The movie was based on the **Helen Hayes**–star-ring Broadway play and tells the story of an incorrigible flirt (played by Pickford) whose father's incestuous feelings throw "her home into a turmoil which ends in tragedy."[14] To prepare her voice for the part, Pickford trained with the British actress and acting coach Constance Collier, and while her "small" and "reprimand-ing tone" made her seem "even more unfamiliar" to audiences,[15] *Coquette* proved to be one of her biggest box-office hits. Like Chaplin's first "talkie," *The Great Dictator* (1940), more than a decade later, the success of the film largely rested on the public's insatiable curiosity in hearing the most "loved and recognized woman in world history" in her first sound picture.[16]

Nominated for her performance in *Coquette*, Pickford faced a field of Best Actress contenders that included Ruth Chatterton (*Madame X*), Corinne Griffith (*The Divine Lady*), Betty Compson (*The Barker*), fellow D. W. Griffith alumna Bessie Love (*The Broadway Melody*), and posthumous nominee Jeanne Eagels (*The Letter*). But as one of the 36 founding members of the Academy of Motion Picture Arts and Sciences, a cofacilitator of the Academy Awards, and the wife of the Academy's first president (Fairbanks), Pickford was seen as having a clear advantage. She wanted the award, and in an effort to secure it, she invited all five members of the Academy's Central Board of Judges (the sole voting block of the organization) to her Pickfair mansion for tea. While she prevailed in her attempt, her award was generally seen as a tribute to her career, and soon after the second awards presen-tation, Academy voting privileges expanded to the entire membership.

After the box-office failures of *The Taming of the Shrew* (1929; the first talking feature to attempt William Shakespeare), *Kiki* (1931), and *Secrets* (1933), Pickford retired from acting. While falling "out of fashion," she grew disdainful of her films and came close to destroying them so as to prevent them from being ridiculed. But realizing that "silent pictures would be valued in the future," she changed her mind and supported the 1935 creation of the Film Library at the Museum of Modern Art (MoMA)—the "first major cinema archive in the United States."[17] Like **Norma**

With her trendy new flapper bob, Mary Pickford (seen here with costars John St. Polis and Louise Beavers) shocked audiences by playing a southern temptress in her first sound picture, *Coquette* (1929). (United Artists/Photofest)

Shearer, she declined to come out of retirement to play the fictitious silent-movie star Norma Desmond in the stylish 1950 film noir *Sunset Boulevard*. Instead, as an industry mascot, she continued to "cut ribbons, [lead] parades, [give] speeches," and even play "an instrumental role in supporting numerous attempts to erect" a film museum in Hollywood.[18] Crippled by alcoholism in her final years, she grew more reclusive and remained out of sight.

However, three years before her death in 1979, the legendary star—"the most popular, powerful, prominent, and influential woman in the history of cinema"[19]—made a final, prerecorded appearance at her Pickfair mansion to receive the Academy Honorary Award (an award that would be bestowed on only one other Best Actress Oscar winner: **Sophia Loren**). Handed her statuette, Pickford simply and affectionately stated, "You've made me very, very happy."[20]

Norma Shearer

The coming of sound, as the silent film star William Haines once put it, was like "the night of the Titanic all over again."[1] What had required "almost three decades of silent movie making to develop—the freedom of the camera, the richness of the lighting, and the unhampered ability for the director and actor to tell a story in delicate, moving nuance—was undone by the technical advancement of putting words to storytelling."[2] On the technical side, and restricting the possibility of on-location filming, microphones (concealed in lamps, in flowerpots, or "even in an actress's décolletage")[3] had to be positioned close to the performer to reduce residual sound. At a huge expense, theaters worldwide had to pay for new projectors and be wired for sound, necessitating the termination of theater organists, orchestras, and other musicians who had performed live in conjunction with silent movies. On the talent side, many silent film stars—including Norma Talmadge, Colleen Moore, the heavy-accented Emil Jannings, the stuttering Marion Davies, and the high-pitched John Gilbert—were unable to adequately cross over into sound, as their voices did not match their romanticized public image. Others lost their jobs too, including title writers, animal trainers who used verbal commands, and owners of small production companies who could not afford to make sound movies.

But the actress **Norma Shearer** was conversely blessed with a cultured voice, strong diction, and an older brother (Douglas Shearer) who happened to be Hollywood's "leading technical wizard" of sound production (a position in the early years of sound that enjoyed almost complete "control over directorial functions like camera placement and actor movement"). These factors helped Shearer

The Divorcee (1930)

In pursuit of the lead role in *The Divorcee* (1930), Norma Shearer had her image revamped by photographer George Hurrell to reveal a more sensuous and seductive persona. (George Hurrell/Photofest)

to become the first star of her home studio of Metro-Goldwyn-Mayer (MGM) to successfully "break the sound barrier."[4]

Given that Shearer had been told that she would never make it in the movies, her ascent to the forefront of sound is somewhat astonishing. The actress was born on August 10, 1902, and comfortably raised in the affluent Westmount neighborhood of Montréal, Quebec, Canada, until her father (the president of a construction company) lost his assets in an economic depression. Suddenly impoverished, Shearer sought work as a piano player in local nickelodeons before moving to New York to pursue acting and modeling. During this time, she once posed nude for the acclaimed photographer Alfred Cheney Johnston.

Shearer eventually found work as an extra on the D. W. Griffith production of *Way Down East* (1920). Dazzled by the meticulousness of its star, Lillian Gish, she nervously approached the legendary director for the tiniest morsel of encouragement. Alas, Griffith haplessly informed her that her clear, slightly crossed eyes "were too blue to be photographed."[5] Self-driven, Shearer later embarked on a stage career under the tutelage of the Broadway producer Florenz Ziegfeld—the "supreme authority" on beautiful, "scantily clad showgirls."[6] But he, too, chastised her for her "bad legs, poor figure, and a cast in one eye."[7] At a time when the "typist" became "a recognized profession" for women,[8] Shearer, with the little money that she had, tenaciously went to an optometrist and had her defect corrected.

By 1927, after years of climbing through the ranks beginning as an extra, Shearer married the MGM "Boy Wonder" Irving G. Thalberg—the studio's physically fragile production head who, with "a physician's skill for diagnosis and prescription," engineered the highest production standard in all of Hollywood while leading movies "way up past the range and power of the theatre."[9] His early career highlights included *The Hunchback of Notre Dame* (1923), *The Big Parade* (1925), and *Ben-Hur: A Tale of the Christ* (1925).

As a result of her marriage to Thalberg, Shearer was nicknamed the "First Lady of MGM" and was forced to tiptoe around certain jealousies, resentments, and "complaints of nepotism."[10] Following their corporate, Jewish wedding, the notorious Hollywood gossip columnist Louella Parsons "complimented" the actress for giving "her most realistic performance" to date.[11] Meanwhile, Shearer's MGM rival **Joan Crawford** (who later costarred with Shearer in 1939's *The Women*) branded the marriage as "a calculated move."[12] "She doesn't love him," accused **Crawford**. "She made a sacrifice for what she can get out of him, knowing he's going to die."[13]

With the aim of turning Shearer into the "Great Lady of the Movies"—the equivalent to what the great Broadway luminaries represented onstage, Thalberg indeed scoured "for the right stimulants among Broadway plays, Book-of-the-Month Club novels, magazine fiction, and the occasional classic" in order to procure for his wife the best roles that he could find.[14]

Shearer, however, was growing tired of having to play virtuous characters and was unable to convince Thalberg that she was "glamorous enough" for sexy, provocative roles. Therefore, upon the recommendation of her former costar Ramon

Novarro, she pulled up in her "cream-colored Rolls-Royce" to the independent studio of the "talented but little-known 24-year-old photographer" George Hurrell.[15] Much like **Joan Crawford**'s partnership with the photographer Ruth Harriet Louise or the later partnerships between **Katharine Hepburn** and Cecil Beaton, **Audrey Hepburn** and Richard Avedon, and **Grace Kelly** and Howell Conant, Shearer was photographed looking sensuous, sinful, and "siren-like," with disheveled hair "cascading over one eye."[16] With the photographs, she not only managed to persuade her husband to reevaluate her public image but also helped to land Hurrell a full-time job at MGM.

Ultimately, Shearer was cast in the desired role of a woman who exposes the hypocrisy of marriage in *The Divorcee* (1930). Amplified by the sound of frank and outspoken dialogue, the film brought to the screen a progressive tale of gender

Depicting double standards within an open marriage, MGM's *The Divorcee* (1930) saw Norma Shearer playing a sophisticated, self-sufficient woman whose romantic decisions inadvertently wreak havoc on the lives of others. (Metro-Goldwyn-Mayer Inc./Photofest)

inequality and double standards within the framework of an open marriage. Based on novelist Ursula Parrott's *Ex-Wife*—the "popular paean to sexual freedom"[17] at the time—the film explores the life of Shearer's Jerry Martin, a New York City commercial artist. Offering an antithesis to the limiting, household-bound lives that women were conditioned to endure prior to World War I (1914–1918), the film represents Jerry as a sophisticated, self-sufficient woman who is willing to challenge the social and behavioral norms, including the notion that a woman cannot enjoy her own sexual freedom without turning into a kind of wanton victim. After being confronted with her husband's disclosure of an extramarital affair—a casual, allegedly justified male dalliance that "doesn't mean a thing"—a vengeful Jerry "goes out . . . and has sex with [her husband's] best friend."[18] "I've balanced our accounts," she later admits, to which her outraged husband—once expecting to be forgiven—punishes Jerry with divorce.

At a time when "90 million Americans were attending the movies each week" (with female audiences representing the majority), portrayals of strong, independent women implicated in morally vexing situations "became the winning box-office formula."[19] These situations ranged from premarital sex to unwed motherhood, illegal abortions, adultery, and divorce (a contentious issue at the time, as the legal dissolution of a marriage in the United States was incrementally being obtained). Seen as a ringleader to this operation alongside the actresses **Claudette Colbert**, **Joan Crawford**, Marlene Dietrich, Greta Garbo, Jean Harlow, Miriam Hopkins, Barbara Stanwyck, Mae West, and the risqué cartoon character Betty Boop, Shearer was hailed as an early feminist icon for taking the "ingénue into the bedroom and [making almost] everybody like it."[20]

At the November 1930 Academy Awards, Shearer, whose husband was "rumored to have pressed his employees to vote for her" as Best Actress,[21] found herself among an impressive rivalry. Solidifying her status, she went on to beat the Swedish screen star and her MGM rival Greta Garbo (*Anna Christie* and *Romance*), Gloria Swanson (*The Trespasser*), Nancy Carroll (*The Devil's Holiday*), Ruth Chatterton (*Sarah and Son*), and herself in *Their Own Desire* (another drama dealing with the issue of infidelity).

Shearer's success, however, was not universally fêted. With Hollywood seen by puritanical America as "a modern Sodom and Gomorrah,"[22] the Motion Picture Production Code (censorship guidelines adopted by the film industry in 1930 but not enforced until July 1934) threatened the further development of roles that provided women onscreen with influence, leverage, and authority. In tandem, the National Legion of Decency—a Catholic organization against immoral movie content—began to recruit thousands of members who pledged to stay away from such objectionable films. To many people in charge, self-empowered women signified emasculated men, and soon the emulated examples distributed by Hollywood worldwide were sequestered. Not until the 1950s and '60s, in films such as *The Rose Tattoo* (1955; with **Anna Magnani**), *I Want to Live!* (1958; with **Susan Hayward**), and

BUtterfield 8 (1960; with **Elizabeth Taylor**), did American audiences once again see women grappling with the same sorts of issues and having the same kind of fun.

With the Production Code forcing Shearer to return to her onscreen virginity (a setback, as the actress enjoyed using her acting as a way to carry out her erotic fantasies with male costars), she went on to make *The Barretts of Wimpole Street* (1934), *Romeo and Juliet* (1936; playing Juliet at 35), and her favorite of her films, *Marie Antoinette* (1938). But with Thalberg's passing in 1936 at the age of 37—a death that paralyzed the film industry and galvanized "the kind of funeral usually reserved for heads of state"[23]—Shearer's career began to fade.

Haunted by both her older sister's mental illness (which the actress had gone "to great lengths to keep . . . out of the press")[24] and her mother's stern directive not to be seen in public after turning 35, Shearer retired in 1942 and descended into a Norma Desmond–like reality of excessive vanity and reclusiveness. While she remarried in 1948 to the Sun Valley ski instructor Martin Arrougé, the former star, an inattentive mother of two, reportedly "suffered a nervous breakdown" before entering the "same sanatorium as [her sister] for shock treatments."[25] Battling depression, failing memory, and the loss of her sight, the onetime screen idol—and, indeed, the first effective voice of women's cinema—passed away in Room D133 at the Motion Picture Country Home in Woodland Hills, California, in 1983.

Marie Dressler

Described as old, bulky, and even gargoyle-like, **Marie Dressler** defied all odds and became—at a time when the United States needed less glamour and more laughter—the biggest and most unlikely box-office star. During the downward-spiraling years of the Great Depression following the devastating stock-market crash of 1929, the actress offered downtrodden moviegoers a stark, stylistic contrast to tactless Hollywood renderings of extreme power, beauty, and wealth by providing a more reassuring, down-to-earth presence interlaced with her trademark blend of rambunctious and sentimental humor.

In a roller-coaster life that included VIP receptions with seven U.S. presidents (beginning with Grover Cleveland in the 1890s) as well as destitute moments of living directly hand to mouth, Dressler never would have predicted that her hard-fought career would reward her with an honor as prestigious as the Academy Award.

Dressler was born Leila von Koerber on November 9, 1868, to a family temporarily stationed in Cobourg, Ontario, Canada. Leaving her unstable home life behind at age 14 and at a time for women when placing "a career before marriage violated virtually every late-Victorian norm,"[1] Dressler bid farewell to her beloved mother and her violent father (an Austrian émigré who taught music and played the church organ). Against the jeers of her community, she set out to pursue a career as a theatrical tragedienne. While many girls in her situation would have landed in factory sweatshops, Dressler, who once fainted in a restaurant while being served "a steaming bowl of tomato soup" that she could not afford,[2] found a way to succeed in her professional attempt.

In the mid-1880s, a time when ragtime, blackface minstrel shows, slapstick knockabout comedy acts, and European-style operettas were the most popular

Min and Bill (1930)

Marie Dressler as the matronly innkeeper Min Divot in MGM's surprisingly successful, Depression-era comedy *Min and Bill* (1930). (Metro-Goldwyn-Mayer Inc./Photofest)

MG-12246

forms of entertainment, Dressler found a niche as an $8-a-week chorus girl for a traveling theater company. At the insistence of the Broadway star Maurice Barrymore (father to Lionel, Ethel, and John), she then switched to comedic burlesque. With her buxom, 200-pound figure and commanding, comical stage presence (which she pulled together at the last minute due to her "never-ending fight against stage fright"),[3] she soon became a larger-than-life personality in vaudeville and a top-headlining Broadway star. Before long, Dressler joined the ranks of such contemporary luminaries as Lillian Russell, Fay Templeton, May Irwin, Anna Held, W. C. Fields, and the Marx Brothers.

In 1914, the Canadian film director Mack Sennett—the most successful producer of comedy shorts in the silent era—approached Dressler to join his slapstick ensemble, which included Roscoe "Fatty" Arbuckle, Ben Turpin, Mabel Normand, and the up-and-coming Brit Charlie Chaplin. Intrigued by "this new plaything" called motion pictures,[4] Dressler descended upon the Los Angeles neighborhood of Edendale, a sparsely populated country hamlet bursting with blue sky, eternal sunshine, and flower-scented air. There, the actress appeared in what became the world's first-ever feature-length silent comedy—the 82-minute *Tillie's Punctured Romance* (1914; based on Dressler's character from the 1910–1911 hit Broadway play *Tillie's Nightmare*).

Although Dressler was one of the first major theater stars to engage in film, her relationship with the fledgling medium did not last for long. Just as she understood her "impact beyond the realms of entertainment" as a suffragist who had performed in the feminist writer Marie Jenney Howe's satirical stage play *An Anti-Suffrage Monologue* (1912), Dressler "canceled [her] bookings" and plunged herself into war-related work for Uncle Sam upon the United States' involvement in World War I.[5] With her career on hold, she appeared in a number of government-financed propaganda films and entertained spiritually and "mortally wounded" soldiers with her healing laughter. "At first I sang gay songs. Loud cheerful ditties to make them forget. But one day a boy . . . pulled at my hand as I sat by his wheeled chair. 'Miss Dressler,' he whispered, 'sing something sad, so we can cry.'"[6]

In addition, Dressler, who spoke "on Wall Street to an estimated 50,000 people," helped "the federal government sell Liberty Bonds as part of the U.S. Treasury's Liberty Loan campaign."[7] Underscoring the tremendous fund-raising power of the celebrity movie star, she exhaustively toured the country with Chaplin, Douglas Fairbanks, then–U.S. Assistant Secretary of the Navy Franklin D. Roosevelt, and **Mary Pickford**, who, in opposition to her sweet image, "sternly" spoke to the massive, unprecedented crowds of men, women, and children hoping to catch a glimpse of the Hollywood contingent. "I'm a silent actress," **Pickford** shouted. "Maybe you think a blonde curly-haired girl can't be serious, but . . . if you could hear the things I've heard from wounded soldiers, . . . you'd know just how serious I can be."[8]

By the time the war ended in November 1918, the public demanded a more youthful brand of star power, and for years Dressler's future began to look dim.

At this 1931 handprint ceremony in front of Grauman's Chinese Theatre in Hollywood, *Min and Bill* costars Marie Dressler and Wallace Beery—two of the era's most popular screen actors—leave their mark in cement. (Metro-Goldwyn-Mayer Inc./ Photofest)

Exacerbating her career headaches was her involvement in the controversial chorus girls' strike of 1919, which resulted in her election as "president of [the] newly formed Chorus Equity Association, a subsidiary of the Actor's Equity Association [labor union]."[9] Consequently blacklisted by theatrical producers and widely regarded as a relic of the past, Dressler clung to the end of her rope. Dejected, she considered the prospect of retiring from acting to become a full-time maid as well as the notion of suicide—an act attempted years later by the likes of **Jennifer Jones**, **Susan Hayward**, **Elizabeth Taylor**, and **Halle Berry**.

But with the support from her longtime acquaintance Frances Marion (Hollywood's highest-paid screenwriter and one of a legion of women—including Marion Fairfax, Elinor Glyn, Anita Loos, and June Mathis—who, allegedly, "collectively wrote half of the films copyrighted between 1911 and 1925"),[10] Dressler was given a second chance.

After Dressler failed to regain her magic in the 1927 silent comedy *The Callahans and the Murphys* (a film censored for its ill-received portrayal of the Irish), she seized on the new opportunities afforded by sound. Inexplicably, she soon found herself upstaging the thickly accented Greta Garbo in the screen adaptation of Eugene O'Neill's Pulitzer Prize–winning stage play *Anna Christie* (1930; the first Garbo "talkie").

That same year, Dressler earned an Oscar nomination for her role in *Min and Bill* (1930) as a poor "waterfront hotel proprietress" who sacrifices herself to protect a prostitute's child whom she has raised as her own daughter.[11] Similar to the forceful, fear-provoking characters later portrayed by **Anna Magnani** in *The Rose Tattoo* (1955), **Elizabeth Taylor** in *BUtterfield 8* (1960) and *Who's Afraid of Virginia Woolf?* (1966), **Glenda Jackson** in *Women in Love* (1969) and *A Touch of Class* (1973), **Cher** in *Moonstruck* (1987), **Julia Roberts** in *Erin Brockovich* (2000), **Sandra Bullock** in *The Blind Side* (2009), and **Frances McDormand** in *Three Billboards Outside Ebbing, Missouri* (2017), Dressler brought to the screen an alpha female on equal, if not superior, terms with her male counterpart. Cowritten by Frances Marion and Marion Jackson, *Min and Bill*, with its rough-and-tumble brand of physical comedy punctuated by an epic, three-minute combat sequence between its two leads, elevated Dressler and her frequent costar Wallace Beery to superstar status. At a time when the movie industry experienced a downturn in business (with theaters shutting down and more people choosing to see fewer pictures or staying at home to listen to the radio for free), the phenomenal success of *Min and Bill* kept MGM in the black and helped to make it the only major studio in Hollywood never to lose "money during the Great Depression."[12]

Squaring off at the fourth Academy Awards (1931) against a younger, more conventionally attractive show of contenders that included the German screen star Marlene Dietrich (*Morocco*), Irene Dunne (*Cimarron*), Ann Harding (*Holiday*), and the previous year's winner, **Norma Shearer** (*A Free Soul*), Dressler "winked back the tears" upon the announcement of her name.[13] Becoming the third straight Canadian performer to earn the Academy Award for Best Actress, Dressler—ill from what she was soon to discover was terminal cancer—clutched her statuette to thunderous applause. She then received a congratulatory kiss from **Shearer**, her former costar from 1930's *Let Us Be Gay*, who saluted the 63-year-old as the "grandest old trouper of them all."[14]

Undoubtedly, Dressler's road to Oscar glory is something of a marvel. Acutely aware of her undesirable, bulldog-like appearance that contradicted the stereotype of a beautiful Hollywood star, the actress strived instead to be funny. "It was pleasanter to have folks laugh at you than to have them ignore you," she once explained.[15] Recognizing that moviegoers "needed to go and laugh for a few hours just to get away from dark times,"[16] Dressler subsequently appeared in *Reducing* (1931; with her frequent comedic partner Polly Moran), the all-star *Dinner at Eight* (1933; with Beery, Lionel and John Barrymore, and Jean Harlow), and the box-office hit *Tugboat Annie* (1933; the spiritual sequel to *Min and Bill* also costarring Beery). While her prankster, "banana-peel sense of humor" threw audiences into welcomed fits of laughter, Dressler could also move them to tears with her "magical transference of humanity."[17] As a result, a rarely seen display of public adoration enveloped the actress, who once stopped New York City Christmas-season traffic as well-wishers fought to see her and touch her extending hand.

On the day of her deeply mourned passing in 1934, Dressler remained MGM's reigning queen and one of the world's biggest box-office draws. Flags were reportedly "flown at half-mast and production stopped" during her jam-packed Hollywood funeral,[18] which included guests such as Lionel Barrymore, Polly Moran, **Norma Shearer**, Jean Hersholt, and Frances Marion. There, her casket was "overwhelmed with the orchids and gardenias ordered by [MGM studio head] Louis B. Mayer," who would later admit that "he only ever had three great actors: Garbo, [Spencer] Tracy, and Dressler."[19]

Helen Hayes

Helen Hayes was born Helen Hayes Brown on October 10, 1900, in Washington, DC. As the first Best Actress Oscar winner born in the 1900s, Hayes came into a world that was discovering film, aviation, ragtime, and Einstein's special theory of relativity. An only child born to lower-middle-class parents via an accidental pregnancy, Hayes grew up in a provincial, turn-of-the-century Washington of "horse drawn victorias and landaus, electric and gasoline motor cars, taxicabs, and nearly every type of carriage."[1] At the time, the average age of death in the United States was 47, only one in 13 homes had a telephone, and more than nine million immigrants began to enter the country.

Hayes's middle-class parents were determined to give their "petite, sweet-featured, but plain-looking" daughter a cultured upbringing, so they took her to baseball games, "the Glen Echo amusement park," plays, museums, matinees, "tea at the Willard Hotel," and public concerts, including John Philip Sousa conducting "the U.S. Marine Corps Band" on the National Mall.[2] Hayes's mother, a "former actress who saw the theatre as a glamorous alternative to the tedium of workaday life,"[3] subsequently pushed her five-year-old daughter into stage productions at the National Theatre in Washington. By the age of nine, Hayes was delighting audiences with her natural and unspoiled acting. By way of a contract from the theater producer Lew Fields, she made it all the way to Broadway—the mecca of entertainment that attracted over 20 million theatergoers every year by the 1920s.

Throughout a dazzling stage career that covered "more than 70 major roles,"[4] Hayes tackled the works of every notable playwright. Required to age 60 years in two and a half hours for a total 969 performances, she appeared as Queen Victoria in her magnum opus *Victoria Regina* (1935–1938; opposite Vincent Price as Prince

The Sin of Madelon Claudet (1931)

Behind the scenes of the pre-Code drama *The Sin of Madelon Claudet* (1931). In the film, Helen Hayes plays the part of a French farmer's daughter who falls in love with a visiting American and becomes pregnant. (Metro-Goldwyn-Mayer Inc./ Photofest)

"First Lady of the American Theatre" Helen Hayes won the Best Actress Oscar for her first feature-length film role, *The Sin of Madelon Claudet* (1931), in which she plays a fallen woman who turns to prostitution. (Metro-Goldwyn-Mayer Inc./Photofest)

Albert). The challenging performance cemented her status as the "First Lady of the American Theater"—a superlative she found embarrassing, as alongside Ethel Barrymore, Ina Claire, Katharine Cornell, Lynn Fontanne, Alla Nazimova, and Laurette Taylor, there were many other "first ladies" around. Incidentally, at a time when the prestige of the theater triumphed over the movies, these women were considered the "official elite of the acting profession."[5] "Off-stage, their influence was equally commanding. The clothes they wore, the fashionable restaurants where they were seen, [and] the way they graciously submitted to [an] interview as if doing the press a favor . . . became an education in star behavior" that Hollywood took note of.[6] As Hayes once put it, "An actor is [really] a public servant"—a figure who should be "unendingly generous" to his or her fans and who should never refuse an autograph or decline an interview.[7]

While her love for theater ran deep, Hayes found herself ambivalent toward the exacting, jigsaw-puzzle-like process of filmmaking. "Determined by a set of complicated scheduling mechanisms," the filmmaking process, as she discovered, required "endless takes" and "endless waits" and wore away at her patience.[8] "I've never been happy with anything I've ever done that I could see later," she once said.[9] Nonetheless, beginning as early as 1910, Hayes dipped her toe into filmmaking's adolescent waters. At a time when many highbrow theater personalities regarded the movies as a horrific fate worse than "starvation or walking the streets,"[10] the juvenile actress, accompanied by her financially persuaded mother, trekked to Brooklyn to appear in a silent two-reeler made on location at Vitagraph Studios. The experience proved to be neither here nor there but provided Hayes with an understanding of the medium while underscoring that the intimacy and immediacy of the stage was indeed her true calling.

By the time the Great Depression took its toll on the United States in the early 1930s (when an astounding six in ten Americans were living in poverty and 25 percent of the U.S. labor force was unemployed), Hayes was conversely at the top of her game. But with daily breadlines beginning to form and lengthen across the country and with the number of Broadway shows diminishing, a slow trickle of New York theater talent made their way to California.

Although the movie industry experienced a downturn in business, many Americans still needed a unifying and inexpensive form of escapism to evade their worries. Exhibitors responded with an emphasis on tactics such as contests, giveaways, and the two-films-for-the-price-of-one "double feature" phenomenon. Posters and advertising became more risqué in order to lure audiences into movie theaters. Even as several of the major studios instituted salary cuts for employees and nearly faced bankruptcy, Hollywood producers (and their new, sound-era financial backers from Wall Street) continued to loot the best of the best from theater, opera, vaudeville, radio, and beyond. Performers "who had been looked at by casting bureaus for their physical appearance . . . were now being considered in terms of their vocal abilities as well as vocal peculiarities."[11] This growing cavalcade of talent included the Marx Brothers, Will Rogers, Maurice Chevalier, Eddie

Cantor, Humphrey Bogart, James Cagney, Henry Fonda, and Fredric March; the future Best Actress Oscar winners **Claudette Colbert**, **Bette Davis**, and **Katharine Hepburn**; and such celebrated writers and playwrights as Herman J. Mankiewicz, Dorothy Parker, Ben Hecht, and Hayes's husband, Charles MacArthur.

Nevertheless, Hayes, who possessed "a remarkable ability to establish a relationship with her audience," was determined to remain in New York, "where her fresh beauty and insouciant charm had brightened one hit play after another."[12] With MacArthur restless to return home to his beloved wife and their baby daughter, Mary (who developed infantile paralysis and died in 1949 at the age of 19), MGM's production head, Irving G. Thalberg, made Hayes a lucrative offer to join her husband in Hollywood. Reluctantly, she obliged. But unable to compete with the formidable glamour and sex appeal of MGM idols Greta Garbo, Jean Harlow, and her eventual "best friends" **Joan Crawford** and **Norma Shearer**, the "ordinary" 5-foot-1 stage star was forced to find her own niche.[13] Eventually, studio head Louis B. Mayer made the decision to promote Hayes as "The Great Actress," and living up to such lofty expectations, Hayes captured the Oscar in her first feature-film role.

Challenging the draconian tenets of the adopted-but-not-then-heavily-enforced Production Code, Hayes's Oscar-winning performance as the title character in *The Sin of Madelon Claudet* (1931) situated the actress in a conflict-ridden drama about a farmer's daughter, who, in early 20th-century France, falls in love with a visiting American medical student and becomes pregnant. At a time when it was taboo for unwed women to be in such a state, Madelon is compelled to place her child in the custody of friends. After being wrongly imprisoned for ten years for her connections to a jewel thief, she spends the remainder of her life as a fallen woman. Limited in her abilities, she anonymously procures for her son's education by way of prostitution—a profession that proliferated in major cities during and after World War I and became a common role for women in film. Portrayals of prostitutes can be seen in six Best Actress Oscar–winning performances, beginning with **Janet Gaynor** in *Street Angel* (1928) and continuing with **Susan Hayward** in *I Want to Live!* (1958), **Elizabeth Taylor** in *BUtterfield 8* (1960), **Jane Fonda** in *Klute* (1971), and **Charlize Theron** in *Monster* (2003).

Disdainful of *Claudet*'s overemotional tenor despite MacArthur's earnest doctoring of the script and Thalberg's "judicious" postpreview weekend retakes,[14] Hayes, who wanted to buy the film from MGM so she could destroy it, nevertheless found herself nominated in the Best Actress category ahead of the fifth Academy Awards (1932). Her competition included fellow Broadway luminary Lynn Fontanne (*The Guardsman*) and the previous year's winner, **Marie Dressler** (*Emma*). Victorious, Hayes celebrated all night at Thalberg's Santa Monica beachfront home. The following morning, she reported for duty on set at Paramount for her next movie—the screen adaption of Ernest Hemingway's *A Farewell to Arms* (1932). When asked by her costar Gary Cooper to show off her freshly bequeathed statuette, Hayes altogether panicked. After a set of frantic phone calls to decipher its whereabouts, she ultimately found the elusive Oscar in the trunk of her car.

Although lauded for her "cinematic artistry,"[15] Hayes never became a popular screen actress (in part, because of her constant disdain for the camera). Like the future Best Actress Oscar recipients **Shirley Booth**, **Vivien Leigh**, **Helen Mirren**, **Geraldine Page**, **Maggie Smith**, and her close friend **Jessica Tandy**, she characterized the theater as her primary love. As a result, she made only an occasional reappearance in such films as *Anastasia* (1956; which brought **Ingrid Bergman** a second Best Actress Oscar), *Third Man on the Mountain* (1959; with her beloved adopted son, James MacArthur), and *Candleshoe* (1977; opposite a 15-year-old **Jodie Foster**). Representing the longest gap in Oscar history between acting honors, Hayes—at the age of 70 and 38 long years after her initial win—won a second Academy Award for her supporting role in the all-star disaster-drama and box-office hit *Airport* (1970). For this, she became the only female performer to have prevailed in each acting category (lead and supporting) with a 1–0 winning record.

As someone who merely became an actress at the insistence of her mother, Hayes was duly honored with a namesake theater, a namesake theater-acting award, a namesake hospital, and the U.S. Presidential Medal of Freedom (an honor given in part for her work for the March of Dimes and bestowed to only three other Best Actress Oscar winners—**Audrey Hepburn**, **Meryl Streep**, and **Barbra Streisand**). On the day of her passing in 1993, the lights of Broadway were dimmed to pay tribute to her remarkable 80-year career.

KH-347

NY-8-107

Katharine Hepburn

I n *Morning Glory* (1933), a young, stage-struck actress with the falsified-to-impress name of Eva Lovelace arrives in New York City broke, close to starvation, and with the single goal of becoming *the* next great actress. In the opening scene, Eva wanders out from the cold and into an empty theater lobby. There, in total awe, she gazes up at the lobby portraits of such revered stage idols as Maude Adams, Ethel Barrymore, and the legendary Sarah Bernhardt. Will she one day join their ranks? Or, like countless aspiring hopefuls, will she simply wither away like a morning glory flower before the midday sun?

Katharine Hepburn, in just her third motion picture, brought to the role of Eva Lovelace her trademark blend of aristocratic self-assuredness, wit, intelligence, and vulnerability. As the film critic David Thomson later observed, "Nobody on the screen could be so funny and so moving in making a fool of herself, or so touching in reclaiming her dignity."[1] Exemplifying such qualities, Hepburn's performance in *Morning Glory* earned her the first of *four* Academy Awards for Best Actress (still a record).

A natural-born rebel and one of a growing host of female stars to shun the Academy's "stuffy and clubbish" awards banquet (at which "V.I.P.'s in penguin suits" were often less than charming toward women),[2] Hepburn became the first Best Actress Oscar winner *not* to show up to collect her prize. In absentia, she beat the Australian actress May Robson (*Lady for a Day*) and the British actress Diana Wynyard (*Cavalcade*) at the sixth Academy Awards (1934). Citing a personal indifference to awards in general, Hepburn's continued absence from the Oscars persisted throughout her entire career despite a total of 12 Best Actress nominations. The lone exception occurred in 1974, when she presented the Irving G. Thalberg Award to her former producer Lawrence Weingarten. Wearing an informal pantsuit and

Morning Glory (1933)

Guess Who's Coming to Dinner (1967)

The Lion in Winter (1968)

On Golden Pond (1981)

A portrait of Katharine Hepburn by photographer Ernest Bachrach taken around the time that she won her first Oscar for *Morning Glory* (1933). (Ernest Bachrach/Photofest)

Katharine Hepburn portrays the aspiring actress Eva Lovelace (opposite Adolphe Menjou) in her third feature film, *Morning Glory* (1933). (RKO Radio Pictures Inc./Photofest)

clogs, she demonstrated (after a long standing ovation) that "a person can wait 41 years to be unselfish."[3]

Hepburn was born in Hartford, Connecticut, on May 12, 1907, and was reared in an academic, liberal-leaning, and well-to-do family that encouraged individuality and an "ever-expanding mind."[4] Throughout her childhood, her father, a prominent doctor, taught her the virtues of maintaining a healthy body through exercise and activity. Meanwhile, her mother, Katharine Martha Houghton Hepburn, an early feminist, suffragist, and birth-control advocate, carted her off to important meetings, lectures, and large-scale demonstrations. There, the young Katharine (the second eldest of six Hepburn children) experienced firsthand the "great temperament and authority" of the supposed "weaker sex."[5] Referring to her mother's circle of activist friends (comprising the sex educator Margaret Sanger, lesbian college associates, and other bohemian Greenwich Village artists and intellectuals), Hepburn once declared that she "knew so many fabulous women growing up" that "it never occurred to [her] that they were in any way inferior to men."[6] Hepburn's interest in acting developed at Bryn Mawr College, a women's liberal arts college in Lower Merion Township, Pennsylvania, that became the first of its kind to offer a PhD. Before long, the determined, aspiring actress made her way to Broadway. Despite a series of early-career firings due to her lack of experience, she learned her craft and soon became a breakout star.

Recruited by then–RKO Radio Pictures production head David O. Selznick for the sum of $1,500 per week, Hepburn arrived in Hollywood in 1932—the year the Great Depression cut "deep into [the film industry's] box-office receipts."[7] With her angular, freckled face, frizzy auburn hair, and a mannish, gender-bending attire consisting of tailored slacks that allowed her tall and sturdy frame to move faster and with a more purposeful and athletic stride, Hepburn, as the movie magazines of Hollywood declared, was "more modern than tomorrow."[8]

While Hepburn was hired to bring a new level of sophistication to RKO, the tomboy actress presented a unique challenge to the Hollywood star-system machinery. Clearly, Hollywood was not accustomed to articulate, college-graduate star performers dictating the parameters of their own star image. In particular, Hepburn's home studio of RKO had a difficult time with her eccentric, outspoken Yankee behavior; her insistence on always wanting to do her own hair and makeup; her refusal to grant interviews, comply with autograph seekers, or "pose for pinup pictures";[9] and her overall avoidance of the Hollywood establishment, public venues, or industry-related events where she would be seen and hounded by photographers. There were also questions about her estranged, uncommitted five-year marriage (1928–1934) to the East Coast businessman Ludlow Ogden Smith (which ended with a quick "Mexican divorce"), as well as her ties to her live-in friend and rumored partner, the American Express heiress Laura Harding. Moreover, she was castigated for supporting the controversial Socialist Party candidate Upton Sinclair in the 1934 California gubernatorial election.

"As a notable offender on the verge of committing 'star suicide,'" Hepburn was eventually "singled out" by the powerful fan magazine *Photoplay*, which alleged that she had alienated fans by displaying too much intelligence by way of her "artificial" speech patterns.[10] The Independent Theatre Owners of America concurrently labeled her "box-office poison." Following a string of sophisticated, overly "important" film appearances that failed to connect to the average Depression-era moviegoer (including the 1936 historical period drama *Mary of Scotland* and the 1938 screen adaptation of the pre-stock-market-crash hit stage play *Holiday*), Hepburn packed her bags and retreated from Hollywood. "She . . . left town quite defeated," recalled **Olivia de Havilland**. "The industry was confused by what I would call her New England pride. [Others] called it arrogance."[11]

Crushed and irritated, Hepburn bought out her RKO contract and returned to Broadway. In a "powerhouse cast" that included Joseph Cotten, Van Heflin, and **Shirley Booth**,[12] the actress originated the role of the marriage-seeking Tracy Lord in the long-running, Philip Barry–authored hit stage play *The Philadelphia Story* (1939–1941). With the play singlehandedly reviving her career, Hepburn, with the assistance of the producer and multimillionaire Howard Hughes, secured the film rights and sold them to MGM in exchange for script consultation and

In a film that daringly tackles the prospect of interracial marriage, Katharine Hepburn's liberal-minded character welcomes her daughter (played by real-life niece Katharine Houghton) and her possible new in-laws (played by Sidney Poitier, Roy E. Glenn Sr., and Beah Richards) in a scene from *Guess Who's Coming to Dinner* (1967). (Columbia Pictures Industries Inc./Photofest)

cast-and-crew-selection veto power (beyond **Mary Pickford**, still a rare position for a woman). She then starred in the triumphant 1940 screen adaptation opposite Cary Grant and Best Actor Oscar recipient James Stewart.

Forging a new partnership with MGM, Hepburn was famously brought into contact with Spencer Tracy—a two-time Best Actor Oscar winner, married Roman Catholic, and father of two with whom she concealed an offscreen relationship. Over the span of the next 25 years, the duo appeared in nine films together, including the feminist-leaning *Woman of the Year* (1942), *Adam's Rib* (1949; featuring **Judy Holliday**), and *Desk Set* (1957).

Hepburn and Tracy's final collaboration—the groundbreaking love story *Guess Who's Coming to Dinner* (1967)—put their liberal principles to the test. Taking cues from such interracial-themed movies as *Island in the Sun* (1957; starring **Joan Fontaine**, who received hate mail after kissing the African American actor Harry

Stanley Kramer (*center*) directs Katharine Hepburn and Spencer Tracy in *Guess Who's Coming to Dinner* (1967). Seventeen days after completing the film, Tracy died. Hepburn, his real-life partner, reportedly could never bring herself to watch the film. (Columbia Pictures Industries Inc./Photofest)

Belafonte), *Sayonara* (1957), *Imitation of Life* (1959), *Hiroshima mon amour* (1959), *West Side Story* (1961), and *A Taste of Honey* (1961), *Guess Who's Coming to Dinner* tackled the taboo subject of interracial marriage at a time in the United States when civil rights and the laws to protect voting rights had been extended to African Americans. (Antimiscegenation laws, however, were still upheld in 17 states.)

In the film, Hepburn is placed in the role of Christina Drayton—an idealized, "color-blind" San Francisco wife, mother, and art-gallery owner. After an abbreviated trip to Hawaii, her daughter (played by her real-life niece Katharine Houghton) returns home with the man that she plans to marry: a handsome, polite, sexually chaste, and successful Ivy League medical graduate, Nobel Prize laureate, and World Health Organization bigwig who happens to be Black. Buoyed by Hepburn's practical acceptance that love can conquer all, the controversial story, with Sidney Poitier as the Black man in question and Tracy as the daughter's skeptical father, ignited sporadic picketing among the Ku Klux Klan despite the film's overwhelming success as the third-highest-grossing film of 1967.

Hepburn, for her performance, at age 60, won her second Best Actress Oscar despite serious competition from former recipients **Audrey Hepburn** (*Wait until Dark*) and **Anne Bancroft** (*The Graduate*), the up-and-coming **Faye Dunaway** (*Bonnie and Clyde*), and the British actress and New York Film Critics Award winner Edith Evans (*The Whisperers*). Unsurprisingly, she was absent from the 1968 Academy Awards, which, in the midst of the most conflict-ridden period in "American history since the Civil War,"[13] had been postponed for two days as a sign of respect owing

Set around the Christmas Yuletide in the year 1183, Katharine Hepburn's Queen Eleanor of Aquitaine assists her husband, King Henry II (played by Peter O'Toole, seated in the middle) in determining which of their three sons will inherit the throne. From left to right, actors Anthony Hopkins, Jane Merrow, Nigel Terry, Timothy Dalton, and John Castle round out the cast. (Embassy Pictures Corporation/Photofest)

The vast majority of women in the Middle Ages held the positions of wife, mother, peasant, artisan, and nun. In contrast, *Lion in Winter* star Katharine Hepburn played one of the wealthiest and most powerful women of this period: Queen Eleanor of Aquitaine. (Embassy Pictures Corporation/Photofest)

to the recent assassination of Dr. Martin Luther King Jr. in Memphis, Tennessee. "I suspect my award was really given to the two of us," she later said,[14] referring to Tracy, who had died just 17 days after completing *Guess Who's Coming to Dinner* (a film the actress could never bring herself to watch).

Pouring her grief into acting, Hepburn traveled to Ireland, Wales, and France for the literary screen adaptation of the 1966 play *The Lion in Winter* (1968). Often castigated in her career for a lack of onscreen versatility, the actress researched everything there was to learn about the cruel, long-suffering Queen Eleanor of Aquitaine (ca. 1122–1204)—the estranged wife of England's King Henry II (and an ancestor to Hepburn herself). Upon her ostentatious arrival by boat at the Château de Chinon in southwestern France, Eleanor, who has just been released from confinement, bluntly greets her three sons by telling them that if she had managed sons for her previous husband, King Louis VII, she would "still be stuck with being Queen of France" and would not have known them. "Such, my angels, is the role of sex in history."[15] Set around the Christmas Yuletide in the year 1183 and wedged within an anxious 24-hour period during which time Henry's successor must be chosen, *The Lion in Winter* placed Hepburn in a vicious, chess-like tête-à-tête with the British-Irish actor Peter O'Toole, who had already performed the role of Henry II in the 1964 film *Becket*.

For her noble, emotionally naked performance, Hepburn earned a third (and second consecutive) Academy Award and the combative nickname of "Katharine of Arrogance."[16] In an unprecedented tie for Best Actress, she shared the honor

As the thoughtful and gregarious foil to Henry Fonda's cantankerous codger in *On Golden Pond* (1981), Katharine Hepburn earned a
record fourth Academy Award, thus becoming the most honored
actor—male or female—in Academy history. (Universal Pictures/
Photofest)

with the debut screen sensation **Barbra Streisand** (*Funny Girl*) and collectively defeated Vanessa Redgrave (*Isadora*) and past recipients **Joanne Woodward** (*Rachel, Rachel*) and **Patricia Neal** (*The Subject Was Roses*).

Acting as a sort of bookend to a phenomenal career (that officially continued for yet another decade), Hepburn went on to star in the sleeper hit *On Golden Pond* (1981). Based on the 1979 stage play by Ernest Thompson, the intergenerational story teamed Hepburn with both **Jane Fonda** and her real-life father, Henry Fonda—another survivor from Hollywood's classical era but one Hepburn had remarkably never met before. Holding her hand out to greet the elder Fonda on their first day together on set, the punctual star, with her hereditary shake and tremulous, often-parodied Bryn Mawr accent, emphatically asserted, "Well, it's about time."[17] She then presented him with Spencer Tracy's "lucky" hat (a tender, poignant gift that Fonda wore throughout filming).

In *On Golden Pond*, which looks "at the fear of approaching death" while offering a "beautiful elegy for a way of life quickly disappearing,"[18] Hepburn played Ethel Thayer, the devoted wife of an old and cantankerous retired professor (Henry Fonda) who is suffering from memory loss. Set at the picturesque New England lakeside cabin that the family has enjoyed for close to half a century, Hepburn's caring, mediating character attempts to bridge the deep emotional gap between her husband and their daughter (**Jane Fonda**) over the course of what is likely to be their final summer together.

On Golden Pond, which was later produced in 2001 as a live television event starring **Julie Andrews**, went on to become the second-highest-grossing film of 1981 after *Raiders of the Lost Ark*. The 76-year-old Henry Fonda, who passed away the following year, won his only Best Actor Oscar for his performance. Meanwhile, Hepburn, at 74, secured her fourth statuette, thus becoming the most honored actor—male or female—in Academy history (Daniel Day-Lewis, with three lead-actor awards, places second). In doing so, she beat former recipient **Diane Keaton** (*Reds*), Marsha Mason (*Only When I Laugh*), **Susan Sarandon** (*Atlantic City*), and early frontrunner **Meryl Streep** (*The French Lieutenant's Woman*).

"Equally capable of dominating the screen in sweeping epics, harrowing dramas, and sparkling comedies,"[19] Hepburn proved to be superlative throughout her epic, nearly 70-year career. Indeed, at the time of her death in 2003 at the age of 96, public opinion embraced her as one of the greatest actresses—if not *the* greatest—of the 20th century.

But beyond her performances and the countless awards that she accumulated, Hepburn, who was portrayed to Oscar-winning success by **Cate Blanchett** in *The Aviator* (2004), was additionally revered for her bold, tough-minded, and for some people, irreverent and forward-thinking views. "Things are getting worse," she once proclaimed, in reference to political wranglings targeted at Planned Parenthood (the provider of pregnancy testing and emergency contraception that her mother had helped to establish in the early 1920s and at which Hepburn herself had worked for many years). "Now they've even changed the rules about when a fetus is alive—although I've never seen a religious service for a miscarriage, have you?"[20]

Claudette Colbert

At the 1989 Kennedy Center Honors in Washington, DC, the American actor Gregory Peck warmly saluted honoree **Claudette Colbert** as "the best thing we've gotten from France since the Statue of Liberty."[1]

Intriguingly, the spirited star could have easily looked back at her long, 60-plus-year career as one that came close to never happening. When she was eight years old, Colbert and her family immigrated to New York City from the Saint-Mandé suburb of Paris. Only drawn into acting at the 11th hour after an ill classmate was forced to forfeit a French-speaking role in a high school theater workshop, Colbert consequently acquired the "acting bug."[2] Before long, the bilingual "apple-cheeked ingénue"[3]—who had initially seen herself pursuing an artistic career in fashion or becoming a secretary—began to make money as a French tutor, a stage actress, and a subsequent Broadway regular.

Born "Lily" Émilie Chauchoin on September 13, 1903, but ultimately constructing her own stage name, Colbert first dabbled with film in the Frank Capra–directed silent feature *For the Love of Mike* (1927). Surprisingly, she came away from the experience feeling disgruntled and apathetic, as "there were no lines to memorize."[4] But with the coming of sound, coupled with the Great Depression's debilitating effect on Broadway, which dwindled ticket sales and halted productions, Colbert gave the motion picture industry a second chance.

With a sophisticated voice of "worldly amusement" stylishly "peppered with her signature, slangy 'No kidding!'" jargon,[5] Colbert attracted legions of fans. Many, indeed, marveled at her "modern marriage" to the actor Norman Foster, who lived in a separate house "for their entire seven-year arrangement."[6] As a glamorous, sexually ambiguous product of the Roaring Twenties, the actress remained the source

It Happened One Night (1934)

Virtually stripped of everything that guarantees her position in a money-defined society, Claudette Colbert's affluent character surrenders to a threadbare newspaper reporter (played by Clark Gable) in director Frank Capra's cross-class romantic comedy *It Happened One Night* (1934). (Columbia Pictures Industries Inc./Photofest)

The Hollywood star system put an emphasis on image rather than acting, and women—like Claudette Colbert, who gave marching orders on how best to be lit and photographed after years of experience—were expected to never leave the house without makeup and stylish clothes. (Photofest)

of much speculation. Although she was married twice, Colbert was known to have "formed her closest and most sustained" relationships with other women,[7] including fellow painter, travel companion, and chauffeur Verna Hull. Like **Katharine Hepburn**, Greta Garbo, and Marlene Dietrich, Colbert was frequently spotted in tailored slacks, perceived by many people at the time as "a code for lesbianism or at least sexual rebellion."[8]

Signing on with Paramount Pictures and shooting such films as *Young Man of Manhattan* (1930; opposite Foster and the newcomer **Ginger Rogers**), *The Big Pond* (1930), and *The Smiling Lieutenant* (1931) at Paramount's Astoria studio annex in Queens, Colbert initially remained in New York and stayed connected to Broadway. Forever fiscally minded, she doubled her salary at Paramount by reprising her screen roles in the simultaneously filmed French-language versions. (Capitalizing on her French, she later starred in two French film productions from 1954, *Destinées* and *Si Versailles m'était conté*.)

While light comedies remained Colbert's specialty, her titillating makeover in director Cecil B. DeMille's biblical epic *The Sign of the Cross* (1932) proved to supply the missing ingredient needed to turn the actress into a bona fide star. In a pre-Code drama that broke a number of sexual taboos, Colbert, similar to the boundary-pushing performances of **Sophia Loren** in *Boy on a Dolphin* (1957), **Julie Christie** in *Don't Look Now* (1973), **Helen Mirren** in *The Cook, the Thief, His Wife & Her Lover* (1989), **Holly Hunter** in *Crash* (1996), and **Nicole Kidman** in *Eyes Wide Shut* (1999), found herself "stimulated by the chance to be provocative."[9] "Filled to the brim" with sex, sadism, orgies, and a lesbian pagan dance scene casually cloaked "under the trappings of religion and history," *The Sign of the Cross* helped "to step up [the] enforcement" of the Production Code and the formation of the National Legion of Decency.[10] Colbert had previously ruffled conservative feathers by way of her "Jazz Up Your Lingerie" sequence from 1931's *The Smiling Lieutenant* (in which she edifies a dim Miriam Hopkins on the virtues of liberated sexuality). However, her naked milk bath from *The Sign of the Cross* altogether paralyzed the censors by "exposing more of her breasts than section VI, part 3 of the Production Code" had ever allowed.[11]

By the time Colbert reteamed with Capra to star in the romantic screwball comedy *It Happened One Night* (1934), the era of pre-Code cinema was coming to an end. Religious and puritanical protest to the hedonistic liberation of 1920s Hollywood warranted the strict enforcement of the Production Code in July 1934, mandating that all filmmakers submit their films for approval to the Production Code Administration before release. Depictions of profanity, sex perversion, suggestive nudity, miscegenation, the illegal trafficking of drugs, the defeated law, the ridiculing of the clergy, and a myriad of other "thou shalt nots" were comprehensively banned, fundamentally robbing women in particular of the power that they had gained in regards to personal and career fulfillment.

Based on a short story that first appeared in the pages of *Cosmopolitan* magazine, *It Happened One Night* offered moviegoers a provocative final glimpse of

P1090-1086

adult-minded fare that did not return to American cinema for several decades. Oozing with "snappy dialogue," thinly decorated euphemisms, double entendres, and sublimated forms of eroticism,[12] the film centers on Ellie Andrews (played by Colbert), an elite socialite who jumps ashore from the yacht of her moneyed, disapproving father to reunite with the pilot and fortune hunter with whom she eloped. Carrying little money and at one point "forced to forage in the woods like an animal for carrots,"[13] Colbert's character discreetly travels from Miami to New York. Along the way, she encounters the brash, threadbare newspaper reporter Peter Warne (Clark Gable), who shelters her from the authorities in exchange for her story.

In the film's famous, sexual tension-building "Walls of Jericho" scene, the characters share a motel room on a rainy night (at the time, a scandalous act for two unmarried people of the opposite sex). After draping a blanket over a clothesline to create a makeshift wall between their twin beds, Peter playfully undresses in front of Ellie as she stands frozen and fixated on his bare and muscled chest. A few moments later, silhouetted against a backlit window, she undresses in comparative privacy, tossing her undergarments over the top of the blanket as he smokes a cigarette on his bed and sings, "Who's Afraid of the Big Bad Wolf?" The scene is later referenced at the end of the film, when the Walls of Jericho—an obvious metaphor for sexual inactivity—finally come tumbling down.

With the movie's satirizing of the rich, elevation of the poor, and straightforward depiction of cross-class romance, *It Happened One Night* became an international word-of-mouth smash-hit sensation that resonated with Depression-era audiences, not to mention the likes of Joseph Stalin and Adolf Hitler. But to Colbert, who was paid $50,000 out of a tightfisted $325,000 budget after Constance Bennett, **Bette Davis**, Miriam Hopkins, Carole Lombard, Myrna Loy, and Margaret Sullavan had all turned down the part of Ellie, the film's popularity remained a mystery.

On her last day on set, Colbert, who had already worked on pictures with similar themes, characterized *It Happened One Night* as the worst film that she had ever made. Throughout shooting, she had been repeatedly subjected to Gable's womanizing ways and sexual pranks (one involving a hammer, the other an upright potato masher placed underneath a blanket). Unpopular with the crew as a result of her standoffishness, her need for regular hours ("By five in the afternoon I am tired and my face shows it"), and her marching orders on how best to be lit and photographed (from her left!), the self-directed actress nevertheless soldiered on with the charming assertion, "I've been in the Claudette Colbert business a long time."[14]

While Colbert completed 1934 with two other high-grossing successes—*Cleopatra* and *Imitation of Life*—it was her performance in *It Happened One Night* that landed her a Best Actress nomination ahead of the seventh Academy Awards (1935). Her competition included former winner **Norma Shearer** (*The Barretts of Wimpole Street*) and the operatic soprano Grace Moore (*One Night of Love*).

Excluded, however, was **Bette Davis**, whose Cockney-accented depiction of an ill-mannered London tearoom waitress in *Of Human Bondage* had prompted

Life magazine to declare it "the best performance ever recorded on screen by a U.S. actress." With growing pressure to overturn the omission, the Academy of Motion Picture Arts and Sciences authorized voters to "write on the ballot [their] personal choice for the winners."[15]

Colbert viewed **Davis** as the probable victor. On the night of the awards, she consequently boarded the *Super Chief* en route to New York. But summoned at the last minute to the nearby downtown Los Angeles Biltmore Hotel (where winners' names had been announced to the press just prior to the ceremony), the actress hurriedly jumped into a taxi and within minutes was presented the Best Actress Oscar by the six-year-old child star Shirley Temple. Dressed in a traveling coat and hat while assured that her train would not leave the station without her, Colbert told the audience, "I'm so happy enough to cry. But I can't take the time to do so. A taxi is waiting outside with the engine running."[16]

Impressively, *It Happened One Night* became the first film to win the Oscar for writer, actor, actress, director, and picture. On top of that, Colbert's salary jumped from $50,000 to $150,000 per picture. By 1938, despite "Depression-era cutbacks," she became the "second-highest wage earner in Hollywood" behind only MGM studio head Louis B. Mayer.[17]

In the late 1950s, after Colbert had added to her résumé such hits as *Boom Town* (1940; reuniting her with Clark Gable), *The Palm Beach Story* (1942), *Since You Went Away* (1944; costarring Shirley Temple and **Jennifer Jones**), and *The Egg and I* (1947), the actress gradually retreated from film acting. She subsequently returned to the stage, continued to participate in Cecil B. DeMille's popular *Lux Radio Theater*, and even hosted her own CBS television talk show geared toward women and examining such issues as "teenage marriage and divorce."[18] Later, Colbert retired to her home in Barbados, where she died in 1996 at the age of 92.

Bette Davis

Dangerous (1935)

Jezebel (1938)

When the Hollywood gossip columnist Hedda Hopper asked **Bette Davis** what she would want to be if she had not become an actress, the iconic superstar, known for her "clipped staccato voice," "penetrating stares," and taking "intense drags on cigarettes," bluntly answered, "a man."[1] Indeed, as a woman who fought tooth and nail to succeed in a man's world with her rule-breaking flamboyance, Davis could easily recall the economic discrimination, social pressure, and sexist double standards that she encountered—and repeatedly triumphed over—all along the way.

Branded by the film industry with a reputation for being haughty, moody, sometimes vulgar, and disruptive, Davis—the ultimate Hollywood prima donna who many celebrities felt unsafe "to have around"[2]—fundamentally lived a lonely life in which she seemed inept at almost everything except her work. While a few of her screen characters were observed as "vulnerable victims," the vast majority were "cold-hearted, calculating bitches" willing to articulate an assertiveness, intelligence, and strength that young female moviegoers responded to and admired.[3] Off camera, she was equally forthright, refusing "to genuflect to the boys in the front office or [those] in the director's chair."[4] Davis recognized that negative portrayals of women in film have broad societal effects (e.g., legitimizing inequality, confirming gender stereotypes, and so forth), and she sought to eradicate such depictions by fostering and maintaining a purposeful "sense of self."[5] By doing so, and to her everlasting credit, she left an indelible cinematic imprint that—to this day—continues to inspire.

Davis was born in Lowell, Massachusetts, on April 5, 1908. At the age of five, she changed her name from Ruth Elizabeth to the Balzac-inspired "Bette." The

Bette Davis, in character and wearing a voluminous white evening gown, poses for a publicity photo for *Jezebel* (1938). (Warner Bros. Pictures Inc./ Photofest)

daughter of a Harvard Law School graduate father (who abandoned the family) and a determined mother hell-bent on seeing at least one of her two girls get "into the theatre,"[6] Davis grew up with a strong feeling of where her life might be headed. Envious of the likes of the actors **Mary Pickford**, Alice Terry, Greta Garbo,

A 1930 portrait of Bette Davis holding a cherry blossom branch. The stage actress was asked by Universal Studios in December 1930 to come to Hollywood, where she felt lost in a sea of hypersexualized blondes. (Photofest)

Jeanne Eagels, Ruth Chatterton, her childhood friend turned screen idol Charles Farrell, and the Welsh stage actress Peg Entwistle (who jumped to her death from the "H" of the Hollywoodland sign in 1932), Davis committed herself to acting. Under the training of the modern dance choreographer Martha Graham and the theater director John Murray Anderson, she studied the finer points of her craft, including movement, gesture, posture, elocution, staging, lighting, and wardrobe. Before she made her New York stage debut at the Provincetown Playhouse in 1929, Davis—as she did throughout her legendary 60-year career—rigorously analyzed her character and spent hours in makeup to ensure that her appearance was right for the role.

Simultaneously, Hollywood was undergoing a tectonic shift with its employment of sound technology, and a large-scale recruitment of distinguished faces with competent voices from the New York and London stage and radio brought a fresh new batch of dream people to Hollywood. As part of this shift, Davis was asked by a Universal Studios talent scout to join the cavalcade in December 1930. But upon her arrival in Hollywood, she immediately felt lost in a sea of hypersexualized platinum blondes. Dismissed for a purported lack of sex appeal, the actress was later retained by Warner Bros., whose Best Actor Oscar–winning star George Arliss was instrumental in landing Davis her first lead role in *The Man Who Played God* (1932). With Davis seen as possessing a "life-force . . . beyond ordinary human animation" and big, "pulsing eyes,"[7] as glorified in the 1981 hit song "Bette Davis Eyes" by Kim Carnes (which **Gwyneth Paltrow** later covered), Arliss became the first to recognize what the entire world was soon to discover.

Helping to break the lingering belief that stage acting was "superior" to film acting, Davis, on loan to RKO, eventually starred as a "boozy, Cockney shrew of a waitress" in the screen adaptation of W. Somerset Maugham's *Of Human Bondage* (1934).[8] The performance was unanimously praised. However, when the actress's name did not appear as a contender for the Academy Award, all hell broke loose. The former Best Actress Oscar winner and nominee **Norma Shearer** stepped in to campaign on Davis's behalf, and the Academy of Motion Picture Arts and Sciences (which had been castigated by the *Hollywood Citizen News*) ultimately acquiesced by granting—for the only year in its history—write-in ballot entries.

Nonetheless, Davis's home studio of Warner Bros. was not about to allow its "contract player to win the Academy Award in a competing studio's film" and put the kibosh on her chances.[9] The actress ultimately lost to **Claudette Colbert**, and, while Davis "was never able to prove it," she later stated "that [studio president] Jack Warner had sent instructions to his personnel not to vote for her,"[10] setting off a colossal feud that drove the first nail into the studio star-system coffin.

The following year, in a new era of conservative cinematic mores brought on by the Production Code (whose "seal of approval" caused many big-city audiences to boo and hiss when it "flashed onto the screen"),[11] Davis played the role of a fallen, jinx-provoking Broadway actress in the unevenly received Warner Bros. production of *Dangerous* (1935; costarring Franchot Tone). Loosely based on the tragic life of Jeanne Eagels (1890–1929), the film captured Davis's frequently drunk character without makeup and with her hair awry. So caustic was Davis's depiction that it even led one reviewer to suggest that her character would "have been burned as a witch . . . if she had lived two or three hundred years" before.[12]

Nonetheless, for her grim, overmannered, but rule-abiding performance, Davis found herself nominated for Best Actress ahead of the eighth Academy Awards (1936). Her competition included Miriam Hopkins (in the groundbreaking, three-strip Technicolor production of *Becky Sharp*), Merle Oberon (*The Dark Angel*), the German actress Elisabeth Bergner (*Escape Me Never*), and former winners **Claudette Colbert** (*Private Worlds*) and **Katharine Hepburn** (whose performance in *Alice Adams* Davis had cited as the best).

Initially planning to skip the ceremony as a way to rebuff the Academy for snubbing her the previous year, Davis was later ordered by Jack Warner to show up and collect what was generally seen as a consolation-prize statuette. Underscoring her resentment and knowing that her photo would be published around the world, the actress made a bold "'anti-fashion' statement" and arrived at the ceremony "like the hired help" in a "suitably dowdy" picnic party costume.[13] To that, her glamorous, lifelong rival **Joan Crawford** (then married to Franchot Tone, "with whom Davis was secretly in love") could not help but make a spiteful remark: "Dear Bette," she said, "what a *lovely* frock."[14]

Davis's stunt, however, proved to backfire. Unresponsive to her Oscar victory, Warner Bros. "refused to increase her salary."[15] Additionally, studio heads "informed the actress that she wouldn't be loaned out again."[16] Embarrassingly, they "leased the use of her face for breakfast cereal ads" and cast her in a succession of mediocre roles that Davis was forced to play.[17] Operating in a fear-based industry of frequent layoffs and suspensions, where "careers often begin by chance" and can "evaporate just as quixotically," Davis began to recognize that "further compliance would only [destroy] the career [she] had so far built."[18] As a result, she packed her bags, "ignored her contract," and in 1936 "accepted an offer to work in England."[19]

In one of 15 Best Actress Oscar–winning roles to portray a performer, Bette Davis stars as Joyce Heath, a fallen, jinx-provoking Broadway actress whose past performance as Juliet deeply affected Franchot Tone's character in *Dangerous* (1935). (Warner Bros. Pictures Inc./Photofest)

Having to pay $50,000 in legal fees "out of her own pocket," Davis was eventually sued by Warner Bros. in a London courtroom adjacent to the one in which "an American woman named Wallis Simpson was suing for divorce."[20] Although she lost the battle and would "return to work without any [initial] modifications,"[21] Davis—with her court case further dramatizing her self-empowered image—ultimately won the war. Before long, she received a new option contract, an increased salary, "defacto script approval,"[22] and starring roles in such acclaimed box-office hits as *Dark Victory* (1939; her personal favorite of her films), *The Little Foxes* (1941), *Now, Voyager* (1942), *Old Acquaintance* (1943), *Mr. Skeffington* (1944), and *A Stolen Life* (1946).

But the film that made Davis an overnight superstar, won her a second Academy Award, and served as "a testament to the studio's faith in her abilities both as an actress and as a personality" was 1938's *Jezebel*.[23] Helmed by Davis's most beloved director, William Wyler (who would guide *five* women—Davis, **Greer Garson**, **Olivia de Havilland**, **Audrey Hepburn**, and **Barbra Streisand**—to Best Actress Oscar victories), *Jezebel* examines the lying, scheming ways of Davis's character—an 1850s

Disdainful that her home studio of Warner Bros. suppressed her chances of winning the Oscar the year before for *Of Human Bondage* (for which she had been loaned out to RKO), Bette Davis was ordered to collect what was seen as a consolation prize Best Actress Oscar for her performance in the unevenly received Warner Bros. production of *Dangerous* (1935). Seeking revenge, the actress—pictured here with presenter D. W. Griffith and Best Actor recipient Victor McLaglen—showed up to the eighth Academy Awards in a picnic party costume. She later sued Warner Bros. in a London courtroom. (© A.M.P.A.S.®/ Photofest)

New Orleans southern belle "who did evil in the sight of God."[24] The film takes its title from a biblical term referring to "wicked" women, who, to this day, are persecuted around the world "for 'shaming' [their families] by acting in ways deemed disobedient and immodest."[25] The film was made "amid the highly publicized and lengthy preproduction planning of *Gone with the Wind* (1939)" and drew "inevitable comparisons with [the "semi-liberated"] Scarlett O'Hara."[26] Essentially flaunting her sexuality, Davis's character of Julie Marsden wears a sleeveless red dress to an all-white cotillion ball and ends up losing not only the respect of her community but also the man she loves, Preston "Pres" Dillard (played by Henry Fonda).

For her superficial-turned-sacrificial performance that culminates with Julie accompanying an ailing Pres to a former leper colony used during a yellow fever outbreak, Davis overcame the likes of former winner **Norma Shearer** (*Marie Antoinette*), New York Film Critics Award winner Margaret Sullavan (*Three Comrades*), the British actress Wendy Hiller (*Pygmalion*), and *Jezebel* Best Supporting Actress winner Fay Bainter (*White Banners*) to clinch her second statuette at the 11th Academy Awards (1939).

Said to have "coined the term 'Oscar' in honor of her first husband's ass,"[27] Davis, two years later, became the first female president of the Academy of Motion Picture Arts and Sciences. But after studying the Academy laws and starting a program of "reform," she was told that "that much participation was not expected" and therefore resigned.[28] Instead, she volunteered her time as the cofounder of the Hollywood Canteen, a club providing free food and entertainment for World War II–era service members.

In a 19th century story set four years after women laid the ground-work for women's rights at the 1848 Seneca Falls Convention in upstate New York, Bette Davis's New Orleans–based character tests the loyalty of the man she loves (played by Henry Fonda) in *Jezebel* (1938). (Warner Bros. Pictures Inc./Photofest)

Davis, who starred in such further highlights as *All About Eve* (1950) and *What Ever Happened to Baby Jane?* (1962; opposite **Joan Crawford**), became the first woman to earn ten Best Actress Oscar nominations. As one of only five women (with **Elizabeth Taylor**, **Barbra Streisand**, **Meryl Streep**, and **Shirley MacLaine**) to be honored by the Film Society of Lincoln Center, the Board of Trustees of the Kennedy Center, and the American Film Institute, the industrious actress was ostensibly sanctified as a cinematic saint. Although she suffered a series of strokes in the early 1980s that slurred her speech, partially paralyzed her face, and made her exceedingly thin, she continued to make television talk-show appearances and — unlike the vast majority of her peers — "remained a working actress almost until the day she died" in Paris in 1989.[29] Determined to fight the status quo and its long-standing representation of women as unperceptive, passive, weak, and naïve, Davis — whose gravestone fittingly reads, "She did it the hard way" — set perhaps the highest standard of professionalism in acting. In doing so, she changed the cinematic image of women forever.

Luise Rainer

Luise Rainer was born on January 12, 1910, into an upper-middle-class
Jewish family and came of age in a post–World War I Germany of "depression, starvation, and revolution."[1] Against the wishes of her father (an oil
and soybean importer-exporter), she decided on the "low and vulgar profession"
of acting and embarked on a successful stage career under the darkening clouds
of Nazism.[2]

Much like **Audrey Hepburn** two decades later, Rainer was celebrated for having
an instinctive approach to acting that she achieved without any formal training. A
fragile, "pencil slim" beauty known behind the scenes for her enigmatic, nonconformist nature,[3] Rainer soon performed in such progressive plays as George Bernard
Shaw's *Saint Joan* and Frank Wedekind's *Spring Awakening (Frühlingserwachen)* — a
candid and frequently banned social critique that featured nudity and dealt with
such issues as rape, suicide, child abuse, masturbation, homosexuality, and abortion. She later joined the esteemed theater director and producer Max Reinhardt
and his "insular," seemingly fascist-"protected" acting troupe in Vienna, becoming "part of an impressionistic acting tradition [that] emphasized [the director's]
rejection of the naturalistic style."[4]

Performing in Berlin on February 27, 1933 (less than one month after Adolf
Hitler became Chancellor of Germany), Rainer witnessed Germany's Parliament
building, the Reichstag, go "up in flames" and light up the night sky.[5] The arson
attack sent a strong, chilling message to many people. At a time when "German
soldiers thronged the streets and people were heiling Hitler all over the place"
(as filmed by the visiting actress **Ingrid Bergman** in 1938 on her personal 16 mm
camera), the Nazis began to arrest "thousands of people" in what "turned into a

The Great Ziegfeld (1936)

The Good Earth (1937)

In the MGM superspectacle *The
Good Earth* (1937), Luise Rainer
plays a Chinese peasant. For her
performance, Rainer became
the first actor (male or female)
to win back-to-back Oscars. But
disdainful of the Hollywood star
system, the actress terminated
her option contract with MGM
the following year. (Metro-
Goldwyn-Mayer Inc./Photofest)

875-X-155

The German Jewish actress Luise Rainer escaped the grips of Nazi fascism by accepting a long-term contract with MGM. Here, Robert Z. Leonard directs Rainer and costar William Powell in a scene from *The Great Ziegfeld* (1936), the Best Picture Oscar–winning movie in which Rainer plays the Belle Époque–era stage performer Anna Held. (Metro-Goldwyn-Mayer Inc./Photofest)

'frenzy' of political purges."[6] Even though Rainer was raised "wild with no religion at all,"[7] she began to realize that her Jewish heritage was now a serious threat to her security.

In 1934, Rainer was "discovered in Vienna by an MGM scout who saw her on stage in *An American Tragedy*."[8] Despite having little interest in film before finding herself moved by the performances of **Helen Hayes** and Gary Cooper in 1932's *A Farewell to Arms*, the distinguished stage actress hastily signed a long-term option contract with MGM, provided that she be "allowed to bring her beloved Scottish terrier, Johnny, with her from Europe."[9] With Hollywood boasting "the largest film industry in the world," Rainer, in conjunction with a sizable influx of "German-speaking film emigrants" including Marlene Dietrich, Fritz Lang, Peter Lorre, and Billy Wilder, fled Nazi fascism and found her way to the great melting pot of America.[10]

As Rainer sailed across the Atlantic on the SS *Île de France*, the famed Russian violinist Mischa Elman serenaded her on her 25th birthday. Upon her arrival at the Beverly Wilshire Hotel in Beverly Hills, the actress spotted Gary Cooper and "nearly fainted."[11] But as she took her place at MGM alongside **Joan Crawford**, Greta Garbo, Jean Harlow, Myrna Loy, Jeanette MacDonald, and **Norma Shearer**, she began to see her glamorous new surroundings as a place that she did not belong.

Rainer replaced Myrna Loy in the sophisticated, Vienna-set *Escapade* (1935; her first American picture) and came to discover the rigid and elaborate "machinery" of the Hollywood star system, in which she was typecast as a "woman scorned" and felt reduced to the status of "a bolt."[12] Exasperated by the studio subjecting her to incessant interviews and public appearances, makeup tests, dress codes, and wardrobe fittings while reappropriating her image as "Viennese" so as to "avoid growing anti-German sentiment,"[13] Rainer inevitably bumped heads with MGM's autocratic studio head Louis B. Mayer over her purported lack of obedience and docility. "Why do you not sit on my lap when we talk contracts, like my other stars do?" Mayer once inquired.[14] Unwilling to "play the game" and "don an artificial façade of amiability" in a manipulative and misogynistic environment, Rainer assertively responded, "I am an actress. I am not a movie star!"[15] But as Rainer came to learn of the blatant double standards that plagued Hollywood, it was acceptable for a male star to thumb his nose at convention or argue "over his salary or a role he disliked," while "the same show of self-determination from a star actress became 'temperament' or 'going grand.'"[16] As **Olivia de Havilland** explained, "Sexism was a fact of life. Men felt threatened and mistrustful of women who had good ideas, and one had to employ immense tact when dealing with directors and producers."[17]

Rejecting the glitter and glamour of Hollywood, Rainer—a "shy, music-loving [intellectual]"[18]—remained a perpetual outsider to the Hollywood crowd. At a time when all of the great artists from Europe were emigrating to America, she kept company with the likes of the architect Richard Neutra and the writers Bertolt Brecht, Thomas Mann, and Anaïs Nin. To her, Hollywood people were conversely "shallow, absurdly materialistic, and politically naïve, particularly in what she called its apathy toward the rise of fascism in Europe and Asia, and labor unrest and poverty in Depression America."[19]

For her second movie in Hollywood, Rainer was cast in the "lengthy, sentimental musical biopic" *The Great Ziegfeld* (1936).[20] In the first of 20 Best Actress Oscar–winning films to portray a real-life person (as of early 2019), Rainer played Anna Held (1872–1918), the Polish-born showgirl and common-law wife to the Broadway impresario extraordinaire Florenz Ziegfeld (portrayed by William Powell). The 179-minute film chronicles Ziegfeld from his early career promoting the scantily clad bodybuilder Eugen Sandow at the 1893 world's fair to his grandiose, Folies Bergère–inspired theatrical revues. It additionally touches on the master showman's creative campaign to turn Held into an American-embraced sensation (just as MGM was attempting to do with Rainer herself). Laying the foundation for 1968's *Funny Girl* (starring Walter Pidgeon as Ziegfeld and Best Actress Oscar winner **Barbra Streisand** as his subsequent protégé, Fanny Brice), Rainer's comparatively abbreviated performance culminates with "the most famous telephone scene in film history."[21] The scene is derived from Jean Cocteau's one-act theater monologue *La voix humaine* (1930) and shows Rainer's character—a "quivering bundle of suppressed grief"[22]—collapsing in a Niagara of tears after congratulating Ziegfeld on his new marriage. The emotive scene fittingly earned Rainer the nickname of the "Viennese teardrop."

Acting awards for supporting characters were first introduced to the awards schedule ahead of the ninth Academy Awards (1937), but Rainer, winner of the New York Film Critics Award, found herself nominated in the lead actress category despite a performance almost equal in length to that of inaugural Best Supporting Actress recipient Gale Sondergaard (winner for *Anthony Adverse*). For Best Actress, Rainer's competition included Irene Dunne (*Theodora Goes Wild*), Gladys George (*Valiant Is the Word for Carrie*), Carole Lombard (*My Man Godfrey*), and former winner and recent widow **Norma Shearer** (*Romeo and Juliet*). Like **Katharine Hepburn**, **Claudette Colbert**, and **Bette Davis** before her, Rainer initially decided not to go to the "stuffy" event but was later summoned by MGM to attend.[23]

With Rainer receiving her award the same night as the Austrian-born Best Actor winner, Paul Muni (*The Story of Louis Pasteur*), MGM was given a "great public-ity coup."[24] Its brand-new prestige picture *The Good Earth* (1937) had just been released and conveniently starred both Rainer and Muni.[25] Based on the Pulitzer Prize-winning novel by Pearl S. Buck and the 1932 Broadway adaptation starring Claude Rains and Alla Nazimova, *The Good Earth*, which is set in the early 20th century during the end of China's Qing Dynasty and thereafter, became MGM's most expensive film since *Ben-Hur: A Tale of the Christ* (1925). It also marked the "last great achievement" brought to the screen by Irving G. Thalberg, who had died during production of "pneumonia stemming from a rheumatic heart condition."[26]

In *The Good Earth*, Rainer plays O-Lan—a submissive but resourceful Chinese kitchen slave turned peasant farmer's wife. As a result of the Production Code's "strict anti-miscegenation rules" that "prohibited a Chinese woman from playing opposite a white man,"[27] the German actress was awarded the role over the Chinese American movie star Anna May Wong, who many people felt would have been a better fit. In an early effort to secure the role for Wong, the Los Angeles press even launched an aggressive publicity campaign on her behalf. But akin to the whitewashing of such non-Asian performers as **Mary Pickford** (*Madame Butterfly*, 1915) and **Loretta Young** (*The Hatchet Man*, 1932) and later **Katharine Hepburn** (*Dragon Seed*, 1944), **Jennifer Jones** (*Love Is a Many-Splendored Thing*, 1955), **Shirley MacLaine** (*My Geisha*, 1962), **Halle Berry** (*Cloud Atlas*, 2012), and **Emma Stone** (*Aloha*, 2015), Rainer committed herself to the part amid a sea of Chinese extras. Although she refused to wear a mask, she was replete in yellow-face makeup then befitting a Hollywood film industry that still believed that "audiences wouldn't pay money to see a movie with an Asian lead."[28]

Portraying a woman who, like many still today, is trapped in old-world tradi-tions that forbid girls from seeking an education, allow for such things as child brides and arranged marriages, and thereby deny a life of meaning and purpose, Rainer plays a stoic, virtually dialogue-deprived character who suffers through drought, famine, poverty, war, floods, polygamy, childbirth, and an astonishing plague of locusts. The actress was deeply moved by her character's miserable circumstances and, off camera, was oftentimes reduced to tears. On one such occasion, **Joan Crawford** approached the actress and inquired as to why she was crying. As Rainer recalled, "I did not want to sound like a phony about acting, so I told her that I had received terrible news from Europe about my family."[29] Rainer later returned to her Brentwood home to find that "a large bouquet of flowers from **Crawford** [had] arrived."[30]

For *The Good Earth*, Rainer won her second Academy Award. Following her victory from the year before, she became the first actor (male or female) to win *two* Oscars and the first of five performers (prior to Spencer Tracy, **Katharine Hepburn**, Jason Robards, and Tom Hanks) to win back-to-back statuettes. While many observers attributed her victory as "a vote for Thalberg's legacy and the production he lovingly oversaw until his sudden death,"[31] Rainer nevertheless prevailed over inaugural winner **Janet Gaynor** (*A Star Is Born*), Irene Dunne (*The Awful Truth*), New York Film Critics Award winner Greta Garbo (*Camille*), and frontrunner Barbara Stanwyck (*Stella Dallas*). Refusing to attend the ceremony, the actress, once again, was later summoned and grudgingly arrived at the Biltmore Hotel with her then-husband—the leftist, antiestablishment playwright Clifford Odets.

Once described by **Jane Fonda** as "the best actress that Hollywood ever had," Rainer, not yet 30 but already feeling "stifled by the frivolous roles that . . . Mayer forced upon her,"[32] termi-

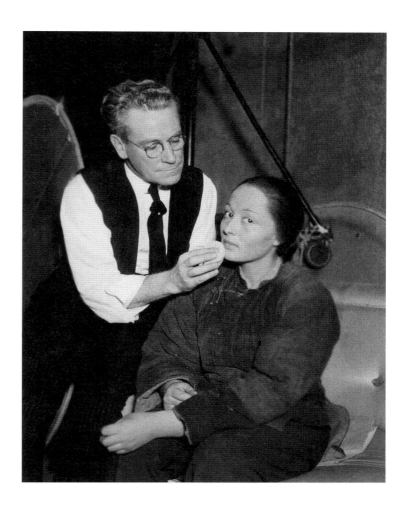

Refusing to wear a mask, Luise Rainer is replete in yellow-face makeup in this off-camera shot from *The Good Earth* (1937), a story set during the end of China's Qing Dynasty and thereafter. (Metro-Goldwyn-Mayer Inc./Photofest)

nated her option contract with MGM in 1938. "We made you, and we are going to kill you!" Mayer warned. Walking out, the actress matter-of-factly replied, "Mr. Mayer, you did not make me. God made me. You are an old man. By the time I am 40 you will be dead."[33] Although she yearned to play in such films as *Madame Curie* and *For Whom the Bell Tolls*, Rainer's meteoric career, as the film critic David Thomson once put it, "crumbled so completely" that her two Oscars "might have been voodoo dolls."[34] After leaving Hollywood, the actress returned to Europe, studied medicine, aided refugees of the Spanish Civil War, entertained Allied troops, rebuilt a stage career, raised a daughter, and later traveled to such countries as India, Thailand, and China with her second husband—the wealthy New York publisher Robert Knittel. Before she died in 2014 at the age of 104, Rainer was the oldest living recipient of an Academy Award.

Vivien Leigh

A ravishing beauty, a stage and screen luminary, and, for 20 years, the distinguished Lady Olivier, **Vivien Leigh** was a star like no other. Similar to **Helen Hayes** and **Barbra Streisand**, Leigh made only 19 films—eight more than **Grace Kelly** but still a comparably modest sum for an actress of her stature. Among her short list of screen credits, however, two legendary, Oscar-winning roles stand out and are destined to withstand the test of time. As Scarlett O'Hara in *Gone with the Wind* (1939) and Blanche DuBois in *A Streetcar Named Desire* (1951), Leigh brilliantly personified a pair of widowed southern belles both struggling in their own way to find stability in a world that is fast leaving them behind.

Born in Darjeeling, Colonial India, on November 5, 1913, on the festive, fireworks-laden Guy Fawkes Day, Leigh was raised by her British father (an officer in the Indian Cavalry) and her strict Catholic mother (who may have been part Indian). As Mahatma Gandhi organized peasants, farmers, and urban laborers to nonviolently protest the rampant discriminations imposed by British rule, the future actress comfortably grew up amid the fragrance of jasmine and sandalwood in a genteel environment reminiscent of a Rudyard Kipling novel.

In 1920, while her parents remained in Calcutta, Leigh moved to England to be convent educated. After an apprenticeship at London's Royal Academy of Dramatic Art (RADA), she became an overnight success by way of her appearance in the 1935 play *The Mask of Virtue*. Opposite the established Laurence Olivier (with whom she fell in love), she subsequently starred in a succession of Shakespeare plays and as Queen Elizabeth I's lady-in-waiting in the film *Fire Over England* (1937).

Nevertheless, Leigh was largely unknown to 1930s Hollywood when the producer David O. Selznick began working on his colossal, Technicolor, and

Gone with the Wind (1939)

A Streetcar Named Desire (1951)

Revolutionary in the era of the Motion Picture Production Code (which enforced censorship and ensured penalties for women who stepped out of line), Vivien Leigh's portrayal of Scarlett O'Hara in *Gone with the Wind* (1939) became a significant symbol of growth, determination, resilience, and self-empowerment. (Metro-Goldwyn-Mayer Inc./Photofest)

Under the guidance of George Cukor (*left*)—the first of three directors to helm *Gone with the Wind* (1939), Vivien Leigh's recently widowed Scarlett O'Hara controversially dances with gambler Rhett Butler (played by Clark Gable) in this off-camera shot from the Atlanta Bazaar sequence. The film's second director, Victor Fleming, later reshot the sequence. Metro-Goldwyn-Mayer Inc./ Photofest)

ultimately 238-minute American Civil War epic *Gone with the Wind* (1939). Based on Margaret Mitchell's 1,037-page Pulitzer Prize–winning novel, *Gone with the Wind* is told almost entirely from the perspective of the lovely, lovable, willful, spoiled, self-absorbed, manipulative, and resilient Scarlett O'Hara. In a film that would cast 50 speaking roles and 2,400 extras, the frenzied search for Scarlett captivated the world's attention. Undoubtedly, it was the most sought-after role in cinema history: 1,400 hopefuls were considered for the part, including **Katharine Hepburn**, **Joan Crawford**, **Claudette Colbert**, **Helen Hayes**, **Loretta Young**, **Luise Rainer**, **Janet Gaynor**, and **Ginger Rogers**. **Susan Hayward**, a New York City fashion model then known as Edythe Marrener, was brought to Hollywood only to be told to return home. **Bette Davis**, who wanted the role, purportedly got *Jezebel* (1938) instead. And after Selznick "toyed with the idea of handing" the role to **Norma Shearer** (whose "fans disapproved of her playing a 'bad woman'"),[1] finalists Joan Bennett, Jean Arthur, and Charlie Chaplin's then-wife, Paulette Goddard, were tested.

But in dramatic 11th-hour fashion, during second-unit photography for the famous Burning of Atlanta sequence, Selznick's brother Myron (who acted as Laurence Olivier's American agent) introduced Leigh to the "brash and audacious" producer.[2] Seeing Leigh's "face in the firelight,"[3] Selznick had a revelation, and after a quick screen test, reportedly told the actress that the role of Scarlett was hers on Christmas Day 1938.

During production, Leigh worked for two hours every morning to achieve Scarlett's aristocratic southern accent and petulant, "fiddle-dee-dee" temperament before reporting for endless fittings, rehearsals, and photographic tests.[4] Suffering through the grueling shoot in constricting antebellum hoop skirts and corsets and with her breasts squeezed "together with adhesive tape," the actress worked "95 percent of the whole 125 days."[5] Whether concerning her character's fiery skirmishes with Rhett Butler (played by Clark Gable), the love triangle between Ashley Wilkes and Melanie Hamilton (Leslie Howard and **Olivia de Havilland**), or her efforts to salvage her beloved homestead of Tara, Leigh was featured in nearly every scene and persisted through three separate directors (George Cukor, the film's Best Director Oscar recipient Victor Fleming, and Sam Wood). For her participation, she received $25,000. (Illustrating the enormous gender pay gap in Hollywood, her costar, the established Clark Gable, worked for 71 days and earned $120,000.)

The character of Scarlett was revolutionary in the era of the Production Code, and echoing the immense popularity of the novel, she became a significant symbol of growth, determination, resilience, and self-empowerment. With World War II escalating at the time of *Gone with the Wind*'s release, Scarlett's defiant attitude inspired women throughout the United States. In a still-controversial story taking place within a racist society that is criticized and ultimately overthrown, Leigh encapsulated Scarlett's transformation from wealthy slave owner to one of the thousands of southern women forced by the war "to expand their definitions of 'proper' female behavior" and take on the duties of cook, seamstress, and untrained nurse.[6] While portraying a "Commandment-breaker,"[7] who, in one carriage scene, asks to put her cold hand in the pocket of her sister's beau, Leigh additionally portrayed Scarlett as a woman who is not above using her sexuality as a tool to advance and survive.

In December 1939, *Gone with the Wind* had its world premiere after three days of celebration in the city of Atlanta. Two months later, the celebrating continued at the 12th Academy Awards (1940) held at the Ambassador Hotel in midtown Los Angeles. For the final time in Oscar history, winners' names were leaked to the press in advance with a warning not to publish anything until each award had been presented. In a surprise victory, Best Supporting Actress winner Hattie McDaniel became the first Black performer to be presented an Academy Award. There was little question, however, as to who would win the Best Actress Oscar. Despite strong competition from the previous year's winner, **Bette Davis** (*Dark Victory*), as well as **Greer Garson** (*Goodbye, Mr. Chips*), Irene Dunne (*Love Affair*), and, in her first comedy, Greta Garbo (*Ninotchka*), Leigh was virtually guaranteed the Oscar and graciously took to the podium upon the announcement of her name. "Ladies and gentlemen," she said, "please forgive me if my words are inadequate in thanking you for your very great kindness. If I were to mention all those who have shown me such wonderful generosity with *Gone with the Wind*, I should have to entertain you with an oration as long as *Gone with the Wind* itself."[8]

For the final time in Oscar history, winners' names were leaked to the press in advance with a warning not to publish anything until each award had been presented. Still, there was no question that *Gone with the Wind* star Vivien Leigh, who was featured in nearly every scene, would prevail. The actress is pictured here at the 1940 Academy Awards at the Cocoanut Grove at the Ambassador Hotel in midtown Los Angeles with costar Olivia de Havilland, producer David O. Selznick, and fiancé Laurence Olivier (*right*). (© A.M.P.A.S.®/Photofest)

With a record-breaking 13 nominations and eight wins including Best Picture, *Gone with the Wind*—in a year teeming with cinematic masterpieces—came to represent the pinnacle of Hollywood's Golden Age. In addition, the film became the most successful motion picture in history by earning an adjusted-for-inflation worldwide box-office gross of $3.7 billion (ahead of *Avatar* [2009], *Titanic* [1997; starring **Kate Winslet**], *Star Wars* [1977], *Avengers: Endgame* [2019], *The Sound of Music* [1965; starring **Julie Andrews**], *E.T. the Extra-Terrestrial* [1982], *The Ten Commandments* [1956], and *Doctor Zhivago* [1965; starring **Julie Christie**]).

With her Best Actress Oscar in hand, Leigh cemented her status as an international superstar, and with Olivier (her fiancé and a first-time Best Actor nominee that evening for *Wuthering Heights*), she became part of one of the world's most fashionable celebrity couples. Draped for the Oscars in a spaghetti-strapped floral-print gown designed by Irene Lentz-Gibbons (then known as the Coco Chanel of America), the actress set the stage for Oscar fashion and developed into one of the most revered and emulated women. At 26, she was "the biggest movie star in the world."[9] And yet, despite Selznick's "efforts to get her to do more films" in Hollywood, Leigh, seemingly ungrateful, only appeared in *Waterloo Bridge* (1940; her personal favorite of her films) and *That Hamilton Woman* (1941; opposite Olivier) before returning "swiftly to wartime London."[10] There, she reembraced the theater, London's intellectual and literary circles, and her new 12th-century Buckinghamshire home with Olivier, Notley Abbey.

A fierce, tenacious actress on the outside, Leigh began to show signs of mental fragility. By the time she performed the role of the "weak-minded fantasist" Blanche DuBois in the screen adaptation of Tennessee Williams's Pulitzer Prize–winning play *A Streetcar Named Desire* (1951),[11] it became clear to many people that Blanche's psychiatric problems were all too similar to Leigh's own manic-depressive disorder.

While **Jessica Tandy** had originated the role on Broadway in 1947, Leigh—evoking a twisted and torn Scarlett O'Hara aching for a kinder, more chivalrous bygone era—was chosen to star in the movie after **Olivia de Havilland** turned the part down. Having played Blanche in the 1949 London West End production of the play directed by Olivier, Leigh ultimately teamed up with nine original Broadway cast members including Marlon Brando, Kim Hunter, and Karl Malden (the latter two of which went on to receive Oscars for their supporting work).

With Tennessee Williams and the director and Actors Studio cofounder Elia Kazan helping to "usher in a form of American filmmaking that was unabashedly literary," "unconcerned with glamour," and "less afraid of offending traditional pieties,"[12] *Streetcar* presented audiences with a perverse portrait of southern culture. Set in New Orleans, the film follows Leigh's penniless, delusional, and high-minded character as she comes to live with her sister, Stella (Hunter), and Stella's husband, Stanley (Brando), whose barbaric, sexually charged masculinity "depends on the subjection" of others.[13]

Unsurprisingly, the film alerted numerous censorship boards of the time. With the Production Code Administration and the National Legion of Decency demanding the removal of six minutes of fragmented material deemed too overt for audience consumption, a firestorm of controversy erupted. Ultimately, Warner Bros. acquiesced and slashed the film of virtually every reference to Blanche's promiscuous past, her nymphomania (including a flirtation with a visiting paperboy),

Gone with the Wind star Vivien Leigh holds up her freshly bequeathed statuette for photographers at the 12th Academy Awards (1940). Dressed in a spaghetti-strapped floral-print gown designed by Irene Lentz-Gibbons, the Indian-born British actress helped to set the stage for Oscar fashion. (© A.M.P.A.S.®/Photofest)

her nonvindicated rape at the hands of her brother-in-law, and details pertaining to her deceased husband's homosexuality and suicide. In 1993, 42 years after the film's release, an uncensored version of *Streetcar* containing Kazan's original vision was finally made available.

In a role that paralleled aspects of her own life, *Streetcar Named Desire* star Vivien Leigh won her second Best Actress Oscar for playing Blanche DuBois, a tragic character marred by mental illness. (Warner Bros. Pictures Inc./Photofest)

At a time when treatment for manic-depressive disorder was rudimentary, Leigh, throughout the 36-day film shoot for *Streetcar*, reportedly felt alienated from the Broadway cast, with Kazan exploiting her mental condition to enhance her desperate, emotionally intricate performance. In doing so, he had the walls on the set built to move in as the film progressed, contributing to a sense of claustrophobia. A rumored sighting of Brando kissing Olivier in a swimming pool outside Leigh's Hollywood mansion only complicated things further. Leigh followed up her work on *Streetcar* with a frenzied theatrical experiment on Broadway, alternating each night as Cleopatra in two separate plays (Shakespeare's *Antony and Cleopatra* and George Bernard Shaw's *Caesar and Cleopatra* [both 1951–1952]). Although most critics hailed her performances, one reviewer lambasted her, teetering the actress to the brink of collapse.

However, on Oscar night 1952, with competition that included former winners **Katharine Hepburn** (*The African Queen*) and **Jane Wyman** (*The Blue Veil*), Shelley Winters (*A Place in the Sun*), and Eleanor Parker (*Detective Story*), Leigh, masked in theatrical Cleopatra makeup, rejoiced when her name was broadcast over a radio backstage as the Best Actress of the year for her performance in *Streetcar*.

As the years passed on, Leigh's film appearances became more infrequent as her stage work accelerated. At the same time, her mental illness worsened, and her turbulent marriage to Olivier came to a sorrowful end, with Olivier unable to cope with his wife's increasingly outrageous mood swings. "I would rather have lived a short life with Larry than face a long one without him," she once said.[14] As fate would have it, the actress had her way. Survived by her daughter Suzanne (the child from Leigh's first marriage to the attorney Herbert Leigh Holman), Leigh died in 1967 at the age of 53, and the world bid farewell to a true acting legend.

Showcasing two contrasting styles of acting, Vivien Leigh (a queen of the British theater and Shakespeare) and Marlon Brando (an explosive disciple of the Method acting approach) converge in a climactic moment from *A Streetcar Named Desire* (1951). (Warner Bros. Pictures Inc./Photofest)

Ginger Rogers

Kitty Foyle (1940)

Feeling more valued for her looks than for her ability to act, the movie-musical star **Ginger Rogers** grew frustrated by the typecasting limitations of her field, which forced her to fight for dramatic roles. Wanting the part of Queen Elizabeth I opposite **Katharine Hepburn**'s doomed Mary Stuart in *Mary of Scotland* (1936), Rogers disguised herself for an "anonymous" screen test. Alas, when RKO studio heads "realized that it was Ginger" behind the opulent Elizabethan-era façade, they grinned and shook their heads. The actress, after all, "was their song-and-dance comedy [showgirl]."[1] How could she be imagined in any other way?

Before ascending to the heights of superstardom by dancing backward in high heels opposite Fred Astaire, Rogers, who was born Virginia McMath in Independence, Missouri, on July 16, 1911, got her start with the ongoing support of her mother. Indeed, Lela E. Rogers, who had twice rescued her daughter from childhood abduction (carried out by Ginger's father), was a paramount figure in Ginger's life. While Lela criticized her daughter for marrying at 17, she cautioned Ginger—a Charleston dance-craze champion—not to pursue vaudeville until she had labored to learn her craft as a singer, dancer, and comedienne. Having previously worked in Hollywood as a scenario writer for such silent-era stars as Theda Bara and Baby Marie, Lela knew show business. As a "buffer, negotiator, chaperon, and general advisor" to Ginger, she was able to safeguard her daughter "from many snags" and help to navigate her career in the same manner as the mothers of **Mary Pickford**, **Elizabeth Taylor**, and **Jodie Foster**.[2] However, many observers, including **Bette Davis**, who had worked with Lela and "other powerful Hollywood women to build the Hollywood Studio Club, where young actresses coming to town to pursue acting careers had somewhere safe to live,"[3] saw Lela as the archetype of

Ginger Rogers, as she appears in *Kitty Foyle* (1940), one of the most successful examples of the "woman's picture" genre. (RKO Radio Pictures Inc./Photofest)

the relentless stage mother (a term Ginger furiously objected to). As mimicked in the 1943, Ida Lupino–starring movie *The Hard Way*, Lela ultimately left her job as a newspaper reporter to accompany her daughter to New York in 1928. There, Ginger, who was admired for "her long, muscular legs,"[4] soon found herself in bit parts at Paramount's Astoria studio annex in Queens and on Broadway in the George and Ira Gershwin hit musical *Girl Crazy* (1930–1931).

With an excessive studio focus on movie musicals at the dawn of sound, Ginger, with Lela by her side, subsequently moved to Hollywood (a "town somehow immune to the suffering of the Great Depression").[5] As Ginger took up residence at the small, family-like RKO — the youngest and fifth largest of the major studios in Hollywood — the studio appointed Lela as an acting coach who helped to develop the talents of Lucille Ball, Jack Carson, Tyrone Power, and others. Meanwhile, Ginger, with her hair dyed bright blond, was assigned to the surreal cinematic chorus lines of the director-choreographer Busby Berkeley, who gave new life to the movie-musical genre by tracking "his salacious camera" between the legs of hundreds of identical chorus girls while underscoring Hollywood's penchant for presenting women as "objects of the male gaze."[6] Making her big break in *Gold Diggers of 1933* (1933), which used the adventures of Broadway chorus girls to reflect the realities of life during the Depression, Rogers was asked to dress down as a scantily clad gold coin while singing the opening hit theme song, "We're in the Money."

Graduating to the next level, Rogers partnered with the urbane, "skinny, [and] plain-faced" dancer, singer, actor, and choreographer Fred Astaire.[7] "Easy on both the eye and the ear,"[8] their nine films together at RKO, beginning with *Flying Down to Rio* (1933), kicked the heyday of the Hollywood musical into high gear. Variously set against the music and lyrics of Irving Berlin, Cole Porter, Jerome Kern, Dorothy Fields, Oscar Hammerstein II, and George and Ira Gershwin, their films drew on the same basic plotline formula, "with Fred falling for the girl, diffidently wooing her and finally getting her, [and] Ginger offering merely token resistance."[9] Pushed to perfection by never-ending rehearsals and Astaire's "meticulously exacting" directives,[10] the duo "danced away on the gleaming floors of penthouse nightclubs" while expressing such moods as seduction, exhilaration, "the tragedy of parting," and "the happy recapture of bygone romance."[11] RKO's reigning queen, **Katharine Hepburn**, was reported to have said that "Ginger gave [Fred] sex [appeal] and he gave her class."[12]

But soon after Rogers filmed the musical biopic *The Story of Vernon and Irene Castle* in 1939, she announced that she was ending her partnership with Astaire to pursue more dramatic roles. Although her career had been dotted with the occasional nonmusical, including the 1937 "theatrical boarding house" tearjerker *Stage Door* (opposite rival **Katharine Hepburn**),[13] Rogers had never been given parts considered too far outside her range. Venturing as far outside as possible, she eventually appeared in *Primrose Path* (1940; about a woman entrenched in a family of prostitutes). Then, in the "sanitized-for-the-screen" adaptation of Christopher Morley's 1939 novel (which incorporated an abortion),[14] she landed the role of her

career—that of the title character in *Kitty Foyle: The Natural History of a Woman* (1940).

Kitty Foyle serves as one of the most successful examples of the "woman's picture" genre (in which falling in love, marriage, and motherhood are three major cornerstones). It follows Rogers's character from the underprivileged part of Philadelphia to her industrious life as a secretary turned Manhattan shopgirl. Kitty's jobs—divergent from the fulfilling careers illuminated by **Joan Crawford** in *Mildred Pierce* (1945), **Olivia de Havilland** in *To Each His Own* (1946), **Glenda Jackson** in *A Touch of Class* (1973), **Faye Dunaway** in *Network* (1976), **Frances McDormand** in *Fargo* (1996), and **Julianne Moore** in *Still Alice* (2014)—are depicted as "a means to an end."[15] In addition, they are "secondary in importance" to the romantic relationships that she develops with an adventure-seeking publisher born into money (played by Dennis Morgan) and a young, penniless doctor (James Craig).[16] While

Receiving a cold reception from the elitist family of the man she has secretly married (played by Dennis Morgan), Ginger Rogers's title character—a working-class girl who grew up in a shanty-town—confronts her new in-laws in *Kitty Foyle* (1940). (RKO Radio Pictures Inc./Photofest)

In a lingerie-style dress deemed somewhat risqué for its day (and predating Cher by several decades), *Kitty Foyle* star Ginger Rogers holds her Best Actress Oscar at the 1941 Academy Awards. Standing beside her is Best Actor Oscar recipient James Stewart. (© A.M.P.A.S.®/ Photofest)

the film incorporates Rogers's trademark mockery of upper-class pretentiousness, it presented audiences with a cautionary tale of a woman's "Cinderella fantasies" and reinforced notions that "appearance is . . . central for all women" and that women should embrace the class-structure "status quo."[17]

Kitty Foyle proved to be a major hit and popularized what is still referred to in the garment trade as the "Kitty Foyle dress"—an austere dark dress with white collar and cuffs. With the film additionally containing "a hospital scene actresses kill for" (in which Kitty, alone and out of wedlock, loses her baby), the Academy voting block—eternal pushovers for "unwed-mother roles"[18]—handed Rogers a Best Actress Oscar nomination amid a cutthroat field of contenders. Her competition included the previous winners **Bette Davis** (*The Letter*) and **Katharine Hepburn** (*The Philadelphia Story*), Martha Scott (*Our Town*), and **Joan Fontaine** (*Rebecca*), whose producer, David O. Selznick, held "a second 'premiere' the day after the nominations [were] announced . . . and [orchestrated] the temporary renaming of Hollywood Boulevard to Rebecca Lane."[19] In turn, RKO gathered all of Rogers's good reviews and—in an unprecedented lobbying move designed to capture voters' attention—crammed them in an advertisement in the trade papers with the headline, "It's Unanimous!"[20]

Rogers arrived at the 13th Academy Awards (1941) in a revealing, lingerie-style gown deemed somewhat risqué for its day (and predating the Oscar dresses of **Barbra Streisand**, **Cher**, and **Halle Berry** by several decades). However, with every reason to believe that her chances of winning were slim, she contemplated staying at home to prepare for her early-hour studio call time on the set of *Tom, Dick and Harry* (1941). Upon the surprise announcement of her name as Best Actress inside the ballroom at the Biltmore Hotel, Rogers tearfully looked "at her mother," who escorted her to the stage.[21] "This is the greatest moment of my life," Rogers emoted. "I want to thank the one who stood by me faithfully—my mother."[22]

Capitalizing on her Oscar success, Rogers's career went on to include such box-office hits as *The Major and the Minor* (1942; in which her mother appears), *Week-end at the Waldorf* (1945), and the Technicolor musical *The Barkleys of Broadway* (1949; in which she reunited with Astaire and had to relearn many of her old dance techniques).

A Bible-quoting member of the conservative organization Daughters of the American Revolution, Rogers "spoke vehemently against Democratic President Franklin D. Roosevelt's New Deal policies" and maintained a persona at odds with a film industry likened "to the biblical sin cities of Sodom and Gomorrah."[23] In 1947, her mother, also a staunch conservative, appeared as a friendly witness before the House Un-American Activities Committee (HUAC)—an anti-Communist, subversion-combating branch of the U.S. House of Representatives that had been initially established to investigate Nazi propaganda infiltrating Hollywood films. There, she provided the names of the supposed Communist sympathizers Clifford Odets and *Kitty Foyle* screenwriter Dalton Trumbo (whose "share and share alike, that's democracy!" line from the 1943 film *Tender Comrade* Ginger had refused to say).[24] Lela later prevented Ginger from appearing in the 1952 film *Carrie* (eventually starring **Jennifer Jones** alongside Laurence Olivier) as a result of the film's "open propaganda" pertaining to bigamy.[25]

Aside from politics, Rogers remained a lifelong swimmer and tennis player who "never drank or smoked" and had a bar in her home that "served ice cream sundaes and sodas rather than liquor." She additionally advocated for film preservation and became a strong adversary against "the colorizing of classic black and white movies," which "made her feel 'painted up like a birthday cake.'"[26] The actress, who married five times and never had children, later rebuilt a stage career and toured internationally with the nightclub act Ginger Rogers & Co. She died in 1995 at the age of 83.

Joan Fontaine

Opting not to attend the 14th Academy Awards (1942) as a result of her early-hour studio call time the following morning, Best Actress Oscar nominee and New York Film Critics Award winner **Joan Fontaine** received a demanding, last-minute phone call from her older sister and fellow nominee, **Olivia de Havilland**, who unwaveringly insisted that Fontaine show up. According to **de Havilland**, who knew that the most anticipated moment of the night centered on the curious coincidence of the two famous sisters competing for the same highly coveted prize, "my absence would look odd," Fontaine later wrote.[1]

Acquiescing, Fontaine arrived at the ceremony with her husband, the actor Brian Aherne, as if she were attending a funeral or greeting the pope. With the Japanese attack on the U.S. naval base at Pearl Harbor less than three months prior and with the West Coast experiencing power blackouts and paranoia about more attacks coming, Fontaine, like **de Havilland**, had been put under surveillance by the U.S. government as a result of having been born in Japan (a country more loathed by Americans at the time than even Nazi Germany). As a result, Fontaine decided to dress up for the ceremony in a black mantilla veil—a decorative head-dress seen by many attendees as an overstep in style from the general dress-code modifications prescribed by the Academy out of respect for the United States' entrance into World War II.

In the Best Actress category, Fontaine faced competition from **de Havilland** (*Hold Back the Dawn*), **Greer Garson** (*Blossoms in the Dust*), Barbara Stanwyck (*Ball of Fire*), and the recent Academy president and former winner **Bette Davis** (*The Little Foxes*). Nominated for her performance in Alfred Hitchcock's *Suspicion* (1941; just as she had been nominated the previous year for Hitchcock's *Rebecca*), Fontaine

Suspicion (1941)

Joan Fontaine in a dramatic moment from director Alfred Hitchcock's *Suspicion* (1941), for which she became the only actor—male or female—to ever win the Oscar for a performance in a Hitchcock film. (RKO Radio Pictures Inc./Photofest)

froze upon the announcement of her name. Staring across the banquet table at her seemingly happy, loudly hand-clapping sister, Fontaine's reality began to blur, with a "kaleidoscopic" rush of "savage" childhood memories thwarting her ability to move, speak, or even blink. "We've won!" shouted **de Havilland**.[2] Nervously accepting her Oscar from presenter **Ginger Rogers**, Fontaine thanked the "ladies and gentlemen that voted" for her, acknowledged producer David O. Selznick, and eschewed any mention of her older sister. "And if Alfred Hitchcock were here tonight, I'd like to say to him, 'thank you, Hitch, with all my heart.'"[3]

The de Havilland sisters were separated in age by one year and three months and became natural-born adversaries from the start. While some people have claimed that their legendary feud was a publicity-driven hoax, their decades-long refusal to speak to each other (after the 1975 death of their mother, the British actress Lillian Fontaine) indicates otherwise. Early in her career, Fontaine wanted to follow her "big sister's hard-earned career path," but was banned from her sister's studio (Warner Bros.) and barred from being "publicized as **Olivia de Havilland**'s sister."[4] In addition, she was forced to take on a pseudonym (first "St. John," then "Burfield," and finally "Fontaine") so as not to be confused with her more established sibling. "I gave her examples of younger sisters who changed their names and had the best careers," **de Havilland** explained. "**Loretta Young** and Sally Blane, for instance."[5]

Born on October 22, 1917, Fontaine was raised in Tokyo, Japan, where the sisters' eccentric, atheist parents resided before their father (a British patent attorney and professor of French and English at the Imperial University) divorced their mother to marry "his Japanese housekeeper" (who was later subjected to the deplorable conditions of a Japanese American internment camp in Colorado).[6] Fontaine, a bright child with a high IQ of 160, nevertheless grew up to feel utterly second rate—thanks in part to her sister and her oftentimes sickly condition.

When the sisters' rivalry shifted to Hollywood many years later, **de Havilland** continued her dominance. Fontaine, a struggling starlet who was said to lack in "professional self-confidence,"[7] conversely floundered. Cast in the musical comedy *A Damsel in Distress* (1937; starring Fred Astaire), *Quality Street* (1937; starring **Katharine Hepburn**), the adventure drama *Gunga Din* (1939; starring Cary Grant), and the all-female comedy-drama *The Women* (1939; costarring **Joan Crawford** and **Norma Shearer**), Fontaine unrewardingly found herself in small, thankless roles.

But Fontaine capitalized on her shy, fragile, plain, and seemingly "aggressive docility" as part of her screen test for Hitchcock's lush, female gothic melodrama *Rebecca* (1940).[8] In the process, she went on to beat **Vivien Leigh**, **Loretta Young**, **Susan Hayward**, Margaret Sullavan, Anne Baxter, and even her older sister for the coveted role of Laurence Olivier's anonymous new bride, "I" de Winter. As part of her job offer, she became the contractual "property" of the Svengali-like *Gone with the Wind* producer David O. Selznick—a move that she later came to regret, as Selznick consistently loaned the actress out to competing studios for a higher profit. With *Rebecca* (Hitchcock's first American film) winning the Oscar for Best

BT-Pub-A9

Picture and Fontaine earning a nomination in the competitive race for Best Actress, the younger, more delicately attractive sister appeared to be catching up to—and possibly exceeding—her older sibling.

Intriguingly, Fontaine was never Hitchcock's first choice to play the lead in his 1941 follow-up, *Suspicion*. Having had to "coax" and "cajole" Fontaine's performance in *Rebecca* with "painstaking direction,"[9] Hitchcock was reluctant to work with her again and was eager to cast the French star Michèle Morgan instead. But with Fontaine hurled into stardom by the international success of *Rebecca*, the director was persuaded to reteam with his former "pupil," and before long, Fontaine set out to play the part of yet another beleaguered Hitchcock heroine.

Drawn from the genre of gothic romance, the RKO production of *Suspicion* presented Fontaine with the role of Lina McLaidlaw—a young and submissive heiress/spinster whom we first meet on a train reading a book about child psychology while being courted by a dashing but irresponsible playboy/gambler (portrayed

Director Alfred Hitchcock (*seated*) discusses a scene with actors Joan Fontaine and Cary Grant in this off-camera shot taken during the production of *Suspicion* (1941). (RKO Radio Pictures Inc./Photofest)

Vying for the same parts, the same Oscar, and oftentimes the same men, the legendary rivalry between Oscar-winning sisters Joan Fontaine (*left*) and Olivia de Havilland captured the public imagination for three quarters of a century. (Photofest)

by Cary Grant). Attracted to Grant's character and hastily willing to marry him, Lina gradually senses that her new husband may be trying to kill her. As a personification of Hitchcock's typically blond/virgin female lead, Fontaine represents a sensible but apprehensive woman living in silent terror. Like **Ingrid Bergman**, later on, in Hitchcock's *Spellbound* (1945), *Notorious* (1946), and *Under Capricorn* (1949) or **Grace Kelly** in *Dial M for Murder* (1954), *Rear Window* (1954), and *To Catch a Thief* (1955), Lina ultimately becomes the victim of oppressive, misogynistic forces as a result of her suspicion, insecurity, and mistrust.

In light of the Production Code (which demanded that a cinematic killer face punishment by law) and audiences' likely repudiation of Grant as a dangerous and threatening murderer, *Suspicion*, at the last minute and after a total of *four* filmed endings, was given a compromised, studio-imposed finale. In it, Fontaine's character is reconfigured as a wife with unsubstantiated fears and "neurotic imaginings." In accordance with Hitchcock's preferred but discarded ending, Lina, who is seen as "passionate, obsessive, and finally self-destructive,"[10] is willingly killed after drinking a glass of poisoned milk, but not before sending her husband off to the mailbox with a sealed, incriminating letter.

All the same, on Oscar night 1942, Fontaine found herself victorious (and thus monetarily revalued, with her official loan-out fee jumping up from $100,000 to $200,000 per picture). While many people judged her victory as "compensation for her loss in *Rebecca*,"[11] Fontaine nevertheless became the only actor—male or female—to ever win an Academy Award for a performance in a Hitchcock film.

With Fontaine's Oscar victory solidifying her status as one of the most sought-after female stars of the 1940s, she went on to appear in *The Constant Nymph* (1943; her personal favorite of her films), *Jane Eyre* (1943; opposite Orson Welles), and the artistically ambitious *Letter from an Unknown Woman* (1948; for which her company, Rampart Productions, was responsible). In the 1950s, she appeared in films such as *September Affair* (1950; featuring **Jessica Tandy**), the box-office hit *Ivanhoe* (1952; opposite **Elizabeth Taylor**), and *The Bigamist* (1953; directed by her costar Ida Lupino—one of an extraordinarily small teaspoon of women, alongside Dorothy Arzner and Wanda Tuchock, to have directed a Hollywood studio feature between 1930 and 1970). Eclipsed by changes within the film industry that favored more extreme sensibilities, Fontaine ultimately gravitated toward the stage and away from the silver screen beginning in the 1960s. "It's a worldwide public now with Madonna and all of these people," she said in 1987. "It seems that they want to be outrageous, otherwise no one will notice, I guess. It's extraordinary. There's no point being refined or knowledgeable or grammatical today. Oh, no, that's stuffy and pompous."[12]

In her later life, Fontaine, who gave birth to one daughter and adopted another from Peru, "studied cooking at the Cordon Bleu School, earned her pilot's license, [became] an expert golfer and fisherman, and won a championship as a member of a hot air ballooning team."[13] She even hosted her own late-1970s cable television talk show, *The Joan Fontaine Show*, and starred in the 1979 Vienna stage production of *The Lion in Winter* (for which **Katharine Hepburn** had won the Oscar in the film version). While married four times and courted in her day by the likes Howard Hughes, Prince Aly Khan, Joseph P. Kennedy, and, at a White House event, then–U.S. Vice President Lyndon Johnson, Fontaine spent her final years surrounded by dogs in the flower-garden paradise of her Northern Californian villa, half a world away from her estranged older sister. "I married first, won the Oscar before **Olivia** did, and if I die first, she'll undoubtedly be livid because I beat her to it!"[14] At the age of 96, survived by her sister, Fontaine passed away on December 15, 2013.

Greer Garson

Before the December 7, 1941, attack on Pearl Harbor, which precipitated the United States' entry into World War II, Hollywood largely remained reluctant to tackle the evils of fascism. Pressures from foreign governments, fears of losing foreign revenues, and Washington's isolationist stance prompted the Production Code Administration to caution the Hollywood studios (the majority of which were run by Jewish businessmen) from criticizing the Nazis. Only a small handful of anti-Nazi films, including *Confessions of a Nazi Spy* (1939), *The Great Dictator* (1940), *The Man I Married* (1940), *The Mortal Storm* (1940), and *So Ends Our Night* (1941), depicted stories specifically referring to the persecution and murder of the Jews by the Nazis that later escalated with the systematic, Nazi-sponsored genocide of up to 17 million people including six million European Jews. While Hollywood films such as *Hitler's Children* (1943), *Hangman Also Die!* (1943), *The Cross of Lorraine* (1943), *None Shall Escape* (1944), and *The Seventh Cross* (1944; featuring **Jessica Tandy**) continued this trend, it was not until after the war that the full horror of Nazi brutality became understood and all too agonizingly detailed onscreen. Part of this came by way of the "documentary films made by Allied forces after the liberation of [several] German camps."[1] Another part came by means of such feature films as *The Stranger* (1946; with **Loretta Young**), *Kapò* (1959), *The Diary of Anne Frank* (1959), *Judgment at Nuremburg* (1961), *The Pawnbroker* (1964), *Sophie's Choice* (1982; with **Meryl Streep**), *Schindler's List* (1993), *The Pianist* (2002), and *The Reader* (2008; with **Kate Winslet**).

In a film that personified a country, a community, and a family struggling to overcome the threat of fascist aggression and the horrific fate that national defeat would have imposed, the Best Picture Oscar–winning drama *Mrs. Miniver* (1942)

Mrs. Miniver (1942)

A Nazi air pilot (played by Helmut Dantine) nervously holds Greer Garson's character at gunpoint in the top-grossing, morale-boosting drama *Mrs. Miniver* (1942). (Metro-Goldwyn-Mayer Inc./ Photofest)

GREER GARSON - Metro Goldwyn Mayer

GXGX-10

became—in the words of British Prime Minister Winston Churchill—"propaganda worth a hundred battleships."[2] Inspired by the writings of Jan Struther, helmed by Best Director Oscar recipient William Wyler, and starring the Anglo-Irish actress **Greer Garson** in the title role, the film centers on the courageous matriarch of an upper-middle-class British family in Kent protecting her family during the bleak days of the sustained Nazi air bombing of the United Kingdom. While her son goes off to the front and her husband (played by Garson's nine-time costar Walter Pidgeon) "takes part in the Dunkirk evacuation," Mrs. Miniver maintains the home front as "the turmoil of war closes in all around them."[3]

In one harrowing scene, Garson's character, while strolling in her garden one morning, stumbles upon a sleeping Nazi paratrooper, who eventually holds her at gunpoint in her house while demanding food. Weakened and collapsing from utter exhaustion (thus allowing Mrs. Miniver the chance to steal his gun), the indignant pilot (played by the Austrian actor and real-life Nazi concentration camp survivor Helmut Dantine) rises up to proclaim that England will ultimately fall. "We will come," he warns. "We will bomb your cities!"[4] To that, Garson's character—vulnerable yet stoic—slaps him across the face before the police arrive to take him away. Later in the film, as Nazi bombs fall on her village, she huddles in her family's backyard bomb shelter while attempting to calm her children to sleep with a reading of Lewis Carroll's *Alice in Wonderland*.

Mrs. Miniver was "produced in the shadow of headlines" (as described by Garson's costar Teresa Wright) and wrapped soon after the Japanese attack on Pearl Harbor.[5] U.S. President Franklin D. Roosevelt, who saw the film at a special advance screening, ordered it to be rushed into theaters so that audiences could see it as quickly as possible. Just as the German director Leni Riefenstahl had managed to rally Nazi support by way of her 1935 documentary *Triumph of the Will*, *Mrs. Miniver* struck a deep emotional chord with American audiences and helped to inspire and mobilize freedom-loving citizens around the world (including isolationist Americans, in particular).

Born in East Ham, Essex, England, on September 29, 1904, Garson admitted great embarrassment to being in Hollywood and working on a studio soundstage while bombs were dropping on her country and killing an estimated 40,000 British civilians. Two years before the war, Garson—a British and French university literature scholar turned London stage actress, had been tutored by Laurence Olivier. Soon after, MGM studio head Louis B. Mayer discovered her while on a scouting trip to Europe and offered the "richly syllabled," "flame-haired" actress a $500-a-week, seven-year option contract ("the biggest salary ever paid [to] a beginner in pictures").[6] At "the mature age of 33,"[7] Garson subsequently moved to California with her widowed mother. However, because the studio was not certain how to correctly cast her or light her cinematographically, the actress was "groomed and tested" for months upon her arrival.[8] During this tedious time, Garson suffered from malnutrition while attempting to conform to the extreme dieting standards of the slim-line Hollywood figure. In frustration, she asked to be released from

Greer Garson, in character as Kay Miniver, poses for a publicity photo for *Mrs. Miniver* (1942). One of the biggest stars of the 1940s and one of the queens of MGM, Garson, who comparatively became famous late in her career in her mid-30s, embodied a specific vision of a "lady" of class and dignity. (Metro-Goldwyn-Mayer Inc./Photofest) her contract so as to return to England to assist in the British wartime efforts. But like many of her acting peers, she was instructed by her government to remain in Hollywood, where, as an artistic ambassador, her morale-boosting, pro-British patriotism in films such as *Goodbye, Mr. Chips* (1939; in which she made her screen debut), *Pride and Prejudice* (1940), *Mrs. Miniver*, and *Random Harvest* (1942) could be of greater value. In addition, she volunteered her time with the British Red Cross and the American Red Cross, raised funds through war bonds, and entertained soldiers at the famed Hollywood Canteen.

As a result of *Mrs. Miniver*'s massive success, Garson emerged as an international superstar, a top box-office attraction, and above all, a beloved, idealized symbol of stalwart female heroism. "You made us feel more brave than we actually were," wrote the queen of England in a letter to the actress. "To you, we will all be eternally grateful."[9] Humbled by her overwhelming embrace, Garson, much like **Julie Andrews** and **Emma Thompson** several decades later, continued to be typecast in charming and virtuous roles that stayed close to the "dignified perfect lady" persona. Although she yearned to play for once a "real bitch," she understood her place in "the present time and the fact that [she was] fighting for the retention of certain values."[10]

At the politically charged 15th Academy Awards (1943), which were held for the last time in a private ballroom, Gary Cooper solemnly reminded the audience that it was "possible to have this banquet only because men in uniform are being shot and killed on foreign battlegrounds."[11] With the ceremony extending into the midnight hours, **Joan Fontaine** presented the award for Best Actress at roughly 1:00 a.m. A virtual shoo-in, Garson clinched the Oscar for *Mrs. Miniver* (which had been nominated for a total of 12 awards). In the process, she knocked out former recipients **Katharine Hepburn** (*Woman of the Year*) and **Bette Davis** (*Now, Voyager*), as well as Rosalind Russell (*My Sister Eileen*) and *Mrs. Miniver* Best Supporting Actress winner Teresa Wright (*The Pride of the Yankees*). Taking the stage, Garson, in front of a heavy-eyed audience, delivered a five-and-a half-minute speech (one of the longest in Oscar history). With her "vibrant speaking voice,"[12] she praised the Allied forces, disparaged the need to compete for Oscar glory, and thanked nearly everyone including her childhood pediatrician.

While Garson's career was at its peak, her personal life soon became an issue. In the summer of 1943, just as she was wrapping production on the film *Madame Curie*, Garson alarmed the MGM publicity department and aroused Hollywood gossip columnists Louella Parsons, Hedda Hopper, and Sheilah Graham by marrying Richard Ney, the young American actor—12 years her junior—who had played her son Vin in *Mrs. Miniver*. Alas, their difficult, four-year marriage did not survive. Accordingly, Ney (along with his *Mrs. Miniver* character) was shut out of the commercially disastrous sequel, *The Miniver Story* (1950), in which Garson's once-vivacious matriarch faces terminal illness.

Ironically, the demise of the Mrs. Miniver character coincided with the financial misfortunes of MGM and the termination of Louis B. Mayer. Coupled with the rise of television and the public demanding a new, postwar brand of movie-star charisma, Garson, like Greta Garbo and **Norma Shearer** before her, stepped down from her MGM throne to make way for the likes of Ava Gardner, Deborah Kerr, and Lana Turner. Though she continued to work sporadically and earned a seventh Best Actress Oscar nomination for portraying First Lady Eleanor Roosevelt in the 1960 film *Sunrise at Campobello*—a nomination that ultimately placed her behind **Meryl Streep** (with 17 Best Actress nominations), **Katharine Hepburn** (with 12), and **Bette Davis** (with 10), Garson's star largely faded from the silver screen.

A regal actress who always insisted on four o'clock tea, Garson personified the wartime era like no other female star (with the exception of the million-dollar-legged Betty Grable). Between 1941 and 1945, she matched **Bette Davis**'s record of five consecutive Best Actress nominations. In addition, she became the only Best Actress winner of the World War II era to win the Academy Award for a film specifically about that war. With a string of noble parts that she once described as "walking cathedrals," Garson, who epitomized a time when "railroad stations . . . were crowded with men in uniform, . . . giving a last embrace before [departing] for a distant port,"[13] undoubtedly left an indelible mark on the hearts and minds of many people. The actress died in 1996 at the age of 91.

Jennifer Jones

The Song of Bernadette (1943)

Bernadette Soubirous (1844–1879) was a Catholic peasant from Lourdes—a small town "in a deeply inconvenient corner of southwest France."[1] On February 11, 1858, while gathering firewood with her sister and a friend, the sickly, impoverished, and illiterate 14-year-old—who would die of tuberculosis at 35 and later be canonized by Pope Pius XI as *Saint* Bernadette—"suddenly felt a gust of wind."[2] Looking up, she claimed to have had a vision of the Blessed Virgin Mary. Following her impulses, she then reported a series of subsequent visions that drew a mixture of suspicion and hope. During the reign of Louis-Napoléon, Bernadette's visions purportedly led to the discovery of a holy water spring and a long sequence of "miraculous" cures. To this day, more than six million worshipers travel every year to "the religious theme park" of Lourdes, passing by the "kitsch stores that line the road" to the legendary spring to fill their "five-galloon jugs with faith."[3]

Fast-forward some 80-plus years to 20th Century-Fox casting its lead in *The Song of Bernadette* (1943), the director Henry King's inspirational drama based on the best-selling novel by the Austro-Hungarian writer Franz Werfel. For the principal role, hundreds of proven young actresses were tested and considered, including Anne Baxter, Gene Tierney, Teresa Wright, and Linda Darnell (who appeared in the film, uncredited, as the Virgin Mary). But in the end, despite Werfel's desire to see his close friend **Luise Rainer** in the lead, the part of Bernadette went to a complete unknown. An "American **Vivien Leigh**" with a flawless complexion, big and credulous eyes, and a child-like simplicity and earnestness that could hardly be faked,[4] **Jennifer Jones**—a shy, eerily sensitive Catholic girl from Tulsa, Oklahoma—seemed the perfect embodiment of the teenage prophet from Lourdes.

Launched to stardom by Hollywood producer David O. Selznick, Jennifer Jones stars in the religious drama *The Song of Bernadette* (1943), in which her character reacts calmly and reverently to visions of the Virgin Mary. (Twentieth Century Fox Film Corporation/Photofest)

Jones was born Phylis Lee Isley on March 2, 1919, to a family of proprietors who ran a traveling circus as well as vaudeville houses and independent movie theaters. She studied at Northwestern University before moving to New York in 1938 to attend the American Academy of Dramatic Arts, the oldest sustained school for acting "in the English-speaking world,"[5] where she met her first husband, the actor Robert Walker. Although she appeared in two films in 1939 under the name Phylis Isley, the actress was soon rechristened as the more exotic-sounding "Jennifer Jones" by the man responsible for launching her career: the Pygmalion-like, iron-willed Hollywood producer David O. Selznick.

Under Selznick's tight control, little information regarding Jones was initially revealed, and a news blackout was enforced, with no photos or interviews granted until *The Song of Bernadette* had had its premiere. To be sure, Selznick, who understood the value of publicity and its ability to generate as much impact on an actor's career as his or her performance onscreen, was replicating the blueprint that he had adopted for **Vivien Leigh** on *Gone with the Wind* (1939). In that situation, Selznick "wanted his Scarlett to be the perfect little virgin southern belle." He therefore decided that Leigh and her then-fiancé, Laurence Olivier, should not live together during production, and he "put 24-hour guard service around [the actress's] house so that no one would come near her to try to take pictures of maybe [Olivier] coming in or coming out."[6]

Despite such similar efforts, an aura of mystery around Jones began to feed the public's insatiable curiosity, and ultimately Selznick was coerced into revealing the tiniest scrap or tidbit pertaining to his "newfound" protégé. While concealing the fact that Jones's reality was that of a struggling married mother of two—a stinging revelation that could damage the unblemished studio image that he was carefully constructing for her—Selznick paralleled the actress's life with her virginal (and much-younger) title character. In an effort to make the public believe that she was just "discovered," her screen credit even read, "And Introducing Jennifer Jones As Bernadette."[7]

Selznick saw "stardom very clearly as a construct that's been created in order to sell things,"[8] and his gamble with Jones initially paid off. *The Song of Bernadette* earned 12 Oscar nominations and became one of the highest grossing films of the World War II era. Ahead of the 1944 Academy Awards (which fell, incidentally, on Jones's 25th birthday), Jones was touted as the Best Actress Oscar frontrunner. Having already captured the inaugural Golden Globe Award, she went on to beat former winners **Joan Fontaine** (*The Constant Nymph*) and **Greer Garson** (*Madame Curie*), Jean Arthur (*The More the Merrier*), and box-office champion **Ingrid Bergman** (*For Whom the Bell Tolls*), who reportedly "cried all the way through *Bernadette*" because she realized that she had "lost the award."[9] After the proceedings, which, out of respect for World War II, were held for the first time in a public theater (Grauman's Chinese in Hollywood) as opposed to a lavish ballroom, **Bergman** rushed backstage to congratulate Jones, who, drying tears, made an earnest apology

for her win. But the Swedish screen star graciously retorted, "No, Jennifer. Your Bernadette was better than my Maria."[10]

In hindsight, Jones's tears had less to do with her Oscar victory and more with the dissolution of her marriage to Robert Walker (with whom she was costarring in Selznick's 1944 super-production of *Since You Went Away*). Signifying all too well the conspiratorial aspects of the Hollywood star system, which relied on the creation and maintenance of a "more interesting, more exotic, or more acceptable-than-the-truth" star persona (in order to turn actors, literally, into gods and goddesses removed from the realities of life),[11] the false impression surrounding Jones was eventually exposed. In a town comprising hundreds of movie reporters, where flash bulbs "greeted stars when they arrived for dinner at a restaurant," and where "restaurant owners always kept some of the best seats in the house for the press,"[12] the Hollywood gossip industry zeroed in on the truth, with its feared queen bee, Louella Parsons, finally detecting Selznick's great lie. As **Helen Hayes** explained, "Everyone lived in deadly fear of incurring the displeasure of Louella Parsons [and] her arch-rival Hedda Hopper. These two women were tough, mean monarchs, reigning over the movie colony with their viper tongues or typewriters."[13] As self-appointed censors of Hollywood, Parsons and Hopper "turned fear into a profitable business."[14] "It was almost blackmail," **Joan Fontaine** said.[15] Using their syndicated, internationally read columns, "they had the power to make or break deals, and ruin careers and marriages. Nothing about the lives of the stars— their politics, friends, family, health, or love affairs—was sacred."[16]

Jones, in a desperate effort to rectify her situation and salvage her public image, filed for divorce on the day following her Oscar victory. Eventually the actress, who already possessed an uncomfortable presence in the limelight, accepted Selznick's proposal of marriage and dazzling guarantee of "unimaginable personal success."[17] Like Norma Talmadge (the wife of the studio executive Joseph M. Schenck) and **Norma Shearer** (Mrs. Irving G. Thalberg) before her, Jones became the protected consort of a Hollywood king and consequently circumvented many of the trappings of the Hollywood studio system.

Over the next two decades, Selznick micromanaged Jones's career. Ignoring the principle of "being recognizable" onscreen as the guiding key to movie popularity,[18] Selznick conversely paraded Jones in a carousel of chameleon-like characters and appearances that preceded **Meryl Streep** and **Cate Blanchett** by several decades. In *Duel in the Sun* (1946), for example, she plays a half-Hispanic temptress. In *Portrait of Jennie* (1948), she plays a ghost. In *We Were Strangers* (1949), she plays a Cuban revolutionary. In *Gone to Earth* (1950), she plays a half gypsy turned fox. And in *Love Is a Many-Splendored Thing* (1955), she plays a China-born Eurasian doctor.

Interfering in how the actress should be costumed, photographed, and directed, not to mention whom she should be paired up with romantically onscreen, Selznick made Jones his primary concern. That concern, however, turned into an obsessive preoccupation, and after producing the disastrously received Technicolor remake of *A Farewell to Arms* (1957; with Jones paired up with Rock Hudson), Selznick, who suffered from mental breakdowns, altogether retired.

After Selznick's death in 1965, Jones semiretired from acting herself and suffered a period of emotional instability that culminated with an attempted suicide-by-drowning at a beach in Malibu. But with her third marriage in 1971 to the millionaire industrialist and renowned art collector Norton Simon, she found new purpose and helped to transform Simon's Pasadena, California–based Norton Simon Museum into one of the most revered private art collections west of Chicago. Under her influence, the museum underwent a major renovation. Inspired by Jones's fascination with Eastern philosophy by way of her spiritual journeys to India, it began to house a growing collection of Indian, Southeast Asian, and Himalayan art. Following the attempted suicide of Jones's second son and the tragic 1976 suicide of her daughter, Mary Jennifer Selznick (who jumped to her death from a building in Los Angeles), the actress additionally lent her voice and money to mental health issues.

Jones, "in the throes of dementia,"[19] died in 2009 at the age of 90. In looking back at her career, which earned a total of five Oscar nominations (an astounding number, considering her purported narrow range and torturous relationship with acting), she is likely to be best remembered for the luminous and ethereal quality that she engendered to create Bernadette. Her calm, reverential reaction to the Marian apparitions—which initially turned her character into the laughingstock of Lourdes—gives warrant to the film's befitting prologue: "For those who believe in God, no explanation is necessary. For those who *do not* believe in God, no explanation is possible."[20]

Ingrid Bergman

At the 31st Academy Awards (1959), held at the RKO Pantages Theatre, **Ingrid Bergman** presented the prestigious Oscar for Best Picture, marking her first return to Hollywood in nearly a decade. As she walked onstage to present the award, the audience leapt to its feet in a rousing ovation. Here again was the woman who—once idolized as a saint and then vilified as a sinner—still remained a dignified, gracious, and unpretentious superstar.

Originating from a liberal country that was among the first to end "a husband's legal power over his wife" and to grant women "a universal and equal right to vote and to stand as candidates in national elections,"[1] Bergman was born in Stockholm, Sweden, on August 29, 1915. Unfortunately, her childhood was marred by tragedy: her German-born mother died when she was three, and her beloved artist father, who owned a photography shop and instilled in his shy daughter a lifelong passion for filmmaking, died when she was 12. Possessed with a combination of natural grace, beauty, and raw emotion, Bergman veered into acting by way of working as a film extra at the Råsunda film studio. She eventually received a scholarship to attend the Royal Dramatic Theatre School in Stockholm. Although it "was the stage that drew her on,"[2] Bergman returned to the movies and ultimately emerged as a leading force in Swedish cinema in films such as *Intermezzo* (1936) and *En kvinnas ansikte* (1938; later remade in Hollywood in 1941 as *A Woman's Face* with **Joan Crawford**).

But Bergman felt limited in Sweden and wanted to get out in the world. Towering at 5-foot-10 (alongside the future actresses **Louise Fletcher** and **Charlize Theron** and the 5-foot-11 **Nicole Kidman**), Bergman left her native country to star in the UFA production of *Die vier Gesellen* (1938) in Nazi Berlin. Although Joseph Goebbels—the Nazi minister of propaganda and overseer of the German film industry—wanted to retain Bergman for her perceived superior exemplification

Gaslight (1944)

Anastasia (1956)

As the victim of an insidious form of abuse, Ingrid Bergman's character is confronted with contradictory evidence by her scheming husband (played by Charles Boyer) in *Gaslight* (1944). (Metro-Goldwyn-Mayer Inc./ Photofest)

of Aryan beauty, she caught the eye of the Hollywood producer David O. Selznick and was happily brought to California to appear in the 1939 remake of *Intermezzo*. While Selznick saw in the young starlet a warmer, more accessible Greta Garbo, he nevertheless wanted Bergman to change her allegedly unpronounceable, too-German-sounding name, go on a "slimming diet,"[3] and have her thick eyebrows and crooked teeth adjusted. However, after Bergman refused and got "ready to fly back to Sweden,"[4] Selznick acquiesced. Although the actress was still required to undergo accent modification (under the guidance of the same speech therapist who would help **Loretta Young** achieve her Swedish accent for 1947's *The Farmer's Daughter*), Bergman became the first studio actress since **Janet Gaynor** to simply be promoted by way of her fresh, natural, and nonartificial beauty.

Within three years, Bergman had crept "into the affection of the American public" and starred in one of the most popular and iconic and movies of all time: *Casablanca* (1942).[5] Within five years, she took home her first Best Actress Oscar for *Gaslight* (1944) for her haunting, layered performance as Paula Alquist—a controlled wife driven to near insanity and ultimate vengeance by a deceptive husband (played by Charles Boyer) who suggests that "the things she sees and hears are all figments of her imagination."[6] Based on Patrick Hamilton's tension-building, late-Victorian-era-set stage play, *Gaslight* contributed to a growing host of thrilling female gothic melodramas including *Wuthering Heights* (1939), the **Joan Fontaine**–starring films *Rebecca* (1940) and *Jane Eyre* (1943), *Experiment Perilous* (1944), and a few years later, the **Olivia de Havilland**-starring movies *The Heiress* (1949) and *My Cousin Rachel* (1952). Historically observed, these dark-themed dramas, which featured women in innocent and often victimized roles (i.e., stripped of their rights, curbed in their participation, and limited in their ability to make their own decisions), offered audiences a stark contrast to the vast number of women in real life partaking for the first time in a wartime economy.

As in previous ceremonies and out of respect for the ravaging war abroad, guests of the 17th Academy Awards (1945) refrained from tuxedos, full dress suits, excessive jewelry, and décolletage. Bergman, who, like many stars, undertook "trips and tours to entertain the [American] troops,"[7] arrived at the ceremony in an austere black dress similar to the one she had worn the year before. With the Oscar trophy up for grabs in what was seen as a wide-open year for lead actresses, Bergman found herself among a group of contenders that included Barbara Stanwyck (*Double Indemnity*) and former winners **Claudette Colbert** (*Since You Went Away*), **Bette Davis** (*Mr. Skeffington*), and **Greer Garson** (*Mrs. Parkington*). After losing to the Swedish star, Stanwyck admitted to the press that she did not "feel at all bad about the Award because [her] favorite actress won it."[8]

Despite the accolades, Bergman increasingly grew bored of Hollywood's "synthetic" brand of filmmaking and wrote a letter of introduction to the Italian neorealist filmmaker Roberto Rossellini,[9] whose gritty wartime dramas *Roma, città aperta* (1945) and *Paisà* (1946) had profoundly moved her. To her delight, the actress

A portrait of Ingrid Bergman, in character, from director George Cukor's Hitchcock-influenced female gothic melodrama *Gaslight* (1944). (Metro-Goldwyn-Mayer Inc./Photofest)

received an invitation from Rossellini to collaborate on the film *Stromboli* (1950). With that, she conscientiously suspended her Hollywood career and relocated to Italy.

When news leaked in 1950 that Bergman and Rossellini were romantically involved and had borne a son out of wedlock, a wrath of anger, betrayal, and moral turpitude was unleashed internationally. In India, the country's first prime minister, Jawaharlal Nehru, lambasted Rossellini as "a scoundrel."[10] In Italy, the headline-dominating scandal gave life to the ravenous and pervasive paparazzi, which relentlessly followed Bergman and Rossellini everywhere. The Italian actress **Anna Magnani**—Rossellini's longtime muse and lover—simultaneously begged newspaper reporters to leave her alone with her "tragedy" before promising to "break every plate of spaghetti in Rome over his head."[11]

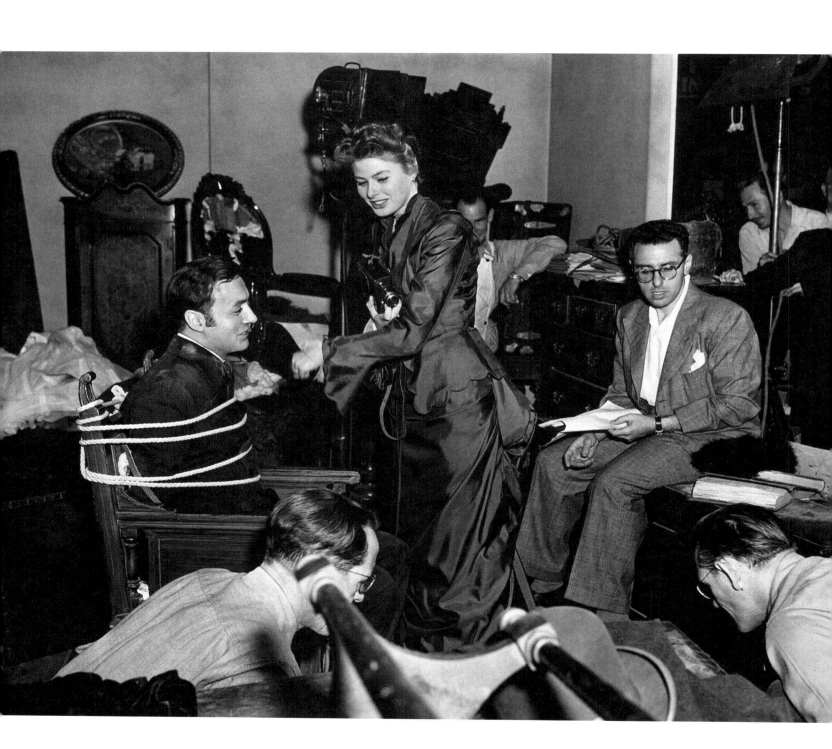

In the United States, the reaction was even more severe. For having previously denied pregnancy rumors to the conservative Hollywood gossip columnist Hedda Hopper, who—with her ties to the FBI director J. Edgar Hoover—had already tried to have Charlie Chaplin "thrown out of the country" for his "subversive" views,[12] Bergman appeared to be the latest celebrity target. Exemplifying a dark period in American history when Hollywood was under fire by the Republican U.S. Senator Joseph McCarthy and the House Un-American Activities Committee (HUAC), the once-beloved star, who had a husband and an 11-year-old daughter at home, was instantly branded "a powerful influence for evil."[13] Having allegedly "perpetrated an assault upon the institution of marriage," Bergman was additionally branded as an "apostle of degradation" and a "danger to American womanhood."[14] "It seemed I had corrupted the human race," she later said,[15] having no idea that her personal life (which included previous affairs with Gary Cooper, Gregory Peck, the photographer Robert Capa, and her *Joan of Arc* director Victor Fleming) could be perceived as so important. In many parts of the world and especially in the most religious corners of the United States, her "adultery-glorifying" films were boycotted, and her scheduled appearance on the popular *Ed Sullivan Show* was famously canceled. Although the dust finally did settle (in effect, paving the way for the Vatican-condemned but hardly career-derailing love affair between **Elizabeth Taylor** and Richard Burton 15 years later), Bergman's remaining working life largely transpired in Europe.

Despite some studio resistance (and Rossellini's strong disapproval), the catalyst for Bergman's Hollywood return came by way of the Ukrainian director Anatole Litvak's screen adaptation of the 1954 stage play *Anastasia* (1956). The lavish 20th Century-Fox / CinemaScope / DeLuxe Color production, which was shot in London, Paris, and Copenhagen, once again touched on the theme of female madness, centering on a suicidal and amnesiac refugee who bears a striking resemblance to the Russian Grand Duchess Anastasia. Based on the real-life impostor Anna Anderson (1896–1984), Bergman's character is hired by the scheming, fortune-seeking General Bounine (played by Yul Brynner) to impersonate Anastasia—the youngest daughter of Russia's murdered Czar Nicholas II, who may or may not have survived the July 1918 Romanov family execution ordered by the Bolsheviks.

Anastasia, which Bergman prepared for by spending time in a mental asylum, proved to be a moral testing ground for the Swedish star after years of being excommunicated. While the film's producer, Buddy Adler, enlisted the "moral and upright reputation" of Bergman's costar **Helen Hayes** (as the skeptical Dowager Empress) to buttress the film from any lingering resentment that audiences may still have harbored toward Bergman,[16] the film ultimately proved to be a genuine hit. At long last, in January 1957, Bergman terminated her exile and made "her first return to American soil" since 1949 to collect the New York Film Critics Award for her performance in the film. With a strong spirit of "sentimental forgiveness" in

At a time when films were rehearsed like stage plays, *Gaslight* star Ingrid Bergman, who is seen here holding the 16 mm camera that she carried everywhere she went, enjoyed a light moment on set with costar Charles Boyer (*left*) and women's-point-of-view director George Cukor. (Metro-Goldwyn-Mayer Inc./Photofest)

the air and "fond crowds [coming] out to welcome her,"[17] the actress's notorious fall from grace had ostensibly been absolved.

Bergman was nominated for Best Actress for *Anastasia* ahead of the 29th Academy Awards (1957) and was seen as the prohibitive favorite. She faced a short list of contenders consisting of the veteran winner **Katharine Hepburn** (*The Rainmaker*), Carroll Baker (*Baby Doll*), Nancy Kelly (*The Bad Seed*), and the British actress Deborah Kerr (*The King and I*). Already scheduled to appear in Paris in the play *Tea and Sympathy*, the actress won her second Oscar in absentia, with her friend and former costar Cary Grant accepting it on her behalf. Soaking in a Paris bathtub at the Hôtel Raphael, where the actress—in the midst of her divorce from Rossellini—resided with her three Italian children (including the future model, actress, and filmmaker Isabella Rossellini), Bergman heard the joyous news of her victory over the radio. "Dear Ingrid," Grant stated. "If you can hear me . . . I want you to know that each of the other nominees and all of the people with whom you worked on *Anastasia* . . . and every one of us here tonight . . . send you our congratulations, our love, our admiration, and every affectionate thought."[18]

With the ability to act in five languages (Swedish, English, German, Italian, and French), Bergman became one of the most international performers in the history of entertainment. When she won her third Oscar (for her supporting role in the 1974 film adaptation of the Agatha Christie novel *Murder on the Orient Express*), she additionally became one of the most elite, trailing the four-time Best Actress Oscar winner **Katharine Hepburn** and drawing even today with **Meryl Streep**.

Besides working with Rossellini on five feature films including *Europa '51* (1951) and *Journey to Italy* (1954), Bergman, during the course of her long career, expanded her artistic growth and technical acting know-how by working with three of cinema's all-time directing greats: Alfred Hitchcock, Jean Renoir, and Ingmar Bergman.

Taking cues from **Joan Crawford** in *Female on the Beach* (1955) and *Autumn Leaves* (1956), **Vivien Leigh** in *The Deep Blue Sea* (1955) and *The Roman Spring of Mrs. Stone* (1961), and **Simone Signoret** in *Room at the Top* (1959), Bergman additionally helped to validate concepts of romance linked to older women. Before the likes of **Anne Bancroft**, **Julie Christie**, **Diane Keaton**, **Cher**, **Susan Sarandon**, and **Helen Mirren** burst onto the scene in desirable older-women roles opposite younger men, Bergman venturesomely did so in films such as *Goodbye Again* (1961), *The Yellow Rolls-Royce* (1964), and *Cactus Flower* (1969).

Right up until her mournful death in 1982 on her 67th birthday, the legendary, adventure-seeking star—who once attributed her ability to overcome life's troubles to "a bad memory"[19]—continued to sustain a glittering and prolific career that encompassed film, television, radio, and numerous stage successes.

In *Anastasia* (1956), Ingrid Bergman portrays a woman hired to impersonate the youngest daughter of Russia's murdered Czar Nicholas II. After years of being excommunicated, the film proved to be a catalyst for Bergman's Hollywood return. (Twentieth Century Fox Film Corporation/ Photofest)

638-530

Joan Crawford

"Allegedly suffering from a 104-degree temperature,"[1] **Joan Crawford**, a first-time Oscar nominee for her spectacular, career-revitalizing performance in *Mildred Pierce* (1945), remained in bed with pneumonia during the radio broadcast of the 18th Academy Awards (1946). Up against Gene Tierney (*Leave Her to Heaven*) and immediate past recipients **Ingrid Bergman** (*The Bells of St. Mary's*), **Jennifer Jones** (*Love Letters*), and **Greer Garson** (*The Valley of Decision*), Crawford—seemingly cured by the announcement of her name as the Best Actress winner—sent for her hairdresser, makeup man, and the gaggle of reporters and photographers gathered outside her Brentwood, Los Angeles, mansion. Sitting up in bed in her shimmering, diaphanous nightgown with her hands lovingly clutched around her freshly bequeathed Oscar statuette, she told the reporters, "This is the greatest moment of my life."[2] The next day, Crawford's in-bed photograph (and hers alone!) appeared on the covers of the morning papers.

A shrewd mastermind in self-promotion, Crawford, who would orchestrate a similar feat 17 years later when she accepted the Best Actress Oscar for an absent **Anne Bancroft**, initially learned the art of publicity from her early days at MGM. There, she began to inform the press of her schedule, lavish attention on photographers, and—with assembly-line proficiency—answer and autograph her deluge of daily fan mail. For *Mildred Pierce*, Crawford—alongside her producer, Jerry Wald, and her publicist, Henry Rogers—weaved together "a winning Oscar campaign." By "feeding items" to the press and keeping her "name in the papers from the first day of shooting through the Oscars,"[3] she beguiled journalists and industry insiders including the gossip columnist Hedda Hopper, who began to forecast that she would win.

Appearing in a movie supplied with a film-noir veneer, Joan Crawford's title character strikes back in this dramatic publicity still for *Mildred Pierce* (1945). (Warner Bros. Pictures Inc./ Photofest)

A purportedly sick Joan Crawford is photographed in bed at her Brentwood mansion after winning the Best Actress Oscar for *Mildred Pierce* (1945) and having it delivered to her on Oscar night 1946 by the film's director, Michael Curtiz. (© A.M.P.A.S.®/Photofest)

Considering Crawford's Dickensian childhood, her ascendance to the apex of Hollywood is astonishing. Crawford was born Lucille LeSueur in San Antonio, Texas, on, allegedly, March 23, 1905, to parents who separated before she was born and was raised by a "seamstress mother liable to beat her daughter without motive." "Treated like a slave and fondled by her mother's boyfriend," she "worked as a laundress, waitress, and shop assistant before taking up dancing after winning a Charleston [dance] contest."[4]

In spite of her mopish red hair, freckled face, and gangly figure, Crawford escaped to New York and was ultimately discovered by MGM vice president Harry Rapf in 1924. Similar to the early career trajectory of **Ginger Rogers**, the 18-year-old Charleston dance-craze sensation turned Broadway chorus girl was then offered a $75-a-week option contract and given the nicer-sounding stage name of "Joan Crawford" by way of a name-the-star contest sponsored by the fan magazine *Movie Weekly*. While nude pictures and soft-core pornographic films of her were rumored to be circulating (a rumor allegedly thrust forward by MGM to propagate her "tramp"-like image), Crawford nonetheless managed to impress nearly everyone with an "insatiable hunger" and "limitless drive" that seemed "to be devouring the future."[5] Her first assignment was to double for **Norma Shearer** in *Lady of the Night* (1925). Before long, she was arresting jazz-age audiences with the quintessential dance film of its time, *Our Dancing Daughters* (1928).

A modern, "sexually frank," "gum-chewing dame" "without inhibitions," Crawford was quick to accommodate an industry in which Hollywood producers were often "looking for . . . starlets they could put under contract [and] who would be available, both night and day."[6] As her rival **Bette Davis** once "carped bitterly," Crawford "slept with every male star at MGM except Lassie."[7]

To be sure, Crawford wholly embraced the star system construct, unlike **Davis**, who had "fought it," or **Katharine Hepburn**, who "was too well off personally to need it."[8] In doing so, she religiously watched her dailies and went off to other MGM soundstages to observe big-name stars (including her idol, Greta Garbo) as a means to better understand her craft. A newcomer to acting, she surrendered to French, English, history, and elocution courses while subjecting herself to major dental work, brutal exercise regimens, and cold showers (to toughen her skin). Having signed a morality clause in her option contract, she additionally submitted to 24/7 studio control over her personal weekly schedule, which included "public appearances," behavioral standards, and instructions on "when she should go to bed."[9]

At the same time, Crawford formed an unprecedented actress-designer partnership with MGM's master couturier, Adrian, who fashioned her in spangly gowns, cinched-waist suits, and shoulder pads. Glamour photographers George Hurrell and Ruth Harriet Louise concurrently captured her in "languorous postures" and as "near to goddess-stature as mortals were likely to achieve in modern times."[10] While the actress was recognized for her fierce, penciled eyebrows and a thick mouth line, she reinvented her look throughout the years "in the hope of devouring even more love next time."[11]

In her quest "to tear up the world," Crawford married Douglas Fairbanks Jr. in 1929. At first, the reigning king and queen of Hollywood—Douglas Fairbanks Sr. and **Mary Pickford**—disapproved of the marriage and banned Crawford from attending "Sunday luncheons and pool parties" at their Pickfair mansion in Beverly Hills.[12] Still, Crawford's ascent to the zenith of Hollywood stardom would not be derailed.

According to the American author F. Scott Fitzgerald, Crawford was unable to "change her emotions in the middle of a scene without going through a sort of Jekyll and Hyde contortion of the face."[13] She nevertheless generated an enormous fan base. Excelling at a time when films about women "dominated at the box office," the actress appeared in movies "in which the Crawford character triumphs over poverty, class, and a dubious past."[14] Conveying to millions of working-class women that a refined exterior was critical to social advancement, these redemptive

"Cinderella stories," as Crawford called them,[15] included *Possessed* (1931), the all-star Best Picture Oscar–winning *Grand Hotel* (1932), and *Sadie McKee* (1934).

But with the censorship guidelines of the Production Code enforced in July 1934, Crawford found herself in chaste, formulaic-type roles. Coupled with her increasingly suffocating brand of exaggerated glamour, she soon became labeled as box-office poison. Considered "washed up" and not working for almost three years after MGM (her home studio for 17 years) "declined to renew her contract,"[16] Crawford, in 1943, "received a new lease on life" by joining forces with Warner Bros.[17] At the time, Warner Bros. (the home studio of Crawford's archrival, **Bette Davis**) was in the process of casting the title character for *Mildred Pierce* (1945). After **Davis** had turned down the role and the likes of Barbara Stanwyck, Ida Lupino, and Rosalind Russell had all been considered, Crawford—refusing "to be thrown on the ash heap"[18]—agreed to submit to a humiliating screen test. For her efforts, she was ultimately awarded the much-sought-after role (her first for portraying not only a mother but—like **Greer Garson**'s character in *Mrs. Miniver*—a mother to *grown* children).

Mildred Pierce was based on the racy 1941 novel by James M. Cain and supplied with a film-noir veneer that was absent from the 2011 TV miniseries starring **Kate Winslet**. Set in Depression-era Los Angeles, the film, which presented post–World War II audiences with a cautionary tale of a woman's place in American society, opens with Crawford's self-sacrificing character elegantly dressed in furs while flirting with suicide from the edge of a pier. In flashback, we learn that she was once beholden to her husband until he abandoned her for another women. Mildred then strikes out on her own and, while transcending gender stereotypes, moves forward in life from a lowly waitress and single mother to a successful restaurant entrepreneur.

Feminist themes of social and political equality, however, were suppressed after World War II. During the war, as evinced in the femme fatales of the burgeoning film-noir period, filmgoers witnessed a number of strong, sexual, deviant, but ultimately punished female characters who articulated fears surrounding the loss of control, stability, and identity for American men. In keeping with these fears, Mildred—a self-empowered woman—is reprimanded for her "patriarchal transgression" in the workplace.[19] Her youngest daughter consequently dies of pneumonia, as her spoiled and manipulative teenage daughter, Vida, inches her way into the arms of her mother's second husband. In the end, Crawford's character is relegated, "sadder but wiser,"[20] to her traditional housewife role, serving as a metaphor to the six million women galvanized to fill the U.S. labor market during World War II before being let go, demoted, or urged to step aside for returning, job-seeking male military personnel.

With her Best Actress Oscar for *Mildred Pierce* enshrined "at the foot of the stairs in her home,"[21] Crawford, entering her 40s, capitalized on her success with *Humoresque* (1946), *Possessed* (1947), and *Sudden Fear* (1952; which she produced). But while her male counterparts appeared with actresses whom they could have fathered, such as **Patricia Neal**, **Audrey Hepburn**, or **Grace Kelly**, Crawford, who still battled "to project a sexual image," was forced "to settle for second-rank names such as Sterling Hayden and Cliff Robertson."[22] Before long, Crawford was consigned to lonely spinsters, neurotic career women, or "horror queens or caricatures" of herself in "hag movies" including *Strait-Jacket* (1964), *Berserk!* (1968), and *Trog* (1970).[23]

Crawford, who died on May 10, 1977, was later castigated for her abusive parenting in her adopted daughter Christina's best-selling memoir, *Mommie Dearest* (1978). Indeed, the book, as well as the 1981 **Faye Dunaway**–starring adaptation, painted a picture of the actress as a publicity-obsessed, clean-freak alcoholic uneasily associated with uneaten steak, bed harnesses, and the inappropriate use of wire hangers.

Remarkably, **Bette Davis**, who costarred with Crawford in the camp-horror *What Ever Happened to Baby Jane?* (1962) and whose own daughter had written a scathing, divisive memoir, defended Crawford. As someone who "carved a monumental career out of nothing," Crawford, as **Davis** put it, "did not deserve . . . that detestable book."[24] "I wouldn't piss on [her] if she were on fire," admitted **Davis**.[25] "[But] to me, she is the personification of the Movie Star. I have always felt her greatest performance is Crawford being Crawford."[26]

Olivia de Havilland

"If I were a young actress today, I wouldn't go into the [movie] business," **Olivia de Havilland** said in 1987. "The only career that would interest me is the kind that **Meryl Streep** is having. But who else has that kind of career anymore?"[1]

While still at the top of her game, de Havilland largely bid farewell to Hollywood in the mid-1950s. With the rise of television "casting a terrible shadow on the film industry,"[2] the two-time Best Actress Oscar winner fled to Paris. "I love living among the French," said the actress, who has since lived in a three-story house in the chic 16th arrondissement. "They are very independent, intelligent, well-educated, and creative. They are a people full of feeling, which they express."[3]

The same could be said of de Havilland herself. Born on July 1, 1916, in Tokyo, Japan, before relocating with her mother and younger sister, **Joan Fontaine**, to the warmer surroundings of Saratoga, California, de Havilland went on to receive an education in music, elocution, and the performing arts with an emphasis on Shakespeare. Although she once harbored aspirations of becoming a schoolteacher and even turned down a scholarship to Mills College (the first women's college west of the Rocky Mountains), de Havilland could not escape "the acting bug" after performing "in school plays as a teenager."[4]

At age 18, and not dissimilar to **Shirley MacLaine**'s "most legendary break in show business" 20 years later, de Havilland "wrangled the part of the second understudy for the role of Hermia" in the celebrated theater director Max Reinhardt's innovative outdoor production of *A Midsummer Night's Dream* "at the . . . Hollywood Bowl during the summer of 1934."[5] Filling in for both Gloria Stuart and her understudy, de Havilland caught the attention of Warner Bros. and ultimately signed a seven-year option contract with the studio.

To Each His Own (1946)

The Heiress (1949)

Described by Olivia de Havilland as "the first women's lib film," *The Heiress* (1949), which was adapted from Henry James's short novel *Washington Square* (1880), was set at a time when women were entirely excluded from any political involvement, had no serious or meaningful job opportunities, had little education, and had no civil rights, voting rights, community property rights, or employment rights. (Paramount/Viacom/Photofest)

In one of only five Best Actress Oscar–winning performances to portray a female business owner, Olivia de Havilland's character becomes a cosmetics firm executive as a means of financially supporting her illegitimate son in *To Each His Own* (1946). (Paramount/Viacom/Photofest)

Despite Jack Warner's management of "an economy-minded studio known primarily for gangster melodramas" geared to the working class,[6] de Havilland—a descendant of two English kings (Edward II and Henry VIII)—nevertheless experienced a regal world as she joined the cavalcade of Warner stars including James Cagney, her close friend **Bette Davis**, Edward G. Robinson, and the newcomer Errol Flynn. As de Havilland described, "Stars had enormous dressing rooms decorated to their taste," where, according to **Joan Fontaine**, you "had your own maid, your own kitchen. You had people to lunch and served wine. **Jennifer Jones** . . . had a lovely dressing room . . . [with] oil paintings [by] Manet, Monet, [and] Renoir."[7] "You went out every night," de Havilland continued. "Not only in long gowns, but wearing long gloves!" On weekends, "you rode in limousines, and the gentlemen who escorted you wore a white tie and tails, and there were four elegant night-clubs where you danced until dawn. There was the opera, and concerts, and lovely manners, a certain civilized elegance."[8]

Spearheading "the crusade to capture" the "educated middle-class" market (members of which "attended the movies . . . as little as once a year or only for special pictures"),⁹ Warner Bros. produced *A Midsummer Night's Dream* (1935)—the second talking feature to attempt Shakespeare after the disastrous results of *The Taming of the Shrew* (1929; starring **Mary Pickford**). The film, which marked de Havilland's screen debut, became a "succès d'estime" and led the actress "to expect [that] her film career would be 'Shakespeare all the way.'"[10]

On the contrary, de Havilland worked "like a circus pony" six days a week, regularly "playing second fiddle" as the romantic love interest.[11] Opposite the heart-throb Errol Flynn, she appeared in nine films including the costume-adventure dramas *Captain Blood* (1935), *The Adventures of Robin Hood* (1938), and *Dodge City* (1939). "Generally thought of as nice, decent, amiable, [and] a good trouper,"[12] the actress was subsequently loaned out to Selznick International Pictures to appear as the prideful Melanie Hamilton in the epic production of *Gone with the Wind* (1939).

The role of Melanie, "the tenderhearted foil to [**Vivien**] **Leigh**'s scheming Scarlett O'Hara,"[13] earned de Havilland her first Oscar nomination. She ultimately lost to her costar Hattie McDaniel in the Best Supporting Actress category and had to be dragged into "the kitchen at the Cocoanut Grove," where she "cried into a bowl of consommé."[14] "When I returned home on Oscar night, . . . I was convinced there was no God," de Havilland recalled. "About two weeks later, I woke up and thought, 'Oh, how wonderful! I wasn't a supporting actress, and Hattie was, and she won! . . . I'd rather live in a world where someone who is a supporting actress wins against someone who, instead, is a star playing a starring role!'"[15]

With empowered confidence and the quest for roles that "cracked the super-ficial ingénue mold,"[16] de Havilland returned to her home studio of Warner Bros. But to her dismay, she continued to find herself relegated to a never-ending barrage of one-dimensional parts that she was obliged to play. After she refused to accept any more of these roles, studio president Jack Warner—who had battled a defi-ant **Bette Davis** in 1937—retaliated. In doing so, he suspended de Havilland for a total of six months, informally blacklisted her by demanding that no other studio in town hire her, and argued that when her seven-year contract did expire, she should give him back an additional six months of employment.

In the midst of this drama, de Havilland's former costar and Screen Actors Guild board member Ronald Reagan informed her of "an old Californian statute that claimed contracts exceeding seven years amounted to slavery."[17] With the same conviction that would propel her at the age of 101 to take unsuccessful legal action against the producer Ryan Murphy for his depiction of her as a "petty gossip" in the **Bette Davis–Joan Crawford** TV miniseries *Feud* (2017), de Havilland, entirely fed up with studios ignoring "the feelings of their talent,"[18] decided to sue. To her credit, the actress was handed a victory ruling in December 1944, known to this day as the de Havilland Decision. The victory generated a defining moment in Hollywood history that ultimately contributed to the downfall of the studio system by limiting option contracts to seven years.

The victory additionally altered "the pattern of [de Havilland's] career."[19] The actress won free-agent status, artistic freedom, and the respect of her peers, and she wasted no time in selecting her own scripts. Becoming "the doyenne of the Hollywood woman's picture," she subsequently stepped into the daring role of an unwed mother forced to give up her illegitimate son before attempting to adopt him back in the "four-hankie weepie" *To Each His Own*.[20] A box-office hit in 1946 when two-thirds of the American population attended the movies every week, the film traces the life of Josephine Norris—a shamed, middle-aged spinster impregnated during World War I by a fighter pilot who is soon killed in action. Not unlike the **Helen Hayes**–starring drama *The Sin of Madelon Claudet* (1931), *To Each His Own* illuminated social issues that the church did not want to have discussed and became one of the last in a long rotation of then-cutting-edge melodramas dealing with the toll of unrequited mother-love and "the stigma of illegitimacy."[21] Despite a convoluted story line that finds Josephine operating a successful transatlantic cosmetics firm as a means of supporting her son, de Havilland secured a Best Actress Oscar nomination ahead of the 19th Academy Awards (1947).

Arriving at the ceremony, de Havilland sparkled in a flower-accented gown (by the African American designer Ann Lowe) that epitomized a return to fashion after World War II. In the Best Actress category, her competition included former winner **Jennifer Jones** (*Duel in the Sun*), Ronald Reagan's wife, **Jane Wyman** (*The Yearling*), Rosalind Russell (*Sister Kenny*), and the British actress and New York Film Critics Award winner Celia Johnson (*Brief Encounter*). De Havilland had already endured splashes of Madeira sauce flicked onto her dress at a preceremony dinner, and upon the announcement of her name, she was forced to muscle her way past an apathetic, exiting Louis B. Mayer and his gaggle of MGM cohorts as she made her way to the stage.

But one more obstacle remained. Two weeks before the ceremony, de Havilland's sister, **Joan Fontaine**, made an offhanded remark to the *Hollywood Reporter*, pointing out that de Havilland was the *fifth* wife to her then-husband, Marcus Goodrich. "It was in the press, and the whole town took it up, so I was deeply embarrassed," de Havilland remembered. "I didn't understand that kind of behavior, and I expected her to apologize."[22] Backstage at the Oscars, a teary-eyed **Fontaine** approached her sister in front of "50 photographers" who captured the "fireworks" as an insulted de Havilland "turned her back" on **Fontaine** and made her way to the winner's room.[23] "I simply couldn't change my attitude," de Havilland explained. "I deserved a happy evening, and I didn't have it."[24]

Three years later, though, de Havilland won again. For her role in the director William Wyler's *The Heiress* (1949), she was unanimously hailed for giving the year's finest performance. Having already collected the New York Film Critics Award, she went on to beat former winner **Loretta Young** (*Come to the Stable*), Jeanne Crain (*Pinky*), **Susan Hayward** (*My Foolish Heart*), and Deborah Kerr (*Edward, My Son*) for the Best Actress Oscar. "Your Award for *To Each His Own* I took as an incentive to venture forward," she gleefully told the audience at the 1950 Academy Awards. "Thank you for this very generous assurance that I have not failed to do so."[25]

For her performance in a film that illuminated social issues that the church did not want to have discussed, *To Each His Own* star Olivia de Havilland celebrated her Best Actress Oscar victory backstage with presenter Ray Milland at the 1947 Academy Awards. (© A.M.P.A.S.®/ Photofest)

Described by de Havilland as "the first women's lib film,"[26] *The Heiress* was adapted from Henry James's short novel *Washington Square*. The story is set amid the Greek-columned brownstones of mid-19th-century Manhattan and centers on the matrimonial prospects of the meek, wealthy, and psychologically tormented Catherine Sloper—a classic ugly-duckling spinster whose blind adoration for the dashing fortune hunter Morris Townsend (played by Montgomery Clift) threatens to undermine her financial security. Taking cues in human cruelty from her stern, heartless father ("I have been taught by masters," she concludes),[27] Catherine ultimately comes to her senses and exercises a manipulative, self-empowered ploy to rid Morris from her life once and for all. With the story taking place at a time when marriage was seen as a societal requirement for women, *The Heiress* asks whether Catherine

William Wyler directs Olivia de Havilland in a scene from *The Heiress* (1949), which centers on a New York City spinster whose blind adoration threatens to undermine her financial security. (Paramount/Viacom/Photofest)

should marry and how her community will regard her if she decides not to. As de Havilland herself put it, "Sometimes it's more important to remain unfulfilled in love and preserve your integrity, your independence, [and] your personal honor."[28]

After moving to Paris, de Havilland appeared onscreen only occasionally. In 1965, she became the first of only ten women (including **Sophia Loren**, **Ingrid Bergman**, and **Cate Blanchett**) to be appointed jury president of the Cannes Film Festival.

While celebrating her 100th birthday on July 1, 2016, de Havilland, one "of the last direct links to one of the most glorious chapters in film history,"[29] candidly "disclosed her true feelings about her late sister," **Joan Fontaine** (who passed away in 2013). "'Dragon Lady' . . . was a brilliant, multi-talented person," de Havilland revealed, "but with an astigmatism in her perception of people and events which often caused her to react in an unfair and even injurious way."[30] Surpassing anything even remotely concocted by the sisters Gish, Talmadge, Bennett, Young, Lane, Gabor, Redgrave, or Fanning, the legendary rivalry between de Havilland and **Fontaine** continues to capture the public imagination.

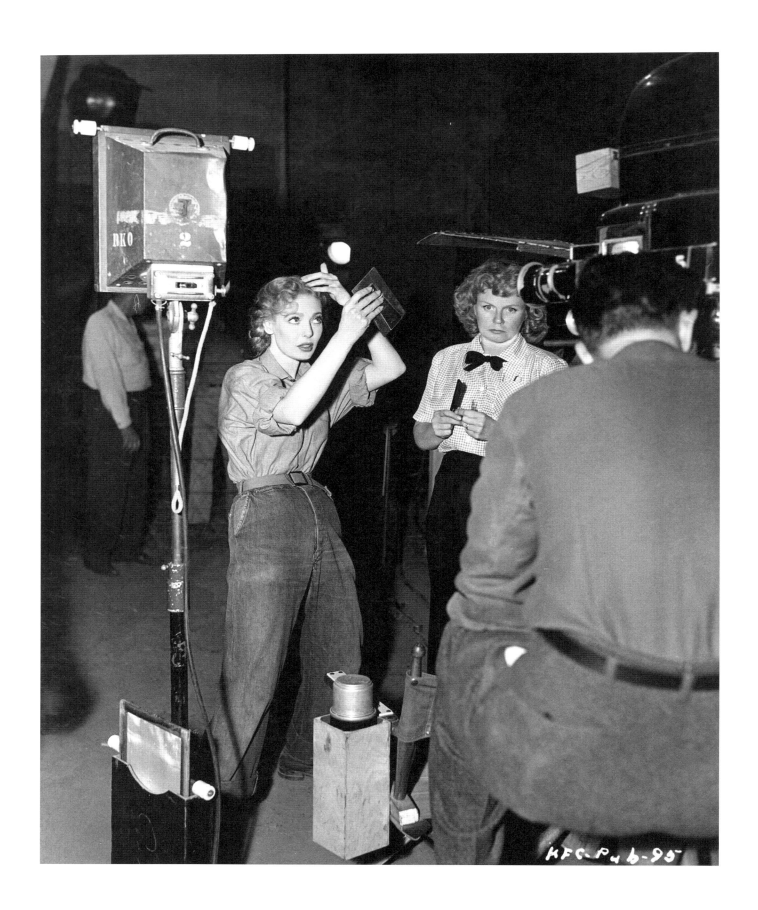

KFC-Pub-95

Loretta Young

When the Best Actress Oscar winner **Loretta Young** decided to abandon the movies for the fertile fields of television in 1953, an astounded Hollywood branded her as a traitor. Imploring Young to reverse her course of action, the former MGM studio head Louis B. Mayer "took it upon himself" to personally telephone the actress. "Television is considered the enemy," he warned.[1] "You'll never be offered another movie script."[2]

Indeed, by 1948, thousands of American households were equipped with television sets, and viewers were choosing to stay home to watch them. By 1951, the number increased to around ten million. With the Paramount Decision (a 1948 antitrust ruling that divorced exhibition from distribution) contributing to the "breakdown of the studio system itself," Hollywood was living through an "unbelievably morbid" time.[3] Implementing large layoffs and salary reductions, studios that had once made over 75 pictures a year were now making ten. Consequently, movie palaces began to shut their doors. In an effort to win back moviegoers, Hollywood began to target the teenage audience while pumping out horror and science fiction thrillers, rock-and-roll movies, and such television-competing offerings as the widescreen format, stereophonic sound, 3-D, the expansion of color films and drive-in theaters, and such "mercifully short-lived" gimmicks as Smell-O-Vision and Aroma-Rama.[4] Following in the footsteps of movie stars Gloria Swanson (*The Gloria Swanson Hour*, 1948), **Helen Hayes** (*Pulitzer Prize Playhouse*, 1950), and Lucille Ball (*I Love Lucy*, 1951), who each created "new contexts for their waning [star] images" by way of early television, Young made her move and never looked back.[5] "If my movie career is over," she told David O. Selznick, "[then] so be it."[6]

As Young was approaching 40 and recognized that her "days of portraying ingénues" were behind her,[7] her audacious move ultimately proved rewarding. After years of feeling objectified by movie-studio bosses as just another star on which "to hang some furs," the actress—with the television success of her pioneering anthology series *The Loretta Young Show* (1953–1961)—finally enjoyed complete control over her "schedule, salary, image, and material."[8]

Born Gretchen Young on January 6, 1913, in Salt Lake City, Utah, Young moved to Los Angeles with her "cash-strapped" family at the age of three. Influenced by her older actress sisters, Polly Ann Young and Sally Blane, she first broke into the movies as a tenacious child extra, "weeping on an operating table" in *The Only Way* (1919) and appearing as an Arab child in the Rudolph Valentino romance-drama *The Sheik* (1921). Whenever there was an opportunity, Young ran "to the front of the pack during crowd scenes to make sure her face flashed prominently before the cameras."[9] With her "skinny and somewhat gawky" "ballerina figure," "high cheekbones," and "distinctive doe eyes," she attracted the attention of the silent-screen star Colleen Moore, who not only "prevailed upon [First National Pictures] to give the . . . girl a screen test" but also played a role in the creation of her stage name.[10] As the actress would soon discover by opening the pages of her local newspaper, the old, clunky-sounding "Gretchen" was now the new "Loretta Young."

Before long, Young—who went on to make nearly 100 films during her career and posed for an estimated 125,000 photographs between 1928 and 1953—starred in such movies as *Laugh, Clown Laugh* (1928; opposite Lon Chaney), *Man's Castle* (1933; opposite her onetime paramour Spencer Tracy), and the director Cecil B. DeMille's *The Crusades* (1935). Like the future Best Actress Oscar winner **Cher**, she suffered from dyslexia and compensated for her learning difference by practicing her lines incessantly. Labeled by some colleagues as a perfectionist and a demanding artist—"attributes that, had she been a man, might have earned her respect"—Young "studied every aspect of filmmaking, asking serious questions about lighting and camera angles" while "making herself the master of her own makeup."[11] Because of her tough business acumen and persistent directives on how best to enhance her ethereal beauty, she was nicknamed the "Steel Butterfly" and the "Iron Madonna."[12]

Yet, in an industry in which the preservation of a star's expensively publicized image accounts for everything, Young soon found herself navigating dangerous waters. Eighty-some years before the #MeToo movement dominated "the conversation around Hollywood" in regard to unwanted sexual advances and sexual assaults, Young, at the age of 23, became pregnant with the child of her married costar Clark Gable, who purportedly date-raped the actress on an "overnight train [ride] back to Hollywood" after filming 1935's *The Call of the Wild* in the State of Washington.[13] Struggling with a moral and professional dilemma, Young—a devout Roman Catholic raised without a father but mentored by visiting priests—went to great lengths to hush up the facts surrounding her career-damaging, morality-clause-contract-violating, out-of-wedlock pregnancy. Feigning exhaustion and

illness, she managed to hide the pregnancy and circumvent the likes of Louella Parsons, whose gossip column was "avidly followed in cities ranging from Los Angeles to Peking, from New York to Beirut."[14] But "when [the actress] missed her sister's wedding, reporters went into a frenzy of speculation." As a result, an emergency 20-minute interview with the gossip columnist Dorothy Manners was arranged, in which Young "remained in a bed piled high with strategically placed pillows and blankets."[15] Repulsed by the notion of an abortion (something the Hollywood studios were known to illegally prearrange), the actress secretly gave birth to a daughter in November 1935 before fabricating an "adoption" to get the child back.

While Young's "adoption" generated lasting rumors, her ability to pull off such a convoluted cover-up and keep the would-be scandal at bay underscored the steel interior beneath her poised and gracious façade. Shocking the industry even more, and predating **Olivia de Havilland**'s 1944 victory ruling against Warner Bros.

In *The Farmer's Daughter* (1947)—a film bursting with political overtones that foreshadowed the fear-of-change-based Americanism ushered into society by U.S. Senator Joseph McCarthy, Loretta Young (pictured here with costar Joseph Cotten) plays a Swedish immigrant who leaves her family's Minnesota farm and ultimately ends up winning a seat in the U.S. House of Representatives. (RKO Radio Pictures Inc./ Photofest) that "ceased the practice of adding suspension time onto a seven-year contract," Young, in 1939, "rejected a five-year, $2 million-contract with 20th Century-Fox" and made the self-directed, risk-taking jump into freelance work.[16] Her new goal was to select a crowd-pleasing part that would earn her the respect of her peers and land her an Oscar.

In 1946, that part materialized when the message-conscious RKO producer Dore Schary approached Young to star in *The Farmer's Daughter*—the 1947 screen adaptation of the hit Finnish play *Juurakon Hulda*, which was written under a male pseudonym by the Estonian playwright Hella Wuolijoki (who had "a direct link to [the Soviet leader Joseph] Stalin and his secret police").[17] The story centers on a Swedish immigrant named Katie Holstrom. "Determined, headstrong, [and] fiercely principled,"[18] Katie leaves her family's Minnesota farm to pursue a career in nursing. But after she is swindled out of her money, she takes a job as a maid to a political power broker (played by Ethel Barrymore) and her U.S. congressman son (Joseph Cotten). Akin to such women-in-government-themed movies as *Politics* (1931; with **Marie Dressler**), *State of the Union* (1948; with **Katharine Hepburn**), *Key to the City* (1950; reuniting Young, as a city mayor, with Clark Gable), *A Woman Called Golda* (1982; with **Ingrid Bergman**), *Marie* (1985; with **Sissy Spacek**), *Primary Colors* (1998; with **Emma Thompson**), *The Iron Lady* (2011; with **Meryl Streep**), and *Game Change* (2012; with **Julianne Moore**), Katie finds herself at odds with a candidate's questionable voting record and ends up running for election herself.

At a time in the United States when left-wing sympathizers were soon black-listed for their political beliefs, *The Farmer's Daughter* managed to ruffle conservative feathers. Bursting with political overtones that would foreshadow the xenophobic, homophobic, anti-Communist, fear-of-change-based Americanism ushered into society by the Republican U.S. Senator Joseph McCarthy, the film showcased an immigrant daughter's ability to participate in the political process while issuing a plea for more integrity and honesty ahead of the 1948 U.S. presidential election. In addition, it paid tribute to the progressive insights of former U.S. president Woodrow Wilson, who supported the League of Nations—the precursor to the newly formed United Nations. Released a few months before the directors and screenwriters of the "Hollywood Ten" were imprisoned for refusing to cooperate with the House Un-American Activities Committee (HUAC), *The Farmer's Daughter*, which was otherwise seen as a "bright comedy,"[19] came to represent the advent of a dim and mistrustful new era. "Fear of spies, threats of Communist takeover, and paranoia about nuclear war" contributed to this period marked by reckless and unsubstantiated accusations, as well as the aggressive questioning of certain Americans' patriotism and psychological balance.[20]

Nonetheless, *The Farmer's Daughter*, alongside Young's other 1947 offering—*The Bishop's Wife* (which premiered in London surrounding the festivities of Princess Elizabeth's wedding)—became one of the year's biggest box-office hits and proved to be what the Oscar-seeking actress had been looking for. RKO lauded Young's performance and first-time Oscar nomination (which was seen by many people as a shock). In doing so, in the weeks leading up the 1948 Academy Awards, the studio placed what was deemed to be the first official, campaign-style "For Your Consideration" advertisement in the Hollywood trades. Although the *Los Angeles Times* erroneously printed the headline "Roz Russell Wins Oscar," Young, up against her close friend Rosalind Russell (*Mourning Becomes Electra*), Dorothy McGuire (*Gentleman's Agreement*), **Susan Hayward** (*Smash-Up, the Story of a Woman*), and former winner **Joan Crawford** (*Possessed*), was "stunned into numbness when she heard *her* name called."[21] The actress, dressed in "yards upon yards of emerald green silk taffeta,"[22] took the stage and tapped on the microphone three times to imitate the pounding sound of her heart. She then congratulated each of her fellow nominees before gushingly turning to her Oscar. "As for you," she said, "at long last!"[23]

For her deeply religious nature, Young became a satirized source of "hilarity in Hollywood."[24] She "refused to utter the word 'divorce'" in any movie and commonly set up a charity "swear box" on set (in which a blasphemous Robert Mitchum once "rammed a five dollar bill").[25] Nonetheless, as a virtuous woman who did things her own way, she worked exhaustively in her final years with underprivileged youth, homeless women, and the mentally ill in downtown Los Angeles's Skid Row. In 2000, Young died at the age of 87.

Jane Wyman

Languishing in film roles as a virtually invisible presence for 15 years before landing her first big break, **Jane Wyman** "had one of the slowest and most tortuous ascents to stardom on record."[1]

Born Sarah Jane Mayfield in Saint Joseph, Missouri, on January 5, 1917, to parents who split up when their daughter was four, Wyman was subsequently raised under the care of neighbors Richard and Emma Fulks. Their harsh disciplinarian ways and ruthless necessity for achievement generated in her a severe inferiority complex that she was forced to overcome.

At the age of eight, Wyman was trotted off to Hollywood to fruitlessly audition for child roles in silent films. As a young adult, she tried her hand again. After working as a model under the name Jane Durrell, she was given a seemingly futile contract at Warner Bros. While the contract system offered her the chance to learn her craft and maintain steady employment, the frustrated actress continued to be cast in a long succession of B-movies.

Seen as a "Plain Jane," Wyman never went after the glamour roles. Thus, unlike **Bette Davis** or **Olivia de Havilland**, she never had to fight the studio executives at Warners to get the parts that she wanted. On the contrary, the actress found herself in the position of having to push "against roles unworthy of her." "I simply refused to play a prostitute [or] a drug addict," she later explained. "Non-exposure is better than appearing in the wrong thing."[2]

When success finally did come knocking, Wyman never stopped to catch her breath. Capitalizing on her recognized talent after appearing as the patient girlfriend to an alcoholic in the Best Picture Oscar–winning drama *The Lost Weekend* (1945), Wyman captured a Best Actress nomination for the Technicolor box-office

Johnny Belinda (1948)

In this picture taken in the early 1940s, Jane Wyman picnics with her husband, actor Ronald Reagan, who became the president of the United States four decades later. (Warner Bros. Pictures Inc./Photofest)

hit *The Yearling* (1946). Two years later, she took home the industry's top acting prize for her gripping turn in *Johnny Belinda* (1948), which earned a total of 12 Oscar nominations.

At the time of her victory, home was not a very happy place for Wyman. Her eight-year marriage to fellow Warner Bros. contract player and future president of the United States Ronald Reagan (which commenced in 1940 at an intimate wedding ceremony hosted by the Hollywood gossip columnist Louella Parsons) began to grow fallow. Despite the "Warner Bros. publicity machine . . . churning out press releases touting them as the new all-American couple" and one of the happiest pairs in 1940s Hollywood,[3] little was left to sustain their crumbling marriage. Following the devastating loss of their prematurely born baby daughter, Wyman, who was criticized by the Hollywood press for choosing an ambitious career over her marriage, filed for divorce. "I just couldn't stand to watch that damn *Kings Row* one more time,"[4] she was later overheard as saying, caustically referring to Reagan's acclaimed 1942 movie.

Though Wyman and Reagan costarred in four films (including 1938's *Brother Rat*, on the set of which they met), their time together was constantly interrupted. For starters, the demanding dictates of the studio system had them working six days a week (sometimes 18 hours a day) and appearing in at least five movies a year, leaving little time besides Sundays to enjoy a personal life.

Exacerbating problems, Reagan's acting career began to falter after World War II. Simultaneously, his interest in politics (a subject that bored Wyman to no end, in part because her own opinions were never considered important) steadily increased. As a "budding politician in Hollywood's acting community," Reagan soon became president of the Screen Actors Guild (SAG) and "took great satisfaction from his work with the FBI."[5] In the fall of 1947, he appeared as a friendly witness before the House Un-American Activities Committee (HUAC). At the time of his testimony, fear of communism was "so palpable" in the United States "that college students turned in professors whose views were perceived as too liberal and therefore possibly communistic in nature, while others began to disassociate themselves from anyone accused of communist ties, real or imagined."[6] While Reagan "declined to identify anyone as a Communist," he later went along with the blacklist and insisted that all SAG "officers sign a loyalty oath . . . affirming that they were not members of the Community Party."[7] A 1985 article in the *San Jose Mercury News*, however, painted a different picture. Through FBI documents obtained in a freedom-of-information request, it reported that both Reagan *and* Wyman "gave the FBI the names of [SAG] actors they believed to be members of a faction that was sympathetic to Communists."[8]

Ironically, any turmoil brought on by Wyman's marriage during these angst-ridden times may have helped her achieve the emotional gravitas required for *Johnny Belinda* (1948), the screen adaptation of the Elmer Harris play that, unusual for its time, featured a Deaf character in the central role. In the dark social-issue drama set along the rugged landscapes of a Nova Scotia fishing village, Wyman plays

For her performance as a Deaf rape victim in *Johnny Belinda* (1948), Jane Wyman became the first of three Best Actress Oscar winners to capture the Academy Award for a post-silent-era nonspeaking part. In the following decades, portrayals of people with disabilities would become an Oscar staple. (Warner Bros. Pictures Inc./Photofest)

689-98

Belinda McDonald, a young woman featured in soiled and tattered clothing and regarded as mentally deficient by the local townspeople because she cannot hear or speak. In keeping with the sexually assaulted characters portrayed by **Vivien Leigh** in *Gone with the Wind* (1939; involving implied marital rape) and *A Streetcar Named Desire* (1951), **Sophia Loren** in *Two Women* (1960), **Jodie Foster** in *The Accused* (1988), **Hilary Swank** in *Boys Don't Cry* (1999), **Charlize Theron** in *Monster* (2003), and **Brie Larson** in *Room* (2015), Wyman's character is raped by a drunken fisherman. Echoing the "fear of sex crimes [from returning military personnel] that dominated the headlines of the time,"[9] Belinda consequently becomes pregnant. Months later, after her illegitimate baby is born, her assailant comes back to retrieve the child (who is named Johnny), but Wyman's character refuses to comply. After a hostile skirmish, she kills him before standing trial for murder.

Well before **Marlee Matlin** starred in *Children of a Lesser God* (1986) and **Holly Hunter** in *The Piano* (1993), Wyman's performance in *Johnny Belinda* became the first to capture the Academy Award for a post-silent-era nonspeaking part. What is more, her performance set a trend that ultimately confirmed the Academy's penchant for characters who cope with a disability, as later evinced in the Best Actress Oscar–winning performances of **Joanne Woodward** in *The Three Faces of Eve* (1957), **Anne Bancroft** in *The Miracle Worker* (1962), **Marlee Matlin**, and **Julianne Moore** in *Still Alice* (2014).

To prepare for her role in *Johnny Belinda*, Wyman received guidance from the Mary E. Bennett School for the Deaf in Los Angeles and spent time with a Deaf girl who was just learning to communicate through sign language. Once production began, the actress sealed her ears with wax while ostracizing herself from fellow cast and crew so as to better understand her character's isolation. But as the Deaf actresses **Marlee Matlin** and Linda Bove later pointed out, Wyman's methodology—while effectively generating an interior dialogue that conveys both tragedy and joy—personifies a Deaf person in a way that is neither truthful nor authentic. In a reflection of the stereotypes of disability commonly depicted in film at that time, the character of Belinda can be observed as a "victimized" master lip-reader, who, as if "her mouth were sewn shut,"[10] cannot even make a sound while being raped.

Coupled with a wave of voter sympathy following her much-headlined divorce, Wyman, who was escorted to the 1949 Oscar ceremony by her *Johnny Belinda* costar Lew Ayres, nonetheless found herself victorious for her concentrated performance. Despite strong competition from the likes of former winner **Ingrid Bergman** (*Joan of Arc*), Barbara Stanwyck (*Sorry, Wrong Number*), Irene Dunne (*I Remember Mama*), and the previous year's winner, **Olivia de Havilland** (*The Snake Pit*), the actress made her way to the Oscar stage at the Academy's own 985-seat theater on Melrose Avenue. There, taking a cue from her silent performance, she delivered an acceptance speech largely noted for its brevity. "I accept this very gratefully for keeping my mouth shut for once," she said. "I think I'll do it again."[11]

Following her Oscar victory, Wyman starred in such films as Alfred Hitchcock's *Stage Fright* (1950), *The Blue Veil* (1951; her personal favorite of her films), and the

Walt Disney Studios production of *Pollyanna* (1960). She additionally appeared in *Magnificent Obsession* (1954; in which she plays a blind woman) and *All That Heaven Allows* (1955)—a pair of Douglas Sirk–directed melodramas that contained biting social commentary on the "conformity and consumerism of the postwar era."[12] Like her close friend **Loretta Young**, Wyman also turned her attention toward the new medium of television—the domestic symbol of unparalleled prosperity and consumption in American culture that coaxed women into shopping centers and back into kitchen aprons with its skillful advertising of consumer products that underscored "the good life." Between 1955 and 1958, the actress hosted and coproduced the anthology TV series *Fireside Theatre* and, decades later, starred in *Falcon Crest* (1981–1990)—the prime-time television hit soap opera that largely coincided with Reagan's eight-year White House term.

Incidentally, Wyman made a point never to speak to the press about Reagan, their failed marriage, or his subsequent marriage to fellow American actress and First Lady Nancy Reagan. However, upon Reagan's death in 2004 (three years before her own passing), she broke her silence. "America lost a great president," she said, "and a great, kind, and gentle man."[13]

Although *Johnny Belinda* is not as well remembered today as perhaps her later projects are, Wyman's greatest role may nevertheless have been the one for which she won the Oscar, for after years of struggle it finally cemented her place among Hollywood's most distinguished stars.

Judy Holliday

Born Yesterday (1950)

In 1951, one of the closest races in Oscar history centered on the battle between the two-time winner **Bette Davis** and the silent-screen legend Gloria Swanson. After **Davis** had gained autonomy from her Warner Bros. contract, she replaced an injured **Claudette Colbert** and secured the role of the aging Broadway luminary Margo Channing in *All About Eve*. Similarly, after **Mary Pickford** and **Norma Shearer** turned down the role of the aging, reclusive, and excessively vain silent-screen star Norma Desmond in *Sunset Boulevard*, Swanson secured the fictitious part. Rounding out the list of Best Actress contenders that year were Eleanor Parker (*Caged*), **Davis**'s *All About Eve* costar Anne Baxter, and *Born Yesterday*'s **Judy Holliday**, who had just been thrown into an awards-season witch hunt as a result of her "leftist tendencies."[1]

Holliday was a New York City native who first became known to moviegoers by way of her small but pivotal role opposite **Katharine Hepburn** and Spencer Tracy in the feminist comedy *Adam's Rib* (1949). She remained in New York for the radio broadcast of the 1951 Academy Awards, and at the invitation of the actor José Ferrer, she joined in on the Oscar festivities at a simultaneous Gloria Swanson birthday party held in midtown Manhattan. Tensely anticipating the announcement of her category (which followed Ferrer's exuberant Best Actor win for *Cyrano de Bergerac*), Holliday was said to have "looked lost" in the shock of her ultimate victory.[2] Before the popping flashbulbs of a dozen photographers, her emotions ranged from sheer sickness to pure astonishment to overwhelming guilt.

An only child to working-class parents of Russian-Jewish descent, Holliday was born Judith Tuvim on June 21, 1921. With an extraordinarily high IQ of 172, she excelled at school. However, after receiving a rejection letter from Yale University, she changed course and set her sights on playwriting and directing. In this pursuit, she accepted a backstage switchboard-operator position at Orson Welles's Mercury Theatre so she could observe its groundbreaking theatrical activities. Alongside

Judy Holliday, in character, posing for a publicity photo for *Born Yesterday* (1950). (Columbia Pictures Industries Inc./ Photofest)

In this scene still from *Born Yesterday* (1950), Judy Holliday's character—the epitome of the "dumb blonde"—is physically assaulted for attempting to liberate herself via an education. (Columbia Pictures Industries Inc./Photofest)

Adolph Green, Betty Comden, and the piano-accompanying Leonard Bernstein, Holliday subsequently found herself in the satirical cabaret act The Revuers, which maintained a long-standing residence at the bohemian Greenwich Village hangout the Village Vanguard. The Vanguard provided Holliday and her troupe with a perfect venue to test out their self-written songs and comedic spoofs "to patrons who had come mainly to drink and converse."[3] One of their performances included a mock documentary burlesque pertaining to a **Joan Crawford** fan club.

Catching the attention of 20th Century-Fox, The Revuers (minus Bernstein) ventured to Hollywood to participate in what became an insignificant cameo in the Carmen Miranda–starring musical *Greenwich Village* (1944). While Holliday hated the whole idea of being an actress, she returned to New York and soon gained attention in her Broadway debut, *Kiss Them for Me* (1945). She was then called on to replace an ailing Jean Arthur three days before curtain in the comedic Garson Kanin stage production of *Born Yesterday* (1946). On an invigorating diet of coffee and Benzedrine, Holliday learned the part and for an astonishing 1,642 performances played the endearingly ditzy, platinum-blonde character of Billie Dawn to thunderous applause.

Equipped with superb comic timing, a technical instinct of knowing how to "interpret a text with the subtlest detail," and a raspy New York City accent that was once described by the comedian Lenny Bruce as sounding like a "Jewish seagull,"[4] Holliday seemed the perfect choice for *Born Yesterday*'s 1950 screen adaptation. However, only after **Katharine Hepburn** sang her praises and after lead contender Rita Hayworth bowed out to marry Prince Aly Khan did a reluctant offer by Columbia Pictures studio head Harry Cohn come through. With Cohn referring to his new star as "that fat Jewish broad,"[5] Holliday repeatedly locked horns with her new boss. Castigating Cohn for his lewd sexual advances and systemic misogyny (just as Hayworth and **Ginger Rogers** had done), the actress was reported to have once "reached inside her blouse" and "retrieved her falsies" before furiously declaring, "Here's what you're after!"[6]

Long before **Barbra Streisand** "came out of hiding" in the 1960s and '70s and made "her unruly Jewishness physically appealing and sexually desirable to a mainstream audience,"[7] Jewish actresses found the rules of the game in Hollywood to be less than hospitable. Despite the industry's long-standing control by the eastern European Jewish immigrants "who came to California in the late 1910s and '20s," "established the major Hollywood studios," but refused to have their own women participate in the "prostitution" of acting,[8] actresses such as Holliday were forced to assimilate. More often than not, they were required to alter their ethnic identities and Jewish-sounding names from the likes of "Judith Tuvim," "Shirley Schrift," and "Betty Perske" to the more Americanized "Judy Holliday," "Shelley Winters," and "Lauren Bacall." In addition, they frequently had to relinquish the dream of acquiring the dramatic lead for the more commonly prescribed appearance in a musical or comedy, in which they were "caricatured as loud-mouths with shrieking laughs."[9]

In *Born Yesterday*—a film lambasted by some people for its "Marxist satire,"[10] Holliday depicts such a character while adding to it a spectacular mixture of ignorance and naïveté. The film was adapted to the screen by the gay, women's-point-of-view director George Cukor, who previously guided **Vivien Leigh** and **Ingrid Bergman** to Best Actress Oscar victories in *Gone with the Wind* and *Gaslight*, respectively. The film, which was widely referenced during the 2016 U.S. presidential election in relation to then-Republican candidate Donald Trump, examines Holliday's character as she accompanies her petulant, tyrannical mobster boyfriend (played by Broderick Crawford) to Washington, DC, to coerce congressional votes. In keeping with other filmic "versions of the Pygmalion legend"[11] including *Anastasia* (1956; with **Ingrid Bergman**), *My Fair Lady* (1964; with **Audrey Hepburn**), and *Pretty Woman* (1990; with **Julia Roberts**), Billie, a social liability trapped inside a conservative place and time, ultimately experiences an awakening via an introduction to history, literature, and the arts. Through this process, she gains an informed and empowered sense of self.

Before the examples set forth by Marilyn Monroe (*How to Marry a Millionaire*, 1953), Jayne Mansfield (*Will Success Spoil Rock Hunter?*, 1957), Goldie Hawn (*Cactus Flower*, 1969), Madonna (*Who's That Girl*, 1987), Cameron Diaz (*There's Something About Mary*, 1998), and **Reese Witherspoon** (the *Legally Blonde* series, 2001–2003), Holliday helped to crystallize the archetypal "dumb blonde" and show that such ignorance and naïveté can actually outsmart the sharpest brains in the business.

Ironically, Holliday's competence in playing such a dim-witted role proved vital in more ways than one. At a time in the United States defined by paranoia, suspicion, and rampant character assassinations, the word "communism" was "being used as a description of not only the Soviet system but for anyone . . . who wanted to change their way in their country."[12] In many situations, "people unconnected to Communism *per se*, including labor union activists and gay men and lesbians, were targeted."[13] Similarly, Lela E. Rogers, the mother of **Ginger Rogers** and a friendly witness to HUAC in 1947, accused the Cary Grant–starring drama *None but the Lonely Heart* (1944) of being a perfect example of Communist propaganda simply because it was "moody and somber throughout in the Russian manner."[14] Listed in the notorious publication *Red Channels* as an alleged entertainment-industry Communist, Holliday was summoned before HUAC in 1950 to answer questions about her patriotism. Indeed, the committee had already "judged hundreds of Hollywood people as un-American, triggering a mass exodus of the film community to safer ports," including New York (the international center of the avant-garde after World War II), Paris, London, and Mexico City. In light of this reaction, Holliday, like many others called to testify, "understood that if [she] made a mistake, had a slip of the tongue, [or] got angry or silly, [then she] could jeopardize [herself], [her] family, [and] even go to jail, as the 'Hollywood Ten' had."[15]

Appealing to the committee's understanding of female ignorance and imperceptivity by channeling her *Born Yesterday* character, Holliday "was able to deny knowledge or memory of any wrongdoing, despite her genius level IQ."[16] Although she managed to flummox the committee (which failed to uncover any associations between her and the Communist Party), the actress—alongside Leonard Bernstein, Luis Buñuel, Charlie Chaplin, José Ferrer, John Garfield, Lillian Hellman, Lena Horne, Kim Hunter, Burl Ives, Arthur Miller, Dorothy Parker, Larry Parks, Anne Revere, Paul Robeson, Edward G. Robinson, Orson Welles, and more than 300 others—was ultimately blacklisted by right-wing forces and banned from performing on television and radio for three years. Oddly enough, "the irascible Harry Cohn"—the unwitting inspiration behind *Born Yesterday*'s obnoxious mobster tycoon—"purchased" certain clearances for Holliday so as to allow the actress to carry on with her film work and thus remain a big Columbia Pictures moneymaker.[17]

During this creatively stagnated time, when filmmakers largely "refrained from making any but the most conservative motion pictures" and thereby avoided "controversial topics or new ideas,"[18] Holliday, who refused to live in Los Angeles, kept herself at bay from the Hollywood publicity machine. In doing so, she only associated with old and trusted New York City friends such as the novelist Patricia Highsmith and her jazz collaborator and boyfriend, Gerry Mulligan. When not spending her free time "reading authors like Stendhal and Proust,"[19] Holliday continued to act in four more plays and six more films, including *It Should Happen to You* (1954), *The Solid Gold Cadillac* (1956), and *Bells Are Ringing* (1960; for which she had won the Tony Award for Best Actress in a Musical). Tragically, the actress ultimately succumbed to breast cancer in 1965 at her Upper West Side Dakota apartment—the future site of the 1968 film *Rosemary's Baby* and John Lennon's 1980 assassination. The youngest Best Actress Oscar winner to die, Holliday, at 43, was survived by her 12-year-old son.

Shirley Booth

In describing the actress **Shirley Booth**, the German screen legend Marlene Dietrich uncharacteristically gushed, "She comes on stage, says 'Hello,' and I [begin] to cry."[1] Operating in the 1950s, when, as **Simone Signoret** put it, "star quality was almost entirely flamboyance, pretense, [and] ostentation," Booth—a soft-spoken "introvert by nature" who made only four movies—offered audiences instead a nuanced depiction of the ordinary "everywoman."[2]

Booth was raised in the Morningside Heights neighborhood of Manhattan before moving with her family to Brooklyn. She set out to pursue a career in acting against the wishes of her strict father (a tobacco salesman turned IBM manager). Altering her name (from Marjory "Thelma" Ford) and falsifying her age by removing eight years from her August 30, 1898, birth date, she began to secure professional character-actor roles onstage in the early 1920s. Possessing, in the words of **Helen Hayes**, "perfect timing," "perfect reading," and a "complete control of herself, her part, and her audience,"[3] Booth leapt from one stage play to another. In 1925, she made her Broadway debut opposite Humphrey Bogart in *Hell's Bells* and later appeared in the 1939 smash hit *The Philadelphia Story* opposite **Katharine Hepburn**.

By 1950, Booth had won the first of her three Tony Awards and landed the role that was to become the crowning achievement of her career: that of the "limited, . . . dull-witted," and "inexplicably child-like" housewife Lola Delaney in the playwright William Inge's *Come Back, Little Sheba*.[4] At the time, Inge was on the precipice of becoming one of America's most celebrated dramatists. A "hard-drinking, deeply secretive homosexual," he began to write *Come Back, Little Sheba* after attending "AA meetings" to cope with his "full-blown alcoholism."[5] "Punishingly

Come Back, Little Sheba
(1952)

In a dramatic moment from *Come Back, Little Sheba* (1952), Shirley Booth's character finds her alcoholic husband (played by Burt Lancaster) in a state of rage. (Paramount/Viacom/Photofest)

compared" in life to his "friend and one-time lover" Tennessee Williams, Inge similarly explored the conservatism and "narrowness of provincial American life" while quaintly confronting issues of sexual frustration, failed relationships, repression, alcoholism, and "the ravaging effects of time on human destiny."[6] Before a new generation of taboo-breaking playwrights began to examine these issues head-on in the late 1950s, Inge continued to write with a more minimalist style, crafting "lonely, unfulfilled" characters with "unfeigned sympathy"[7] as he avoided the temptation to caricature them.

In the *New York Times*, the theater critic Brooks Atkinson described *Come Back, Little Sheba* as "terrifyingly true . . . with a kind of relentless frankness."[8] Set in a midwestern American college town, the story centers around Booth's character Lola, who whiles away her days in the ill-kept middle-class house that she shares with her husband, Doc (an "emotionally remote recovering alcoholic" and "failed MD"),[9] and Marie (a flirtatious college boarder). Saddled with a similar sense of confinement, loneliness, and disappointment that the characters of **Jessica Lange** and **Halle Berry** struggle with in *Blue Sky* (1994) and *Monster's Ball* (2001), respectively, Lola—an aging woman of "limited mental resources"[10]—retires to bed without washing her face and sleeps until noon. In an era barely predating the proliferation of daytime television soap-opera dramas, she additionally subjects the mailman to long, meaningless conversations, spies on her "boarder's busy love life,"[11] and bemoans the disappearance of her beloved, eponymous dog. As Booth herself put it, "All I had to do was prove to the audience that Lola was a colossal bore—without boring the audience."[12]

Reflecting the surge of postwar hostility against women, as seen in such films as *Johnny Belinda* (1948; with **Jane Wyman**), *Born Yesterday* (1950; with **Judy Holliday**), and *A Streetcar Named Desire* (1951; with **Vivien Leigh**), *Come Back, Little Sheba* harrowingly culminates with Doc—drunk and dissatisfied with his "fat slut" of a wife—attempting to strangle Lola in a "frenzied rage."[13] "Holler," he shouts, "so the neighbors will think I'm beating you!"[14]

In spite of Booth's tremendous stage success with *Sheba*, the Paramount producer Hal B. Wallis remained undecided on her for the studio's screen adaptation. For starters, she had never worked in film. Also, with television seen as a new and commanding competitor to cinema, Wallis wondered whether moviegoers would buy "tickets to see a downbeat drama" starring an actress not known for her beauty and completely unheard of outside of Broadway.[15] Having seen Booth perform *Sheba* onstage, **Bette Davis**, who was mesmerized by the performance and its "wonderful words," turned down the initial offer, wryly admitting, "no one will ever believe me as someone who would spend their life mourning for a dog."[16] **Judy Holliday** was subsequently approached. As she grumbled to a friend, "They spend two years trying to find out who should play *my* part in *Born Yesterday*. And then they spend two years trying to figure out who should play Shirley's part in *Sheba*. And then they decide I should play her part. Can you imagine?"[17]

After several other actors insisted that the Broadway star was the only one to play the character, Booth—in the days when stage professionals still "looked down on screen people as 'hacks' and had no desire to subvert their art to be like them"[18]—conditionally signed on with Paramount. At the time, the practice of the studios placing actors under contract was beginning to wane, and agent-represented actors were beginning to jump from lot to lot "depending on where the best material—and paychecks—resided."[19] Thus, Booth ironed out a deal with Wallis that gave her partial authority to choose her own projects without interfering with her work on Broadway.

Filming *Sheba* in early 1952, Booth was forced to adapt to the subtleties of acting for the camera, which invasively recorded each and every wrinkle. In addition, she had to learn how to deliver her lines at a quieter pitch, adjust to her new and significantly younger costar Burt Lancaster (as Doc), and acclimate to the use of a kitchen knife (as opposed to an axe) as the weapon with which he tries to kill her. But ultimately committing Lola to celluloid with equal aplomb, Booth, who had already won the Tony for her "histrionic tour-de-force" performance,[20] picked up a special mention at the Cannes Film Festival, the New York Film Critics Award, and a Best Actress nomination ahead of the 25th Academy Awards (1953).

In the weeks leading up to the Awards presentation, the Academy of Motion Picture Arts and Sciences made the decision to telecast its bicoastal ceremony for the first time and capitalize on the 25 million television sets in American households. For many stars, including the Best Picture presenter **Mary Pickford**, the event marked a television-appearance debut. Intriguingly, with star image accounting for everything, many studios contractually restrained their stars from appearing on television, and with "no assurance that [the] studios would relax this rule,"[21] many celebrities decided not to attend. For Booth—aged 54 and primarily operating outside the image-grooming factories of Hollywood—no such rule ever applied.

On Oscar night, Booth was performing on Broadway in the Arthur Laurents play *The Time of the Cuckoo*. After her performance, she made "a mad dash" to the East Coast site of the Oscar telecast.[22] There, her competition included an array of big-name stars: **Susan Hayward** (*With a Song in My Heart*), fellow stage actress Julie Harris (*The Member of the Wedding*), and former winners **Joan Crawford** (*Sudden Fear*) and **Bette Davis** (*The Star*; a film, incidentally, about a bankrupt Oscar-winning actress). At the anticipated announcement of her name, Booth took the stage to thunderous applause. "It's been a long, long climb," she admitted. "I guess this is the peak. But the view has been wonderful all along the way."[23]

With her victory for *Come Back, Little Sheba* (which was later made for television in 1977 with **Joanne Woodward** and Laurence Olivier), Booth became the first of four Best Actress Oscar winners to capture the most coveted prize in international show business by way of her film debut. (Screen newcomers **Julie Andrews**, **Barbra Streisand**, and **Marlee Matlin** followed suit.) Booth's triumph, however, was not universally celebrated. Like **Judy Holliday** (*Born Yesterday*) and **Vivien Leigh** (*A Streetcar Named Desire*) in the two preceding years, the actress had performed her Oscar-winning role onstage, and many critics felt that she had had an unfair advantage, with which the actress concurred. "There is all the difference in the world," she said, "between playing a character more than a thousand times, as I did, and getting your lines on the set in the morning and having to face the camera with them in the afternoon."[24]

With the box-office failures of Booth's three cinematic follow-ups, the disappointment in losing two screen roles to **Katharine Hepburn** that she had originated onstage (1955's *Summertime* and 1957's *Desk Set*), and Wallis consequently turning his attention to the likes of **Anna Magnani**, Jerry Lewis, **Shirley MacLaine**, and the "King of Rock and Roll," Elvis Presley, Booth, in her own sad words, became "last year's rose."[25] Constructively following the leads of **Loretta Young** and **Jane Wyman**, however, the actress managed to find further success in the long-running TV sitcom *Hazel* (1961–1965). Before voice acting for animated films helped to augment the careers of **Geraldine Page** (*The Rescuers*, 1977), **Sandra Bullock** and **Helen Mirren** (*The Prince of Egypt*, 1998), **Holly Hunter** (*The Incredibles* series, 2004–2018), **Julie Andrews** (*Shrek 2*, 2004), **Nicole Kidman** (*Happy Feet*, 2006), **Kate Winslet** (*Flushed Away*, 2006), **Meryl Streep** (*Fantastic Mr. Fox*, 2009), **Emma Thompson** (*Brave*, 2012), **Frances McDormand** (*The Good Dinosaur*, 2015), **Diane Keaton** (*Finding Dory*, 2016), and countless others, Booth additionally provided the voice of Mrs. Claus for the animated Christmas TV special *The Year Without a Santa Claus* (1974).

After an extended retirement in Cape Cod, where she lived next door to her friend and former rival Julie Harris, Booth, who never had children and whose two marriages had ended by the early 1950s, died in 1992 at the age of 94. Her Oscar statuette, which was seen by some people as a jinx but by others as a fitting tribute to an undervalued talent, currently resides in the lobby of the Cape Playhouse in Dennis, Massachusetts—the "oldest professional summer theater" in the United States[26] where **Bette Davis** once worked as an usher.

Audrey Hepburn

Audrey Hepburn died on January 20, 1993, but in many ways she is still with us. Since her mournful passing, countless writers and filmmakers have lovingly documented her life, while advertisers worldwide have cashed in on her gentle, sublime, and graceful image. Holding "the record for magazine covers (she appeared on 650 of them),"[1] Hepburn remains the ultimate yardstick on which style is measured. For her clean, "less is more" aesthetic, she has been emulated by women internationally and by such actresses as **Halle Berry**, **Marion Cotillard**, Mia Farrow, Anne Hathaway, Keira Knightley, Rooney Mara, **Natalie Portman**, Jean Seberg, Audrey Tatou, and Emma Watson. Regarded "as one of the most beautiful women who ever lived,"[2] Hepburn captivated the world with a rare and benevolent beauty that emanated from the inside out. For that and for raising awareness and badly needed funds for the scores of children dying needlessly each year from gross malnutrition, her name has become synonymous with charity, graciousness, and goodwill.

Once describing her life as "much more than a fairy tale,"[3] Hepburn experienced both the brightest and most terrifying aspects of humankind. The future actress was born on May 4, 1929, to a mother of Dutch aristocracy and an Anglo-Irish father who abandoned the family when his daughter was six. When World War II broke out, Hepburn's mother "made the fateful decision to return to her home town of Arnhem, believing that Holland would remain neutral."[4] But ultimately trapped under the five-year Nazi occupation, the property and bank accounts of Hepburn's family were seized. An aspiring ballerina who smuggled secret notes "to the British and American fliers who'd been shot down over Holland," delivered "the Resistance newspaper to Dutch loyalists," and staged "clandestine ballet recitals . . . to raise money for the Dutch resistance," Hepburn "risked her life" and suffered malnutrition

Roman Holiday (1953)

Audrey Hepburn, around the time she appeared in *Roman Holiday* (1953). Almost overnight, the actress—known for her "less is more" aesthetic—transformed into a style and fashion icon. (Photofest)

In her first major screen role in *Roman Holiday* (1953), Audrey Hepburn became a global phenomenon. Sensing this beforehand, her already-established costar Gregory Peck generously demanded that Hepburn be given equal star billing. (Paramount/Viacom/Photofest)

after the Nazis halted food supplies.[5] As a result, she was forced to bake grass into bread and cook tulip bulbs to a pulp in order to survive. Five weeks older than Anne Frank, the Jewish teenage diarist who hid from the Nazis in Amsterdam for 25 months and died in a concentration camp at age 15, Hepburn additionally bared witness to some of the most brutal and horrifying Nazi atrocities. "More than once," she remembered, "I was at the station seeing trainloads of Jews being transported, seeing all the faces over the top of the wagon. We saw reprisals. We saw young men put against the wall and shot, and they'd close the street and then open it and you could pass by again. If you read the diary, I've marked one place where [Frank] says, 'Five hostages shot today.' That was the day my uncle was shot."[6]

To be sure, the nightmare of World War II rendered Hepburn physically delicate, with "acute anemia, respiratory problems, and edema-swelling of the limbs."[7] Remarkably, it also instilled in her a strength, a compassion, and a deepness of character that carried forth throughout her life and in every film she made. As she oscillated between black-and-white and "the alluring gloss and polish" of Technicolor in films such as *Sabrina* (1954), *Funny Face* (1957), *The Nun's Story* (1959), *Breakfast at Tiffany's* (1961), *The Children's Hour* (1961), *Charade* (1963), *My Fair Lady* (1964), *Two for the Road* (1967), and *Wait until Dark* (1967),[8] the entire world seemed to fall in love with Audrey Hepburn.

In *Roman Holiday* (1953), Hepburn's first major film and personal favorite of all her movies,[9] she plays a lonely young princess who visits Rome on an official goodwill tour. Under sedative and passing as a commoner, she sneaks away from the suffocating protocols of her royal duties. For the next 24 hours, she wanders the picturesque ruins of the Eternal City, has her hair chopped short, drinks, smokes, drives around erratically on a Vespa, and subsequently gets arrested, all while falling in love with the penniless, Rome-based American newspaper reporter Joe Bradley (played by Gregory Peck). Alas, as in many fairy tales, their love can never be. And at the end of the film, after the princess returns to the embassy and greets members of the press, she turns to Peck's character for the final time, looks into his eyes, and conveys—as only Audrey Hepburn can—the deepest-felt love, gratitude, and regret before disappearing forever.

While Hepburn never had any formal acting training and even admitted that her career was "a total surprise since the first day,"[10] her natural poise and warm, sprightly authenticity caught the right attention. She was immediately offered the title role in the stage adaptation of *Gigi* (1951) after the celebrated French novelist Colette discovered her in Monte Carlo. Hepburn was subsequently introduced to the producer and director William Wyler, who had already started production on *Roman Holiday*. Wyler refused to shoot the movie in Hollywood or anywhere except Rome, and his budget was consequently slashed. He therefore had to forgo the expensive use of Technicolor and the option to cast a big-name star such as **Elizabeth Taylor** or Jean Simmons for the principal role. In his search for an unknown, non-American actress to play the part of Princess Ann, the director offered the inexperienced Hepburn a screen test. In it, after the cameras had theoretically stopped running, Hepburn's natural-born charms emanated from the screen—qualities that later propelled the already-established Gregory Peck to demand that she be given equal star billing.

Roman Holiday was released "in the year of Queen Elizabeth's coronation,"[11] and it proved to be a major international hit. Earning ten Oscar nominations, the film turned Hepburn into a global phenomenon. As publicists pored "over their dictionaries" for new words to describe her composed and ethereal beauty (e.g., "elfin," "gamine," "gazelle-like," and so forth),[12] Hepburn offered the world a stylistic alternative to such voluptuous contemporaries as **Sophia Loren**, **Elizabeth Taylor**, and Marilyn Monroe (who had just appeared as the centerfold model in the 1953 inaugural issue of *Playboy*).

After securing the New York Film Critics Award for her performance in *Roman Holiday*, Hepburn, at 24, was seen as the shoo-in for Best Actress on Oscar night

Wearing her "lucky dress," *Roman Holiday* star Audrey Hepburn delivers her Best Actress Oscar acceptance speech. Having earlier performed that evening as a water sprite in the Broadway play *Ondine*, Hepburn raced six blocks by police motorcycle escort to the East Coast sister ceremony of the 1954 Academy Awards. (© A.M.P.A.S.®/ Photofest)

On Oscar night 1954, Audrey Hepburn celebrates her Best Actress Oscar victory for her performance in *Roman Holiday* (1953). (© A.M.P.A.S.®/Photofest)

1954. In the same manner as **Shirley Booth** the year before, Hepburn was performing onstage that evening in Alfred Lunt's Broadway production of *Ondine*. Masked in theatrical makeup and sporting a chunky, pixie-like haircut, she raced six blocks by police-motorcycle escort to attend the East Coast sister ceremony at NBC-TV's New York City theater. There, she changed into her "lucky dress"—a chic, belted floral gown adapted by the French designer Hubert de Givenchy from the Edith Head costume she had worn in *Roman Holiday*'s final scene.

Hepburn arrived to her seat just in time to hear the roll call of Best Actress nominees, which included the French actress Leslie Caron (*Lili*), Ava Gardner (*Mogambo*), Maggie McNamara (*The Moon Is Blue*), and her close friend Deborah Kerr (*From Here to Eternity*). After her name was predictably announced, she took to the podium and graciously acknowledged both the audience and the intrusive television cameras. "It's too much," she said. "I want to say thank you to everybody who in these past months and years have helped, guided, and given me so much. I'm truly, truly grateful and terribly happy."[13]

In September 1954, Hepburn returned to Rome on her honeymoon with her *Ondine* (and later *War and Peace* [1956]) costar Mel Ferrer. Like **Ingrid Bergman** and **Sophia Loren**, she later became a "Roman housewife" in the late 1960s with her second husband, the Italian psychiatrist Andrea Dotti.[14] As she turned her attention and devotion toward her two sons and away from motion pictures, Hepburn's exciting new life in Rome was plagued by the constant barrage of roving freelance photographers and the all-too-genuine threat of kidnap. Toward the end of her life, she "lived quietly in Switzerland with her companion, [the Dutch actor] Robert Wolders, gardening, playing with her dogs, and reading."[15]

But beginning in 1988, Hepburn, with no obvious division between her public and private persona, began to repay the organization that had once saved her as a child during World War II. Demonstrating great compassion and conviction, she followed in the footsteps of such celebrities as Danny Kaye and Harry Belafonte by traveling the world for the United Nations Children's Fund (UNICEF). As a Goodwill Ambassador for UNICEF, she made the journey to such countries as Somalia, Sudan, Ethiopia, India, and Bangladesh. There, she visited, touched, held, fed, immunized, educated, and embraced countless numbers of weak, suffering, and undernourished children at UNICEF-assisted feeding centers. Appealing to the public in the variety of languages that she knew (English, Dutch, French, Spanish, and Italian), Hepburn "made public service announcements, gave press conferences, appeared at fundraisers, testified before the U.S. Congress, launched reports, [and] gave numerous speeches and press interviews."[16] She also helped to "tell Anne Frank's story . . . as narrator in a special concert tour of the London Symphony Orchestra."[17] "I've seen it happen," she told one journalist of her experiences. "And I'm filled with a rage, at ourselves. I don't believe in collective guilt, but I do believe in collective responsibility."[18]

For her enormous efforts in pushing the world to awaken to the grave epidemic concerning the millions of children suffering from malnutrition, Hepburn was awarded the U.S. Presidential Medal of Freedom and, posthumously, the Academy of Motion Picture Arts and Sciences' Jean Hersholt Humanitarian Award—a prestigious Oscar given only to Hollywood's most generous and magnanimous. Inadvertently, and long before actor-celebrities began to augment their star-brand identities with causes outside their comfort zones, Hepburn inspired a "transformative era of [international] celebrity diplomacy."[19] Genuine in her philanthropic efforts by avoiding public praise, donating substantial time, and only receiving a salary of one dollar a year, she set a high bar that successive Goodwill Ambassadors such as **Emma Thompson**, **Jessica Lange**, and **Susan Sarandon** have aspired to match. "I don't know how Audrey did it," admitted a sleep-deprived **Sarandon**, "rummaging in her bag for some rosemary-scented wipes" after arriving in India. "She always looked immaculate."[20]

Grace Kelly

The Country Girl (1954)

A year after receiving the Best Actress Oscar for *The Country Girl*, **Grace Kelly** presented Ernest Borgnine with the Best Actor Oscar for *Marty* at the March 21, 1956, Academy Awards. But before leaving the stage, Oscar host Jerry Lewis led the actress back to the podium, where he bid Kelly a public farewell on behalf on the entire movie industry. Within days, the 26-year-old star would complete her final film, *High Society*, and move away from the constant sunshine of Hollywood that she had long despised to set sail for her new home of Monaco—the hilly Mediterranean principality that is roughly the same size as New York's Central Park.

Following an eight-day transatlantic voyage on the SS *Constitution* accompanied by an entourage of family, friends, and Kelly's beloved dogs, the American actress arrived in Monte Carlo harbor on April 12. There, she was enthusiastically greeted by church bells, ship horns, distinguished yachts, an overflow of "red and white carnations," and a mob scene of 20,000 well-wishers, representatives of the international press, and "a band [playing] 'The Star-Spangled Banner.'" On board "a yacht owned by billionaire shipping magnate Aristotle Onassis,"[1] Kelly was additionally welcomed by her soon-to-be-husband, the Sovereign Prince of Monaco, Rainier III, whom she had met during a 1955 Cannes Film Festival–related visit to Monaco orchestrated by **Olivia de Havilland**'s husband, the *Paris Match* editor Pierre Galante.

After a "stilted, formal courtship" that lasted less than two weeks, arrangements for the royal wedding were under way.[2] In a deal with Kelly's father, Rainier was given a $2 million dowry, and Kelly agreed to "submit to an examination by his physician to prove that she was capable of bearing him an heir."[3] In a separate deal

Director George Seaton, shown seated, sets up a shot for *The Country Girl* (1954) as his glamorous star, Grace Kelly, watches on. (Paramount/Viacom/Photofest)

with MGM that freed Kelly from her seven-year option contract, Rainier allowed the studio to film and chronicle the entire April 19 wedding and its surrounding festivities, which was later released in cinemas as an exclusive 30-minute documentary in CinemaScope and color entitled *The Wedding in Monaco*. Providing a "sparkle of Mediterranean sunshine in a world in the grips of Cold War," the royal wedding—"one of the most publicized events of the 20th century"[4]—was additionally watched by 30 million television viewers worldwide. Radiant in an $8,000 ivory wedding dress designed by the MGM couturier Helen Rose, the poised and dignified actress, who had made only 11 pictures in her brief six-year movie career, bid a final good-bye to her former life and profession and became Her Serene Highness, the Princess of Monaco.

Unquestionably, Kelly had already experienced a life of great privilege. Born on November 12, 1929—just days after the most disastrous stock-market crash in Wall Street's history, Kelly was raised with the help of a Black servant in a "lovely 17-roomed house" in Philadelphia affixed with a tennis court and elaborate gardens.[5] Growing up, she attended private Catholic schools and "wore only the finest seasonal wardrobes."[6] Since her father—a 1920 Olympic gold medalist turned contractor—kept his money in liquid cash and bonds, Kelly and her three siblings "were deprived of nothing" during the economic collapse of the Great Depression.[7]

Gravitated to the arts, mentored by her openly gay, Pulitzer Prize–winning uncle, the playwright George Kelly, and inspired by the performances of **Ingrid Bergman**, Kelly was encouraged to pursue her dream of acting despite her parents' general disapproval. Like **Joan Crawford** and later Sylvia Plath, Joan Didion, Candice Bergen, and **Liza Minnelli**, the aspiring actress took up residence at New York's Barbizon Hotel—an Upper East Side safe haven for career-seeking women that barred its doors from men after 10:00 p.m. With the help of her uncle, Kelly simultaneously gained late admission to the American Academy of Dramatic Arts in Manhattan. In her graduation performance, she played the lead role of Tracy Lord in *The Philadelphia Story* before going on to study at the Neighborhood Playhouse with Sanford Meisner, who taught his "students to be truthful, spontaneous, and emotionally credible and to act with other actors, not against them."[8]

After working in theater and as a print and television model for cigarettes, soaps, and cosmetics, Kelly was eagerly approached by Hollywood. But the actress was forever mindful of her uncle's cautionary warning of the "feudal studio system,"[9] and she signed a seven-year contract with MGM only after its executives acquiesced to her conditions of allowing her to primarily live in New York and to continue to act on the stage. "I never believed in the studio system," Kelly later admitted. "The idea of being owned by a studio was offensive to me."[10]

Celebrated as a paragon of style, fashion, and flawless beauty in an era that worshiped the merger of "prosperity, family ties, and hard work to achieve the American dream," Kelly came to epitomize "the perfect lady of the 1950s." While "her image was carefully molded to appeal to a male audience, she was also

presented as a respectable, white-gloved girl who could be admired by women. She was therefore featured in magazines like *McCall's*, *Ladies Home Journal*, and *Mademoiselle*" and was later used as an inspiration for the Barbie fashion doll, which first appeared in 1959.[11] Similar to **Audrey Hepburn**, she became the very product of the marriage between Hollywood and haute couture, and with a slightly foreign-sounding accent that reflected a "love affair with continental women," she mastered a star image that "depended on a mysterious amalgam of presence and reserve."[12]

Ironically, Kelly ultimately took home the Oscar for playing a character entirely "different from the public's perception" of her. Having already captured a Best Supporting Actress Oscar nomination for 1953's *Mogambo*, the actress ached to play "more than a supporting [role] for the leading man,"[13] and she threatened to quit Hollywood altogether if MGM did not loan her out to Paramount to star in *The Country Girl*—the screen adaptation of Clifford Odets's Tony Award–winning play. In a role that **Joan Fontaine** campaigned for, that **Jennifer Jones** agreed to play until she became pregnant, and that **Faye Dunaway** tackled for television decades later in 1982, Kelly deglamorized herself for the part of Georgie Elgin, a bereaved New York City housewife conditioned to an unhappy marriage after the accidental death of her five-year-old son. Once a "hopeless drunk" who "set fire to [a] hotel

Holding her freshly bequeathed statuette, *Country Girl* star Grace Kelly is congratulated by 1955 Oscar host Bob Hope before leaving the stage at the RKO Pantages Theatre in Hollywood. The next day, Kelly celebrated her victory at Paramount Studios with a cake decorated with the figure of an Oscar. (© A.M.P.A.S.®/Photofest)

In what seemed like a fairy-tale wedding to the millions of viewers who watched it on TV, Grace Kelly, just one year after winning her Best Actress Oscar, married Prince Rainier III of Monaco in April 1956 while saying good-bye to her Hollywood career. (Photofest)

suite" in a fit of depression and was found "stretched out across the bed . . . with her wrists cut and bleeding."[14] Georgie is forced to step up in her marriage and safeguard her husband (a former Broadway star played by Bing Crosby) from the same kinds of debilitating experiences.

For going outside her comfort zone, Kelly received a Best Actress Oscar nomination for *The Country Girl*. However, just days before the 1955 Academy Awards, the actress found herself in a fierce battle with her home studio of MGM. Like **Bette Davis** and **Olivia de Havilland** before her, Kelly refused the bad roles that were being handed down to her and was consequently told "that her salary would be withheld until she came back to work on assignment." In response, she angrily informed "the press about Metro's action against her" and was subsequently barred from the studio and its wardrobe consultants.[15] Irritated and provoked, she then turned to the designer Oleg Cassini and the Paramount couturier Edith Head and, in preparation for the Oscar ceremony, was classically adorned in an aquamarine spaghetti-strapped gown that she modeled for the pages of *Life* magazine.

Although Kelly won the New York Film Critics Award for her trio of 1954 box-office-hit performances (*The Country Girl*, *Dial M for Murder*, and *Rear Window*), she was locked in a tight race for Best Actress. Her competition included the previous year's winner, **Audrey Hepburn** (*Sabrina*), former recipient **Jane Wyman** (*Magnificent Obsession*), first-time Black Best Actress nominee Dorothy Dandridge (*Carmen Jones*), and frontrunner Judy Garland (*A Star Is Born*)—who, "recovering from an emergency Caesarean," had "television cameras set up in her hospital ward" in case of her victory.[16] But at the surprise announcement of Kelly's name by her former paramour and *Country Girl* costar William Holden, the deeply moved, 25-year-old actress made her way to the stage. "The thrill of this moment keeps me from saying what I really feel," she warmly but ambiguously acknowledged.[17]

Following the ceremony, Kelly was the star that "everyone wanted to meet and congratulate." But in the throws of a disagreement that prevented her then-boyfriend, Oleg Cassini, from accompanying her, the actress retired to her room at the Hotel Bel-Air and later characterized the evening as "the loneliest moment of [her] life."[18]

Ultimately Kelly adjusted to her seemingly isolated new life as Monaco's princess-consort, busying herself with hosting charities, "distributing the prizes at the Monaco Grand Prix,"[19] and raising her three children—Princesses Caroline and Stéphanie and the Hereditary Prince, Albert II. As later depicted in the divisive film *Grace of Monaco* (2014), starring **Nicole Kidman**, the princess even accepted an offer by her former Pygmalion, Alfred Hitchcock, to star in the film *Marnie* (1964). But when her subjects got word that their princess was planning to appear in a psychological thriller and play a traumatized thief, they protested and "appealed to the Vatican to support their cause."[20] As a result, the former actress, whose films were already banned in Monaco, gave up the role and purportedly spiraled into a depression.

Shockingly, in September 1982, on the same mountain road on which she drove in the 1955 Hitchcock film *To Catch a Thief*, the 52-year-old princess was killed after her car plunged "down a steep embankment" near Monaco.[21] As her daughter Princess Stéphanie recovered from the crash in a Monte Carlo hospital, "nearly 100 million people watched the funeral" on TV and mourned a cinematic icon whose incomparable style continues to keep the world in awe.[22]

Anna Magnani

The Rose Tattoo (1955)

The Italian actress **Anna Magnani** arrived in Hollywood in 1954 like a fish out of water. In Italy, she had acquired the beloved nicknames "Nannarella" and "Mother Tiber" because of her defiant depictions of working-class mothers, widows, and prostitutes. In 1945, she turned into an international cult celebrity for her passionate death scene in the Italian director Roberto Rossellini's *Roma, città aperta*. Filmed during the final months of World War II and marking an end to life under Benito Mussolini's fascist rule (when elections "were abolished," "freedom of speech . . . disappeared," and slogans such as "Believe! Obey! Fight!" "covered public buildings"),[1] the film epitomized the Italian neorealist style, which was characterized by location shooting, natural lighting, and the frequent use of nonprofessional actors. As part of an emerging group of "actors and directors . . . beginning to explore a more unaffected, less glamorous view of humanity,"[2] the actress helped to bring about an enormous change in the perception of film stardom.

A few years later, Magnani again caught moviegoers' attention for her portrayal of a "demented goat-tender" who "thinks she is carrying the child of Christ" in Rossellini's 1948 Italian film *Il miracolo* (aka *The Miracle*).[3] Condemned as sacrilegious by the Catholic Church when it was shown in New York, the film eventually led to the "Miracle Decision"—a landmark 1952 ruling by the United States Supreme Court that triggered a decline in film censorship by recognizing that film is an artistic medium entitled to free speech under the First Amendment.

At this time, foreign films were coming into vogue in America, with the rise of a postwar international art cinema that introduced audiences that were dissatisfied "with the entertainment model of commercial cinema" to the works of Ingmar

Unlike any American actress at the time, and a far cry from the traditional beauties groomed by Hollywood, *Rose Tattoo* star Anna Magnani—one of the faces of the Italian neorealism movement—provided something new to filmgoers of the 1950s with her striking persona, temper, and intensity. (Photofest)

Representing a new take on the sexual dynamics of the 1950s, Anna Magnani and costar Burt Lancaster pose for this erotically charged publicity still from *The Rose Tattoo* (1955). (Paramount/Viacom/Photofest)

Bergman, Federico Fellini, Akira Kurosawa, and others.[4] Concurrently in Rome, Magnani came into contact with the American playwright Tennessee Williams. The two shared a fearlessness "in their determination to live unconventional lives,"[5] and Williams eventually invited Magnani to the United States to star in his 1951 stage production *The Rose Tattoo*—the follow-up to his groundbreaking Broadway plays *A Streetcar Named Desire* (1947) and *Summer and Smoke* (1948). But Magnani, for whom the role of the widowed Sicilian immigrant and mother Serafina Delle Rose had specifically been written, turned down the part, recoiling at the thought of performing in English (a language that she barely spoke).

Magnani's outlook, however, changed. For starters, liberated Italian audiences were growing tired of the "taxing emotional workouts" conveyed in her work. As "the celluloid icon of postwar reconstruction," she and her films—in direct opposition to a new breed of "rose-tinted" dramas and comedies featuring Vittorio Gassman, Marcello Mastroianni, Gina Lollobrigida, and **Sophia Loren**—were increasingly seen as "living reminder[s] of hard times past."[6] Moreover, Magnani—driven to threats of suicide over the professional and romantic betrayal of Rossellini, who had ditched her and sabotaged his own dreams of "living in Beverly Hills" to run away with a married **Ingrid Bergman**[7]—warmed to the idea of a Hollywood career as a subtle form of revenge. After she appeared in the director Jean Renoir's English-based *The Golden Coach* (1952), in which she plays an 18th-century actress performing in a commedia dell'arte acting troupe (historically, the first troupes to hire female actors), Magnani finally agreed to star in the 1955 screen adaptation of *The Rose Tattoo*.

Helping to enliven Tennessee Williams's adult-minded script "for a Hollywood desperate to win back its customers" from "their living room televisions,"[8] Magnani joined the cadre of actors who would become associated with the playwright's work—including Marlon Brando, Montgomery Clift, **Katharine Hepburn**, **Vivien Leigh**, Paul Newman, **Geraldine Page**, **Jessica Tandy**, **Elizabeth Taylor**, **Joanne Woodward**, and **Jane Wyman**. *The Rose Tattoo* focuses on the discontents of life among a group of Sicilian immigrants living on the Mississippi Gulf Coast, and it provided Magnani with a tailor-made character whose mercurial, hot-tempered foreignness seemed to ignore the dictates of a chauvinistic American male society. Magnani's character of Serafina uses "her body to tell us what her devoutly Catholic character will not" (and *could not* under the Production Code).[9] She grapples with her tortured new reality after the death of her unfaithful husband, with whom she shared an enormous appetite for sex. In time, she struggles to fight off her attraction to a brutish truck driver (played by Burt Lancaster) and break free from "Old World institutions" including "fidelity to her late husband."[10]

The Rose Tattoo was partially filmed next door to the Key West, Florida, property owned by Williams (who was then writing *Cat on a Hot Tin Roof*) and proved to be a difficult shoot. Known for having "big strong teeth" that always seemed ready "to bite" and a voice that could "make the simplest word sound like an expletive,"[11] Magnani reportedly caused Lancaster to walk off set and threaten not to return until the domineering actress stopped attempting to direct him. What is more, Magnani, who declined to wear makeup to cover "the black circles under her eyes" or permit the studio's stylist to work on her disheveled hair ("This is not Magnani!" she insisted), inadvertently broke the ribs of supporting actress Virginia Grey while shooting a fight scene. "Script say [*sic*] fight—so we fight!" she bluntly reasoned.[12]

Much like *A Streetcar Named Desire* (1951), *The Rose Tattoo* posed "significant challenges" to the weakening Production Code.[13] As a consumer product, the film was lambasted by the National Legion of Decency for "provoking sexual desire,"[14] as seen in titillating publicity stills featuring Magnani ogling Lancaster and the rose tattoo painted on his naked chest.

Despite the film's controversy, Magnani received the New York Film Critics Award and was nominated in the Best Actress category ahead of the 1956 Academy Awards. Nonetheless, she did not believe that she would win the Oscar. Wanting to be measured only on her performance and not on "her handshaking ability," the "anti-diva," "anti-bourgeois" actress refused to budge from her home base in Rome.[15] Her competition included former winners **Katharine Hepburn** (*Summertime*) and **Jennifer Jones** (*Love Is a Many-Splendored Thing*), Eleanor Parker (*Interrupted Melody*), and **Susan Hayward** (*I'll Cry Tomorrow*). Marisa Pavan, who played Magnani's daughter in *The Rose Tattoo*, ultimately accepted the Best Actress Oscar on her behalf. With her Oscar victory, Magnani became the first Italian actress to win the internationally coveted prize. At a press conference at Paramount's office in Rome the following day, she was amusingly presented with a life-size substitute Oscar until the real one arrived from Hollywood.

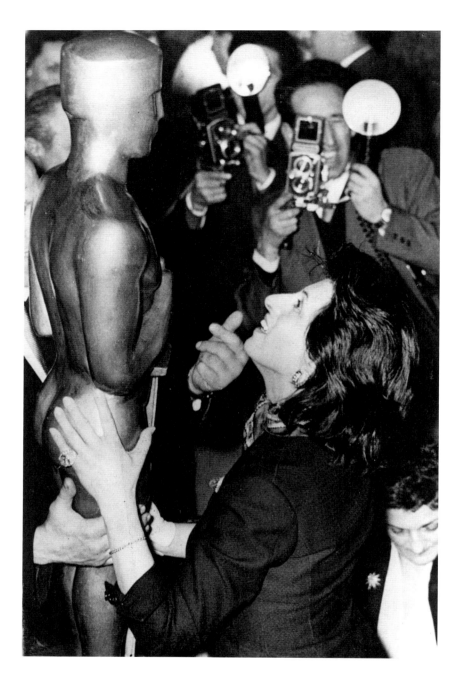

Soon after winning the Best Actress Oscar for her performance in *The Rose Tattoo* (1955), Italian star Anna Magnani was presented with a substitute Oscar at a 1956 press conference in Rome until the real one arrived from Hollywood. (© A.M.P.A.S.®/ Photofest)

Certainly, Magnani could never have predicted her good fortune. Born out of wedlock on March 7, 1908, to an Egyptian father who disappeared and an Italian-Jewish mother who worked as a seamstress and eventually moved to Alexandria, Egypt, Magnani was largely raised in the Porta Pia slum district of Rome by her maternal grandparents. She eventually attended a local convent school, where her passion for acting blossomed by way of the school's lavish Christmas pageants.

In 1925, Magnani trained in Rome at the Eleonora Duse Royal Academy of Dramatic Art, an institution that she was barely able to afford. She survived "for long stretches on black coffee and cigarettes" while working with her "hand outstretched . . . until she held her day's pay."[16] Gaining a reputation as a hot-tempered actress with a "wounded yet driven face,"[17] Magnani began to perform in cabarets and nightclubs before venturing into film and theater. Despite her training, she relied on an instinctual acting approach that transformed her volatility into a raw, "natural-as-life" performance style.[18] "Most movies show only beautiful, well-dressed women," lamented the actress about the "arousing display of the female form" that both Hollywood and the bourgeois, Mussolini-era "white telephone" movies had long been exploiting.[19] "Why not ordinary, down-to-earth women for a change?"[20] For her practical style and candid resolve, Magnani—operating at a difficult time that was brightened to some extent by Italian women's newfound right to vote in 1946—affected legions of female fans who finally felt validated, liberated, and singularly understood.

Capitalizing on her Oscar success, Magnani went on to star in such Hollywood productions as *Wild Is the Wind* (1957; for which she received the anatomically correct "Italian Oscar," the David di Donatello) and *The Fugitive Kind* (1959; based on the Tennessee Williams play *Orpheus Descending* and costarring Marlon Brando and **Joanne Woodward**). Entering her 50s and feeling overshadowed by the likes of **Sophia Loren** (the Italian "slum kitten packaged for international consumption . . . as a younger, domesticated, sexualized version of Magnani"),[21] the actress largely retreated to the stage while appearing in such Italian film productions as *Risate di gioia* (1960; opposite Totò, her friend and longtime collaborator) and the director Pier Paolo Pasolini's allegedly immoral *Mamma Roma* (1962).

Magnani was diagnosed with pancreatic cancer and died in 1973 at the age of 65, survived by her son (her only child from a short-lived affair with the Italian actor Massimo Serato). Her jam-packed funeral at the Basilica of Santa Maria sopra Minerva—just steps away from her terrace overlooking the Pantheon and its surrounding Roman "monuments where . . . she had walked at night, alone, in the company of her dog"[22]—generated the kind of fanfare that was commonly held in reserve for religious leaders. Symbolizing the soul of her country, Magnani— whom **Bette Davis** lauded as "the greatest actress" for possessing a technique that "matches Vermeer['s] for clarity and delicacy"—was laid to rest in the family mausoleum of her former collaborator Roberto Rossellini, with whom she shared a lasting bond "that couldn't be replaced."[23] Undoubtedly, her legacy represents an integral feminism that, however loud, intense, and eruptive, helped to fracture not only film censorship but also the institutionalized shackles of female oppression.

Joanne Woodward

When **Joanne Woodward** arrived in Hollywood, studio executives were unsure of what to do with her. "The problem is you have no image," explained **Shirley MacLaine** while pointing out the actress's varied range of screen roles.[1] In spite of her extensive acting training and "apple-cheeked wholesomeness," Hollywood tried to "transform [Woodward] into yet another femme fatale"—an attempt to which the actress "reportedly hissed at executives" with a stern and unwavering "forget it!"[2] Indeed, Woodward never sought to become a screen goddess in the mold of **Elizabeth Taylor**, Marilyn Monroe, Joan Collins, or Kim Novak, and it soon became clear that the multifaceted thespian—who possessed an obvious disdain for stardom in general—was fundamentally motivated by "movie roles that required trained skills more than tight skirts."[3]

Even as Woodward devoured movie magazines as a child and tried, as an obsessive fan, to climb into the limousine that carried **Vivien Leigh** and Laurence Olivier to the star-studded 1939 Atlanta premiere of *Gone with the Wind*, she never saw acting as anything less than a respected craft.

Born on February 27, 1930, in Thomasville, Georgia, Woodward began acting as a child. As a teenager, she successfully entered beauty contests before majoring in theater at Louisiana State University. When her divorced father (a former educator) moved to New York City to become a publisher, Woodward followed suit and enrolled at New York's Neighborhood Playhouse (where she was taught by Sanford Meisner) and the Actors Studio (where she was instructed by Lee Strasberg).

Under the influence of the Method actors Montgomery Clift and Marlon Brando (whose raw and electric portrayal of Stanley Kowalski in Tennessee Williams's *A Streetcar Named Desire* astounded Broadway in 1947), Woodward eagerly learned the

The Three Faces of Eve (1957)

Joanne Woodward shows three separate personalities in this wardrobe test shot triptych from *The Three Faces of Eve* (1957). (Twentieth Century Fox Film Corporation/Photofest)

Method—a collection of techniques first "developed by Konstantin Stanislavsky in the Moscow Art Theatre in the early 20th century."[4] In the process of studying these techniques, Woodward rubbed shoulders with "a new breed" of actors that included **Anne Bancroft**, James Dean, **Geraldine Page**, and Anthony Perkins.[5] Deviating from classical acting, the Method enabled actors "to draw out naturalistic emotions by exploring the complex psychological motivations of the character they were playing and to forge a personal identification with the role."[6] "Driven by artistic [and] not commercial aspirations," these actors "brought a new, edgy realism to their work, more internal and personal than the standard theatrical fare audiences were accustomed to."[7] But as **Shirley Booth** noticed, there was also a flip side to this detailed preparation, as Woodward—during rehearsals for the play *By the Beautiful Sea* (1954)—reportedly "spent too much time . . . questioning her motivation for every step she took, and not enough time learning her lines." After putting up with this for several days, **Booth**, at the end of her rope, finally uttered, "She's gotta go!"[8]

In the midst of this education, Woodward encountered the shy, handsome, and "genuinely humble" Paul Newman, a budding actor who had studied with Strasberg and "majored in directing at the Yale Drama School."[9] Woodward and Newman initially met at the office of a mutual agent before striking up a platonic friendship. They soon found themselves cast (she as a permanent understudy) in the 1953 Broadway production of William Inge's Pulitzer Prize–winning play *Picnic*.

The strength of Woodward's subsequent performances onstage and on television earned her a seven-year contract with 20th Century-Fox. She eventually learned that the popular nonfiction book *The Three Faces of Eve, a Case of Multiple Personality* was to be made into a film with Judy Garland mentioned as a possible star. The film afforded "one of the most extraordinary opportunities" for any young actress to show off her "talent [and] versatility." After Garland failed to follow through, Woodward jumped at the chance to play "three of the best parts of the year"[10] and eventually studied the book in preparation for her "psychologically daring" role.[11]

Released the same year as the similarly themed, Eleanor Parker–starring drama *Lizzie*, *The Three Faces of Eve* (1957) delved deep into the topic of dissociative identity disorder, with Woodward, as the sad and withdrawn Georgia housewife Eve White, ultimately assuming the part of "three distinct women connected tenuously by a single psyche."[12] After Eve endures a series of "splitting headaches and spells of amnesia,"[13] not to mention exhibiting bizarre behavior that results in the attempted strangulation of her young daughter, she is sent to a psychiatrist (played by Lee J. Cobb). Under hypnosis, over the course of many sessions, two alternate personalities emerge: the "upright [and] straightforward" Jane and the "tartish" Eve Black, who "sneers at her [abusive but ultimately aroused] husband . . . and takes up with any male who will give her a big hello."[14]

Woodward utilized the Method for a performance that was unanimously well received and even praised by one reviewer as so masterfully projected that "you

One of Hollywood's first power couples: Joanne Woodward celebrates her Best Actress Oscar victory with husband Paul Newman at the 30th Academy Awards (1958). (© A.M.P.A.S.®/ Photofest)

will be sorry to see at least one of them go when her personality is successfully coordinated."[15] For her acting efforts, Woodward found herself nominated in the Best Actress category ahead of the 30th Academy Awards (1958).

Less than two months prior, Woodward and Newman, who had reconnected on the set of *The Long, Hot Summer* (1958) and were romantically cohabitating with the gay writer and intellectual Gore Vidal and his boyfriend, Howard Austen, in "**Shirley MacLaine**'s old house in Malibu,"[16] quietly married in Las Vegas. "Like a young Sicilian couple seeking the matrimonial blessing of the local Mafia don before heading to the altar," the couple instantly "rang [the Hollywood gossip columnist] Hedda Hopper with the news"—a mandatory, Hollywood star-system ritual "disguised as a courtesy."[17]

As one of the most attractive and talked-about items in Hollywood, Woodward and Newman arrived at the Academy Awards at the RKO Pantages Theatre with

Woodward predicting that the New York Film Critics Award winner, Deborah Kerr, would win for *Heaven Knows, Mr. Allison*. Her additional competition included former winner **Anna Magnani** (*Wild Is the Wind*), **Elizabeth Taylor** (*Raintree County*; who "stayed away . . . because her husband, Mike Todd, had been killed in a plane crash [four days] before"),[18] and Lana Turner (*Peyton Place*; whose boyfriend, "Johnny" Stompanato, would be stabbed to death by her daughter nine days later). Wearing an elegant, emerald-green taffeta gown that she had designed herself and worked on for two weeks with fabric "that cost her all of $100," Woodward inadvertently "caused a minor uproar among the fashion conscious Hollywood set."[19] "[She] is setting the cause of Hollywood glamour back twenty years," ranted **Joan Crawford**, "for whom Joanne had been named."[20]

Nevertheless, on a night that saw the first (and only) female Asian performer (the Japanese actress Miyoshi Umeki) win an Oscar (for her supporting role in *Sayonara*), Woodward's name was surprisingly announced as the winner for Best Actress. Hurrying to the stage without so much as giving Newman a kiss, Woodward glowingly clutched her statuette and confessed that she had "been daydreaming about this since [she] was nine years old."[21] As a result of her victory, any reprimand over her dress was forgiven. "I suddenly became 'acceptable,'" she acknowledged before admitting that she was "almost as proud of that dress" as she was of her Oscar.[22]

After her Oscar triumph, Woodward "settled into a pattern of working only with [Newman]."[23] She additionally excelled under his direction in "a new generation of films in which women's interior lives" are explored,[24] starring in the dramas *Rachel, Rachel* (1968) and *The Effect of Gamma Rays on Man-in-the-Moon Marigolds* (1972). Woodward largely lived outside of Hollywood like fellow American actresses **Helen Hayes, Judy Holliday, Anne Bancroft, Sissy Spacek, Meryl Streep, Frances McDormand, Julianne Moore**, and **Jessica Lange** (who later emphasized how this separation allows one to "actually see how real life progresses").[25] In doing so, she conversely embraced a more "contemplative life" in Westport, Connecticut, and New York City.[26] There, she and Newman, who remained together for 50 years until his death in 2008, raised three daughters in addition to Newman's three children from his previous marriage. "My life was a frenzy of diapers and bottles and scripts and half-sorted clothes," explained the actress,[27] who recognized the discrepancy between parenthood and acting's self-involving nature.

On top of everything, Woodward, like **Nicole Kidman** during her 11-year marriage to the superstar Tom Cruise several decades later, discovered how difficult it was to escape the enormous shadow cast by her husband and his "alarming beauty."[28] Just as the mythological Greek character "Orpheus was torn to bits by women in love with his voice," Newman's "freaky," Adonis-like magnetism propelled autograph hounds to knock at their door and insist on "seeing Paul and his [trademark cornflower] blue eyes."[29] In public, "women would [even] try to tear his clothes off."[30]

But even with Woodward's distinction as the first performer to be given a star on the Hollywood Walk of Fame (in 1960), she professionally resigned herself to second fiddle. An important star despite her amorphous star image, the actress largely retreated into television work, once playing a psychiatrist to a woman with 13 different personalities (played by **Sally Field**) in the TV miniseries *Sybil* (1976). She later earned a final Best Actress Oscar nomination for her performance (opposite Newman) in the Merchant-Ivory production *Mr. and Mrs. Bridge* (1990). A "participant in . . . third-party politics,"[31] Woodward additionally dedicated her time to philanthropic work pertaining to the theater, children with serious illnesses (via the Hole in the Wall Gang Camp), Planned Parenthood, and AIDS research—a subject near to her heart as evinced in her involvement in the landmark gay-themed drama *Philadelphia* (1993).

Susan Hayward

I Want to Live! (1958)

The French writer, philosopher, and existentialist Albert Camus once said, "It is the job of the thinking people not to be on the side of the executioners."[1] In Hollywood's most arresting petition for the elimination of the death penalty, not to mention one of its most stinging indictments of post–World War II misogyny, 1958's *I Want to Live!*, starring **Susan Hayward**, offered the conservative, wholesome, and conformist era of 1950s America a "social problem" movie unlike anything seen before. At a time when the United States experienced a tremendous spike in the criminal behavior of young people reacting to the blandness and rule-abiding hypocrisy of middle-class culture, *I Want to Live!*—with its rebellion-articulating jazz score and "assertive, exclamatory demand"—probed the tensions and "anxieties simmering beneath the surface."[2] Comparable to *Gun Crazy* (1950), *The Wild One* (1953), *Blackboard Jungle* (1955), *Rebel Without a Cause* (1955), and *Touch of Evil* (1958), the film tackled issues of corruption, violence, alienation, drug addiction, and generational conflict and presented audiences with characters living on the edge of society. As the bishop and early-television evangelist Fulton J. Sheen complained throughout the 1950s, these kinds of young people were increasingly seeking new types of thrills such as "alcohol, marijuana, and murder."[3]

I Want to Live! is a gripping portrait of an insubordinate woman who is excessively punished for living "beyond the boundaries that had been carefully set out" under the pastel façade of white-picket-fence America.[4] The movie is squarely centered on Hayward's character—the real-life party girl, battered wife and mother, and hardened criminal Barbara Graham (1923–1955). Convicted of murder after her involvement in the "pistol whipping of a 62-year old Burbank, California woman,"[5] Graham—a media sensation mockingly dubbed "Bloody Babs" by the

In this rare color image from director Robert Wise's anti-death-penalty film noir *I Want to Live!* (1958), Susan Hayward portrays the real-life criminal Barbara Graham, the third woman to be executed by the state of California. (United Artists/Photofest)

tabloid press—ultimately became the third woman to be executed by the state of California despite evidence that she may not have been guilty.

I Want to Live! was controversially brought to the screen by the independent producer and former Academy of Motion Picture Arts and Sciences president Walter Wanger, who had served a four-month prison sentence in 1951 for wounding the lover of his then-wife, the actress Joan Bennett, with a gun. Affected by his experience in jail, Wanger went on to make the prison drama *Riot in Cell Block 11* (1954). He then turned his attention to *I Want to Live!*—a film noir made in fierce "opposition to pressures from police, politicians, [the] press, as well as the studios"[6] because of the questionable police procedures that led to Graham's conviction and gas-chamber execution on June 3, 1955.

For Hayward, *I Want to Live!* solidified her persona as a tenacious "women's-picture" heroine. More than anything else, after four heartbreaking Oscar losses, it additionally provided her with what she had wanted most—the Academy Award for Best Actress.

Born Edythe Marrener on June 30, 1917, to a poor, Brooklyn-based family, Hayward, whose father worked as a subway lineman, grew up with few advantages and no serious acting ambitions whatsoever. In 1937, she nevertheless attracted the attention of the original *Gone with the Wind* director, George Cukor, and the producer David O. Selznick when her pert, pinup features were spotted in a modeling-agency advertisement in the *Saturday Evening Post*. Immersed in the famous "Search for Scarlett" that ultimately resulted in the casting of **Vivien Leigh**, Selznick brought Hayward out to California to test for the coveted role. But after a lackluster audition due to Hayward's brusque Brooklyn accent, thorough lack of acting experience, and a subtle limp that she acquired from a childhood accident, Selznick recommended that the glamorous, copper-haired beauty pack her bags and return home.

Stubborn, self-ruled, and determined to succeed, Hayward conversely cashed in her return train ticket, moved into a cheap Hollywood bungalow, and enrolled in elocution classes. In due course, she signed on with Warner Bros. (which gave her her new name) before moving on to Paramount Pictures, plugging away in secondary roles under the established likes of **Ingrid Bergman**, Paulette Goddard, and **Loretta Young**. Walter Wanger saw in Hayward a youthful **Bette Davis**, and he eventually intervened by buying the remainder of her contract and later selling it to 20th Century-Fox, where the actress starred in such biblical box-office-hit epics as *David and Bathsheba* (1951) and *Demetrius and the Gladiators* (1954).

Throughout her career, Hayward rejected taking part in the "routine sweet and sticky characterizations the average star insists upon" and was met with one suspension after another.[7] Like **Sissy Spacek**, **Jessica Lange**, and **Hilary Swank** several decades later, the risk-taking actress was drawn instead to gritty, marginalized characters of lower-class means who were "marked in some way by tragedy."[8] As **Jessica Lange** acknowledged, "I always found it easier to play those parts. I just think the larger the character, the easier it is. More than anything, though, as an actor, they're just fun to play."[9]

After four previous losses and a 1955 suicide attempt, Susan Hayward, for her performance in *I Want to Live!*, celebrates her Best Actress Oscar victory alongside Best Actor recipient David Niven at the 31st Academy Awards (1959). (© A.M.P.A.S.®/Photofest)

While Hayward gained a reputation in Hollywood as a "tough broad" who was unwilling to play by the rules,[10] she experienced a difficult life at home, where her breadwinning abilities and box-office status bruised her husband's delicate ego. Hayward's idle husband—the actor Jess Barker—once referred to his famous wife as "a good meal ticket,"[11] and he flinched at the notion of becoming a subservient "Mr. Mom" in the 1950s "Father Knows Best" era of patriarchal authority. His jealousy and resentment unhappily set in motion a chain of domestic violence. One episode included Barker throwing his wife into a swimming pool, with Hayward retaliating by pushing a lit cigarette into his face. The upheaval led to Hayward's alcoholism, sleeping-pill dependency, and a bitter custody battle over their twin sons. It also led to her 1955 suicide attempt, immediately after which her unconscious body was carried out to an ambulance in front of a dozen photographers for the entire world to see.

But however stormy her private life, Hayward bounced back and, like Barbara Graham in the chillingly detailed execution climax of *I Want to Live!*, refused to surrender any shred of remaining dignity.

Unlike any other biographical film depicting female capital punishment, including *Mary of Scotland* (1936; with **Katharine Hepburn**), *Marie Antoinette* (1938; with **Norma Shearer**), *Joan of Arc* (1948; with **Ingrid Bergman**), and *The Other Boleyn Girl* (2008; with **Natalie Portman**), *I Want to Live!*, which was made only three years after Graham's death, showed "no compromise of reality."[12] Marking one of the first instances in which a complete execution was depicted "on the commercial screen," the film, in an "almost minute-by-minute account" of Graham's final moments,[13] harrowingly conveyed the tortured mental state of Hayward's character after a jolting seesaw of last-minute stays. Ultimately, she is escorted into the gas chamber wearing a blindfold, as "a horde of fifty onlookers, all of them middle-aged men, [crowd] into the [observation] room" as if to benefit from a "voyeuristically sexualized" peep show.[14] Graham is strapped into her chair and then advised by the prison captain to "count to ten" and "take a deep breath" when she hears "the [cyanide] pellets drop." "It's easier that way," he insists. "How would you know?" she sardonically hammers back.[15]

Hayward campaigned for the Best Actress Oscar by going along with Walter Wagner's extravagant publicity for the film, which included a stirring quote from Albert Camus equating Graham's situation to when "witches were burned."[16] Hayward had already secured the New York Film Critics Award for her shattering performance, but she still faced a challenging field of contenders ahead of the 31st Academy Awards (1959). Her competition included **Shirley MacLaine** (*Some Came Running*), Rosalind Russell (*Auntie Mame*), Deborah Kerr (*Separate Tables*), and **Elizabeth Taylor** (*Cat on a Hot Tin Roof*). Upon the announcement of her name and to "sustained applause," cheers, and whistles,[17] the beaming actress rushed to the stage and dotingly accepted her shining prize. "Thank you very much," she told the audience in her famously versatile voice ("feathery and kittenish at times; gravelly, guttural, and brassy at others").[18] "And thank you, ladies and gentlemen of the

Academy, for making me so very, very happy tonight."[19] After she left the stage, in an unprecedented move giving emphasis to the win that she had "been fighting for with a clinched fist for the past 20 years," Oscar host Jerry Lewis "asked Hayward to come back out and take another bow."[20] Savoring the moment and "convinced that she now had everything she had ever wanted in life," the actress graciously obliged. "I used to make pictures for Academy Awards," she later confessed, "but now I'll act for the joy of it and for the money."[21]

After her Best Actress Oscar victory, Hayward, who had happily settled down with her second husband, the rancher Floyd Eaton Chalkley, returned to her new home in Carrollton, Georgia, where locals greeted her with a splashy ticker-tape parade. Although she was diagnosed with brain cancer (attributed to her proximity to nuclear testing during the 1956 Utah desert production of *The Conqueror*, from which 91 of 220 cast and crew members were affected), Hayward made a brave final appearance at the 46th Academy Awards (1974). Despite her frail condition, which rendered her bald and "down to just 85 pounds . . . after [several rounds of] cobalt treatments," Hayward, sporting a red wig but glowing "over her peers' loving reception,"[22] presented to an absent, Oscar-winning **Glenda Jackson** the Best Actress award that had meant so much to her. The following year, Hayward died at the age of 57.

Simone Signoret

During the Nazi occupation of France (May 1940–December 1944), **Simone Signoret**, who was raised agnostic despite her paternal Jewish roots, endured cold winters, air raids, and a lack of food and clothing, not to mention the constant fear of being rounded up and deported. Nevertheless, she somehow managed to maintain her delight in simply being alive.

Signoret was born Simone Kaminker on March 25, 1921, in Wiesbaden, Germany, and was raised in the affluent Parisian suburb of Neuilly-sur-Seine. Her father, a skilled journalist who "covered Hitler from the time he became Chancellor of Germany" in 1933, encouraged the discussion of politics and art in the house while sharing with his daughter "the stories of Wagner operas and Greek myths."[1] Developing an adolescent passion for the cinema, Signoret frequently sneaked out of the house as a child and managed to see such life-altering films as *The Jazz Singer* (1927), Fritz Lang's *M* (1931), and *Little Women* (1933; starring **Katharine Hepburn**). To the prying delight of her two much-younger brothers, she additionally displayed her "flair for the dramatic" "in front of the mirror" at home by imitating the French actresses Annabella and Danielle Darrieux.[2]

Signoret, who adopted her French Catholic mother's maiden name and entered her 20s just as World War II broke out, began to mix with a very male-centered Parisian art community in cafés along the Boulevard Saint-Germain. Although the streets of Paris were so dangerous during the occupation that most "people feared leaving their homes," these Left Bank cafés proved to be a safe haven. As Signoret explained, "No Germans came in . . . because there were no prostitutes, no black market alcohol, no music, only coffee with saccharin and talk, talk, talk."[3] By virtue of her intelligence, verve, and striking facial appearance consisting of

Room at the Top (1959)

Simone Signoret and costar Laurence Harvey engage in a doomed romance in the groundbreaking British New Wave drama *Room at the Top* (1959). (Continental Distributing/ Photofest)

"sensual bee-stung lips and heavy-lidded blue eyes,"[4] Signoret caused herself to be instantly noticed and — exceptional for a woman of her time — equally esteemed. In Paris, she came in contact with celebrated writers, artists, musicians, and film-makers including Jean Cocteau, Jean-Paul Sartre, the feminist author Simone de Beauvoir, Alberto Giacometti, Django Reinhardt, and her first husband, the French film director Yves Allégret (16 years her senior).

During this time, even as "the Nazis . . . expanded the definition of Jewry" to include "non-religious Jews and those married to Jews," Signoret confirmed her love for cinema by assisting Cinémathèque Française founder Henri Langlois "in his efforts to hide forbidden films slated for destruction by the Nazis." To this end, Signoret "transported films in a baby carriage to undisclosed locations" and became partly "responsible for saving thousands of films."[5]

Signoret worked without a permit because of her Jewish status and used her café contacts as an entrée into acting. After a fleeting appearance in Marcel Carné's *Les visiteurs du soir* (1942), she went on to collaborate with such leading directors working in France as Luis Buñuel, Henri-Georges Clouzot, and Max Ophüls. While she often played prostitutes in films rooted in misogyny, her assertive looks and tough, opinionated manner broke with "the constraints of feminine representation." In an era when French women had only obtained the right to vote beginning in 1944, Signoret, in films such as *Manèges* (1950), *Casque d'or* (1952), and *Les diaboliques* (1955), strove for a sexual politics that rejected a traditional hierarchy, freeing her to move more easily within both "male and female spheres."[6]

But Signoret was shunned by the *Cahiers du cinéma* film magazine critics turned filmmakers of the French New Wave, who perceived her (and many of the directors with whom she had worked) as too old and too attached to a previous school of cinema that lacked originality. As a result, Signoret shifted gears. Accepting a small but pivotal role that had originally been offered to **Vivien Leigh**, the sensuous, husky-voiced actress packed her bags for England to star in the small-budgeted, antibourgeois-themed *Room at the Top* (1959). In the film, Signoret plays Alice Aisgill, the intelligent, nurturing, and unhappily married mistress to a poor young man ten years her junior (portrayed by Laurence Harvey), who wants to climb his way to "the top" of a Yorkshire mill town by any means necessary. Alice is precariously drawn further into their emotionally and sexually fulfilling relationship and is eventually discarded in favor of a rich industrialist's daughter (Heather Sears). In the end, she is left grief stricken and driven to self-destruction and possible suicide in an alcohol-related car-accident death.

While *Room at the Top* helped to launch the angst-driven British New Wave (a social-realist movement that drew attention to the domestic struggles of the working class and challenged the status quo by focusing on such issues as poverty, abortion, race, sexuality, disability, and nonconservative households), it also helped to further enfeeble the barriers of film censorship. Directed by Jack Clayton from John Braine's best-selling novel, the film was banned from the city of Atlanta and earned an "X" certificate (which in England between 1951 and 1970 deemed a

French actress Simone Signoret celebrates her Best Actress Oscar victory with husband Yves Montand at the 32nd Academy Awards (1960). (© A.M.P.A.S.®/ Photofest)

film suitable only for people aged 16 and over), which deeply fueled its box-office success. At a time when foreign films were unbound by the weakening Production Code and consequently gained in popularity in the United States (something that is rarely the case anymore), the film, with its frank and explicit dialogue, realistically addressed adultery, prostitution, and out-of-wedlock pregnancy while leaving audiences "feeling [like] they were voyeurs in the bedroom."[7] In addition, more than a generation before the age-defying romances enjoyed by **Cher** in *Moonstruck* (1987) and **Kate Winslet** in *The Reader* (2008), the film offered audiences a rare example of an older woman taking charge sexually.

Room at the Top earned Signoret the top acting prize at the 1959 Cannes Film Festival and consecrated her status as an international star. Signoret, who did not "owe her career to Hollywood" in any way,[8] became both a surprise frontrunner in the Oscar race for Best Actress and a near Oscar-night absentee. As a politically controversial figure whose opinions were "highly regarded by intellectuals, artists, and . . . the working class" and whose stance after the United States' atomic bombings of Hiroshima and Nagasaki led to her signature on the 1950 nuclear-arms-banning Stockholm Appeal, Signoret became inextricably linked to the French Communist Party (which she never joined) and its peace-movement demonstrations. In addition, due to her "tour of Russia and the Eastern Bloc" and her involvement in the film adaptation of the playwright Arthur Miller's implicitly anti-HUAC play *The Crucible* (1957),[9] a paranoid, Cold War–era U.S. government came close to denying Signoret a visa to enter the country and thereby attend the Academy Awards.

Further complicating the matter was the "fearsomely powerful, right-wing gossip columnist Hedda Hopper," who had locked horns with Signoret on the topic of free speech as part of Edward R. Murrow's "first all-lady symposium" for his television talk show *Small World*.[10] Seeking vengeance, Hopper later attempted to stop Signoret from winning the Oscar by omitting the actress's name from a published list of nominees and fabricating a tale of her supposed meeting with the Soviet leader Joseph Stalin.

But under "the crisscrossing beams of two enormous searchlights sweeping the sky" in Hollywood,[11] Signoret arrived at the 32nd Academy Awards (1960) with her second husband—the French actor-singer Yves Montand. There, she faced a star-studded short list of Hollywood-manufactured actresses including veteran winner **Katharine Hepburn** (*Suddenly, Last Summer*), **Elizabeth Taylor** (*Suddenly, Last Summer*), Doris Day (*Pillow Talk*), and former recipient and New York Film Critics Award winner **Audrey Hepburn** (*The Nun's Story*). Upon the announcement of her name by presenter Rock Hudson, Signoret took to the stage in pure astonishment. "You can't imagine what it means to me, being French," she graciously acknowledged.[12]

As the first woman to win the Best Actress Oscar by way of a non-American film and the only French citizen to have received this particular honor until **Marion Cotillard**'s victory for *La Vie en Rose* (2007), Signoret's name was written into the history books. But perhaps more importantly, her win also "scored a victory" for Hollywood, proving once and for all that the conservative era of McCarthyism and blacklisting, which compromised the lives and careers of **Ingrid Bergman**, **Judy Holliday**, and countless others, was now "in the past."[13] In response to Signoret's win, an "irate" Hedda Hopper "got so mad, [she] upped and resigned from the Academy."[14]

Not unlike the scandal that hit **Sandra Bullock** in 2010, Signoret suffered a post-Oscar blow when it was rumored that Montand (a former protégé and lover to Édith Piaf) was carrying out an adulterous affair with Marilyn Monroe on the set of *Let's Make Love* (1960). Two years later, similar rumors surrounded his working relationship with **Shirley MacLaine** on the set of *My Geisha*. While the Monroe scandal took a noticeable toll on Signoret, it additionally won her a wave of sympathy that helped to elevate her popularity.

A French cinematic icon, Signoret worked virtually nonstop up until her death in 1985. Shocking some fans by neglecting her degenerating, swollen appearance (caused, in part, by chain-smoking and excessive drinking), she continued her acting by taking advantage of her "ugliness" in a series of textured performances in such films as *Le chat* (1971) and the Best Foreign Language Oscar–winning *Madame Rosa* (1977). Hardly concerned with glamour or even stardom, Signoret, who became a best-selling writer and novelist, ignored the cultural value placed on maintaining the "proper" weight and refused the notion of undergoing a facelift—a procedure that had gained enormous popularity in the 1970s. "There is nothing sadder," she said, "than an actress of my age trying, through artifice, to appear thirty years old. I haven't lost the hours I could have spent looking after my figure. I have spent them living. And it's from having lived that an actor can evolve."[15]

Elizabeth Taylor

In the kingdom of Hollywood, **Elizabeth Taylor** reigned supreme as a leading actress for a quarter century and as a superstar phenomenon for nearly her entire life. As the first female actor to be awarded a record-setting $1 million contract (for 1963's *Cleopatra*—an easy role that she was "not dumb enough" to turn down),[1] Taylor exercised her power with unrelenting conviction while captivating a world that she was deliberately helping to change.

Taylor mesmerized everyone with her astounding beauty, consisting of thick eyebrows, raven-colored hair, and violet-gray eyes. She was born in the London suburb of Hampstead Garden on February 27, 1932, the younger of two children brought up by American parents temporarily residing in England. "As war clouds gathered over Europe," Taylor's parents (her father was an art dealer, and her mother was a former actress) returned their family to the United States, settled in Los Angeles, and were soon persuaded to present their daughter to the film studios of Hollywood. With her "immaculate English [accent]" and attention-grabbing charisma,[2] Taylor almost immediately landed a contract with MGM and roles in such films as *Lassie Come Home* (1943), *Jane Eyre* (1944; starring **Joan Fontaine**), and *National Velvet* (1944), which skyrocketed her to fame at the age of 12.

Taylor operated during "the last gasp of the old studio system," when "self-contained film factories with their own armies of craftsmen, filmmakers, and stars turned out movies by the score."[3] She ultimately endured a rigorous, whirlwind career of "working days and nights on end."[4] Unlike fellow child star **Jodie Foster**, who, decades later, came out of the "Hollywood star production line" remarkably unscathed, Taylor, within the confines of MGM, was "pampered in artificial surroundings" and "corralled into a life of bogus glamour."[5] Upon reflection, she

BUtterfield 8 (1960)

Who's Afraid of Virginia Woolf? (1966)

Elizabeth Taylor waits to be properly lit in this off-camera shot from *BUtterfield 8* (1960). Playing the assertive prostitute Gloria Wandrous, the actress offered audiences a bold antithesis to images of victimized women that were commonly projected. (Metro-Goldwyn-Mayer Inc./Photofest)

owned up to having experienced an "awful," schizophrenic adolescence in which reality and illusion were virtually indistinguishable.[6] "My toughest role is trying to grow up," she once explained.[7]

By the time Taylor took home her first Oscar at age 29, she had already been married *four* times, divorced twice, and widowed once, and she had given birth to three children. Additionally, she had appeared in 30 films, effortlessly transitioning from adolescent star to ingénue to leading lady.

But for all the excitement Taylor generated onscreen, her films were often no match for the tabloid-selling dramas unfolding in her own life. Altogether, she had eight marriages to seven men, numerous affairs, epic struggles with prescription drugs and alcohol, and "more than 70 illnesses, injuries, and accidents requiring hospitalization."[8] She additionally celebrated friendships with the likes of Montgomery Clift, James Dean, Rock Hudson, **Liza Minnelli**, Malcolm Forbes, Colin Farrell, and fellow child stars Roddy McDowall and Michael Jackson. Indeed, her jet-set, jewelry-consumed reality, which crisscrossed the globe between Hollywood, New York, London, Rome, Puerto Vallarta, Botswana, Sardinia, Monte Carlo, and Gstaad, Switzerland, appeared to operate at a fever pitch. Besieged by both roving photographers and a persistent, frenzied mob scene of fans pushing and shoving to get closer to her, Taylor undoubtedly reached a threatening, **Mary Pickford**-like level of celebrity stardom in which she often had to rely on police escort to get from point A to point B. But she was rarely blinded by the glare of such attention and never needed to sentence herself to a life of isolation as a result of that glare. Even decades after her acting career began to fade, she managed to maintain her power of celebrity by knowing how to keep a gossip-obsessed public craving for more.

Captivating the world's attention, Taylor suffered a near-fatal bout with pneumonia that—just weeks before the 1961 Academy Awards—required an emergency tracheotomy procedure. As many film scholars have argued, her well-publicized, "Lazarus-like" return from the dead earned her a wave of voter sympathy that was probably responsible for her first Oscar victory for *BUtterfield 8* (1960).[9]

Based on the 1935 novel by John O'Hara and directed by Daniel Mann (who had guided **Shirley Booth** and **Anna Magnani** to Best Actress Oscar victories), *BUtterfield 8* tells the story of the nymphomaniac New York City model and prostitute Gloria Wandrous. A critically reviled but commercially successful Metrocolor drama that Taylor made "under contractual duress" and was said to deplore,[10] the film, more recently examined, has been hailed for Taylor's self-respectful "brand of pro-sex feminism."[11] At a time when many Hollywood movies showed female sex symbols as a "creation of male oppression" and a mere object for men to "live out [their] fantasies and obsessions" (e.g., Hope Lange in *Peyton Place* [1957], **Shirley MacLaine** in *Some Came Running* [1958], Martha Hyer in *The Best of Everything* [1959], Susan Kohner in *Imitation of Life* [1959], Janet Leigh in *Psycho* [1960], Yvette Mimieux in *Where the Boys Are* [1960], and Tippi Hedren in *The Birds* [1963] and *Marnie* [1964]),[12] Taylor's assertive performance offered audiences a bold antithesis

For her performance in *BUtter-field 8* (1960), Elizabeth Taylor celebrates her Best Actress Oscar victory backstage at the 33rd Academy Awards (1961). Weeks before, the actress—shown here with a tracheotomy scar on her neck—was in the hospital with a life-threatening bout of pneumonia. (© A.M.P.A.S.®/Photofest)

to depictions of victimized women that were commonly projected. In one scene, her character defiantly scrawls "No sale!" with lipstick on the living room mirror of her wealthy married lover (played by Laurence Harvey) after he leaves "her a promissory note for $250."[13] In another scene, after a heated quarrel, she "grinds her stiletto heel into his elegant shoe." As the feminist critic Camille Paglia later observed, "It's male v. female—a ferocious equal match. He's strong, but she's strong, too."[14]

Weeks following Taylor's tracheotomy, and with a visible scar "snaking down one side of her windpipe,"[15] the actress—frail but beautifully draped in Christian Dior—made her way down the first comprehensive, publicity-driven red-carpet procession preceding the 33rd Academy Awards (1961) held at the Santa Monica Civic Auditorium. In a race for Best Actress in which all four of her fellow nominees had won a lead-up award, Taylor managed to come away as the sentimental victor by beating former winner **Greer Garson** (*Sunrise at Campobello*), Greek actress Melina Mercouri (*Never on Sunday*), New York Film Critics Award winner and six-time nominee Deborah Kerr (*The Sundowners*), and **Shirley MacLaine** (*The Apartment*), who later joked that she had "lost to a tracheotomy!"[16] Escorted to the stage by Taylor's fourth husband and *BUtterfield 8* costar, Eddie Fisher (whom she had scandalously stolen away from actress Debbie Reynolds in 1959), the actress took to the podium amid rousing, thunderous applause. "I don't really know how to express my gratitude for this," she quietly stated. "I guess all I can do is say thank you, thank you with all my heart."[17] Overwhelmed, she then proceeded to a backstage bathroom and fainted.

Six years later, Taylor secured her second Best Actress Oscar for *Who's Afraid of Virginia Woolf?* (1966), but this time her victory had little to do with voter condolences. Lauded as one of the most towering performances ever committed to film, Taylor's boozy, bitchy, and embittered Martha—the festering, sadistic wife to a failed New England university associate professor named George (played by Richard Burton)—revealed a raw and novel side of her acting that proved to doubters just how compelling she could be. For the coveted role, Taylor signed on for $1.1 million after knocking out the likes of **Patricia Neal**, Rosalind Russell, and **Bette Davis** (whose "What a dump!" line from 1949's *Beyond the Forest* is notably used in the film). To prepare for the part, the 34-year-old Taylor, who was "a good fifteen years younger than her character,"[18] aged her face with makeup, donned a frumpy gray wig, and even gained a staggering 25 pounds.

Based on the controversial 1962 Edward Albee hit stage play, *Who's Afraid of Virginia Woolf?* takes place late one evening at the home of George and Martha. There, a young college professor and his wife (George Segal and Best Supporting Actress Oscar recipient Sandy Dennis) join their hosts for drinks, only to witness a verbal sparring match that explodes after years of masked resentment and silent rage. With its bold and vulgar use of profanity and sexual insinuation, the film contributed to the "downfall of screen censorship" in the United States while leaving audiences uncomfortable and satisfyingly drained.[19] In addition to showing Taylor utilizing the middle finger, the film featured "eleven 'goddamns,' seven 'bastards,' a 'screw you,' a 'hump the hostess,' [an] 'up yours,' and a reference to 'monkey nipples.'"[20] The film eventually forced the Motion Picture Association of America to replace the Production Code Seal with the lenient but age-restrictive dictates of the new film-rating system, which acclimated to the tastes of a less naïve, late-1960s demographic. Owing much to Taylor's "viperish-then-vulnerable" performance,[21] *Who's Afraid of Virginia Woolf?* thus became the first movie to be given the disclaimer, "No one under 18 will be admitted unless accompanied by his parent."

In this rare color image, Elizabeth Taylor—widely regarded as one of the most beautiful women in the world—was transformed into an aging, spiteful, and alcohol-driven associate professor's wife in *Who's Afraid of Virginia Woolf?* (1966). (Warner Bros. Pictures Inc./Photofest)

Ahead of the 39th Academy Awards (1967), Taylor, the corecipient of the New York Film Critics Award (with Lynn Redgrave), was nominated amid an international field of Best Actress contenders. Her competition included the French actress Anouk Aimée (*A Man and a Woman*), the Polish actress Ida Kaminska (*The Shop on Main Street*), and the British sisters Lynn (*Georgy Girl*) and Vanessa Redgrave (*Morgan—A Suitable Case for Treatment*). Taylor was regarded as the heavy favorite for her performance in *Who's Afraid of Virginia Woolf?* (a movie read by many viewers as a parallel to her own volcanic marriage to her fifth husband and 11-time costar, Richard Burton). Ultimately, the actress clinched the Oscar, with former recipient **Anne Bancroft** accepting it on her behalf. But furious that Burton had not also won for his performance, she was reportedly unable to fully appreciate her second Best Actress Oscar victory.

Although Taylor was never able to recapture the critical glory that she had previously achieved, she nevertheless continued to forge ahead in more daring, campy, and experimental projects that allowed her to live out her self-indulgent fantasies and get paid for doing it. But as the years passed on, Taylor's film career (and side profession as a successful marketer of high-priced perfumes) was eclipsed

In a quiet moment of script analysis for the bombastic drama *Who's Afraid of Virginia Woolf?* (1966), Elizabeth Taylor is photographed off-camera with costar (and fifth husband) Richard Burton. (Warner Bros. Pictures Inc./Photofest)

by an urgent call to action. The AIDS crisis, which was first recognized in 1981 and began as a quiet, deadly pandemic, became her paramount concern. At a dark time when the "gay plague" became a shameful casualty of government neglect, Taylor, even before the 1985 AIDS-related death of her *Giant* (1956) costar Rock Hudson, decided to use her fame in a constructive way and "emerged as a powerful voice for tolerance and compassion."[22] "Shocked when many of her Hollywood colleagues refused" to risk "their fame on a cause shrouded in such a social stigma" that "gay people stopped being [seen as] human beings and started becoming the enemy,"[23] Taylor redoubled her courageous activism. "Giving her cause immense publicity,"[24] she frequently visited AIDS hospices, held gala fund-raising events, testified before Congress to plead for funding, cofounded the American Foundation of AIDS Research (amfAR), and persuaded the reluctant U.S. President Ronald Reagan to finally discuss the issue openly. Defying the law, she even "ran an underground network to provide experimental HIV medication to patients."[25]

Appropriately, Taylor's activism earned her many accolades, including the Academy's Jean Hersholt Humanitarian Award in 1993. Accepting the award from the very industry that had created her, Taylor called on the audience "to draw from the depths of [their] being to prove that we are a human race. To prove that our love outweighs our need to hate. That our compassion is more compelling than our need to blame. That our sensitivity to those in need is stronger than our greed. That our ability to reason overcomes our fear. And that at the end of each of our lives, we can look back and be proud that we have treated others with the kindness, dignity, and respect that every human being deserves."[26] An icon of beauty, glamour, and unwavering humanitarianism, Taylor died on March 23, 2011, at the age of 79.

Sophia Loren

Two Women (1960)

When the international superstar **Sophia Loren** was nominated for her performance in the Italian director Vittorio De Sica's *Two Women* (1960; aka *La ciociara*), she was "shocked to be in the running" for the English-language-centric Academy Award.[1] Prior to Loren, no actor or actress had ever won a competitive Oscar for a performance in a foreign-language film. In the Best Actress category alone, only the Greek actress Melina Mercouri (for her performance in 1960's *Never on Sunday*) had even been nominated for a foreign-language film. Nevertheless, Loren had already picked up top honors from the Cannes Film Festival and the New York Film Critics for her "stunningly honest" performance in *Two Women*.[2] Soon after, she found herself in a competitive rivalry ahead of the 1962 Academy Awards alongside former recipient **Audrey Hepburn** (*Breakfast at Tiffany's*), Piper Laurie (*The Hustler*), Natalie Wood (*Splendor in the Grass*), and **Geraldine Page** (*Summer and Smoke*).

Capitalizing on Loren's chances of winning "the ultimate movie prize," the veteran film distributor Joseph E. Levine got her booked on American TV shows. Levine "even talked NBC into creating a special around her [entitled] *The Life of Sophia Loren*." In addition, he went on to buy "ads in trade newspapers and [hold] private screenings for voters . . . in L.A., . . . New York, Chicago, London, Paris, and even Rome."[3]

Despite Levine's efforts, Loren was too "fear-stricken to fly out to Hollywood."[4] Without access to television or radio to see or hear **Greer Garson** accept the award on her behalf, Loren—drinking, smoking, and eating spaghetti to overcome her anxiety—stayed close to the telephone in her Rome apartment in case of any news. By six o'clock in the morning, the actress "knew the ceremony was

Sophia Loren, around the time she appeared in *Two Women* (1960). While known for her sex appeal, the actress—under the guise of her producer-husband, Carlo Ponti—broadened her scope to be taken more seriously. (Photofest)

The lead character of the widowed shopkeeper Cesira in the World War II–era drama *Two Women* (1960) was originally intended for Anna Magnani. But when Magnani backed out, the part went to Sophia Loren. For her tour-de-force performance, Loren (pictured here with costar Eleonora Brown) became the second Italian actress (after Magnani) to win the Best Actress Oscar. (Embassy Pictures Corporation/Photofest)

over and was sure she had not won."[5] But then, 40 minutes later, the telephone rang. Receiving word from Hollywood by way of the "pleasant voice" of Cary Grant (Loren's former love interest and costar from 1957's *The Pride and the Passion* and 1958's *Houseboat*), Loren's producer, paramour, and future husband, Carlo Ponti, relayed the announcement of her groundbreaking victory in "an explosion of joy."[6] "You have won!" he shouted.[7] "I could hardly believe it," the actress recalled. "It was incontestably the greatest thrill of my life."[8]

Born Sofia Villani Scicolone on September 20, 1934, in a Rome hospital "charity ward for unwed mothers," Loren grew up exceedingly poor in Pozzuoli — a "little seaside town on the outskirts of Naples."[9] As a child, she "lived off bread and sugar and meager bowls of pasta," "never slept in a bed with fewer than three family members," and once "watched . . . her mother [standing] in the street begging for money."[10] At school, she wore clothes made from curtains and sat "in the back row among the orphans" so as not to be picked on for her "tall and terribly thin" frame and her "illegitimate" status.[11]

Comparable to the experiences of **Audrey Hepburn** and **Simone Signoret** during World War II, Loren frequently overheard her "grandparents talking about deportations and Jews, torture and pulled-out fingernails, retaliation and betrayal."[12] The area of Naples and Pozzuoli became one of the heaviest-hit targets throughout the war because of its nearby munitions factory. During the nightly Allied aerial assaults that killed an estimated 25,000 local civilians, Loren and her family were forced to take shelter in the dark and often cold railway tunnels before rushing "out to avoid being run over by the early [4:00 a.m. trains]."[13] "Everywhere," she recalled, "there were babies crying, couples making love, people being bitten by huge rats, sickness, laughter, drunkenness, [and] even death."[14] "My life is not a fairy tale," she explained, "and it's painful still to speak about it."[15]

After the war, Loren "caught a glimpse of her future career when Pozzuoli's only movie theatre reopened" and started showing Hollywood films starring the likes of Tyrone Power, **Joan Crawford**, Betty Grable, and Carmen Miranda.[16] Intriguingly, Sophia's mother — a Greta Garbo look-alike — almost went to Hollywood in the early 1930s to do a screen test with MGM until her mother put a stop to the idea, believing her daughter "would be killed in America" just as the Italian superstar Rudolph Valentino "had been murdered there by the Black Hand."[17] With Sophia's mother eventually "channeling all her frustrated ambition into her own daughter's career," Loren was pushed into an endless cycle of beauty pageants, where wealthy men often looked for their "female possessions."[18] Unexpectedly, this effort resulted in a life-changing encounter with the up-and-coming film producer Carlo Ponti.

Just as the Hollywood producers Irving G. Thalberg and David O. Selznick had shaped the careers of their respective wives, **Norma Shearer** and **Jennifer Jones**, Ponti, who had already helped to mold the careers of Alida Valli, Silvana Mangano, and Gina Lollobrigida, guided Loren from B-pictures to more sophisticated fare. While she refused Ponti's advice to lose weight and get her nose fixed, she agreed to learn English so as not to "limit herself to Italian films." In

addition, she agreed to change her name to "the more internationally-sounding Sophia Loren" (which caused great confusion among those she knew, since the *ph* in Italian "is not pronounced F but P").[19]

At the same time that Loren's career began to fully blossom, Italy became a top "showcase of elegance, modernity, sophistication, license, and style." With Rome as its epicenter, the country, in just 15 years after the Second World War, "galvanized the world's attention" by hosting the 1960 Summer Olympic Games and bringing the "vitality that had invigorated Paris and Berlin and New York in previous

With her Oscar in hand, Best Actress winner Sophia Loren appears with producer Joseph E. Levine (*left*) and Geoffrey Shurlock at a special event in Rome subsequent to the 1962 Academy Awards (which the actress did not attend). (© A.M.P.A.S.®/ Photofest)

decades." "Between the bomb and the Beatles," it functioned "with new vigor" and gave rise to a chic and alluring culture of "Fiat convertibles, . . . sharp lapels, . . . plunging necklines, . . . big sunglasses, and endless cigarettes." Here, Italian "fashion designers and street photographers" collided with international filmmakers and stars (including Tyrone Power, **Ingrid Bergman**, Gregory Peck, **Audrey Hepburn**, Ava Gardner, Charlton Heston, and **Elizabeth Taylor**), many of whom had come to be filmed at the enormous and cost-efficient Cinecittà studio in Rome.[20]

Loren epitomized "the ultimate in sultry, Italian sex appeal" and was not in the least bit "uncomfortable about the attention" that her God-given assets drew.[21] In one film after another, she regularly appeared as the earthy, exotic screen seductress. Hailing from a flesh-worshiping country where, as **Helen Mirren** put it, "women of all ages, shapes, and sizes walk around in bikinis, free, self-confident, and without a care or judgment,"[22] Loren appeared topless in *Era lui . . . sì! sì!* (1951) and swam naked in *Due notti con Cleopatra* (1953). After she arrived in Hollywood, she arrested audiences internationally with her wet, see-through attire in *Boy on a Dolphin* (1957; her English-language debut).

But Loren began to realize that her talent was being eclipsed by her cat-eyed image as an Italian sex goddess, and her movie career soon required a fundamental change. In the midst of a tabloid-exacerbated drama pertaining to her "proxy marriage" to the already-married Carlo Ponti, the sudden reemergence of her estranged father, and the impending marriage of her younger sister (to Benito Mussolini's son), Loren was strategically cast as a widowed shopkeeper "trying to shield her daughter from the horrors of war" in *Two Women* (1960).[23]

Based on the 1958 novel by Alberto Moravia, *Two Women* was initially conceived with the "Oscar-winning powerhouse" **Anna Magnani** placed in the role of the single mother opposite the "mature and voluptuous" Loren as her young daughter.[24] "I was amazed," **Magnani** recalled. "I asked [the filmmakers], 'Did you read the book?' In the book the daughter is small and ugly as a child. I'm ready to play a mother—but to *this* kind of daughter, not Sophia! But if you insist that Sophia play my daughter, I must refuse." Unhappily bowing out of the project, **Magnani** underlined that "there is only one thing left: if Sophia has the courage to play the mother, she should."[25]

A "searing drama" of displacement and the "inhumanity of war" "set in Italy during the final weeks of World War II," *Two Women* traces the arduous journey of Loren's Cesira (a widowed shopkeeper) and her 13-year-old daughter, Rosetta, from the debris of Rome to the "comparative safety" of Cesira's native village and back.[26] The characters intersect with "Nazi collaborators, American soldiers, Italian refugees, pacifists, and prisoners of war," not to mention a "howling mob" of 16 Moroccan soldiers from the Allied forces who savagely gang-rape them inside a bombed-out church.[27] The film, which was remade with Loren in 1989 as a TV movie, echoed the loss of personal dignity and endless sorrow suffered by real-life wartime rape victims of the Ciociaria region of central Italy. It gave the star an opportunity to display her acting range and pay tribute to her own "mother's courage during the years of deprivation and danger." "Before I made *Two Women*, I was a performer," Loren summarized. "Afterward, I was an actress."[28]

In a career that has spanned 60 years and included such further highlights as *El Cid* (1961), *Marriage Italian Style* (1964), and *A Special Day* (1977), Loren came to personify her country, much like its famous national monuments. Forever linked to the "Dolce Vita" era of 1950s and '60s Italy, as commemorated in her participation in the musical *Nine* (2009; costarring **Nicole Kidman** and **Marion Cotillard**), Loren has additionally found success as a devoted mother of two, a Goodwill Ambassador for the United Nations, a cookbook author, and a celebrity marketer of the high-priced perfume Sophia.

Still, "in the center of everything" remains Loren's Oscar for *Two Women*— the very symbol of Hollywood's apparent openness to a more diverse, global, and multilingual cinema. "The chandelier light hits it so it's always shining," the actress divulged. "Of course I dust it every day."[29]

Anne Bancroft

W hen **Joan Crawford** learned that she had not received a Best Actress Oscar nomination for *What Ever Happened to Baby Jane?* and that her rival and costar **Bette Davis** had, the legendary star took it upon herself to "[campaign] against **Davis** . . . in favor of . . . all of the other nominees."[1] In keeping with her penchant for publicity and self-promotion, **Crawford** offered to "accept the award for any winner who couldn't attend."[2] The strong field of nominees ahead of the 1963 Academy Awards also included **Katharine Hepburn** (*Long Day's Journey into Night*), Lee Remick (*Days of Wine and Roses*), **Geraldine Page** (*Sweet Bird of Youth*), and **Anne Bancroft** (*The Miracle Worker*), who gladly accepted Crawford's offer, as she was unwilling to interrupt her Broadway run of Bertolt Brecht's *Mother Courage and Her Children* to attend the Oscar ceremony. Later "watching the [ceremony] on TV with her then-fiancé Mel Brooks,"[3] Bancroft cried with joy as **Crawford** enthusiastically collected her award in what **Davis** perceived as an epic, feud-driven display of passive-aggressive upstaging. (For the record, **Davis** purportedly sought retribution by tormenting **Crawford** on the set of their next project, 1964's *Hush . . . Hush, Sweet Charlotte*.)

The next month, Bancroft finally received her prize when **Crawford** attended a performance of *Mother Courage* and presented the actress—fresh offstage and still in full makeup—with her Best Actress Oscar. When Bancroft was "asked by a reporter if she deserved to win," she openly replied, "Well, if that means I was better than anyone else, [then] the answer is yes!"[4] But despite her pridefulness, her universal acclaim, and her new Academy Award–winning credentials lifting her to the pantheon of acting royalty, Bancroft's "intelligence and fierce independence ensured that she [would never conform] to movie stardom" again.[5]

This opposition, however, was not congruent to Bancroft's way of thinking when she first set out on her long and winding path. Born Anna Maria Louisa

The Miracle Worker (1962)

In this rare color image from *The Miracle Worker* (1962), Anne Bancroft, as the sight-impaired teacher Annie Sullivan, interacts with her pupil Helen Keller (played by Patty Duke) as Helen's mother (Inga Swenson) looks on. (United Artists/Photofest)

Italiano on September 17, 1931, to Italian immigrants, the actress subsequently grew up in the Bronx during the height of the Great Depression. While her mother saved money as a Macy's department store telephone operator, her father worked as a dress pattern maker in New York's garment district. But even when her father became unemployed, Anna—an "irrepressible performer" who learned to sing and dance at the age of two[6]—took tap dance lessons and regularly walked up to strangers to ask if they wanted to hear her sing. As the actress later reasoned, "Why play with dolls when you can sing . . . on the street corner?"[7]

To be sure, Bancroft possessed "an extraordinary body of raw emotion" that "she didn't quite know how to work."[8] After she graduated from high school in 1948, she appeared as Anne St. Raymond on a Peekskill, New York, radio station, supplemented her income by working as a salesgirl and teaching English to the noted Peruvian singer Yma Sumac, and, at her mother's urging, eventually followed in the footsteps of **Jennifer Jones** and **Grace Kelly** by enrolling at the American Academy of Dramatic Arts. Although her graduation performance opened doors for her in television, the fledgling actress ultimately yearned to break into the movies "for the sole purpose of becoming famous." "I thought Hollywood was just the cat's meow," Bancroft explained. "I thought it was the best thing that could happen to a little girl from the Bronx."[9]

Inadvertently, Bancroft received an offer to sign with 20th Century-Fox as a contract player after helping "a fellow actor with a screen test."[10] "Willing to endure anything Hollywood threw at her," including Fox studio head Darryl F. Zanuck's requirement that she select a new name from a list of options given to her, the actress consequently relinquished her stage name of Anne Marno and adopted the more WASPy-sounding "Anne Bancroft," since it "was the only [name] that didn't sound like a stripper."[11]

While groomed "to be a sex symbol" by the womanizing Zanuck (who "routinely summoned" actresses "to a small part of his large, green-paneled office suite" for "afternoon trysts"),[12] Bancroft made a promising debut in *Don't Bother to Knock* (1952; opposite Marilyn Monroe). Alas, she subsequently found herself in a long succession of B-movies, including the 3-D horror *Gorilla at Large* (1954) and *The Girl in Black Stockings* (1957). At first, the entire Hollywood experience seemed "terrific" to the actress: "somebody did my hair every morning [while] somebody else brought me coffee and gave me a Kleenex when I sneezed."[13] But going "downhill in terms of self-respect and dignity" while realizing that she had "learned nothing" in a Hollywood run by Wall Street businessmen who loved their women to have depth, but only when it pertained to their cleavages,[14] Bancroft began to take serious stock of her career.

After divorcing her first husband in 1957, Bancroft moved back to New York, went to psychotherapy three times a week, and attended classes at the Actors Studio. During this time, she discovered "that acting was about more than perks" and began to work with the director Arthur Penn.[15] Under Penn's direction and because of her "funny and authentic" performance style, Bancroft "changed the face of theater" in the William Gibson play *Two for the Seesaw* (1958; opposite Henry Fonda).[16] After she won the Tony Award for Best Featured Actress in a Play, Gibson was "inspired to write *The Miracle Worker* [specifically] for her."[17]

Set in 1887 Alabama, *The Miracle Worker*—a true-life tale of triumph over adversity—centers on the efforts of the 20-year-old teacher Annie Sullivan (played by Bancroft) to "reach" into the world of her six-year-old pupil, Helen Keller, who was left Deaf and blind at 19 months old as a result of a serious illness. Keller—terrified, confused, and unable to communicate—reacts to life with ferocious outbursts and temper tantrums. Only by way of Sullivan's effective teaching of the manual alphabet of sign language is Keller released from her dark and silent "prison."

The 1959 Broadway production of *The Miracle Worker* costarred Patty Duke as Keller (and initially **Patricia Neal** as her pampering, pitying mother) and proved to be a massive hit, fundamentally altering Bancroft's career with a second Tony. In one long, physically demanding scene that escalates into a food-throwing/water-tossing battle of the wills that required

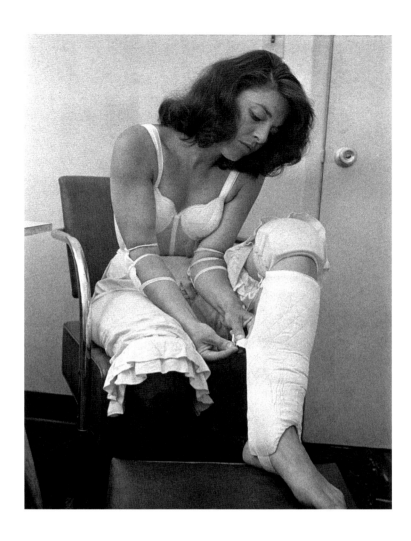

In this off-camera shot, Anne Bancroft applies protective padding to her legs for the physically demanding role of teaching the Deaf, blind, and frustrated six-year-old Helen Keller in *The Miracle Worker* (1962). (United Artists/Photofest)

both actresses to wear protective padding underneath their period costumes, Sullivan attempts to teach Keller the behavioral standards of dining-room-table etiquette. Haphazardly on opening night, Duke—about to "toss a pitcher of water on Bancroft"—overshot her costar "and drenched Rosalind Russell, who was sitting in the first row."[18]

To prepare for the role of Annie Sullivan (1866–1936), Bancroft, who was "known for [her] intensive research," blocked her ears "for long periods of time," learned the manual alphabet of sign language, and observed blind children at New York's Institute of Physical Medicine and Rehabilitation.[19] She even taped bandages over her eyes during a stay in an unfamiliar city, allowing her to better understand Sullivan's own damaged eyesight.

Still, when it came time to adapt the play to the screen in 1962, United Artists wanted to cast either **Audrey Hepburn** or **Elizabeth Taylor** in the title role. Insisting instead on hiring and reteaming Bancroft with the eventual Best Supporting Actress Oscar recipient Patty Duke, director Arthur Penn, who had "been trained in the medium of television,"[20] was ultimately given the green light but only with a budget slashed from $5 million to $500,000.

At a time when television and the rise of TV soap operas took a "toll on the motion picture industry" and helped "to kill off the kind of melodramas that sustained many of the actresses of the 1940s and '50s,"[21] *The Miracle Worker* proved to be as big of a hit in movie theaters as it was on Broadway. Simultaneously, it brought "the sensibility of 1960s European art films to American movies" and paved "the way for the new generation of American directors who came out of film schools."[22] *The Miracle Worker*—with its television aesthetic of close-ups filmed on constricted sets and "insanely long . . . dissolves"[23]—additionally captured Bancroft's hardened character in a way that had not otherwise been seen or experienced onstage.

Capitalizing on her Oscar success, Bancroft worked "at her own pace and inclination" while taking on new, unconventional challenges.[24] She turned down *Funny Girl* onstage (which ultimately made **Barbra Streisand** a star) and instead appeared as an "emotionally abused wife" in the British film *The Pumpkin Eater* (1964; featuring **Maggie Smith**), as a sexually obsessed medieval nun in the 1965 play *The Devils*, and as the bored, middle-aged Mrs. Robinson in the "anti-establishment" box-office sensation *The Graduate* (1967).[25] Predating **Barbra Streisand** (*Yentl*, 1983), **Jodie Foster** (*Little Man Tate*, 1991), **Diane Keaton** (*Unstrung Heroes*, 1995), **Sally Field** (*Beautiful*, 2000), **Shirley MacLaine** (*Bruno*, 2000), **Helen Hunt** (*Then She Found Me*, 2007), **Natalie Portman** (*A Tale of Love and Darkness*, 2015), and **Brie Larson** (*Unicorn Store*, 2017), Bancroft additionally went on to direct her own feature-length film, *Fatso* (1980), a comedy about overeating in Italian American culture.

In light of the intimidating women Bancroft played, which seemed to prevent men from approaching her in real life, she was surprised and delighted when the comedic actor, writer, and director Mel Brooks aggressively courted her. As polar opposites equally fascinated by each other, the fellow Manhattanites enjoyed a long, inseparable union that commenced with Bancroft telling Brooks "the story of [her] life" and then "[acting] out *The Miracle Worker*—the entire play—because he hadn't seen it."[26] Before Bancroft's sudden and deeply mourned passing in 2005, the couple bore a son, collaborated on the 1980 drama *The Elephant Man*, costarred in the 1983 comedy *To Be or Not to Be*, and shared an enormous appetite for Chinese food, foreign films, and their Fire Island beach-house getaway. "He makes me laugh a lot," Bancroft once said of her husband. "I get excited when I hear his key in the door. It's like, 'Ooh! The party's going to start!'"[27]

Patricia Neal

Hud (1963)

After suffering through an "almost Biblical succession of calamities," **Patricia Neal**, who was scarcely known to have ever played weak characters, painfully admitted to having once entertained the idea of suicide. "I'd like to," she told *Life* magazine in October 1965, "but I don't know how."[1]

Five years earlier, just months after Neal had costarred with **Audrey Hepburn** in *Breakfast at Tiffany's* (1961), her infant son, Theo, while under the supervision of a nanny, was hit by a speeding New York City taxi and flung from his carriage 40 feet into the air. Simultaneously shopping at a nearby store, the unknowing Neal "heard the wail of an approaching ambulance" and reportedly "said a silent prayer."[2]

In November 1962, Neal experienced yet another tragedy. At the family's new home in Buckinghamshire, England ("a place where you don't get hit by taxis"), and with Theo "still in peril," having sustained neurological damage,[3] the actress's seven-year-old daughter, Olivia, died of a rare form of encephalitis after returning home with a note to parents warning of the school's detection of measles.

As if these misfortunes were not enough, Neal, with a "black cloud" seemingly hovering over her head,[4] suffered a massive stroke in February 1965 that caused a ruptured aneurysm in her brain. The 39-year-old actress had won the Best Actress Oscar for her performance in *Hud* (1963) less than a year before. Now, three months pregnant with her fifth child, she entered into "a coma for more than two weeks and [was] on the critical list for three."[5] Jumping to conclusions, the American trade magazine *Variety* and several other newspapers erroneously printed her obituary.

But Neal, who became half paralyzed, partially blind, and had no memory to speak of, pulled through. With the loving but nonpitying support of her husband, Roald Dahl—the British author of such acclaimed children's novels as *James and the Giant Peach* (1961), *Charlie and the Chocolate Factory* (1965), and *Fantastic Mr. Fox* (1970), the actress was soon undergoing extensive rehabilitation with memory "flash cards originally intended for her brain-damaged son."[6]

The daughter of a coal company manager, Neal was born on January 20, 1926, in the present-day ghost town of Packard, Kentucky. The aspiring actress was "enthralled by performing from a young age" and showed great "talent in reciting monologues at church gatherings."[7] One Christmas, she wrote a letter to Santa Claus asking for drama lessons. Her wish was granted, and before long, Neal, like **Jennifer Jones**, was studying theater at Northwestern University in Evanston, Illinois under the guidance of the legendary acting professor Alvina Krause. With a "burning ambition," she moved to New York City in 1945. There, cash-strapped and subsisting on "tuna fish dishes, doughnuts, and popcorn,"[8] she shared a crammed Upper West Side apartment with three other women. Throughout this time, she slogged her way through auditions, accepted "occasional understudy work,"[9] and toiled as a part-time waitress at a Greenwich Village diner.

In the days before air-conditioning offered a respite from the sweltering New York summer heat, the long-lasting tradition of summer stock theater (in places like Westport, Connecticut, and Dennis, Massachusetts) provided audiences with a cool and frequently open-air forum from which to discover new Broadway talent. For Neal, summer stock proved especially fortuitous, as it led the American playwright Lillian Hellman to offer her a lead in her 1946 production of *Another Part of the Forest*, the prequel to her triumphant 1939 stage play *The Little Foxes*. Demonstrating a powerful command onstage, Neal's performance garnered her the first-ever Tony Award for Best Featured Actress in a Play. She was additionally elevated by advanced-level training alongside Montgomery Clift and Marlon Brando at the newly formed Actors Studio. Almost instantly, Neal was approached by Hollywood with numerous job offers. One of the first came from the Hollywood producer David O. Selznick, who, desperate to sign the actress, indecently promised Neal "an Academy Award for her first part" while unsuccessfully attempting "to get [her] into bed."[10]

But Hollywood, which has been acerbically described by the playwright Clifford Odets as "The Big Knife," by **Julie Christie** as "a throwaway society run by publicity machines," and by **Sandra Bullock** as a place that "can rip people completely apart,"[11] proved to be an uneasy fit for Neal. As **Grace Kelly** attested, the "only value [in Hollywood] seemed to be money, and it seemed to me that many friendships and even marriages were often based on wealth and how a relationship could benefit someone's career. I saw so many unhappy people [there]."[12] Clearly, Neal's initial interface with Hollywood supported this view. The actress was first introduced to the Hollywood film community at a New Year's Eve party where she met Ronald Reagan, with whom she eventually starred in her motion picture debut, *John Loves Mary* (1949). Later that evening, Neal happened to notice Reagan "on the terrace with an older woman," apparently "weeping" over his collapsed marriage to his soon-to-be-ex-wife, **Jane Wyman**.[13]

In the midst of personal tragedies, Patricia Neal earned a Best Actress Oscar for her plain-spoken performance as Texan housekeeper Alma Brown in *Hud* (1963). (Paramount/Viacom/Photofest)

It was not long before Neal joined this unhappy chorus herself. Operating in an industry in which female stars, in the words of **Loretta Young**, "are in intimate daily contact with the most emotionally appealing men in the world," Neal, whose onscreen sexuality "left teenage males of the day lusting after her,"[14] succumbed to a passionate, five-year romance with the screen idol Gary Cooper — her married costar from *The Fountainhead* (1949) and *Bright Leaf* (1950). While Cooper's "off-screen . . . affairs with many of his leading ladies" (including Clara Bow, Marlene Dietrich, **Ingrid Bergman**, and **Grace Kelly**) often overshadowed his own film successes,[15] his scandalous affair with Neal nearly cost him his marriage when the actress discovered that she was pregnant. In view of the fact that **Ingrid Bergman** had "recently had a baby out of wedlock and [had consequently been] locked out of any further work in Hollywood,"[16] Neal and Cooper decided that a then-illegal abortion was the only logical course of action. Ultimately rejected by Cooper, publicly censured, and "suspended by Warner Bros. for refusing to star in a Western with Randolph Scott," Neal left Hollywood and returned to New York on the verge of "a nervous breakdown."[17]

"Ragged from the bitterness [that she] had endured," Neal plunged herself into darker and more introspective projects.[18] This included the Broadway revival of Lillian Hellman's lesbian-themed drama *The Children's Hour* (opposite Kim Hunter) and the original stage productions of *Cat on a Hot Tin Roof* (1956; substituting for Barbara Bel Geddes), *Suddenly, Last Summer* (1958), and *The Miracle Worker* (1959).

By the time Neal set out to play the role of the "cynical, world-weary" housekeeper Alma Brown in 1963's *Hud*,[19] she had little emotion left to uncover. Agreeing to the part six months after the death of her daughter and just as her son had "undergone his seventh operation," the hard-bitten actress nevertheless poured into her character a "quiet ferocity" tough enough to withstand the callous, womanizing ways of Paul Newman's Texas cattle rancher, Hud Bannon.[20] Based on the 1961 novel by Larry McMurtry (who cowrote the screenplays for such comparable modern westerns as 1971's *The Last Picture Show* and 2005's *Brokeback Mountain*), *Hud* captures the "Texas landscape in all its loneliness and emptiness," with Neal's character straying "about on the edge of the action like a forlorn panther."[21] As the "only woman of consequence in the script"[22] opposite Hud, Brandon deWilde's Lonnie, and Best Supporting Actor Oscar recipient Melvyn Douglas's Homer, Alma, who was originally conceived as a Black woman, attends to the Bannon family's individual needs before packing her bags and jetting out of town the instant Hud attempts to rape her. "No thanks," she says in her grown-up southern drawl, "I've done my time with one cold-blooded bastard. I'm not looking for another."[23]

Despite appearing onscreen for a mere 25 minutes and thus winning the Cleveland Critics Circle Award for *supporting* actress, Neal ultimately captured the New York Film Critics Award for *lead* actress as well as a Best Actress Oscar nomination ahead of the 36th Academy Awards (1964). Her competition included **Shirley MacLaine** (*Irma la Douce*), Natalie Wood (*Love with the Proper Stranger*), and British New Wave representatives Rachel Roberts (*This Sporting Life*) and Leslie Caron (*The

L-Shaped Room), the latter of whom Neal had projected to win. At the time, Neal was pregnant with her fourth child and unable to attend the ceremony, but from her home in England, she received word of her victory by way of an early-morning flood of telephone calls. In the middle of this great excitement, Neal's son, Theo, inquisitively asked, "What is an Oscar, Mummy?" "It's a great golden boy," the actress replied, "who whispers in your ear what you've known all your life."[24]

After Neal had fetched her Oscar amid a barrage of reporters and photographers at Marylebone Station in London ("Good heavens," she exclaimed, "I feel just like **Elizabeth Taylor!**"),[25] she enjoyed a post-Oscar hike in salary. In spite of her subsequent stroke, the resilient actress landed a second Best Actress Oscar nomination for *The Subject Was Roses* (1968). Following the leads of the Chesterfield and Lucky Strike cigarette representatives **Claudette Colbert**, **Bette Davis**, and **Jane Wyman**; the Lux Soap models **Olivia de Havilland**, **Joan Fontaine**, and **Judy Holliday**; the soft-drink ambassador **Joan Crawford**; and the Lustre Crème Shampoo delegate **Grace Kelly**, Neal additionally used her celebrity in print and television commercials for Maxim coffee and the headache-relief medicine Anacin. The actress, who was honored with a namesake hospital for her work in the field of rehabilitation, continued to perform up until her death in 2010 at the age of 84. Her resilient story was movingly portrayed in the 1981 television drama *The Patricia Neal Story*, starring fellow Best Actress Oscar winner **Glenda Jackson** as Neal and Dirk Bogarde as Roald Dahl.

Julie Andrews

Mary Poppins (1964)

Possessed with a freakishly "pure, light, and agile" voice capable of spanning five octaves, **Julie Andrews** first demonstrated her great talent "during a singsong in a [World War II] air-raid shelter when she was eight years old."[1] Five years later, she became a preteen sensation after winning over the British royal family at a Royal Command Performance.

Although Andrews eventually beguiled generations of children with a "lady-like purity" in the colossal hit musicals *Mary Poppins* (1964) and *The Sound of Music* (1965), underneath her façade resided a gifted performer with "demons and a lot of depressing memories" stemming from a childhood of "grinding hardship and poverty."[2] "There's got to be a lot of rage down there,"[3] her second husband, the director Blake Edwards, once said.

Andrews was born Julia Elizabeth Wells on October 1, 1935, in the London-adjacent town of Walton-on-Thames. She was subsequently raised by loud, alcoholic vaudevillians "in a series of squalid digs, sleeping in a room where rats crept along the pipes and having her scalp scrubbed and rinsed with vinegar to remove lice."[4] Her mother was a frustrated pianist who took "a factory job to make ends meet."[5] Her "hated stepfather" was a tenor who provided his stepdaughter with singing lessons (under the great opera singer Madame Lilian Stiles-Allen) and "twice drunkenly tried to get into bed with her."[6] Despite her "acute shyness and reserve," Andrews joined her parents onstage, toured the country, enchanted BBC radio listeners with her coloratura soprano range, and took "on the role of the breadwinner to her family of five."[7] At the time, her life became "a bleak and tacky repetition of drafty dressing rooms and cheap hotels in crumbling resort towns."[8]

In this picture revealing what the film *Mary Poppins* (1964) looks like before animation and special effects are applied, Julie Andrews leads her young charges and chimney-sweeping boyfriend (played by Dick Van Dyke) on a psychedelic musical adventure. (Walt Disney Studios Motion Pictures/Photofest)

After Andrews had an unimpressive screen test in London by MGM talent scouts at which she was deemed "unphotographable,"[9] she began to work in West End musicals and, at age 18, was chosen for the lead in the Broadway production of *The Boy Friend* (1954–1955). Out of this success, the gawky and "exceedingly plain" performer was selected to create the role of Eliza Doolittle (opposite Rex Harrison's Professor Henry Higgins) in what became the longest running Broadway production of its day: Lerner and Loewe's *My Fair Lady* (1956–1962).[10] However, when it came time to cast the lead in the 1964 screen version, Andrews was bypassed. Warner Bros. studio president Jack Warner offered the role of Eliza to the Oscar-winning star **Audrey Hepburn**, in spite of a technically inferior singing voice that had to be dubbed. Andrews, meanwhile, had little choice but to sit on the side, where she prepared "a very unprintable reply" in the off chance that she was "offered the dubbing job" herself.[11]

Enjoying Broadway success again as Queen Guenevere in *Camelot* (1960–1963), as well as increasing exposure on American television in such specials as *Julie and Carol at Carnegie Hall* (1962; with the actress and comedian Carol Burnett), Andrews, who had yet to appear in a film, was simultaneously approached by Walt Disney to star as the eponymous Edwardian-era nanny in *Mary Poppins* (1964). She accepted Disney's offer with the caveat that she be released from the project if the opportunity to do *My Fair Lady* arose. Outshining the likes of **Bette Davis**, Mary Martin, and Angela Lansbury for the title role, she soon equipped herself with a "magical satchel and [a] flying umbrella" while learning the pronunciation of a 34-letter word.[12]

The story of *Mary Poppins* focuses on the healing of a dysfunctional family. In the film, Andrews's magical character descends from the London skies to teach Mr. Banks (a workaholic bank manager) and Mrs. Banks (an engaged First Wave feminist) to "better appreciate their own children."[13] Andrews's character occupies herself in a Technicolor world of psychedelic musical adventures comprising live-action, animation, Audio-Animatronics, special effects, and Monet-inspired set designs. She additionally wiles away "her billable hours with her [chimney-sweeping] boyfriend" (played by Dick Van Dyke) as she whips her young charges into shape with her "spit-spot demeanor."[14]

Mary Poppins was based on the popular P. L. Travers book series (1934–1988), which—alongside *Anne of Green Gables* (1908), *Nancy Drew* (1930–2003), *Little House on the Prairie* (1932–1943), *Wonder Woman* (1942–), and *Eloise* (1955; modeled after a young **Liza Minnelli**)—contributed to the small quantity of early 20th-century literature for girls. To be sure, Travers (whose misgivings with Disney were spelled out by **Emma Thompson** in the 2013 film *Saving Mr. Banks*) conceived Mary Poppins as a "conceited and unpredictable" nanny who "never wasted time on being nice."[15] Against Travers's wishes, Andrews's character was generally softened. And against the emerging voices of second-wave feminism and its focus on workplace inequalities, the film—much like 1945's *Mildred Pierce* with **Joan Crawford**—came to be

After losing the lead role in the film version of *My Fair Lady* to Audrey Hepburn, Julie Andrews enjoyed payback at the 37th Academy Awards, where she captured the Best Actress Oscar for her performance in the Walt Disney Studios production of *Mary Poppins* (1964). In this photograph, Hepburn congratulates Andrews backstage amid a crowd of reporters, photographers, and presenter Sidney Poitier (*left*). (© A.M.P.A.S.®/ Photofest) seen as a "coded appeal to women" to restore "the ideal . . . family structure of breadwinning father [and] stay-at-home mother."[16]

Andrews arrived at the August 1964 world premiere of *Mary Poppins* at Grauman's Chinese Theatre — a "glittering extravaganza even by Hollywood standards" — and was greeted by Mickey Mouse, Goofy, Snow White and the Seven Dwarfs, and an assemblage of "entertainers who gestured toward the movie's Edwardian setting."[17] Guaranteed awards-season recognition, Andrews went on to win the Golden Globe for her performance. There, she lightheartedly thanked the man who had rejected her as Eliza Doolittle and "made all this possible in the first place: Mr. Jack Warner." It was "grand fun," Andrews later said. "I hope I didn't sound too bitchy."[18]

Shored up by *The Americanization of Emily* (1964; her personal favorite of her films, which received an X certificate in Britain) and the March 1965 premiere of *The Sound of Music* (the biggest box-office hit since *Gone with the Wind* and a triumph in every market outside West Germany), Andrews became seen as the Oscar frontrunner for *Mary Poppins*, which was nominated for 13 Academy Awards. With *My Fair Lady* star **Audrey Hepburn** notably absent among the contenders, Andrews's competition at the 37th Academy Awards (April 1965) included former winners **Sophia Loren** (*Marriage Italian Style*) and **Anne Bancroft** (*The Pumpkin Eater*), Debbie Reynolds (*The Unsinkable Molly Brown*), and New York Film Critics Award winner Kim Stanley (*Séance on a Wet Afternoon*).

Following **Audrey Hepburn**'s presentation of the Best Actor Oscar to her *My Fair Lady* costar Rex Harrison (who expressed his "deep love to . . . *two* fair ladies"),[19] Sidney Poitier announced Andrews's name as the Best Actress Oscar winner. Draped in a floor-length lemon-yellow chiffon gown and accessorized with long white gloves and a sparkling crystal bib necklace, Andrews received a kiss from her then-husband, Tony Walton (who had been nominated for Best Costume Design for *Mary Poppins*), and took to the stage to accept her award. "I know you Americans are famous for your hospitality," she said, "but this is really ridiculous."[20]

Although *Mary Poppins* became the second-highest-grossing film (after *Gone with the Wind*) to feature a Best Actress Oscar–winning performance, Andrews's reign at the top of the box office was extraordinarily short-lived. Despite her successes, she struggled to disassociate herself from her character in *Mary Poppins* and Maria von Trapp in *The Sound of Music* and soon saw her "stock plummet and [her wholesome, saccharine-sweet] image become twisted and ridiculed as the early 1960s gave way to 'The Sixties.'"[21] Against the backdrop of political assassinations, Vietnam War demonstrations, the Black civil rights movement, Second Wave feminism (as sparked by Betty Friedan's 1963 book *The Feminine Mystique*), drug experimentation, and the widespread use of the birth-control pill, Andrews became a victim of a changing and rapidly dividing culture. To be sure, she operated at a time when the draconian rules of the Production Code evaporated (rules that, for nearly 40 years, "prohibited anything that couldn't be seen by the whole family"),[22] and her audiences consequently drifted to harder-edged forms of entertainment.

Alas, mixed reviews came with her appearance in Alfred Hitchcock's *Torn Curtain* (1966). By 1968, with the anticipated success of Andrews's musical *Star!*, the box-office tills were only "alive with the sounds of silence."[23]

Teetering "on the brink of a nervous breakdown," Andrews "found solace in psychotherapy" with the "analyst to the stars" Milton Wexler.[24] In the process, she participated in group therapy sessions alongside **Jennifer Jones**, Bud Cort, and the architect Frank Gehry and simultaneously met Blake Edwards, "one of the hottest writer-producer-directors" in Hollywood.[25] "Are you going where I just came from?" inquired Edwards,[26] after crossing paths with the actress week after week, at the same time and at the same place. Sharing a similar kind of "wicked wit," Andrews and Edwards married in 1969.[27] Much like **Joanne Woodward**'s partnership with her husband, Paul Newman, the couple worked together almost exclusively as they tried to eradicate Andrews's squeaky-clean image. "I hope I am not as square as some people might think," said the actress, who was once photographed smoking a cigarette on the set of *Mary Poppins* and drove a car with the bumper sticker "Mary Poppins Is A Junkie" on it.[28] Testing the limits, she then went on to bare her breasts in *S.O.B.* (1981) and cross-dress in *Victor Victoria* (1982) before hitting "the sack with her lesbian maid" in *Duet for One* (1986).[29]

Andrews has been unable to sing following a 1997 throat surgery, but the mother of three has since published numerous children's books, appeared in Disney's *Princess Diaries* franchise (2001–2004), and brought attention to the performing arts for children by way of her educational TV series *Julie's Greenroom* (2017). While serving as a Goodwill Ambassador for the United Nations Development Fund for Women (a post later filled by **Nicole Kidman** and **Reese Witherspoon**), she raised awareness for women's human rights including the right to vote and live free from violence. With the ongoing popularity of *Mary Poppins* and *The Sound of Music*, she additionally became the beloved centerpiece of numerous tributes and sold-out sing-along events.

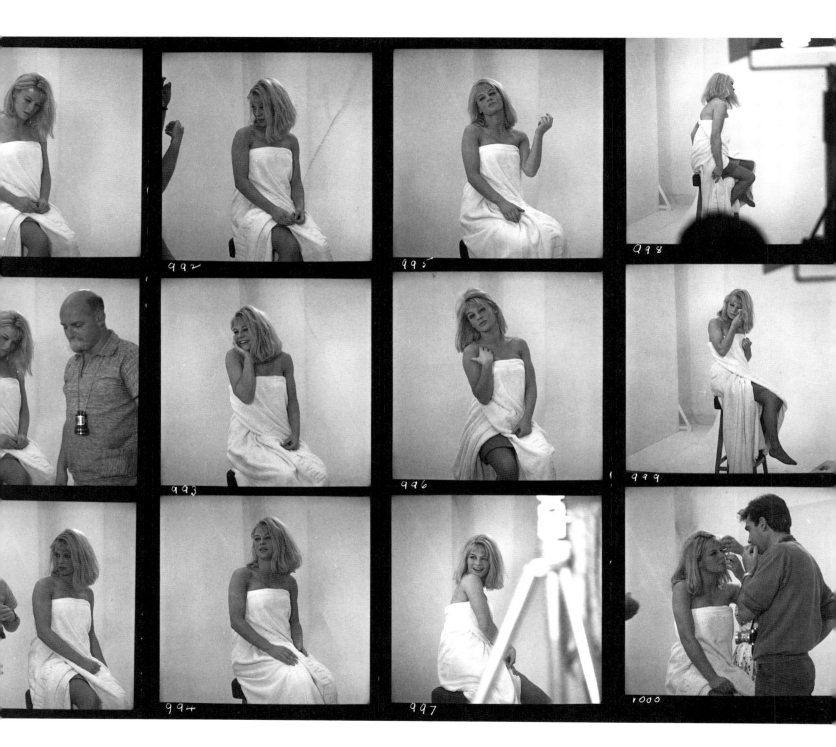

Julie Christie

Darling (1965)

Arresting audiences with her blond and luminous beauty, the 25-year-old British actress **Julie Christie** became an overnight sensation in 1965. In addition to her performances that year in *Young Cassidy* (costarring **Maggie Smith**) and the internationally successful epic drama *Doctor Zhivago* (in which she plays Lara, mistress and muse to the film's title character), Christie's Best Actress Oscar–winning turn in the socially groundbreaking *Darling* solidified her worldwide popularity.

A throwback to the spirit of independence and adventure embodied by such actresses of the 1930s pre-Code era as **Norma Shearer** and **Claudette Colbert**, Christie came to signify the face of a new generation as well as a transitional period marked by revolutionary change. Alongside the Beatles, the Rolling Stones, Marianne Faithfull, and the Who; the fashion models Jean Shrimpton and Twiggy; and such actors as Michael Caine, Terence Stamp, and the sisters Lynn and Vanessa Redgrave, Christie became part of the widespread, antiestablishment youth cultural rebellion of 1960s "Swinging London" that was producing some of the most innovative, exciting, and provocative music, art, fashion, theater, and cinema in the world. The hedonistic London of Christie's existence was a "mecca for mods" situated against the backdrop of joints, orgies, antinuclear protests, and "eroding traditional class distinctions."[1] It astonished conservatives worldwide. Here emerged the unisex look, which consisted of long hair for men, miniskirts (arguably "the most sexualized clothing item in history")[2] for women, and hip-hugger pants for both genders. Meanwhile, the twist, a sexually provoking, rock-and-roll-inspired dance deemed "vulgar" by the likes of **Ginger Rogers**,[3] became a popular craze.

Julie Christie in a proof sheet from 1965's *Darling* (featuring director John Schlesinger in the left-hand column). In the film, Christie plays the neurotic, social-climbing model Diana Scott. Challenging the social mores of its day, the film addressed such issues as abortion and homosexuality while making Christie the first Best Actress Oscar winner to have appeared without clothing. (Embassy Pictures Corporation/ Photofest)

A beaming Julie Christie shows off her newly collected Best Actress Oscar at an Academy Awards after-party in 1966. (© A.M.P.A.S.®/Photofest)

Christie was accustomed at the time to lugging her air mattress across town and sleeping on the floors of her artist friends' apartments. She derived from a specific social set in which being wealthy was not the "in" thing and the "lost paradise" of the British Empire was not something that concerned her at all.[4]

Born in British Colonial India on April 14, 1941, Christie was raised by a Welsh mother who painted and an English father who owned a 900-acre tea plantation in the "lush beauty of the Himalayan foothills."[5] She was "never rich but never poor." Nonetheless, she "grew up in an atmosphere of nannies and governesses" and went to the same "Darjeeling girls academy for daughters of ex-pats" that **Vivien Leigh** had attended in the 1910s.[6] During World War II, her family was protected from the Japanese by soldiers of the United States Army as "riots and killings" took place nearby.[7] After India's transfer to independence in 1947 following nearly 200 years of British rule, Christie moved to England. There, she attended convent school (at which she rebelled by not standing to "God Save the King") before studying abroad for a year in Paris.

Christie had "always wanted to be an actress,"[8] and she eventually made her way to the University of London's Central School of Speech and Drama, where she caught the eye of the up-and-coming gay British director John Schlesinger by way of her starring performance in a stage production of *The Diary of Anne Frank*. Schlesinger immediately noticed her romantic beauty as well as an "angsty intensity,"[9] and he approached her to appear in his offbeat, British New Wave comedy *Billy Liar* (1963). Two years later, bypassing **Shirley MacLaine**, he offered the actress her first lead role in the blisteringly cynical production of *Darling* (1965).

Appearing in practically every scene, Christie labored on *Darling* for "three and a half months" without a weekend break and for a paycheck of $7,500.[10] In the film, she portrays the superficial model, actress, and "gold-digging *it* girl" Diana Scott, an ambitious woman who climbs the ladder to high society and becomes (à la **Grace Kelly**) the "loveless wife of an Italian prince."[11] Only when it is too late, however, does she learn that her shallow, self-centered ways have contributed to an empty life "miserably misspent."[12]

While challenging conventional social mores, *Darling* became a box-office success. For starters, the movie shocked audiences with a decadent view of the British nouveau riche, who had come of age since the repressed 1950s, "had money, and wanted to spend it."[13] Sexually frank, it additionally addressed the issue of abortion at a time when the procedure was still illegal and backstreet operations remained the only viable option available to women. "Providing clues to the next logical step in the perception of homosexuality on screen," the film also showed Christie's character freely associating with well-adjusted gay men and women at a time when "homosexuality was an imprisonable offence in Britain" (and punishable by two years of hard labor).[14] What is more, the film includes brief, distantly shot nudity (making Christie the first Best Actress Oscar winner to have appeared without clothing) and a hedonistic Parisian party scene, in which beatniks sit

around and watch live copulation before engaging in a musical-chairs/cross-dressing game of cinema verité.

Christie was exhausted from "the harsh demands of sudden and unbidden fame" and was reluctant to attend the 38th Academy Awards (1966). As the actress explained, "The promotion tour for the American premiere of *Doctor Zhivago* — ten days of non-stop rushing from one taxi to another, endless interviews, photographs, 'Pose this way, Miss Christie . . . a smile please, Miss Christie' finally wore me out. I could think of nothing but wanting to go to bed and sleep forever."[15] In part, her reluctance also had to do with her general disdain for Hollywood and her concern about feeling "completely out of place among the Hollywood elite" (with which she was unfamiliar).[16]

But soon after Christie had wrapped up on the set of the sci-fi thriller *Fahrenheit 451* (1966), she was given a birthday party/send-off soirée by the French director François Truffaut before boarding a flight to Los Angeles. As the actress recalled, "[The] only reason I went is because I wanted to go to the desert and the producers promised to pay for a holiday there afterwards."[17] Hospitably, fellow Brit and Best Actress Oscar nominee **Julie Andrews** invited Christie to stay at her Los Angeles home. However, with *Darling*'s American publicists playing up the "Battle of the Julies," Christie was persuaded instead to book a room at the Beverly Hills Hotel.

Exercising a detached "feminine cool" that contrasted with the pompousness and vanity of old Hollywood (as epitomized by the orchestrated "media blitz that preceded **Joan Crawford**'s Oscar-winning comeback" in 1945).[18] Christie ultimately arrived at the 1966 Academy Awards with all heads turning. Operating at a time when the "manufacturing [of] movie stars" became less of a priority in Hollywood as a result of the crumbling studio system,[19] the shy actress, who modestly wore a sleeveless gold lamé pantsuit designed by a personal friend, walked past a line of news photographers dotting the red carpet and answered a few questions. She then nervously made "her way to her seat among the 3,000 show business luminaries packed into the . . . [Santa Monica Civic] Auditorium,"[20] where, throughout the night, the orchestra played "Lara's Theme" from *Doctor Zhivago*.

As the winner of the New York Film Critics Award for her performance in *Darling*, Christie was seen as the prohibitive Oscar favorite. In the midst of a three-year period that saw 28 Oscar nominations for British performers, her Best Actress competition included the British actress Samantha Eggar (*The Collector*), Elizabeth Hartman (*A Patch of Blue*), former recipient **Simone Signoret** (*Ship of Fools*), and the previous year's winner, **Julie Andrews** (*The Sound of Music*). Christie reacted in genuine disbelief to the announcement of her name, and at the first ceremony broadcast in color, she ran across the stage, embraced presenter Rex Harrison, and burst into tears. "I don't think I can say anything except to thank everyone concerned, and especially my darling John Schlesinger for this wonderful honor."[21] After the ceremony, Christie and her then-boyfriend, the artist Don Bessant, were "taken to hear The Four Tops play at a club" before traveling to Palm Springs for a much-needed vacation.[22]

In 1967, Christie returned to Hollywood to present the Best Actor Oscar. Cited by *Time* magazine that year as having "more real impact on fashion than all the clothes of the 10 Best Dressed Women combined," the actress "panicked censors" when she walked out onstage in a "barely-there," long-sleeved miniskirt that rose way above her thigh.[23] In reaction—before the distinctive Oscar fashion statements of **Barbra Streisand** and **Cher**—the alarmed Academy president, Gregory Peck, requested future attendees to help "reinstate a sense of dignity."[24]

In keeping with Christie's overall discomfort in the limelight and ongoing assessment of celebrity success as "a trap" (an opinion further punctuated by the gruesome 1969 murder of her close friend, the actress Sharon Tate), she has "shied away from" personal interviews.[25] But the actress came to recognize that her lack of self-confidence prevented her from being as active as she could have been at events such as the 1968 anti–Vietnam War demonstration outside the American embassy in London. Over time, she learned to "beat her crisis . . . by studying the issues that she wanted to talk about in public."[26] Since then, she has "campaigned vocally" and volunteered her time for animal rights, for environmental protection, for nuclear disarmament, to combat global poverty (via Oxfam International), and to protest the 2005 De Beers–sponsored *Diamonds* exhibition at the Natural History Museum in London.[27] In addition, she has come to embrace the symbol of her success. "For a long time, I didn't put [my Oscar] anywhere. I was too embarrassed by it. Then, I grew up a little bit more and thought, 'Wonderful, look what I've got!'"[28]

Barbra Streisand

An eclectic group of celebrities dubbed "Friends of Oscar" jointly hosted the 41st Academy Awards (1969) at its new location, the Dorothy Chandler Pavilion in downtown Los Angeles. In a rare display of male-targeted finger-pointing during the presentation of the Best Director Award, the former Best Actress winner **Ingrid Bergman** explained that she and her female cohosts were "assembled, somewhat reluctantly, to give the Award for Best Director."[1] "This year the nominated directors have done their best," **Jane Fonda** stated. "To make female stars obsolete," continued Rosalind Russell. "Only one of the four," Natalie Wood concluded, "even had a lady star in his picture, and that was *Lion in Winter*."[2]

Later **Bergman** returned to the stage to present the Oscar for Best Actress. Opening the envelope and generating astonishment from an audience in disbelief, she gasped, "It's a tie! The winners are **Katharine Hepburn** for *The Lion in Winter* and **Barbra Streisand** for *Funny Girl*."[3]

With **Hepburn** and Streisand beating out Vanessa Redgrave (*Isadora*) and past recipients **Joanne Woodward** (*Rachel, Rachel*) and **Patricia Neal** (*The Subject Was Roses*), Streisand was escorted to the stage by *The Lion in Winter*'s director, Anthony Harvey (who accepted for the habitually absent **Katharine Hepburn**). In front of television cameras that broadcast the show live for the first time to an unprecedented 37 countries, the actress tripped up the stairs in a sequined Arnold Scaasi–designed bell-bottom pantsuit whose derrière became see-through "as the flashbulbs went off."[4] Streisand became the last of five women (after **Vivien Leigh, Judy Holliday, Shirley Booth,** and **Anne Bancroft**) to have won the Best Actress Oscar for a role originally performed onstage. After cradling her statuette with the now-famous greeting, "Hello, gorgeous," she expressed amazement

Funny Girl (1968)

Reprising her 1964 Broadway stage success, Barbra Streisand took Hollywood by storm in her first motion picture, the screen adaptation of *Funny Girl* (1968). (Columbia Pictures Industries Inc./Photofest)

In this off-camera shot, William Wyler directs Omar Sharif and Barbra Streisand in *Funny Girl* (1968). In the Arab world, eyebrows were raised over the film's controversial casting when publicity stills—featuring the Egyptian actor and the Jewish actress—were released. (Columbia Pictures Industries Inc./ Photofest)

in being in the same "company as **Katharine Hepburn**." "It's kind of a wild feeling," she confessed. "Sitting [here] tonight I was thinking that the first script of *Funny Girl* was written when I was only eleven years old. And thank God it took so long to get it right!"[5]

Indeed, when the *Funny Girl* producer Ray Stark hired Ben Hecht, the "Shakespeare of Hollywood," to write an ultimately rejected screenplay based on the life of his mother-in-law, Fanny Brice (1891–1951), Streisand was still attending yeshiva and living in near poverty in the Yiddish-speaking "Williamsburg part of Brooklyn."[6] Born on April 24, 1942, to a Columbia University PhD graduate who died when his daughter was 15 months old and an unsympathetic mother who worked long hours to make ends meet, Streisand was forced to embrace a self-sufficient childhood. Growing up, she shared a crammed apartment with her mother, brother, and grandparents. As an undisciplined teenager aggravated by a "hostile stepfather [brought] into the household," she babysat and earned money at her "home away from home"—the Brooklyn-based Chinese restaurant Choy's Oriental.[7] "When I come back to New York, I always think about [proprietress] Muriel Choy," Streisand has said. "I've tried to find her a couple of times, but I never can."[8]

After Streisand saw *The Diary of Anne Frank* on Broadway when she was 16, she ultimately set out to pursue an acting career. Although her mother did "everything to discourage" her unconventionally beautiful daughter by finding her work as a typist,[9] Streisand camped out in the living rooms of various friends' Manhattan apartments. But unable to fit in with the "WASP stereotypes"[10] and thereby find serious work as an actress, Streisand, who removed the middle *a* from her first name to be unique, began singing in gay bars and Beat Generation–era clubs. These included the Bon Soir and the Village Vanguard, where **Judy Holliday** got her start in the late 1930s.

Riveting audiences with her clear and emotive soprano voice, Streisand quickly ascended the ladder of fame while defiantly wearing "her Jewishness like a badge of honor."[11] At a time when "a lot of girls were having their noses 'fixed'" and conforming to Hollywood standards of beauty, she refused to alter her prominent "Nefertiti nose" or hide her "intense Brooklyn accent."[12] When Streisand was asked why "she appeals so strongly to homosexuals" and has been classified as a gay icon among the likes of **Julie Andrews**, **Joan Crawford**, **Bette Davis**, **Audrey Hepburn**, **Liza Minnelli**, **Maggie Smith**, **Meryl Streep**, **Elizabeth Taylor**, and **Cher**, she replied, with her tendency to "fly in the face of conventional wisdom," "I suppose because I'm different."[13]

A year after Streisand released her debut album (*The Barbra Streisand Album*, 1963) and performed on *The Judy Garland Show*, she became the toast of Broadway, singing 12 Jule Styne/Bob Merrill songs per show, eight shows per week, in the physically and emotionally demanding Ray Stark stage production of *Funny Girl* (1964). Incorporating such songs as "People" and "Don't Rain on My Parade," the musical traces the life story of the actress, singer, and Ziegfeld Follies comedienne Fanny Brice between 1910 and 1925, when the single-minded Jewish girl from New

York became a "paragon of female independence" by conquering Broadway with her coarse comic delivery, self-deprecation, and unexpected touch of pathos.[14] "*Funny Girl* is [really] about me," Streisand once explained. "It just happened to Fanny Brice earlier."[15]

Hollywood was "the next logical step" for Streisand.[16] However, in an era when studios were absorbed by conglomerates, the actress was dismissed by Gulf+Western/Paramount's CEO, Charles Blühdorn, who, at the prospect of a Barbra Streisand–starring film adaptation of *Funny Girl*, "could not satisfactorily answer his own question, 'Who wants to hear this Jewish girl singing?'" Nonetheless,

At the 41st Academy Awards (1969), *Funny Girl* star Barbra Streisand poses with her Best Actress Oscar, which she captured in an unprecedented tie with Katharine Hepburn (for *The Lion in Winter*). (© A.M.P.A.S.®/ Photofest)

when Columbia Pictures picked up the $35 million project (and bypassed **Shirley MacLaine** for the principal role), Streisand—who had no formal acting training, had never "faced a camera," and was nervous about doing so—became the most electrifying personality to arrive in the film capital since Elvis Presley.[17]

In her film debut at age 26, Streisand easily adapted her role to the screen but recalled that Hollywood did not adapt as easily to her. Cut off from the previous era when *Photoplay* (the "most powerful of the [movie fan] magazines") published guidelines for star actresses that recommended "'good manners and sincerity' as essential aids to success,"[18] Streisand conversely "insisted on creative control, clashed with fellow cast members and directors," and was "accused of being anti-social."[19] "She was downright rude," reported *Funny Girl* assistant director Jack Roe.[20] But as Streisand clarified, "I wasn't part of a mold. I didn't fit in, . . . and right from the first day I was off on a bad foot."[21]

Written for the screen by Isobel Lennart, *Funny Girl*—a spiritual sequel to *The Great Ziegfeld* (1936; for which **Luise Rainer** captured the Best Actress Oscar)—became the second-highest-grossing film of 1968 after Stanley Kubrick's *2001: A*

Space Odyssey. Still, it was not universally embraced. When publicity stills from the film were "wire-photoed around the world," featuring Streisand's Egyptian costar Omar Sharif romantically "associating with a Jewish woman," eyebrows were raised, and the film was "ultimately banned in the Arab [world]" for purportedly "furthering Zionist objectives."[22] Having already received a death threat for supporting Israel during the 1967 Arab-Israeli War, Streisand became identified as a Jewish entertainer with enormous political sway, much like the internationally renowned Jewish stage star Sarah Bernhardt (1844–1923), who stood up against anti-Semitism in 1890s France.

Streisand was influential at a time when other Jewish women such as Betty Friedan, Bella Abzug, Shulamith Firestone, and Gloria Steinem were spearheading Second Wave feminism. Using her power, she became a progressive activist for civil rights and women's issues. Consistent with her first single—a rerecording of the hit theme song for Franklin D. Roosevelt's 1932 U.S. presidential election campaign, "Happy Days Are Here Again"—as well as her 1963 performance for U.S. President John F. Kennedy at a Washington Press Correspondents Dinner, Streisand also became the "largest single celebrity donor to political campaigns." "I was taught about charity," she explained. "I was taught to invite a stranger to share your Sabbath dinner."[23]

With her Best Actress Oscar victory expanding her horizons, Streisand went on to become the top female box-office star of the 1970s while conquering the worlds of songwriting and producing. She wanted to control her own art and consequently followed in the footsteps of United Artists cofounder **Mary Pickford** by coforming the production company First Artists (with Sidney Poitier and Paul Newman) in 1969. Under First Artists, she extended her range in the feminist-driven *Up the Sandbox* (1972) and, at the peak of her fame, in the rock-music retelling of *A Star Is Born* (1976; for which she won the Best Original Song Oscar for "Evergreen"). Often defined as "the voice of the century,"[24] Streisand additionally remained the top-selling female artist of all time until the likes of Madonna, Rihanna, Mariah Carey, Céline Dion, and Whitney Houston dethroned her in the decades that followed.

With men "ensconced in [Hollywood's] primary power roles" and few female directors entrusted with major, big-budget productions (an imbalance cited in 2015 by the *New York Times* film critic Manohla Dargis as "immoral, maybe illegal"),[25] Streisand also ventured into the traditionally male domain of "giving orders [and] mastering not only people but machinery" to direct *Yentl* (1983), *The Prince of Tides* (1991), and *The Mirror Has Two Faces* (1996).[26] In the process of persisting, she faced both criticism for her "ardent—some have said arrogant—interest in wearing more than one hat" and resistance from men, in general, who "did not like taking orders from a woman."[27] As she later stated with bitterness and exactitude, a "man is [seen as] forceful; a woman is pushy. A man is assertive; she's aggressive. He strategizes; she manipulates. He shows leadership; she's controlling. He's committed; she's obsessed. It's been said that a man's reach should exceed his grasp. Why can't that be true for a woman?"[28]

Maggie Smith

In opposition to a traditional mixed-gendered classroom, in which the teacher will more often call and heap praise on male students, interrupt them less, and thereby erode the confidence of female students, who are then conditioned to take a back seat, a typical all-girls school offers its students an encouraging and empowering environment. Filmic examples of the all-girls-school setting include *All This, and Heaven Too* (1940; with **Bette Davis**), *The Children's Hour* (1961; with **Audrey Hepburn** and **Shirley MacLaine**), *Heavenly Creatures* (1994; with **Kate Winslet**), and *Mona Lisa Smile* (2003; with **Julia Roberts**). Each of these films portray schools that are "genuinely intent on opening up . . . girls' lives; on heightening their awareness of themselves and their world; and on breaking free of restrictive, conventional ways of thinking, feeling, and being."[1]

The Prime of Miss Jean Brodie (1969) is another film from the all-girls-school canon as well as one of three teaching-related Best Actress Oscar–winning movies, alongside *The Miracle Worker* (1962; with **Anne Bancroft**) and *Still Alice* (2014; with **Julianne Moore**). In the film, **Maggie Smith** plays the title character—an influential teacher in her "prime" who prides herself on her extreme, colorful individualism. Based on Muriel Spark's 1961 novel of the same name and written for the screen by Jay Presson Allen (one of the few successful female screenwriters at the time), the story is entirely set in a staid 1930s Edinburgh. There, Miss Brodie, who spends her summer holidays in Italy absorbing art and intermingling with "large formations of Il Duce's Fascisti,"[2] implores her students to be aware of all of life's possibilities while stirring thoughts of emancipation. In doing so, she encourages one of her "gels" to fight for Franco in the Spanish Civil War and facilitates for another student a romantic entanglement with the

The Prime of Miss Jean Brodie (1969)

Schoolteacher Jean Brodie (played by Maggie Smith) sophisticatedly smokes a cigarette as she arrives by bicycle to the Marcia Blaine School for Girls in Edinburgh, Scotland in this publicity still from *The Prime of Miss Jean Brodie* (1969). (Twentieth Century Fox Film Corporation/Photofest)

school's dashing art instructor (played by Smith's real-life husband at the time, Robert Stephens).

For *Jean Brodie*, Smith turned in a screen performance of great pathos and complexity, punctuated by comic elements of haughty absurdity and Scottish affectation. In a role originally offered to **Julie Andrews**, Smith personifies Miss Brodie in such a way that it is difficult at first to recognize her character's reckless underpinnings. When she is asked to resign by the austere and intimidating headmistress, Miss Mackay (Celia Johnson), Miss Brodie ultimately explodes into an emotionally charged, masterfully acted rage worthy of any performance-study examination. "I am a teacher, first, last, always!" she asserts. "Do you imagine that for one instant I will let that be taken from me without a fight?"

The daughter of an Oxford University pathologist, Margaret Natalie Smith was born on December 28, 1934, in Ilford, Essex, England, and grew up alongside her older twin brothers in a British household described as Spartan and at times even suffocating. Despite her mother prohibiting her from attending the cinema and her grandmother's stern opinion "that she wasn't pretty enough to be an actress and should [therefore] learn to type," the craft of acting remained "a childhood obsession."[3]

Undeniably, this strict upbringing led Smith to approach her craft with a "brutal, scientific precision and persistence" that has made her one of the most accomplished, revered, and honored stage and screen actresses of all time.[4] In a career that has covered a great deal of Shakespeare as well as J. M. Barrie, Anton Chekhov, Jean Cocteau, Noël Coward, Henrik Ibsen, and Eugène Ionesco, she has remained meticulously attentive to the nuances of performance, including the proper modes of expression associated with the period-piece characters that she has long inhabited.

Unlike her British contemporary **Julie Christie**, Smith has refrained from characterizing the working collaboration of film actors as "one long cocktail party without the drinks."[5] During rehearsals, she will instead "withdraw from the company coffee break and be found poring over the script at the back of the room."[6] As **Jessica Lange** has pointed out, "Most film scripts . . . are practically illiterate. You have to figure out a way . . . just to make it sound human-like. You spend half your energy doing that."[7]

While Smith's focus on set is always professional and "about the work," she gained the nickname "Acid Queen" for her vexation toward other actors and—like the honest and sometimes cutting **Ingrid Bergman**, **Sissy Spacek**, or **Julianne Moore**—for asking directors a lot of questions.[8] "[Smith] can get impatient with people," the director William Gaskill explains. "She does outclass a lot of the [actors] she plays with, particularly the men. To find someone who can stand up to her is not easy." As the playwright Ronald Harwood elaborates, "If Maggie likes another actor's kind of acting, she'll do anything to help that performance. [But] if she finds it in any way boring or tedious, that other actor might as well not exist."[9]

Maggie Smith with costars Gordon Jackson and Celia Johnson during a contentious scene on the set of *The Prime of Miss Jean Brodie* (1969). (Twentieth Century Fox Film Corporation/Photofest)

Smith first cut her teeth at 16 as a repertory actor at the Oxford Playhouse School of Theatre (where she made her professional debut as Viola in *Twelfth Night*). Very quickly, she adjusted to the relentless Playhouse schedule of performing one play in the evening while rehearsing for the next one during the day. In direct opposition to the myriad of gifted but formally untrained actors ranging from **Norma Shearer** to **Audrey Hepburn**, **Gwyneth Paltrow**, and **Jennifer Lawrence**, the experience ensured that Smith would not miss out on the "essential building blocks of [her] profession." "I find it sad that people have to go straight into television and film now," Smith later said. "Lots of them are thrown into a West End production without having the grounding."[10]

In the "days when everybody [in England] was impersonating [Laurence] Olivier," Smith stood out for "not speaking that kind of Oxford theatrical voice" and ultimately found a road to London's West End by way of the "now-dormant art form [of] revue."[11] There, she teamed up with the flamboyant British actor and comedian Kenneth Williams, who is credited for conferring on the fine-boned, red-headed actress the wicked timing, wry, piercing wit, and droll, "cut-glass British" tics, mannerisms, and eccentricities that fans have come to love.[12] In the early 1960s, Smith subsequently joined Britain's prominent National Theatre Company, working alongside (and often overshadowing) Olivier himself in such celebrated stage productions as *The Recruiting Officer* (1963) and *Othello* (1964).

Even so, by the time *The Prime of Miss Jean Brodie* premiered in 1969, Smith was still establishing her star presence in the United States. At the time, she had only appeared onscreen in "a succession of inconsequential cameos"[13] and supporting roles, including the 1965 screen adaptation of *Othello*, for which she received an Oscar nomination. Regardless of her excellent reviews for *Jean Brodie*, Smith—nominated for Best Actress—was not at all expected to win the top honor at the 42nd Academy Awards (1970). For starters, *Jean Brodie* had come and gone from theaters roughly an entire year before. Additionally, her competition that year included **Liza Minnelli** (*The Sterile Cuckoo*), fellow Brit Jean Simmons (*The Happy Ending*), and rival frontrunners **Jane Fonda** (*They Shoot Horses, Don't They?*) and the Canadian actress Geneviève Bujold (*Anne of the Thousand Days*), who had won the New York Film Critics Award and the Golden Globe, respectively. But due in part to Smith's pre-Oscar stage success in the Los Angeles production of *The Beaux' Stratagem* (1970), not to mention the enormous popularity of the lyrical theme song "Jean" (a number-one Billboard hit), Smith's chances were given a boost.

Unable to attend the Tuesday-night Oscar ceremony in Los Angeles, Smith received the news of her ultimate victory "when the telephone shrilled in her Chelsea home [in central London] early Wednesday" morning.[14] "I'm thoroughly delighted and very stunned," Smith gushed. "I did not imagine it would happen."[15] Before appearing "Wednesday night in the first night of *The Beaux' Stratagem* at London's Old Vic Theater," Smith was asked by journalists to further comment on her Oscar victory, but she confided that she was "more nervous about tonight's opening."[16] Twelve days later, the actress Lauren Bacall presented Smith with her Best Actress Oscar statuette at the 24th Tony Awards in New York City.

Largely appearing in supporting roles, Smith continued to act in a mixture of commercial and literary art-house films before landing the most widely seen role of her career: the beloved Professor Minerva McGonagall in the top-grossing *Harry Potter* series (2001–2011). In a role she once described as "Miss Jean Brodie in a wizard's hat,"[17] the actress once again worked her magic, expanded her fan base to a whole new generation, and consequently became the highest-grossing Best Actress Oscar winner of all time with a total of more than $8 billion for her cumulative film work. As if that were not enough, the actress—reaching the peak of fame in her late 70s—became something of a scene-stealing global phenomenon in the British television period drama *Downton Abbey* (2010–2015), in which she arrested audiences with her amusing, quintessential class-conscious snobbery as the elderly Dowager Countess.

Nevertheless, Smith herself has remained comparatively anonymous. For an actress of her stature and the first of six Best Actress Oscar winners to have received the prestigious honor of Dame Commander of the British Empire (the others being **Julie Andrews**, **Elizabeth Taylor**, **Helen Mirren**, **Olivia de Havilland**, and **Emma Thompson**), she has defined her star image strictly and entirely by way of her acting. Despite international acclaim, Smith has been said to "behave at all times as if she has no power or status whatsoever."[18] She does little publicity and zero awards-season campaigning, goes to few parties, equates giving interviews to "testifying in court,"[19] and is exceedingly modest and fiercely protective of her private life (she has two sons and was married to the late English playwright Beverley Cross). As a result, she has sometimes been confused by autograph seekers with a different actress altogether. "I used to write '**Glenda Jackson**,'" she once admitted. "It saves time, if that's who they think you are."[20]

Glenda Jackson

When **Glenda Jackson**'s name was announced as the winner of the Best Actress Oscar in 1971, many viewers asked, "Who *is* Glenda Jackson?"[1] Three years later, when she won again, her aloof, individualistic persona continued to mystify Hollywood. At a time when young performers were criticizing the star system and when attending the Academy Awards was even considered déclassé (as evinced in the number of empty seats at the Dorothy Chandler Pavilion), the serious, sharp-witted British actress seemed to exemplify the antithesis of a glamorous Hollywood star. To be sure, Jackson eschewed not only the Oscars but also the concept of celebrity stardom and the many trappings that go with it. Possessing "the grittiness of [her idol] **Bette Davis** and the same independence of spirit one associates with **Katharine Hepburn**,"[2] her aim was never to be adored but simply to become a master of her craft.

Jackson was born on May 9, 1936, in the staid seaside village of Hoylake, England (18 kilometers outside the Beatles' hometown of Liverpool). As the eldest of four daughters to a mother who cleaned houses and a father who laid bricks, she grew up during the hardships of World War II and would bare witness to tremendous changes in relation to men's and women's roles in society. "I am of a generation," she later said, "who was raised by women. The men had all gone to war to defend our freedoms, . . . and the women that I knew . . . ran our factories and our businesses [and] put out the fires when the bombs dropped."[3]

Over time, Jackson managed to dig her way out of limiting circumstances. She initially "started appearing in amateur theater productions" and soon landed a scholarship in 1954 at London's Royal Academy of Dramatic Art (RADA).[4] Entering into the hard life of a theater student, she rigorously trained the instrument of her voice and body while gaining connections to people of similar interests for the first time. To make ends meet, she worked for years in department stores,

Women in Love (1969)

A Touch of Class (1973)

Glenda Jackson's character dances in front of a herd of highland cattle in director Ken Russell's *Women in Love* (1969), a story set in presuffrage England. (United Artists/Photofest)

offices, and "every coffee bar in London" before making her first professional stage appearance in 1957.[5]

At a time in Britain when "there was a feeling in the air" that "your class and background need not hold you back,"[6] Jackson went on to join the distinguished Royal Shakespeare Company in 1964. In her audition, she was told by the company's directors, Peter Brook and Charles Marowitz, to prepare a piece "within the context of a woman who opens her front door and is immediately bundled into a straightjacket and taken off to a lunatic asylum." "No one had ever asked me to do that kind of work in my life before," Jackson admitted, appreciative of finally feeling properly challenged as an actor, who, by definition, should be able to do "absolutely anything that was demanded." In keeping with the company's repugnance toward the "literary exposition of emotion," Jackson was subsequently cast as both First Lady of the United States Jacqueline Kennedy and the controversial, high-class prostitute Christine Keeler in an experimental skit in which she appeared naked onstage.[7]

Drawn to less conventional material in the same manner as **Luise Rainer, Helen Mirren, Nicole Kidman, Frances McDormand,** and **Cate Blanchett,** Jackson went on to garner attention for her role as a schizophrenic who believes that she is the French Revolution–era assassin Charlotte Corday in the visceral 1964 stage production of *Marat/Sade* (otherwise known by its lengthy title, *The Persecution and Assassination of Jean-Paul Marat as Performed by the Inmates of the Asylum of Charenton under the Direction of the Marquis de Sade*). As part of Peter Brook's "Theatre of Cruelty" season, the play was based around the ideas of the French dramatist Antonin Artaud (1896–1948), who argued that the "theatre should assault the senses of the audience" to expose "the existential horror behind all social and psychological façades."[8] In 1967, Jackson made her film debut in the play's esoteric screen adaptation.

Tough, blunt, and with a "militant intelligence,"[9] Jackson was the logical choice to later play the sexually curious, perversely independent, and emasculating sculptress Gudrun Brangwen in the director Ken Russell's provocative, Baroque-inspired *Women in Love* (1969). Adapted from the once-controversial D. H. Lawrence novel and dealing with many of the same issues taken up by the counterculture movement of the late 1960s (e.g., freedom from traditional modes of authority, women's rights, and gay liberation), the film tells the story of two educated but unfulfilled sisters (played by Jackson and Jennie Linden) living in the Midlands in presuffrage/post–World War I England. Undeniably, Jackson, who consulted the novel throughout filming, constructed a character that audiences had never seen before. In one scene, she "stands her ground" and "dances defiantly" in front of a herd of highland cattle before driving them away,[10] just as she rejects the manhood of her lover—the chauvinistic heir to a wealthy coal mine owner (Oliver Reed) who is ultimately led to torment and despair.

Women in Love was released just months after the breakthrough American film *Easy Rider* (1969), which, alongside such "New Hollywood" productions as *Bonnie and Clyde* (1967) and *2001: A Space Odyssey* (1968), helped to dilute the impact that foreign films had long enjoyed in the United States. Taking the movie business "completely off guard," these films caught the mood of their young, disaffected audiences by looking "inward at their characters," by replacing content with "style and attitude,"[11] and by doing so to critical acclaim often without the use of a major star. *Women in Love* was made during a transgressive period that "dealt explicitly with human sexuality in ways unthinkable only a few years before."[12] It not only featured Jackson's naked breasts but additionally stunned moviegoers and critics alike with "its homoerotic subtext and depiction of male frontal nudity" as part of an extended nude wrestling scene between costars Oliver Reed and Alan Bates.[13]

Despite—or perhaps as a result of—these bold and revolutionary steps, Jackson, who had already secured the New York Film Critics Award, became the Best Actress Oscar front-runner ahead of the 43rd Academy Awards (1971). In the same year that the Beatles won their only Oscar for *Let It Be* (for Best Original Score), Jackson found herself victorious in an unusual field of never-before-nominated actresses including Jane Alexander (*The Great White Hope*), Ali MacGraw (*Love Story*), fellow Brit Sarah Miles (*Ryan's Daughter*), and Carrie Snodgress (*Diary of a Mad Housewife*). Filming in England, the actress received word of her stun-

ning victory by way of an exuberant early-morning phone call from **Bette Davis**. "You've won! You've won!" screamed the legendary two-time Best Actress Oscar winner. "Thank you very much," Jackson replied in her "distinctively low, richly textured voice"[14] before returning back to bed. Weeks later, she collected her Oscar with the misprinted inscription "*Woman in Love*."

Unlike many of her British predecessors (including **Greer Garson** and **Julie Andrews**) who "were expected to take up residence in the Hollywood Hills alongside their [Oscar statuettes]," Jackson chose to retain her "overseas residence" in England after winning her Academy Award.[15] Similar to **Maggie Smith**, whose "selection of roles [is] perhaps the most purely English" of any of the Best Actress winners,[16] Jackson—in one British production after another—largely followed in the same path. She was disheartened, however, by the number of weighty scripts being sent her way that dealt "with the darker side of human nature,"[17] and she eventually shifted gears to try her hand at comedy—a genre that many actors regard as far more difficult than drama. There is "no immediate guideline as to whether

In *Women in Love* (1969), Glenda Jackson offered audiences a sexually curious, perversely independent, and emasculating heroine who had no issue standing up to the men around her, including the heir to a wealthy coal mine owner (played by Oliver Reed). (United Artists/Photofest)

Glenda Jackson and George Segal enjoy a sex holiday in Spain in the screwball-comedy-inspired *A Touch of Class* (1973), for which Jackson pulled out a second Best Actress Oscar victory in a highly competitive year. (AVCO Embassy Pictures/Photofest)

you're getting a laugh," the actress explained of filmic comedy, "because there is no audience."[18]

For her "artful . . . one-liners" in the surprise-hit comedy *A Touch of Class* (1973), Jackson unexpectedly clinched her second Best Actress Oscar at the 46th Academy Awards (1974).[19] In a year that saw the ceremony's first-ever streaker, not to mention the first female producer (Julia Phillips) win the Oscar for Best Picture (for *The Sting*), Jackson's provocative, adultery-glorifying performance struck a feminist chord with Academy voters. Certainly, the Academy was mindful of such recent milestones as Title IX, *Roe v. Wade*, the publication of *The Joy of Sex*, and Billie Jean King's "Battle of the Sexes" tennis victory (as later depicted by both **Holly Hunter** and **Emma Stone**).

Nominated for five Oscars including Best Picture, *A Touch of Class* examines the life of Jackson's Vickie Allessio—a London designer, mother of two, and divorcée looking for an uncomplicated, no-strings-attached sexual relationship with a male equal (played by George Segal) who will not be "a pain in the ass when it's all over."[20] Compared to the screwball comedies of the 1930s and '40s that featured **Katharine Hepburn**, Carole Lombard, and **Claudette Colbert**, the film separated itself from its predecessors in its nonjudgmental treatment of infidelity and its candid conversation on the topic of recreational sex. As a woman in control of her own sexual destiny, Jackson's character willfully enters into an adulterous affair on her terms (which includes a sex holiday in Spain followed by the purchase of a "love nest" apartment in London's Soho). In one scene, Vickie is represented reading the feminist writer Germaine Greer's 1970 international best-seller *The Female Eunuch*, and, throughout the film, she fittingly turns her back on all things that repress women sexually. In doing so, her liberated character helps to modernize and democratize the notion of sex and relationships between men and women.

For her performance in *A Touch of Class*, Jackson provided her mother with a pair of Best Actress Oscar "bookends."[21] To do so, she bested former winner **Barbra Streisand** (*The Way We Were*), Marsha Mason (*Cinderella Liberty*), and the visibly astounded nominees **Ellen Burstyn** (*The Exorcist*) and veteran recipient **Joanne Woodward** (*Summer Wishes, Winter Dreams*), the latter of whom had won the New York Film Critics Award.

In a "blazing career" that never shied away from controversial material,[22] Jackson played everything from Queen Elizabeth I to Sarah Bernhardt to the "female Hamlet" of the theater world, Hedda Gabler. She additionally portrayed "a nymphomaniacal . . . groped to orgasm by asylum inmates"[23] in Ken Russell's *The Music Lovers* (1970) and a sadomasochistic housemaid in the film adaptation of Jean Genet's *The Maids* (1974). In 1989, the actress reteamed with Russell for *The Rainbow*—the film in which she played the mother of her character from *Women in Love*.

But Jackson recognized that prominent roles for women of advancing age were few and far between and began to disengage from acting altogether. Unlike **Anne Bancroft**, who admitted in 1992 to taking parts "even if they're one page" since "there are very few good scripts [in the first place], even for **Julia Roberts**,"[24] Jackson maintained a different outlook. "I don't fancy hanging around to play Nurse in *Romeo and Juliet*," she once explained.[25] Instead, she raised a son, taught courses in acting, and, at 55, entered politics as a leftist, Labour Party member of an almost entirely male-dominated British Parliament. Initially spurred into politics "by a hatred of Thatcherism" and a conservative government that she felt only looked out for "the top people,"[26] the two-time Oscar-winning actress became a Parliamentary Under-Secretary of State for Transport, "an outspoken critic of the war in Iraq,"[27] and a staunch crusader against homelessness. Jackson served her constituents for 23 years before returning to the London stage at age 80 to perform as the title character in a 2016 production of Shakespeare's *King Lear*—"one of the most demanding roles in theater."[28] Two years later, and showing no signs of slowing down, she took home the Tony Award for Best Actress in a Play for her performance in Edward Albee's *Three Tall Women*.

Jane Fonda

Jane Fonda was born with the uppity and self-admittedly pretentious name of Lady Jayne Fonda on December 21, 1937. At the time of her birth, her father, the internationally acclaimed actor Henry Fonda, was working with **Bette Davis** on the set of 1938's *Jezebel*. Fonda was ultimately raised in a privileged but laughter-deprived family alongside her younger brother, Peter. Their mother "slit her throat with a razor . . . when Jane was 12,"[1] and Fonda dealt early on with eating disorders and various insecurities while learning the truth about her mother's suicide by way of a movie magazine.

Growing up as part of the international jet set, Fonda came into close contact with the likes of Pablo Picasso, Jean Cocteau, Ernest Hemingway, Jacqueline Kennedy, the gossip columnist and socialite Elsa Maxwell, Charlie Chaplin, and the Swedish screen legend Greta Garbo. One summer while swimming in the Mediterranean Sea, Garbo asked Fonda—a self-doubting teenager at the time—whether she planned to follow in the footsteps of her famous father. Over time, Fonda would do so. Sidestepping the egregious advice of breaking her jaw and removing back teeth so as to achieve the classical sunken-cheek look that many actresses were pressured to attain, she eventually appeared onstage opposite her father in *The Country Girl* (1954) before starring in her first movie, *Tall Story*, in 1960. "Obviously having a famous parent helps," she later acknowledged,[2] a sentiment echoed by the likes of second-generation actors including Beau and Jeff Bridges, Michael Douglas, Carrie Fisher, Melanie Griffith, **Liza Minnelli**, **Gwyneth Paltrow**, Lynn and Vanessa Redgrave, and Isabella Rossellini.

Throughout her life, Fonda struggled to construct a meaningful relationship with her father—the honorable movie star of such American classics as *The*

Klute (1971)

Coming Home (1978)

For *Klute* (1971), Jane Fonda (pictured here with costar Donald Sutherland) became the fifth of six women to win the Best Actress Oscar by portraying a prostitute. To prepare for the role, the actress spent time with real-life New York City sex workers. (Warner Bros. Pictures Inc./ Photofest)

Jane Fonda, protesting the Vietnam War around the time she starred in *Klute* (1971). Throughout her life as an activist, Fonda, who was put on U.S. President Richard Nixon's list of political opponents, additionally battled to recognize the rights of immigrants and indigenous peoples, people with disabilities, and disadvantaged youth. (Photofest)

Grapes of Wrath (1940) and *12 Angry Men* (1957). Only after attending Vassar College and living in France for seven years in the 1960s did she begin to appreciate the dignified, salt-of-the-earth American values that her father embodied in his films.

During her time in France, Fonda's political ideologies first began to bloom. Much of this had to do with her associations with the French movie star, leftist activist, and former Best Actress Oscar winner **Simone Signoret**, who took Fonda "under her wing" and "always insisted on being a human first, a star second."[3] Unfortunately, with the release of *Barbarella* (1968; a film directed by Fonda's first husband, Roger Vadim, that "caused a certain generation of men to have their first erections"),[4] Fonda began to notice that her burgeoning activist efforts were being overshadowed by her image as a spoiled Hollywood sex kitten.

To remedy the situation, Fonda overhauled her image by darkening her hair and styling it in a more modest feathered shag. She additionally pared down her wardrobe so as not to alienate herself from fellow antiwar demonstrators with whom she marched in solidarity against the war in Vietnam, the secret United States–led invasion of Cambodia, the 1970 Kent State and Jackson State college shootings, and an untrustworthy Nixon administration. As an outspoken activist in a divided America, Fonda appeared on American television and on college campuses to warn the public that U.S. President Richard Nixon was lying to the American people. For her actions, she was placed on Nixon's list of political opponents alongside liberal Democrats George McGovern and Edward Kennedy, the Black Panther Party, the academic Noam Chomsky, and the actors Paul Newman, Gregory Peck, and **Barbra Streisand**.

Under surveillance, Fonda put her activism on hold to star in *Klute* (1971)—a dark, claustrophobic murder-mystery thriller that exemplified the repercussion of the Sixties when utopian dreams were replaced by "alienation and disillusionment."[5] *Klute* was intensified by the cinematographer Gordon Willis's composition of numerous shots that mask "off much of the frame width to emphasize" the themes of isolation and paranoia.[6] It additionally offered filmgoers a frightening glimpse into the "spiritual malaise" of Fonda's strong but self-destructive urban

outsider. As Bree Daniels—a New York City call girl "skilled in determining the fantasies" of her male clients while stalked by a homicidal man,[7] Fonda elevated her acting to a new level of theatrical realism. Internalizing the psychological makeup of her character by way of employing her sense-memory training at Lee Strasberg's Actors Studio, the actress excelled at depicting Bree as a "victim of every crime men commit against women: physical and sexual abuse, economic oppression, and abandonment."[8] In preparation for the part, Fonda mixed with real-life city prostitutes and spent a night alone in Bree's creaking apartment (built on a New York studio soundstage). She additionally let her nose drip wet with snot in a key crying scene, jolting audiences who were unaccustomed to such unsightly fare.

Having already captured the New York Film Critics Award, Fonda was the heavy favorite and the only American in an otherwise British field of Best Actress contenders including former recipient **Julie Christie** (*McCabe & Mrs. Miller*), the South African/British actress Janet Suzman (*Nicholas and Alexandra*), Vanessa Redgrave (*Mary, Queen of Scots*), and the previous year's winner **Glenda Jackson** (*Sunday Bloody Sunday*). Suffering from the flu, Fonda arrived at the 1972 Oscars in a "counterculture cool" Yves Saint Laurent "Mao" pantsuit.[9] Upon the announcement of her name, Fonda walked onstage, bowed, and delivered a restrained acceptance speech recommended by her father to a somewhat contemptuous audience bracing themselves for a political diatribe about the war in Vietnam. "There's a great deal to say and I'm not going to say it tonight," she said. "I would just like to really thank you very much."[10] Overwhelmed, she found a small corner backstage where she sobbed in gratitude before addressing the press, which inquired as to why she did not use her victory speech to pontificate about her politics. "I was thinking," Fonda reflected, "that while we're all sitting there giving out awards, . . . there are murders being committed in our name in Indochina, and . . . I think everyone wants it to end as much as I do, and I didn't think that I needed to say it."[11]

Alongside Harry Belafonte, **Julie Christie**, **Shirley MacLaine**, Paul Newman, Vanessa Redgrave, **Barbra Streisand**, Donald Sutherland, and **Joanne Woodward**, Fonda was one of a few big-name Hollywood celebrities at the time to contest or even discuss the war in Vietnam—the first major war to be televised. In contrast to many of the pro-Nixon Republican supporters of the old Hollywood guard—including **Claudette Colbert**, **Helen Hayes**, Charlton Heston, Bob Hope, **Mary Pickford**, **Ginger Rogers**, James Stewart, and John Wayne—this younger generation appeared to be far more radical and outspoken. The opposing sides came to a point of contention during the Nixon-versus-McGovern 1972 election and found themselves in "the most Hollywood-inflected presidential election ever," with Fonda situated as a leftist "Hollywood Freedom Fighter" and feminist.[12]

In this capacity, Fonda established the Indochina Peace Campaign and produced and starred in *F.T.A.* (as in "Fuck the Army")—a 1972 political documentary that aspired to persuade soldiers to declare their opposition to Nixon and the Vietnam War. Controversially, she also accepted an invitation from the North Vietnamese to travel across U.S. enemy lines and use her celebrity to direct attention toward the

imminent American bombing of dikes, levees, and dams, which, if executed, would
have flooded rice paddies and led to the starvation of close to a quarter million
peasant civilians. "How can you say that we're defending freedom if the man that
we're keeping in power has . . . closed off all the freedoms of speech, press, and
assembly in Saigon?" questioned Fonda upon her return.[13] But while her daring
efforts were motivated by peace, the actress's self-acknowledged lapse in judgment
in standing on a North Vietnamese antiaircraft shooter unleashed a wrath of anger.
In the midst of an election year, two Republican congressmen "demanded she be
convicted for treason,"[14] and much like the vilified **Ingrid Bergman** two decades
before, Fonda's image among political conservatives (who chose to disparage her
as the treasonous "Hanoi Jane") was severely, if not irreparably, damaged.

Met with a combination of blinded patriotism and antifeminist resistance,
Fonda was informally blacklisted in Hollywood as she continued her activism.
Unsurprisingly, her detractors labeled *Introduction to the Enemy* (a 1974 docu-
mentary that she produced with her activist husband, Tom Hayden, about the

Jane Fonda celebrates her second Best Actress Oscar victory for *Coming Home* at the 1979 Academy Awards. (© A.M.P.A.S.®/Photofest)

lives of Vietnamese people after years of wartime struggle) as nothing more than "Communist propaganda."[15] But after she cohosted the 1977 Academy Awards and won, two years later, her second Best Actress Oscar for her role in the director Hal Ashby's antiwar love story *Coming Home* (1978), Fonda's respectability, in Hollywood at least, was restored.

Coming Home turned Fonda's real-life associations with returning veterans (including the antiwar activist Ron Kovic) into one of the first movies to tackle the aftereffects and opposing attitudes of the Southeast Asian conflict. The film proved to be for the Vietnam War what *The Best Years of Our Lives* (1946) was for World War II. *Coming Home* was developed by the actress's production company, IPC Films, and contained a soundtrack featuring the Rolling Stones, Bob Dylan, and Jimi Hendrix. In the movie, Fonda plays Sally Hyde—a military wife whose Marine Corps captain husband (portrayed by Bruce Dern) goes off to fight in Vietnam.

Horrified by the insensitive treatment and neglect of the wounded veterans returning home, she becomes a hospital volunteer and falls in love with a recuperating paraplegic veteran (Best Actor Oscar recipient Jon Voight).

On her way to capturing her second Best Actress Oscar, Fonda, at the 51st Academy Awards (1979), faced a formidable short list that included former winner **Ellen Burstyn** (*Same Time, Next Year*), Jill Clayburgh (*An Unmarried Woman*), **Geraldine Page** (*Interiors*), and veteran recipient and New York Film Critics Award winner **Ingrid Bergman** (*Autumn Sonata*). Taking the stage, Fonda showcased enormous compassion and conviction by accepting her award partially in sign language so as to acknowledge Deaf viewers in particular but also to underscore "the problems of the handicapped,"[16] which was illustrated by the more than 21,000 permanently disabled American Vietnam War veterans. "I'm so happy," she beamed. "I wanted to win very much because I'm so proud of *Coming Home*. And I want many people to see the movie."[17]

Over the course of Fonda's multifaceted career, which rarely found her playing second fiddle to male costars, she engaged in battles to recognize the rights of immigrants and indigenous peoples, people with disabilities, and disadvantaged youth (for whom she operated a summer camp). At the 2018 United State of Women Summit, she additionally addressed the effects of white privilege in relation to the roots of racism. In 1982, at a time when few gyms catered to women, Fonda not only helped to improve women's health and fitness worldwide but also popularized the videocassette recorder (VCR) by selling and distributing over 17 million copies of her best-selling exercise videos. "One reason I started my workout was because I knew that to be fully empowered, I needed to feel strong in my body," she explained.[18] A mother of three, Fonda also became a best-selling author and cofounder of the Women's Media Center—a nonprofit with the goal of helping women to become more "visible and powerful in the media."[19]

In a career that has spanned more than 60 years, Fonda has proven to be much more than an Oscar-winning star and the daughter of a Hollywood icon. At the expense of her own career and at the risk of her personal boundaries (in 2005, she was angrily approached by a Vietnam veteran who spat "tobacco juice into her face"),[20] the actress stepped down from her ivory tower to stand up against the moral corruption that she experienced in front of her. In the process, she touched hearts, opened minds, and showed the world what a major difference a single individual can make.

Liza Minnelli

The year 1972 signaled a radically new era of acceptance and open-minded-ness, with the top-grossing pornographic films *Deep Throat* and *Behind the Green Door*, Ralph Bakshi's X-rated cartoon *Fritz the Cat*, Alfred Hitchcock's "sexually explicit" *Frenzy*,[1] and Woody Allen's *Everything You Always Wanted to Know about Sex* (*But Were Afraid to Ask)*.

The dark and provocative musical *Cabaret*, seedy and decadent in its own way, became one of the top-grossing films of 1972 and earned ten Oscar nominations. The film not only gave moviegoers a peek into the "thriving laboratory of art and culture" that existed in Germany's Weimar Republic before the political extrem-ism of the Nazi era but also transformed its star—the actress, singer, and dancer **Liza Minnelli**—into an international icon.[2]

Nominated for the Best Actress Oscar, Minnelli arrived at the 1973 Academy Awards with her proud father, the Oscar-winning director Vincente Minnelli. On a night when the 27-year-old activist and National Native American Affirmative Image Committee president Sacheen Littlefeather "stole the thunder" for refus-ing the Best Actor Oscar on behalf of *Godfather* star Marlon Brando (before being threatened backstage by an angered John Wayne),[3] Minnelli listened absorbedly as the Best Actress category was called out. Her competition included former winner **Maggie Smith** (*Travels with My Aunt*), Cicely Tyson (*Sounder*), the Norwegian actress and New York Film Critics Award winner Liv Ullmann (*The Emigrants*), and sing-ing superstar Diana Ross (*Lady Sings the Blues*), whose Motown producers "ran nine full-page ads over an intense two-and-a-half-week" campaigning period while lauding her performance as Billie Holiday.[4] Upon the announcement of her name, Minnelli—clad in a Halston-designed yellow cashmere dress and jacket with match-ing shoes and a "woven gold and copper choker"[5]—smiled brightly and showed

Cabaret (1972)

An off-camera shot from *Cabaret* (1972), for which Liza Minnelli managed to amaze even nonmu-sical fans with her show-stopping performance. (Allied Artists/ Photofest)

enormous relief before taking the stage. "Thank you very much," she told the audience. "And thank you for giving *me* this award. You've made me very happy."[6]

Emphasizing her appreciation in receiving the Oscar on the basis of her own merits and not for nepotistic ties, Minnelli emerged as her own person with an award that her late mother, the legendary Judy Garland, had "never won" and "always regretted."[7] (For the record, Garland, the star of *The Wizard of Oz* [1939], received a special, noncompetitive Oscar in 1940 for her outstanding performance as a screen juvenile.)

Much like **Jane Fonda**, Minnelli grew up in Hollywood aristocracy. Born in Hollywood on March 12, 1946, Minnelli was raised in a household where the likes of Irving Berlin, Oscar Levant, and her godfather, Ira Gershwin, would "drop by to socialize" and "take turns singing and playing a few songs" at the piano.[8] "After school or on vacations," Minnelli roamed her personal "playground" of MGM, exploring "the prop and costume rooms" "the way any other kid might go to her father's office."[9] "I got so that I knew every inch of it," she said, "all the shortcuts to different stages and all the underground passages" previously used by Greta Garbo, **Norma Shearer**, **Marie Dressler**, and **Joan Crawford**. "I used to go over to Rehearsal Hall B or C and watch Cyd Charisse, Fred Astaire, and Gene Kelly, and I'd learn all their numbers. Then I'd go home and practice for hours in front of the mirror."[10]

Minnelli first appeared onscreen with her mother at age three in the MGM musical *In the Good Old Summertime* (1949). Years later, the mother-daughter duo teamed up to record a live album in 1964 at the London Palladium. Minnelli—seemingly from the start—was branded as the ultimate Judy Garland "impersonator."[11] While many people felt that she "could never hold a candle to her mother" vocally,[12] it soon became clear that Minnelli possessed the same masterful display of vulnerability and raw emotion that Garland had employed for decades.

Nonetheless, Minnelli "refused to rely on her [mother] for direction" and instead turned to her godmother, Kay Thompson, and the French singer Charles Aznavour for inspiration.[13] Like **Anne Bancroft**, **Geraldine Page**, and later **Jessica Lange**, Minnelli additionally received her acting training from Uta Hagen and Herbert Berghof at the HB Studio in Greenwich Village. In 1965, at the age of 19, she won the Tony Award for Best Actress in a Musical for her performance in the John Kander–Fred Ebb production *Flora the Red Menace*. Despite the acclaim, Minnelli did not get the part of Sally Bowles when she auditioned for *Cabaret*—Kander and Ebb's 1966 Broadway musical based on the 1951 play *I Am a Camera*, which was adapted from Christopher Isherwood's short, semiautobiographical novel *Goodbye to Berlin* (1939). Several years later, however, the director-choreographer Bob Fosse saw the "petite Piaf américaine" at the Olympia music hall in Paris, where Minnelli happened to perform *Cabaret*'s title song.[14] The buoyant actress—with her "bobbed shag hair" and "cartoonishly thick eyelashes"—was offered the role of Sally and "became the first person cast in the film version."[15]

At the time, the movie musical, which had enjoyed box-office success since the early days of the choreographer Busby Berkeley and the pairing of Fred Astaire and **Ginger Rogers**, was "low on filmgoers' lists."[16] In the musicals *Star!* (1968) and

Set during the last days of the Weimar Republic before the Nazi Party dominated German society, Liza Minnelli plays American expatriate Sally Bowles in *Cabaret* (1972). (Allied Artists/ Photofest)

Darling Lili (1970), for example, **Julie Andrews** failed to recapture her former brilliance. Similarly, after **Barbra Streisand**'s Oscar-winning turn in *Funny Girl* (1968), she barely broke even with *Hello, Dolly!* (1969) and the Vincente Minnelli–directed *On a Clear Day You Can See Forever* (1970). Consequently, **Streisand** stayed away from the movie-musical genre for the next five years.

But Fosse approached *Cabaret* from a unique perspective. Having suffered a major flop with the **Shirley MacLaine**–starring musical *Sweet Charity* (1969), he purposefully crafted a musical "for people who hate them." In doing so, he kept the songs site-specific and eschewed the artificially integrated musical style of the 1950s and '60s—in which characters spontaneously break out into song and "dance gracefully" in "color-coordinated costumes." In addition, Fosse, who would win the Best Director Oscar for his work, made his cabaret dancers look harsh, ghoulish, sleazy, and lurid, carving an "image of pre-Hitler Germany into the popular imagination with even greater force and flair than the grotesque cartoons" of New Objectivity painters George Grosz, Otto Dix, and Jeanne Mammen.[17]

Written for the screen by Jay Presson Allen and shot on location in Bavaria and around the then-divided city of Berlin, *Cabaret* (1972) traces the friendship between the flighty and delusional Kit Kat Club performer Sally Bowles and the bisexual Isherwood character Brian Roberts (played by Michael York)—two expatriates "frittering their brittle lives away" in Berlin "on the brink of [Hitler's] fascist revolution."[18] Symbolizing the liberated "New Woman" of the Weimar Republic (who obtained the right to vote and run for office in 1919), Minnelli depicted Sally as a fashionable and flamboyant figure. She rejects traditional notions of gender and sexuality, has an abortion after envisioning herself as a bored housewife, and chooses to work outside the home. There, in her seedy, smoke-filled nightclub of endless revelry (led by Best Supporting Actor Oscar recipient Joel Grey as the "Master of Ceremonies"), she "explodes in giggles and squeals, dances like a sex tornado, and sings like a siren."[19] To prepare for the role of Sally (a part that has been performed over time by the likes of Julie Harris, Judi Dench, Natasha Richardson, Michelle Williams, and **Emma Stone**), Minnelli worked with her father, a former costume designer, and researched such dark-haired actresses of the Weimar period as Asta Nielsen, Louise Brooks, **Luise Rainer**, Lotte Lenya, and Lya De Putti.

Cabaret drew on the "practices of sexual and social transgression established in *Pandora's Box* (1929) and *The Blue Angel* (1930)," and with Minnelli's character squarely situated at the center of action, it entered into the canon of works classified as part of the "Fascinating Fascism" fad of the 1970s.[20] Fitting in with such films as *The Damned* (1969), *The Conformist* (1970), and *The Night Porter* (1974); New York City S&M chic; and *Station to Station*–era David Bowie, *Cabaret* transformed Minnelli into a token of free-spirited feminism and alternative culture. With the hit Bob Fosse–directed concert *Liza with a "Z"* later televised in 1972, the actress was seen as virtually unstoppable.

However, by the late 1970s, in an echo of the tolerant moral attitudes of Weimar Berlin, Minnelli began to travel down the slippery road of drug and alcohol addiction and became "a heartbreakingly close replica" of her mother, who died of an accidental drug overdose at the age of 47.[21] As Andy Warhol recorded in his diary in 1978, Minnelli once turned up at Halston's house imploring him to "give [her] every drug [he had]," with Halston "obligingly handing over coke, marijuana, Valium, and four Quaaludes."[22] Alongside Halston, Warhol, Truman Capote, and **Elizabeth Taylor**, Minnelli additionally became a late-night regular at Studio 54—the legendary New York City nightclub "dedicated to the most extreme form of pleasure."[23] There, alcohol and massive amounts of psychoactive drugs were consumed, while "boys with boys, girls with girls, girls with boys, black and whites, [and] capitalists and Marxists" partied under a spinning disco ball.[24]

But buoyed by the support of the gay community (whose fight against police oppression coincidentally escalated outside the Greenwich Village gay bar the Stonewall Inn just hours after her mother's June 1969 funeral), Minnelli "engaged in the painstaking task of reversing years of bad habits."[25] "My whole life, this disease has been rampant," she once said of her alcoholism. "I inherited it, and it's been horrendous, but I have always asked for help."[26]

While Minnelli never recaptured the glory of *Cabaret*, she later starred in the Vincente Minnelli swansong *A Matter of Time* (1976; opposite **Ingrid Bergman**), *New York, New York* (1977; featuring the legendary Kander and Ebb–written title theme song), and the box-office hit *Arthur* (1981) before appearing as herself in a string of cameos. Having dealt with the loss of many gay friends including her former husband Peter Allen as a result of the AIDS pandemic, Minnelli additionally contributed her time and money to amfAR. Continuing to sell out concerts internationally, she remains a symbol of survival and a lasting connection to classical Hollywood.

Ellen Burstyn

"I really wanted an Oscar when I was a kid," **Ellen Burstyn** once admitted. "That was the Holy Grail."[1] "I wrote my first Academy Award acceptance speech at the age of seven."[2] But unable to deliver a speech at the 47th Academy Awards (1975) as a result of her commitment to the hit Broadway play *Same Time, Next Year*, Burstyn—a nominee for her performance in *Alice Doesn't Live Here Anymore* (1974)—watched the show on television at the home of New York City friends. In a wide-open year for lead actresses, her competition included Diahann Carroll (*Claudine*), **Faye Dunaway** (*Chinatown*), Valerie Perrine (*Lenny*), and frontrunner Gena Rowlands (*A Woman Under the Influence*). Upon the joyous announcement of Burstyn's name, the three-times-divorced, 42-year-old actress and single mother found herself in the midst of "screaming," "hugging," and "[back]-slapping," which hindered her ability to hear Martin Scorsese, the film's director, accept the Oscar on her behalf. She later withdrew to "a small dark meditation room," where, in a quiet state, she "lit a candle" and sat, eyes closed, "for half an hour."[3] There, she reflected on the long and tumultuous journey that she had traveled from her poor, Depression-era childhood to her new state of grace as an internationally respected Best Actress Oscar winner.

Burstyn was born in Detroit, Michigan, on December 7, 1932, into a working-class Catholic family. Like **Marie Dressler**, **Joan Crawford**, **Elizabeth Taylor**, **Julie Andrews**, **Sally Field**, **Halle Berry**, and **Charlize Theron**, her childhood was marred by an abusive parent (in her case, her tormenting mother). At age 18, Burstyn dropped out of high school to marry her first husband. She subsequently purchased a bus ticket to Dallas in a desperate effort to get out of Detroit and "see the world." "I thought it would be unpatriotic if I went to Europe before seeing my own country," she later said.[4]

Alice Doesn't Live Here Anymore (1974)

Bouncing between cities (Dallas, Detroit, Montréal, Los Angeles, and New York), names (Edna Rae, Keri Flynn, Erica Dean, and Ellen McRae), and professions (modeling, dancing, and acting—for which she made her debut in a U.S. Navy film about venereal diseases), Burstyn began to land small parts on television. But after she had appeared on such late-1950s and early-1960s programs as *Gunsmoke*, *Perry Mason*, *The Jackie Gleason Show*, *The Loretta Young Show*, and *The Many Loves of Dobie Gillis*, the determined actress wanted to develop her craft and enrolled at Lee Strasberg's Actors Studio. Ultimately, she settled on the surname of "Burstyn" by way of her third husband (a schizophrenic who stalked his ex-wife for six years following their 1972 divorce) and began to attract attention, earning a Best Supporting Actress Oscar nomination for her role in the coming-of-age drama *The Last Picture Show* (1971).

Burstyn worked in an era when the "phony glamour industry" of Hollywood was "losing touch" with its audience, just as the "movie business became departments of multinational conglomerates."[5] She thus rode in on a wave of independent American film that introduced the world to such art-cinema-influenced directors as Robert Altman, Hal Ashby, Peter Bogdanovich, Francis Ford Coppola, and Steven Spielberg. Ushering in the "second golden age in American filmmaking,"[6] these directors replaced Hollywood's sleek production values, "sanitized virtues," and familiar narrative conventions with tonally sharper, cinema-verité-like depictions of life while employing a new generation of actors who looked like the boy or girl next door. For women, however, this colossal cinematic shift signified the loss of "much of their economic leverage."[7] To be sure, "there were no studio contracts forcing [independent] directors and producers to hire certain stars or to employ actresses at all."[8] Therefore, the vast majority of roles for women were "subordinated to or upstaged by" their male counterparts.[9] Unlike the 1930s, '40s, and '50s, when "many of the box-office hits . . . were driven by their female leads" and when studios, as a result, meticulously manufactured their female stars and protected their expensively publicized images, actresses such as Burstyn were now more or less on their own. On one hand, this provided them with an opportunity to control their own image and to "take jobs as they choose."[10] On the other hand, without the studio system in place to support them, they were often saddled with the extra burden of having to pay for their own agents, publicists, stylists, lawyers, and so forth. "Committed as ever to their craft" but only finding a paucity of female-driven story lines to choose from,[11] many stars and emerging female talent began to realize that their craft was simply not as committed to them.

Showing enormous ambition in furthering her career, Burstyn soon approached the director William Friedkin to star in the horror-thriller *The Exorcist* (1973), after the likes of **Audrey Hepburn**, **Anne Bancroft**, **Jane Fonda**, **Shirley MacLaine**, and **Geraldine Page** (who "read the book and . . . wanted to throw up")[12] dropped out of contention. As Friedkin recalled, Burstyn "was passionate, intense, focused, and highly intelligent. She told me about her Catholic girlhood and how she had left the church and was now studying to become a Sufi. We discussed the novel for

In *Alice Doesn't Live Here Anymore* (1974), a rare female-driven film by Martin Scorsese, Ellen Burstyn plays a submissive housewife who is given a second chance at life following her husband's traffic-collision death. The film played a key role in galvanizing the women's liberation movement. (Warner Bros. Pictures Inc./Photofest) a couple of hours, and I thought she had an acute understanding of [the part of the mother to a demonically possessed child]. Yet, [because she had never played a lead before] I didn't think the studio would approve her."[13] Ultimately, Friedkin secured Burstyn for the lead, and *The Exorcist* became one of the highest-grossing movies of all time, igniting a mass hysteria not seen in theaters since Alfred Hitchcock's *Psycho* (1960).

Like **Mary Pickford** and **Katharine Hepburn** before her, the enormous success of *The Exorcist* placed Burstyn in the rare position of having cast-and-crew-selection veto power over her subsequent Warner Bros. project, *Alice Doesn't Live Here Anymore* (1974). In her pursuit of "someone young and fresh to direct,"[14] she came across the up-and-coming film director Martin Scorsese, who had impressed the actress with his interest in wanting to examine the interior lives of women. From there, Burstyn helped to assemble a crew with as "many women in positions of authority as possible."[15] Reflecting the aspirations of second-wave feminism and the women's liberation movement, her goal was to achieve a certain "level of reality" and a more truthful depiction of women from what was "afforded by conventionally conceived Hollywood stereotypes."[16]

To this end, *Alice Doesn't Live Here Anymore* offered audiences—and female audiences in particular—one of the first stories in years to prominently feature a woman who does not end up getting punished in the process of self-awareness, self-reliance, and self-liberation. In the film, Burstyn portrays Alice Hyatt, a submissive housewife and mother conditioned to living her mundane life in suburban New Mexico for her dictatorial husband but not knowing how to do so for herself. Trapped in an abusive marriage, she fantasizes with her best friend, Bea, about the size of Robert Redford's penis. But after her husband dies in a traffic collision, Alice is given a chance to rebuild her life and fulfill her childhood dream of becoming a nightclub singer. As the American cultural anthropologist Margaret Mead observed, "The only women allowed to be dominant and respectable at the same time are widows. You have to [have] . . . a husband who dies, and then have power thrust upon you,"[17] much like the widows portrayed by **Vivien Leigh** in *Gone with the Wind* (1939), **Anna Magnani** in *The Rose Tattoo* (1955), **Sally Field** in *Places of the Heart* (1984), **Cher** in *Moonstruck* (1987), and **Jessica Tandy** in *Driving Miss Daisy* (1989). For Alice, however, numerous roadblocks still await: the "hovering threat of male violence";[18] the unwanted influence on her young son, Tommy, by a local preteen (played by **Jodie Foster**); and—just as she is gaining her sense of freedom—a blossoming romance with a handsome rancher (Kris Kristofferson) who is eventually willing to compromise *his* goals in support of *her* dreams.

While made during one of the most sexist periods in American cinema, when women, according to Burstyn, were portrayed as "whores, boring wives, [or] insipid, frightened little Jane Austen characters,"[19] *Alice Doesn't Live Here Anymore* became an instant feminist classic. Expressing the idea of female independence and agency ("It's *my* life," declares Alice. "Not some man's life that I'm here to help him out with"),[20] the film emboldened women and helped to galvanize the women's liberation movement. At the time, thousands of women (both straight and gay) were leaving their husbands after discovering what feminism stood for. Indeed, a year after the film's release, the National Organization for Women (NOW) sponsored "Alice Doesn't Day," which encouraged women across America to force husbands, businessmen, and other men to take seriously their demands for equal rights. In doing so, women refrained from shopping; boycotted work and school; wore arm bands to demonstrate their solidarity; demanded full social, political, and economic equality via passage of the Equal Rights Amendment; and attempted to show to a chauvinistic American society what a vital role they serve.

For Burstyn, *Alice Doesn't Live Here Anymore* transformed her into the "frazzled but unbeaten icon of single motherhood."[21] It additionally helped to bolster a long career that included *Resurrection* (1980; her personal favorite of her films, in which she plays a faith healer), the short-lived TV sitcom *The Ellen Burstyn Show* (1986; in which she plays a "beleaguered widow"),[22] and *Requiem for a Dream* (2000). Endowed "with an aura of spirituality,"[23] Burstyn was initiated into the mystical Islamic religion of Sufism and was ordained as a priest in the mid-1980s. After Lee Strasberg's passing in 1982, she additionally went on to become the Actor Studio's co-artistic director as well as the first female president of the Actors' Equity Association.

Louise Fletcher

From Clint Eastwood to Charles Bronson, Burt Reynolds, Robert Redford, and Steve McQueen, the macho male movie star dominated the films of the 1970s. With "an emphasis on the increasingly violent nature of men," the "era's male protagonists tended to be rebels and anti-heroes while the women in their lives wound up in supporting roles," often playing victims, irritants, or "quivering neurotics."[1] Along these lines, **Julie Christie**, while reflecting on her performances in *Shampoo* (1975) and *Heaven Can Wait* (1978), later admitted that she didn't even "know what those films were about. The women in them were not very empowered."[2] The era did produce remarkable new talent including **Ellen Burstyn**, Gena Rowlands, **Sissy Spacek**, and **Diane Keaton**, but only one actress—**Barbra Streisand**—consistently reigned at the box office and was thereby offered the best roles before anyone else. While **Jane Fonda** and Vanessa Redgrave were "too busy as political activists to devote themselves [full-time] to movie careers,"[3] a dichotomy between the emerging voices of the 1970s women's liberation movement and the evaporation of strong cinematic roles for women in general became seen as problematic.

Indeed, this dichotomy reached a startling boiling point ahead of the 48th Academy Awards (1976), which marked, according to many observers, "one of the weakest years in Oscar history for female performances."[4] At a time when film studies increasingly found its way into university curriculums and feminist film scholars such as Laura Mulvey, Teresa de Lauretis, and Molly Haskell began to call attention to the marginalized depictions and mistreatment of women in film, a sizable number of secondary roles for women underscored the 1976 Best Actress Oscar category. Representing this imbalance were contenders **Louise Fletcher**

One Flew Over the Cuckoo's Nest (1975)

In *One Flew Over the Cuckoo's Nest* (1975), the relatively unknown actress Louise Fletcher played Nurse Ratched, a controlling, patronizing villain capable of projecting a convincing smile. (Saul Zaentz Company/ Photofest)

(*One Flew Over the Cuckoo's Nest*), Ann-Margret (*Tommy*), Carol Kane (*Hester Street*), former recipient **Glenda Jackson** (*Hedda*), and the French actress and New York Film Critics Award winner Isabelle Adjani (*L'histoire d'Adèle H.*).

Incensed by "the lack of substantial roles for women,"[5] **Ellen Burstyn**—the previous year's Best Actress Oscar winner—went on television to urge Academy voters to boycott the Best Actress category altogether. While **Burstyn** was motivated by a sense of social purpose, she nevertheless stole some thunder from the ultimate victor, Louise Fletcher, who had to defend herself against the allegation that only a light year afforded her the Oscar. Fletcher expressed her bitterness, reportedly telephoning **Burstyn** "to tell her it would have been nicer if she had made the suggestion in a year in which **Burstyn** was up for a nomination" herself.[6]

Despite winning for what was regarded as a supporting role (a detail also attributed to the Oscar victories of **Luise Rainer** for *The Great Ziegfeld* [1936], **Simone Signoret** for *Room at the Top* [1959], **Patricia Neal** for *Hud* [1963], and, decades later, **Nicole Kidman** for *The Hours* [2002]), Fletcher's performance—weak year or not—ingrained itself into the public psyche. As Nurse Mildred Ratched—a chillingly quiet, passive-aggressive spinster so depraved that audiences "stood up and cheered" when she was nearly choked to death[7]—Fletcher managed to craft one of the most memorable cinematic villains of all time.

One Flew Over the Cuckoo's Nest (1975) was adapted from the 1962 social-protest novel by Ken Kesey. Kesey, who had once been "paid seventy-five dollars a day to ingest hallucinogens" for a federally funded research program, directly delved into what the American writer saw as the "sorry state of psychiatric hospitals of his day."[8] Coinciding with the rise of American films dealing with "the fallout of immense social and political upheaval" from the Vietnam War era and Watergate, *Cuckoo's Nest* tackled the common theme of "the fragility of the human psyche" while forcing audiences to "really question what sanity is."[9] Representing the rigid, power-abusing inhumanity of the U.S. government is Fletcher's autocratic head nurse—a "person you recognize as being perfectly nice" but who calmly delivers "her care . . . in a killing manner."[10] For Nurse Ratched, "insubordination and disobedience are signs of illness that must be cured."[11] Nobody knows this better than the defiant Randle McMurphy (played by Jack Nicholson)—a crusader of anti-authoritarian freedom who fakes his insanity so he can serve out his prison term for battery and statutory rape in the seemingly more comfortable surroundings of Nurse Ratched's psychiatric ward. Disrespectful to the mind-numbing, life-denying reality that Nurse Ratched implements, McMurphy ultimately pays a terrible price when he is subjected to electroconvulsive therapy.

After several auditions and after **Anne Bancroft**, **Ellen Burstyn**, **Jane Fonda**, Angela Lansbury, and **Geraldine Page** had all turned down the role of Nurse Ratched (partly because they found the character too grotesque), Fletcher, who was virtually unknown to Hollywood at that time, was offered the part for $10,000. The towering 5-foot-10 actress was given one week of rehearsals before shooting, and she additionally prepared by observing group therapy sessions at the

Louise Fletcher celebrates her Best Actress Oscar victory alongside *One Flew Over the Cuckoo's Nest* costar (and Best Actor recipient) Jack Nicholson at the 1976 Academy Awards. (© A.M.P.A.S.®/Photofest)

Oregon State Hospital, where *Cuckoo's Nest* was filmed. Throughout the 11-week shoot, in the midst of "dozens of . . . patients at the hospital [who] were drafted in as extras," Fletcher, with her hair "turned under in a perfect Page Boy" cut, was "totally isolated" from her "crazy" cast mates as a result of the severe character that she was playing.[12]

With *One Flew Over the Cuckoo's Nest* becoming the third-highest-grossing film of 1975 (after *Jaws* and *The Rocky Horror Picture Show*) and the second film (after 1934's *It Happened One Night*) to win all five of the Academy's top filmmaking honors (writer, actor, actress, director, and picture), Fletcher was thrown into a Cinderella-like experience. After sprinting to the podium to accept her Best Actress Oscar, she informed the audience that she "loved being hated" by them and thanked Jack Nicholson and the other actors involved for making "being in a mental institution [feel] like being in a mental institution." She then broke into sign language to express her gratitude to her Deaf parents: "For my mother and my father, I want to say thank you for teaching me to have a dream. You are seeing my dream come true."[13] But as if somehow casting an omen over Fletcher's subsequent career, Nicholson and *Cuckoo's Nest* director Miloš Forman jokingly predicted backstage, "Now, we're all going to make flops!"[14]

Born on July 22, 1934, Fletcher grew up in a "poor, primitive, [and] fundamentalist" Alabama.[15] As the second of four children to an Episcopalian minister who pioneered 40 Deaf ministries throughout the region, Fletcher was surrounded by Deaf congregations but nevertheless experienced a childhood "marked by a sense of loneliness and separation." "If I fell down and hurt myself," she said, "I never cried. There was no one to hear me."[16]

Fletcher was first introduced to acting by way of a doting theatrical aunt who taught her "prohibitively shy" niece "how to show off."[17] She soon began to perform at home in order to make her parents laugh. She eventually studied drama at the University of North Carolina and then in the late 1950s moved to Los Angeles, where she sporadically appeared on television in modest bit parts. But just as she was offered a lead film role in the 1960 coming-of-age drama *Where the Boys Are*, Fletcher turned her back on acting to marry the Hollywood agent and producer Jerry Bick. Together, they raised two sons and relocated to London—a move, she recalls, that ultimately "added up to a sense of disappointment." "The women's movement had been sort of seeping in through my pores, and I was beginning to get the idea that I [didn't] have to do things because other people [expected] me to."[18]

After more than ten years, Fletcher made her acting return in the Robert Altman–directed, Jerry Bick–produced *Thieves Like Us* (1974), handing in a performance that eventually caught the attention of Miloš Forman.

But denied a starring role in Altman's *Nashville* (1975) due to a personal conflict with the director over a character that she had helped to create (that of a mother of Deaf children, eventually played by Lily Tomlin), Fletcher began to notice a growing pattern of missed opportunities and career-derailing setbacks that stubbornly failed to relent. Even after her sanctifying Oscar victory for *Cuckoo's Nest* at the age of 41, the actress was unable to capitalize on her success and was instead typecast in lesser-quality roles in a Hollywood that had "little use for middle-aged women."[19] Exacerbating problems when "the '70s ended and Hollywood switched from star-driven pictures to special effects blockbusters,"[20] the actress repeatedly found herself in such critically reviled films as *Exorcist II: The Heretic* (1977), *Mama Dracula* (1980), *Brainstorm* (1983), and *Firestarter* (1984).

Unlike "many Oscar winners who blame agents [and] studio executives . . . for failing to exploit [their triumphs]," Fletcher, who never achieved any true measure of stardom, maintained a more levelheaded perspective: "[Winning an Oscar will] make you wonderfully happy for a night," she once said, "but don't expect that it'll do anything for your career."[21] Similar to **Marlee Matlin**, who won the Best Actress Oscar without becoming a household name, Fletcher continued to seek work where she could find it. In an industry of fleeting successes, trends, and uncertainties, she found out "the hard way" that rejection is something to learn from and should never be taken so seriously.[22] Forever associated with Nurse Ratched (a character she can no longer "bear to watch"), Fletcher additionally learned that some "parts win [the] Oscars" as opposed to the actual actors who play them.[23]

Faye Dunaway

Faye Dunaway never played the ingénue. In fact, there is nothing really simple or innocent about her. "I was born an old soul," the actress once acknowledged,[1] and in life as well as in her movies she has demonstrated that repeatedly.

Born on January 14, 1941, and subjected to a nomadic upbringing as a result of her father's roving military career, Dorothy Faye Dunaway grew up with little stability and few circumstantial advantages in places as diverse as Texas, Utah, backwoods Florida, and West Germany. At age 12, the "poor Southern girl from the wrong side of the tracks" ultimately had to pick up the slack at home when her father "left in a divorce."[2]

But with hard work, determination, and "a series of patchwork scholarships,"[3] Dunaway quickly advanced. "Tall, willowy, and [with] porcelain[-like features]," she went on to win "a beauty contest at the University of Florida" before studying drama at Boston University and joining the original Repertory Theatre of Lincoln Center.[4] In 1967, she made her screen debut in *The Happening*, and the next year, she became a top trendsetting icon and a Best Actress Oscar nominee for *Bonnie and Clyde* (1967)—a watershed crime drama that produced one of the most violent endings in film history.

Although Dunaway played a fashion designer in *A Place for Lovers* (1968), a former fashion model in *Puzzle of a Downfall Child* (1970), and a fashion photographer in *Eyes of Laura Mars* (1978), she never appeared on the fashion runways, even though her severe, supermodel beauty blew the hinges off the door. In line with such famous actress-designer pairings as Adrian and **Joan Crawford**, Hubert de Givenchy and **Audrey Hepburn**, Edith Head and **Grace Kelly**, Arnold Scaasi and

Network (1976)

Reviving a female self-empowerment not seen since Joan Crawford, Bette Davis, and Katharine Hepburn reigned supreme in the 1930s, Faye Dunaway portrays a TV programming executive with stainless-steel ambition in *Network* (1976). (Metro-Goldwyn-Mayer Inc./Photofest)

Barbra Streisand, Halston and **Liza Minnelli**, and Bob Mackie and **Cher**, Dunaway formed an impressive collaboration with Theadora Van Runkle. Sparking a world-wide fashion phenomenon, Van Runkle designed Dunaway's complete on- and offscreen wardrobes. Her "Bonnie look" alone brought long skirts, belted cardigans, and the French beret into high-level vogue. As Dunaway explained, "I came in on the tail end of the [studio] star system. The costumes, for example . . . for *Bonnie and Clyde*, they were all handmade. It was still like the old Hollywood. . . . I'm sort of a 'bridge' character in a funny way, you know."[5]

It was not *Bonnie and Clyde*, however, that garnered Dunaway the Oscar. Nor was it her spectacular turn as a daughter with secrets in *Chinatown* (1974). It was for *Network* (1976)—a powerful film that is best remembered for its electrifying Peter Finch / Howard Beale proclamation: "I'm as mad as hell, and I'm not going to take this anymore!"[6] The line resonated with American audiences of the time, echoing the anger, mistrust, and moral ambiguity of an era still reeling from the political assassinations of the 1960s, the debilitating war in Vietnam, Chappaquiddick, inflation, the Patty Hearst kidnapping, and Watergate.

Based on Paddy Chayefsky's prophetic, satirical screenplay about the degenerating state of television news, *Network* featured Dunaway in the role of the TV programming executive Diana Christensen. Offered the role after Chayefsky had vetoed **Jane Fonda** because of her political views, Dunaway—who was braless in every scene—brought to her character a "stainless steel ambition" not observed since **Joan Crawford**, **Bette Davis**, and **Katharine Hepburn** enjoyed "the upper hand on their male leads" in the 1930s and '40s.[7] Even though we learn that Diana's husband "ran off with his boyfriend" and that her psychotherapist told her that she was "the worst lay he'd ever had," Diana, who is "inept at everything except [her] work," operates "like a machine"[8] with the exactitude of **Louise Fletcher**'s Nurse Ratched. As a "cobra-like," ratings-hungry Machiavellian, she "digs [her] way into the top professional ranks" and "lays out a template for the coming age of 'disinfotainment' and canned news-porn."[9] In the process, she manages her male and female staff with arresting confidence and determination. "By the way," she warns from her towering New York City corner office, "the next time I send an audience research report around, you'd all better read it, or I'll sack the fucking lot of you. Is that clear?"

As Dunaway explained, this "was the mid-seventies, and if you wanted to succeed as a woman in a man's world, you had to be able to beat them at their own game."[10] To be sure, it was a time when the women's liberation movement was impacting society; when *Ms.* magazine, "the bible of the movement," was celebrating its fifth anniversary; and when Dunaway's talent agent, Sue Mengers, and MGM executive story editor turned 20th Century-Fox president Sherry Lansing became two of "the first truly powerful [businesswomen] in Hollywood."[11] In accordance with these cultural shifts, Dunaway's performance underscored "the growing pains as men and women adjusted to changing roles."[12] Divergent from the 37 percent of Best Actress Oscar–winning performances featuring women without any form of a job or a career, Dunaway's character is seen as a woman of leadership, influence, and authority. Incidentally, her character is part of the small 6.6 percent of female executives or business owners portrayed to Oscar-winning success by **Marie Dressler** in *Min and Bill* (1930), **Vivien Leigh** in *Gone with the Wind* (1939), **Joan Crawford** in *Mildred Pierce* (1945), **Olivia de Havilland** in *To Each His Own* (1946), and **Katharine Hepburn** in *Guess Who's Coming to Dinner* (1967). Bolstered by these attributes, Diana stays secure within herself when giving orders, decides on "what is important enough to report,"[13] and thereby determines the content of the news (a role still vastly underrepresented by women working in the media industry today).

On Oscar night 1977, which celebrated the first woman ever nominated in the Best Director category (the Italian director Lina Wertmüller for *Seven Beauties*), *Network* was ultimately honored with four Oscars including Best Actor (Peter Finch), Best Supporting Actress (Beatrice Straight), and Best Original Screenplay. Arriving at the ceremony in a casual, "karate-style pant-suit" designed by Geoffrey Beene,[14] Dunaway was locked in a tight race for Best Actress. A third-time's-the-charm nominee, she faced a pack of contenders including the French actress Marie-Christine Barrault (*Cousin, cousine*), box-office champions Talia Shire (*Rocky*) and **Sissy Spacek** (*Carrie*), and rival frontrunner Liv Ullmann, whose angst-ridden performance in Ingmar Bergman's *Face to Face* earned her the New York Film Critics Award. But turning in a topical performance that paralleled many of the issues driving the women's liberation movement (e.g., workplace rights and economic equality), Dunaway was seen to have the added edge and accepted her Oscar from the previous year's winner, **Louise Fletcher**. "I didn't expect this to happen quite yet," she told the audience. "But I do thank you very much and I'm very grateful."[15]

Early the next morning, Dunaway, with an "expression on her face that conveys the confusion of a fatigued mountaineer who has finally reached the summit only to be disappointed by the view," was photographed by her future husband, Terry O'Neill, poolside at the Beverly Hills Hotel, staring "at her Oscar and piles of newspapers headlining her victory."[16]

As an actress "strongly identified with tough, cold movie roles," Dunaway, who was criticized by the media for "allegedly showing too little reverence for

Not expecting to have won, Faye Dunaway holds her Best Actress Oscar backstage at the Dorothy Chandler Pavilion in downtown Los Angeles at the 49th Academy Awards (1977). (© A.M.P.A.S.®/ Photofest)

her nearby statuette" in O'Neill's photograph,[17] ultimately came to personify the archetype of the "Great American Bitch."[18] As women began to crack the corporate glass ceiling, this epithet was increasingly used to define women who (a) did not need a man to complete them and (b) threatened the status quo of male dominance by entering "the labor markets in ever-growing numbers, penetrating such male sanctuaries as law, medicine, banking, and business."[19] Gaining a reputation for sometimes having a temper, being "over-insistent on her interpretation of a role," and being "unprofessional" (according to **Bette Davis**, her costar in the 1976 TV movie *The Disappearance of Aimee*),[20] Dunaway found herself relegated to inferior projects. Moreover, much like her character from *Network*, her devotion to her career in the eyes of many of her male counterparts began to affect perceptions of her femininity.

Dunaway was additionally derided by some people for her "brilliant but lynching impersonation" of the late **Joan Crawford** in *Mommie Dearest* (1981)—a film about child abuse that "incensed the entertainment community, which felt [that too much had been revealed] about one of their own and the system that had created her."[21] Dunaway, who was held responsible, recoiled. "My focus was not on my work," explained the actress.[22] "I had been through the star machine and was ready to get out."[23] In the process of doing so, Dunaway moved to London in the early 1980s to escape the glare of Hollywood and to raise her son. Like **Joan Crawford** and **Bette Davis** in the later stages of their careers, the actress started to get "offers [to play] only overstrong women, even weird women,"[24] in movies such as *The Wicked Lady* (1983) and *Supergirl* (1984).

But Dunaway defined her era as few other actresses did. At a time when American women battled against a "toxic brew of fear and sexism" for a measure of equality in the workplace (where they represented a labor-force participation level of only 43 percent, made "59 cents for every dollar made by men," and typically aspired to become no more than "a nurse, a secretary, a schoolteacher, or maybe a librarian"),[25] the actress played her part with unrelenting conviction. Operating in a world that has historically embraced "the idea of women's inferiority" and encouraged women "to pursue advanced education [only as] long as they don't forget their paramount destiny to marry and become mothers,"[26] Dunaway conversely showed audiences a self-assured woman who demanded "a seat at the table rather than to reset the table" itself.[27] With *Network* sardonically speaking "to the Seventies the way *Dr. Strangelove* (1964) spoke to the chaotic Sixties,"[28] she stepped up to the plate and, like her cinematic role models, began to question the preconceived notions of gender, power, and sexuality that helped to promote further activism and social change.

In her towering New York City corner office, Faye Dunaway's character in *Network* (1976) contemplates her next move in a tenacious, male-driven executive workforce. (Metro-Goldwyn-Mayer Inc./Photofest)

Diane Keaton

Annie Hall (1977)

Set in Los Angeles and New York, the life and career of **Diane Keaton** could be characterized as a tale of two cities. Born Diane Hall on January 5, 1946, to a father working in real estate and a mother concentrating in visual arts, Keaton, the oldest of four children, was raised under the sunshine of Highland Park, Los Angeles. After a year in college, she moved to the gritty, crumbling mayhem of late-1960s New York City—a near-bankrupt metropolis teetering "on the verge of a nervous breakdown." With New York's real estate affordable "even for artists and aspiring deadbeats,"[1] Keaton—equipped with a zany charm and an openhearted likability—determinedly pursued a career in show business. Like **Grace Kelly** and **Joanne Woodward** before her, she enrolled at New York's Neighborhood Playhouse, where she received a thorough training in Sanford Meisner's "observe-and-respond" acting technique.

In 1968, Keaton auditioned for a part in the original Broadway production of *Hair*—the "seminal hippie," antiwar rock musical that hit the stage "like a thunderclap at the height of the Vietnam War."[2] Becoming the first Broadway show to feature both male and female nudity and containing such counterculture anthems as "Aquarius," "Let the Sunshine In," "Sodomy," and "Black Boys," *Hair* proved to be a genuine hit that "straight America was not ready for."[3] In a cast "filled with unknowns,"[4] Keaton landed a small role but she refused to disrobe despite a $50 incentive offered to all cast members who did. She was also "ordered to lose 10 pounds"—an all-too-common provision for women in entertainment that pushed the struggling actress into a "bulimia nightmare."[5]

Around this time, Keaton caught the attention of the actor, director, and comedian Woody Allen, with whom she first worked on his 1969 Broadway stage

In an amusing, self-deprecating gush of continuous dialogue, Woody Allen's Alvy Singer and Diane Keaton's title character forge a loving, unconventional, and transformative relationship in *Annie Hall* (1977). With her chic, androgynous wardrobe, Keaton helped to change the rules on how a woman could dress. (United Artists/Photofest) production, *Play It Again, Sam*. Allen credited Keaton for her impeccable comic timing and for "opening his eyes to the potential of female characters" without conforming to "simplistic stereotypes." He began to cast his new romantic muse in one project after another while making complex and memorable women a "hallmark of his movies." "Often you can write more closely about your own perspective and experience of the world through a character of a different gender," observed **Cate Blanchett**, who decades later won the Best Actress Oscar for her performance in Allen's *Blue Jasmine* (2013). "People criticized me for being a self-hating Jew . . . but not being able to create good women was not aimed at me very often," said Allen,[6] who has additionally worked with **Kathy Bates**, **Marion Cotillard**, **Jodie Foster**, **Helen Hunt**, **Geraldine Page**, **Natalie Portman**, **Julia Roberts**, **Meryl Streep**, **Charlize Theron**, and **Kate Winslet**.

As Keaton reflected, "The thing I remember about Woody is that he always wanted people to behave and look sort of like they did in real life. He . . . liked the idea of overlapping and loosening up the dialogue."[7] Impressively, Keaton proved competent in handling Allen's difficult, daffy, and excessively talky scripts as well as more serious parts such as Kay Corleone in the Best Picture Oscar–winning dramas *The Godfather* (1972) and *The Godfather Part II* (1974). Alongside **Jane Fonda** and 1970s box-office queen **Barbra Streisand**, Keaton became one of the few bankable female stars of her generation.

Two years after Keaton ended a romantic relationship with Allen, she attained the signature role of her career. In her Oscar-winning part, she starred as the endearingly scatterbrained, eclectically dressed, cannabis-loving, and psychoanalysis-seeking title character of Allen's revisionist romantic comedy *Annie Hall* (1977). "That was a movie that was *completely* effortless," Keaton later admitted. "It was about the easiest thing I've ever done in my life."[8] With the film partly using her real name (Diane Hall) in its title and blending biographical details of her life with her onscreen persona, Keaton personified the modern American urban woman of the 1970s as a free-spirited "la-di-da" nonconformist who juggles her search for a meaningful relationship with the overriding need to maintain and make use of her personal freedom.[9] Abandoning traditional gender roles by circumventing societal pressures to marry, settle down, and bear children, the character of Annie Hall— much as Keaton did herself— moves to New York to pursue a career in singing. In the process, she stumbles upon Woody Allen's Alvy Singer—a neurotic Jew "born in an apartment under a roller coaster in Coney Island."[10] Adventuring together through New York (and briefly Los Angeles) "in a perpetual state of emotional contradiction[s],"[11] the couple—in an amusing, self-deprecating gush of continuous dialogue—forge a loving, transformative relationship that is only sabotaged by their nervous, behaviorally funny insecurities.

Annie Hall—with its universal theme of falling in and out of love, not to mention its striking contrast to the grim and tiresome offerings of Vietnam-era cinema— became a top-grossing hit with hordes of addicted fans lining up to see it over and over again. At a time "when the women's liberation movement was at its height"[12]

In one set depicting two different psychotherapy office locations, the characters portrayed by Diane Keaton and Woody Allen in *Annie Hall* (1977) each attempt to better understand themselves. (United Artists/Photofest)

and had achieved a great deal in helping to increase workplace opportunities, liberalize divorce laws, mandate the legality of abortions, equalize educational and athletic opportunities, spur on the creation of women's studies courses, and empower women in serving on juries and using their own credit cards, the film additionally epitomized a new way of feeling, reacting, and dressing. As a result, Keaton, with her hand-selected, thrift-store wardrobe for the film, consisting of Chaplinesque bowler hats, "masculine shirts,"[13] raffish neckties, and baggy chino trousers, turned into an unexpected fashion icon. In keeping with "the disregard of gender rules by the . . . musical forerunners of punk, the New York Dolls, Roxy Music, and David Bowie,"[14] she changed the rules on how women could dress in public, making her chic, androgynous bad-taste-is-good-taste look become a popular trendsetting force in fashion. Although **Claudette Colbert**, Marlene Dietrich, and **Katharine Hepburn** (to whom Keaton's bohemian star image has sometimes been compared) all raised eyebrows by donning menswear beginning in the late 1920s, Keaton was able to appropriate the look "without causing a stir."[15] In direct opposition to the "stereotypic Californian blonde image [that then] dominated certain areas of the media,"[16] her forward-thinking attire started a political-sexual revolution in one of the most sexist periods in U.S. history and became for many women the "ensemble de rigueur." Moreover, it conveyed the powerful message, "I'm the same as him."[17]

While Keaton turned in a stunning performance as a doomed New York City schoolteacher in *Looking for Mr. Goodbar* (1977), she clinched the New York Film Critics Award for her performance in *Annie Hall* and was soon nominated for the Best Actress Oscar. Eclectically layered in high heels, rolled-up stockings, a jacket, a scarf, and a stripy dress covering up a pair of slacks, the actress arrived at the 50th Academy Awards (1978). In one of only three instances in which every Best Actress–nominated film was also nominated for Best Picture, Keaton found herself in a field of contenders that included Marsha Mason (*The Goodbye Girl*), **Shirley MacLaine** (*The Turning Point*), and former recipients **Anne Bancroft** (*The Turning Point*) and **Jane Fonda** (*Julia*). At an event that was perhaps best remembered for Vanessa Redgrave's controversial, antiauthoritarian remarks tethered to her support for the Palestine Liberation Organization, *Annie Hall* was ultimately honored with four Oscars, including Best Picture, Best Director, Best Original Screenplay, and Best Actress. Unlike the absent, awards-wary Woody Allen (who later "forbade the film's publicists from advertising the movie as having won the Oscars within 100 miles of New York"),[18] Keaton graciously accepted her Oscar from the presenter and inaugural winner **Janet Gaynor**. "Mercy," she gushed to the audience. "This is terrific. It's simply terrific!"[19]

While balancing her acting career with such diverse, far-reaching films as *Reds* (1981), *The Little Drummer Girl* (1984), *Baby Boom* (1987), and *Something's Gotta Give* (2003), not to mention several other Woody Allen–directed vehicles, Keaton has managed to allocate time to other projects. Her ancillary activities consist of directing (including the singer Belinda Carlisle's 1987 "Heaven Is a Place on

Earth" music video and the 1995 feature film *Unstrung Heroes*), producing (Gus Van Sant's school-shooting-related drama *Elephant* [2003]), photography, animal advocacy, and—in the city of Los Angeles in particular—historic preservation. Setting her sights on such architectural wonders as Frank Lloyd Wright's crumbling Ennis House (built in 1924), the ill-fated Ambassador Hotel (host to six Academy Award ceremonies), the Century Plaza Hotel, and Lloyd Wright's art deco Samuels-Novarro House (once home to the silent-film idol Ramon Novarro before Keaton herself took residence half a century later),[20] the actress has used her celebrity and passion for restoring old Hollywood to underscore the fragility of these overlooked cultural relics. "We've treated old buildings like we once treated plastic shopping bags—we haven't reused them, and when we've finished with them, we've tossed them out," said Keaton,[21] who has worked for both the Los Angeles Conservancy and the National Trust for Historic Preservation.

Maintaining much of the same spirit of independence that fans of *Annie Hall* first came to love, Keaton has continued to forge her own way. In doing so, she has rejected preferential treatment often accorded to celebrities, shunned the possibility of marriage, and opted to adopt two children as a single parent in her 50s. In addition, she has proudly appeared regularly on worst-dressed lists while remaining a beacon of individuality for those who do not like their culture delivered straight up.

Sally Field

In a pair of roles centered around southern American family values, back-breaking labor, cotton, and the challenge and struggle to find the confidence needed to overcome enormous adversity, **Sally Field** won the Best Actress Oscar for *Norma Rae* (1979) and *Places in the Heart* (1984). At the time of Field's victories, the home-video era of Betamax and VHS was giving "viewers immediate access to . . . an unprecedented universe of films."[1] Simultaneously, Hollywood was increasingly relying on sequels, remakes, and franchises in the wake of such colossal, moneymaking blockbusters as *Jaws* (1975), *Rocky* (1976), *Star Wars* (1977), *Superman: The Movie* (1978), and *Raiders of the Lost Ark* (1981). With a greater number of films financed by foreign presales, the major studios were additionally exporting "more movies to international markets."[2] "There was a decision at some point in Hollywood that the audience for film, the broadest audience, were young, international males between 18 and 24," said **Julianne Moore**, who slammed "movie studios for producing action pap instead of art."[3] By the time Ronald Reagan took office as the 40th president of the United States in 1981, Second Wave feminism was being disparaged, and films began to reflect "the beliefs of . . . the conservative former movie star who [now] occupied the White House."[4] As a result, director-driven films were brought to an end, and the financial backers of the Hollywood studios took control over the content of the films being made. Social and political comment and "themes dealing with that which was ugly, threatening, or cautionary were, for the most part, left to independent filmmakers."[5]

With Hollywood believing that "men tend to have more value in foreign sales,"[6] female actors of the late 1970s and 1980s were barely promoted overseas. Meanwhile, hypermasculine stars such as Sylvester Stallone and Arnold Schwarzenegger

Norma Rae (1979)

Places in the Heart (1984)

As the textile worker (and title character) Norma Rae, Sally Field turns against terrible work conditions and scrawls the word "UNION" on a piece of cardboard, ultimately setting in motion a movement formed to protect and further their workers' rights. (Twentieth Century Fox Film Corporation/Photofest) enjoyed worldwide popularity. As **Meryl Streep** began to notice, female characters were "eclipsed by Rambo and his testosterone-driven successors" and were simultaneously portrayed onscreen "getting slapped, kicked, and asking for help."[7] The trend left talented actresses with fewer opportunities to create indelible screen images for younger female viewers to look up to and admire. According to **Streep**, what exacerbated the problem were not only "the economic factors" that "skewed film production toward the [male-dominated] action blockbuster," but also a resistance among men in general to imagine, adapt to, and empathize with a strong screen persona "if that persona is a she."[8] "It's harder for men to imagine themselves as the girl in the movies than it is for me to imagine myself as Daniel Craig bringing down the building," **Streep** underlined.[9]

For Field, who was considered a kind of "national joke" as a result of her starring roles in the trite, late-1960s television sitcoms *Gidget* and *The Flying Nun*,[10] the prospect of ever being promoted or taken seriously as an actress was once difficult to imagine. "I was a walking sight-gag," explained Field, who was known at the time for her cute, animated girlishness. "Everybody was taking acid and dropping out and protesting the [Vietnam] War and I was the Flying Nun! As far as my generation was concerned, I represented the establishment that they were rebelling against. I represented organized religion and commercial television. They were wearing miniskirts [while] I was wearing a habit."[11] But ultimately showcasing a spectacular range and grit that made use of her "pert [and] sulky face,"[12] Field surprised audiences and critics alike and became one of the most esteemed actors of her generation.

Field was born on "a different side of the track" in Pasadena, California, on November 6, 1946.[13] Alongside her older brother and half sister, she grew up under precarious financial conditions with working-class actor parents who struggled to pay the rent. Her divorced mother, the actress Margaret Field, had once "signed a contract with Paramount Pictures" and appeared in such B-movies as *The Man from Planet X* (1951) and *Captive Women* (1952) before giving up "her career . . . to raise her children."[14] With a charismatic but cruel stepfather in the picture (the actor and stuntman Jock Mahoney), Field was literally forced to "jump through hoops" and was once thrown "across the yard in a fit of temper." In high school, she "landed in the drama department," and as the actress explained, "It just kind of saved me."[15] But unlike her brother, "college was not presented to [her] as a possibility," and following her appearance in the poorly received *Gidget* (1965–1966), her stepfather "frightened her into accepting the starring role" in *The Flying Nun* (1967–1970). "He said I probably wouldn't work again if I didn't take it. The assumption was that I wasn't good enough."[16]

After three seasons on the show, Field attempted to shed her *Flying Nun* image in order to be taken more seriously. But facing two and a half years of unemployment, the dispirited actress "fired her agent" after being told that "she'd never break out of TV." Self-determined, she eventually followed in the footsteps of **Anne Bancroft, Ellen Burstyn, Jane Fonda, Patricia Neal, Geraldine Page, Sissy Spacek,**

and **Joanne Woodward** by enrolling in "acting classes under the leadership of the legendary teacher Lee Strasberg."[17] Equipped with Strasberg's Method acting training, Field soon made her mark in the acclaimed TV miniseries *Sybil* (1976; in which she portrayed a woman with 13 personalities, opposite **Joanne Woodward**). Field was seen neither as "glamorous and haughty like an old-fashioned star" nor as "clenched and hyper-conscious in the new **Glenda Jackson**–**Jane Fonda** style." Nonetheless, with "her wiry little body, [Jeanne] Moreau–like down-turned mouth, and rumpled manner," the actress continued to surprise skeptics with her "portrait of valor" in the socially conscious drama *Norma Rae* (1979).[18]

Overseen by the female producers Tamara Asseyev and Alexandra Rose and directed by Martin Ritt (a "victim of the Hollywood blacklist" who had guided **Patricia Neal** to Oscar-winning success in 1963's *Hud*),[19] *Norma Rae* tells the story of textile laborers from a poor, inward-looking Baptist community in Alabama. Based on the life of the union organizer Crystal Lee Sutton (1940–2009), the film centers on Field's title character, a young, uneducated mother who is held in virtual "slavery at the local cotton mill"[20] where she works alongside her parents. The factory laborers are afraid to demand higher pay and are blocked from critical information needed to improve the health-hazardous conditions contributing to brown lung

Faced with the challenge of keeping her family together and saving her farm during the Great Depression, Sally Field's widowed character takes in a Black vagrant (played by Danny Glover) and a war-blinded boarder (John Malkovich) as a means to survive. (Colubmia TriStar/Photofest)

Giving an acceptance speech that is well remembered (and often parodied), *Places in the Heart* star Sally Field celebrates her second Best Actress Oscar victory at the 1985 Academy Awards. (© A.M.P.A.S.®/ Photofest)

disease. They carry on with their daily grind until a New York Jewish labor-union organizer (played by Ron Leibman) arrives in town. Norma Rae, whose mother has gone "nearly deaf from the din of the machinery" and whose father collapses and dies from a heart attack after being denied an early 15-minute break, is persuaded to take action and throws her "heart and soul into the cause" of unionizing her factory "in spite of horrific harassment" from the company heads.[21] In one of the most iconic scenes in cinema history, she "scrawls the word 'UNION' on a piece of cardboard,"[22] climbs on top of a table, and flashes her sign in front of a sea of coworkers until each worker, one by one, shuts off his or her machine, resulting in a defiant and powerful silence.

Allied with such labor-themed movies as *Strike* (1925), *Modern Times* (1936), *How Green Was My Valley* (1941), *On the Waterfront* (1954), the blacklisted feminist political drama *Salt of the Earth* (1954; which was banned until 1965), and *Tout va bien* (1972; with **Jane Fonda**), *Norma Rae* had a difficult time finding a Hollywood distributor because "it had to do with unions" and union activism.[23] Despite its theme, however, the film scored four Oscar nominations including Best Picture. Field, who researched her role by working in a factory, had already secured top acting prizes from the Cannes Film Festival and the New York Film Critics, and she soon became the Best Actress Oscar frontrunner. At the 52nd Academy Awards (1980), she went on to beat Jill Clayburgh (*Starting Over*), Marsha Mason (*Chapter Two*), Bette Midler (*The Rose*), and the previous year's winner, **Jane Fonda** (*The China Syndrome*). When Field reached the stage to collect her statuette, she told the audience, "Oh I'm gonna be the one to cry tonight. . . . No matter how many awards I win, if it weren't for [my family] I wouldn't be worth a damn. Thank you very much."[24]

Five years later, Field would strike gold again by starring in *Places in the Heart* (1984). Akin to the **Luise Rainer**-starring drama *The Good Earth* (1937), the parable-like film placed Field in the role of Edna Spalding, an uneducated Christian widow and mother of two young children living in Great Depression–era Texas. After the accidental killing of her sheriff husband by a drunken Black boy (whose lynched body is dragged in front of the Spalding house for Edna to see), Edna is faced with the seemingly impossible challenge of keeping her family together and saving her farm. Forced to make socially controversial decisions in order to avoid foreclosure, she takes in a war-blinded boarder (played by John Malkovich) and a Black vagrant (Danny Glover) and races against time to see if her parched, Dust Bowl–era land will grow cotton and cultivate urgently needed profit. Additionally battling the local bank, a devastating tornado, and provocation from the Ku Klux Klan, Field's character sheds blood, sweat, and tears under the sweltering Texan sun while demonstrating that great challenges often reveal extraordinary things in ordinary people.

For her performance in *Places in the Heart*, Field triumphantly overcame former winner **Sissy Spacek** (*The River*), Vanessa Redgrave (*The Bostonians*), the Australian actress Judy Davis (*A Passage to India*), and **Jessica Lange** (*Country*) to clinch her second Best Actress Oscar at the 57th Academy Awards (1985). Taking the stage, the ecstatic actress told the audience that she had "wanted more than anything to have [their] respect." In a deeply heartfelt and highly imitated and misquoted acceptance speech, she then continued, "The first time I didn't feel it, but this time I feel it. And I can't deny the fact that you like me. Right now, you like me!"[25]

Like her character in *Norma Rae*, Field has long been an activist in her own right. Although she believes that "nothing will change" in regard to gender disparity "as long as the men are the ones who are funding and producing films,"[26] she has used her celebrity to attract attention to causes that she supports. Having performed in the playwright Eve Ensler's *The Vagina Monologues* (an episodic feminist play that deals with such issues as rape, menstruation, and female genital mutilation), the actress participated in corresponding V-Day events aimed at ending violence against women—a subject near to her heart as evinced in her involvement in the films *Not Without My Daughter* (1991) and *Eye for an Eye* (1996). One particular V-Day event included an awareness-raising protest (alongside **Jane Fonda** and others) in the Mexican border city of Ciudad Juárez, where, between 1993 and 2003, approximately 4,000 women were mysteriously murdered while 400 others simply disappeared in what has been called a "femicide." As a sufferer of osteoporosis, Field has additionally lent her voice for the improvement of women's health in television commercials for the prevention drug Boniva. Moreover, as the mother of a gay son, Field, like other celebrities with LGBTQ+ children (including **Barbra Streisand**, **Cher**, and **Susan Sarandon**), has been honored for her strong stance against homophobia. Proving that her trademark vulnerability is only a façade, she addressed the issue while accepting the Ally for Equality Award in 2012 from the political advocacy group the Human Rights Campaign. Some children are gay, she explained, "and so the *fuck* what?"[27]

Sissy Spacek

As a result of an assassination attempt against sitting U.S. President Ronald Reagan, the 1981 Academy Awards was postponed by 24 hours. Reagan's would-be-assassin, John Hinckley Jr., told police that he was motivated by worship of the movie star **Jodie Foster** and her appearance in 1976's *Taxi Driver*, a film about a Vietnam veteran who attempts to assassinate a politician. Ironically, Robert De Niro, the star of *Taxi Driver*, won the Best Actor Oscar that evening for *Raging Bull*.

Immediately following, the Best Actress presenter, Dustin Hoffman, delivered an edifying speech that underscored the state of women in a post-studio-system era. "The actresses who are nominated tonight . . . are characteristic of a new actor," he said. "The studio system is dead, . . . [and therefore actors are no longer] handed a number of roles . . . by the studio. [Instead], *they* pick. So, each actress tonight . . . has been a part of the inception of the part—the writing, the re-writing, a part of the production of it, the selection of the other actors, the post-production of it, and even the promotion of the film. Most of these actresses . . . have probably been with this one role for one, two, or three years."[1]

Up against a group of contenders that included Mary Tyler Moore (*Ordinary People*), Gena Rowlands (*Gloria*), Goldie Hawn (*Private Benjamin*), and former recipient **Ellen Burstyn** (*Resurrection*), the frontrunner and New York Film Critics Award winner **Sissy Spacek** listened absorbedly as the Best Actress category was called out. Nominated for her role in *Coal Miner's Daughter* (1980) but still immortalized in the minds of many people as a ridiculed prom queen with telekinetic powers in *Carrie* (1976), Spacek waited "for the bucket of blood to drop" upon the announcement of her name as the winner.[2] Taking the stage in a modest polyester

Coal Miner's Daughter (1980)

Sissy Spacek as the poverty-stricken 1940s Appalachian mountain girl Loretta Webb in the Loretta Lynn biopic *Coal Miner's Daughter* (1980). In the film, Spacek's character is married at age 13, a mother of four by 19, and a grandmother by 29. (Universal Pictures/Photofest)

jumpsuit, she thanked her cast, crew, and family, as well as the woman whom she had portrayed to Oscar-winning success: the legendary country singer Loretta Lynn (1932–), who smiled beamingly from her seat inside the Dorothy Chandler Pavilion.

Based on the singer's 1978 factually-incorrect-at-times autobiography, *Coal Miner's Daughter* chronicles Lynn's life from a poverty-stricken Appalachian mountain girl raised alongside a gaggle of siblings in a crowded shack on her father's coal-mining salary to her remarkable ascent as one of country music's most distinguished superstars. At the heart of the story is Lynn's marriage to her philandering, alcoholic husband (played by Tommy Lee Jones), who falsely promises not to "hit her" or "take her far from home" before buying her a guitar and pushing her into a life of show business—a profession, in her estimation, that is tantamount to prostitution.[3] Championed by the country singing star Patsy Cline, Spacek's timid, insular character—who, according to the film, is married at age 13, a mother of four by 19, and a grandmother by 29—ultimately takes ownership of her plight as a woman. In doing so, she juggles marriage, motherhood, and a burgeoning career that elevates her to national fame by way of the "very personal nature of her songs."[4]

In playing Lynn, Spacek took her place in the pantheon of actors depicting real-life singers, alongside **Luise Rainer** (as Anna Held in *The Great Ziegfeld*, 1936), **Barbra Streisand** (as Fanny Brice in *Funny Girl*, 1968), **Reese Witherspoon** (as June Carter Cash in *Walk the Line*, 2005), and **Marion Cotillard** (as Édith Piaf in *La Vie en Rose*, 2007). To prepare for the role, Spacek, whom Lynn specifically requested to play her, followed the country legend on tour and studied with her for an entire year at the singer's Civil War–era mansion outside Nashville, Tennessee. The two became "as close as sisters," and the actress soon began to "speak Loretta" and sing "along with her phrase by phrase until she made . . . Lynn's inflection her own."[5] Her efforts paid off, with Spacek able to convincingly perform her own live singing, consisting of such Loretta Lynn classics as "You Ain't Woman Enough (to Take My Man)" and the film's celebrated title track.

Spacek promoted *Coal Miner's Daughter* as far away as Beijing, China, conveying to audiences that were not otherwise accustomed to country music a strong, indelible impression of an outspoken country star who sang about child rearing, relationships, and even birth control and, in the process, became a major feminist role model. As Dolly Parton later wrote to the actress, "I hope you make millions of dollars from *Coal Miner's Daughter* so that you can get a boob job and do *The Dolly Parton Story*."[6]

Intriguingly, Spacek "never set out to be an actress."[7] The daughter of a father who worked as a county agricultural agent and a mother who worked in the local courthouse, Spacek was born Mary Elizabeth Spacek on Christmas Day 1949. Like the character of Scout from her favorite movie, *To Kill a Mockingbird* (1962), the 5-foot-2 tomboy with "big, blue eyes," strawberry-blond hair, and a distinctively pale and freckled face was lovingly raised alongside her two older brothers (who nicknamed her "Sissy") amid the frog-hunting, horseback-riding "joys of rural life" in Quitman, Texas.[8] Growing up, Spacek recalled rushing home from school

In *Coal Miner's Daughter* (1980), Sissy Spacek's character juggles marriage, motherhood, and a burgeoning country-music career that elevates her to national fame and transforms her into a major feminist role model. (Universal Pictures/Photofest)

"clutching book-club order forms." "I wanted to order the books about Clara Barton, Helen Keller, and Joan of Arc," she explained. "I've always been attracted to women in adverse situations who find strength within themselves."[9]

In the summer of 1967, Spacek, at age 17, was required to find her own inner strength when her parents sent her to New York City as a way of sparing "her from the grief of watching [her beloved 18-year-old brother Robbie] die of leukemia."[10] Marking what would become a defining moment in her life, Spacek, "who had rarely been out of Texas on her own," set out to pursue a singing career with the help of the "show-biz bad boy" Rip Torn (her older cousin) and his "funny and elegant" wife, **Geraldine Page** (the future Best Actress Oscar winner who was then considered one of the greatest performers of the American stage).[11] While Spacek

At the 1981 Academy Awards, *Coal Miner's Daughter* star Sissy Spacek celebrates her Best Actress Oscar victory alongside country music legend Loretta Lynn, who specifically requested that Spacek portray her in the film. (© A.M.P.A.S.®/Photofest)

was gaining special backstage access on Broadway and rubbing shoulders with a who's who of film and theater greats by way of her famous relatives, she spent the summer "traipsing between record companies with her acoustic guitar by day and gigging in Greenwich Village coffeehouses by night" under the pseudonym "Rainbo."[12] Although she was determined to become "the next Joni Mitchell,"[13] she was ultimately told by record company VIPs to return when she learned to sing—an incident that she laughs about now in light of her Oscar-winning performance in *Coal Miner's Daughter*.

After Decca Records turned Spacek away because she sounded, ironically, too much like Loretta Lynn, she was encouraged to study acting instead and was subsequently introduced by **Page** to the acting guru Lee Strasberg. Before long, Spacek, who once admitted that her pale, seemingly translucent complexion would have kept her out of the movies if motion pictures had not already transitioned to color from black and white, was riding in on a wave of independent American cinema that put her in contact with the directors Terrence Malick, Brian De Palma, Robert Altman, and David Lynch. "I think I represented something in a generation as opposed to being some great trained actor," Spacek later acknowledged.[14]

Despite Spacek's cinematic successes (including six Best Actress Oscar nominations), she has maintained a levelheaded relationship with her celebrity status. Long separated from her 11 years living in Hollywood, she has since spent the majority of her time with her husband (the longtime Terrence Malick production designer Jack Fisk) and their two daughters on a 210-acre ranch outside Charlottesville, Virginia. "I'm sure there are things we miss out on," she said, "but what we gain is more important."[15]

In addition, ever since Spacek read an "inflammatory full-page ad denouncing [U.S. President John F. Kennedy] . . . in the *Dallas Morning News* on the day the President was [assassinated]" less than 90 miles from her childhood home on November 22, 1963, she has remained informed and politically active. Tackling issues she believes are important, the actress starred in such political dramas as *Missing* (1982), *Marie* (1985), and *JFK* (1991), and in reaction to childhood memories of racial segregation in the Jim Crow South, where she witnessed African Americans "line up outside a separate [movie theater] side entrance and sit in the balcony,"[16] she appeared in *The Long Walk Home* (1990) and *The Help* (2011). In the tradition of **Helen Hayes** (who, in 1939, urged the U.S. Congress to admit 20,000 homeless children from Nazi Germany), **Elizabeth Taylor** (who pushed Congress to spend more money on AIDS research), **Audrey Hepburn** (who called on Congress to help impoverished children worldwide), **Meryl Streep** (who warned Congress about the dangers of Alar in food), and **Helen Mirren** (who implored Congress to help return art stolen by the Nazis), Spacek—alongside **Jane Fonda** and **Jessica Lange**—additionally testified before a 1985 House Agriculture Committee. All three actors had "portrayed farm wives facing hardships in movie roles," and although they were derided by one congressman, who did not "have time to play 'Hollywood Squares,'"[17] they spoke passionately about America's failing farm economy.

In spite of being described as a "woman trapped inside the body of a yearling,"[18] Spacek has proven to be a "strong-willed . . . performer who doesn't fit the homespun image she has weaved for herself in the media." "Sissy gives the impression that she goes along with everything," said the director Costa-Gavras. "On the contrary, she demands that a director do his job and explain himself. And the explanation better be good. The best thing about her is that she gives you everything she's got."[19]

Meryl Streep

In a world where data can be instantaneously retrieved, **Meryl Streep**'s Oscar victory at the 84th Academy Awards (2012) broke "the barrier of 20,000 tweets per minute" and became "the highest spike of the night."[1] Streep was locked in a tight race for Best Actress after clinching the New York Film Critics Award (for a record fourth time). Her competition included rival frontrunner Viola Davis (*The Help*), Glenn Close (*Albert Nobbs*), and two performers who "were not even conceived" when the actress won her first Oscar: Michelle Williams (*My Week with Marilyn*) and Rooney Mara (*The Girl with the Dragon Tattoo*).[2] Nominated for her performance as the British prime minister Margaret Thatcher in *The Iron Lady* (2011), Streep, who was visibly astounded upon the announcement of her name, went "into a sort of white light."[3] "I had this feeling I could hear half of America going, 'Oh no. Come on, why? Her? Again?'" Streep told the audience before drolly interjecting, "But, whatever."[4]

Having already overtaken **Katharine Hepburn**'s previous record of 12 Oscar nominations, Streep entered the record books in 2018 with 21 nominations overall (including four in the Best Supporting Actress category). With her third Oscar for *The Iron Lady*, Streep matched **Ingrid Bergman**'s tally of three Oscar victories, two in the lead category and one, *Kramer vs. Kramer* (1979), in the supporting category.

As a result of the enormous praise that Streep has received throughout her career (substantially more than any other actress of her generation), she has admitted to understanding "Streep fatigue."[5] Labeled a genius—a concept seldom attributed to women but upheld for the likes of Shakespeare, Beethoven, Einstein, and Picasso—the actress-technician has accordingly been offered the crème de la crème of available roles as her peers have scrambled from "Batgirl one day" to "Madame Curie the next."[6] While she has sustained a "fragile, fleeting beauty that allows her to travel the spectrum between earthily plain and ethereally

Sophie's Choice (1982)

The Iron Lady (2011)

Bringing to the screen a raw and horrifying depiction of the Holocaust, Meryl Streep stars as an Auschwitz concentration-camp prisoner and survivor in *Sophie's Choice* (1982). Four years earlier, Streep had starred in the ground-breaking American TV miniseries *Holocaust*, which opened many eyes to the Nazi's Final Solution. (Universal Pictures/Photofest)

Meryl Streep waits to be filmed in this off-camera shot from *Sophie's Choice* (1982). The movie was based on one of the most acclaimed novels of the era and written with Swiss actress Ursula Andress in mind. Alan J. Pakula initially envisioned Norwegian actress Liv Ullmann before Streep fell to her knees when soliciting the director for the part. (Universal Pictures/ Photofest)

glamorous and radiant," it is her "astonishing versatility," deftly conveyed manner-isms, and total-immersion "chameleonism" that has beguiled audiences worldwide.[7] Stretching beyond the behavioral patterns of the typical Method actor, her cere-bral and instinctive approach to her craft was once characterized by her *Mamma Mia!* (2008) costar Colin Firth as "unreasonably good."[8] "It's more akin to chan-neling than anything else," explained **Shirley MacLaine**,[9] who costarred with the actress in *Postcards from the Edge* (1990).

But aside from knowing "the tricks of screen acting better than almost anyone," Streep—whose "solemn acting" has progressively lightened in tone but never in technique—is perhaps most identified with her "uncanny ability" to produce accents.[10] In nondubbing regions of the world, where "actors are expected to be masters of accents," she is regarded as the standard against which "other accented performances are measured."[11] In *The Deer Hunter* (1978), she produced a western Pennsylvanian accent. In *Out of Africa* (1985), *A Cry in the Dark* (1988), *The Bridges of Madison County* (1995), *Dancing at Lughnasa* (1998), and *Doubt* (2008), she respec-tively produced spot-on Danish, Australian, Italian, Irish, and Bronx accents. She additionally nailed Julia Child's distinctive upper-class patter in *Julie & Julia* (2009).

Demonstrating her proficiencies, Streep not only learned to speak Polish (by way of Berlitz training) but also English and German with a Polish accent for her

In a role tackling the topic of survivor's guilt, Meryl Streep learned to speak not only Polish but also English and German with a Polish accent for her Oscar-winning performance in *Sophie's Choice* (1982). (Universal Pictures/Photofest)

heartbreaking, Oscar-winning performance in the sober adaptation of William Styron's novel *Sophie's Choice* (1982). In the film, Streep portrays Zofia "Sophie" Zawistowski, a Polish Catholic immigrant and concentration camp survivor living in Brooklyn in the summer of 1947 and attempting to reinvent her life after the ravages of World War II. A young writer named Stingo (played by Peter MacNicol) takes a room in the same boardinghouse as Sophie and her beloved, wild-mood-swinging boyfriend, Nathan (Kevin Kline). Stingo befriends the couple and slowly learns of Sophie's battle with survivor's guilt.

In one of the most emotionally devastating scenes ever committed to film, Sophie—as seen through a flashback as she explains her life story to Stingo—arrives

In the Margaret Thatcher biopic *The Iron Lady* (2011), Meryl Streep explores the controversial life of the first woman to have risen through the ranks of the British political system to become prime minister. (The Weinstein Company/Photofest)

at the Auschwitz concentration camp at night with her two small children. She catches the eye of a Nazi officer who is entranced by her Aryan beauty but only half forgiving of her non-Jewish, "Polack" status. As a result, Sophie is given an impossible choice: to keep only one of her two children (otherwise both will be sent to their immediate gas-chamber deaths). In this depiction of the "ultimate in sacrificial horror,"[12] Streep reportedly nailed the "choice" scene in one take. With the scene being exceedingly painful and emotionally exhausting to perform, she refused to do it again.

Previously, Streep had starred in the groundbreaking American TV miniseries *Holocaust* (1978)—"a much-anticipated media event" broadcast on West German television.[13] To be sure, the miniseries "contributed to intense public and private debate . . . of Germany's National Socialist past" at a time when "the shadow of the World War . . . [still hung] over the country."[14] The miniseries, in conjunction with New German Cinema offerings such as *The Marriage of Maria Braun* (1978), *Die Patriotin* (1979), and *Germany, Pale Mother* (1980), facilitated an act of "remembering" for shame-scarred Germans who began to deal with their Nazi past while demonstrating "how larger cultural conversations operate in relation to films."[15] By bringing to the screen a raw and horrifying depiction of the most "unique crime in the history of mankind," *Holocaust* not only influenced the German legislature "to vote to continue the hunt for [Nazi criminals]" but also inspired a number of directors to depict the Nazi era in a manner that had not been attempted before.[16]

Streep once admitted to having fallen to her knees when soliciting director Alan J. Pakula to consider her for the title role in *Sophie's Choice*. For her impactful performance, she won the New York Film Critics Award and ultimately found herself as the biggest shoo-in in the Best Actress Oscar category since **Vivien Leigh** won for *Gone with the Wind* (1939). Her competition ahead of the 55th Academy Awards (1983) included previous recipients **Julie Andrews** (*Victor Victoria*) and **Sissy Spacek** (*Missing*), Debra Winger (*An Officer and a Gentleman*), and **Jessica Lange** (*Frances*). Although Streep had already won the Best Supporting Actress Oscar for *Kramer vs. Kramer* (and "famously left [that statuette] on top of a toilet" at the Dorothy Chandler Pavilion), when she was honored for her leading role, she sweetly informed the audience that "no matter how much you try to imagine what this is like, it's just so incredibly thrilling, right down to your toes."[17]

Streep was born Mary Louise Streep in Summit, New Jersey, on June 22, 1949. Her father worked as a pharmaceutical executive, and her "big-hearted" mother worked as a commercial artist and encouraged her daughter "to do something valuable and interesting with [her life]."[18] Growing up in well-to-do surroundings, Streep, the eldest of three children, first developed an interest in opera before realizing that she was singing something that she did not easily comprehend. Inspired as a child by the powerful presence of such female movie stars as **Katharine Hepburn** and **Bette Davis**, Streep soon decided to turn her attention to acting and starred "in all three of [her] high school musicals."[19] Educated in an era when female students debated what a woman's role in society should and should not be, she enrolled at Vassar College—a women's liberal arts college that was just becoming coeducational. She eventually received a master of fine arts degree in drama at Yale University, where she "appeared in 30 to 40 productions with [the] Yale Repertory Theater."[20] Attracting the attention of New York producers, she made her screen debut at the comparatively late age of 28 in the 1977 film *Julia* (starring **Jane Fonda** and Vanessa Redgrave).

In the 1980s, Streep became a perennial Best Actress Oscar nominee. But despite her tremendous output, she began to complain that cinema had not succeeded in measuring up to the standards that Hollywood established in earlier decades, when strong female performers, whose appeal "often equaled or surpassed those of their male counterparts,"[21] existed onscreen. In 1980, for example, four of the ten top box-office stars were women: **Sally Field**, **Jane Fonda**, **Sissy Spacek**, and

Meryl Streep, celebrating backstage at the 84th Academy Awards (2012), matched Ingrid Bergman's Oscar-victory tally with three Oscars (two in the lead category and one in supporting). (© A.M.P.A.S.®/Photofest)

Barbra Streisand. By 1990, however, there was only one: **Julia Roberts**. Speaking at the Screen Actors Guild's first National Women's Conference in 1990, Streep addressed the cultural issue at stake. "Three years ago, women were down to performing only one-third of all the roles in feature films. In 1989, that number slipped to 29 percent. If the trend continues, . . . we will [be] eliminated from the movies entirely."[22]

But after Streep starred in a string of films featuring strong women in positions of power—first as a politician in the 2004 remake of *The Manchurian Candidate*, then as a steely magazine editor in chief in *The Devil Wears Prada* (2006)—she began to notice a change in the way audiences, and men in particular, responded to her work. Her observation was further validated when she took on the biographical role of the "hawkish, militaristic" Margaret Thatcher (1925–2013) in *The Iron Lady* (2011).[23] Directed by Phyllida Lloyd and written by Abi Morgan, the film examines the groundbreaking life of the first woman to have risen through the ranks of the "class bound and gender phobic" British political system and become the "first woman to lead a major political party in the West."[24] Spanning 35 years of Thatcher's life and aided by a "discreetly applied ton of [Oscar-winning] geriatric makeup,"[25] Streep's performance served to expose the "Pygmalion process" that Thatcher, who kept office for 11 years (1979–1990), had to undergo in order to look and sound authoritarian in a political arena in which men were not at all accustomed to female counterparts.[26]

The Iron Lady was made at a time when women still accounted for a dismal percentage of female legislative representation but were stepping into higher levels of political authority (e.g., German Chancellor Angela Merkel, Brazilian President Dilma Rousseff, and so forth). The film helped to underscore Thatcher's larger-than-life persona as a divisive figure who, for better or worse, became the absolute model for women in power. While Streep's performance was widely admired, many Britons felt that, as an American actress, she had delivered a "rather sympathetic portrayal" and approached Thatcher "with an innocence denied [to] those . . . who lived through her [time] as prime minister."[27] Upon Thatcher's death in April 2013, the two-time Best Actress Oscar winner **Glenda Jackson**, who subsequently served as a member of British Parliament, delivered a stirring reminder to fellow lawmakers concerning what **Jackson** considered the travesties that were committed under Thatcher's rule. "To pay tribute," she said, "to the first prime minister deputed by female gender? Okay. But a woman? Not on my terms."[28]

Having taken on such issues as AIDS research, reproductive rights, the prevention of food adulteration, arts and literacy improvement, the development of the National Women's History Museum in Washington, DC, and the creation of a screenwriters lab for women writers over 40, Streep has indeed played an important role in the social and political arenas. During the 2016 U.S. presidential election, she slathered on a fake tan to impersonate Donald Trump and, while accepting the Cecil B. DeMille Award, disparaged the president-elect at the 2017 Golden Globes for using his power to bully others; in response, Trump tweeted that Streep was "one of the most over-rated actresses in Hollywood."[29] But "at a time when most of her female peers have been shoved into early quasi-retirement,"[30] Streep has conversely gained in popularity. In the process, she has been embraced by women and men alike as the most revered actress of her generation and as one of the most incomparable acting greats to ever exist.

Shirley MacLaine

Terms of Endearment (1983)

Two years before filming the tearjerker *Terms of Endearment* (1983)—the "last Best Picture winner [to pass the gender-equality-measuring] Bechdel Test with flying colors,"[1] **Shirley MacLaine** predicted to friends that the role of the possessive, prickly, and tightly wound Texas matriarch Aurora Greenway might land her the Oscar. Given the convoluted path by which the role found its way to the actress, MacLaine's clairvoyant sixth sense proved to be on point. Initially, the veteran Best Actress winner **Jennifer Jones** had acquired the rights to the project as a vehicle for her never-to-happen screen return. Told, however, that she was too old to play the lead by the writer and director James L. Brooks, **Jones** sold the rights to Paramount. The actresses Janet Leigh, **Louise Fletcher**, and frontrunner **Anne Bancroft** were then considered. But after MacLaine had a lunch date with Brooks that was specifically rigged to test her erupting response to the restaurant's terrible food and lack of service, MacLaine—who, in the words of **Meryl Streep**, does not "sentimentalize or soften" her characters[2]—was awarded the role.

Akin to the complicated mother-daughter relationships explored in *Mildred Pierce* (1945; with **Joan Crawford** and Ann Blyth) and later *Black Swan* (2010; with Barbara Hershey and **Natalie Portman**), *Terms of Endearment* chronicles the "defects and imperfections" of such a relationship over the course of many years in the late 1970s.[3] The film paints a portrait of Aurora as an uptight mother who believes that her "not-always-endearing" advice is paramount[4]—advice that her headstrong daughter (played by Debra Winger) disregards. As a result, MacLaine's character deliberately fires back. In doing so, she diminishes her daughter's unsuitable husband, the couple's excessive number of children, and their life purposely lived far outside her Houston base. Additionally unwilling to accept her arrival at middle

Shirley MacLaine and costar Debra Winger run their lines in this off-camera shot from *Terms of Endearment* (1983). At times, the working relationship between the two stars was acrimonious. (Paramount/Viacom/Photofest)

age (a topic MacLaine has tackled in one successful film after another), Aurora begins to crumble. But soon Aurora is dealing with her daughter's terminal cancer diagnosis and learns to let go of her narcissism and conceit in order to embrace the inconveniences that her family's tragedy has created.

Despite threatening to quit *Terms of Endearment* after reportedly putting up with Debra Winger's "off-camera antagonism," MacLaine—over the course of her long, more-than-60-year career—has been a permanent mainstay in "female-relationship movies."[5] In *The Children's Hour* (1961; opposite **Audrey Hepburn**), she plays a "self-loathing lesbian" who commits suicide.[6] In *The Turning Point* (1977; opposite **Anne Bancroft**), she plays "a woman whose old ballerina dreams intrude in the life of her daughter."[7] And in *Postcards from the Edge* (1990; opposite **Meryl Streep**), she plays a famous actress mother to a drug-addicted actress daughter. "Women working together on films do not 'cattily' compete with each other," MacLaine insisted. "On the contrary, they bond together, usually against an insensitive male in power. On *Steel Magnolias* [1989; costarring **Sally Field**], our director Herb Ross was consistently unkind to Dolly Parton and to newcomer **Julia Roberts**. The rest of us called him on it."[8]

Born Shirley MacLean Beaty on April 24, 1934, and named after the 1930s child superstar Shirley Temple, MacLaine was raised with the help of a Black nanny in a drab, middle-class neighborhood in Richmond, Virginia. Because of her dull childhood surroundings, she never would have dreamed that both she and her younger brother (the actor and director Warren Beatty) would go on to "become A-list movie stars."[9] Growing up, MacLaine was "embarrassed by [her] red hair and freckles" and by a "complicated" schoolteacher father "who still called Black people 'niggers' and saw nothing demeaning in it."[10] With the encouragement of her mother (a former actress turned drama coach), she eventually left her home at age 16 to become a ballet student and chorus dancer in New York City.

Before long, MacLaine experienced what many people consider to be "the most legendary break in show business" history when she filled in for an injured Carol Haney in the original Broadway production of *The Pajama Game* (1954).[11] Capitalizing on the moment, the aspiring dancer caught the attention of the film producer Hal B. Wallis and was offered a five-year contract at Paramount. Without any formal acting training whatsoever or even the goal of wanting to become an actor, the zany and vivacious free spirit moved to Hollywood and soon had a dressing room next to the likes of **Shirley Booth**, **Anna Magnani**, Jerry Lewis, Dean Martin, and Elvis Presley. She simultaneously made her screen debut in Alfred Hitchcock's black comedy *The Trouble with Harry* (1955).

In direct opposition to the wholesome, conservative, and conformist era of President Dwight D. Eisenhower's 1950s America, MacLaine took on a bohemian approach to life. At the time, she was involved in "a very open marriage" with Steve Parker[12]—an older international businessman who principally raised the couple's only child, Sachi, while in Japan. "I find myself preferring relationships with men that give me a lot of space," MacLaine admitted.[13] With her marital status protecting her from being discussed in the tabloid pages of *Hush-Hush* and *Confidential* regarding the people she was with, the actress enjoyed a stunning array of "serial monogamous relationships." At the same time, she was "adopted as the female 'mascot'" of the Rat Pack, which included Frank Sinatra, Dean Martin, Sammy Davis Jr., and "visiting dignitaries from the Kennedy clan."[14] While partying "as hard as the guys," MacLaine developed a keen political consciousness as part of the group's "chorus of cheerleaders" behind the presidential campaign of Senator John F. Kennedy.[15] "Before he was President," the actress recalled, "we'd go to Mulholland Drive, look out over the lights of [Los Angeles], and talk. [Kennedy] never made a pass at me. In fact, I wondered what was wrong with me."[16]

Twelve years later, MacLaine essentially "put her career on hold" to campaign for the Democratic presidential nominee, U.S. Senator George McGovern.[17] As issues such as women's rights, abortion, and—for the first time—gay rights were raised at the 1972 Democratic National Convention, MacLaine spoke about her fierce opposition to the Vietnam War. She additionally hosted celebrity fund-raisers in Hollywood and helped to surround McGovern "with 'hip' stars to attract young voters."[18] Her actions put her on the cover of *Newsweek* magazine. But in the midst of political rancor with the Nixon administration, her apartment, like that of **Jane Fonda**'s, "was ransacked beyond recognition and [her] telephone lines [were] cut to ensure that [she] got the message."[19]

Despite the harassment and McGovern's eventual loss, MacLaine continued to tackle important political issues. She wrote "about the Cultural Revolution in China" and, after meeting with Cuban President Fidel Castro in Havana in 1978, the equal constitutional rights given to women in Cuba.[20] MacLaine was later romantically linked to the former Canadian prime minister Pierre Trudeau, the former Swedish prime minister Olof Palme (who was assassinated in 1986), and the former foreign minister of Australia, Andrew Peacock.

After MacLaine had suffered four defeats in the Best Actress Oscar category (in addition to a loss for her nominated 1976 political documentary, *The Other Half of the Sky: A China Memoir*, about the mistreatment of women in China), "a vindicated MacLaine" finally came home a winner from the 56th Academy Awards

As a self-absorbed mother wanting to control her daughter's life, Shirley MacLaine stars in *Terms of Endearment* (1983). (Paramount/Viacom/Photofest)

(1984).[21] Locked in a Best Actress Oscar battle with her *Terms of Endearment* costar Debra Winger, the British actress Julie Walters (*Educating Rita*), Jane Alexander (*Testament*), and the previous year's winner, **Meryl Streep** (*Silkwood*), MacLaine, who had clinched the New York Film Critics Award, rushed up the aisle upon the boisterous announcement of her name by presenter **Liza Minnelli**. Along the way, she stopped and "whispered to Winger, 'You deserve half of this,'" to which her costar responded, "I'll take it."[22] In her speech, MacLaine thanked "the turbulent brilliance of Debra Winger," "the comic chemistry" of Best Supporting Actor recipient Jack Nicholson, and the "passion" of Best Director winner James L. Brooks. The actress, who many observers felt had won for her entire body of work, gleefully admitted that she had "wondered for 26 years what this would feel like. Thank you so much for terminating the suspense." "You know," she went on, "if *Terms of Endearment* had happened to me five years ago, I think I would have called it a thrilling, commercial, artistic accident. But . . . I don't believe there's any such thing as accident. I think that we all manifest what we want and what we need. I don't think there's any difference really between what you feel you have to do in your heart and success. They're inseparable."[23]

As a traveler to such far-off corners of the world as Africa, South America, the Middle East, and India, where Hinduism taught her the spiritual sciences of "yoga, meditation, diet, reincarnation, and the power of passive resistance,"[24] MacLaine, who played a globetrotting photographer in the short-lived TV series *Shirley's World* (1971–1972), has since written extensively on such topics. Risking public ridicule by relating her theories and experiences concerning out-of-body travel, the actress published her candid autobiography *Out on a Limb* in 1983 and helped to "birth a New Age spiritual movement."[25]

Since then, MacLaine has continued to act in such films as *Guarding Tess* (1994) and *Bruno* (2000; marking her directorial debut for a fiction film) and as the title character in the 2008 TV movie *Coco Chanel*. In addition, just as **Greer Garson** (in *The Miniver Story* [1950]) and **Barbra Streisand** (in *Funny Lady* [1975]) returned to the characters that they had portrayed to Oscar-winning success, MacLaine revisited the role of Aurora Greenway in the *Terms of Endearment* sequel, *The Evening Star* (1996), which examines Aurora 13 years after her daughter's untimely death.

In 2012, MacLaine received the American Film Institute Life Achievement Award, an award given to 36 men but only eight other women: **Bette Davis**, Lillian Gish, Barbara Stanwyck, **Elizabeth Taylor**, **Barbra Streisand**, **Meryl Streep**, **Jane Fonda**, and **Diane Keaton**. During her acceptance speech, the actress used the occasion to make "a heartfelt plea." While encouraging women "to take a stronger part in shaping cinema and the world," she underlined that "it is the feminine—including the feminine within men—that will make the world a better place."[26]

Geraldine Page

A t the 1987 memorial service for the actress **Geraldine Page**, held at the midtown Manhattan Neil Simon Theatre, fellow actors including **Sissy Spacek**, Al Pacino, Paul Newman, **Joanne Woodward**, Cicely Tyson, James Earl Jones, Jason Robards, Shelley Winters, Angela Lansbury, **Marlee Matlin**, William Hurt, and F. Murray Abraham arrived to pay their respects. Already in fragile health but wanting to spend what was to be "her final day doing what she loved,"[1] Page, who had performed at the Simon on a Friday evening alongside Richard Chamberlain and Blythe Danner in a revival of Noël Coward's *Blithe Spirit*, "failed to show up for a [Saturday-afternoon] matinee performance."[2] With her heart having given way, the 62-year-old actress, whose "magisterial" approach to acting "could blow the gods off Olympus," was found lifeless in her cluttered townhouse apartment in Chelsea, where "boxes of theater memorabilia [were commonly] stacked everywhere [next to] unwashed dishes stewing in the sink."[3] Page's widower, the actor Rip Torn, delivered his eulogy to a standing-room-only gathering of friends, family, and colleagues. His marriage to Page had seen its fair share of "wild parties," philandering, and jealousy-induced fights, but now he "gazed at the several thousand people who filled the theater's seats and aisles" and said, "Yeah, Gerry would like this," to which the entire audience "rose to its feet" in a long, bravo-filled ovation.[4]

Page had been hailed as the "Method's greatest actress," but throughout her long and prolific career both onstage and onscreen, she remained "remarkably unsung" for an actress of such great talent and stature.[5] Equipped with a "mild and manageable face" much like **Joanne Woodward** or **Jessica Tandy**, she was known for hiding "behind the mask of a character," and she frequently succeeded in going

Returning to her childhood home for the final time, a contemplative Geraldine Page stars as Carrie Watts in *The Trip to Bountiful* (1985). (Island Pictures/Photofest)

unrecognized. "I love to fool people," she once admitted.[6] But as Page flirted with movie stardom in an industry that likes its stars to adhere to a particular star image from "one role to the next," her "priceless anonymity" undeniably "had its costs."[7]

Page was born in Kirksville, Missouri, on November 22, 1924. The daughter of an osteopathic medical physician, she first discovered a talent in art as an amateur sketch artist. However, after participating in a church play, she set out instead to pursue acting. Moving to Chicago to attend courses at the Goodman School of Drama at DePaul University, Page spent a lengthy three years of study and five years performing in stock companies before being "booted . . . out of the Midwest." "Will you just go to New York?" her drama teacher exasperatingly implored.[8]

At last, Page moved to New York in the late 1940s. Between the few off-Broadway pocket-stage jobs that she could find, she earned a scanty living as a hat-check girl, a lingerie model, and—while reading Shakespeare to pass the time—a spool winder in a thread factory. "The first rule of survival was to stretch every penny," she once said. "I'd eat in a restaurant that featured soup and free rolls for 15 cents and I'd stuff my pocket with rolls. Fortunately, food didn't mean much to me."[9]

During these years of hardship, Page trained at the HB Studio (under the guidance of Uta Hagen) and at the Actors Studio, where she studied alongside Marilyn

Monroe, Kim Stanley, and **Patricia Neal**. Sharpening her abilities to "convey the complex traits and impulses that make up a person and to respond to events in an honest way," the actress began to demonstrate "just how versatile the Method [acting techniques] could be."[10] Eventually, she got her first big break. By virtue of a magnificent tip from a fellow Goodman alumnus, Page made her way to the Circle in the Square Theatre in Greenwich Village. There, she landed the part of a sexually frustrated southern spinster in the 1952 off-Broadway hit revival of the 1948 Tennessee Williams play *Summer and Smoke*. Although she earned only $40 a week for her performance (a meager increase from the $25 weekly salary she had made while winding thread), the actress became an overnight success.

When it came time, however, for Page to sign a "dream [seven-year] contract" in Hollywood after she had received a supporting Oscar nomination for her role in the 1953 John Wayne hit western *Hondo*, Page's deal fell through. "It was during the McCarthy era," the actress explained, "and I had studied with Uta Hagen," who, like **Judy Holliday** and other alleged entertainment-industry communists, had been listed in the notorious publication *Red Channels*.[11] In addition, Hagen had shocked conservatives by starring with the African American singer and actor Paul Robeson in the fabled Broadway production of Shakespeare's *Othello* (1943–1944). Guilty by association in an era resistant to change and defined by rampant character assassinations, Page was branded as politically suspect and "didn't work in films again for seven years."[12]

Returning to New York, Page starred in such plays as *The Rainmaker* (1954) and the stage adaptation of André Gide's *The Immoralist* (1954). In the latter production, she played the wife of a closeted homosexual archeologist (Louis Jourdan) whose lust is aroused by a gay Arab boy (played by a brazenly suggestive James Dean, with whom Page had an affair before his movie breakthrough). But after the success of her idiosyncratic performance in the original stage production of Tennessee Williams's *Sweet Bird of Youth* (1959; costarring Paul Newman and her eventual husband, Rip Torn), the Broadway actress finally returned to the screen in the film adaptations of *Summer and Smoke* (1961) and *Sweet Bird of Youth* (1962). Throughout the remainder of her career, she who would "resort to movies as a relaxation from the stage."[13]

By the time Page was approached to star in the ruminative screen adaptation of the Horton Foote play *The Trip to Bountiful* (1985), she had already earned seven Oscar nominations (three in the lead category and four in supporting) and knew that she had another critical hit on her hands. First performed on television in 1953 before its original star, Lillian Gish, took it to Broadway, *The Trip to Bountiful* became one of the "most distinguished independent films" of the 1980s.[14] Produced by FilmDallas Pictures, the film tells the story of Carrie Watts, an elderly, hymn-singing widow who longs to "return to her rural hometown before she dies."[15] Set in 1947, "when Coke, beauty shops, and sleek Greyhound buses were in full vogue," the film traces Carrie's determined escape from the cramped confines of the Houston apartment that she shares with her "loving but timid son and his nagging shrew of a wife" to her hometown of Bountiful—a present-day ghost town enveloped by grass that few people have even heard of.[16] The story is "structured as an odyssey" and anchored by Page's "strange, sad, [and] rapturous" acting.[17] It underlines "the need to square up memories with reality before completing one's life journey."[18] "I guess when you've lived longer than your house and your family, then you've lived long enough," her character reasons.[19]

Page believed that the role of Carrie allowed her "to use all the things [she had ever] learned about acting."[20] Although the oddsmakers predicted her victory ahead of the 58th Academy Awards (1986), she was nevertheless convinced that she would not win the Best Actress Oscar. In part, this had to do with her previous loses, but it was also related to the ceremony's seating plan, which had her blocked behind the director John Huston and his "two large oxygen tanks."[21] "I don't care," Page admitted. "Either way will be just fine with me. It's all accidental, like a roulette game or something."[22] But having secured the inaugural Independent Spirit Award for Best Female Lead (a lead-up honor that has produced ten Best Actress Oscar winners in its first 33 years), the veteran actress had less reason for self-doubt against a field that included **Jessica Lange** (*Sweet Dreams*), Whoopi Goldberg (*The Color Purple*), and previous recipients **Meryl Streep** (*Out of Africa*) and **Anne Bancroft** (*Agnes of God*; whose part Page had originated onstage). Before the announcement of Page's name, and ushering in an era when independent films such as *Kiss of the Spider Woman* (1985), *A Room with a View* (1986), and *My Left Foot* (1989) began to successfully compete for Academy Awards, Best Actress Oscar presenter F. Murray Abraham effusively gushed, "I consider this woman the greatest actress in the English language."[23] To that, the audience surrounded Page in a standing ovation as she finally—on her *eighth* attempt—made her journey to the Oscar stage.

Speaking at Page's memorial service 15 months later, **Sissy Spacek** recalled her "star-struck summer in New York" in 1967, when—largely on Page's account—she got to experience "a side of the city most 17-year olds never dreamed of."[24] "I had the good fortune to have Gerry marry my cousin Rip," she told the audience. "After that summer, I couldn't imagine being anything other than an actress."[25] "They were artists," she later said. "I can remember being included in many evenings with their artist and actor friends [including Tennessee Williams, Terry Southern, Paul Newman, and **Joanne Woodward**] and they'd be talking about creative things I knew nothing about but that were just so exciting."[26]

Page, who in 1963 was invited to Hyannis Port, Massachusetts, by President and Mrs. Kennedy to discuss plans for building a national theater in the United States, is best remembered for "her indelible images of delicate women refusing defeat."[27] In real life, however, she proved to be "unpretentious and straightforward when speaking her mind." "I wish they would up the pay a little," the actress once complained about her work, "but I'd rather have the experience."[28]

Marlee Matlin

Children of a Lesser God (1986)

"Like stepping into an imaginary world that [she'd] seen at a distance for years,"[1] the Best Actress Oscar contender **Marlee Matlin** anxiously arrived at the 59th Academy Awards (1987) at the Dorothy Chandler Pavilion. Draped in a lavender laced gown and accessorized with tortoise-shell glasses and a sprig of baby's breath in her hair, Matlin was nominated for her first-ever film performance in *Children of a Lesser God* (1986). The actress was escorted to the ceremony by her costar and then romantic companion William Hurt, who was scheduled to present the Best Actress Oscar since he had won the Best Actor Oscar the year before. Facing a rivalry of far more seasoned performers, Matlin's competition included frontrunner Kathleen Turner (*Peggy Sue Got Married*), Sigourney Weaver (*Aliens*), and former recipients **Jane Fonda** (*The Morning After*) and **Sissy Spacek** (*Crimes of the Heart*), the latter of whom had clinched the New York Film Critics Award.

Deaf since she was 18 months old (after coming down with the disease Roseola), Matlin "couldn't hear any of the names being called nor the pin-drop silence that followed."[2] But upon Hurt's groundbreaking announcement of her name as the winner (immediately before he signed toward her and tenderly smiled), the actress made her way to the stage as her challengers "looked on in apparently sincere appreciation."[3] After a long and sustained applause, Matlin, alongside her interpreter, Jack Jason, addressed the audience in sign language. "I just want to thank a lot of people," she signed before acknowledging the Academy, her fellow cast and crew, and specific members of her family. "I love you."[4]

Hardly a household name, Matlin was catapulted into "sudden fame" by her Best Actress Oscar victory.[5] Sharing the evening's top acting honors with the Hollywood

In *Children of a Lesser God* (1986), the first Best Actress Oscar–winning film to be directed by a woman (Randa Haines), Marlee Matlin plays a former student turned campus janitor at a residential school for the Deaf. With major film roles for Deaf actors exceedingly few and far between, Matlin saw the lead role of Sarah Norman as a golden, once-in-a-lifetime opportunity. (Paramount/Viacom/Photofest)

legend Paul Newman, the actress was approached backstage by a whirlwind of well-wishers including the superstar **Elizabeth Taylor**. But the next morning, Matlin opened the newspapers and was smeared with attacks that reframed her victory as both a "waste" and merely brought about by way of "a sympathy vote."[6] One critic wrote that even though Matlin "won the award *this* time, there wouldn't be another" because she would "never work in Hollywood again." "It was the first time in my life I felt handicapped," Matlin recalled. "I felt that people were hand-icapping me. I didn't handicap myself."[7]

Rebutting "an unfortunate attitude that's kept a lot of very talented people from working" in Hollywood,[8] *Children of a Lesser God*'s director, Randa Haines—the first woman, before Jane Campion, Kimberly Peirce, Patty Jenkins, and Phyllida Lloyd, to have directed a Best Actress Oscar–winning performance—came to Matlin's defense. In doing so, she called attention to a form of prejudice that has been an issue in Hollywood from the very start and, regrettably, has remained ingrained in the institution despite advances in society when it comes to diversifying. As the recipient of the "first and only [Oscar] given to a Deaf person,"[9] Matlin, much like **Halle Berry** (the only performer from a racial minority to have won the Best Actress Oscar), understood that planting the seeds of change into the minds of Hollywood's gatekeepers would require an enormous amount of collective determination.

Matlin was born in the Chicago suburb of Morton Grove, Illinois, on August 24, 1965, to a Jewish family that owned a used-car dealership. She was raised with the belief that "no opportunity should be denied her because of her handicap."[10] Matlin grew up in tandem with the successes of the disability rights movement of the 1970s, and she quickly learned American Sign Language (ASL) and devel-oped the ability to read lips. She enjoyed such children's television programs as *The Electric Company* and *ZOOM* but became frustrated with the popular TV show *Sesame Street* because "she didn't understand the puppets."[11] In an era before home video and without closed captioning (the display of interpretative screen text that Matlin advocated for in the years to come), the actress, like millions of other Deaf individuals at the time, looked forward on television to "a subtitled film or a silent Charlie Chaplin" movie. Unfortunately, as she later recalled, those moments "didn't happen very often."[12]

Matlin was determined to become an actress, despite her mother's firm belief that such a dream "would only end in a life of disappointment and rejection."[13] Early on, she began to perform in such roles as Dorothy in *The Wizard of Oz* and the title character in *Mary Poppins* at the Chicago-area Children's Theater for the Deaf. Her world, however, drastically changed after seeing the 1980 Tony Award–winning play *Children of a Lesser God*, which starred (and had been written for) the Deaf actress Phyllis Frelich.

Subsequently appearing in "a small role in the Chicago stage production" of the play, Matlin learned that Paramount Pictures intended to adapt *Children of a Lesser God* to film. With major film roles for Deaf actors exceedingly few and far between, the actress, like so many members of the "small, close-knit" Deaf acting

Deaf since she was 18 months old, *Children of a Lesser God* star Marlee Matlin accepts her Best Actress Oscar at the 1987 Academy Awards. After a long and sustained applause, the actress, alongside her interpreter, addressed the audience in sign language. (© A.M.P.A.S.®/ Photofest)

community.[14] saw the lead role of Sarah Norman as a golden, once-in-a-lifetime opportunity. Flying to Los Angeles for a screen test (which marked her first time on or within sight of a studio soundstage), the 19-year-old actress was eventually offered the part for $50,000 (nude swimming scene included). Almost as instantly, and setting the stage for an unusual and extra-challenging atmosphere on set, Matlin found herself in a torrid, drug- and alcohol-fueled romance with her celebrated, 35-year-old costar William Hurt.

As if that were not enough, the preparation for *Children of a Lesser God* got off to a rocky start and was "dead in the water at least 15 times."[15] With the "logistical nightmare" of having a cast comprising both Deaf and hearing actors, a long list of accomplished male directors ("twenty-five names" in total) delicately sidestepped the project, many because they "didn't believe" in the movie's money-making potential.[16] As a result, Paramount turned its attention to the television director Randa Haines, one of a shamefully small group of 1980s female directors entrusted with a major Hollywood production.

Set at a residential school for the Deaf in a remote town in coastal Maine, *Children of a Lesser God* centers on the school's new "maverick speech therapist" (played by Hurt).[17] Over time, he encounters the mysterious and reclusive Sarah

Norman, a former student turned campus janitor. Sarah is proud and unwilling to accept anybody's patronizing sympathy. She would rather "remain soundless than lose [her] dignity by attempting to mimic the speech of a hearing person."[18] Ultimately, she is coerced out of her insular shell by way of a "stormy affair" with Hurt's equally stubborn and expressive character.[19]

Matlin was acclaimed for acting "with her eyes" in the subtle "way the stars of the silent era did," and she eventually found herself in the "strange new terrain" of having to promote *Children of a Lesser God* during the frenzied state of awards-season campaigning, in which there is "publicity to do, photo shoots to line up, magazine covers to consider, [and] TV talk shows to book."[20] In the midst of this process, she entered into the fray of awkward questions by members of the press who seemingly had never "talked to a Deaf person before."[21] But overcome by her self-admitted drug use, Matlin suspended her campaign. Like **Elizabeth Taylor** and **Liza Minnelli** before her, she checked into rehab at the Betty Ford Center, the prestigious chemical-dependency recovery hospital in Rancho Mirage, California. There for 26 days, the actress had to miss the London premiere of *Children of a Lesser God*, which Britain's Prince Charles and Princess Diana attended. One morning at the center, Matlin awoke to learn that she had been nominated for the Best Actress Oscar by way of a telecommunications device for the Deaf (TDD).

At 21 years and 218 days, Matlin ultimately overtook inaugural recipient **Janet Gaynor**'s long-held record and became the youngest woman to win the Best Actress Oscar. She additionally became the second performer with a physical disability to take home the film industry's most coveted honor. But reminiscent of Harold Russell, who, 40 years before, had won the Best Supporting Actor Oscar for portraying an amputee Army veteran, like himself, in *The Best Years of Our Lives* (1946), Matlin soon discovered the prejudicial barriers of the Hollywood institution at large. Despite her breakthrough Oscar victory, being "female and hearing-impaired in a realm controlled by hard-driving men" rendered her "low on the 'take me seriously' scale."[22] Even when she pursued the role of the mute Ada McGrath in *The Piano* (1993)—a part that ultimately earned **Holly Hunter** the Best Actress Oscar, the director Jane Campion dismissed the idea because she "didn't think anyone in the audience would be able to forget [that Matlin] was Deaf."[23]

Finding a wider breadth of opportunity on American television, Matlin, the crusader for Deaf children who was once predicted to have only a short-lived acting career, flummoxed many people by remaining a steadfast fixture in the entertainment industry. While she was never offered another signature leading role in film, she sporadically appeared in minor but rewarding film projects such as the AIDS-related *It's My Party* (1996) and the existential documentary/drama *What the #S*! Do We (K)now!?* (2004). As the actress later reflected, the "greatest barrier" she faced in Hollywood was not "her deafness as much as the many closed minds" that she encountered[24]—an obstruction that has erased many possibilities and has surely diminished the universality of the human experience onscreen.

Cher

In 1985, **Cher** won the Cannes Film Festival's Prix d'interprétation féminine for her emotionally devastating performance in *Mask* (1985), in which she plays a biker mom to a son with a rare form of skull deformity. But when the Oscar nominations were announced several months later, her name was surprisingly absent among the contenders. "They didn't nominate me," she said to her friend the designer Bob Mackie.[1]

Nevertheless asked to present the Oscar for Best Supporting Actor that year, Cher—in an act of calculated rebellion guaranteed to generate headlines for the sake of self-promotion—decided to have some "fun."[2] Requiring her to "sit on the floor of [her] limo" so as to "avoid damaging [her two-foot] headpiece,"[3] the singer/actress later concealed her nervousness and came out onstage in a black, almost entirely see-through, gothic, "Zulu-princess-on-her-wedding-day" Mackie gown, which was topped with a thousand feathers "gathered by hand from rooster farmers in France." "As you can see, I did receive my Academy booklet on how to dress like a serious actress," she informed the audience in a charming effrontery encased in her trademark deadpan humor.[4]

Well before the onslaught of other monosyllabic names that came into high-level vogue, with Adele, Beyoncé, Björk, Eminem, Madonna, Moby, Morrissey, Prince, Rihanna, and Sting, Cher was "striking gold in music, movies, and television" while challenging the stereotypes of race, age, and beauty.[5] Wearing the most extravagant, attention-grabbing array of fashion this side of Liberace, she epitomized the cutting-edge trends from her early days as a 1960s mod/beatnik/hippie to her 1980s reign as a "MTV rock diva" with big, crinkly hair.[6] By way of her wardrobe hits, which have included a "red Pocahontas outfit," a "Louis XIV corset," feathered frocks, jingling skirts, and a constant "barely-there couture" of outerwear

Moonstruck (1987)

Cher poses for a publicity photo for *Moonstruck* (1987), a film that validated the star as a serious actress. (Metro-Goldwyn-Mayer Inc./Photofest)

lingerie,[7] she additionally became a stylistic godmother to the likes of Björk, Lady Gaga, and countless numbers of worshiping drag queens.

Cher was born Cherilyn Sarkisian in the city of El Centro, California, on May 20, 1946. She grew up poor and once remembered "going to school with rubber bands around [her] shoes to keep [her] soles on."[8] Her parents were married and divorced three times. Her mother (of European and possibly Cherokee descent) was once an aspiring actress, and her largely absent Armenian American father worked as a truck driver.

Cher was once suspended from high school for sneaking out to see *Breakfast at Tiffany's* (1961) and returning to class in rebellious **Audrey Hepburn**/Holly Golightly–inspired sunglasses. She "never wanted to fit in" and eventually quit school altogether.[9] Attempting "to escape her poverty" and pursue her film-acting ambitions, she entered the entertainment industry as a go-go dancer and became part of the growing counterculture scene along the bohemian Sunset Strip in present-day West Hollywood.

There, the tall, lean, raven-haired 16-year-old met and moved in with the diminutive, 28-year-old Italian American Salvatore Phillip "Sonny" Bono—an enthusiastic musician, songwriter, and protégé to the "Wall of Sound" record producer Phil Spector. Initially, the couple "slept in separate twin beds" since Sonny "didn't find [Cher] particularly attractive."[10] "Completely and voluntarily under Sonny's domination"[11] in the same way that **Norma Shearer**, **Jennifer Jones**, and **Sophia Loren** permitted their husbands to manage their careers, Cher, as instructed, kept "the apartment clean," did "the cooking," and, with her husky contralto vocal range, sang backup with Sonny "on almost everything Spector recorded for a year."[12] Before long, the couple—adorned in bell-bottoms, fur boots, and "matted-dog-fur vests"[13]—rose to the top of the record charts with their own 1965 hit single, "I Got You Babe." Perceived as folksy "weirdos" analogous to such contemporary Los Angeles–based hit makers as Buffalo Springfield, the Byrds, and the Doors, the monogamous, drug-free duo eventually expanded their range and recognition. In doing so, they disastrously ventured into filmmaking with the box-office failures *Good Times* (1967) and *Chastity* (1969; which coincided with the year of their marriage and the birth of their eponymously named daughter).

Television proved to be the couple's best medium. Their variety show, *The Sonny & Cher Comedy Hour* (1971–1974), was a major success and featured a diverse list of guests ranging from Ronald Reagan to the Jackson 5. But like many show-business marriages, theirs was a contractual hell. "It's impossible to explain Sonny's hold on me," Cher later reflected.[14] "For five years before I left him, I wanted to leave, but [the show] was so popular that I was afraid. And when I finally did leave, he said, 'America will hate you. You'll never work again.'"[15] In 1975, four days after divorcing Sonny, Cher went on to marry the musician Gregg Allman. While she was "fearful of becoming 'the next Dinah Shore,'"[16] she unhappily carried on with her ex-husband in the new but similarly formatted *The Sonny & Cher Show* (1976–1977) until breaking free and taking control over her own career.

Pictured here with Best Actor recipient Michael Douglas, Cher—in this famously risqué Bob Mackie–designed gown—celebrates her Best Actress Oscar victory for *Moonstruck* at the 1988 Academy Awards. (© A.M.P.A.S.®/Photofest)

Aware of her self-described "narrow range" ("I've never tried anything more than playing who I am").[7] Cher nevertheless poured herself into a series of raw screen performances that separated this new phase of her career from anything that she had done before. For her role as **Meryl Streep**'s butch lesbian roommate in *Silkwood* (1983), she earned a supporting Oscar nomination. At a time when feminism was under siege in America, she followed up her success with *Mask* (1985) by kicking off the banner year of 1987 with a platinum-selling album and three successful films (*Moonstruck*, *Suspect*, and *The Witches of Eastwick*).

A magical-realist fairy tale of sorts, *Moonstruck* centers on Cher's unfulfilled Loretta Castorini, a dowdy, romantically resigned, family-devoted Italian American bookkeeper and widow who is convinced that her life is plagued by bad luck. But transformed by a "mischievous [New York City] moon" and displaying certain "affinities" with the characters from the Puccini opera *La bohème*, the film's protagonists (including Loretta's mother, played by Best Supporting Actress Oscar recipient Olympia Dukakis) are individually "gripped by the heart's great distemper."[18] Consequently, Loretta struggles to fight off the affections of her fiancé's much-younger brother (a "passionate one-handed baker" played by Nicholas Cage).[19]

Although **Sally Field** was initially offered the starring role in *Moonstruck*, Cher, who had trouble imagining herself as Loretta, ultimately secured the lead and helped to shine an unusual spotlight on the issue of ageism. Going "against the Hollywood grain, where older men–younger women pairings" are almost always the norm,[20] the film offered audiences a provocative alternative while finding the character of Loretta dying her gray hairs away. In real life, Cher—after **Greer Garson**, **Ginger Rogers**, and **Louise Fletcher** but before the likes of **Elizabeth Taylor**, **Susan Sarandon**, **Sandra Bullock**, and **Julianne Moore**—captivated the world's attention by engaging in a number of age-defying romances that coincidentally paralleled with her character's situation. As a quintessential "cougar" (a term used to define women who seek sexual relationships with younger men), the singer/actress was seen with Bon Jovi guitarist Richie Sambora, Val Kilmer, and fellow superstar Tom Cruise—years before his marriage to **Nicole Kidman**.

Cher was nominated for her performance in *Moonstruck* ("the first movie" of hers that she had "ever watched without wanting to throw up").[21] Escorted by her 18-years-her-junior boyfriend, Rob Camilletti, she arrived at the 60th Academy Awards (1988) in a Mackie-designed "sheer black body stocking" only "a few sequins shy of requiring television censors."[22] In a tight race for Best Actress, her competition included former winner **Meryl Streep** (*Ironweed*), Sally Kirkland (*Anna*), Glenn Close (*Fatal Attraction*), and New York Film Critics Award winner **Holly Hunter** (*Broadcast News*). While Kirkland's publicist had gone so far as to hand out copies of her client's film to entertainment journalists and Academy members, Cher, in the months preceding the ceremony, simultaneously managed to keep herself in the public eye. One notable appearance occurred on the American comedy talk show *Late Night with David Letterman*, where she was musically reunited with Sonny in what the *Village Voice* referred to as "an amazing piece of psychodrama."[23]

Nevertheless, upon Paul Newman's announcement of her name as Best Actress, Cher—"capping an extraordinary rise from ridiculed pop star to respected leading lady"[24]—ascended to the podium amid a rousing standing ovation. "When I was little my mother said, 'I want you to be something,'" she reflected in her acceptance speech. "I don't think [this award] means that I am somebody, but I guess I'm on my way."[25]

Subsequently hindered by chronic fatigue syndrome, Cher appeared in fewer movies, including *Mermaids* (1990), the abortion-themed TV movie drama *If These*

Walls Could Talk (1996; her directorial debut), and *Tea with Mussolini* (1999; opposite **Maggie Smith**). "I think I act really great, but I don't think of myself as an actress," she once admitted. "I don't like making movies. I like acting and if I never make another movie I will be proud of the movies — except for *Witches* — that I've made."[26]

Over the course of her career, Cher has proved to be more than an entertainer. As evinced by her enormous fan base worldwide, the 100 million albums that she has sold, and the biennial Cher Convention, she is indeed a personality whose sum is greater than her parts. Cher has additionally lent her voice to such humanitarian projects as Operation Helmet, a Kenyan school for orphans, PFLAG (Parents, Families, and Friends of Lesbians and Gays), and the Children's Craniofacial Association. Despite ongoing sexism and misogyny, Cher's libertarian sensibility and freedom from male control helped to carve out a space for third-wave feminism in the early 1990s, with its emphasis on individual empowerment, diversity (related to race, class, age, body type, gender identity, and sexuality), and sexual entitlement (free of sexual harassment). Adventurous, curious, sexual, and still having fun, Cher's influence today appears to be as strong as ever.

Jodie Foster

Before being given permission to play the role of the wayward, scantily clad New York City child prostitute in Martin Scorsese's *Taxi Driver* (1976)—a character who "bears obvious marks of exploitation and abuse,"[1] the 12-year-old **Jodie Foster** had to undergo a series of psychological examinations to prove that the experience would not leave her emotionally scarred. For most child actors, such a precaution might seem to be imperative, but for Foster—the "breath-takingly gifted" tomboy prodigy who began performing in front of the camera at the age of three[2]—the assessment of her mental faculties merely presented a frivolous exercise before she clinched the controversial role and earned her first Academy Award nomination for it.

To be sure, Foster's mental prowess has become a thing of legend. When she was 18 and attending Yale, she received love letters from a deranged *Taxi Driver*–obsessed fan by the name of John Hinckley Jr. After Hinckley learned that the young actress was a student at Yale, he "enrolled in a writing course" on campus and began to stalk Foster with a gun.[3] When she did not reciprocate his attention, Hinckley, like the Robert De Niro character in *Taxi Driver*, "turned to the idea of assassinating a president to impress her." At first, Hinckley targeted U.S. President Jimmy Carter "before focusing on [Ronald] Reagan after he took office in January 1981."[4] Sixty-nine days into Reagan's term, Hinckley ambushed Reagan "as the president left the Washington Hilton Hotel after a speech," managing "to fire six shots from the .22-caliber revolver he had purchased at a pawn shop for $29."[5] As Reagan recuperated from a bullet wound to his lung, Foster's world was turned upside down. Agitated by the shooting and finding "herself unpleasantly in the spotlight" with a blitz of media attention, she nevertheless managed

The Accused (1988)

The Silence of the Lambs (1991)

Jodie Foster, with a bloodshot eye, poses for a publicity photo for *The Accused* (1988). (Paramount/Viacom/Photofest)

A generation before intimacy coordinators were hired to protect actors from psychological trauma, abuse, and harassment during scenes connected to sexual intimacy and sexual violence, Jodie Foster appeared in one of the first (gang) rape sequences explicitly depicted onscreen, as seen in this contact sheet from *The Accused* (1988). Foster insisted that female costar Kelly McGillis be present throughout the five-day, closed-set shoot despite the fact that McGillis was not in the scene. (Paramount/Viacom/Photofest)

to remain calm. Instead of triggering "further headlines by fleeing into seclusion," she "quietly continued appearing with classmates in a school play."[6]

Foster, like **Julianne Moore**, has since become a gun control advocate, but she has rarely touched on the incident regarding Hinckley (who was incidentally released from a psychiatric hospital in 2016). In fact, she is said to walk out on interviews if the subject is ever raised. But through a back-to-back pair of psychologically grueling screen performances, Foster made constructive use out of her nightmarish experience by transforming her vulnerable characters into fearless victors and earning two Best Actress Oscars along the way.

Turning her attention toward the most underreported violent crime concerning women, Foster first took on the role of the rape victim Sarah Tobias in *The Accused* (1988). The film is based on the true story of a woman who was gang-raped at a bar in New Bedford, Massachusetts. In the scene leading up to the rape, Foster's character is portrayed as a "party animal"—a woman with a crude and checkered personality who is legally drunk, high on marijuana, provocatively dressed, and overtly flaunting her sexuality as she "dirty dances with a man in [the back room of a] bar."[7] The scene, which is excruciating to watch, culminates with the film's distressingly visceral, three-minute gang-rape that features three men raping Sarah over a pinball machine while a group of cheering male bystanders egg on her brutal assault and help to keep it going.

To be sure, the scene is a far cry from the implied rapes depicted in *Johnny Belinda* (1948) and *A Streetcar Named Desire* (1951), in which the fates of the characters portrayed by **Jane Wyman** and **Vivien Leigh** are visually represented by a falling shadow, "a shattered mirror," "a swinging light bulb," and a sinister fade-out. *The Accused* conversely leaves us "with the unspeakable horror" of what we actually see.[8] During the meticulously rehearsed scene, Foster was instructed to cry on cue so many times that—throughout the five-day, closed-set shoot (at which costar Kelly McGillis was present, per Foster's request)—she burst the blood vessels in her eyes. Savvy and forever balanced, she nevertheless withstood the challenge, watched the dailies, and made an occasional joke. Much like **Hilary Swank** on the set of *Boys Don't Cry* (1999), Foster even offered comfort and reassurance to her male costars, who, take after take, remorsefully wound themselves into a crying mess.

Foster's performance in *The Accused* was a "pop-culture turning point" and "prompted serious study of the prevalence and causes of rape."[9] In a world in which police and various governments have been known to turn a blind eye to such acts of violence (e.g., discouraging women from reporting rape and advising many even to marry their rapists so as to avoid "irreversible" stigmatization), the film served as a disavowal of victim blaming as well as an important "warning to men who do nothing to stop rape."[10] Fanning the flames of Third Wave feminism, it additionally challenged the notion that a flirtatious woman "of questionable character" is somehow complicit in her own assault.[11]

Foster, who read newspaper articles about rape experiences, attended support groups, and spoke with rape crisis counselors in preparation for her performance, ultimately found herself as a Best Actress Oscar contender ahead of the 61st Academy Awards (1989) for what many people considered to be her "first full-scale, grown-up performance."[12] At a ceremony marred by a misogynistic opening song-and-dance number featuring Snow White and the young, sexualized Hollywood heartthrob Rob Lowe, Foster's strong field of competition included Glenn Close (*Dangerous Liaisons*), Sigourney Weaver (*Gorillas in the Mist*), Melanie Griffith (*Working Girl*), and former recipient and New York Film Critics Award winner **Meryl Streep** (*A Cry in the Dark*). Upon the announcement of Foster's name, she took to the podium and, in her distinctive, throaty alto, thanked her mother and manager, Brandy, for teaching her as a child that all of her "finger paintings were Picassos, and that [she] didn't have to be afraid."[13] Refocusing the spotlight on the issues of violence and accountability, she then went on to underscore that "cruelty might be very human, and it might be very cultural, but it's not acceptable."[14]

In her first role after winning the Oscar for *The Accused*, Foster ramped up the issue of violence against women in the director Jonathan Demme's screen adaptation of the Thomas Harris novel *The Silence of the Lambs* (1991). In the film, Foster plays Clarice Starling, an earnest special-unit FBI agent-in-training (later played

by **Julianne Moore** in the 2001 sequel *Hannibal*), who is pushed to confront evil in the form of "Buffalo Bill," a grotesque serial killer and abductor of young women whose flesh he adorns as fashion. Unearthing clues to the killer's whereabouts by way of heady counsel from another notorious murderer, the incarcerated but still threatening Dr. Hannibal "The Cannibal" Lecter (played by the Best Actor Oscar recipient Anthony Hopkins), Clarice is led to the killer's dungeon-like cellar. There, in a suffocating, panic-stricken game of cat and mouse that is chillingly shot through the greenish, filtered perspective of the killer's night-vision goggles, a groping Clarice is blindly stalked and traumatized in complete darkness.

While some moviegoers hailed Foster's portrayal of Clarice, the film's graphically detailed violence troubled, disturbed, and offended others. It was released in the United States on Valentine's Day 1991, at a time when the average American child was reported to "have seen 200,000 violent acts on television."[15] The film's depiction of "sadism, torture, brutality, and human suffering—all in the name of entertainment"—made many audiences cringe. In an era of escalating bloodshed in motion pictures, many people speculated that this trend could lead to "the desensitization of viewers" and have violent "real-life ramifications."[16]

Moreover, at a time of increased gay bashing and paranoia stemming from the AIDS pandemic, the repellent, effeminate personification of "Buffalo Bill" and general outrage concerning Hollywood's homophobic stereotyping of gay men and women galvanized dozens of Queer Nation demonstrators outside the Dorothy Chandler Pavilion on Oscar night 1992. Further incensed by objectionable depictions in films such as *JFK* (1991) and *Basic Instinct* (1992), demonstrators—many aware of Foster's own closeted sexual orientation—"struggled behind police barriers, blasting whistles" and holding signs that read "Stereotypes + Hatred = Violence."[17]

Despite the film's controversies, and despite having had its premiere more than one year before, *The Silence of the Lambs* tied *It Happened One Night* (1934) and *One Flew Over the Cuckoo's Nest* (1975) by winning the Oscars' "big five" awards (writer, actor, actress, director, and picture). Wearing both a Giorgio Armani pantsuit and a red ribbon as "a symbol of solidarity with AIDS sufferers,"[18] Foster, who had already clinched the New York Film Critics Award, electrified the Oscar ceremony by becoming the 11th woman (and, at 29, the second youngest after **Luise Rainer**) to win the Best Actress Oscar more than once. In doing so, she bested Bette Midler (*For the Boys*), Laura Dern (*Rambling Rose*), and Geena Davis and **Susan Sarandon** for their roles in the hit feminist road movie *Thelma & Louise*.

Throughout her life, Foster, born in Los Angeles on November 19, 1962, and unpretentiously raised alongside the glitz and glitter of Hollywood by her mother and three significantly older siblings, has managed to maintain a strong-centered, down-to-earth persona, deemphasizing her fame as best as she can while relishing her fiercely guarded privacy. As the film industry's "most staid and no-nonsense . . . power player,"[19] Foster, the mother of two, long refrained from addressing the persistent rumors surrounding her sexual orientation—the same rumors that,

Silence of the Lambs star Jodie Foster, in character and surrounded by a wreath of moths, poses for a portrait by photojournalist Ken Regan. (Ken Regan/Photofest)

Wearing an Armani-designed ivory jacket with kimono sleeves, beaded trousers, and an AIDS ribbon, *Silence of the Lambs* star Jodie Foster mesmerized the film industry at the 1992 Academy Awards by becoming the second youngest woman (after Luise Rainer) to win the Best Actress Oscar more than once. (© A.M.P.A.S.®/Photofest)

generations before, surrounded the likes of **Claudette Colbert**, **Joan Crawford**, Marlene Dietrich, **Marie Dressler**, Greta Garbo, **Janet Gaynor**, **Katharine Hepburn**, and many others. Undoubtedly, Foster came of age at a radically different time, when the role of the arts and the AIDS pandemic played a major part in the evolution of the perception of homosexuality, leading many gay men and women to no longer feel the need to keep quiet. Foster, however, was still operating in a film industry in which "scandals and marketing strategies [forced] the private lives of film actors to fit narrow standards," and she initially opened up only to "trusted friends and family."[20] But at a Hollywood event in 2007, she "referred lovingly to her longtime partner Cydney Bernard" and acknowledged the issue again at the 2013 Golden Globes, publicly thanking Bernard (her "ex-partner-in-love" and "righteous soul sister in life") while lighting up the blogosphere.[21] The following year, she married the photographer Alexandra Hedison. Although Foster's sexuality was widely speculated on for years, her coming-out revelation—which coincided with the public disclosures of other female stars including Kelly McGillis, Cynthia Nixon, Ellen Page, Anna Paquin, Kristen Stewart, and Evan Rachel Wood—proved to many people that lesbian identity is now taken more seriously in mainstream American popular culture, despite its challenges to "the moral, sexual, and psychic authority of men."[22] To others, her revelation was simply viewed as a shrewd, headline-generating career move—a "cagey bid for attention by a former box-office champ who hasn't had a hit" since 2005's *Flightplan*.[23]

With Foster's magna cum laude degree in English literature, fluency in French, and penchant for film producing and directing (to date, she has four films in the director's chair), her acting—a craft that she once observed as not very intellectual[24]—has been occasionally relegated to the back burner. Still, as one of the most revered actresses of her generation, and certainly one of the most heroic, her place in the pantheon of movie history is assured.

Jessica Tandy

In a youth-obsessed industry that once asked the 34-year-old **Bette Davis** to play a spinster in *Now, Voyager* (1942) and the 36-year-old **Anne Bancroft** to portray Mrs. Robinson in *The Graduate* (1967), the 80-year-old **Jessica Tandy**'s Oscar-winning turn in the Best Picture–winning drama *Driving Miss Daisy* (1989) marked a bold milestone in Hollywood's uneasy relationship with aging. On the heels of two "distinguished, gray-haired veterans" collecting Best Actress Oscars (the 74-year-old **Katharine Hepburn** for *On Golden Pond* [1981] and the 61-year-old **Geraldine Page** for *The Trip to Bountiful* [1985]),[1] Tandy's victory helped to galvanize the film industry to more often tackle the issues surrounding the physical, psychological, and social changes pertaining to old age.

Although a 70-year-old **Shirley MacLaine** criticized the film industry "for failing to make enough" movies on these subjects,[2] there has actually been an increase in the number of projects *for* and *about* older people that have made money since *Driving Miss Daisy*'s "careful, graduated,"[3] and ultimately successful release. Examples include *Grumpier Old Men* (1995; featuring **Sophia Loren**), *Woman in Gold* (2015; starring **Helen Mirren**), *The Best Exotic Marigold Hotel* series (2012–2015; starring **Maggie Smith** and Judi Dench), and *Amour* (2012; featuring the oldest Best Actress Oscar nominee, the 85-year-old Emmanuelle Riva). What is more, a number of older actresses, including **Barbra Streisand**, **Jane Fonda**, and **Glenda Jackson**, have returned to acting in their 60s, 70s, and 80s, proudly appearing onstage or onscreen while re-creating careers that might have been blocked to them before.

A far cry from the grotesque "human gargoyles" of the post–*What Ever Happened to Baby Jane?* (1962) "hag movies" that gave former leading ladies **Bette Davis** and

Driving Miss Daisy (1989)

Driving Miss Daisy (1989) centers on the unanticipated friendship between Jessica Tandy's racist, stubborn character and her illiterate "Negro" chauffeur (played by Morgan Freeman). For her performance, Tandy—at 80 years and 292 days—became the oldest recipient of the Best Actress Oscar. (Warner Bros. Pictures Inc./Photofest)

Joan Crawford a second career in horror pictures (while keeping others, such as **Claudette Colbert**, far away from Hollywood),[4] Tandy's performance in *Driving Miss Daisy* (1989) offered filmgoers a peek into the life of an elderly woman who is squarely situated at the center of action. Set in Atlanta between 1948 and 1973, the film zeroes in on the deep, unanticipated friendship between Tandy's "sassy sourpuss" of a character—the racist, Jewish widow Daisy Werthan—and her illiterate "Negro" chauffeur (played by Morgan Freeman).[5] Over the course of two and a half decades, during which the bigotry-propelled laws of the Jim Crow South gave way to the civil rights movement and desegregation, the characters begin to discover "parallels between their stories due to the anti-Semitism and racism [that] they face."[6] But although the film presents a thought-provoking message on "the need to overcome racial prejudice," it was largely seen as being too simplistic and adherent "to a moonlight-and-magnolias vision of the South, where life was gracious and Black people were childlike and cheerful."[7] Next to the director Spike Lee's blunt race-relation drama *Do the Right Thing*, which opened the same year and stirred a fear among theater owners nationwide of possible riots, *Driving Miss Daisy* seemed restrained and unchallenging in its safe, "rose-tinted view of the past" that rarely let "Freeman or the other African-American actors break out of stereotype." "When *Driving Miss* motherfucking *Daisy* won [the Best Picture Oscar], that hurt," said Lee, whose film was controversially snubbed in the Best Picture category.[8]

Despite a long career, Tandy had never been given a signature leading role in a film before and *Driving Miss Daisy* was a sudden and unexpected piece of good fortune for her: a rare quality part for an established older actress who was more accustomed to being offered small "character [roles] as an extra added attraction."[9] Having recently appeared in *Cocoon* (1985) and *Cocoon: The Return* (1988) for the *Driving Miss Daisy* producers Richard and Lili Zanuck, Tandy landed the coveted role after the likes of **Katharine Hepburn**, **Joan Fontaine**, **Loretta Young**, and **Bette Davis** had all expressed interest. "I'd like just one more of the kind of part I once played," said **Davis**,[10] who died in late 1989 at the age of 81 after appearing in such unevenly received swan songs as *The Whales of August* (1987) and *Wicked Stepmother* (1989). Ultimately thanking her "lucky stars," Tandy happily joined forces with the Australian director Bruce Beresford and her costar Morgan Freeman, who had previously appeared in the Pulitzer Prize–winning stage version of *Driving Miss Daisy* by Alfred Uhry.[11]

A product of Edwardian England, Tandy was born in London on June 7, 1909, not long before the introduction of feature-length films and the pioneering of sportswear for women (who, at the time, were still largely constricted in corsets and huge, feathered hats). Alongside her two older brothers, she grew up in a life of poverty. At age 12, her traveling-salesman father died. But despite the family's misfortunes, Tandy's mother—a strict woman who believed that time was never to be wasted—routinely took her children "to plays, pantomimes, and museums" while remaining resolute that they should each make their mark in the world. "It sounds terribly snobbish," explained the actress, "but she raised us to be intellectually above our neighbors" as a way to break out "of our bleak life."[12]

Tandy was too young to stay at home alone, so she tagged along to the night school for adults where her mother worked as a teacher. There, with fellow students "more than twice her age,"[13] she enrolled in a course on Shakespeare just to pass the time. With her mother supplementing the family's income with extra clerical jobs, Tandy, at the age of 15, was able to enroll at the Ben Greet Academy of Acting. At age 18, she was expected to provide her own costumes as she made her professional debut in London's West End, where she first gained recognition in Christa Winsloe's lesbian-themed stage play *Children in Uniform* (1932). The actress then appeared as Ophelia in *Hamlet* (1934; starring and directed by John Gielgud), as Katharine in *Henry V* (1937; opposite Laurence Olivier), and as Cordelia in *King Lear* (1940; opposite Gielgud again).

A portrait of Jessica Tandy from the late 1920s, when the teenage actress began to appear in a number of plays in London's West End. (Photofest)

With the outset of World War II, Tandy—divorced from her first husband (the actor Jack Hawkins) and realizing that theater work in England was about to dry up—accepted an invitation to go to America. "I had to support myself and a daughter," she explained. "But so many of us had come over from Europe, and everybody who had said 'we long to have you here' disappeared into the woodwork. So it was tough for a while."[14]

After Tandy landed a role in the play *Jupiter Laughs* (1940), she was greeted backstage by the Canadian actor Hume Cronyn, whom she ultimately accompanied to Hollywood, married, and remained married to for 52 years. At the time, Cronyn was in demand as a screen character actor, and he was able to arrange for his wife to appear in a succession of small but essentially thankless movie roles that failed to bring her serious attention, including *The Seventh Cross* (1944; a Spencer Tracy suspense drama about Nazi concentration camp escapees) and *The Valley of Decision* (1945; with **Greer Garson** and Gregory Peck).

Feeling "rather unused,"[15] Tandy returned to the theater to star in Tennessee Williams's landmark stage production of *A Streetcar Named Desire* (1947). In the play, her experience as a Shakespearean actor sharply contrasted with costar Marlon Brando's innovative Method approach. In over 800 performances and to great acclaim, she poured her "heart and soul and physical body and mind" into the haunting, "emotionally taxing" character of Blanche DuBois.[16] Despite originating the role, the disappointed actress remained the only principal player not to be hired for the 1951 screen adaptation (which landed **Vivien Leigh**, as Blanche, a second Academy Award).

Forging ahead in a "strange [and uneven] career," Tandy nonetheless garnered a total of three Tony Awards.[17] But with the notable exception of her memorable turn in Alfred Hitchcock's *The Birds* (1963), she continued to be cast in the same types of forgettable film roles that she had been seen in before.

By the time that Tandy was nominated for Best Actress for her performance in *Driving Miss Daisy*, she had finally ascended to the upper echelon of movie stardom and became "the surest bet" ahead of the 62nd Academy Awards (1990).[18] At the Dorothy Chandler Pavilion in downtown Los Angeles, her much-younger competition included **Jessica Lange** (*Music Box*), Isabelle Adjani (*Camille Claudel*), Pauline Collins (*Shirley Valentine*), and New York Film Critics Award winner Michelle Pfeiffer (*The Fabulous Baker Boys*). When her former costar Gregory Peck read her name as the winner, Tandy elegantly made her way to the stage to a sustained standing ovation that she could hardly believe. "I never expected in a million years that I would ever be in this position. It's a miracle," she said. "Thank you, the Academy, and all of you. I am on cloud nine!"[19]

After winning the Oscar, Tandy spent a few days blissfully and unrecognizably strolling the Hudson River–adjacent village of Nyack, New York, while visiting her close friend **Helen Hayes**—the winner of the Best Actress Oscar 58 years before. Although Tandy faced her final years in a superficial culture that embraces the concept of age as something to be cured, the oldest woman to ever win the Best Actress Oscar nevertheless went on to star in such successful films as *Fried Green Tomatoes* (1991; for which she received a Best Supporting Actress Oscar nomination) and *Nobody's Fool* (1994; opposite Paul Newman). Unlike **Bette Davis**, who, in 1961 at the age of 53, placed "a 'Job Wanted' ad in the Hollywood trade papers,"[20] Tandy effectively demonstrated that age can bolster one's warmth, charm, and individuality. On September 11, 1994, at the age of 85, Tandy passed away, survived by her husband.

Kathy Bates

In a film genre that first represented women attempting "to wriggle out of their bonds as a train barreled down on them" or depicted them screaming "as a psycho slashed them in the shower,"[1] **Kathy Bates** became an anomaly as the first horror-movie queen to win the Best Actress Oscar. Taking cues in human cruelty from the likes of **Louise Fletcher** in *One Flew Over the Cuckoo's Nest* (1975), the actress appeared as the psychotic, homicidal nurse Annie Wilkes in the 1990 screen adaptation of the Stephen King novel *Misery*. In doing so, she helped to crystallize the dark and demented side of female self-empowerment, where men, in rare displays of gender reversal, are cast as the objectified targets of terror. In direct opposition to the countless numbers of female characters abducted in film, including the victim saved by **Jodie Foster** in *The Silence of the Lambs* (1991) or **Brie Larson**'s routinely raped character in *Room* (2015), Bates brought the screen an unusual type of character whose deranged obsession unleashes a terrorizing form of power and control. So edgy and extreme is her Annie that today she rests in the pantheon of the all-time cinematic villains, which includes Darth Vader, Norman Bates, Dr. Hannibal Lecter, Nurse Ratched, and the Wicked Witch of the West.

Certainly, Bates would never have guessed that she would one day be linked to one of the greatest villains in movie history. Born on June 28, 1948, to a middle-class family in Memphis, Tennessee, Bates grew up feeling "much like an only child" as a result of having two significantly older sisters as well as middle-aged parents who "didn't always see eye to eye" with her. "I was playing guitar and they were pulling their hair out," she once said of her grandparent-like parents.[2]

Bates caught the acting bug early on and was bequeathed the nickname of "Sarah" (after the French actress Sarah Bernhardt). She decided to major in theater

Misery (1990)

Number-one fan and psychopath Annie Wilkes (played by Best
Actress Oscar winner Kathy Bates) contemplates her good fortune
after having come to the rescue of her favorite author (James
Caan) in *Misery* (1990). (Castle Rock Entertainment/Photofest)

at Southern Methodist University in Dallas before trying her hand at acting in New York City. "My parents went to see me do a play at [the] university," she recalled. "They talked to my acting teacher. They were concerned."[3] Nobody from her family had ever ventured to early-1970s New York—a city that "reeked" at the time "of angst, mistrust, fear, and insecurity" as a result of "stagflation, rotting infrastructure, sanitation workers' strikes, and rampant crime."[4] Much like the buxom **Marie Dressler**, Bates was professionally reminded that she was "not conventionally beautiful." Still, after seeing her perform, her father (a mechanical engineer) reluctantly gave her his blessing and the gift of $500, and upon graduation, Bates made her way to the "dangerous" and "unfriendly" Big Apple.[5]

Bates was pigeonholed for being "round, pudgy, and overweight," and with her soft alto "Tennessee twang,"[6] she found New York City and its cutthroat show-business industry to be tough to endure. "This business is so perplexing," she explained. "You try not to get bitter or cynical about the breaks."[7] While scrounging for bit parts, Bates worked at "the cash register at the Museum of Modern Art gift shop and as a singing waitress in the Catskills."[8] She and her friends even "staged theatre in a disused porno cinema off Times Square."[9] Finally, after having to return to Tennessee for a year out of sheer frustration, she landed her first regular gig: that of a quacking duck in a traveling children's theater troupe. "It's hard to make a living and even harder to make an artistically satisfying living," she added.[10]

Eventually appearing in both *The Doctors* and *All My Children*, Bates dipped her toe in daytime television soap operas (much like the *Search for Tomorrow* player **Susan Sarandon**, the *Ryan's Hope* and *General Hospital* guest stars **Joan Fontaine** and **Elizabeth Taylor**, and the *As the World Turns* regular **Julianne Moore**). Soon after, she received small film parts and a succession of stage roles that caught New York theatergoers' attention. Despite earning a Tony Award nomination for *'night, Mother* (1983) and an Obie Award for her performance as Frankie in the off-Broadway production of *Frankie and Johnny in the Clair de Lune* (1987), Bates was bypassed altogether when each production was adapted for film (ultimately starring **Sissy Spacek** and Michelle Pfeiffer, respectively). "**Geraldine Page** didn't get to do *Agnes of God* and Ethel Merman didn't get to do *Gypsy*," she pointed out with an air of realism. "It happens at all levels."[11]

But soon Bates's luck changed when the director Rob Reiner saw her perform onstage in *Aunt Dan and Lemon* (1987) opposite his then-girlfriend, Elizabeth McGovern, at the Mark Taper Forum in downtown Los Angeles. In the midst of his search for a brawny-looking woman to play the lead role in his film adaptation of *Misery* (1990), Reiner, who had first considered Bette Midler, made the "risky and unorthodox choice" of casting Bates—a 40-year-old woman whom nobody really knew.[12] Filmed with the actress "in looming, full-body shots as if she were a bull bearing down on [the audience]," *Misery* tells the story of a famous writer (played by James Caan) who is badly injured in a car crash and nursed back to health by his number-one fan: the "aggressively doting," borderline-personality-disorder-suffering Annie Wilkes.[13] Caan's character is imprisoned in Annie's tucked-away home in the blizzardy Colorado Rockies and comes to realize that Annie—the hermit owner of a pet pig, a keen follower of the American game show *Love Connection*, and a former nurse who killed victims in her care—is the only person he can turn to for help. As the *Village Voice* put it, "it's [James] Stewart in *Rear Window* [1954] with Raymond Burr in the same room and in drag."[14]

For Bates, the enormous success of *Misery*—which was widely embraced by male audiences and became infamous for its sledgehammer scene—was a complete surprise. "I had no idea it would take off," she admitted. "In fact, when I saw the first screening, I was horrified. I thought, 'Oh dear God, I'm on a limb and I'll never be able to crawl back.'"[15]

With *Misery* addressing the "dark side of success" and every celebrity's "worst nightmare,"[16] Bates, who cried after filming a fight scene "because of the amount of violence" it contained,[17] nonetheless managed to create an indelible portrait of a person who seems nice until her deranged, morally reprehensible personality sets in. Incidentally, in the year of *Misery*'s 1990 release, in reaction to an escalating number of celebrity-stalking occurrences connected to John Lennon, **Jodie Foster**, and the 1989 murder of the 21-year-old actress Rebecca Schaeffer, the state of California passed its first antistalking law. Over time, however, with the Internet facilitating new ways to survey celebrities, a new wave of stalking has since transpired, often subjecting young, typically female celebrities to death threats (e.g., **Halle Berry**, **Marion Cotillard**, and **Kate Winslet**), lurking trespassers (e.g., **Nicole Kidman**, **Sandra Bullock**, and **Natalie Portman**), pornographic letters (e.g. **Gwyneth Paltrow**), and, in the case of **Julia Roberts**, online pictures of a man who was so infatuated with the actress that he tattooed her image 82 times over his body.

Ahead of the 63rd Academy Awards (1991), Bates, for her frighteningly disturbing role, found herself in a strong group of Best Actress contenders that included past recipients **Joanne Woodward** (*Mr. and Mrs. Bridge*) and **Meryl Streep** (*Postcards from the Edge*), **Julia Roberts** (*Pretty Woman*), and rival frontrunner Anjelica Huston (*The Grifters*). But Bates sensed that she might win and ultimately received "sweet payback" after her early-career disappointments.[18] In victory, she became the first woman of her physical size to win the Oscar for a lead role since **Marie Dressler** 60 years before. "I'd like to thank the Academy," she warmly told the audience. "I've been waiting a long time to say that." She then saluted her cast and crew before managing to hold back the tears as she thanked her family, friends, and her deceased father, whom, she said, "I hope is watching somewhere."[19]

For Bates, winning the Best Actress Oscar "changed everything," including "better salary, working with better people, better projects, more exposure, [but] less privacy."[20] However, aside from her title performance in *Dolores Claiborne* (1995; her favorite of her films, for which Stephen King adapted the screenplay with her in mind), the actress, similar to **Frances McDormand**, primarily returned to a pattern of smaller, well-crafted character-actor roles following her Oscar victory. "To be out there scrabbling for [lead] roles is very difficult," admitted Bates. "I keep reading about older actresses who have to sell their houses because they can't get hired."[21] In an "art form that coaxes much of its expressiveness from the display and deployment of the human body" and that often ostracizes hefty performers for supposedly "living on pure appetite" and lacking in self-control,[22] Bates, whose "weighty looks denied her the typical route of [an] ingénue,"[23] managed to get the most out of her size-driven roles. In addition, the actress has refused to shy away from crass, raunchy, or tasteless material, by way of her participation in the *American Horror Story* TV series or as a "nasty, give-no-fucks woman . . . who'll take a shit with the door open" in the black comedy *Bad Santa 2* (2016).[24] "When I was younger, I wished I was more beautiful, more conventionally attractive," she said. "But now I feel really happy that I didn't have to go through that aging process that a lot of [big-name] movie stars [go] through."[25]

Emma Thompson

ominated for her performance as the "proto-feminist and suffragette" Margaret Schlegel in *Howards End* (1992),[1] the British actress **Emma Thompson** arrived at the 65th Academy Awards (1993) in a sea-foam-green pantsuit. On the red carpet, she remembered hearing one "fashionista" rudely snicker, "Gawd love her, she looks dowdy in anything."[2] Once describing herself as "a horse with a permed fringe,"[3] the straightforward, openly atheist, and refreshingly self-deprecating actress has freely admitted to feeling at times unattractive, talentless, insecure, and clinically depressed. But as the only Best Actress Oscar winner to have also won the Academy Award for Best Writing (which she received for adapting the Jane Austen novel *Sense and Sensibility* for the 1995 Ang Lee–directed film), Thompson has continually projected an image of wide-ranging achievement in a world that still struggles to see women as anything more than the "fairer sex."

At the 1993 Academy Awards—a ceremony at which **Elizabeth Taylor** and the late **Audrey Hepburn** were honored with the Jean Hersholt Humanitarian Award—the Academy of Motion Picture Arts and Sciences devoted the evening to the celebration of "women and the movies." Drawing sneers, the show opened with a "patronizing" montage of Hollywood's female stereotypes (the mother, the temptress, the working girl, and so forth) that covered everything from Scarlett O'Hara in *Gone with the Wind* (1939) to *Thelma & Louise* (1991). **Liza Minnelli** subsequently took the stage to perform a campy, "specially written tune" by John Kander and Fred Ebb entitled "Ladies Day," which included such lyrics as "We're taking a Senate seat" and "Hillary [Clinton] will lead the way!" Before the closing credits rolled, with the "orchestra . . . playing 'Thank Heaven for Little Girls,'"[4] **Barbra Streisand** eloquently addressed the audience with a charming rebuff. "Tonight the Academy honors women and the movies," she said. "That's very nice, but I look

Howards End (1992)

At a time in England when women were increasingly arrested, jailed, beaten, or thrown out of their homes for demanding equality, Emma Thompson's Edwardian-era character of Margaret Schlegel begins to challenge the rigid social hypocrisies of her husband (played by Anthony Hopkins) in *Howards End* (1992). (Merchant Ivory Productions/Photofest) forward to the time when tributes like this will no longer be necessary, because women will have the same opportunities as men in all fields, and will be honored without regard to gender but simply for the excellence of their work."[5]

In a year that was ironically criticized for the "paucity of substantive roles" for female actors and that saw "the ultimate man's man,"[6] Clint Eastwood, dominate the awards season with his film *Unforgiven*, Thompson, the recipient of the New York Film Critics Award, found herself victorious in the Best Actress Oscar category. Her competition included distant frontrunner **Susan Sarandon** (*Lorenzo's Oil*), Mary McDonnell (*Passion Fish*), Michelle Pfeiffer (*Love Field*), and French screen icon Catherine Deneuve (*Indochine*). Taking the stage, Thompson expressed her gratitude to the Academy (an organization with female membership at around 20 percent) before humorously thanking the following: "[author] E. M. Forster, for creating 'Margaret Schlegel'; . . . [*Howards End* director] James Ivory, for asking me to play her; . . . [and producer] Ismail Merchant, for paying me to play her, which feels very unnecessary at this moment." She then concluded by dedicating her Oscar "to the heroism and the courage of women, and to hope that it inspires the creation of more true screen heroines to represent them."[7]

In an industry that is evidently lacking in gender equality, therefore resulting in "51 percent of the population" unable to "see themselves [equally] represented" in the "hugely influential" medium of film, Thompson's dedication cannot be underestimated. As **Jane Fonda** later explained, "When we are not present or when we are seen through the lens of men, . . . our essence, our sensibilities, are not there. So without even being conscious of it, we don't feel that we're important."[8]

In the same manner, as the centerpiece of *Howards End* (1992), Thompson's character of Margaret Schlegel is initially perceived as a compliant spinster of seemingly no great importance beyond the boundaries of her own family. Despite her cheery demeanor, she is often made to feel invisible. Representing the themes of "forgiveness and connection," *Howards End* concentrates on the convoluted relationship between Margaret's family (members of London's intellectual bourgeoisie), the Wilcoxes (members of the aristocracy-displacing social class), and Leonard Bast (a "near destitute" but "high-minded" clerk whom Margaret and her sister have taken on as a protégé).[9] The movie is set in 1907 Edwardian England, when the "spread of the motorcar industry, the growth of the Labor Party, and the appearance of a militant suffragette movement" led by the activist Emmeline Pankhurst (played by **Meryl Streep** in the 2015 film *Suffragette*) suddenly "brought into question all the comfortable faiths and assumptions that Englishmen had lived by."[10] It examines the delicate issues surrounding class and gender relations in changing times, issues that, to be sure, are brought to the surface upon the marriage of Margaret and the widowed Mr. Wilcox (played by Anthony Hopkins), who rejects the notion of a more equal partnership and clings to the definition of marriage as a "relationship between the dominant, bread-winning husband and the subordinate, child-rearing wife."[11] As the film moves forward, Margaret is imprisoned between the rigid social hypocrisies of a bygone era and the progressive ideas of

early feminism (which increasingly saw women activists arrested, jailed, beaten, thrown out of their homes, and stigmatized for fighting for civil rights, voting rights, employment rights, community property rights, financial rights, contractual rights, and so forth). As a result, she begins to challenge her husband, and for her actions, she ultimately emerges as an early feminist standing on "the brink of major social change."[12]

Howards End is based on E. M. Forster's 1910 novel and was adapted to the screen by the literary art-house triumvirate of the Indian producer Ismail Merchant; his professional and romantic partner, the American director James Ivory; and the German-born Jewish screenwriter Ruth Prawer Jhabvala. Thompson, who had been suggested for the part by the Merchant-Ivory alumnus Simon Callow, was offered the role of Margaret after the British actresses Joely Richardson, Miranda Richardson, and Tilda Swinton were tested and considered. Thompson auditioned not by way of reading the script but instead by reading "directly from the novel." "And from that moment on," as Ivory recalled, "there was no question" as to who would play the part.[13] Thompson worked 55 out of 59 days on shoot, "often putting in 16 hours at a stretch."[14] Like the other Merchant-Ivory heroines portrayed by **Maggie Smith**, **Julie Christie**, **Jessica Tandy**, Helena Bonham Carter, Judi Dench, **Joanne Woodward**, **Gwyneth Paltrow**, and **Julianne Moore**, she was sumptuously captured in elegant period costumes and lavish sets. The film catapulted Thompson to transatlantic fame, and before long, she became one of Britain's best-known actresses and a doyenne of the costume-drama genre, "often playing haughty or matronly characters with a sense of irony."[15]

Similar to her *Howards End* costar Vanessa Redgrave, Thompson (born in London on April 15, 1959) grew up in a bohemian family immersed in the theater. Her parents—the actress Phyllida Law and the actor-director Eric Thompson—"both

. . . had to work" in order to support Emma and her younger sister, the actress Sophie Thompson. "Sometimes there was money and sometimes there wasn't," Thompson recalled. "They weren't particularly famous."[16]

Thompson was an English literature major at Cambridge University and "never had any formal training in acting beyond the neighborhood drama workshop she attended as a child." She began "writing and performing comedy sketches" for the university's first all-female revue. Working alongside fellow acting students Hugh Laurie and Stephen Fry in the university's Footlights sketch-comedy troupe, she eventually caught "the eye of the BBC."[17] But after the actress was eviscerated by television critics for her short-lived BBC comedy series *Thompson* (1988), she shifted gears to work with the Shakespearian actor and director Kenneth Branagh. The couple was married for six years beginning in 1989 and became Britain's "golden couple" in the same manner as Laurence Olivier and **Vivien Leigh** decades before. Together, they appeared in such Shakespeare film adaptations as *Henry V* (1989) and *Much Ado about Nothing* (1993). In 1995, they divorced, some say because Branagh — like the famous ex-husbands of **Jane Wyman** (Ronald Reagan), **Cher** (Sonny Bono), and **Reese Witherspoon** (Ryan Phillippe) — could not cope with his wife's ballooning professional success.

In 2003, Thompson married her *Sense and Sensibility* (1995) costar, the British actor Greg Wise. Together, they raised a daughter and an adopted son from Rwanda, whom the actress first met as part of her work with the United Kingdom's Refugee Council. Fashioning herself as more than the "Oscar-winning empress of high-tea cinema," Thompson has additionally served as an activist for Palestinian human rights, freedom and democracy in Burma, AIDS awareness, and the campaign against the trafficking of women in the sex industry (for which she "curated and championed an art installation" in London's Trafalgar Square).[18] She has also sailed to the Arctic as part of "a Greenpeace mission to highlight global warming" and once took part "in an anti-fracking demonstration" that provoked an angry local English farmer to spray liquid manure at her.[19]

At the 2014 National Board of Review gala, **Meryl Streep**, Thompson's former costar from the 2003 TV miniseries *Angels in America*, praised the British actress for her political efforts and achievements as "a rabid, man-eating feminist, like I am." "She's a thinker," gushed **Streep**. "She's a living, acting conscience. Emma considers carefully what the fuck she is putting out into the culture. Emma thinks, 'Is this helpful?' Not, 'Will it build my brand?' . . . 'Will I get a sequel out of it, or a boat? Or a perfume contract?'"[20] Thompson, who once appeared as a fictitious Hillary Clinton in the political satire *Primary Colors* (1998) and whose stand-up-comedy-like interviews are "packed with feminist views and critiques of the male-dominated Hollywood" and the "centuries of entitlement" that men have enjoyed, then took the stage.[21] Boldly and barefooted, she addressed the audience. "I've taken my heels off as a feminist statement," she said. "Because why do we wear them? They're so painful. And pointless, really."[22]

Holly Hunter

Holly Hunter, according to Steven Spielberg (who directed the actress in 1989's *Always*), is never happy "unless she is on treacherous terrain."[1] Wanting to go beyond the clichéd status quo, Hunter, who once described her career trajectory as horizontal as opposed to vertical, predicted that she would not have a very "long life on anybody's A-list" as a result of her "odd" tastes.[2] As she has commuted between film, theater, and television, those tastes have manifested themselves in the hit black comedy *Raising Arizona* (1987), the TV movie *Roe vs. Wade* (1989), the psychosexual film *Crash* (1996), the perpetual split-screen experimentation *Time Code* (2000), and the multicultural romantic comedy *The Big Sick* (2017). But throughout her adventure-seeking career, the motivating force behind these decisions has remained the same: namely, a determined drive to deeply explore the interior lives of the various women whom she inhabits.

The youngest of seven children, Hunter was born on March 20, 1958, and raised on a 250-acre farm in Conyers, Georgia. After Hunter performed as Helen Keller in a fifth-grade production of *The Miracle Worker*, her parents encouraged their petite, tomboyish daughter to pursue her acting ambitions. She went on to study drama at Carnegie Mellon University in Pittsburgh, where she was unsuccessfully persuaded to lose her melodious Georgian accent. Like **Meryl Streep** and **Frances McDormand**, she then attended the Yale School of Drama before moving to New York City. As a struggling actor, she waitressed and shared a Bronx (and then Greenwich Village) apartment with **McDormand** while falling in "with a cutting-edge group of young artists."[3] Around this time, Hunter met the playwright Beth Henley in a stalled elevator. Marking the first of several collaborations that Hunter has had with a female writer or director (which also include partnerships

The Piano (1993)

In *The Piano* (1993), Holly Hunter stars as a 19th-century mail-order bride who arrives to New Zealand alongside her illegitimate, nine-year-old daughter (played by Anna Paquin). Directed by a woman (Jane Campion), produced by a woman (Jan Chapman), and told from a feminist perspective, the film became an important benchmark in women's cinema. (Miramax/Photofest)

with **Jodie Foster**, Catherine Hardwicke, and Diablo Cody), the actress was cast in Henley's hit Broadway play *Crimes of the Heart* (1982),

By the time Hunter had made *The Piano* (1993), she was already a household name via her Best Actress Oscar–nominated performance in *Broadcast News* (1987). Set in the 1850s, *The Piano* tells the story of Ada McGrath, a woman who is "obligated by her Scottish father to marry" a wealthy and insensitive English landowner (played by Sam Neill) "living in colonial New Zealand." As a strong-willed mail-order bride, Ada, who has inexplicably willed "herself not to speak since she was six,"[4] arrives to New Zealand's savage shores alongside her illegitimate, nine-year-old daughter/interpreter, Flora (played by Anna Paquin). On the beach, she is forced to leave her too-cumbersome-to-carry piano—"her chief mode of self-expression"— before traveling through bush and mud in a period hoop skirt to the desolate, "stunted pioneer community" that she and her daughter apprehensively join.[5] Constrained by her husband (and his control of all of her personal possessions), Ada is finally permitted to reunite with her piano by giving "lessons" to the illiterate, Māori-indoctrinated local plantation worker George Baines (Harvey Keitel).

The Piano hails from the same narrative time frame as *Jezebel* (1938; with **Bette Davis**), *Gone with the Wind* (1939; with **Vivien Leigh**), *The Song of Bernadette* (1943; with **Jennifer Jones**), and *The Heiress* (1949; with **Olivia de Havilland**), but the film offered audiences a bold, personal, and far more liberal depiction of mid-19th-century female sexuality than was previously projected. In one of the most nuanced portrayals of female sexual gratification since **Jane Fonda** "acted in a breakout scene . . . on the receiving end of oral sex" in *Coming Home* (1978), Hunter's Ada eventually participates in sexual acts with Baines, knowing "that the consequences for doing so will mean a great sacrifice for herself in a social sense."[6] A community theater production of the French literary folktale *Bluebeard* (about a psychopathic multiple-wife-murdering husband) foreshadows the film's harrowing climax, in which "tragedy follows faster than Cathy can follow Heathcliff to the moors of Brontë country."[7] After spying on the illicit lovers, Ada's husband subjects his wife to attempted marital rape and barricades her as a prisoner in their home. Driven by rage after he learns that she has continued to disobey him, he chops "off one of her fingers in a fruitless attempt to control her."[8] But strangely liberated following a flirtation with suicide, Ada begins life anew. "George has fashioned me a metal finger tip," her inner voice reveals at the end. "I am quite the town freak, which satisfies!"[9]

Taking place in a country (New Zealand) that became the first to grant women the right to vote in 1893, *The Piano* is told from a feminist point of view. Its story unfolds at a time when women throughout the world were exceedingly limited by social, cultural, and/or legal factors and instilled with the notion of their own inferiority. Not only did women yield ownership of their property to their husbands once they married, but they were restricted in their movements and could not vote, file lawsuits, sign contracts, or have their own money. While the principles of the women's rights movement were first conceived at the 1848 Seneca Falls Convention in upstate New York and were bolstered by the likes of the social activists Elizabeth Cady Stanton and Susan B. Anthony, women at this time were excluded from any political involvement and had practically no serious job or educational opportunities. Moreover, female writers such as Amantine Lucile Aurore Dupin (aka George Sand), Mary Anne Evans (aka George Eliot), the Brontë sisters, and Louisa May Alcott were forced to publish under masculine pseudonyms; Jane Austen's name, in fact, "never appeared on . . . any of her . . . novels until after her death in 1817."[10]

Intriguingly, *The Piano* proved to be an important benchmark in women's cinema in its own right. The film was written and directed by the New Zealand–born, Sydney, Australia–based director Jane Campion, who, for her work, became the first (and only) woman director to win the prestigious Palme d'Or at the Cannes Film Festival. Although she ultimately lost to Steven Spielberg for *Schindler's List*, Campion later became the second of only five female directors ever to be nominated for the Best Director Oscar (after the 1977 nominee Lina Wertmüller and before Sofia Coppola, 2010 winner Kathryn Bigelow, and Greta Gerwig).

In casting the role of Ada, Campion considered the likes of Jennifer Jason Leigh, the French actresses Juliette Binoche and Isabelle Huppert, and the former Best Actress Oscar winner **Marlee Matlin**. Undeniably, Campion "had some reservations" when Hunter doggedly pursued the central role, since the actress had established herself as a loud, talkative "fireball of energy" associated with characters who use "language as their weapon against the world."[11] But in masterfully portraying a hearing woman who communicates with simple gestures (e.g., "the tightness of lips," a certain "expression in the eyes"), Hunter not only secured the part but also developed "an original sign language" for her character with the assistance of an American Sign Language instructor.[12] What is more, Hunter, who had once hoped to become a concert pianist, performed original pieces written by the film's composer, Michael Nyman, onscreen. As the crew set up for a scene, she would often be heard practicing nearby.

For her efforts, Hunter went on to become the fifth woman, after **Shirley Booth** (who received a special mention), **Simone Signoret**, **Sophia Loren**, and **Sally Field**, to capture both the Oscar and the Cannes Film Festival's Prix d'interprétation feminine for the same role. At the 66th Academy Awards (1994)—the first Oscar ceremony hosted exclusively by a woman (Whoopi Goldberg), the actress, alongside **Emma Thompson**, found herself as a double nominee, as she was additionally nominated in the Best Supporting Actress category for her performance in *The Firm*. (She lost to her 11-year-old *Piano* costar Anna Paquin.) Although Hunter took virtually "every other major acting accolade" in the world for her lead performance in *The Piano*,[13] she still faced a formidable field of Best Actress contenders, including the previous year's winner, **Emma Thompson** (*The Remains of the Day*), Debra Winger (*Shadowlands*), Stockard Channing (*Six Degrees of Separation*), and Angela Bassett (*What's Love Got to Do with It*), who "emerged as a strong sentimental favorite" for her performance as the battered singer/superstar Tina Turner.[14]

Hunter, who met her future (and now former) husband, the *Schindler's List* cinematographer Janusz Kamiński, by way of awards-season-related events, accepted her Oscar from the presenter Al Pacino and graciously addressed the audience. "I'm so overwhelmed," she said. "To be with that group of actresses just slays me." She then went on to thank her parents, her first piano teacher, and everyone involved in *The Piano* before delivering a poignant note of gratitude to Miramax cofounders Bob and Harvey Weinstein, whose 1981 horror/slasher *The Burning* marked not only the beginning of their successful film distribution company but also Hunter's feature-film debut. Thirteen years onward, after the releases of such prosex, feminism-leaning Miramax productions as *sex, lies, and videotape* (1989), the documentary *Madonna: Truth or Dare* (1991), and *The Crying Game* (1992), Hunter underscored her appreciation. "You . . . break my heart with your uncensored passion and support for this movie. Thank you . . . for letting this movie in."[15]

Following her Oscar success, Hunter began to notice lead roles for women of her age gradually evaporating. As a result, she began to produce her own starring vehicles and, for three seasons beginning in 2007, played the alcoholic police detective Grace Hanadarko in the television crime drama *Saving Grace*. In 2013, Hunter additionally reteamed with Campion for the TV miniseries *Top of the Lake*, in which she played a women's camp guru. "I've been straddling . . . two worlds," the actress admitted. "That's always offered me my own advantages and my own challenges."[16]

At the age of 47, Hunter, with her romantic partner, the British actor Gordon MacDonald, became a first-time mom by giving birth to twin sons.

Jessica Lange

When the film producer Dino De Laurentiis was evaluating the newcomer **Meryl Streep** as part of the audition process for the 1976 remake of *King Kong*, he dismissively asked his assistant/son in Italian, "Why do you bring me *this*?"[1] Consistent with casting decisions that misjudge "women on the way they look" or callously subject them to questionable, misogynistic protocols (including intimidation and sexual harassment), **Jessica Lange**—a model and New York City barmaid "living in [a condemned] apartment in the West Village that had no hot water"[2]—was in turn rejected by the producer for appearing too gawky. However, when De Laurentiis was told that Lange's screen test showed attributes that she had not projected in person, the director, who had been castigated by **Streep** in Italian for his offensive remarks, hired her for the part that was once made famous by Fay Wray as the movie monster's cheesecake love interest. Although Lange was "derided by critics and [seemingly] condemned to the purgatory of bimbohood"[3] with the commercial success of *King Kong* and its groundbreaking, pre–*Star Wars* (1977) merchandising tie-ins, she became an overnight sensation. Unpredictably, she went on to become one of the most revered actors of her generation.

Born in the rural surroundings of Cloquet, Minnesota, on April 20, 1949, Lange was raised in a "tumultuous family" of Polish and Finnish descent. Her "restless, hard-drinking" father (a traveling salesman) moved his wife and four children at least "12 times by the time Jessica reached her last year of high school."[4] As a child, Lange entertained herself by imitating the movements, gestures, and expressions of characters from old movies that she had seen on TV (such as **Vivien Leigh**'s Scarlett O'Hara and **Olivia de Havilland**'s Melanie Hamilton). Additionally, she

Blue Sky (1994)

Jessica Lange, in character, poses for a publicity photo for *Blue Sky* (1994), a film that had been shelved for three years due to the bankruptcy of Orion Pictures. (Orion Pictures Corporation/ Photofest)

watched programs such as the conventional, American-nuclear-family sitcom *The Donna Reed Show* (1958–1966) that, in the words of the actress, "created a totally false image of what family was" and made her think "that what was going on in [her own] family was absolutely nightmarish."[5]

"At a provocative time" in late-1960s America,[6] Lange enrolled on a scholarship as a photography and art history student at the University of Minnesota before ditching college altogether for a life on the road with her new husband, the 26-year-old Spanish photographer, filmmaker, and university professor Francisco "Paco" Grande. Reflecting on their "hippie odyssey,"[7] the actress affectionately recalled moving "from town to town" across the United States, South America, and Europe. "For no reason at all you'd get in the car and drive across [the country] with strangers. You'd spend nights in houses where you didn't even know who lived there." However, with her marriage unraveling and the "things that had galvanized [her] generation" steadily evaporating,[8] Lange moved to Paris in the early 1970s. There, she took dance courses with the Opéra-Comique, worked as a street performer, and—inspired by the film director Marcel Carné's *Les enfants du paradis* (1945)—studied classical mime with Étienne DeCroux.

At a pivotal moment in her career, Lange was additionally discovered in Paris by the Karl Lagerfeld associate Antonio Lopez, a "virtuosic illustrator" who had become known for using Black models and spearheading such popular trends in fashion as "mohawks, oversized jewelry, and pierced ears for men."[9] For a specific advertising assignment, Lopez needed a "young Marilyn Monroe type." Having spotted Lange "somewhere around the rue de Seine," he obsessively "put notes on every single . . . lamppost in the area," hoping that "the blonde American girl" would somehow respond.[10] After two weeks, Lange showed up at Lopez's studio with his note in hand, and before long, she was sharing a flat in the Saint-Germain-des-Prés with fellow Lopez models Jerry Hall and the gender-bending, soon-to-be disco/reggae/new-wave icon Grace Jones. Fully engaged in the Parisian nightlife and rarely having to pay for anything, the flatmates partied at such venues as the gay-oriented Club Le Sept, where **Sophia Loren**, Roman Polanski, Yves Saint Laurent, Giorgio Armani, Karl Lagerfeld, and "all the top models would have a table."[11] "It was a really strange time," remembered Jones, "because we felt free to be what we wanted to be."[12] "We had brazen appetites and desires. If we went to a straight club, every man in the room would approach us. Sometimes they would drink to pluck up the courage."[13]

By the time Lange returned to the United States in the mid-1970s and became a part-time model at the Wilhelmina Agency, the dust of Watergate and the Vietnam War were barely beginning to settle. "Artistically restless" and uncomfortable with being branded as a superficial sex symbol via *King Kong*, Lange, with her "fragile vulnerability" and "distant air,"[14] eventually shifted gears. "Given full credence as an actor,"[15] she subsequently floored audiences in the director/choreographer Bob Fosse's *All That Jazz* (1979) and in the erotic-thriller remake of *The Postman Always Rings Twice* (1981). Making history, she became the first female performer

Jessica Lange's character sets out to flaunt her sexuality in front of military personnel and their wives in *Blue Sky* (1994). (Orion Pictures Corporation/Photofest)

since Teresa Wright (in 1943) to land *two* Oscar nominations in the same year, ultimately winning in the Best Supporting Actress category for the box-office hit *Tootsie* (1982) while being nominated in the lead category for her schizophrenic portrayal of the 1930s Hollywood star Frances Farmer in *Frances* (1982; her personal favorite of her films). Lange, who ended her relationship with the Russian ballet dancer Mikhail Baryshnikov to begin a new one with the American actor and playwright Sam Shepard, in a short time became a perennial 1980s Oscar nominee by way of playing a wide range of "gutsy and wonderfully intuitive" roles that explored the "catastrophic misery" of "complex women given a raw deal."[16]

In keeping with this tendency, Lange signed up in 1989 for the part of Carly Marshall in *Blue Sky* (1994). Set in the "litter box" of early-1960s Alabama, the drama centers on the turbulent inner conflict of her character—an isolated, sex-crazed, manic-depressive army housewife and mother "tormented by pressure to conform."[17] Carly, whom we first see "roaming half nude on a beach,"[18] models her appearance on Marilyn Monroe, **Elizabeth Taylor**, and Brigitte Bardot. Much like the rebellious, free-spirited characters portrayed by **Bette Davis**, **Judy Holliday**, and **Nicole Kidman** in *Jezebel* (1938), *Born Yesterday* (1950), and *The Hours* (2002), respectively, Carly is agonizingly trapped inside a repressed and stodgy world in which she does not belong. While she fears that she is "losing her looks" and "disappearing altogether,"[19] she yearns for her personal freedom. Bearing similarities to the scene from *Jezebel* in which **Bette Davis**'s character scandalously arrives in a sleeveless red dress to an all-white cotillion ball, Carly—drunk and also wearing a sleeveless red dress—flirts openly on the dance floor at a military party with a base commander (played by Powers Boothe) before her army-major husband (Tommy Lee Jones) picks her up and tosses her in a swimming pool.

Lange recollected her own contempt for the confining postwar conventionality that she experienced as a child as she plunged herself into the character of Carly. Distinct from the acting processes of, say, **Anne Bancroft** (who mysteriously pulled "a small, folded-up piece of paper out of her pocket," read it, and "then carefully [refolded] the note and [tucked] it away"), **Diane Keaton** (who listened to music before immersing herself into a role), or **Sissy Spacek** (who stayed "in character . . . on and off the set"),[20] Lange often accomplished her acting goals in part with the restorative use of aromatherapy.

Blue Sky was completed in 1991 but was forced to sit "on a shelf in a bank vault in New York City" due to the bankruptcy of Orion Pictures.[21] After Lange made her Broadway debut as Blanche DuBois in *A Streetcar Named Desire*, the film was finally released in September 1994 and grossed only $3.4 million (the lowest for any Best Actress Oscar–winning movie). Indeed, the film was scarcely seen in theaters by anybody, including its director, Tony Richardson—a prominent member of the 1960s British New Wave movement who died from AIDS in late 1991.

Nevertheless, in a wide-open year for lead actresses, Lange found herself nominated as a dark-horse contender ahead of the 67th Academy Awards (1995). Her competition included **Susan Sarandon** (*The Client*), Winona Ryder (*Little Women*), the British actress Miranda Richardson (*Tom & Viv*), and former winner **Jodie Foster** (*Nell*). Lange fittingly characterized her ultimate victory as an "unexpected treat."[22] "I want to thank the Academy so much," she told the audience. "This is such a wonderful honor, especially for a little film that seemed to have no future."[23]

Once described by Jack Nicholson as a "cross between a fawn and a Buick" for her instinctual ability to "displace . . . vulnerability with steely reserve,"[24] Lange has continued to appear in demanding and far-reaching film, stage, and television projects. When she is not performing, she has allocated much of her time as a Goodwill Ambassador for UNICEF, focusing on HIV/AIDS reduction in countries such as Russia, the French-speaking Democratic Republic of the Congo, and other areas where "few pampered Hollywood celebrities would even consider" going to. "Jessica has a lot of courage and compassion," explained fellow UNICEF Goodwill Ambassador **Susan Sarandon**. "It's not everyone who can deal with the physical and emotional toll these trips take."[25]

In an echo of Lange's early days as a photography student, she has chronicled her travels by way of her own black-and-white photographs, which have been published and exhibited at the International Museum of Photography and Film at the George Eastman House. "I find photography to be the opposite of acting. It gives me balance. [The people I have met around the world] have no idea who I am," she said, laughing. "I am just a crazy white woman on the street taking pictures."[26]

Susan Sarandon

Susan Sarandon was raised as "a good Catholic girl" who never tried to "make waves."[1] Born Susan Abigail Tomalin on October 4, 1946, the future actress grew up as the eldest child to working-class parents of Welsh and Italian heritage and was "designated babysitter to eight [younger] siblings."[2] She left her hometown of Edison, New Jersey, to attend the Catholic University of America in Washington, DC, and came of age in the 1960s, when turbulence led to political engagement. She soon developed a deep social and political consciousness and engaged as an activist against the war in Vietnam and a Nixon administration that was lying to the American people. "I think the whole purpose of having youth is to challenge the status quo," said Sarandon, who, for her activism, has been arrested numerous times. "Before they started doling out Prozac in college, the point of being 20 was that you asked questions and were irate and you wanted to change things and you believed you could."[3] Following in the footsteps of **Jane Fonda**— who was "once the most controversial woman in the United States,"[4] Sarandon has since become one of Hollywood's most vocal left-wing activists. While she is noted for her "gentle, low-key presence" onscreen, she has conversely "maintained so consistent a tone of disciplined [political] rage" that she was actually "kicked out of the Academy of Motion Picture Arts and Sciences" in 1993.[5]

Sarandon had no personal acting ambitions while growing up, and she never would have predicted that she would one day become a such a beloved—and yet polarizing—Hollywood figure. In 1967, she married the aspiring actor Chris Sarandon and one day followed her husband to an acting audition, only to come away with her own acting contract. Although her initial projects enabled her to pay off her student debts, the devastation of being sexually assaulted on a casting

Dead Man Walking (1995)

After promising to keep politics out of her acceptance speech, Best Actress Oscar winner Susan Sarandon addressed the press backstage at the 1996 Academy Awards. Three years prior, the actress had been ejected from the Academy for having used her presentation of the Best Film Editing Oscar for political purposes. (© A.M.P.A.S.®/ Photofest) couch during her early days in New York left a lasting and deeply unsavory impression. "It was really disgusting," explained the aggrieved actress in 2012. "I just went into a room, and a guy practically threw me on the desk."[6] While **Barbra Streisand** grew out "her signature nails as [a form of] protection,"[7] other actresses, including **Jennifer Lawrence**, **Helen Mirren**, **Charlize Theron**, **Reese Witherspoon**, and **Gwyneth Paltrow**, have come forward with similar stories. At the commencement of her career, **Paltrow** "recalled her shock" when the film producer Harvey Weinstein "suggested [they] finish a meeting in the bedroom" of "his suite at the Peninsula Beverly Hills Hotel,"[8] where the actress could give him a massage. Aware of the games that many powerful men in Hollywood play in an industry overflowing with desperate actors clamoring to make it big, **Paltrow** later admitted that she "could see how someone who didn't know better might worry, 'My career will be ruined if I don't give this guy a blow job!'"[9]

Acknowledging, in her own words, that she was never "skinny enough or charismatic enough to be a **Julia Roberts** kind of actress—somebody who sells a movie on the basis of her personality,"[10] Sarandon instead offered audiences a confident and self-respectful brand of female sexuality in one film after another. Specializing in "erotic rule-breakers," she appeared in 1975's *The Rocky Horror Picture Show*—the ultimate cult classic/midnight feature that helped to keep many art-house theaters alive. She then appeared as a New Orleans prostitute in the banned and vilified *Pretty Baby* (1978) before starring as a "lesbian vampire victim" opposite Catherine Deneuve and onetime beau David Bowie in *The Hunger* (1983).[11] But as she continued to project an image of sexual assuredness in such films as *Bull Durham* (1988) and *White Palace* (1990), the actress, who conceived her first child "on the Spanish Steps in Rome sometime after midnight" in 1984, additionally came to be defined by her progressive social and political beliefs.

Sarandon received a taste of what Vanessa Redgrave had gone through for supporting the Palestine Liberation Organization at the 1978 Academy Awards when she (alongside the actor, director, and her real-life partner at the time, Tim Robbins) ignited a firestorm at the 1993 ceremony. In their presentation of the Best Film Editing Oscar, the couple took an additional 28 seconds "to decry the internment at Guantanamo Bay of [250] Haitian [refugees] afflicted with AIDS" and to call for "government officials to admit the refugees into the United States."[12] While Sarandon and Robbins heard "people screaming . . . in the wings" for them to wrap it up,[13] they managed to effectively make their case in front of half a billion TV viewers in a succinctly worded speech that had been vetted by the Center for Constitutional Rights.

When Sarandon and Robbins retook their seats inside the Dorothy Chandler Pavilion, Sarandon remembered all the "people wearing little red [AIDS] ribbons" refusing to make eye contact with them,[14] and so they left. As **Emma Thompson**—the evening's Best Actress Oscar recipient—attempted to explain, "There is something very uncomfortable about taking this strange, ephemeral thing called fame and plunking it in some other arena and shaking it about saying, 'look at this, look at

Dead Man Walking (1995) earned Susan Sarandon the Best Actress Oscar for her striking performance as a nun who controversially agrees to become the spiritual adviser to a killer (played by Sean Penn). (Miramax/Photofest)

this.' I didn't take it amiss, but others were deeply offended."[15] Among the naysayers were the veteran actor Charlton Heston, who characterized Sarandon and Robbins as having "peed on the carpet."[16] The ceremony's producer, Gil Cates, meanwhile, declared that he wouldn't "invite them to a future show."[17] But having clinched four Best Actress Oscar nominations between 1991 and 1996 for her work in the feminist-outlaw drama *Thelma & Louise* (1991), *Lorenzo's Oil* (1992), *The Client* (1994), and *Dead Man Walking* (1995), the actress/activist, who had received a ton of bigotry-laced hate mail for her outspokenness, was ultimately assured reentry.

For *Dead Man Walking*, Sarandon stepped into the biographical role of the New Orleans–based Roman Catholic nun Sister Helen Prejean (1939–). Based on Prejean's 1994 book and adapted to the screen by the director Tim Robbins, *Dead Man Walking* presented audiences with a moral tale "of everything wrong with a society that takes an eye for an eye."[18] The film is set in the United States (where the death penalty still exists), and much like the **Susan Hayward**–starring drama *I Want to Live!* (1958), it simulates the cruel and unusual "machinery of capital punishment meticulously, clinically, [and] even to the point of representing the condemned man's final half hour in something close to real time."[19]

At the center of this drama is the killer Matthew Poncelet (played by Sean Penn), whose brutal murder of two high school sweethearts finds him marching to an execution chamber. Sarandon's character is morally opposed to both capital punishment and the fervent desire of the victims' families to seek retribution, and she controversially agrees to become Poncelet's spiritual adviser, an official "act never before attempted by a woman."[20] "I want the last face you see in this world to be the face of love," she tells Poncelet. "So you look at me when they do this thing."[21] Poncelet is then "strapped to a vertical table, his arms outstretched for his lethal injection."[22] With Sister Prejean looking on, he ultimately addresses the parents of his victims to deliver a political diatribe that underscores the film's most fundamental theme. "I just wanna say I think killin' is wrong," he declares, "no matter who does it, whether it's me or y'all or your government."

Sarandon became the first woman since **Jennifer Jones** to win the Best Actress Oscar for portraying a nun, and at the 68th Academy Awards (1996), she found herself triumphant against a pack of contenders that included Sharon Stone (*Casino*), Elisabeth Shue (*Leaving Las Vegas*), and former recipients **Emma Thompson** (*Sense and Sensibility*) and **Meryl Streep** (*The Bridges of Madison County*). Sarandon promised to keep politics out of her acceptance speech and took to the stage amid rapturous applause and a standing ovation. After thanking her cast and crew, her three children, and Sister Prejean (who was seated in the audience), the actress concluded her speech with an expression of hope. "May all of us find in our hearts and in our homes and in our world a way to nonviolently end violence and heal," she warmly told the audience.[23]

Over the course of her long career, Sarandon has continued both to speak her mind ("I don't vote with my vagina," she said of her decision not to back Hillary Clinton for president in 2016) and to raise money for "political issues that she believes are significant."[24] These issues include tackling AIDS discrimination, donating farm animals to poor countries, providing services to homeless youth, and launching a "worldwide petition to lobby state governments for 'safe harbor' laws that protect victims of sex trafficking."[25] In December 2015, Sarandon, as part of her role as a UNICEF Goodwill Ambassador, additionally traveled to the Greek island of Lesbos to greet Syrian refugees "as they [arrived] from the nearby coast of Turkey."[26]

As a trendsetting, eco-conscious celebrity, Sarandon earlier partnered with the environmental organization Global Green USA and arrived at the 2003 Academy Awards in a fuel-efficient vehicle. There, "she took a bag of white dove badges" and, in protest of President George W. Bush's post-9/11 war against Iraq, tried to pass them out. "People didn't want to wear them," she recalled. "They said, 'Oh, it's such a confusing time, and then, you know, my dress.' One person said it didn't go with her necklace."[27] As Sarandon later explained, "Hollywood isn't political. [Instead], Hollywood is about profit . . . and is more upset about people getting fat and old than it is about what party they support."[28]

Frances McDormand

The French artist and filmmaker Jean Cocteau once said, "Film will only become an art when its materials are as inexpensive as pencil and paper."[1] With modern technology affordably offering consumers not only digital cameras that rival the quality of 35 mm film but also easy-to-use computer editing software, the world has moved into an era when the craft of filmmaking is within the reach of nearly anyone. The lead-up to this point has involved the constant push and pull among the art, technology, and commerce of filmmaking, which has often pitted monopolistic patent holders and major studios against small independent production companies. Created by artists and *not* business people, the United Artists Corporation was founded in 1919 by Charlie Chaplin, Douglas Fairbanks, D. W. Griffith, and **Mary Pickford** and provided a home for independent producers for decades. In 1942, Chaplin, **Pickford**, Walt Disney, Samuel Goldwyn, David O. Selznick, Orson Welles, and others launched the Society of Independent Motion Picture Producers, which progressed the interests of independent filmmakers in an industry overpowered by "the five major film studios, who controlled the production, distribution, and exhibition of films."[2] This monopoly came to an end with the 1948 Paramount Decision, a landmark U.S. Supreme Court antitrust ruling that forced studios to sell off their theater holdings, thus providing opportunity for independent filmmakers and art-house theaters. It was not, however, until the late 1980s that a wave of independent cinema, as evinced by the lucrative Cannes Film Festival Palme d'Or winner *sex, lies, and videotape* (1989), began to see a significant cash flow at box offices worldwide.

This David-vs.-Goliath battle came to a head in 1997 when independently made movies garnered—for the first time in Oscar history—the lion's share of top-category nominations prior to the 69th Academy Awards. In the race for Best Actress

Fargo (1996)

Three Billboards Outside Ebbing, Missouri (2017)

Codirectors Joel and Ethan Coen (standing in the middle) discuss a scene with actress Frances McDormand in this off-camera shot taken during the production of *Fargo* (1996). Costar Bruce Bohne (*left*) looks on. (Gramercy Pictures/Photofest)

In a film that inspired real-life protest signage worldwide, Frances McDormand's character thinks outside the box in steering attention to her teenage daughter's rape and murder in *Three Billboards Outside Ebbing, Missouri* (2017). (Fox Searchlight Pictures/Photofest)

alone, all five nominees, including ultimate victor **Frances McDormand** (*Fargo*), former recipient **Diane Keaton** (*Marvin's Room*), the British actress Kristin Scott Thomas (*The English Patient*), and the rival British frontrunners and respective Cannes and New York Film Critics Award winners Brenda Blethyn (*Secrets & Lies*) and Emily Watson (*Breaking the Waves*), were honored for their work in modestly budgeted, independent productions that exceeded commercial expectations.

Upon the surprise announcement of her name as Best Actress, McDormand could hardly believe her good fortune as she defiantly strode onto the stage to a standing ovation in a victory that was understood as both an indictment against mainstream Hollywood and a "celebration of the fact that there [had] been a shift in the age and tastes of Academy voters."[3] "What am I doing here?" she asked before thanking independent producers "for allowing directors to make autonomous casting decisions based on qualifications and not just market value."[4]

McDormand had prepared for a career in theater, and so her path to Best Actress Oscar glory is something of a miracle. The actress was born in Gibson City, Illinois, on June 23, 1957, to a birth mother whom she describes as "white trash."[5] She was subsequently adopted by a Disciples-of-Christ minister and his receptionist wife and spent her childhood trekking from town to town across the "Bible Belt" of America with a revolving gaggle of foster children. Because her family moved so frequently, the shy, stern-looking girl with glasses rarely had the opportunity to form new friendships. Like the childhood-roving **Faye Dunaway**, **Jessica Lange**, **Sandra Bullock**, and **Julianne Moore**, she consequently made constructive use out of her station in life as an adaptable outsider who studied the social behavior of the people around her.

McDormand zeroed in on acting "after playing Lady Macbeth in high school" and went on to pursue a master of fine arts degree from the Yale School of Drama.[6] There, she bonded with fellow student **Holly Hunter** on "a very dramatic night" that neither actress is willing to discuss in full. "It's a secret," said **Hunter**. "We saw each other in the midst of this chaos and we became friends right then."[7] Before long, the friends joined forces and moved to New York. There, in a chain of events that changed McDormand's life forever, the "two-headed" writing/directing team of Joel and Ethan Coen saw **Hunter** in the play *Crimes of the Heart* and asked if she would appear in their debut film, *Blood Simple* (1984), a small "indie" with a virtually nonexistent budget.[8] **Hunter** was committed to another project but suggested that they audition her roommate instead. In the end, McDormand got the part, and later in 1984, she married Joel.

McDormand moved to Los Angeles and shared a three-bedroom house in Silver Lake with Joel, Ethan, the *Evil Dead* director Sam Raimi (who kept "weird creatures" in his room),[9] **Hunter**, and at one point **Kathy Bates**. Around this time, McDormand started to make a name for herself professionally. In 1988, she appeared in *Mississippi Burning* (for which she received a Best Supporting Oscar nomination), and she followed up in Raimi's *Darkman* (1990), Robert Altman's *Short Cuts* (1993), and various Coen brothers projects.

In an unprecedented move during her second Best Actress Oscar acceptance speech at the 90th Academy Awards (2018), *Three Billboards Outside Ebbing, Missouri* star Frances McDormand asked all of the female nominees in every category to stand up in recognition of gender inequality in Hollywood. (© A.M.P.A.S.®/Photofest)

In the Coens' S7 million film *Fargo* (1996), McDormand signed on to play Marge Gunderson, a cheerful small-town Minnesota police detective who, six months pregnant, waddles her way through the region's bleak, snow-covered tundra to solve a host of gory murders. McDormand had initially rejected the role of Marge out of fear of looking like "a big brown turd in a white field."[10] Ultimately changing her mind, she prepared for the role by shadowing a pregnant officer from the St. Paul, Minnesota, vice squad. On the heals of **Jodie Foster**'s Oscar-winning portrayal of the FBI agent Clarice Starling in *The Silence of the Lambs* (1991), McDormand not only offered a competent depiction of a uniformed policewoman but also tickled audiences' funny bones with her deadpan humor, her lilting litany of "alrightys" and "you betchas," and her shocked, "poker-faced" reactions to the "wicked things people do."[11] The film profited from the Coen brothers' dark, unorthodox, and absurdist sense of humor, which sprayed the screen with graphic violence while satirizing the folksy cadence of the Norwegian American accent of McDormand's character, who comes across the most violent of acts, including a man being "fed into a wood-chipping machine."[12] All the way through, her character, while representing a profession still entrenched within a male domain, shows that it matters little who fires a gun—male or female—so long as the gun can be fired in a straight line.

Fargo was based on the true story of a perfect kidnapping plot gone horribly wrong, and it was widely embraced by male audiences, earning more than $60 million at the box office. In addition, *Fargo* went on to spawn an acclaimed TV series in 2014, similar to the remade or reconfigured Best Actress Oscar–winning films *7th Heaven* (1927), *It Happened One Night* (1934), *Kitty Foyle* (1940), *Suspicion* (1941), *Mrs. Miniver* (1942), *Mildred Pierce* (1945), *The Farmer's Daughter* (1947), *Johnny Belinda* (1948), *The Heiress* (1949), *Born Yesterday* (1950), *Come Back, Little Sheba* (1952), *Roman Holiday* (1953), *The Country Girl* (1954), *I Want to Live!* (1958), *Room at the Top* (1959), *Two Women* (1960), *Guess Who's Coming to Dinner* (1967), *The Prime of Miss Jean Brodie* (1969), *Alice Doesn't Live Here Anymore* (1974), *On Golden Pond* (1981), and *Howards End* (1992).

But even "after the monetary success of *Fargo*," McDormand and the Coen brothers "were still considered outsiders by Hollywood." Refraining from "conforming to expectations,"[13] McDormand skipped the typical post-Oscar promotional circuit and continued to forge an offbeat career. She uniquely capitalized on her "glorious moment" while dissolving "into near invisibility,"[14] opting for smaller character-actor roles in children's films such as *Sesame Street*'s direct-to-video *Big Bird Gets Lost* (1998) and *Madeline* (1998). "I'm trying to use the clout [of the Oscar] in my way," the actress admitted, "not someone else's prescribed way."[15]

Untrustworthy of celebrity fame, unwilling to sign autographs or attend press junkets, and weary of being "trademarked" as an Oscar-winning actress,[16] McDormand became the antithesis of, say, **Joan Crawford**, who devoured the glitz and glitter of Hollywood while reinventing her look all along the way. "Being a movie star is a very specific job and takes a very large group of people to help

happen," explained McDormand. On the other hand, with some "good representation," a regular "actor can work in movies all by themselves."[17]

McDormand is often cast in "magnetic but thorny" roles, and 21 years after *Fargo*, she went on to star in another independent, local-law-enforcement-oriented black comedy—the "cartoonish," revenge-driven *Three Billboards outside Ebbing, Missouri* (2017),[18] for which she won her second Best Actress Oscar. In the role of Mildred Hayes, the mother to a teenage daughter who was raped and murdered by an unknown assailant seven months prior, McDormand brought to the screen a grieving, rancorous personality at odds with an incompetent police force (epitomized by Best Supporting Actor Oscar recipient Sam Rockwell's Officer Dixon). Mildred, who works at a rustic gift shop and is often seen wearing industrial coveralls and a bandana, vents her rage by renting three derelict billboards outside town and posting aggressively confrontational comments on each one before they are obliterated by arson. In response, channeling the grit and ferocity of a **Marie Dressler** or an **Anna Magnani**, she "beats up teenagers, . . . tells off priests,"[19] and eventually—with Olympic precision—throws a Molotov cocktail into the window of the police station.

Three Billboards inspired real-life protest signage worldwide while questioning law enforcement's commitment to protecting women against violence. Under these circumstances, McDormand uniquely found herself as the voice of revolutionary change at the 90th Academy Awards (2018). There, she was victorious against the Australian actress Margot Robbie (*I, Tonya*), the Irish American actress and New York Film Critics Award winner Saoirse Ronan (*Lady Bird*), the British actress and rival frontrunner Sally Hawkins (*The Shape of Water*), and veteran recipient **Meryl Streep** (*The Post*). At a time when the #MeToo and Time's Up movements dominated "the conversation around Hollywood," McDormand used her acceptance speech as a "chance to advocate for increased gender equality."[20] After thanking *Three Billboards* director Martin McDonagh and her family, the actress—with presenters and former winners **Jodie Foster** and **Jennifer Lawrence** to her side—"set her Oscar statuette down on the floor" and sought to gain "some perspective."[21] "If I may be so honored to have all the female nominees in every category stand with me in this room tonight. The actors—**Meryl**, if you do it everybody else will, c'mon! The filmmakers. The producers. The directors. The writers. The cinematographers. The composers. The songwriters. The designers. C'mon!" With the audience dotted with standing female nominees (including *Mudbound*'s Rachel Morrison, the first woman ever to receive an Oscar nomination for Best Cinematography), McDormand went on to implore the film industry to finance women-led and women-centric projects. "Don't talk to us about it at the parties tonight. Invite us into your office in a couple of days—or you can come to ours . . . and we'll tell you all about them."[22] Boldly, she then concluded her speech with two words: "inclusion rider," which refers to a "contractual clause requiring racial and gender diversity on film sets."[23]

Aside from a flirt with mainstream Hollywood via *Transformers: Dark of the Moon* (2011), McDormand has taken pride in working on "riskier, less star-driven, [and] more writer-oriented" projects. While "testing her theatrical range through avant-garde adventures with the Wooster Group [and other] Off-Broadway forays,"[24] she has routinely collaborated with marginalized female directors including Lisa Cholodenko (*Laurel Canyon*, 2002), Nancy Meyers (*Something's Gotta Give*, 2003), Niki Caro (*North Country*, 2005), Karyn Kusama (*Æon Flux*, 2005), and Nicole Holofcener (*Friends with Money*, 2006). Alongside **Nicole Kidman**, **Julianne Moore**, and others, McDormand has additionally been identified with helping to spur on the "indie film" movement of the 1990s, which has since inspired major studios to compete with the independent market by way of creating specialty film divisions that produce and distribute independent films and documentaries. The indies are the "most fun," **Kathy Bates** admitted. "But they tend to have a $5 million budget and you're working for scale."[25] As **Jodie Foster** observed, "Independents are not so much a financial state of mind, but a creative state of mind. Studios . . . want the most risk-averse films. Quality films that studios used to make aren't on their agenda. That's where the independents come in." In discussing *Fargo*, McDormand reflected that the film would never "have been made at a studio." "They would have wanted a star," she said cheerfully. "They would have wanted someone less pregnant than I was. They would have wanted someone with a different accent. And they would have wanted a shoot-'em-up ending."[26]

Helen Hunt

Helen Hunt is not known for being a prima donna. She was once voted as "women's number one role model" and "the nation's new definition of beauty" in 1990s America. Nonetheless, the "deeply introverted" actress would prefer to talk about anything but herself and has remained "a bit of a puzzle."[1] Representing a consumer image that is thought of as unintimidating and "downright plain," Hunt, the first television star since **Sally Field** to successfully transition to film and capture the Best Actress Oscar, has made it clear that she "has no intention of helping" strangers get to know her any better.[2]

Born in Culver City, California, on June 15, 1963, Hunt subsequently grew up in the "personal playpen" of Manhattan.[3] There, she attended the theater two or three times a week before moving back to the West Coast at the age of nine when her father, Gordon E. Hunt, became the casting director of the prestigious theater, the Mark Taper Forum, in downtown Los Angeles.

As a child, Hunt received acting lessons from her father and began to perform in plays such as *The Bad Seed* and *The Children's Hour* before landing minor "guest gigs" on 1970s and early-1980s television programs such as *The Mary Tyler Moore Show*, *The Bionic Woman*, and *The Facts of Life*. But never groomed for film possibly due to her resemblance to child star **Jodie Foster**, Hunt was conversely held back. Eventually relegated to a seemingly never-ending barrage of teenage-driven TV movies, she famously jumped out of a window while freaking out on the drug PCP in *Desperate Lives* (1982) and battled sexism as a young girl yearning to play quarterback for her high school football team in *Quarterback Princess* (1983). Although she was constantly "told she was not pretty enough," "not sexy enough," or "too mature" to break into film,[4] Hunt ultimately got her first big break when the director

As Good as It Gets (1997)

Helen Hunt, as she appears in *As Good as It Gets* (1997). For her performance, Hunt became the first television star since Sally Field to successfully transition to film and capture the Best Actress Oscar. (Columbia TriStar/Photofest)

Francis Ford Coppola cast her in a supporting role in the romantic comedy *Peggy Sue Got Married* (1986).

Though Hunt was happy to have finally broken through in movies, she quickly discovered both the difficulties that women face within a male-dominated film industry, as well as the "strange sort of omertà" of even talking about gender disparity. "Women who say it's not O.K. are [considered] wet blankets or sore losers," she acknowledged.[5] Plugging away in an industry with "fewer women in leadership roles than other . . . industries [such] as tech, finance, and the military," the actress began to connect the continual struggle for women to achieve box-office clout with the major film studios' "reluctance to green-light female driven" projects.[6]

Unfortunately, as Hunt would learn, the problem of gender disparity in Hollywood is even more multifaceted. "There have always been great roles for men," **Anne Bancroft** explained. "But there have [always] been great roles for men in real life."[7] As **Glenda Jackson** remarked, the "lack of equal opportunities is compounded by the bias towards male parts." "If you're lucky and you're talented as a man," she said, "you can go all the way from . . . Hamlet to Lear. There is no equivalent for women."[8] In addition, as **Helen Mirren** irritably addressed, many gender-neutral roles that could have been filled by women are automatically given to men. "You look at a scene and it's going to be all men around a table and you think at least half of those could have been women," she said.[9] This situation is only made worse by the "persistent age discrimination that narrows [women's] opportunities once they reach 40" and leaves them in limbo until they are "old enough to play the matriarch, the witch, or grandmother."[10] "We live in a society," **Charlize Theron** pointed out, "where women wilt and men age like fine wine."[11] As the director Billy Wilder was once reputed to have confirmed, "There's only one thing for an actress in Hollywood to do [at that age]: leave town."[12]

For these reasons and against the advice of Hollywood agents who felt that television could be "detrimental after a client's film career takes off" (a sentiment echoed from the days of **Loretta Young** in the early 1950s),[13] Hunt daringly returned to the small screen to star in *Mad About You*, a hit TV show about a newly married couple living in New York City.

But continuing to search for films that fit in with her annual hiatus from television, Hunt appeared in the high-grossing disaster drama *Twister* (1996) before learning about the part of the no-nonsense waitress Carol Connelly in the romantic comedy-drama *As Good as It Gets* (1997). Akin to the waitresses portrayed by **Joan Crawford** in *Mildred Pierce* (1945), **Ellen Burstyn** in *Alice Doesn't Live Here Anymore* (1974), **Halle Berry** in *Monster's Ball* (2001), **Hilary Swank** in *Million Dollar Baby* (2004), and **Emma Stone** in *La La Land* (2016), Carol is a "thirtyish single mom" who lives in a "depressing apartment with her mother and [her severely asthmatic] son" and ekes out a living at a New York City diner.[14] There, she encounters Melvin Udall (played by the Best Actor Oscar recipient Jack Nicholson), an obsessive-compulsive, "rabidly homophobic, racist, and anti-Semitic" best-selling novelist and misanthrope who habitually emerges from his "anti-social cocoon" with his own

set of utensils to eat at the diner where Carol works.[15] With Carol gently chiding him for his unhealthy eating habits, Melvin tactlessly and heartlessly responds, "We're all going to die soon. I will, you will, and it sure sounds like your son will." To that, Hunt's character is stunned into silence before delivering a penetrating rebuke. "If you ever mention my son again," she says, "you will never be able to eat here again. . . . Do you understand me, you crazy *fuck*?"[16] While trying to teach Nicholson's character the many virtues of kindness, Carol is eventually caught off guard when Melvin undergoes a catharsis and sends a pediatric allergy specialist to her rescue. From there, an unlikely cross-class romance begins to bloom.

After **Holly Hunter** and Courtney Love turned down the role of Carol (the latter for feeling too young to play opposite the 61-year-old Jack Nicholson), Hunt, at age 34, eagerly auditioned *twice*. "I was finally given [the part]," the actress explained, "but not with the greatest enthusiasm."[17] Even as Hunt changed her "hair from

As the only American in an otherwise British field of contenders, Helen Hunt surprised many people by capturing the Best Actress Oscar by way of her thoughtful portrayal of a struggling New York City mother, waitress, and foil to Jack Nicholson's misanthropic character in *As Good as It Gets* (1997). (Columbia TriStar/Photofest) straight blond to shorter dark, curly hair" and wore "clothes that made [her] seem older," the age difference between herself and Nicholson took many viewers "out of the picture."[18] Alas, in a youth-driven industry that gives its male stars "casting approval over their [female] co-stars" and consequently creates "May–December romances in acute disproportion to reality," Hunt had little choice but to play her part while supplying Nicholson with an "aura of invincibility" and "enough sex appeal" for them both.[19] To be sure, the "coupling of older men with much younger women" is nothing new to Hollywood.[20] **Audrey Hepburn**, for example, "often teamed with . . . older male co-stars," while a twenty-something-year-old **Grace Kelly** was "wooed by everyone from Gary Cooper to Cary Grant to Bing Crosby, all in their 50s."[21] Soon after appearing in *A Perfect Murder* (1998) opposite Michael Douglas, **Gwyneth Paltrow** admitted her discomfort. "It was weird kissing him," she said, "because he was an old friend of my father's and I used to call him uncle."[22] As **Meryl Streep** later stated, "I wish Hollywood would stop feeding the myth that it's a good fantasy for a girl to want to grow up, stop eating, and at 25 marry a 60-year-old and have a fabulous 10 years escorting him into his dotage. That's a time-honored fantasy for him. What's hers?"[23]

Riding the zeitgeist of commercial appeal, exacerbated by her familiarity with television viewers accustomed to seeing her every week in the comfort of their own living rooms, Hunt found herself as the only American in an otherwise British field of Best Actress contenders for her performance in *As Good as It Gets*. In a lean year, her competition included box-office champion **Kate Winslet** (*Titanic*) and rival frontrunners Helena Bonham Carter (*The Wings of the Dove*), Judi Dench (*Mrs. Brown*), and veteran recipient **Julie Christie** (*Afterglow*). Arriving at the 70th Academy Awards (1998) in a "subdued blue" Gucci gown, the actress, who had recently hosted the Academy's Scientific and Technical Awards, was amazed both to have "a very good seat in the front row next to Jim Carrey" and to hear her name announced as the ultimate winner.[24]

However, in the minds of many observers, Hunt "had difficulty stepping up a gear" after winning the Oscar. "I suddenly had an embarrassment of riches and did not know what to take," the actress admitted.[25] Operating at a time when the 50-inch television set began to compete with megaplex screens and when the line between film and television started to blur with films such as *The X-Files* (1998), *Charlie's Angels* (2000), and *Bewitched* (2005), Hunt signed up for a final, 22-episode season of *Mad About You*. Not only did this move earn her a salary of $1 million per episode and a fourth-consecutive comedy-actress Emmy Award, but it also proved to supply the actress with more "complicated and interesting" material. "We're getting to do work and explore issues in a way you never could in a movie," she explained.[26] This sentiment was soon echoed by a cavalcade of Oscar-winning actresses turned TV stars, including **Marlee Matlin** (*The West Wing*; *The L Word*), **Holly Hunter** (*Saving Grace*; *Here and Now*), **Kathy Bates** (*Harry's Law*; *American Horror Story*), **Jessica Lange** (*American Horror Story*), **Maggie Smith** (*Downton Abbey*), **Sissy Spacek**

(*Bloodline*), **Jane Fonda** (*Grace and Frankie*), **Reese Witherspoon**, **Nicole Kidman**, and **Meryl Streep** (*Big Little Lies*), and **Julia Roberts** (*Homecoming*).

Since her Best Actress Oscar victory, Hunt "has kept a lower profile."[27] She appeared in the box-office hits *Cast Away* (2000) and *What Women Want* (2000) and later earned a Best Supporting Oscar nomination for her moving performance as a professional sex surrogate in *The Sessions* (2012). Additionally, in a gender-biased industry where, in 2013, only "1.9 percent of directors of Hollywood's 100 top-grossing films were female,"[28] she went on to direct and star in the movies *Then She Found Me* (2008) and *Ride* (2014).

Gwyneth Paltrow

In an effort to secure higher ratings and avoid weekday-evening traffic, the 1999 Academy Awards were held on a Sunday for the first time in Oscar history. With the expectation of increased viewership tuning in early, the show's famous red-carpet arrivals were given extensive, fashion-show-level coverage like never before. Indeed, the switch to Sunday from the long-held Monday-night tradition changed the red carpet forever. Whereas before "the nominees would get out of a car, walk past the news photographers, maybe answer a few questions, and then duck into the ceremony," the new format, as **Julie Christie** pointed out, had everybody "milling around like dogs in a pen at a dog show . . . passed from one dog judge to another . . . and all asked silly questions—totally stupid questions."[1] "There are actual signs outside the ceremony which say 'Turn around.' Why? Because they want you to advertise."[2]

Wearing a $160,000 Harry Winston diamond choker, $25,000 diamond earrings, and a chiffon, pretty-in-pink Ralph Lauren designer gown evocative of **Grace Kelly**'s dress worn on the night that she won the 1955 Best Actress Oscar for *The Country Girl*, a svelte **Gwyneth Paltrow** arrived at the 1999 ceremony with all heads turning. Exquisitely assembled with the help of a stylist, a makeup artist, and a hairdresser who had slicked her shimmering blond hair back in a tight-looking bun, Paltrow entered into the blinding light of swirling cameras while facing "a huge, hungry pack of reporters."[3]

Paltrow was the first in a long, consecutive line of supermodel-like recipients of the Best Actress Oscar. Hailed as a cinema princess and courted by most every major designer," she suddenly found herself in a new, exceedingly commercialized era when "artistic achievements" and "endorsement achievements" would be

In her Best Actress Oscar–winning role, Gwyneth Paltrow's Elizabethan-era noblewoman is attended to by her nurse (played by Imelda Staunton). During the Renaissance, marriage or the cloister were the only options for women from the upper classes. However, in *Shakespeare in Love* (1998), Paltrow's character seeks an alternative path. (Miramax/Photofest) bound together into a forced marriage.[4] "[The Oscars now] have much less to do with cinema," explained **Glenda Jackson**. "They are about frocks and the whole shebang of nonsense."[5] "The Academy has now become . . . a spectacle for television," said **Joan Fontaine** in 1991. "It was originally to honor the profession . . . and I have given up watching them."[6] With designers and jewelers reaping the Oscar PR bonanza and paying top actresses "between $100,000 and $250,000" to advertise their creations on the red carpet (an exorbitant fee that offsets the "income lost in choosing, say, a small indie film to bolster [one's] acting [credibility]"),[7] the elongated arrivals portion of the ceremony came to be seen as just as important, if not more important, than the award show itself.

In spite of Paltrow's having crisscrossed the globe like an international ambassador to attend pre-Oscar events and promote her nominated film—the independent dramatic comedy *Shakespeare in Love* (1998), she was locked in a tight race for Best Actress. Her film earned a total of 13 Oscar nominations, and Miramax Films producer Harvey Weinstein launched an unusually expensive, aggressive, and ultimately successful publicity buildup campaign unlike anything seen before. Elevating Paltrow's chances while "raising questions about the legitimacy of lavishing so much money on an awards process [that] is supposed to focus on artistic excellence,"[8] Miramax spent a reported $15 million on movie trailers; magazine, newspaper, radio, and TV advertisements; product collaborations; and high-profile sit-down interviews.

In the Best Actress Oscar category, Paltrow's competition included veteran recipient **Meryl Streep** (*One True Thing*), the Brazilian actress Fernanda Montenegro (*Central Station*), Emily Watson (*Hilary and Jackie*), and rival frontrunner **Cate Blanchett** (*Elizabeth*), the latter of whom, as Queen Elizabeth I, presented a divergent view of England's Golden Age. But in the end, much to the chagrin of Montenegro, who accused Hollywood of favoritism and characterized Paltrow's victory as "an investment,"[9] Paltrow took to the stage upon the announcement of her name by presenter Jack Nicholson. Choking back tears, the actress then delivered an effusive acceptance speech that, years later, she would admit evoked both embarrassing and traumatic memories. "I would not have been able to play this role had I not understood love of a tremendous magnitude, and for that I thank my family," she gushed.[10]

While many of Paltrow's films have earned bountiful praise, including *Emma* (1996), *The Talented Mr. Ripley* (1999), *The Royal Tenenbaums* (2001), *Proof* (2005), and the *Iron Man* series (2008–2013), her Oscar-winning turn in the Best Picture–winning *Shakespeare in Love* (1998) remains her magnum opus. In it, she plays the luminescent Viola De Lesseps, a highly educated, poetry-obsessed Elizabethan-era noblewoman who dreams of becoming an actor in spite of the ban that prevented women from performing onstage. In an era when acting was considered dishonorable for women and when roles for women in society were limited irrespective of the culturally flourishing reign of Queen Elizabeth I (r. 1558–1603; played by Best Supporting Actress Oscar recipient Judi Dench), Viola circumvents the "feminine

While acting troupes connected to Italy's commedia dell'arte became the first to hire women as actors beginning as early as the 1560s, stage acting in England at the time was restricted to men regardless of the role. In *Shakespeare in Love* (1998), Gwyneth Paltrow's character circumvents such restrictions both onstage and off. (Miramax/Photofest)

'virtues' of pliability, passivity, submission, [and] even wistfulness" in order to overcome the existing gender barriers.[11] In doing so, Viola emerges from behind the latticed screens from which ladies of her stature observed the daily life of the streets below without being noticed and daringly disguises herself as a man. With her beautiful enunciation of William Shakespeare's playful, intricate language, she goes on to read the part of Romeo in the Bard's brand-new production of *Romeo and Juliet*.

With the exception of **Katharine Hepburn**'s 12th-century Queen Eleanor of Aquitaine in *The Lion in Winter* (1968), no other Best Actress winner has ever won the Oscar for portraying an individual dating back so far in history. Additionally, no winner has ever done so by delivering as much spoken Shakespeare. "I think it's especially intimidating for American actors," said **Jessica Lange**, who starred in *Titus*, a film adaptation of Shakespeare's *Titus Andronicus*, in 1999. "There's such a spin put on the language, you know? [But] once you start, it's much easier doing Shakespeare than bad dialogue."[12] Through Viola, a spirited though fictionalized character, Paltrow infused a measure of modernity into late 16th-century England, passionately unlocking Shakespeare's writer's block while lighting up the screen with her whimsical creativity, intelligence, and charm. In the end, Viola proves to be not only a self-emancipating muse but, much like Paltrow herself, a forward-thinking woman of dynastic privilege.

Paltrow was embraced as a media darling the instant her acting career took off, and she has lived a charmed life that few others will ever know. Born in Los Angeles on September 27, 1972, to the actress Blythe Danner and the TV producer-director Bruce Paltrow, the actress—like **Jane Fonda** and **Liza Minnelli**—grew up on studio sets in pampered Hollywood surroundings. With the fortune of having

At the 1999 Academy Awards, Gwyneth Paltrow delivered her Best Actress Oscar acceptance speech in an iconic pink dress designed by Ralph Lauren that many people compared to the spaghetti-strapped gown worn by Oscar winner Grace Kelly 44 years before. (© A.M.P.A.S.®/ Photofest)

the director Steven Spielberg as her godfather, she eased into film acting with a small role in the Spielberg-directed, Peter Pan–themed motion picture *Hook* (1991; featuring **Julia Roberts** and **Maggie Smith**). Enjoying friendships with the likes of Madonna, Jay-Z, Beyoncé, and the fashion figureheads Tom Ford, Stella McCartney, Donatella Versace, and Anna Wintour, Paltrow has since maintained an elite status among the bellwethers of modern culture as the celebrity face of Calvin Klein, Estée Lauder, Coach, and Bean Pole International.

But in a shifting film industry in which actors, according to the *Vanity Fair* editor Graydon Carter, "are not making anywhere as much money as they used to" in view of the fact that "Hollywood is not making the kinds of movies that require gifted performers," Paltrow, like other celebrities, has had to harness new ways to make up her income. Spurred on by "the rise of social media and the ease of setting up a business online," the actress moved from "endorsing products to *being* the product," à la Martha Stewart, Oprah Winfrey, Kim Kardashian, Nigella Lawson, and Ivanka Trump. At a time when virtually "every Oscar winner [began to secure] a cosmetics contract" (minus **Meryl Streep**, who "stayed away"),[13] Paltrow transformed into a shrewd lifestyle maven. In doing so, she followed in the footsteps of **Janet Gaynor** (who sold her own paintings), **Ginger Rogers** (whose mother penned the girls' adventure novel *Ginger Rogers and the Riddle of the Scarlet Cloak*), **Judy Holliday** (who invented "a special rack for . . . phonograph records"),[14] **Jane Fonda** (who launched an exercise-video empire), and **Elizabeth Taylor** and **Sophia Loren** (who sold high-priced perfumes). In September 2008, Paltrow premiered her consumer-culture website and e-newsletter Goop. An instant success, Goop (a play on the actress's initials) has covered everything from macrobiotic recipes to jet-setting travel tips to relationship advice and beyond. In 2015, Goop attracted "nearly 1 million subscribers" and Paltrow launched a corresponding magazine, podcast, documentary series, clothing line, beauty company, and "advertising hub."[15] At the same time, she may have inspired the likes of **Susan Sarandon**, **Diane Keaton**, **Marlee Matlin,** and **Reese Witherspoon** to pursue similar ventures with, respectively, a table tennis nightclub franchise, a signature wine, a mobile app to teach American Sign Language, and a southern-themed home décor and fashion retail brand.

Retaining a look of confidence chic that almost "belongs to a different, superior species,"[16] Paltrow has often been criticized for maintaining a persona that is read as aristocratic, cool, and aloof. "I am who I am," she once said. "I can't pretend to be somebody who makes $25,000 a year."[17] While married to Chris Martin of the British band Coldplay (until the couple's "conscious uncoupling" led to divorce in 2016), Paltrow was named both *People* magazine's "Most Beautiful Woman" and *Star* magazine's "Most Hated Celebrity."

But despite the jeers, Paltrow has forged ahead as a fourth-wave, neoliberal feminist and entrepreneur assisting more women—especially white, middle- and upper-class women—in becoming visible participants in the world. Because of that, her "relative absence from the big screen has left some wondering if her passion for film is waning."[18] "It's our tendency to want to put women in one little category,"[19] Paltrow stated, refuting the idea that women can only manage one career at a time.

Hilary Swank

Hilary Swank did not come from a place of privilege. Growing up poor in a mobile-home trailer park under the frequently gray skies of Bellingham, Washington, Swank was often teased by other kids and made to feel embarrassed, ashamed, and self-conscious by a classist society that valued social standing over individual worth. Her father, a former Air National Guard officer turned traveling salesman, left the family when Swank was six. Her mother, an office secretary who suffered from depression, meanwhile struggled to make ends meet. "I was emotionally unavailable and Hilary was lonely," Swank's mother explained. "She would go out [to nearby Lake Samish] and lay in the lake. I'd see her out there, thinking and dreaming."[1]

Although Swank "swam competitively and was state-ranked in gymnastics,"[2] she turned to the movies as a form of escape. At the age of nine, she began to perform in school plays and community theater. However, it was not until she saw the performances of Patty Duke and **Anne Bancroft** in *The Miracle Worker* (1962) that she came to believe that she could also break into the movies and deliver the same dramatically intense brand of acting. To this end, a 15-year-old Swank, much like **Brie Larson** several years later, persuaded her mother to take her to Los Angeles in the audacious hope of securing a talent agent. By then, her older brother "was on his own,"[3] and her mother was unemployed. Sensing that they had little to lose, her mother, who had always encouraged Swank to follow her dreams, acquiesced.

"Bound for glory or homelessness," Swank dropped out of high school and headed to California with her mother, driving 1,225 miles with less than $100 in the bank in a beat-up Oldsmobile that "they had borrowed from [her aunt]."[4] The

Boys Don't Cry (1999)

Million Dollar Baby (2004)

Following in the footsteps of Best Actor Oscar recipients William Hurt (*Kiss of the Spider Woman,* 1985) and Tom Hanks (*Philadelphia,* 1993), *Boys Don't Cry* star Hilary Swank (pictured here with costar Chloë Sevigny) became the next lead actor to win an Oscar for playing an LGBTQ+ character. (Fox Searchlight Pictures/Photofest) pair slept "in the car all the way down the coast" and ate from vending machines and meals charged on Swank's mother's gas card.[5] They continued to live out of their car during their "first couple of months" in Los Angeles until "a friend, whose house was on the market, let them bathe there at night and sleep on the floor in their sleeping bags."[6] During the day, while Swank went to "more auditions than she cares to remember," her mother stood "at a pay phone with rolls of quarters, calling agents and begging them to see her daughter."[7] After several weeks, "one finally agreed,"[8] setting in motion a Cinderella-like story that would find the young actress astonishing the film industry by winning *two* Best Actress Oscars within 15 years of arriving in Hollywood.

First appearing in small roles on television sitcoms before showing off her athleticism in *The Next Karate Kid* (1994), Swank relied on "focus and discipline" to overcome a "lousy hand"[9] and actively searched for better parts. After playing a single mother in the eighth season of the successful teen TV drama *Beverly Hills, 90210* (1997–1998), Swank learned that the independent film director Kimberly Peirce was interviewing "every butch lesbian and transgender actor she could find" for the principal role in her upcoming biopic *Boys Don't Cry* (1999).[10]

Swank flew to New York to audition for the part of Brandon Teena (1972–1993), the biologically female, pre-op transsexual who finds love in rural Nebraska before getting anally and vaginally gang-raped and murdered. There, Swank disguised herself in the clothes of her then-husband (the actor Chad Lowe), "hid her long hair under a cowboy hat, strapped her breasts down, [and] packed a sock down her pants." When she reached the casting department, "the receptionist announced that a young man had arrived."[11] Although several actresses were considered for the part, including **Reese Witherspoon** and Chloë Sevigny (who ultimately appeared in the film as Brandon's love interest), Peirce envisioned a young, unknown, **Jodie Foster**–like actress for the role. But when she saw a videotape of Swank "dressed as a boy," the director offered her the "part for $75 a day."[12] "Most of the actresses who auditioned . . . seemed to think you couldn't be butch if you smiled," Peirce explained. "But Hilary had . . . the sort of smile that made you understand how all those girls could have fallen in love with [Brandon]."[13]

Ironically, Swank had been born in the same Lincoln, Nebraska, hospital as Brandon on July 30, 1974. To prepare for her role in *Boys Don't Cry*, she submitted herself to "vocal training to deepen her voice" and "a punishing physical work-out routine, which hardened her slim but feminine frame into a more masculine shape."[14] Androgynously strapped and packed, and with her hair cut short, she strolled around her neighborhood in Santa Monica, passing "herself off" as a boy for "four weeks before filming."[15] "When I went out dressed that way," acknowledged Swank, "I knew what it felt like to constantly look into someone's eyes and see whether they believed that I was a boy. And if I didn't fit into a stereotypical definition of a boy or a girl, I was treated very bad."[16] In addition to her physical transformation, Swank "read widely . . . about the real-life case" and visited New York City's Hetrick-Martin Institute, "a safe and supportive environment" for lesbian, gay, bisexual, transgender, and questioning youth.[17] As a result of her visit, she later became a spokeswoman for the community. "[*Boys Don't Cry*] opened up the topic for a big discussion," she said. "One hundred percent of [these kids] were either abused physically or heckled emotionally every day of their lives [for] their sexuality."[18]

Taking the film industry by storm, Swank's performance in *Boys Don't Cry* echoed the gender-bending performances of **Mary Pickford** in *Little Lord Fauntleroy* (1921), **Katharine Hepburn** in *Sylvia Scarlett* (1935), **Elizabeth Taylor** in *National Velvet* (1944), **Joan Fontaine** in *Frenchman's Creek* (1944), **Julie Andrews** in *Victor Victoria* (1982), **Barbra Streisand** in *Yentl* (1983), and the previous year's Best Actress Oscar winner, **Gwyneth Paltrow**, in *Shakespeare in Love* (1998). The film was developed with the assistance of the Sundance Film Institute and was inspired by the lesser-known documentary *The Brandon Teena Story* (1998). It additionally arrived at a time when "people were really starved for [gay] content" and when the unapologetic assertiveness of the independent, late-1980s and early-1990s New Queer Cinema movement was starting to gain acceptance "in mainstream popular entertainment."[19] Ushering in a new era, this movement led to an escalating number of LGBTQ+-related films nominated for Academy Awards, including *Before Night Falls* (2000), *The Hours* (2002; with **Nicole Kidman**, **Julianne Moore**, and **Meryl Streep**), *Monster* (2003; with **Charlize Theron**), *Transamerica* (2005), *Brokeback Mountain* (2005), *Milk* (2008), *The Kids Are All Right* (2010; with **Julianne Moore**), *Black Swan* (2010; with **Natalie Portman**), *Dallas Buyers Club* (2013), *The Imitation Game* (2014), *The Danish Girl* (2015), *Carol* (2015; with **Cate Blanchett**), the Best Picture Oscar–winning *Moonlight* (2016), and *Call Me by Your Name* (2017).

With Fox Searchlight Pictures mounting a marketing campaign that "managed to get the attention of Oscar voters,"[20] Swank woke up on the morning of the Academy Award nominations to her name in the Best Actress Oscar mix alongside **Meryl Streep** (*Music of the Heart*), the British actress Janet McTeer (*Tumbleweeds*), **Julianne Moore** (*The End of the Affair*), and rival frontrunner Annette Bening (*American Beauty*). But the little-known actress was representing a film that was produced by the skin of its teeth and had "made only $11.5 million at the

Hilary Swank's character trains to become a boxer in director (and costar) Clint Eastwood's *Million Dollar Baby* (2004). (Warner Bros. Pictures Inc./Photofest)

At the 77th Academy Awards (2005), *Million Dollar Baby* star Hilary Swank—dressed in a backless navy-blue gown designed by Guy Laroche—surprised many people by winning her second Best Actress Oscar. (© A.M.P.A.S.®/Photofest)

domestic box office."[21] Despite winning almost every pre-Oscar trophy there was, Swank was not at all guaranteed the award.

Arriving at the 72nd Academy Awards (2000) on the same evening that *South Park* creators Trey Parker and Matt Stone shocked the red carpet by cross-dressing in imitation gowns that had previously been worn by **Gwyneth Paltrow** and Jennifer Lopez, Swank made her way into the Shrine Auditorium in a bronze Randolph Duke–designed gown and a $250,000 necklace originally conceived for one of Queen Victoria's daughters. Later that evening, upon the announcement of her name as Best Actress, Swank clasped her hand to her heart and took to the stage. "We have come a long way," she told the audience before thanking her mother, her fellow cast and crew, and the legacy of Brandon Teena (who, against the jeers of Brandon's family, was referred to in the male pronoun).[22]

Following her Oscar victory, Swank, at age 25, found herself facing the realities of sudden success. Almost overnight, her salary rose from the meager $3,000 that she had made on *Boys Don't Cry* "to about $3 million" per picture.[23] But after the disastrous reviews from her turn as a "countess in pre-revolutionary France" in *The Affair of the Necklace* (2001), "whispers about the Oscar 'curse,'" long associated with the likes of **Luise Rainer, Louise Fletcher**, and **Marlee Matlin**, began to circulate. To be sure, Hollywood "didn't quite know what do to with" the tomboy actress, who seemed out of place in traditional feminine roles. Before long, "Swank slipped further and further off Hollywood's radar."[24]

But known for her brutal work ethic, Swank bounced back. Training "six days a week for three months" and consuming 210 grams of protein daily by way of "60 [liquefied] egg whites" and "protein shakes,"[25] the actress put on 23 extra pounds of muscle and reemerged onscreen as a determined boxer in the director Clint Eastwood's *Million Dollar Baby* (2004).

Offering a rare glimpse into the world of female athletes, *Million Dollar Baby* contributed to the tiny quantity of women-in-sports-themed movies such as *National Velvet* (1944; with **Elizabeth Taylor**), *Pat and Mike* (1952; which saw **Katharine Hepburn** compete in both tennis and golf), *A League of Their Own* (1992), *The Next Karate Kid* (1994), *Girlfight* (2000), *Bend It like Beckham* (2002), *Wimbledon* (2004),

Whip It (2009), *I, Tonya* (2017), *Battle of the Sexes* (2017; with **Emma Stone**), and *The Miracle Season* (2018; with **Helen Hunt**). The story follows Swank's character, Maggie Fitzgerald, as she attempts to enlist the mentorship of a sexist trainer (played by Eastwood) and become a champion in women's boxing—a sport that was banned from Olympic competition until 2012 out of antiquated concerns for women's reproductive organs. Often resembling a "victim of a car wreck with blackened eyes, a broken nose, and bloodied tissue stuffed up her nostrils,"[26] Maggie finally reaches her potential, only to be struck down by a paralyzing spinal-cord injury. She is unwilling to accept her fate as a "ventilator-dependent quadriplegic" and begs Eastwood's character "to pull the plug," setting in motion a controversial, allegedly "left-wing diatribe" on the issue of assisted suicide.[27]

At the 77th Academy Awards (2005), Swank was the odds-on Best Actress frontrunner for her performance in *Million Dollar Baby*, which went on to capture four Oscars including Best Picture, Best Director, and Best Supporting Actor (Morgan Freeman). In "a rematch of sorts" against Annette Bening (*Being Julia*),[28] as well as fellow contenders **Kate Winslet** (*Eternal Sunshine of the Spotless Mind*), the Columbian actress Catalina Sandino Moreno (*Maria Full of Grace*), and the British actress and New York Film Critics Award winner Imelda Staunton (*Vera Drake*), Swank once again astonished the film industry by winning her second Academy Award. In doing so, she became the 12th of 14 women to have clinched the Best Actress Oscar more than once, alongside **Luise Rainer**, **Bette Davis**, **Olivia de Havilland**, **Vivien Leigh**, **Ingrid Bergman**, **Elizabeth Taylor**, **Katharine Hepburn**, **Glenda Jackson**, **Jane Fonda**, **Sally Field**, **Jodie Foster**, **Meryl Streep**, and **Frances McDormand**.

Clutching her Oscar in a backless navy-blue gown designed by Guy Laroche, Swank openheartedly admitted to the audience, "I don't know what I did in this life to deserve all this. I'm just a girl from a trailer park who had a dream."[29] The actress later celebrated that night at Astro Burger in West Hollywood, where awestruck customers showered her with applause.

Julia Roberts

There are actors, there are movie stars, and there are superstars, and it is the latter category that applies to **Julia Roberts**. A "star of the highest force" existing at the "top of the Hollywood food chain" since the late 1980s (soon after Hollywood agents gained enormous power and began to demand multimillion-dollar price tags for their top talents), Roberts has long been cherry-picking "the best and most commercial projects" while enjoying "years of jet-set glory."[1] Undoubtedly, the actress is seen as having "smarts, tenacity, and an ability to tune in to what audiences want."[2] Without any female rival, she has remained one of the most bankable, recognizable, and sought-after stars on the planet, alongside Tom Cruise, George Clooney, Johnny Depp, Leonardo DiCaprio, Harrison Ford, Mel Gibson, Tom Hanks, Brad Pitt, Arnold Schwarzenegger, Will Smith, and Denzel Washington. Forty years after **Elizabeth Taylor** became the first actress to make a million dollars for a single film (1963's *Cleopatra*), Roberts—while still earning significantly less than her male counterparts—became the first actress to earn $25 million, for 2003's *Mona Lisa Smile*. Attracting both female *and* male audiences (a feat few actresses can consistently maintain), she additionally became the first actress whose cumulative film work grossed more than $1 billion worldwide (and has since surpassed $5.5 billion).

Roberts is celebrated for her wide, electrifying smile, her ebullient laugh, a "trademark tangle of curls,"[3] and a warm southern-Georgia accent. She skyrocketed to fame at the age of 22 in the astronomically successful *Pretty Woman* (1990) and has long embodied "'that magic something' that transforms actors into international icons." "When you say 'action,' something very odd happens," explained Roger Michell, who directed the actress in 1999's *Notting Hill* (1999). "She comes alive in the lens in the most extraordinary way. It's not quite like life itself, but a sort of super-concentrated superlife."[4]

Erin Brockovich (2000)

In *Erin Brockovich* (2000), Julia Roberts's title character clandestinely gathers contaminated water for evidence for a groundbreaking court case against the Pacific Gas and Electric Company. The film is based on a true story. (Universal Pictures/Photofest)

Despite her future fanfare, Roberts was humbly born in Atlanta, Georgia on October 28, 1967. Similar to **Helen Hayes**, **Joan Fontaine**, **Olivia de Havilland**, **Elizabeth Taylor**, **Sophia Loren**, **Jane Fonda**, **Liza Minnelli**, **Sally Field**, **Shirley MacLaine**, **Cher**, **Emma Thompson**, **Gwyneth Paltrow**, **Marion Cotillard**, **Kate Winslet**, and **Sandra Bullock**, who all had one or more parent involved in performing, Roberts grew up in a bohemian, middle-class environment that fostered theatrical expression as well as freethinking political discourse. Even though her actor parents operated a local theater company (at which Martin Luther King Jr.'s children took lessons), Roberts initially took an interest in veterinary medicine before being bitten by the acting bug "after she was cast in a high school play."[5] Upon graduating from high school in 1985, she moved to New York.

In the same nepotistic manner that a fledgling **Sissy Spacek** benefited from rubbing shoulders with a who's who of film and theater greats by way of her older cousin Rip Torn and his wife, **Geraldine Page**, Roberts followed in the footsteps of her much-older brother—the long-established stage, screen, and television heart-throb Eric Roberts. Although his sister signed up to take acting classes and tried her hand in modeling, Eric helped to expedite her career. In a stunningly simple journey to stardom, she landed her first major role in *Mystic Pizza* (1988) before demonstrating the ability to "evoke vulnerability, humor, and tenderness" (along with a death scene) in the hit comedy-tearjerker *Steel Magnolias* (1989; opposite **Sally Field** and **Shirley MacLaine**).[6]

As many big box-office stars do, Roberts, with her strong, accessible, and down-to-earth personality, cultivated a familiar, reliable, and well-tested star image that fans could not get enough of. In the process, the actress deliberately stayed close to a winning box-office formula, with the notable exceptions of *Mary Reilly* (1996), *Closer* (2004), and *Mirror Mirror* (2012)—three films that diluted her brand name.

True to form in her Best Actress Oscar–winning turn as a novice, in-your-face paralegal combating corporate immorality, Roberts starred as the title character in the director Steven Soderbergh's *Erin Brockovich* (2000). Written by Susannah Grant, the film is based on the true, "pulled-from-the-headlines" story of Brockovich (1960–),[7] a twice-divorced single mother of three who empowers herself by successfully helping to prosecute the Pacific Gas and Electric Company, a $28 billion public utility conglomerate whose toxic, cancer-causing groundwater is killing the local residents of Hinkley, California. Much like **Sally Field**'s blue-collar crusader in *Norma Rae* (1979), Brockovich steps up against the face of adversity and the threat of violence to expose a corruption that no one else is willing to speak of. Balancing a serious social message with another crowd-pleasing character, Roberts delivered an intelligent performance punctuated by her character's penchant for skin-tight miniskirts, push-up bras, and prominently featured cleavage—an attention-grabbing look that propels the story line in more ways than one.

Behind the scenes of *Erin Brockovich*, for which Roberts was reportedly paid $20 million to star, the actress was equally engaged. As an astute businesswoman with a sharp understanding of what it takes to successfully market her own films,

Roberts connected herself to nearly every critical aspect of the film-production pipeline. In doing so, she fraternized with the media, campaigned at industry-related events, made "the personal appearances required to break through a crowded marketplace," and was even involved in the selection of the film's thematic working-class poster. As Soderbergh attested, the actress is a master at publicity. "She's found a way to do it and give people enough stuff that they go away feeling like they got something, and she doesn't feel compromised or violated."[8] Not unlike **Mary Pickford** or **Barbra Streisand**, Roberts has come to exert such power and to command such respect that she has virtually metamorphosed into a movie-making minicorporation unto herself. With the formation of her own production company, Red Om Films, she has gone on to coproduce some of her own movies (including 2010's *Eat Pray Love*) while inspiring this increasingly common practice among other stars.

With her hair dramatically sculpted in a 1960s Jacqueline Kennedy bouffant, Roberts arrived at the 73rd Academy Awards (2001) in a vintage gown with a white Y trim by Valentino. Timelessly breathtaking, she offered the red carpet a stark, stylistic contrast to the avant-garde swan-head concoction coiled around the neck of the Icelandic singer-songwriter Björk. A frontrunner in the Best Actress category against veteran winner **Ellen Burstyn** (*Requiem for a Dream*), Joan Allen

Julia Roberts on the set of *Erin Brockovich* (2000), for which she was reportedly paid $20 million to star. (Universal Pictures/ Photofest)

With her hair dramatically sculpted in a 1960s Jacqueline Kennedy bouffant, *Erin Brockovich* star Julia Roberts—dressed in this vintage black-and-white gown by Valentino—reacts to her Best Actress Oscar victory at the 73rd Academy Awards (2001). (© A.M.P.A.S.®/Photofest)

(*The Contender*), the French actress Juliette Binoche (*Chocolat*), and New York Film Critics Award winner Laura Linney (*You Can Count on Me*). Roberts, overcoming the Oscar curse often attributed to big box-office stars who are deemed "too pretty to be taken seriously,"[9] burst into joy upon the announcement of her name. In what many people in Hollywood considered to be "a coronation long overdue,"[10] the actress took to the stage and delivered a grateful, laughter-filled acceptance speech that ran well beyond the allotted time of 45 seconds. But as the orchestra conductor Bill Conti delicately tried to usher her offstage, Roberts refused to be interrupted. "Sir," she said, "you're doing a great job, but you're so quick with that stick. So why don't you sit, 'cause I may never be here again." After playfully admonishing Conti as "stick man,"[11] Roberts reportedly quelled any bad feelings the following morning by sending the conductor flowers and a box of chocolates.

Operating at the top of an industry that has "relied on star power almost since its inception,"[12] Roberts, whose Oscar victory only solidified and added respect to her superstar status, has often paid a hefty price for her fame. In an era inundated with trash-talk television, "checkout-line journalism," and gossip-based social media, Roberts has long had to withstand, as **Jodie Foster** put it, the increasingly fanatical "gladiator sport of celebrity culture."[13] With an insatiable market for photographs and video footage capturing the offscreen escapades of stars, an influx of paparazzi have carved out lucrative careers. Surprisingly commissioned at times by Hollywood publicists (hoping to "drum up coverage")[14] or the stars themselves (who, in some cases, have been known to develop friendships "in exchange for impeccable images"),[15] these cameramen have followed celebrities (most often younger female celebrities) by foot, boat, helicopter, or speeding car. "When I was with Tom [Cruise]," **Nicole Kidman** recalled, "I don't remember paparazzi sitting outside our house, . . . not like now."[16] "I think I was lucky," acknowledged **Julie Christie**. "God, I'd hate to be really famous now [with these] beastly people [and] their horrible long-distance lenses, making dirt of your normal, developing, evolving life."[17] Just as she has confronted the media when asked a provocative or inappropriate question, Roberts has often been compelled to deal with the paparazzi head-on. In 2007, six years before **Halle Berry** spearheaded a successful legal campaign in California to protect "celebrities' children from paparazzi,"[18] Roberts chased down a photographer in her car, blasted her horn, and forced him to pull over before reprimanding him for trying to take pictures of her children.

Intriguingly, this degree of overexposure has gradually eaten away at the "strength and the mystery of individual starpower."[19] At the same time, Hollywood studios have increasingly turned "their backs on star-driven pictures" and embraced the enormous profits that hinge on special-effects-laden sequels, franchises, and spin-offs.[20] "You really don't want to have a movie star" in large franchises, one senior studio executive explained. "The films will be hits either way, so why pay more?"[21]

Showing just how brazen and self-protective a 21st-century superstar has to be, Roberts—the mother of three and a convert to Hinduism—has increasingly withdrawn from the public spotlight despite her ongoing international appeal. Whenever she is not working, she is said to enjoy the peaceful sanctuary of her faraway ranch in Taos, New Mexico, and her "$20 million eco-friendly compound" in Malibu[22]—just down the way from **Barbra Streisand**'s village-like mansion overlooking the Pacific Ocean.

Halle Berry

For the first time since 1960, the Academy Awards returned to the Hollywood district in Los Angeles for its 74th Awards presentation (2002). Marking the dawn of a new era marred by the September 11, 2001, terror attacks, the ceremony moved into its new home, the Kodak Theatre.

Wowing the red carpet in a risqué Elie Saab–designed dress with an embroidered sheer top, a flawless, pixie-cropped **Halle Berry** made her way into the Kodak on a night that would soon become steeped in historical significance. Berry was nominated for her performance in *Monster's Ball* (2001) and faced a challenging short list of contenders including **Nicole Kidman** (*Moulin Rouge!*), Judi Dench (*Iris*), Renée Zellweger (*Bridget Jones's Diary*), and veteran winner, rival frontrunner, and New York Film Critics Award recipient **Sissy Spacek** (*In the Bedroom*).

Berry shuddered in disbelief upon the surprise announcement of her name and a rousing standing ovation, as she became the first Black woman to win the Best Actress Oscar. On a night made even more poignant by Denzel Washington's victory as Best Actor (for *Training Day*) and Sidney Poitier's Academy Honorary Award, Hollywood bore witness to a remarkable turning point on its long road toward equality, diversity, and inclusion. "This moment is so much bigger than me," Berry exclaimed, as she struggled to fight back tears. "This moment is for Dorothy Dandridge, Lena Horne, Diahann Carroll. It's for the women that stand beside me, Jada Pinkett, Angela Bassett, Vivica Fox. And it's for every nameless, faceless woman of color that now has a chance because this door tonight has been opened!" Surely, the gravitas of Berry's historic win (punctuated toward the end of her speech, as the orchestra tried to play her offstage, with her frantic, almost rage-driven reminder, "[there's] seventy-four years here!") cannot be underestimated.[1]

Monster's Ball (2001)

Making history and generating a rousing standing ovation at the 2002 Academy Awards, Halle Berry became the first (and, to date, only) Black woman to win the Best Actress Oscar. (© A.M.P.A.S.®/Photofest)

A reexamination of Hollywood's representation of Black people clearly illustrates their deprived and marginalized place in the motion-picture industry: first confined "within certain spaces, such as kitchens, and into certain supporting roles, such as criminals" before branching out into self-contained musical interlude numbers where "they could entertain white audiences."[2] As the Hollywood screen legend John Wayne controversially put it in a 1971 interview with *Playboy* magazine, "I believe in white supremacy until the blacks are educated to a point of responsibility."[3] In view of this type of thinking, Hattie McDaniel, who became the first Black performer to be presented an Academy Award for her supporting performance as Mammy in *Gone with the Wind* (1939), was excluded from the *Gone with the Wind* table at the ceremony (where costars **Vivien Leigh** and **Olivia de Havilland** were seated) and had to make a "long walk" to the podium before delivering a studio-prepared acceptance speech.[4] In 1946, the Screen Actors Guild board member Ronald Reagan ineffectively complied with a request from the National Association for the Advancement of Colored People (NAACP), assembling a committee (that included his wife, **Jane Wyman**, and chairman Gregory Peck) to ensure a "policy of presenting Negro characters on the screen in the true relation they bear to American life."[5] Alas, only through Sidney Poitier's dignified and idealized performances of the 1960s, followed by the Blaxploitation "payback" movies of the 1970s,[6] Eddie Murphy's comedy blockbusters of the 1980s, and the director Spike Lee's crossover successes in the 1980s and 1990s, did Black actors, Black directors, and Black viewpoints gain some favor with mainstream audiences.

In the role that ultimately landed Berry in the history books by winning her the Best Actress Oscar, she played the impoverished waitress, mother, and death-row widow Leticia Musgrove in the interracial tragedy *Monster's Ball* (2001). Leticia is evicted from her home and ready to implode after a string of heartbreaking misfortunes. She eventually turns to the only person willing to give her salvation—ironically, the same racist Georgia State Corrections officer (played by Billy Bob Thornton) who had escorted her husband to the electric chair. As depicted in a physically naked love scene rife with reckless, lascivious sexuality, Leticia engages in an alcohol-fueled sexual relationship with Thornton's character as a form of emotional escape. In an earlier scene—cited by Berry as the most difficult to have played—her character beats her feckless, grossly overweight son, whom she refers to as a "fat little piggy." "A Black man in America can't be like that!" she hopelessly declares.[7]

Despite Berry's winning the Oscar for such a raw, wide-ranging performance, her victory was met with great resistance. In an intensely scrutinized performance that managed to stir up a "strange brew of pride and shame in America's still very complicated relationship with race,"[8] her depiction of Leticia represented to some people (including the actress Angela Bassett) a demeaning, objectified stereotype of Black femininity. "I wasn't going to be a 'prostitute' on film," explained Bassett, who was originally offered the role of Leticia. "Film is forever. It's about putting

something out there you can be proud of ten years later. I mean, **Meryl Streep** won Oscars without all that."⁹

With the prestige of Berry's Oscar, coupled with her stunning beauty, her asking price in Hollywood shot up to $10 million per film. However, despite these attributes, the actress's career, as she put it, did not end up materializing "into something magical."¹⁰ Continuing to face a tougher climb in Hollywood as an actress of color, Berry followed up her Oscar victory with a derided appearance as a scantily clad "Bond girl" in the James Bond thriller *Die Another Day* (2002). Donning "faux feline skins," she then starred as the title character in the superhero-action movie *Catwoman* (2004), a critically reviled and commercially disastrous film that nonetheless marked a novel attempt by the "bottom-line-driven . . . studio industry" to cast a Black woman in the lead role for a big-budget film targeted to an international market.¹¹ When the actress was candidly asked if she thought she would ever be regarded in Hollywood outside the context of her race, she thoughtfully

Halle Berry (with costar Coronji Calhoun) in a scene from *Monster's Ball* (2001). In the film, Berry plays an impoverished waitress, mother, and death-row widow evicted from her home and ready to implode after a string of heartbreaking misfortunes. (Lions Gate Films/ Photofest)

replied, "Well, I still think, honestly, we're still living in a time where I'm still Halle Berry, the Black actress first."[12]

Born on August 14, 1966, Berry was raised alongside her older sister in an all-black intercity neighborhood in Oakwood Village, Ohio. When her abusive, African American father abandoned the family when Berry was four, her Caucasian mother, a hospital nurse of British and German descent, kept the family afloat. Similar to the early careers of **Joanne Woodward**, **Sophia Loren**, and **Faye Dunaway**, Berry initially found her footing in the beauty-pageant circuit and was crowned Miss Ohio USA in 1986. She was unsure, however, if she could earn a living as an actress and had once found herself homeless (like **Hilary Swank**) before modeling and studying improvisation at Chicago's Second City. Berry eventually went on to appear in numerous television roles at a time when there were not many Black people on television at all. After catching the film industry's eye, she starred as a homeless crack addict in Spike Lee's *Jungle Fever* (1991) and as a crack-addicted mother in *Losing Isaiah* (1995; opposite **Jessica Lange**). Intriguingly, she went on to foreshadow her own Oscar victory by playing the first Black woman ever nominated for the Best Actress Oscar (in 1955) in the television biopic *Introducing Dorothy Dandridge* (1999; which she produced).

Undeniably, Berry's 2002 Best Actress Oscar victory represented a significant triumph. But while this triumph seemed to have signified a growing shift toward equality during a time of increased diversity in the American moviegoing public, there were still, according to one study, "only 1.1% more Black characters on the big screen [in 2014] than in 2007."[13] In the 73-year history of the Academy Awards prior to Berry's win, Black performers received a scanty, disproportionate sum of 36 acting nominations out of more than 1,300 overall, illustrating an average of less than one nomination every two years and contributing to feelings of institutional racism within the entertainment industry. In the Best Actress Oscar category alone, only 15 non-Caucasian actresses in 90 years have ever been nominated: Merle Oberon, Dorothy Dandridge, Diana Ross, Cicely Tyson, Diahann Carroll, Whoopi Goldberg, Angela Bassett, Fernanda Montenegro, Berry, Salma Hayek, Catalina Sandino Moreno, Gabourey Sidibe, Viola Davis, Quvenzhané Wallis, and Ruth Negga. Among Black actresses, Berry became the seventh of 11 to be nominated, each of whom, incidentally, "played characters who are homeless or might soon become so."[14] Spanning these 90 years, no Latin American–born actress has ever won the award, and unless **Vivien Leigh** (whose mother was rumored to be part Indian), **Anna Magnani** (whose father was Egyptian), or **Cher** (whose mother is rumored to be part Cherokee and whose father was Armenian American) is taken into consideration, no actress of Asian, Native American, or Middle Eastern descent has won either.

Encouragingly, in the decade following Berry's win, the Academy—which is 94 percent Caucasian, is 77 percent male, and represents a median age of 62—has nominated an escalating number of minority actors. At the behest of Academy president Cheryl Boone Isaacs (the third woman and first African American to hold this office), the Academy pledged "to double the number of women and people of color among its membership ranks by 2020."[15] But as the Academy seeks change in an effort to break from "a homogenized picture of the world" (and to add to its 2018 tally of 25 minority-actor victories: one for Best Actress, six for Best Actor, nine for Best Supporting Actress, and nine for Best Supporting Actor), so must the entertainment industry as a whole. "Black women [still] get paid less than everybody in Hollywood," explained the Black comedian, actor, and Academy Awards host Chris Rock. "Talk to Gabrielle Union. If you want to hear stories, talk to Nia Long. Talk to Kerry Washington. They would love to get to **Jennifer Lawrence**'s place, or just be treated with the same amount of respect."[16] Only until then will "these awards result in concrete changes" that genuinely mark a "watershed event."[17]

Nicole Kidman

"It is very rare in movies for stars to be unrecognizable," the film critic David Thomson observed.[1] The silent-screen legend Lon Chaney ("The Man of a Thousand Faces") and Laurence Olivier, Alec Guinness, Robert De Niro, Jim Carrey, and Johnny Depp have often delved into characters by way of extreme appearance makeovers, but few female stars have repeatedly done the same. Among the first 75 Best Actress Oscar–winning performances, only **Luise Rainer**'s yellow-faced representation of a Chinese peasant in *The Good Earth* (1937) and **Elizabeth Taylor**'s frumpy and festering Martha in *Who's Afraid of Virginia Woolf?* (1966) showed radical signs of screen-identity experimentation—that is, until **Nicole Kidman** vanished into the role of the intellectual, mentally suffering, and clinically bipolar "priestess of British modernism," the feminist writer Virginia Woolf (1882–1941), in *The Hours* (2002).[2]

Transforming from "one of Hollywood's most stunning beauties" into "the defiant, damaged spirit of Woolf,"[3] Kidman wore a prosthetic nose, a dark, disheveled wig, dowdy dresses, and heavy makeup "to alter her eye shape."[4] She consequently set a trend that was later evinced in the aesthetically altered Oscar-winning performances of **Charlize Theron** in *Monster* (2003), **Marion Cotillard** in *La Vie en Rose* (2007), and **Meryl Streep** in *The Iron Lady* (2011). As Kidman's *Hours* costar **Meryl Streep** explained, "Sometimes [this physical transformation is] a very liberating thing for an actor. It enables them to do things [the audience] won't let them do . . . unless they change."[5]

For Kidman, who took delight in wearing the prosthetic nose off camera and in private so as to circumvent the hovering paparazzi, the opportunity to play Woolf proved therapeutic. On the heels of her devastating public divorce from the

The Hours (2002)

In *The Hours* (2002), for which she received as much publicity for her brave performance as for her prosthetic nose, Nicole Kidman vanished into the role of the mentally suffering feminist author Virginia Woolf. (Paramount/Viacom/Photofest)

superstar Tom Cruise, Kidman was depressed and initially reluctant to take on the role of the early 20th-century English writer. But she was ultimately coaxed out of her shell, joining a cadre of other actresses who have depicted real-life writers onscreen, including **Olivia de Havilland** as Charlotte Brontë in *Devotion* (1946), **Jane Fonda** as Lillian Hellman in *Julia* (1977), **Glenda Jackson** as Stevie Smith in *Stevie* (1978), **Diane Keaton** as Louise Bryant in *Reds* (1981), **Meryl Streep** as Karen Blixen in *Out of Africa* (1985), **Kate Winslet** as Iris Murdoch in *Iris* (2001), **Gwyneth Paltrow** as Sylvia Plath in *Sylvia* (2003), and **Sandra Bullock** as Harper Lee in *Infamous* (2006). During production, Kidman threw herself into her character, finding solace in this lonely and introspective new "role to hide behind."[6] To prepare, she vigilantly read Woolf's personal letters, reread the novel *Mrs Dalloway* (on which the movie hinges), fiendishly smoked roll-your-own cigarettes, and with "nicotine-stained" fingers, aggressively trained herself to write right-handed.[7] "I lived in this cottage in the middle of the woods like a madwoman," Kidman said of her three-week shoot in England.[8] "I went with Virginia to a place where life might stop for art, and it's a scary place."[9]

The Hours, which interconnects the lives of three women from separate decades, was helmed by the openly gay director Stephen Daldry and adapted from Michael Cunningham's Pulitzer Prize–winning novel. The film dissects Woolf during the "humdrum hours of an average day" in suburban London in 1923 (and briefly during her suicide by drowning in 1941), closely examining a woman with rumored "lesbian tendencies" trapped inside a "suffocating" place and time in which she does not belong as she recovers from a mental breakdown.[10] "My life has been stolen from me," Kidman's character tells her loving but closely monitoring husband. "I'm living in a town I have no wish to live in. I'm living a life I have no wish to live."

Hailing from Australia, a country that produced a spate of male stars (from Errol Flynn to Mel Gibson) but never a major female equivalent, Kidman—several years ahead of countrywoman **Cate Blanchett**—became a national first. The actress was born on the Hawaiian island of Oahu on June 20, 1967, to a biochemist father "studying for his Ph.D." and an active feminist mother who taught nursing.[11] Her family eventually moved to Washington, DC, before returning to suburban Sydney. Averse to the Australian "national obsession with reddening, blistering, and getting bronzed" due to her porcelain complexion, Kidman—the surprisingly tall (at 5-foot-9 by the age of 13) redhead—grew up in the summers covered up in long sleeves and big hats. In addition, similar to the childhood experiences of **Katharine Hepburn**, she was carted off by her liberal parents to political events and often fell into the "doomed duty of handing out Labor Party how-to-vote cards on polling day." "There was always political discussion at our table," Kidman recalled. "We had a sit-down dinner every night, and politics was sort of the thing to discuss."[12]

Kidman was determined to become an actor after starring as Blanche DuBois "in a school production of *A Streetcar Named Desire*." "Safe from the embarrassments of height, politics, and sun," she began to spend her free time "voraciously" reading plays and assisting the stage manager at the downtown Sydney Phillip

At the 2003 Academy Awards, Nicole Kidman struggled to justify the Oscars in the context of the U.S. invasion of Iraq during her Best Actress Oscar acceptance speech. (© A.M.P.A.S.®/ Photofest)

Street Theater.[13] While her parents "presumed that she would go to college," the aspiring actress capitalized instead on her "self-motivated experience in the theater" and went on to appear in low-budget Australian films and TV miniseries before receiving global recognition in the psychological thriller *Dead Calm* (1989).[14]

Filming her first American feature, the box-office hit *Days of Thunder* (1990), Kidman was introduced to her costar Tom Cruise. At age 23 in 1990, she was presented to the Hollywood elite by way of her star-studded Christmas Eve wedding to Cruise. Shy and not usually "the most comfortable person in the room," the actress was rapidly whisked into a life of private jets, limousines, bodyguards, and an "entourage of assistants" while becoming a regular figure in international tabloids.[15] She frequently wore flats so as not to tower over her four-inch-shorter husband.

Although Kidman was told by Hollywood agents that her career was "going to die" once she became Mrs. Tom Cruise, she began to detour from the typical Hollywood-star trajectory by showing an "insatiable appetite to explore new works and characters."[16] To be sure, the actress was attracted to "adventurous material,"[17] and much like the restless **Ingrid Bergman** half a century before, she took her chances and often for little money went on to collaborate with such cinematic auteurs as Gus Van Sant (*To Die For*, 1995), Jane Campion (*The Portrait of a Lady*, 1996), Stanley Kubrick (*Eyes Wide Shut*, 1999), Lars von Trier (*Dogville*, 2003), Jonathan Glazer (*Birth*, 2004), Park Chan-wook (*Stoker*, 2013), Werner Herzog (*Queen of the Desert*, 2015), Yorgos Lanthimos (*The Killing of a Sacred Deer*, 2017), and Sofia Coppola (*The Beguiled*, 2017).

In the aftermath of Kidman's 2001 divorce from Cruise, she received her first Best Actress Oscar nomination for her starring role in the director Baz Luhrmann's lush, hallucinatory musical *Moulin Rouge!* (2001). The following year, she maintained an "amazingly creative streak"[18] for her work in *The Hours* and ultimately found herself in a Best Actress Oscar field that included Renée Zellweger (*Chicago*), the Mexican-American actress Salma Hayek (*Frida*), **Julianne Moore** (*Far from Heaven*), and New York Film Critics Award winner Diane Lane (*Unfaithful*). Although Kidman's screen time as Virginia Woolf accounted for only 28 minutes (versus costars **Julianne Moore** and **Meryl Streep**, who appeared onscreen for 33 and 42 minutes, respectively), the film's distributors, Paramount and Miramax, decided to put Kidman forward as the lead since her character supports "the larger thread of the work."[19]

The 75th Academy Awards (2003) occurred just three days after the post-9/11, United States–led invasion of Iraq. As a result, the Academy of Motion Picture Arts and Sciences scrapped the traditional walk down the red carpet. As "thousands of anti-war protesters . . . gathered outside the [Kodak Theatre]" alongside "the National Guard" and "police marksmen on stand-by," the stars—who refrained from excessive attire—"were ferried straight to the door." Using the Oscars as a platform to appeal "for an end to the conflict," the Best Documentary Feature recipient, Michael Moore, "launched a scathing attack on U.S. President George W. Bush." Later, the Best Actor winner, Adrien Brody, prayed "for a peaceful and swift resolution" after forcibly unleashing a passionate kiss on presenter **Halle Berry**.[20]

Immediately following, Best Actress Oscar presenter Denzel Washington announced Kidman's victory by "a nose."[21] Wearing a black Jean-Paul Gaultier–designed dress with "three thin straps on one shoulder,"[22] the actress took to the stage and briefly turned her back to the audience as she wept. Kidman, who had almost chosen not to attend the ceremony, then asked the audience, "Why do you come to the Academy Awards when the world is in such turmoil?" She then nervously answered, "Because art is important. And because you believe in what you do and you want to honor that. . . . At the same time you say there is a lot of problems in the world. And since 9/11 there's been a lot of pain."[23]

After a 75th Oscar anniversary reunion-finale that gathered 59 past acting recipients onstage (including 15 former Best Actress winners, dating back as far as **Luise Rainer**), Kidman retired to the Beverly Hills Hotel. Much like **Grace Kelly** on Oscar night 1955, she later characterized the evening as "the loneliest I'd ever been." "Winning [the Oscar]," she explained, "caused an epiphany which was, 'This is not the answer.'"[24] Two years later, Kidman's life fundamentally changed upon meeting—and marrying—the Australian country music singer Keith Urban, with whom she now has two children (in addition to her two adopted children with Cruise). "I was going to be like my idol **Katharine Hepburn**, who said you couldn't have a career and a [family]. Then, I thought, 'Fuck it, I'm going to be happy.'"[25]

Charlize Theron

Following **Nicole Kidman**'s virtually unrecognizable rendition of the writer Virginia Woolf in *The Hours* (2002), the South African model turned actress **Charlize Theron**—one of Hollywood's most regal and beautiful stars—morphed from her "usual honey-dripped glam persona" to the frightful, repellent reincarnation of the serial killer Aileen Wuornos (1956–2002) in *Monster* (2003).[1] For the role that the actress was said to be afraid to play, Theron opted not to wear padded costumes and gained 30 pounds instead. With the help of the makeup team behind *The Planet of the Apes* (2001), she then had her hair thinned and her eyebrows severely mutilated. While donning dull brown contact lenses and fake prosthetic teeth, she additionally subjected herself each day of shooting to a layer of liquid-latex tattoo paint sprayed on her face to create the look of blotchy, "sun-damaged skin."[2]

Physically transformed for a role in which no one would have "recognized her . . . without [the film's] credits,"[3] Theron delved deep into the biography of her character—a Florida drifter and prostitute who was convicted and put to death for killing seven men. In the process of her research, Theron spent time with Wuornos's high school friend, watched news and documentary footage, and read letters that had been written by Wuornos right up until her election-season, Governor Jeb Bush–endorsed execution by lethal injection on October 9, 2002.

While mimicking Wuornos's "aggressive physical posture," her "bruised and brutish tenderness,"[4] and a fierce, volcanic rage à la **Anna Magnani**, Theron managed to convey a real-life monster and a supremely damaged madwoman. "I . . . spent a lot of time in front of the mirror trying to pick up five things [that she] kept doing," Theron explained. "She had a waddle, so I put all of my weight on

Monster (2003)

Charlize Theron, portraying the real-life serial killer and sex worker Aileen Wuornos in *Monster* (2003), waits on the side of the road for her next client. (Photofest)

my knees. . . . And then she carried all of her tension in her mouth . . . so it took some work to transfer the tension into a different place."[5]

By all accounts, as Theron's performance in *Monster* details, Wuornos lived a life of desperate survival and "unimaginable abuse."[6] At the age of eight, she was raped by her father's friend and subsequently beaten by her father for supposedly lying about it. At age nine, she was abandoned by her teenage mother and began to barter "sex for cigarettes."[7] At age 13, she gave birth to a baby that was probably "sired by the local pedophile."[8] And at age 15, she was "living on the streets."[9] To be sure, the movie paints a grim and all-too-realistic portrait of gender and class oppression. While addressing several important topics, it closely examines the legal and patriarchal conditions that "frame and constrain women's choices."[10] In one scene, as a result of a life of abject poverty ("living out of a storage shed [and] cleaning up in public restrooms"), Theron's undereducated character is "doomed to be humiliated" during a job interview[11] as she lacks each and every imaginable qualification. In direct response to a world where "one in three women . . . will be raped or beaten in her lifetime,"[12] the film also posits the question of whether Wuornos was a victim of sex crimes and fundamentally acted and avenged in self-defense.

Theron was impressed by the script for *Monster* and its containment of "big, wrenching" moments in every scene (something almost unheard of for most female parts), and she purportedly drew on her own "decades-old family trauma" to additionally prepare for the role.[13] Born on August 7, 1975, to a father who worked as a civil engineer and a mother who ran "the third largest road construction business in South Africa,"[14] Theron was raised with the help of a nanny during the difficult and tumultuous era of apartheid in the backwater farm town of Benoni (25 miles outside Johannesburg). At age 15, she observed her mother shoot and kill "her abusive, alcoholic father" in an act of self-defense after her father drunkenly stormed home and threatened to kill the family.[15] Although the actress was devastated by the incident, she remained adamant in her unwillingness to go through life victimized by what had happened (a decision, incidentally, that may have informed the tough and self-possessed roles that she has gone on to play).

Graced with a powerful blond beauty "that swept up every man in sight,"[16] Theron, at age 16, entered and won a modeling contest with the grand prize of a modeling contract in Milan, Italy. After a year in Europe, she moved to New York City to study dance at the Joffrey Ballet School. But betrayed by a knee injury, she set her sights on movies and flew to Los Angeles. Upon arrival, the aspiring actress checked into the Farmer's Daughter (an hourly motel situated "somewhat close to the Hollywood sign") and spent her first night "scrubbing" her room with "several bottles of bleach" before retiring to bed.[17] "There was something really great about not knowing where I was going to end up next," said Theron, who adopted two dogs within weeks of being in Los Angeles. "Those two dogs, somehow between them and the universe, they knew I was going to stay in L.A., even if I didn't."[18]

In what the actress describes as her "Lana Turner soda fountain moment," Theron—19, food insecure, and with a thick Afrikaans accent—was soon approached and hired by a Hollywood talent agent who "noticed her only because she was engaged in a heated argument" with a bank teller who declined to cash a check that her mother had sent her.[19] Although she refused her agent's offers to appear in the highly sexualized *Showgirls* and *Species*—two 1995 films that, for many people, "set new low standards for [the] demeaning treatment of women"[20]—she accepted a speaking role in the black-comedy crime film *2 Days in the Valley* (1996). But after finding herself on *2 Days in the Valley* movie-poster "billboards towering over Sunset Boulevard in white lingerie,"[21] the actress began to pass on the never-ending barrage of "babe parts" being handed to her.

Undoubtedly, Theron's reasoning was further compounded when nude pictures of the actress—taken during her early modeling days when she was still a struggling nobody—surfaced in the pages of *Playboy* magazine in 1999. Unlike **Joan Crawford** and **Norma Shearer**, whose early careers in the 1920s may have inadvertently benefited from posing nude, or Kim Basinger, who was "grateful for the exposure she got from her *Playboy* spread in 1983,"[22] Theron sued the photographer, claiming that the soft-porn photos were not meant for publishing purposes. In a duplicitous industry in which many actresses are "relegated to the trash heap" after posing nude in magazines while still being asked to push up their bras and show off their cleavage in casting calls,[23] Theron's forceful stand against her violation of privacy was altogether unique. Unfortunately, the issue of privacy in relation to nude celebrity photography once again reached a critical stage when **Jennifer Lawrence**—along with "other famous young women" including Kirsten Dunst, Jessica Brown Findlay, and Kate Upton—woke up on the morning of August 31, 2014, to find sexually compromising photographs of themselves hacked from their iCloud accounts and released across the Internet "for delectation and debauchery."[24] "[This is] not a scandal," **Lawrence** clarified afterward. "It is a sex crime. [And] anybody who looked at those pictures [is] perpetuating a sexual offense."[25]

By the time Theron signed up for *Monster* (2003), she had risen to the ranks of the A-list in Hollywood. With her newfound production company, Denver & Delilah Films, she became the first woman to receive screen credit for producing her own Best Actress Oscar–winning film. (For the record, **Mary Pickford** for *Coquette* [1929], **Ellen Burstyn** for *Alice Doesn't Live Here Anymore* [1974], **Jane Fonda** for *Coming Home* [1978], and **Julia Roberts** for *Erin Brockovich* [2000] fulfilled producer obligations without being given screen credit.) Skilled in both the corporate world and the art world, Theron, who typically does not "like watching herself on screen," locked herself in the editing suite before getting involved in the film's international marketing. "This [film] was easier to watch," she lightheartedly admitted, "because I look so different in it."[26]

Having inhabited her character so convincingly that "three minutes [into the film], you knew she had the Oscar," Theron went on to win "just about every award in the book."[27] Up against the British actresses Naomi Watts (*21 Grams*) and Samantha Morton (*In America*), the New Zealand Māori actress Keisha Castle-Hughes (*Whale Rider*), and veteran winner **Diane Keaton** (*Something's Gotta Give*) at the 2004 Academy Awards, Theron ultimately ascended the stage while wowing audiences "in an almost-nude beaded Gucci gown" designed by Tom Ford.[28] In a self-assured acceptance speech, she paid tribute to her mother, expressed gratitude to her then-boyfriend, the actor Stuart Townsend, and thanked her fellow cast and crew, including the writer and director Patty Jenkins and her onscreen love interest, Christina Ricci. "And if I'm forgetting anybody, please don't kill me," she jokingly stated.[29]

For her performance, Theron was hailed by South African presidents Nelson Mandela and Thabo Mbeki, the latter of whom characterized the former farm girl's life as "a grand metaphor of South Africa's move from agony to achievement."[30] Giving back to her country, the actress went on to facilitate the Charlize Theron Africa Outreach Project, which provides health education and HIV counseling to impoverished South African youth. Largely successful in darting the paparazzi and avoiding all celebrity hangouts, Theron—the mother of two adopted children—has stuck to her guns in declining to "play the [Hollywood publicity] game." As **Shirley MacLaine** put it, "the way to get to know Charlize is to have her cook a meal for you with lots of her friends."[31]

Reese Witherspoon

Walk the Line (2005)

As much as the 2002 Academy Awards "was seen as a celebration of African-American achievement after **Halle Berry** and Denzel Washington won the top acting Oscars," the 78th Academy Awards (2006) was predicted to be a "watershed" moment for "alternative lifestyles."[1] In the Best Picture category, the gay western love story *Brokeback Mountain* was seen as the leading contender, while Felicity Huffman's groundbreaking portrayal of a man "in drag waiting for a transgender operation" in *Transamerica* placed her as the early frontrunner in the race for Best Actress.[2] The Oscar has long been upheld as a symbolic valida-tion of the cultural themes presented in a movie, and LGBT-rights supporters were left stunned when *Crash* (a film about racial tensions in Los Angeles) took home the Best Picture trophy and **Reese Witherspoon** overtook Huffman, the British actresses Judi Dench (*Mrs. Henderson Presents*) and Keira Knightley (*Pride & Prejudice*), and former winner **Charlize Theron** (*North Country*) to claim the Best Actress Oscar.

Having already secured the New York Film Critics Award for her strong but secondary role as the country singer-songwriter June Carter Cash in the Johnny Cash biopic *Walk the Line* (2005), Witherspoon, who had surpassed **Julia Roberts** as the highest-paid actress in Hollywood, conveyed the look of gratitude and breath-less relief upon the announcement of her name by presenter Jamie Foxx. Taking the stage in a metallic-embellished vintage Christian Dior gown that was once owned by an unnamed princess, the actress, in a "dewy-eyed acceptance speech,"[3] thanked her family (including then-husband and *Crash* star, Ryan Phillippe) and her fellow cast and crew before acknowledging the woman whom she had played. "People used to ask June how she was doing," Witherspoon shared. "And she used

to say, 'I'm just trying to matter.' And I know what she means. You know, I'm just trying to matter . . . and make work that means something to somebody. And you have all made me feel that I might have accomplished that tonight."[4]

Witherspoon was known at the time for having sustained a "short but steady career that . . . kept the cash registers ringing" in such lighthearted films as *Pleasantville* (1998) the *Legally Blonde* series (2001–2003), and *Sweet Home Alabama* (2002). But for her role in *Walk the Line*, she conversely brought to the screen a surprising level of "weight and confidence" in her "most serious, fully elaborated performance."[5] While the film principally chronicles the life of the "Man in Black," the country-music icon Johnny Cash (played by Joaquin Phoenix), it additionally unfolds as a love story between "a troubled man haunted by a childhood tragedy" and "a no-nonsense woman from a country-music dynasty."[6] As June Carter (1929–2003), the popular "auto-harping country singer" and twice-divorced mother of two, Witherspoon depicts a woman who, like **Sissy Spacek**'s Loretta Lynn in *Coal Miner's Daughter* (1980), tries "to break out and do things" in the conservative American South of the 1950s and '60s.[7] The film is set during the burgeoning days of rock-and-roll, when "dancing . . . became less connected with courtship, and individual, non-contact dancing led to both men and women dancing on their own."[8] Galvanized, Carter chooses to gain experience, and without compromising her integrity or independence, she tours with the likes of Cash (who is already married but has his mind set on June), Jerry Lee Lewis, and the pre-legendary, pelvis-thrusting Elvis Presley.

As the film makes clear, however, not all of Carter's choices are embraced. Shopping one day at a five-and-dime store, she is scolded by the store's manager, who underlines that "divorce is an abomination." "I'm sorry I let you down, ma'am," Carter earnestly but unyieldingly replies.[9]

Witherspoon had played "Mother" Maybelle Carter in a grade-school play and attended high school with the child and grandchild of the country legends Emmylou Harris and Minnie Pearl, so she seemed the perfect casting fit for June Carter Cash. In addition, the actress was already equipped with the "chirpy twang" and "crack comic timing" associated with her character.[10] To prepare for the role, she darkened her hair and researched everything that she could learn about the spirited daughter of the first family of country music. When she was told that she would need to do her own singing, however, the actress's stomach turned to knots. "I really had no idea when I signed on to this role that I would be spending [six] months taking autoharp lessons, singing lessons, working with professional musicians, and then recording tracks every day," admitted the actress, who purportedly begged the director, James Mangold, "to hire someone like [country singer] LeAnn Rimes to take over."[11]

Although Witherspoon had initially set her sights on becoming a gynecologist or the first female president of the United States, she pursued acting at an early age. Witherspoon, a descendant of the Declaration of Independence signer John Witherspoon, was born in New Orleans on March 22, 1976, to a roving military

Reese Witherspoon (with costar Joaquin Phoenix) in a scene still from the Johnny Cash biopic *Walk the Line* (2005), for which the actress portrayed the country singer-songwriter June Carter Cash. Witherspoon reportedly begged director James Mangold to hire someone else when she discovered that she would need to perform her own singing. (Twentieth Century Fox Film Corporation surgeon father and a mother who worked as a nurse. She began to act in school plays, TV commercials, and community college theater courses for kids. Banned by her parents from wearing black, dressing in bikinis, and applying lipstick outside the shade parameters of peach and pink, the spunky 14-year-old spotted an advertisement in her local Nashville newspaper "calling for extras" to appear in the 1991 drama *The Man in the Moon*. Within days of being unexpectedly asked "to read some lines" at the casting call, Witherspoon received word that she had been given the principal lead.[12] Nicknamed "little **Meryl**" by her *Man in the Moon* costars, the "petite, angelic blonde" subsequently appeared in the **Diane Keaton**–directed TV movie *Wildflower* (1991).[13] Witherspoon continued to lead a normal life as a cheerleader and straight-A student,[14] but after two semesters at Stanford University, she decided to move to Hollywood.

Possessed with a warmth, a charm, and a diminutive, 5-foot-1 frame (proportions uncommonly seen in Hollywood female leads since the days of **Janet Gaynor**, **Helen Hayes**, and **Mary Pickford**), Witherspoon quickly proved herself as both a comedic and dramatic talent with a variety of girlish characters that had not quite developed into full adults. However, at age 23, by virtue of an unintended pregnancy that caused a stir throughout a Hollywood that was no longer accustomed to young, pregnant stars, Witherspoon adjusted her image and become a first-time parent with the Hollywood heartthrob Ryan Phillippe (her costar from the 1999 teen drama *Cruel Intentions*). In a pressure-filled, image-conscious industry in which female stars have been known to adopt children (like **Mary Pickford**, **Joan Crawford**, **Charlize Theron**, and **Sandra Bullock**), postpone their pregnancy (like **Emma Thompson** and **Holly Hunter**), hire a surrogate (like **Nicole Kidman**), or avoid motherhood altogether (like **Katharine Hepburn**, **Ginger Rogers**, **Greer Garson**, **Julie Christie**, and **Helen Mirren**), Witherspoon defiantly embraced her newfound role. In direct opposition to **Simone Signoret**, who confessed to not being "the best example of . . . a mother," someone who "is always there when the child goes to bed . . . [and] gets up in the morning to go to school,"[15] Witherspoon has repeatedly conveyed the picture-perfect image of a young and successful celebrity mom.

However, when an incident in 2013 found the actress arrested for disorderly conduct after mouthing off to an Atlanta state trooper as her second husband, the Hollywood talent agent Jim Toth, was pulled over under suspicion of driving while intoxicated, Witherspoon's seemingly "perfect veneer" was called into question.[16] With footage of her arrest circulating the Internet and showing the star attempting to use her "celebrity as a way out" ("Do you know my name, sir?" "You're about to find out who I am!"),[17] the actress was thrown into the same kind of public-relations nightmare that had previously haunted **Sophia Loren** (jailed for tax evasion), **Halle Berry** (convicted for a hit-and-run), and **Hilary Swank** (lambasted for "renting out" her celebrity to attend a Chechen dictator's birthday).

Within hours of her arrest, Witherspoon, who has often been ridiculed for being excessively conventional and even "boring" as a result of her perky, girl-next-door image, issued an apology. A few days later, she delivered a "self-deprecating [and] earnestly apologetic" act of contrition on the TV show *Good Morning America*.[18] In the minds of many observers, Witherspoon's mea culpa, which clearly demonstrated mastery in the art of damage control, appeared to serve as her most charming and effective performance to date by both salvaging her reputation and beneficially raising her public profile.

But connected to a generation of actors who, in the words of **Shirley MacLaine**, are "too focused on the red carpet" and too caught up in the status of their own celebrity,[19] Witherspoon has had to walk a fine line. In a cynical and superficial era when we hear more about movie studios "hiring young stars because of their social media following" (a "disaster," according to **Emma Thompson**) than we do about the development of technique and artistic growth" (e.g., acting school, "actor-playwright relationships," or "the regular commuting between stage and screen"), Witherspoon has had to rigorously concentrate on avoiding the pitfalls that have soiled the reputations of others.[20] "I'm not passing margaritas out in my trailer after work," said the actress,[21] who rarely drinks, does not smoke, and is not into the club scene at all. Instead, as evinced in her involvement with the Avon Foundation for Women and her participation at the 2010 International Women of Courage Awards (alongside U.S. Secretary of State Hillary Clinton and First Lady Michelle Obama), Witherspoon has focused her remaining energies on solving problems such as ending child poverty and the global epidemic of violence against women.

Helen Mirren

To some people, **Helen Mirren** may have once seemed like an unlikely choice to play, arguably, the most recognized woman of the 20th century: Britain's Queen Elizabeth II (1926–). The rebellious stage star and art-house film favorite early on gained the unwanted nickname of the "Sex Queen of Stratford" and has never shied away from sexually explicit parts in such films as *Age of Consent* (1969), *Savage Messiah* (1972), *Caligula* (1979), *Excalibur* (1981), and *The Cook, the Thief, His Wife & Her Lover* (1989).[1] In a 1975 interview, the British TV host Michael Parkinson deplorably exaggerated this reputation in a "cringe-worthy example of sexism."[2] In doing so, he made continuous reference to Mirren's "physical attributes" and "sluttish eroticism" before asking the actress if her "equipment" ever got in the way of her acting. "Because serious actresses can't have big bosoms, is that what you mean?" Mirren politely but pointedly fired back.[3]

Comforted at the time by a palm reader's prophecy that her "greatest success will come" at middle age,[4] Mirren soldiered past the chauvinism. As forecasted, she entered into the mainstream by playing Detective Jane Tennison in the acclaimed British TV series *Prime Suspect* (1991–2006). Following up with her Oscar-winning, career-defining role in *The Queen* (2006), she ultimately reached her peak.

After a long line of young, supermodel-like recipients of the Best Actress Oscar (including **Gwyneth Paltrow**, **Halle Berry**, and **Charlize Theron**), Mirren, at age 61, circumvented the typical Hollywood sell-by date for women and became, in 2007, the fourth-oldest woman to win the Best Actress Oscar, following **Marie Dressler** (at age 63), **Katharine Hepburn** (at 74), and **Jessica Tandy** (at 80). Soon after, the actress—looking toned, tanned, and smolderingly attractive in a red bikini—was captured by tabloid photographers while holidaying near her 500-year-old vacation

The Queen (2006)

Welsh corgis are photographed with Queen Elizabeth II, as personified by Best Actress Oscar winner Helen Mirren in *The Queen* (2006). (Miramax/ Photofest)

farmhouse in the Salento region of southern Italy. Redefining the very concepts of age and sex-symbol beauty in a sexist, youth-obsessed industry that, according to the actress, worships "at the altar of the 18- to 25-year-old male and his penis,"[5] Mirren subsequently appeared topless and nakedly submerged in bathtub water for a 2010 Juergen Teller photo shoot for *New York* magazine. In a principled next step forward that continued to break down the barriers of ageism, Mirren joined a growing list of older actresses who have signed lucrative contracts for major cosmetic firms (including **Jane Fonda**, **Diane Keaton**, **Jessica Lange**, and **Susan Sarandon**) and became a radiant and defiantly wrinkled spokesmodel for L'Oréal. "My whole life, one had these images of perfect, incredibly youthful girls shoved at you as what you should aspire to," the actress complained. "And we're not even talking about 25-year-olds, incidentally, we are talking about girls of 15. Who looks 15? It's not fair."[6]

Mirren was the heavy shoo-in for Best Actress at the 79th Academy Awards (2007), and essentially turning back the clock, she captivated the red carpet as she arrived in a low-cut, Christian Lacroix–designed gown that underscored her God-given assets. Her competition that evening included former recipient **Meryl Streep** (*The Devil Wears Prada*), the Spanish actress Penélope Cruz (*Volver*), **Kate Winslet** (*Little Children*), and distant frontrunner Judi Dench (*Notes on a Scandal*), who, in light of Mirren's awards-season sweep of roughly 30 individual honors for her towering performance in *The Queen*, did not even bother to attend. Warmly accepting the Best Actress Oscar, Mirren characterized the iconic golden trophy as "the biggest and best gold star that I have ever had in my life." She then turned her attention to "Elizabeth Windsor," the woman who, for more than 50 years, "has maintained her dignity, her sense of duty, and her hairstyle. . . . I thank her, because if it wasn't for her, I most certainly would not be here."[7]

Alongside **Katharine Hepburn** as Queen Eleanor of Aquitaine in *The Lion in Winter* (1968), Mirren became the only other performer as of early 2019 to have captured the Best Actress Oscar for portraying a real-life member of royalty— something that became a notable theme throughout her career. Following her rendition of the Egyptian Queen Cleopatra (also portrayed onscreen by **Claudette Colbert**, **Vivien Leigh**, and **Elizabeth Taylor**), she played the Roman Empress Caesonia, Queen Margaret of Anjou, Queen Elizabeth I (also portrayed by **Bette Davis**, **Glenda Jackson**, and **Cate Blanchett**), Queen Charlotte, and numerous figures of fictional royalty. However, by tackling the role of not just any monarch but a *sitting* monarch situated within a period of collective grief and shock over the death of Diana, Princess of Wales, Mirren, in a scrutinized performance that could have easily devolved into satire or sentimentality, crafted a nuanced portrayal of Queen Elizabeth II that has since transformed the British actress into a major international star.

Culminating with Diana's funeral (which was watched by two billion TV viewers and attended by a Hollywood contingent that included **Nicole Kidman**), *The Queen* centers on the "anxious week" following the paparazzi-triggered car accident in

During production of *The Queen* (2006), director Stephen Frears and Helen Mirren discuss the script in this off-camera moment. (Miramax/Photofest)

Paris that claimed the lives of Diana, her companion Dodi Fayed, and their intoxicated chauffeur on August 31, 1997.[8] In the film, Mirren immerses herself in the role of a seemingly distant and resolute sovereign, who appears "strikingly out of touch" with her heartbroken subjects as "she and [her] family remain hidden . . . in Balmoral Castle."[9] "Bound by tradition and protocol" as her nation's grief intensifies, the queen begins to wrestle with public pressure (and the pressure of her new prime minister, Tony Blair) to shed her "near-impenetrable veil of privacy" and mourn alongside her people.[10]

To prepare for *The Queen* — a film almost entirely based on researched conjecture — Mirren read biographies, examined portraits painted of the ruler, and practiced "certain vowel qualities" to achieve "the stoic royal purr pulsating in [her character's] voice."[11] Mirren was keenly aware of the fact that she was playing a character whose appearance, movements, and gestures are well known to the world, so she took her research one step further to mimic the prim and sometimes playful body language showcased in old film clips of Elizabeth as a young princess. "She doesn't often smile while she's on official duties," Mirren observed. "She's working. She's not a celebrity."[12]

The granddaughter of a Russian army officer turned diplomat who emigrated to Britain with his family after being "stranded by the Russian Revolution in 1917,"[13] Mirren was born Ilyena Mirnoff in London on July 26, 1945. She grew up in Leigh-on-Sea, Essex, in a working-class family of atheists that despised the British monarchy and the divisive social structure of the United Kingdom. While harboring a "pensive wistfulness for the loss of homeland culture," her father "anglicized the family name to Mirren in the 1950s" and worked as a taxi driver and driving-test examiner.[14] Meanwhile, Mirren's plain-speaking British mother, the granddaughter of a butcher who once worked for Queen Victoria, taught her three children that it is "tasteless to talk about yourself."[15]

Nevertheless, Mirren wanted to see her name in lights. She first performed in secondary school. Unable to afford to go to drama school, however, she auditioned at age 18 for the prestigious National Youth Theatre in London. There, the young hippie actress was seen as a phenomenon and was quickly "plucked to join the Royal Shakespeare Company."[16] But wanting "to do something braver and broader," she became part of company director Peter Brook's International Centre for Theatre Research, an experimental, multinational company of actors, dancers, and musicians that "[threw] down a carpet and [improvised] to unpredictable audiences" throughout Africa and the Middle East in the early 1970s.[17] On one such occasion, 2,000 bemused Sahara Desert nomads showed up to watch on camels.

As a free-spirited nonconformist who has tried LSD, once had a penchant for cocaine, and enjoys erotic photography, Mirren found herself in a vexing predicament when, in 2003, she was invited by the royal establishment to become a Dame Commander of the British Empire. Surrendering to pride after a long deliberation, she finally accepted the honor and, though she pulls back from being coined a "royalist," has befittingly referred to herself instead as a "Queenist."[18] "Monarchy is a bit hard for me to get my head around," Mirren admitted. "However, . . . we're very lucky to be living in a country where you are allowed to portray or even satirize the Queen. If you did that in Iran—if you did the Ayatollah Khomeini in a play making fun of him—you'd be executed."[19]

Since her Oscar victory and surprising return to the role of Elizabeth II in the 2013 stage production of *The Audience* (about the queen's meetings with her various prime ministers), Mirren has had to dispel correlations between herself and the actual queen. "I am nothing like her," she insisted. "I may have been appointed Dame . . . but I am not all scones and teacups."[20] For the record, Queen Elizabeth II and her theatrical doppelgänger have come face-to-face before, first at a 2006 polo match and later, in 2011, at a palace event hosted by the queen at which Her Majesty (as seen in a candid photograph) appeared to be inspecting the woman who had played her to Oscar-winning success out of the corner of her eye.

As the queen's biographer Robert Lacey amusingly pointed out in his tutorial on how to present oneself to the queen, "A curtsy or bow is not required. Address the queen as 'Your Majesty' or 'Ma'am.' Don't call her 'Mum,' which suggests she is your mother. And don't call her Helen, either."[21]

Marion Cotillard

Although the British actress and veteran recipient **Julie Christie** had won the New York Film Critics Award and was crowned by many critics for her Best Actress Oscar–nominated performance as an Alzheimer's sufferer in *Away from Her* (2007), she "stayed quiet and out of town for long stretches of the [awards] season."[1] Capitalizing on her absence, the French actress and rival front-runner **Marion Cotillard**, who was virtually unknown to Hollywood at the time, actively worked the circuit in support of her performance as the fierce but fragile French singer Édith Piaf in *La Vie en Rose* (2007; aka *La môme*). In a group of contenders that also included **Cate Blanchett** (*Elizabeth: The Golden Age*), Laura Linney (*The Savages*), and the Canadian actress Ellen Page (*Juno*), Cotillard's efforts ultimately paid off when presenter Forest Whitaker called her name as the winner at the 80th Academy Awards (2008). Cotillard, shimmering in a "mermaid-inspired," "scalloped white gown" designed by Jean-Paul Gaultier,[2] reacted in intense disbelief to the surprise announcement and took to the stage with her hands clasping her mouth. Two days before, the actress had collected the César Award (France's equivalent to the Oscar) for her "technically virtuosic" performance.[3] But on the night of the Oscars, she thanked "life," "love," the "members of the Academy," and her "maestro" (*La Vie en Rose* director Olivier Dahan) in her sweetly accented, endearingly fractured English. "There is some angels [sic] in this city!" she exclaimed before trotting offstage, completely "overwhelmed with joy and sparkles and fireworks."[4]

With her triumph, Cotillard found herself in the annals of Oscar history. In an American-centric industry that prides itself on its promotion of cinema as a global language but still awards its Oscars, first and foremost, to films conveniently and

La Vie en Rose (2007)

Virtually unknown to Hollywood, French actress Marion Cotillard seemingly came out of nowhere to play the fierce but fragile singer Édith Piaf—one of France's most celebrated stars—in *La Vie en Rose* (2007). (Picturehouse Entertainment/Photofest)

almost exclusively presented in English, she became the first Best Actress Oscar winner to capture the Academy Award for a performance in a French-language film. What is more, she became only the second recipient in the history of her category to have won the Oscar for a foreign-language film since **Sophia Loren**'s remarkable performance in the Italian movie *Two Women* (1960; aka *La ciociara*). Awarded the Oscar the same year that fellow European actors Tilda Swinton, Daniel Day-Lewis, and Javier Bardem each won in their respective categories, Cotillard's victory, similar to that of countrywoman **Simone Signoret** in 1960, turned the actress into an overnight international star. In addition, her victory seemed to validate the growing perception that the film community, in general, was indeed "a *global* film community." As the multiple-Oscar-winning Mexican director Alejandro González Iñárritu observed, "It's not anymore about cultural barriers or language barriers. It's [about] emotion and humanity."[5]

But taking a closer look at Hollywood—the global capital of entertainment that once opened its doors to Greta Garbo (Sweden), Marlene Dietrich (Germany), Ramon Novarro and Delores del Río (Mexico); box-office champions Maurice Chevalier (France), Omar Sharif (Egypt), and Hedy Lamarr (Austria-Hungary); and important character actors such as Peter Lorre (Germany), Katy Jurado (Mexico), and Sabu (India)—the current crop of foreign-raised/non-native-English-speaking actors enjoying major Hollywood careers is curiously and substantially less than ever before. In a work-visa-restrictive era when accents are often regarded as a detriment, when foreign actors are stereotypically cast in one-dimensional roles (such as "mystics or terrorists"),[6] and when more opportunities can be found in such places as Mumbai (where more than 1,000 Bollywood films are produced annually), the Hollywood of today is indeed a far cry from the era of Classical Hollywood Cinema. Known for playing "very mysterious characters" and for possessing the quality of a silent-era femme fatale (à la Greta Garbo or Louise Brooks, her style icons),[7] Cotillard, largely due to her Oscar victory, has since been placed in the rarefied company of such actors as Jackie Chan (China), Antonio Banderas, Javier Bardem, and Penélope Cruz (Spain), Selma Hayek (Mexico), Christoph Waltz (Germany), Alicia Vikander (Sweden), and Priyanka Chopra (India). Enjoying "more money, free English lessons, and the global exposure that only the American movie machine can offer,"[8] each of these actors has successfully developed more recent international careers while beating the odds to become an A-list Hollywood star.

Nonetheless, as Cotillard has pointed out, "getting her mouth around [English] words is still tricky." "I tried to do it for a little while without a dialect coach," she said. "[But] I couldn't do it. I have trouble even with a coach. There are so many subtleties in English, just in the way you stress the words. And words are a big part of how you act."[9]

The daughter of middle-class actor parents who performed mime, taught drama, and directed theater to Molière Award–winning success, Cotillard was born in Paris on September 30, 1975, and "began acting at a young age."[10] Having grown up in the French countryside with the backdrop of nature and its ever-changing

After Sophia Loren's victory in 1962, French actress Marion Cotillard became the second Best Actress recipient to have won the Academy Award for a foreign-language film. Capturing the Oscar for her performance in *La Vie en Rose* (2007), Cotillard (*second from the left*) celebrates backstage with fellow European actor-recipients Daniel Day-Lewis (*left*), Tilda Swinton, and Javier Bardem. (© A.M.P.A.S.®/Photofest)

seasons, the shy, elfin beauty cultivated an active imagination as well as an acute ecological awareness that has more recently served her as a global ambassador for Greenpeace. After she became one of the youngest trainees at the Orléans Conservatoire d'Art Dramatique, she appeared in a series of short but promising French-language films before attracting the attention of the established French director and producer Luc Besson, who had turned **Natalie Portman** into a star by way of his English-language French thriller *Léon: The Professional* (1994).

After Cotillard had appeared in Besson's popular but critically reviled *Taxi* trilogy (1998–2003), she starred in *Jeux d'enfants* (2003; opposite her future real-life romantic partner, Guillaume Canet) and played a supporting role in director Tim Burton's *Big Fish* (2003; her first English-language film). She then appeared in 2004's *Un long dimanche de fiançailles* (aka *A Very Long Engagement*), for which **Jodie Foster**, incidentally, took on a small French-speaking role—a linguistic irregularity for almost any American-born actor beyond the French-speaking **Jane Fonda** and the foreign-dialect-gifted **Meryl Streep**.

Before long, Cotillard was shaving her eyebrows off and her hairline back nearly two inches in preparation for her physically and emotionally transcending part as the illustrious chanteuse française in *La Vie en Rose* (2007). The actress saw "another person emerge" throughout "30 days of heavy [Oscar-winning] makeup," and she all but became the manifestation of Édith Piaf (1915–1963), the poverty-born, drug-ravaged songbird whose "wonderfully raspy, tobacco-hardened voice" carried her country's hopes and dreams between two world wars and beyond.[11] Portraying one of only two women (alongside the physicist and chemist Marie Curie) to be ranked among France's "100 most important persons," Cotillard surveyed the Little Sparrow's tortured life to gut-wrenching detail with her "coat-hanger posture, shuffling gait, and toothy grin."[12] While masterfully lip-syncing to such classic Piaf tracks as "La vie en rose," "Non, je ne regrette rien," and "La foule," Cotillard examined Piaf from tawdry street-singing urchin to cabaret entertainer to the morphine-addicted superstar who, like Judy Garland six years later, ended up dead (from liver cancer) at age 47. As one reviewer put it, "this is show-business as martyrdom."[13]

Since winning the Best Actress Oscar, Cotillard has oscillated between French and American movies. Her diverse filmography includes the French national blockbuster *Les petits mouchoirs* (2010); the director Christopher Nolan's *Inception* (2010) and *The Dark Knight Rises* (2012); and *The Immigrant* (2013), which marked her first leading role in the United States. The actress also became a spokesmodel for Dior's Lady Dior Collection. In that position, she musically performed in an advertising campaign with the Scottish rock band Franz Ferdinand. Soon after, like other actresses with low-key recording careers, including **Judy Holliday** and **Brie Larson**, Cotillard set out on her own musical adventure under the pseudonym Simone with the French singer-songwriter Yodelice. In 2013, she even appeared as a scantily clad, suggestively dancing prostitute/Madonna figure who develops a gruesome stigmata in a seedy nightclub in the David Bowie music video for "The Next Day."

While Cotillard epitomizes to American audiences the stereotypical essence of European womanhood, she has additionally come to represent an anomaly in a 21st-century landscape that, despite advances in equality, often remains xenophobic toward outsiders, immigrants, and minorities. A reexamination of Hollywood's overall exclusion of foreign talent provides an unwelcome parallel. For example, since the Swiss-born German/Austrian performer Emil Jannings captured the inaugural Best Actor Oscar in 1929 for the silent pictures *The Last Command* and *The Way of All Flesh*, only six foreign-raised/non-native-English-speaking Best Actress recipients have been honored. That list includes **Ingrid Bergman** (Sweden), **Sophia Loren** (Italy), **Anna Magnani** (Italy), **Luise Rainer** (Germany), and **Simone Signoret** (France; whose daughter, Catherine Allégret, incidentally appeared in *La Vie en Rose*). Moreover, among the 436 performances nominated in the Best Actress Oscar category between 1929 and 2018, only 18 (or 4.1 percent of all nominees) were nominated for foreign-language films (ten of which arrived in the 1960s and '70s). Comparatively, in the Best Actor category, that number is even lower, with only eight such performances ever nominated and only one ever winning (that of the Italian actor Roberto Benigni in 1997's *Life is Beautiful*).

As the sixth such member of the Best Actress Oscar category, Cotillard, who many people felt would never go on to become a serious actress (let alone a major international star), has indeed joined a small, elite, and prestigious group. But with more non-native-English-speaking actors finding the hurdles in Hollywood difficult to jump, Cotillard's Oscar-winning place in cinema history may ultimately be less defined by any growing trend and more by a rare display of exceptional talent exemplified in a performance of magnificent authenticity.

Kate Winslet

Like five goddesses standing before the masses, former Best Actress Oscar winners **Sophia Loren**, **Shirley MacLaine**, **Halle Berry**, **Nicole Kidman**, and **Marion Cotillard** stepped out on stage at the 81st Academy Awards (2009) to a rousing standing ovation and Max Steiner's dramatic score from *Gone with the Wind* (1939). The actresses collectively appeared to present the Oscar for Best Actress in a unique and highly honorific format that had never been used before or since. They each took a turn in saluting one of the nominees, beginning with **MacLaine**'s tribute to Anne Hathaway (*Rachel Getting Married*) and continuing with **Cotillard**'s to **Kate Winslet** (*The Reader*), **Berry**'s to Melissa Leo (*Frozen River*), **Loren**'s to past winner **Meryl Streep** (*Doubt*), and **Kidman**'s to Angelina Jolie (*Changeling*).

The ultimate winner, Kate Winslet, a previous five-time nominee, took to the stage to a standing ovation, holding "in the tears but not the earthy remembrance of standing in front of the mirror as an eight-year-old kid pretending her shampoo bottle was an Oscar."[1] There, she confessed to the audience that she would "be lying" if she said that she had not "made a version of this speech before."[2] Winslet, sublime in an Yves Sant Laurent evening gown, had an urge "to run over to [her] parents and do one of those Wimbledon moments when the person jumps from the court and leaps over the audience and the bleachers," but instead instructed her father to whistle from the audience "so she'd know where he was."[3] To the amusement of everyone, he did just that. Later that night, Winslet "took her parents to a post-Oscar party," where "seeing [her] dad meet Elvis Costello and [her] mom shaking hands with Elton John" provided an added extraordinary thrill.[4]

The Reader (2008)

Unaware of her past as a Nazi concentration-camp guard, 15-year-old Michael Berg (played by David Kross) engages in a seductive romance with Kate Winslet's Hanna Schmitz in *The Reader* (2008). (The Weinstein Company/Photofest)

Winslet had initially hoped to be nominated for *The Reader* in the Best Supporting Actress Oscar category, so as "to clear the way for a lead actress nomination" for her turn in the 1950s "picket-fence-America" drama *Revolutionary Road*,[5] a film directed by her then-husband, Sam Mendes, that had reteamed the actress with her *Titanic* costars Leonardo DiCaprio and **Kathy Bates**. But as the actress half jokingly stated on a 2005 episode of the British TV sitcom *Extras*, "If you do a film about the Holocaust, [you're] guaranteed an Oscar. *Schindler's* bloody *List*, *The Pianist*, Oscars coming out of their ass!"[6]

The Reader (2008) was based on the 1995 international best-seller by Bernhard Schlink and directed by Stephen Daldry (who had guided **Nicole Kidman** to a Best Actress Oscar victory for 2002's *The Hours*). The film "navigates the emotional and psychological contradictions of the generation in Germany that became aware of the extent to which their parents had acquiesced in the war crimes of the Nazi era."[7] The postwar story centers on a 15-year-old West German boy named Michael (played by David Kross), who, in 1958, falls in love with a poor, uneducated, and much-older tram conductor named Hanna Schmitz (Winslet). Michael regularly visits Hanna in her dilapidated apartment, and the twosome engage in sexual intercourse, after which Michael reads "to her from the works of literary giants."[8] Without warning, Hanna disappears and is only to be seen again several years later as a defendant at a 1966 war-crimes tribunal for female Nazi concentration camp guards, at which Michael happens to be observing as a law student. Horrified, bewildered, and disgusted, he agonizingly listens to the testimony accusing Hanna of letting 300 "Jewish women and children burn to death in a locked church" during a winter death march from Auschwitz.[9]

Unlike the victimized mothers portrayed in earlier Best Actress Oscar–winning films dealing with World War II — **Greer Garson** in *Mrs. Miniver* (1942), **Sophia Loren** in *Two Women* (1960), and **Meryl Streep** in *Sophie's Choice* (1982) — *The Reader* tells its story of the war through courtroom testimony while examining "the genocide from the point of view of Germany."[10] The film was criticized by several prominent thinkers for its "cultural pornography," oversimplification of history, and humanizing of a wartime criminal, but it nonetheless offered Winslet an opportunity to play a complex, emotionally stunted character "who understands all too well that she is beyond forgiveness."[11]

A "proper actress" who "prepares with the fastidiousness of a brain surgeon," Winslet, who mastered an English-speaking German accent for the role, has frequently been hailed as the "finest actress of her generation."[12] In an industry inundated with excessive egos, she has additionally been celebrated for her disarming views. Regarding celebrity, for example, Winslet has admitted to feeling like a movie star (a term she loathes to be called) only when she appears "at the Academy Awards or at an important glamorous event."[13] And even then, she is said to feel not much like herself because "you're on show." "Our knickers will still go up our ass at the most inappropriate moment. And we'll still want to flick them out, but you can't, because someone is going to catch you."[14] Regarding

Kate Winslet is photographed backstage at the 81st Academy Awards with past recipients Halle Berry and Marion Cotillard after winning the Best Actress Oscar for her performance in *The Reader* (2008). (© A.M.P.A.S.®/ Photofest)

advertising, for which she has represented such luxury brands as Longines, St. John, and Lancôme, Winslet has been equally forthright. Considered "somewhat controversial for carrying half a handful of body fat" on her curvy, "Rubenesque" figure and for frequently being naked onscreen,[15] Winslet became one of the first major celebrities to speak out against the perils of photo enhancement and digital slimming (an common practice that measures women against an impossible standard of beauty). "We do not look like that," she once complained, in reference to her inhumanly perfect face and body as featured in *GQ* magazine in 2003.[16]

In a youth- and beauty-obsessed industry that expects its performers (*female* performers in particular) to look a certain way despite their actual age, Winslet has additionally taken a strong stand against cosmetic surgery, a divisive and contentious issue within Hollywood. Surgical procedures, alongside the use of Botox and collagen injections, have cast a certain shadow over the careers of stars including **Faye Dunaway**, **Jessica Lange**, and **Nicole Kidman**, the latter of whom purportedly abstained from further treatment in 2010 when she was on the verge of becoming a caricature of herself. But as **Cher**, one of the first celebrities to openly admit to having had cosmetic surgery, boldly asserted, "If I want to put my tits on my back, it's nobody's business but my own."[17] As **Jane Fonda** later confessed, "I wish I'd been brave enough not to do anything, but, instead, I chose to be a somewhat more glamorous grandma."[18] "It's not a normal thing," **Emma Thompson** argued. "And the culture we've created that says it's normal is not normal." "I'd rather have somebody go, 'Wow, that girl has a bad nose' than 'Wow, that girl has a bad nose job,'" **Jodie Foster** said.[19] "It doesn't make them look younger," added **Julianne Moore**. "It just makes them look like they had work done."[20] With an increasing number of directors reluctant to hire older actresses as a result of what is perceived as years of image-altering surgery, some stars (ranging from **Maggie Smith** to **Glenda Jackson** to **Sally Field**) have remained resolute in their determination not to mess with their faces. "There are roles I want to do when I'm an old woman," **Field** said, "and I don't want to look like a weird old woman."[21] "I want to play the way the great ones did, like **Helen Hayes** and Lillian Gish."[22]

Recognizing the negative, confidence-debilitating effects of self-objectification, Winslet, who takes pride in the fact that her Botox-free eyebrows go up and down ("They're supposed to move," she said. "I'm very proud of that"),[23] has come to represent a spirit of self-acceptance. "As a child I never heard one woman say to me, 'I love my body.' . . . So, I make sure to say it to [my daughter], because a positive physical outlook has to start at an early age."[24]

Winslet was born in Reading, England, on October 5, 1975, and derives from a family of stage actors. She got her training at the Redroofs Theatre School before landing a TV commercial for the breakfast cereal Sugar Puffs. She was often "bullied for being 'fat' at school" and was later cast as the daughter of a 300-pound woman in the TV miniseries *Anglo-Saxon Attitudes* (1992).[25] The actress determinedly lost her heavyset frame before bursting "onto the scene" in director Peter Jackson's *Heavenly Creatures* (1994) and getting "picked by **Emma Thompson** at an open audition" for *Sense and Sensibility* (1995).[26] Although James Cameron was searching for "an **Audrey Hepburn**–type" lead in *Titanic* (1997), Winslet "wore [Cameron] down with daily notes from England until he invited her to Hollywood to audition."[27] For her performance as Rose in *Titanic*, she was catapulted into the stratosphere of superstardom. But instead of continuing forward with commercial fare, Winslet, who turned down the lead role that was eventually given to **Gwyneth Paltrow** in *Shakespeare in Love* (1998), "maintained a clarity of vision about the kind of work she wanted to do" and returned to the calmer waters of independent cinema.[28] After winning her Oscar in 2009, Winslet adopted a similar approach by starring in the five-part TV miniseries *Mildred Pierce* (2011), a faithful adaptation of the James M. Cain novel for which **Joan Crawford**, in the 1945 original, had won the Best Actress Oscar.

Never one for "games or vanity or wardrobe freak-outs," Winslet is widely regarded for her unpretentiousness and inner grace.[29] In addition to her acting, she has traveled the world, advocating for both PETA (People for the Ethical Treatment of Animals) and the improvement of the lives of children with autism. Inclusive and kindhearted, she even allowed "her golden boy,"[30] on the day following her Oscar victory, to be passed around her flight, giving passengers and crew the opportunity to hold her freshly bequeathed statuette as she took pictures and celebrated with a bottle of champagne.

Sandra Bullock

Sandra Bullock was born on July 26, 1964, in the Washington, DC, suburb of Arlington, Virginia. Her American father worked in the U.S. Army and gave voice lessons. Her mother, the renowned German opera singer Helga Meyer, simultaneously performed around the world. Bilingually raised in theatrical surroundings and taught never to conform, Bullock spent much of her childhood in Vienna and Salzburg, Austria, and lived in Nuremberg, Germany, until the age of 12. Growing up with "a love of opera, a lack of stage fright, and the passion to be a performer," Bullock and her younger sister, Gesine, were often used as extras. "Every opera has a Gypsy kid," she later explained. Night after night on the stage of the Staatstheater Nürnberg, the sisters would watch their mother "commit seppuku, strip for John the Baptist, and die of consumption." And "every New Year's Eve," they would sit on the top of the stairs in their home and "look down at their parents' boisterous parties," where Helga would belly dance as the sisters fled "to their bedrooms."[1]

Returning to the United States, Bullock enrolled at Washington-Lee High School (the alma mater of **Shirley MacLaine** and Warren Beatty), where she became a cheerleader as a way to meet boys but was incessantly teased about her German accent. "With performing in her blood," Bullock studied theater at East Carolina University (in Greenville, North Carolina) before moving with her dog to New York. There, she landed the lead in an off-Broadway play before relocating to Los Angeles, where she began to land roles in TV movies and feature films such as *Love Potion No. 9* (1992) and *Speed* (1994), the smash-hit action thriller that put her on the map and "changed her life forever."[2] Making a career "out of playing neurotic singletons" in a succession of formulaic romantic comedies that capitalized on

The Blind Side (2009)

Wealthy friends of Tennessee tiger mom Leigh Anne Tuohy (played by Best Actress Oscar winner Sandra Bullock) may not have approved of the addition of Michael Oher, a disadvantaged Black teenager living in the Tuohy family home, as seen in this Christmas-card portrait from *The Blind Side* (2009). *From left to right*, actors Tim McGraw, Lily Collins, Jae Head, and Quinton Aaron round out the cast. (Warner Bros. Pictures Inc./ Photofest)

In what many people considered to be another "white savior" narrative coming out of Hollywood, Sandra Bullock's character in *The Blind Side* (2009) encourages Michael Oher (played by Quinton Aaron) to stay the course. (Warner Bros. Pictures Inc./Photofest)

her "her down-to-earth sensibility,"[3] Bullock soon became a top box-office draw and, for a time, the second-highest-paid actress in Hollywood after the similarly marketed **Julia Roberts**.

In 2009, Bullock starred in *The Blind Side*, a film based on the 2006 book by Michael Lewis. In it, she plays the real-life "iron-willed evangelical Christian" Leigh Anne Tuohy (1960 –),[4] an affluent Memphis, Tennessee, tiger mom and interior designer who dresses in Chanel skirts and Gucci shades, carries her cell phone along with a .22-caliber revolver, and is happily married to the football-obsessed owner of 85 fast-food franchise restaurants. While driving home one frosty night with her family in their SUV, Leigh Anne notices Michael Oher, an "overgrown Black teenager" and football prodigy who, on scholarship, attends the same private Christian academy as her two children.[5] Michael (played by Quinton Aaron) is wandering along the street, dressed only "in shorts and a T-shirt" and "carrying his belongings in a plastic bag."[6] As he lives in poverty in an abusive, gang-ridden slum, Leigh Anne decides to invite him into the gated surroundings of her family's opulent home. Despite the tremendous "differences in their backgrounds,"[7] the Tuohy family help Michael to develop his football skills, hire him a private tutor (**Kathy Bates**) to assist him in getting into college, and eventually adopt him.

The Blind Side was a "smorgasbord of football, faith, and family values" that managed to charm "members of both liberal Hollywood and the conservative Bible Belt."[8] The film was released "two weekends before Barack Obama's inauguration" and proved to be a major hit.[9] After **Julia Roberts** had turned down the starring role, Bullock initially regretted having taken it on herself, but Leigh Anne Tuohy ultimately turned into the defining performance of her career.

For many viewers, however, Bullock's role in *The Blind Side* was seen as yet another example of racial stereotyping within a Hollywood "white savior" narrative. In the same vein as *Imitation of Life* (1934; with **Claudette Colbert**), *Places in the Heart* (1984; with **Sally Field**), *Mississippi Burning* (1988; with **Frances McDormand**), *Driving Miss Daisy* (1989; with **Jessica Tandy**), *Music of the Heart* (1999; with **Meryl Streep**), *Monster's Ball* (2001; with **Halle Berry**), and *The Help* (2011; with **Emma Stone** and **Sissy Spacek**), the movie implied that underprivileged people of color can only rely on well-intentioned white folks as a means of upward mobility. While attempting to open up a "conversation on race that the American public is always supposedly eager to have, but never right now,"[10] the film, according to some analysts, also served "an ideological purpose" with the goal of reinforcing the bonds of institutionalized racism. As Michael Oher (who went on to become a star National Football League tackle for the Baltimore Ravens) put it, the film, even if entertaining, was a source of "wounded pride," as his character is portrayed as dumb, asexual, lacking in opinion, and ignorant to the basic "rules of football."[11]

Having previously appeared in two films that squarely center on race, *A Time to Kill* (1996) and *Crash* (2004), Bullock has been relentless in dealing with the topic. In *Crash*, the Best Picture Oscar–winning drama set in Los Angeles and

inundated with racial epithets, her unlikeable character (the wife to a Los Angeles district attorney who is mugged at gunpoint) comes off as a "seething race-conscious" bigot who disingenuously "hugs the maid she's treated like dirt and says, 'You're the best friend I've got.'"[12] Conversely, her multifaceted character in *The Blind Side* comes across as the picture of strong and dignified womanhood. On the one hand, she can be seen as a fierce protector who is unafraid to confront traditional masculinity, the Memphis slums, and the jeers of her "wealthy white friends."[13] On the other hand, she can be regarded as a "cheerful giver insofar as her [wealthy] husband continues exploiting countless [others] as his underpaid and overworked [fast-food] employees."[14]

Aside from becoming "the highest grossing sports movie of all time" (ahead of *Rocky IV* [1985] and *Million Dollar Baby* [2004; starring **Hilary Swank**]),[15] *The Blind Side* presented Bullock with her first-ever Oscar nomination ahead of the 82nd Academy Awards (2010). In the same year as *The Blind Side*, she additionally starred in the blockbuster hit *The Proposal* and the critically reviled *All About Steve*, for which she won the Golden Raspberry Award for Worst Actress (a dishonor previously given to **Faye Dunaway**, **Liza Minnelli**, and **Halle Berry**). With her goofball, self-deprecating sense of humor, Bullock, a self-described underdog in the Oscar race for Best Actress ("People who do what I do, don't make award-winning films," she once admitted),[16] kept herself in the public eye. In doing so, she appeared on "late-night talk shows, morning TV and radio, and a host of intimate events," all "designed to grab the attention of the 6,000 Academy voter members."[17]

On a historic night that saw the director Kathryn Bigelow become the first woman to win the Academy Award for Best Director (for *The Hurt Locker*), Bullock arrived at the 2010 Oscars with her then-husband, Jesse James, in a shimmering silver gown designed by Marchesa. Her competition in the Best Actress category included former winner **Helen Mirren** (*The Last Station*), the British actress Carey Mulligan (*An Education*), Gabourey Sidibe (*Precious*; a film dealing with similar issues of race, poverty, and discrimination), and veteran recipient and New York Film Critics Award winner **Meryl Streep** (*Julie & Julia*), the latter of whom largely kept quiet during the awards season.

Bullock was ultimately lavished with a standing ovation upon the announcement of her name as Best Actress, and just one night after accepting her Golden Raspberry Award in person, she took to the Oscar stage. With her statuette in hand, she amusingly asked the audience, "Did I really earn this or did I just wear you all down?" Shining a spotlight on "the moms that take care of the babies and the children no matter where they come from," Bullock thanked the Tuohy family (who were seated inside the Kodak Theatre). After a small, emotional pause, she then thanked her late mother, who had reminded "her daughters that there's no race, no religion, no class system, no color, nothing, no sexual orientation, that makes us better than anyone else. We are all deserving of love."[18]

But Bullock had little time to bask in the glory of her success. Just eight days after winning the Oscar, she was blindsided by tabloid reports of her husband's infidelities and a shocking photo of him sporting "a hat with a Nazi insignia and giving a Hitler-style salute."[19] Within days, the public came to learn that the couple had adopted an African American baby from New Orleans, an area in which Bullock and her husband had spent much time after 2005's Hurricane Katrina. Whereas in the old days, the Hollywood studios would have taken care of such a publicity faux pas as her husband's by paying for "media silence" and negotiating "with newspapers and gossip columnists,"[20] Bullock was forced to take matters into her own hands. With the take-charge attitude of her character from *The Blind Side*, she escaped the frenzy of Hollywood, moved to her quieter base in Austin, Texas, with her adopted son in tow, and filed for divorce.

An American Red Cross supporter and major donor to various disaster relief funds, Bullock, who adopted another African American child, has largely remained in Austin whenever she is not working on a film. An active member of the city's vibrant and energetic community, she owned a local bistro and an event-planning business, is involved in property restoration, and can be seen strolling about town several hundred miles away from the relentless glare of the Hollywood paparazzi.

Natalie Portman

In an era steeped in 24/7 media coverage and social networking, the 83rd Academy Awards (2011) tapped into the "multi-tasking tendencies" of modern audiences by offering viewers—for the first time in Oscar history—expanded, exclusive, and unfiltered online access not only to the red carpet but also to the star-studded lobby bar, the green room, the press room, the winners' walk, and the post-telecast, invitation-only Governors Ball.[1] Capturing behind-the-scenes glimpses of stars chatting idly and milling about the Kodak Theatre, cameras cut through the velvet rope like never before, giving audiences the ability to watch their favorite celebrities while diminishing perhaps a particular aura of Oscar mystique.

Locked in a tight race for Best Actress, a very pregnant and composed **Natalie Portman**, who was nominated for her physically and psychologically demanding performance in the ballet-themed, horror-thriller *Black Swan* (2010), listened attentively as her category was called out. Her competition included former winner **Nicole Kidman** (*Rabbit Hole*), Michelle Williams (*Blue Valentine*), **Jennifer Lawrence** (*Winter's Bone*), and rival frontrunner and New York Film Critics Award winner Annette Bening (*The Kids Are All Right*). Upon the announcement of Portman's name, the actress took to the stage in a beautiful off-the-shoulder burgundy gown designed by the sisters Kate and Laura Mulleavy of Rodarte (the same duo who had fashioned her raven-inspired looks for the film). After she delivered a gracious acceptance speech, she chugged a bottle of water near a backstage sign that warned, "You're on Camera."[2]

In her Academy Award–winning performance in *Black Swan*, Portman plays Nina Sayers, a physically disciplined, self-flagellating ballerina vying for the lead in Tchaikovsky's *Swan Lake*. Taking cues from such ballet-themed classics as *The*

Black Swan (2010)

Natalie Portman talks off-camera with director Darren Aronofsky, who instructed the actress to drop as much weight as possible for *Black Swan* (2010) without becoming sick. (Fox Searchlight Pictures/Photofest)

Red Shoes (1948) and *Suspiria* (1977), as well as the Japanese animated psychological thriller *Perfect Blue* (1997), *Black Swan* zeroes in on the themes of perception, identity, and the "tension between control and losing oneself in the pursuit of artistic perfection."[3] The film is set amid the ultracompetitive atmosphere of an elite New York City dance company. Interlaced with mirrored images, lesbian fantasies, masturbation, and doppelgängers, it follows Nina as she elegantly pirouettes to the top of her profession before descending into a surreal, psychosexual nightmare in which she begins to sprout feathers and transform into a swan.

Portman, who met her future husband, the French danseur and choreographer Benjamin Millepied, on the set of *Black Swan*, was confronted with the task of having to attain almost professional ballerina standards, despite having a body double on hand. To prepare for her role, she aggressively trained for more than a year, exercising five to eight hours a day. At one point, she dislocated her rib and drastically lowered her calorie intake so as to achieve and maintain the allegedly more perfect, more accurate, and more photographable size-zero figure. Although *Black Swan*'s director, Darren Aronofsky, never specified just how much weight she should lose for her performance, according to Portman, "he was definitely like, 'How thin do you think you can get without being sick?'" Aronofsky later regretted having asked the question in light of the actress's rapidly "shrinking frame" and dangerous, stick-like proportions.[4]

Disturbingly, the depiction of Nina, who refuses to "even taste a pink-frosted celebration cake her [overbearing] mother has bought her,"[5] all too realistically parallels the poor body image that is surprisingly harbored by many actresses and aspiring hopefuls in Hollywood. Locked in a looks competition and a "system of rewards" in which you are essentially "rewarded for being the most beautiful, the sexiest, and . . . the thinnest,"[6] many female stars, including **Ginger Rogers**, **Greer Garson**, **Audrey Hepburn**, **Jane Fonda**, **Diane Keaton**, **Sally Field**, and **Kate Winslet**, have subjected themselves to bulimia, binge eating, or anorexic diets in order to stay "professionally" thin. "I was raised in the '50s," said **Jane Fonda**. "I was taught by my father [the actor Henry Fonda] that how I looked was all that mattered. . . . He was a good man, and I was mad for him, but he sent messages to me that fathers should not send: Unless you look perfect, you're not going to be loved."[7]

Habitually conforming to the ideals of men, the perfect body image for women has progressively become smaller and smaller and taller and taller, influencing many women around the world to travel down a dangerous road of self-injurious behavior. In Hollywood, this trend has even alerted some actresses not to "be the one . . . whose photo is taken with two skinny actresses" because you end up looking "like [the animated character] Shrek."[8] In addition, as more actresses have sidelined "officially or unofficially as fashion models, more [have appeared] to adopt the aesthetic of the modeling industry, which prefers stick-like figures because they highlight the clothes better."[9]

Remarkably, Portman, who has long been conditioned to a life under the international spotlight, has managed to navigate herself through these hostile waters.

Natalie Portman as she appears in *Black Swan* (2010), a film interlaced with mirrored images, doppelgängers, and lesbian fantasies. (Fox Searchlight Pictures/Photofest)

The only child of a father who worked as a fertility specialist/gynecologist and a mother who worked as an artist turned talent agent, Portman was born Natalie Hershlag in Jerusalem, Israel, on June 9, 1981. The actress grew up in Israel before moving to the United States at the age of three. When she was only nine, she was "spotted by a model scout for Revlon" at a Long Island pizza parlor. "I kept my cool," she recalled. "I told him that I wanted to act."[10]

Like **Jodie Foster**, Portman proved herself capable of playing characters that are wise beyond their years. At age 11, she was cast in the French director Luc Besson's 1994 mafia thriller *Léon: The Professional*, in which she appeared as a cigarette-smoking child orphan. Before long, she was working with some of the top directors in Hollywood, including Woody Allen (*Everyone Says I Love You*, 1996), Tim Burton (*Mars Attacks!*, 1996), and George Lucas (as Queen Padmé Amidala in the three-part *Star Wars* trilogy prequel, 1999–2005). In 1997, she appeared onstage, starring as Anne Frank in the Broadway revival of *The Diary of Anne Frank*. Marking **Meryl Streep**'s first appearance in a stage production in New York in 20 years, Portman additionally costarred with the legendary actress in the August 2001 Shakespeare in the Park production of Anton Chekhov's *The Seagull*. "I always want to return to stage," Portman has said. "It's really an actor's medium, where film is a director's medium, and it's a place where you can learn a lot about yourself as an actor."[11]

Portman is a student of the world, with dual American and Israeli citizenship, a bachelor's degree in psychology from Harvard, and philanthropy work that has taken her to some of the most impoverished developing nations on the map. She speaks Japanese, French, and Hebrew and has undoubtedly developed a star image defined as much by her political and social beliefs as by her acting. In a celebrity era when the "line between public service and self-promotion" can sometimes become "fraught with complications,"[12] she has garnered enormous praise for her dignified actions and ability to raise public awareness. Examples include her animal rights advocacy, her money-raising efforts to lift women out of poverty (via FINCA International), and, as a Miss Dior Chérie fragrance spokesmodel, her 2011 public condemnation of the fashion designer John Galliano's anti-Semitic slurs shortly prior to his termination as Dior's creative director. Additionally, at a 2018 Power of Women event hosted by *Variety*, Portman, a spokesperson for the Time's Up movement and its legal defense fund to cover the costs for workers to pursue lawsuits involving sexual harassment against their employers, rallied the audience. "At Time's Up, we want all people—men and women and those who identify as neither and both—to lead the charge." "Many men," Portman concluded, "are behaving like we live in a zero-sum game. That if women get the respect, access, and value we deserve, they will lose."[13]

As the only Israeli-born performer to have won a competitive acting Oscar, Portman, whose Jewish great-grandparents were killed in Auschwitz, has undoubtedly lived a life consumed with discussions around politics, terrorism, and violence. Channeling her energy both artistically and academically, she starred in *Free Zone* (2005; "an allegorical plea for harmony in the Middle East")[14] and as a freedom fighter in *V for Vendetta* (2006; a film from which the stylized "Guy Fawkes" mask has since become an antiestablishment symbol in real-life protest efforts worldwide). Portman has also delivered university lectures on terrorism and counterterrorism. "I took a class at school," she said in front of a packed audience at Columbia University, "and we read a lot about the Israeli Supreme Court decision on torture and also the United States sending prisoners to other countries to get tortured there. It is something that is very important for us to talk about because there is no discussion about it. [The United States is saying] that 'torture is wrong,' but are actually doing it behind closed doors."[15] Following in the footsteps of **Ginger Rogers**, **Greer Garson**, **Ellen Burstyn**, **Sally Field**, and **Jane Fonda**, who portrayed First Ladies Dolly Madison, Eleanor Roosevelt, Barbara Bush, Mary Todd Lincoln, and Nancy Reagan in *Magnificent Doll* (1946), *Sunrise at Campobello* (1960), *W.* (2008), *Lincoln* (2012), and *The Butler* (2013), respectively, Portman further articulated her interest in politics by starring as a grieving but stoic Jacqueline Kennedy in the 2016 film *Jackie*.

In a 21st century inundated with celebrity overexposure and often featuring leaked photos of celebrity bodies "splayed across the Internet,"[16] Portman has remained modest and unassuming despite her ubiquitous, product-selling image flooding the Internet, magazines, shopping malls, airports, and billboard advertisements worldwide. In a cutthroat industry that breeds narcissism and has intensified its focus on fashion, commercialism, and digitally altered beauty, the actress has seemingly emerged from the static unscathed, circumventing the trappings and pitfalls of modern-day stardom while acing the demands of a modern-day star.

Jennifer Lawrence

For the 85th Academy Awards (2013), a total of 35 women were nominated in all categories alongside 140 men. In a tight race for the Best Actress Oscar, **Jennifer Lawrence** found herself up against the category's youngest-ever nominee (the nine-year-old Quvenzhané Wallis for *Beasts of the Southern Wild*) as well as its oldest ever (the 85-year-old French actress and rival frontrunner Emmanuelle Riva for *Amour*). Also in the running were Naomi Watts (*The Impossible*) and the early favorite Jessica Chastain (*Zero Dark Thirty*).

Quickly becoming known for her candid and self-deprecating sense of humor, Lawrence, who was nominated for her performance in *Silver Linings Playbook* (2012), took the world and the media industry by storm in a series of memorable Oscar-season missteps that made her a charismatic YouTube sensation. Triumphant at the Golden Globes, she jokingly bragged about beating **Meryl Streep**. Victorious at the Screen Actors Guild Awards, she (figuratively) set the room on fire with a purported wardrobe malfunction. And while hosting *Saturday Night Live*, she caused a wave of commotion by disparaging her fellow Best Actress Oscar nominees in a playful opening monologue "designed to skewer the competitive nature of awards." "Jessica Chastain?" she openly questioned. "More like Jessica Chast-*ain't* winning no Oscar on my watch!"[1] In an industry that expects its stars—and its female stars, in particular—to "project the right image," Lawrence's monologue "led to gossip headlines" and managed to turn off some Academy voters who were "not amused."[2] But much like **Julia Roberts** 25 years before, the actress ultimately won over her critics by revealing herself to be a confident lead "whose gorgeousness and talent is hugely amplified" by a "wickedly funny" and "refreshingly unfiltered" brand of deadpan humor.[3]

Silver Linings Playbook (2012)

Although Lawrence had been a Best Actress Oscar nominee two years before for her hard-hitting turn as the daughter of a crystal-meth manufacturer in *Winter's Bone* (2010), the relative newcomer to Hollywood still confessed to tremendous nerves on the red carpet. "I end up getting so nervous," she said. "And I get really hyper!"[4] "My biggest fear is speaking publicly." At a ceremony that was condemned by the likes of **Jane Fonda** and others for a song-and-dance number about topless actresses in film (ranging from **Charlize Theron** in *Monster* to **Kate Winslet** in *The Reader* to **Jodie Foster** in *The Accused*), Lawrence arrived at the 2013 Academy Awards in a ballooning Christian Dior ball gown that "seemed to trail on endlessly behind her."[5]

Unconvinced that she had given the best performance of the year, Lawrence reacted in genuine disbelief upon the announcement of her name as Best Actress. In a moment that cemented her fame and turned her into an international superstar who could be respected and taken seriously, Lawrence, at age 22, became the second-youngest recipient of the Best Actress Oscar (after 21-year-old **Marlee Matlin**). Before reaching the stage to collect her statuette, the actress—encumbered by her dress—tripped over and fell flat on the stairs, eliciting a gasp from the audience. "Thank you," she said as she got to the microphone, to which the audience leapt to their feet in a compassionate show of support. "You guys are just standing up because you feel bad that I fell and that's really embarrassing, but thank you. This is nuts!"[6] She then went on to thank the Academy, her competition, her family, and her fellow cast and crew before wishing Emmanuelle Riva a happy 86th birthday.

During her post-Oscar press interviews, Lawrence continued to make headlines. Bearing "the soul of a comedian" who "can riff on just about anything that crosses her path,"[7] the actress responded to questions about her legendary fall by simply underscoring the voluminous proportions of what she was wearing. "What do you mean 'what happened?'" she asked. "I tried to walk up stairs in this dress." "What went through my mind when I fell down? A bad word that I can't say . . . that starts with F."[8] Before fending "off advances from Jack Nicholson on camera" backstage, Lawrence topped off the evening by "cheekily and good-naturedly" giving one member of the press the middle finger[9]—the bold appearance of which seemed to signify a new and less conservative era in Hollywood.

Lawrence was born on August 15, 1990, and raised alongside her two older brothers in the suburbs of Louisville, Kentucky. Growing up, she worked on her parents' horse farm and during the summer months helped out at the children's summer day camp that her mother managed. A self-described "weirdo" who suffered from anxiety, "didn't fit in" at school, and was consequently sent to a therapist,[10] Lawrence tried her hand at softball, field hockey, cheerleading, and modeling before finding an outlet in acting. Despite having no formal acting training outside the experience that she gained in a few local theater productions, Lawrence, at 14, was able to convince her mother to take her to New York during her spring break. On account of her good looks (which were later compared to

Jennifer Lawrence, as she appears in *Silver Linings Playbook* (2012). For her arresting performance as a young widow suffering from bipolar disorder, Lawrence, at 22 years of age, became the second-youngest recipient of the Best Actress Oscar (after 21-year-old Marlee Matlin). In the process, she beat the oldest- and youngest-ever nominees: 85-year-old Emmanuelle Riva and nine-year-old Quvenzhané Wallis. (The Weinstein Company/Photofest) that of a "1970s California prom queen" or a blond "Malibu Barbie"),[11] a modeling scout approached the aspiring actress in Union Square. Before long, Lawrence found herself in H&M print advertisements and MTV commercials and quit school altogether to move to Hollywood.

Although Lawrence auditioned for the role that was ultimately given to **Emma Stone** in *Superbad* (2007), the role of Bella in *Twilight* (2008), and the role of Lisbeth Salander in *The Girl with the Dragon Tattoo* (2011), she initially found roles on television and in independent movies. Recognized for bringing surprising depth and gravitas to her performances, Lawrence was subsequently cast in a supporting role in *The Beaver* (2011; directed by **Jodie Foster**), as Raven Darkhölme/Mystique in the hit superhero-action adventure *X-Men: First Class* (2011), and as the clever and quick-witted Joan of Arc–like lead, Katniss Everdeen, in the massively lucrative film franchise adaptation of *The Hunger Games* (2012).

Auditioning over Skype, Lawrence was additionally offered the role of the feisty, bipolar, and "sex-crazed widow" Tiffany Maxwell in *Silver Linings Playbook* (2012).[12] Despite feeling far "too young" to pull off the part, the actress managed to morph into character by way of applying heavy makeup, dying her hair black, gaining some weight, and speaking "in a deeper octave to make her sound older."[13] Based on the novel by Matthew Quick, the film centers on a Philadelphia high school teacher (played by Bradley Cooper) who "suffers a breakdown after discovering his wife's affair."[14] Lawrence's character, who first appears 25 minutes into the movie, is "ridden with guilt and grief" over her husband's recent death and chooses to "sleep her way out of depression."[15] She first flings herself onto her coworkers until she is fired from her job. She then aims her attention at Cooper's character, who has just returned from a mental institution. Both characters are erupting from "madness" (and the stigma that surrounds mental illness) and ultimately decide to "face the reality of their situations and do something about it."[16]

While gaining a reputation for being able to stay "loose" and "in the moment" on set—goofing around, hovering about the craft service table, and making off-color jokes—Lawrence openly confessed to having experienced a "meltdown" as she adjusted to her sudden fame.[17] As the director David O. Russell explained, "People didn't really know who she was" when "she first showed up on the set of *Silver Linings*. But by the time the film was released . . . it was like being at a Beatles concert."[18]

In the period that followed Lawrence's Oscar victory, her adjustment to movie stardom did not get any easier. With the demands of movie stars having intensified "to the point where looking good" at premieres, talk shows, press conferences, and various award-related ceremonies has "become a nearly full-time job," the actress has additionally found herself in an era when everyone is capable of emulating the paparazzi with smartphones while capturing celebrities on camera as if they were monkeys "in a zoo."[19]

Three months after nude and otherwise-revealing photographs of Lawrence were hacked from her iCloud account and released across the Internet, she found herself in the midst of another computer-security scandal when hackers leaked confidential data from Sony Pictures that revealed that the actress had earned significantly less money than her male costars for the film *American Hustle* (2013). "After learning how badly Lawrence was underpaid," **Charlize Theron** "demanded and reportedly got a massive bump to her pay" for *The Huntsman: Winter's War* (2016).[20] Later, Patricia Arquette "turned her supporting-actress acceptance speech [at the 2015 Academy Awards] into a 'Norma Rae' moment by demanding equal pay for women,"[21] generating enthusiastic applause from **Meryl Streep, Shirley MacLaine**, and others. While some actresses, such as **Emma Thompson, Helen Hunt, Cate Blanchett, Sandra Bullock** (who said she was "glad Hollywood got caught"), and **Emma Stone** (who claimed "her male co-stars took salary cuts so she could receive equal pay"), helped to move "this controversial issue into the spotlight,"[22] it has remained problematic for others. "Maybe it's a British thing," **Kate Winslet** acknowledged. "I don't like talking about money. It's a bit vulgar, isn't it?"[23]

Buttressed by bodyguards and the sounding board of her close-knit family, Lawrence, who earned $46 million in 2016 and thus became the highest-paid actress in Hollywood, has managed to live up to industry pressures and expectations. Representing a fresh voice and a new and compelling kind of screen heroine, the actress has quickly proven that she can "rack up box-office dollars and critical praise" while simultaneously leaving her fans in stitches.[24]

Cate Blanchett

Just days after **Cate Blanchett** had attended the private funeral service of her friend and colleague, the actor Philip Seymour Hoffman (to whom she dedicated her BAFTA Award for Best Actress), she arrived at the 86th Academy Awards (2014) in a "sparkling nude champagne gown" accented with flower-petal-shaped sequins and crystal baguettes.[1] Able "to command the utmost respect on both the silver screen and the red carpet," Blanchett, whose weighty Armani dress and jewelry came to a combined cost of $18.1 million, appeared to wear her "couture as comfortably as a cotton tee."[2]

In a strong year for female actors, Blanchett, the regal and revered Australian star of the director Woody Allen's *Blue Jasmine* (2013), faced an impressive lineup of Best Actress contenders including former recipients **Meryl Streep** (*August: Osage County*) and **Sandra Bullock** (*Gravity*), Amy Adams (*American Hustle*), and Judi Dench (*Philomena*). But despite the competition, Blanchett, the recipient of the New York Film Critics Award, was seen as the "red-hot Oscar favorite."[3] Not even the controversy swirling around an "allegation of Woody Allen's having sexually abused his adopted daughter" could stop the runaway train of her ultimate win.[4]

Blossoming into a star over a relatively brief span of time, Blanchett advanced in her career the moment she discovered her true love for acting. Born in Melbourne, Australia, on May 14, 1969, the actress was raised the second of three children by a teacher mother and an advertising executive father who died when she was ten. She was bored as a student of fine arts and economics at the University of Melbourne and decided to leave school and travel the world in search of herself. While backpacking in Egypt, she was asked to participate as an extra in an Arabic boxing film. Before long, she returned to Australia to enroll at the prestigious National Institute

Blue Jasmine (2013)

Immaculately dressed in a Giorgio Armani Prive gown embroidered with raised dégradé sequins and baguettes, *Blue Jasmine* star Cate Blanchett holds her freshly bequeathed statuette backstage at the 86th Academy Awards (2014). (© A.M.P.A.S.®/Photofest)

of Dramatic Art in Sydney. Possessed with an "intellectual and emotional curiosity" that found her eavesdropping on conversations while waiting on tables during her student days,[5] Blanchett soon arrested audiences in such plays as David Mamet's *Oleanna* (1992) and as Ophelia in Shakespeare's *Hamlet* (1995). Film work quickly followed, with roles in small Australian productions, a minor part in *Paradise Road* (1997; with **Frances McDormand**), a starring role in *Oscar and Lucinda* (1997), and the title role of Queen Elizabeth I in the internationally acclaimed *Elizabeth* (1998; for which Blanchett earned a Best Actress Oscar nomination).

By the time Blanchett finally captured the Best Actress Oscar for her performance in *Blue Jasmine* (2013), the 44-year-old actress had amassed a stunning array of chameleon-like portrayals that is only eclipsed in modern times by the likes of **Meryl Streep**. Highlights have included *The Talented Mr. Ripley* (1999), *Notes on a Scandal* (2006), *I'm Not There* (2007; for which she played across gender lines as Bob Dylan), and *Elizabeth: The Golden Age* (2007; for which she became the only actress in Oscar history to be nominated twice for playing the same character in two separate films). Just as **Faye Dunaway** (*Mommie Dearest*, 1981) and **Jessica Lange** (*Feud*, 2017) portrayed **Joan Crawford**; **Susan Sarandon** (*Feud*, 2017) portrayed **Bette Davis**; **Glenda Jackson** (*The Patricia Neal Story*, 1981) portrayed **Patricia Neal**; and **Nicole Kidman** (*Grace of Monaco*, 2014) portrayed **Grace Kelly**, Blanchett additionally played **Katharine Hepburn** in 2004's *The Aviator*, for which she won the Best Supporting Actress Oscar. By virtue of her appearance as the ethereal Galadriel in the lucrative *Lord of the Rings* series (2001–2003), the actress maintains a cumulative film gross of more than $7 billion worldwide (second only to the *Harry Potter* star **Maggie Smith** among the Best Actress Oscar winners).

After **Diane Keaton** (*Annie Hall*) and Best Supporting Actress winners Dianne Wiest (*Hannah and Her Sisters*; *Bullets over Broadway*), Mira Sorvino (*Mighty Aphrodite*), and Penélope Cruz (*Vicky Cristina Barcelona*), Blanchett became the fifth woman to win an Oscar by way of a Woody Allen film. In *Blue Jasmine*, Allen's stinging indictment of modern American income inequality, she portrays the "Park Avenue princess" Jasmine French, a deluded, unlikeable trophy wife who falls into financial ruin after her financier husband "is exposed as a fraud."[6] Lacking in self-sufficiency and self-awareness, Jasmine, a broke, homeless, and self-objectifying fantasist unwilling to relinquish her first-class lifestyle, is forced to turn to her cash-strapped, San Francisco–based sister for help. She takes Xanax, frequently babbles to herself, and vacillates between moments of implosion and explosion. Ultimately, she experiences a total mental breakdown.

To prepare for the role, Blanchett met with a vocal coach, conducted an "anthropological study in Manhattan" by observing people in Upper East Side "shops, cafes, and restaurants," and repeatedly watched Robert B. Weide's 2012 documentary on Woody Allen's life and career. In lieu of rehearsals (something Allen does not do), the actress additionally met with costar Sally Hawkins to "make sense" of their characters' complicated sibling relationship.[7] While *Blue Jasmine* draws parallels to the case involving the American stockbroker Bernard L. Madoff and to

Drawing parallels to the plight of Blanche DuBois in *A Streetcar Named Desire*, Cate Blanchett's haughty character of Jasmine French finds herself on the edge of sanity (and possible homelessness) in *Blue Jasmine* (2013). (Sony Pictures Classics/Photofest)

A Streetcar Named Desire (for which **Vivien Leigh** hurled herself toward her own mental breakdown), Blanchett gained further inspiration from Eugene O'Neill's *Long Day's Journey into Night*, from the entitled title character of Shakespeare's *Richard II*, and from having played Blanche DuBois in Liv Ullmann's 2009 stage production of *Streetcar*.

At presenter Daniel Day-Lewis's announcement of Blanchett's name as Best Actress at the 2014 Academy Awards, she made her way to the Oscar stage and became the sixth woman (after **Helen Hayes**, **Ingrid Bergman**, **Maggie Smith**, **Meryl Streep**, and **Jessica Lange**) to have won an Oscar in both the lead and supporting categories. Acknowledging her standing ovation, Blanchett wryly told the audience to "sit down; you're too old to be standing."[8] She then thanked the Academy, her fellow contenders, and her fellow cast and crew before chiding Hollywood for sexism in a pointed acceptance speech that encouraged "studios to make more movies about women."[9] "And to the audiences," she said, "who went to see [*Blue Jasmine*], and perhaps those of us in the industry who are still foolishly clinging to the idea that female films with women at the center are niche experiences: They are not. Audiences want to see them, and, in fact, they earn money. The world is round, people!"[10] As **Meryl Streep** underlined nearly 25 years before, "If we don't have these images of women [that] we feel for, admire, recognize, and esteem, then we stifle the dreams of our daughters."[11]

For a film with a woman squarely situated at the center of action, *Blue Jasmine* enjoyed a long theater run and garnered $97.5 million worldwide (against an $18 million budget). Set apart from the so-called chick-flick genre (a recent, derogatory replacement term for the "woman's picture" genre, which fosters female-centered narratives and is designed to attract a predominantly female target audience), the film resonated with a diversified viewership that was still reeling from the 2008–2012 global recession. In a Hollywood industry "built by women, immigrants, and Jews" but where female protagonists only account for "16% of the general movie output,[12] *Blue Jasmine*'s success is still regarded an exception to the rule. To be sure, white heterosexual men are still "ensconced in the industry's primary power roles" and are therefore more likely to be seen up onscreen—a reality that poses "a serious threat to the industry's ability to serve an increasingly diverse movie-going population."[13] "We all know what we have to do," said **Jane Fonda**, addressing the fact that women behind the scenes account for only "six percent of directors, ten percent of writers, 15 percent of executive producers, 17 percent of editors, and three percent of cinematographers."[14] "We have to keep talking about it. We have to shame the studios for being so gender-biased."[15]

As a self-described feminist coexisting in an era when the auteur director Quentin Tarantino invited "whores" to apply to a casting call via a 2016 Facebook post,[16] Blanchett has openly spoken about these issues and the equality that women have yet to achieve. "Conservatism is affecting the way women perceive who they are in the world," she explained. "I feel that all the steps forward that we've made . . . a lot of those have been rescinded."[17] With many young women under the assumption that the women of the 1970s liberation movement "did all that could or should be done," many today, as the American feminist and political activist Gloria Steinem has pointed out, feel that they "can now relax."[18] But in a world that still "thrives on the hatred of women" and where self-objectification has become an epidemic, women—for the first time in history—are "no longer half the human race."[19] Contributing to this decline are the practices of "son preference, . . . the lethal results of genital cutting, domestic violence, sex trafficking, sexualized violence in war zones, honor killings," and so forth.[20]

As an activist against sexual abuse, substance abuse, depression, and suicide; a supporter of the United Nations' HeForShe gender-equality campaign; and a ringleader in the demand for increased female representation onscreen (as demonstrated in her protest as Cannes jury president in 2018 alongside 82 other female filmmakers including Agnès Varda and Ava DuVernay), Blanchett has used her celebrity status to help and empower. As seen in such films as *Cinderella* (2015), *Carol* (2015), and the all-female *Ocean's Eight* (2018; costarring **Sandra Bullock**), Blanchett's movies continually pass the Bechdel Test, a rating system that determines the "level of gender equality in a film" by assessing whether two women converse about something other than a man.[21] Taking the industry to task on issues concerning pay, roles, and representation, she has additionally articulated the frustration of the thinking woman by imagining a better future in which women are no longer marginalized but are instead embraced by men for their knowledge, their skills, and their multidimensional talents.

Julianne Moore

I n a Karl Lagerfield–designed Chanel dress that took 27 workers and 987 hours to create, **Julianne Moore** arrived at the red carpet ahead of the 87th Academy Awards (2015). Although she was happy to show off the embroidered dress (which included 80,000 white, hand-painted sequins and flowers made of ivory), the auburn-haired actress refused to participate in the so-called Mani-Cam — a short-lived "ladies-only red-carpet ritual" that prompted actresses to place their "well-tended nails into a box with a camera."[1] Her refusal coincided with #AskHerMore, a new "initiative to query actresses about more substantive things than their outfits."[2] "Watch," insisted **Sandra Bullock**, who was also present that night. "We're going to walk down the red carpet [and] I'm going to be asked about my dress and my hair while the man standing next to me will be asked about his performance and political issues."[3]

Against a field consisting of the British actresses Rosamund Pike (*Gone Girl*) and Felicity Jones (*The Theory of Everything*) and past recipients **Marion Cotillard** (*Two Days, One Night*) and **Reese Witherspoon** (*Wild*), Moore was crowned Best Actress for her performance as a woman diagnosed with Alzheimer's disease and subsequently abandoned by her husband in *Still Alice* (2014). Taking the stage, she was given a standing ovation that was largely seen as a recognition of her remarkable career. Intriguingly, in the 87 years of Oscar history up to that point, the 54-year-old star became (after **Shirley Booth**) only the second actress in her 50s to win the Best Actress award — 19 years older than the average Best Actress Oscar–winning age of 35. Addressing the audience, Moore underscored that "there's no such thing as best actress" before shining a spotlight on Alzheimer's disease. "So many people with this disease feel isolated and marginalized, and one of the wonderful things

Still Alice (2014)

Julianne Moore's character of Alice Howland, a respected linguistics professor at Columbia University who has been diagnosed with early-onset Alzheimer's disease, learns by phone that her eldest daughter will one day develop the disease in a crestfallen moment from *Still Alice* (2014). (Sony Pictures Classics/Photofest) about movies is it makes us feel seen and not alone. And people with Alzheimer's deserve to be seen, so that we can find a cure."[4] Moore additionally thanked her managers, her family, and everyone involved in *Still Alice*, including the film's codirectors, the gay married couple Wash Westmoreland and Richard Glatzer (who died of complications from ALS less than two weeks later).

In the process of filming *Still Alice*, the focus on disease was indeed given "extra emotional charge." Based on the self-published 2007 novel by the neuroscientist Lisa Genova and made during Glatzer's "steadily worsening condition," which impaired the director's ability to speak, the film shows the "subtle slippages in time and memory that become commonplace to Alzheimer's sufferers."[5] Moore's brain-ravaged character, Alice Howland, a respected linguistics professor at Columbia University, faces mental decline by way of a "rare strain of the . . . disease that strikes much younger and swifter than usual" and descends into a terrifying spiral of "confusion, anger, and sadness" as her husband and three adult children try to help her.[6] Over the course of the movie, Alice is reduced from a genius to a shell of herself. In one scene, she urinates while attempting to locate the bathroom in her beach house. In another, she unsuccessfully follows the suicide instructions that she left for herself via video several months before. In 1995, Moore played a similar role as a woman with multiple chemical sensitivity disorder in *Safe*. To prepare for *Still Alice* (which was shot over 23 days in nonchronological order), she read extensively on the disease and interviewed National Alzheimer's Association consultants. On set, she took directions from Glatzer by way of an iPad text-to-speech application that allowed him to communicate with his cast and crew.

Known for portraying characters who appear alienated, distressed, and emotionally complex (as evinced in a three-minute YouTube montage from 20 of her films, entitled "Julianne Moore Loves to Cry"), Moore has rarely shied away from soul-baring material. With the exception of her participation in such blockbusters as *The Lost World: Jurassic Park* (1997) and *The Hunger Games: Mockingjay—Part 1 and Part 2* (2014; 2015), she has been attracted to difficult projects that are dependent on "language and nuance" and has consequently remained a queen of independent cinema in acclaimed and often LGBT-related films such as *Far from Heaven* (2002), *A Single Man* (2009), *The Kids Are All Right* (2010), and *Freeheld* (2015). "The movie that plays in Japan, that plays in Germany, that plays in California, that plays in Australia, that goes everywhere and doesn't need to be translated, that's an action movie," she explained. "[But] I'm . . . drawn to ordinary characters in domestic situations because I think that's what our lives are about."[7]

Moore was born on December 3, 1960, in Fort Bragg, North Carolina, and like **Faye Dunaway** and **Reese Witherspoon**, she grew up as a military brat. Her father worked as an army paratrooper during the Vietnam War before serving as a colonel and military judge. Because of her father's roving military career, her family was continually uprooted from one military base to another in places as wide ranging as Alaska, Nebraska, Panama, and West Germany. "We were moving all the time,"

In her Best Actress Oscar acceptance speech at the 2015 Academy Awards, *Still Alice* star Julianne Moore shined a spotlight on Alzheimer's disease while honoring codirector Richard Glatzer, who died of complications from ALS less than two weeks later. (© A.M.P.A.S.®/ Photofest)

recalled the actress, who attended nine different schools throughout her upbringing. To provide a sense of stability, Moore's mother, a Scotland-born psychologist and social worker, regularly took her three children "to the library to check out books." "Literature was a comfort," said Moore. "You pick up a book and you know you're going to get a story."[8]

Although she first toiled with the idea of becoming a doctor, Moore, who was the "star of all her school plays," was encouraged to pursue acting by her theater teacher at the Frankfurt American High School in Germany. "I think it was a surprise even to me that I became an actor," acknowledged Moore, who "had never met an actor or seen a professional play." "I liked television and movies, but I didn't even know there was an industry." While researching colleges, Moore made a deal with her parents that she would only "apply to drama schools that also offered a liberal-arts degree" just in case her acting dreams did not come to fruition.[9]

After a short time, Moore, like **Faye Dunaway** before her, was studying theater at Boston University before moving to New York, where she worked as a part-time waitress while making the rounds in regional theater. Like the dual roles performed onscreen by **Mary Pickford** in *Stella Maris* (1918) and *Little Lord Fauntleroy* (1921), **Norma Shearer** in *Lady of the Night* (1925), **Bette Davis** in *A Stolen Life* (1946) and *Dead Ringer* (1964), **Olivia de Havilland** in *The Dark Mirror* (1946), and **Julie Christie** in *Fahrenheit 451* (1966), Moore soon arrested audiences with the incarnation of good and evil twins on the CBS daytime soap opera *As the World Turns* (1985–1988). Expanding her artistic growth and technical acting know-how, she then committed herself to the theater director Andre Gregory's painstaking five-year workshop exploring the Russian playwright Anton Chekhov's *Uncle Vanya*.

In 1992, marking a major turning point in her career, Moore was approached by the veteran director Robert Altman, who had seen her perform in *Uncle Vanya*. "I called her," said Altman, "[and] I said, . . . 'I have to tell you this character has to play a scene . . . naked from the waist down. . . . It's not a sex scene, it's not about sex, but she has to be there naked."[10] Moore accepted the role in Altman's *Short Cuts* (1993) and was ultimately greeted with positive reviews, even though some people found her nakedness to be contrived, exploitative, and specifically designed (by a male director) to flatter a male audience.

Certainly, in the history of entertainment, this tradition dates back to "the earliest days of the peep shows," but it has since reached an alarming level where "doing a nude scene is almost a rite of passage for actresses."[11] **Kate Winslet**, who posed nude in many of her films including her Oscar-winning turn in *The Reader* (2008), stood up to this trend alongside the Actors' Equity Association and swore "not to repeat her clothes-dropping act in the future following fears of being typecast."[12] **Natalie Portman** similarly "succeeded in getting a nude scene . . . axed" from one of her films, while **Halle Berry** conversely exercised her clout to demand an extra fee of $500,000 for a topless scene in *Swordfish* (2001).[13] For Moore, who went on to star as a drug-addicted porn star in *Boogie Nights* (1997), sex scenes and nudity sometimes go hand in hand with the job. As the actress asserted, "There's almost nothing I wouldn't do while acting, because it's pretend. It's narrative."[14] "I don't have a problem with nudity. I [only] have a problem . . . when it's superfluous and gratuitous—like the nudity I did in *Body of Evidence*" (a 1993 erotic thriller starring Madonna).[15]

But despite her propensity to undress onscreen, Moore, who once posed nude for a Michael Thompson photograph that ethereally captured her in the mode of an Ingres oil painting, tries not to call attention to herself in public. "I don't understand why that would serve you as a person or as an actor," she stated. As *The Hours* novelist Michael Cunningham observed, the actress has an uncanny ability to withdraw her beauty so as not to be noticed. "There [is] a glow," he said, "that she [can emanate] in the living room . . . [and conversely] retract in the street." As David Cronenberg, who directed Moore in *Map to the Stars* (2014), further remarked, duality is fundamentally constructed into her face. "She's more angular from the profile and softer from the full on. So, just by turning her head, she can go from hard to soft. She knows how to use that, too."[16]

Brie Larson

The big question leading up to the 88th Academy Awards (2016) was not "What will you be wearing to the Oscars?" but "Will you actually be going?"[1] For the second year in a row, in spite of a multitude of standout performances from ethnic-minority actors, the Academy of Motion Picture Arts and Sciences failed to nominate a single non-Caucasian in its four acting categories. The Academy was ridiculed on late-night talk shows and social media for a lack of diversity within its membership, and it found itself in a political quagmire exacerbated by the revived OscarsSoWhite hashtag and calls to orchestrate a boycott. Reaffirming that the Oscars broadcast is often more than "an overhyped spectacle" and is "an event of immense political and social importance in the United States,"[2] the actors Will Smith, Jada Pinkett-Smith, and Tyrese Gibson, the rapper Snoop Dogg, the documentary filmmaker Michael Moore, and the freshly minted Academy Honorary Award recipient Spike Lee announced that they would not be attending or watching the ceremony. Others unsuccessfully pressured the Black comedian, actor, and Academy Awards host Chris Rock to drop out. At "Hollywood cocktail parties, Academy screenings, and guild awards ceremonies, the chatter [became] less about who's up and who's down in the Oscar campaign than about thorny questions of race and discrimination in [an] entertainment industry" that is still dominated by the white heterosexual male elite.[3] On Facebook, **Reese Witherspoon** expressed her disappointment while advocating for "a more diverse voting membership."[4] **Halle Berry** also weighed in on the visible lack of opportunity. "To sit here almost 15 years later, and knowing that another woman of color has not walked through that door, is heartbreaking."[5] "As filmmakers and as actors, we have a responsibility to tell the truth," **Berry** emphasized. "The films, I think,

After enduring seven years held captive in a shed, Brie Larson's character of Joy "Ma" Newsome and her five-year-old son Jack (played by Jacob Tremblay) ponder how to survive in the outside world. (A24/Photofest)

coming out of Hollywood aren't truthful. And the reason they're not . . . is that they're not really depicting the importance . . . and the participation of people of color in our American culture."[6] "I think that when everybody's story is told, then that makes better art," U.S. President Barack Obama concluded.[7]

Perhaps tilting the outcome of the Oscar race for Best Actress, the veteran British thespian and first-time nominee Charlotte Rampling caused a stir on French radio by suggesting that "the #OscarsSoWhite controversy was prejudiced against white people."[8] After her comments went viral, the 70-year-old actress, who was nominated for her turn in the film *45 Years*, awkwardly walked back her remarks.

On Oscar night, Rampling's competition included former recipients **Cate Blanchett** (*Carol*) and **Jennifer Lawrence** (*Joy*), New York Film Critics Award recipient Saoirse Ronan (*Brooklyn*), and the ultimate winner, **Brie Larson**, for her performance as a woman held captive and sexually assaulted for seven years in

Room (2015). In an Oscar moment that seemed to mirror the swift ascendance to superstardom by previous relative newcomers **Jennifer Jones**, **Audrey Hepburn**, and **Julie Christie**, Larson, wearing a ruffled royal-blue Gucci gown, hugged her young costar Jacob Tremblay before accepting her Oscar from presenter Eddie Redmayne. At the culmination of a long awards season that found the actress relentlessly promoting *Room*, embarrassingly talking about herself at length, and almost "hallucinating" while doing a roundtable with the likes of **Jane Fonda**, **Helen Mirren**, **Kate Winslet**, **Cate Blanchett**, and **Jennifer Lawrence**,[9] Larson used her acceptance speech to thank the Academy, various film festivals, A24 Films, fellow cast and crew members, and her friends and family.

Backstage, where the #OscarsSoWhite controversy continued to garner attention alongside the sexual-abuse-themed Best Picture winner, *Spotlight*, the actress beamingly revealed that "her feelings about winning could best be summed up with the song 'I'm in Love with My Life' by Phases," a pop band fronted by her boyfriend, Alex Greenwald.[10] Larson, who was earlier seen individually hugging 50 survivors of sexual violence who had accompanied Lady Gaga's Oscar performance of "Til It Happens to You," additionally "touched on what she hoped [*Room*] would do for women in similar situations as her character." "In the core of [the film], we [wanted] to talk about abuse; the many different ways that females can be abused or feel confined. . . . I hope that when people watch this they realize that they have it in themselves to break free of whatever it is that's holding them back."[11]

Based on Emma Donoghue's 2010 novel of the same name and inspired by the real-life account of a woman who emerged from captivity in Austria in 2008 after 24 years of rape and enslavement that resulted in the births of seven children, *Room* tells the story of Joy "Ma" Newsome. While walking home from school in Akron, Ohio, at the age of 17, Joy gets tricked into helping a man with his sick dog, only to find herself abducted and locked in his garden shed. The film begins seven years later inside the tiny and squalid shed that Joy and her five-year-old son, Jack (the product of Joy's captivity, played by Jacob Tremblay), call "Room." Despite suffering from depression, malnutrition, and the trauma of being routinely raped by her psychopathic captor ("Old Nick") while Jack is sleeping, Joy tries to give her son a sense of optimism and, ultimately, a notion of the world that exists outside of "Room," as they plan a bold and successful ruse to escape. Later, as Joy adjusts to life with her reunited family, she agrees to participate in a television interview, in which she is questioned as to why she decided to keep her son in captivity with her. Besieged with guilt and echoing attempts of suicide as seen in such Best Actress Oscar–winning films as *7th Heaven* (1927; with **Janet Gaynor**), *Mildred Pierce* (1945; with **Joan Crawford**), *Anastasia* (1956; with **Ingrid Bergman**), *The Piano* (1993; with **Holly Hunter**), and *Still Alice* (2014; with **Julianne Moore**), Joy is admitted to a hospital before finding the strength to recover by way of Jack's blameless compassion and resilience.

Selected for the lead in *Room* over the likes of Rooney Mara, Mia Wasikowska, Emma Watson, and Shailene Woodley, Larson, who had shown a willingness to get her acting hands dirty as a counselor to troubled teens in *Short Term 12* (2013), went all out to prepare for her role. In doing so, she locked "herself in her apartment for weeks," kept "out of the sun for months," dieted "until she had just 12% body fat," and consulted with a trauma specialist.[12] She also developed a bond with her young costar, with whom she would share (sometimes with as many as eight camera operators) a cramped, 11-by-11-foot soundstage over the course of five weeks.

Larson additionally acknowledged that aspects of her early life helped to prepare her for *Room*. The actress was born Brianne Desaulniers in Sacramento, California, on October 1, 1989. Although her stage name derives from the maiden name of her Swedish great-grandmother, she was raised speaking French by parents who were holistic-medicine practitioners. Larson first took an interest in acting by way of watching, among other things, a scratched VHS tape of **Vivien Leigh**'s performance in *Gone with the Wind* (1939). Before long, her parents divorced, and alongside her mother and younger sister, Milaine, Larson relocated to Los Angeles in pursuit of acting by way of endless auditions, sporadic commercials, and an unsuccessful TV sitcom (*Raising Dad*, 2001–2002). Reflecting on this time, the home-schooled actress painfully recalled "sharing a Murphy bed" with her sister and distressed mother in an overcrowded studio apartment and "not being able to . . . afford a McDonald's Happy Meal."[13] "I had, like, two shirts, a pair of jeans, and that was it," she said.[14] Even as her film career began to take shape with supporting roles, Larson remembered living "off the food in the film-festival welcome gift bags."[15]

But with Larson's newly minted Oscar prestige, her asking price ensured that those days were over. In an age in which actors often "float across and around stardom" without a "single system" in place to define that stardom "for the public's endorsement,"[16] Larson next appeared in the commercially successful *King Kong* franchise reboot of *Kong: Skull Island* (2017). On the heels of the DC Comics success of the first *Wonder Woman* movie (2017), it was announced that Larson—as Captain Marvel—would become "the first woman in the Marvel Cinematic Universe to get a stand-alone film,"[17] shattering yet another glass ceiling and ultimately scoring big at the box office despite a flood of internet trolls who attempted to discredit Larson with sexist reviews.

At the 2017 Academy Awards, Larson became something of a superhero to many people in real life when she remained motionless with her arms drawn to her side after presenting Casey Affleck with the Best Actor Oscar. Standing by the principles that led her to criticize the judge who lightly sentenced a Stanford University student convicted of three counts of sexual assault in 2016, Larson refused to join the chorus of audience applause as Affleck, who had been "sued by two women for sexual harassment in 2010,"[18] prepared to deliver his acceptance speech. "I think that whatever it was that I did on stage kind of spoke for itself," the actress later stated.[19] Sending a strong message to a male-dominated world that such behavior will never go unnoticed, Larson again used her status to draw attention to the 2017 sexual-abuse allegations against the actors Dustin Hoffman, Geoffrey Rush, James Franco, and Kevin Spacey; the directors John Lasseter,

Brett Ratner, Oliver Stone, and Lars von Trier; the fashion photographer Terry Richardson; the TV figures Matt Lauer and Charlie Rose; U.S. Senator Al Franken; and many others, after actresses including Salma Hayek, Angelina Jolie, Ashley Judd, Rose McGowan, and **Gwyneth Paltrow** accused the film producer Harvey Weinstein of sexual harassment. Posting on Twitter in the wake of these accusations, which hastened an international reckoning against sexual harassment with the #MeToo and Time's Up movements, Larson wrote, "As always, I stand with the brave survivors of sexual assault and harassment. It's not your fault. I believe you."[20]

Emma Stone

In an era when audiences watch movies and network, cable, and web TV shows on their televisions, personal computers, cell phones, or "on the back of an airplane seat,"[1] a proliferation of opportunities has seemingly opened up for young and aspiring actors. As these screens continue to shrink in size, the number of streaming and video-sharing platforms continue to grow, presenting many actors with "a million options . . . as long as [they're] cool getting 'famous'" via social media services such as Instagram, Facebook, Twitter, and YouTube.[2] In a hypercompetitive industry that offers "less big-studio auditions," aspiring actors—with their head shots and requisite demo reels—continue to vie for desirable roles as they hone their performance skills at various film schools, improvisational theaters, and acting workshops (the latter of which, in some cities, have been criticized for their exploitative nature as "de facto 'pay to play' casting calls").[3] "To become an actor was a dangerous thing financially," recalled **Helen Mirren** of her fledging career in the 1960s. "But, on the other hand, it was doable and I don't know whether it is anymore. It's gone back to only really posh kids being able to afford to be actors."[4] "I couldn't make it as a young actor today," acknowledged **Maggie Smith**. "I think they are so brave. They seem to have to strip off every second. I can't imagine how they cope with it today, I really don't."[5] "I think it is terrifying being a young actress now," said **Jane Fonda**. "There is even more emphasis on how you look."[6] "I would arrive [to auditions] in sneakers and they'd say, 'Come back in a miniskirt and heels,'" **Brie Larson** added. "I would come back and blow the audition. I felt more in my body when I wasn't dressing as a fantasy for the male gaze."[7]

For **Emma Stone**, who won the Best Actress Oscar for mimicking in *La La Land* (2016) what many struggling young actresses go through, the obstacles

La La Land (2016)

A nostalgic throwback to the Hollywood musicals of the 1930s featuring Ginger Rogers and Fred Astaire, *La La Land* performers Emma Stone and Ryan Gosling dance in a romantic sequence shot at the Griffith Observatory. (Summit Entertainment/ Photofest)

involved in obtaining respect and recognition as an actor today are unmistakable. After persuading her parents to "let her move to Los Angeles" via a step-by-step PowerPoint presentation entitled "Project Hollywood 2004" (featuring the Madonna song "Hollywood"),[8] Stone, a high school freshman, dropped out of school, rented an apartment with her mother in the Miracle Mile, found a part-time job selling dog treats, and dejectedly slogged her way through endless auditions. "It's this strange sort of combination of a job interview and a first date and a breakup on a daily basis," described the actress, whose real-life experiences (including "crying as part of a monologue only to be interrupted by a director taking a phone call about lunch") were "incorporated into the *La La Land* script."[9]

The daughter of a CEO of a general contracting company, Stone was born Emily Jean Stone in Scottsdale, Arizona, on November 6, 1988. Growing up, she suffered from anxiety and panic attacks and ultimately sought solace by way of therapy. "My anxiety was constant. I would ask my mom a hundred times how the day was gonna lay out. What time was she gonna drop me off? Where was she gonna be? . . . At a certain point, I couldn't go to friends' houses any more—I could barely get out the door to school."[10] At the age of 11, Stone discovered another strategy to calm her nerves. Performing "to escape her demons," she "started acting at [the Valley Youth Theatre in Phoenix], doing improvisation and sketch comedy." As she explained, "You have to be present in improvisation, and that's the antithesis of anxiety."[11] With the raspy voice that she acquired from having infantile colic, she appeared in more than a dozen plays including *Alice in Wonderland*, *The Princess and the Pea*, and *Cinderella* as a wicked stepsister. While living on the grounds of the Camelback Inn—a historic resort and spa coowned by her parents that once played host to Clark Gable, James Stewart, **Bette Davis**, and numerous political leaders—Stone, who possesses the independent air of a modern-day **Katharine Hepburn**, bossed her little brother, Spencer, around in homemade skits as she concocted her plans to conquer Hollywood.

By the time Stone sang and danced her way through Los Angeles in the musical-romantic-comedy-drama *La La Land* (2016), she had amassed a significant fan base by way of her roles in *Superbad* (2007; for which she made her screen debut), *Easy A* (2010; for which she made her lead debut), *The Help* (2011), *The Amazing Spider-Man* franchise (2012–2014), and the Best Picture Oscar–winning *Birdman* (2014). Opening with an acrobatic song-and-dance "sequence set on a gridlocked L.A. freeway," *La La Land* tells the story of Mia Dolan (played by Stone), an aspiring actress who works "as a barista in a coffee shop on the Warner Bros. lot not far from the sets where *Casablanca* (1942) was shot."[12] As a "billboard-sized poster of **Ingrid Bergman**" watches over the bed of her shared apartment, Mia—like **Janet Gaynor**'s determined character in *A Star Is Born* (1937)—joins the depressing Hollywood "audition merry-go-round."[13] Antagonistically, she bumps into Sebastian (Ryan Gosling), an aspiring, Paul Newman (à la 1961's *Paris Blues*)–like jazz musician who ekes "out a living as a pianist in a restaurant." In "a world of intrusive cell phones and electronic car keys,"[14] a courtship ensues that finds the couple

traipsing around Los Angeles landmarks (such as Angel's Flight, Watts Tower, and the Colorado Street Bridge) and dancing up amid the stars like **Ginger Rogers** and Fred Astaire in a fantasy sequence at the Griffith Observatory. While *La La Land* pays tribute to classical Hollywood cinema, Bollywood, and the colorful work of the French director Jacques Demy, it ultimately shows Mia and Sebastian—two highly motivated individuals—supporting each other's dreams and holding each other accountable, even if the end result is not conducive to their couplehood.

For Stone's performance in *La La Land* (a role that almost went to the British actress Emma Watson), she found herself in a stiff race for Best Actress ahead of the 89th Academy Awards (2017). Her competition included 20-time Oscar nominee and veteran recipient **Meryl Streep** (*Florence Foster Jenkins*), the French actress, fellow frontrunner, and New York Film Critics Award recipient Isabelle Huppert (*Elle*), the Ethiopian-Irish actress Ruth Negga (*Loving*), and, for her performance as Jacqueline Kennedy, former winner **Natalie Portman** (*Jackie*). But with *La La Land* tying *All About Eve* (1950; with **Bette Davis**) and *Titanic* (1997; with **Kate Winslet**) with the highest number of nominations in Oscar history (14), Stone's chances were given an added boost. After *La La Land*'s director, Damien Chazelle, became the youngest director (at age 32) to win the Best Director Oscar, presenter Leonardo DiCaprio announced Stone's name as Best Actress. Draped in a "sparkling gold [1920s-style] Givenchy Haute Couture gown with a fringe skirt covered in Swarovski

In *La La Land* (2016), the romance between the aspiring actress played by Emma Stone and the struggling jazz musician played by Ryan Gosling ends in heartbreak but allows both characters to realize their career ambitions. Contrary to many films that depict women succeeding only if they sacrifice love, Stone's character ultimately emerges famous, wealthy, and happily married (albeit to someone else). (Summit Entertainment/Photofest) crystals,"[15] Stone hugged her brother before making her way to the Oscar stage. "To . . . everyone that put their heart and souls into this film, I'm gonna find you . . . and hug the hell out of you when the feeling reenters my body," she said. "I still have a lot of growing and learning and work to do, and this . . . is a really beautiful symbol to continue on that journey."[16]

Moments later, marking the 50th anniversary of the groundbreaking film *Bonnie and Clyde* (1967), the actors Warren Beatty and **Faye Dunaway** made their way to the stage to present the Oscar for Best Picture. Unbeknownst to the presenters, the card in Beatty's hand was not for Best Picture but instead a duplicate Best Actress card with Emma Stone's name on it for *La La Land*. Beatty stalled and looked quizzically offstage and at his copresenter and then began to announce the winner. "You're impossible,"[17] **Dunaway** playfully interjected before calling out *La La Land*'s name as the winner, representing the most epic blunder in Oscar history. Over two minutes and two and a half victory speeches in (with Stone and her fellow *La La Land* cast and crew flooding the stage), flustered representatives from the Academy and the accounting firm of PricewaterhouseCoopers finally corrected the jaw-dropping mistake by providing the correct card with the name of the actual winner: *Moonlight*.

Backstage after the show, the confusion and "disbelief continued" as journalists tried to discern what had happened.[18] Speaking to reporters, Stone confirmed that she had been holding her "Best Actress card the whole time" and that "she was authentically happy" for *Moonlight*—the first movie with an all-Black cast to capture the Best Picture Oscar and a powerful symbol of progress in light of the recent #OscarsSoWhite controversy. "I fucking love *Moonlight*," she said while clutching the Oscar that she had humorously characterized to the press as a creepy "naked man."[19] "Of course, you know, it was an amazing thing to hear *La La Land*. I think we all would have loved to win Best Picture, but we are *so* excited for *Moonlight*. I think it's one of the best films of all time."[20]

Earning "$26 million over the 12-month period" between August 2016 and 2017 (incidentally, less than double the amount of her average male counterpart),[21] Stone quickly became one of the highest paid actresses in the world. With her Oscar victory, a ton of free publicity, and top roles dropped at her feet after she won, the down-to-earth actress unquestionably had the "city of stars" (as characterized in the Oscar-winning song from *La La Land*) brightly and boldly shining just for her.

ACKNOWLEDGMENTS

I would like to express my love and gratitude to Aero and Olive, Jeremie Adkins, Farah Afnan, Ellie Blankfort, Christina Bogar Sunstone, Krista Carlson, Peggy Chepeleff, Sarah Blankfort Clothier at the American Film Institute, my late mentor and the longtime photography curator for the Academy of Motion Picture Arts and Sciences Robert Cushman (1946–2009), Atu Darko, Summer Doan, Caroline Drasbæk, Janet Fankhauser-Nyman, Shirley Ferguson, Melissa Gallagher, Sara Greenleaf-Seitz, Miyoko Kinard, Anna Lena Kortmann, Leilani Lamarca, Sheila Lowenbraun, Nathalie Monnet, Linda Pickering, my nephew Brandon Tapert Raimo, Joanne Robertson, John Robertson, Lance Robertson, Jeffrey Rogers, Ingrid Ryberg, Barbara and Kai Sametinger, Vionnette Dover Sellers, Jeremy Simmons, Azalia Snail, Sigrid Solheim, Michelle Sullivan, my father Gary Tapert, Gaye Harris-Tapert, Francesco Vatteroni, Julio Vera, Gloria Vilches, and Stine Sophie Winckel.

I also received invaluable assistance and support from Kaveh Askari, Stephanie Armstrong, Catherine Bainbridge, Lucia Bay, Carrie Beauchamp, Ron Bernstein at ICM Partners, Manoah Bowman, Stephanie Cabot, Heather Carmichael at My Friend's Place, Bruce Carroll, the China brothers: Ben and Paul, Merrianne Couture, Brett Davidson, India Dupre, the Ebell of Los Angeles, Ellen Fontana at The Audrey Hepburn Children's Fund, Kristen Hatch, Catherine Hess at The Huntington Library, Ed Hudeček, Laura Jennings, Jay Jorgensen, Adrià Julià, Judy Karfiol, Andrea Kittelson, Mark Knowles, the late Cecily MacArthur, Andie MacDowell, Liza Minnelli, Sreya Mitra, Sheryn Morris at the Los Angeles Central Library, everyone at Photofest (especially Howard Mandelbaum and Todd Ifft), Brad Roberts, Mark Bruce Rosin, Virginia Saunders, Will Schmenner, Susan Sarandon, Kirsten Schaffer at Women in Film, Christel Schmidt at The Library of Congress, Greg Schreiner, Matt Tunia, Jeffrey Vance, Mark A. Vieira, Heather von Rohr, Beth Werling at the Natural History Museum of Los Angeles County, Wash Westmoreland, Tom Wilson, and Connor Winterton.

At the Museo Nazionale del Cinema in Turin, Italy, I wish to thank Claudia Bozzone, Elena D'Agnolo, Grazia Paganelli, Donata Pesenti, Angela Savoldi, and most especially my co-curators Nicoletta Pacini and Tamara Sillo. At the Deutsche Kinemathek in Berlin, Germany, I thank Kristina Jaspers, Peter Mänz, Daniela Sannwald, Nils Warnecke, and Andrea Wickleder.

I would like to thank my friends and former colleagues at the Academy of Motion Picture Arts and Sciences' Margaret Herrick Library for providing aid and support for this project.

I am additionally grateful to my former professors Susan Fiksdal and Marianne Bailey at The Evergreen State College and Tom Gunning, Yuri Tsivian, and Jacqueline Stewart at The University of Chicago.

I would also like to thank my students at the New York Film Academy; my colleagues, particularly those involved in NYFA's women's studies council (Lexie Helgerson, Anna Hogg, Anastasia Coon, Nedra Gallegos, and Karen Howes); and the chair of NYFA's Liberal Arts and Sciences' department, Mary Samuelson, and associate chairs Vanessa Conte Herse and Nancy Gong, for giving me the opportunity to transform this project into a college course.

This book owes a great debt to Nancy Cymerman, Jessica Davies, Maria Lamarca Anderson, and Andrew Katz for their input in shaping the text; Roxane Gay for contributing her foreword; and Don Kilhefner for helping in ways beyond measure.

Finally, this book would not be possible without the encouraging support and accommodating vision of several key individuals: Denis Rossano (for his incredible friendship, for sharing his vast and nuanced knowledge of film history with me, and for reviewing the manuscript in full); the magnificent Joan Brookbank of Joan Brookbank Projects; Nicole Solano, Micah Kleit, Dayna Hagewood, Courtney Brach, Vincent Nordhaus, and everyone at Rutgers University Press (for taking me and this project on); Museo Nazionale del Cinema director and Venice Film Festival artistic director Alberto Barbera (for being the first to see this project's value and potential); and, lastly, Bill Bednarz (for his thoughtfulness, generosity, encouragement, and enthusiasm for this project from day one).

NOTES

INTRODUCTION

1. B. Williams, "Pharrell: Women's Contribution to History Was Always Erased," *Huffington Post*, November 21, 2016, https://www.huffingtonpost.com/entry/pharrell-hidden-figures-gender-bias_us_583325b9e4b030997bc07e21.

2. "Academy Can Reclaim Auctioned Oscar Statuette for $10," BBC News, August 13, 2015, https://www.bbc.com/news/entertainment-arts-33903795.

3. Speech by Jimmy Carter to the Parliament of the World's Religions, Carter Center, December 2, 2009, https://www.cartercenter.org/news/editorials_speeches/parliament-world-religions-120309.html.

4. C. Rosen, "Keira Knightley, 'Anna Karenina' Star, on How Hollywood Underserves the Female Audience," *Huffington Post*, November 12, 2012, https://www.huffingtonpost.com/2012/11/12/keira-knightley-anna-karenina_n_2115341.html; *Miss Representation*, dir. J. Siebel Newsom (2011); J. Flanagin, "Because We Need More Kathryn Bigelows: Segregate the Oscars by Gender!," *Salon*, January 10, 2014, https://www.salon.com/2014/01/10/and_the_academy_award_for_best_female_director_goes_to_partner/.

5. J. P. Ogilvie, "How Hollywood Keeps Out the Stories of Women and Girls," *LA Weekly*, November 16, 2015.

6. J. A. Glancy, "The Accused: Susanna and Her Readers," in *A Feminist Companion to Esther, Judith, and Susanna*, ed. A. Brenner-Idan (Sheffield, UK: Sheffield Academic Press, 1995); Ogilvie, "How Hollywood Keeps Out the Stories."

7. J. Fontaine, *No Bed of Roses: An Autobiography* (New York: Berkley, 1978).

8. H. Mirren, acceptance speech, February 25, 2007, Academy Awards Acceptance Speech Database, http://aaspeechesdb.oscars.org/.

9. S. Hayward, *Simone Signoret: The Star as Cultural Sign* (New York: Continuum, 2004).

10. B. Weinraub, "Oscar's Glory Is Fleeting: Ask One Who Knows," *New York Times*, March 27, 1995.

11. *Los Angeles Examiner*, March 15, 1953.

12. J. Basinger, *A Woman's View: How Hollywood Spoke to Women, 1930–1960* (London: Chatto and Windus, 1993).

13. J. Basinger, *The Star Machine* (New York: Knopf, 2007).

14. D. Bona, "A Long, Strange History for Your Consideration: Miramax and DreamWorks Are Going All Out on Their Oscar Campaigns, but They Are Hardly the First to Do So," *Los Angeles Times*, March 19, 2000.

15. E. Dutka and R. W. Welkos, "Calendar Goes to the Oscars: A Few Good Words behind the Scenes Backstage," *Los Angeles Times*, March 30, 1993.

16. *Miss Representation*.

17. *Miss Representation*.

JANET GAYNOR

1. C. Billips, *Janet Gaynor: A Bio-Bibliography* (New York: Greenwood, 1992).

2. A. S. Berg, *Wilson* (New York: G. P. Putnam's Sons, 2013).

3. B. Staples, "When the Suffrage Movement Sold Out to White Supremacy," *New York Times*, February 2, 2019.

4. M. LaSalle, *Complicated Women: Sex and Power in Pre-Code Hollywood* (New York: Thomas Dunne Books, 2000).

5. LaSalle.

6. LaSalle.

7. *The Story of Film: An Odyssey*, dir. M. Cousins (2011).

8. J. Basinger, *A Woman's View: How Hollywood Spoke to Women, 1930–1960* (London: Chatto and Windus, 1993).

9. G. P. Williams, *The Story of Hollywood: An Illustrated History* (London: BL Press, 2005).

10. A. Slide, *Inside the Hollywood Fan Magazine: A History of Star Makers, Fabricators, and Gossip Mongers* (Jackson: University Press of Mississippi, 2010).

11. Program notes, *Janet Gaynor: A Centennial Celebration (1906–2006)*, presentation (Los Angeles: Louis B. Mayer Foundation and the UCLA Film & Television Archive, 2006).

12. D. Thomson, *The New Biographical Dictionary of Film* (New York: Knopf, 2010).

13. Program notes, *Janet Gaynor*.

14. "Nonfiction," *Publishers Weekly* 253, no. 49 (2006): 54.

15. T. Gunning, *D. W. Griffith and the Origins of American Narrative Film: The Early Years at Biograph* (Urbana: University of Illinois Press, 1994).

16. Program notes, *Janet Gaynor*.

MARY PICKFORD

1. E. Whitfield, "Laws of Attraction: Mary Pickford, Movies, and the Evolution of Fame," in *Mary Pickford: Queen of the Movies*, ed. C. Schmidt (Lexington: University Press of Kentucky, 2012).

2. T. Gunning, *D. W. Griffith and the Origins of American Narrative Film: The Early Years at Biograph* (Urbana: University of Illinois Press, 1994).

3. A. Slide, *Inside the Hollywood Fan Magazine: A History of Star Makers, Fabricators, and Gossip Mongers* (Jackson: University Press of Mississippi, 2010); D. Spoto, *High Society: The Life of Grace Kelly* (New York: Three Rivers, 2010).

4. K. Brownlow, *Mary Pickford Rediscovered: Rare Pictures of a Hollywood Legend* (New York: Harry N. Abrams, 1999).

5. Whitfield, "Laws of Attraction."

6. B. Thomas, "Rolling the Credits on Cinema's Extraordinary First Century; Movies: They Make Us Giggle, Sob, Even Swoon. And It All Began with a Sneeze. Or Was It a Kiss?," *Los Angeles Times*, April 18, 1999.

7. R. Koszarski, *An Evening's Entertainment: The Age of the Silent Feature Picture, 1915–1928* (Berkeley: University of California Press, 1990).

8. D. Thomson, *The New Biographical Dictionary of Film* (New York: Knopf, 2010).

9. G. P. Williams, *The Story of Hollywood: An Illustrated History* (London: BL Press, 2005); *The Thanhouser Studio and the Birth of American Cinema*, dir. N. Thanhouser (2014).

10. M. Idato, "The Real Deal | Jodie Foster | Mistress of Her Destiny," *Sun Herald*, May 22, 2016; M. Donnelly, "Showbusiness Parents Behaving Very Badly," *Daily Telegraph*, October 22, 2012.

11. Brownlow, *Mary Pickford Rediscovered*.

12. D. Spoto, *Possessed: The Life of Joan Crawford* (New York: William Morrow, 2010).

13. G. Studlar, "Oh, 'Doll Divine': Mary Pickford, Masquerade, and the Pedophilic Gaze," *Camera Obscura* 16, no. 3 (2001): 196–227.

14. J. Zhao, "Talking Was Golden: Actors and the First Talkies in America: 1927–1930," *Atlanta Review of Journalism History* 11, no. 4 (2010): 46–68.

15. C. Schmidt, "Crown of Glory: The Rise and Fall of the Mary Pickford Curls," in Schmidt, *Mary Pickford*.

16. M. LaSalle, *Complicated Women: Sex and Power in Pre-Code Hollywood* (New York: Thomas Dunne Books, 2000).

17. C. Schmidt, "Mary Pickford and the Archival Film Movement," in Schmidt, *Mary Pickford*.

18. Whitfield, "Laws of Attraction."

19. Brownlow, *Mary Pickford Rediscovered*.

20. S. Wulf, "25 Years Ago," *Entertainment Weekly*, February 23, 2001.

NORMA SHEARER

1. B. Thomas, *Thalberg: Life and Legend* (New York: Doubleday, 1969).

2. V. Wilson, *A Life of Barbara Stanwyck: Steel-True 1907–1940.* (New York: Simon and Schuster, 2013).

3. B. F. Dick, *Claudette Colbert: She Walked in Beauty* (Jackson: University Press of Mississippi, 2008).

4. G. Lambert, *Norma Shearer: A Life* (New York: Knopf, 1990); D. Cook, *A History of Narrative Film*, 4th ed. (New York: Norton, 2004); Lambert. *The Trial of Mary Dugan* (1929) was MGM's first all-talking drama.

5. M. Beck, "Persistence Paid Off for Hollywood's Greats," *Wisconsin State Journal*, August 15, 1982.

6. Lambert, *Norma Shearer*; C. Schmidt, "Crown of Glory: The Rise and Fall of the Mary Pickford Curls," in *Mary Pickford: Queen of the Movies*, ed. C. Schmidt (Lexington: University Press of Kentucky, 2012).

7. Lambert, *Norma Shearer*.

8. H. H. Prinzler, *Sirens and Sinners: A Visual History of Weimar Film, 1918–1933* (London: Thames and Hudson, 2012).

9. Lambert, *Norma Shearer*; R. Barton Palmer, *Twentieth-Century American Fiction on Screen* (Cambridge: Cambridge University Press, 2007).

10. D. Kehr, "Critic's Choice," *New York Times*, March 11, 2008; Thomas, *Thalberg*.

11. A. Tapert, *The Power of Glamour* (New York: Crown, 1998).

12. Lambert, *Norma Shearer*.

13. J. Basinger, *The Star Machine* (New York: Knopf, 2007).

14. *New York Times*, December 2, 1938; Lambert, *Norma Shearer*.

15. Lambert, *Norma Shearer*; M. Vieira, *Hurrell's Hollywood Portraits* (New York: Harry N. Abrams, 1997); J. A. Walz, "Film's Early Blue Period: Mark Vieira's Lectures and Screenings Recall 'Pre-Code' Hollywood, When Energetic but Raw Movies Led to Hays Office Crackdowns," *Los Angeles Times*, February 27, 2002.

16. Vieira, *Hurrell's Hollywood Portraits*.

17. J. Vermilye, *The Films of the Thirties* (Secaucus, NJ: Citadel, 1982).

18. *The Divorcee*, dir. R. Z. Leonard (1930); M. LaSalle, *Complicated Women: Sex and Power in Pre-Code Hollywood* (New York: Thomas Dunne Books, 2000).

19. M. Vieira, *Sin in Soft Focus: Pre-Code Hollywood* (New York: Harry N. Abrams, 1999); LaSalle, *Complicated Women*.

20. LaSalle, *Complicated Women*.

21. K. Collins, "Courting Oscar through the Years," *Variety*, November 24–30, 2003.

22. B. Thomas, "Rolling the Credits on Cinema's Extraordinary First Century; Movies: They Make Us Giggle, Sob, Even Swoon. And It All Began with a Sneeze. Or Was It a Kiss?," *Los Angeles Times*, April 18, 1999.

23. Tapert, *Power of Glamour*.

24. Tapert.

25. Tapert.

MARIE DRESSLER

1. M. Duberman, *Hidden from History: Reclaiming the Gay and Lesbian Past* (New York: Meridian, 1989).

2. M. Dressler, *My Own Story: As Told to Mildred Harrington* (Boston: Little, Brown, 1934).

3. Dressler.

4. Dressler.

5. A. Trope, "'Little Mary' Formidable Philanthropist," in *Mary Pickford: Queen of the Movies*, ed. C. Schmidt (Lexington: University Press of Kentucky, 2012); Dressler, *My Own Story*.

6. Dressler, *My Own Story*.

7. K. Brownlow, *Mary Pickford Rediscovered: Rare Pictures of a Hollywood Legend* (New York: Harry N. Abrams, 1999); Trope, "Little Mary."

8. Schmidt, *Mary Pickford*.

9. *New York Tribune*, August 13, 1919.

10. C. Beauchamp, *Without Lying Down: Frances Marion and the Powerful Women of Early Hollywood* (Berkeley: University of California Press, 1998).

11. D. Chan, "Oscar Best Actress Debuts," *Malay Mail*, May 13, 2004.

12. D. Spoto, *Possessed: The Life of Joan Crawford* (New York: William Morrow, 2010).

13. Dressler, *My Own Story*.

14. N. Shearer, presentation of the Oscar for Best Actress, November 10, 1931, Academy Awards Acceptance Speech Database, http://aaspeechesdb.oscars.org.

15. Dressler, *My Own Story*.

16. S. King, "Cine File: When Comedy Ruled the Screen; Because Real Life Was Such a Serious Matter, Hollywood Found Gold by Going for Laughs," *Los Angeles Times*, December 18, 2005.

17. T. Balio, *Grand Design: Hollywood as a Modern Business Enterprise, 1930–1939* (Berkeley: University of California Press, 1993); B. Thomas, *Thalberg: Life and Legend* (New York: Doubleday, 1969).

18. V. Wilson, *A Life of Barbara Stanwyck: Steel-True 1907–1940* (New York: Simon and Schuster, 2013).

19. M. Kennedy, *Marie Dressler: A Biography, with a Listing of Major Stage Performances, a Filmography, and a Discography* (Jefferson, NC: McFarland, 2006); D. Thomson, *The New Biographical Dictionary of Film* (New York: Knopf, 2010).

HELEN HAYES

1. D. K. Goodwin, *The Bully Pulpit: Theodore Roosevelt, William Howard Taft, and the Golden Age of Journalism* (New York: Simon and Schuster, 2014).

2. H. Hayes with K. Hatch, *My Life in Three Acts* (San Diego: Harcourt Brace Jovanovich, 1990); B. Barnes, "Renowned Actress Helen Hayes Dies; D.C.-Born Stage Great Was 9," *Washington Post*, March 18.

3. Barnes, "Renowned Actress."

4. Barnes.

5. G. Lambert, *Norma Shearer: A Life* (New York: Knopf, 1990).

6. Lambert.

7. V. Price, "Vincent/Victoria: For His Daughter, Vincent Price Was Not a Scary Movie Star but the Dad Who Supported Her Coming Out as a Lesbian," *Advocate*, November 9, 1999, 62.

8. D. Spoto, *High Society: The Life of Grace Kelly* (New York: Three Rivers, 2010); Hayes with Hatch, *My Life in Three Acts*.

9. C. Champlin, "Helen Hayes Isn't Ready to Rust: The Actress, Nearing 90, Holds to Her 'Stay Busy' Credo: She's Now Promoting Her Recently Completed Book—Her Third Memoir," *Los Angeles Times*, May 13, 1990.

10. Hayes with Hatch, *My Life in Three Acts*.

11. V. Wilson, *A Life of Barbara Stanwyck: Steel-True 1907–1940* (New York: Simon and Schuster, 2013).

12. Barnes, "Renowned Actress"; B. Thomas, *Thalberg: Life and Legend* (New York: Doubleday, 1969).

13. Barnes, "Renowned Actress."

14. Thomas, *Thalberg*.

15. Barnes, "Renowned Actress."

KATHARINE HEPBURN

1. D. Thomson, *The New Biographical Dictionary of Film* (New York: Knopf, 2010).

2. D. Friend, "Academy Bashes, 1929 to Now: How Did an Intimate Dinner for 300 Turn into Hollywood's Most Exclusive Extravaganza? An Excerpt from the Book *Oscar Night* Looks Back across the Glittering Arc of 75 Enchanted Evenings," *Vanity Fair*, October 10, 2006; B. Cosgrave, *Made for Each Other: Fashion and the Academy Awards* (London: Bloomsbury, 2008).

3. M. Wiley and D. Bona, *Inside Oscar: The Unofficial History of the Academy Awards* (New York: Ballantine Books, 1986).

4. V. Wilson, *A Life of Barbara Stanwyck: Steel-True 1907–1940* (New York: Simon and Schuster, 2013).

5. R. Bergan, *Katharine Hepburn: An Independent Woman* (New York: Arcade, 1996); M. Haskell, *From Reverence to Rape: The Treatment of Women in the Movies* (Chicago: University of Chicago Press, 1987).

6. A. Nordberg, "One and Only," *InStyle*, September 2013.

7. M. LaSalle, *Complicated Women: Sex and Power in Pre-Code Hollywood* (New York: St. Martin's Griffin, 2000).

8. C. R. Pierpont, "Born for the Part: Roles That Katharine Hepburn Played," *New Yorker*, July 14, 2003.

9. Wilson, *Life of Barbara Stanwyck*.

10. G. Lambert, *Norma Shearer: A Life* (New York: Knopf, 1990); A. Edwards, *Katharine*

Hepburn: A Remarkable Woman (New York: St. Martin's Griffin, 2000).

11. W. Stadiem, "Olivia de Havilland and the Most Notorious Sibling Rivalry in Hollywood," *Vanity Fair*, April 2016.

12. D. C. Tucker, *Shirley Booth: A Biography and Career Record* (Jefferson, NC: McFarland, 2008).

13. D. Cook, *A History of Narrative Film*, 4th ed. (New York: Norton, 2004).

14. A. Edwards, *Katharine Hepburn: A Remarkable Woman* (New York: St. Martin's Griffin, 2000).

15. *The Lion in Winter*, dir. A. Harvey (1968).

16. Bergan, *Katharine Hepburn*.

17. S. Gold, "Hearts beneath the Tinsel," *New York Times*, November 4, 1984.

18. *Women's Wear Daily*, November 30, 1981.

19. "The Vulture's Top 100 Actresses," *The Times*, December 23, 2000.

20. Bergan, *Katharine Hepburn*.

CLAUDETTE COLBERT

1. M. Sherrill and K. Swisher, "Curtain Call for Five Arts Greats: Politics Pauses for the Kennedy Center Honors," *Washington Post*, December 4, 1989.

2. Sherrill and Swisher.

3. M. LaSalle, *Complicated Women: Sex and Power in Pre-Code Hollywood* (New York: St. Martin's Griffin, 2000).

4. B. F. Dick, *Claudette Colbert: She Walked in Beauty* (Jackson: University Press of Mississippi, 2008).

5. LaSalle, *Complicated Women*; E. Kendall, "A Wisecracker in the Tropics," *New York Times*, August 11, 1996.

6. Dick, *Claudette Colbert*; W. J. Mann, *Behind the Screen: How Gays and Lesbians Shaped Hollywood, 1910–1969* (New York: Penguin Books, 2001).

7. Mann, *Behind the Screen*.

8. Dick, *Claudette Colbert*.

9. D. Thomson, *The New Biographical Dictionary of Film* (New York: Knopf, 2010).

10. S. King, "Retro Cecil and Claudette: MCA/Universal Video Releases Collections of Two Legendary Hollywood Figures," *Los Angeles Times*, April 2, 1995; Dick, *Claudette Colbert*; J. A. Walz, "Film's Early Blue Period: Mark Vieira's Lectures and Screenings Recall 'Pre-Code' Hollywood, When Energetic but Raw Movies Led to Hays Office Crackdowns," *Los Angeles Times*, February 27, 2002.

11. T. Doherty, *Pre-Code Hollywood: Sex, Immorality, and Insurrection in American Cinema, 1930–1934* (New York: Columbia University Press, 1999).

12. M. C. Smith, "Alternate Screen: 'Citizen Kane,' Filmmaking for All Time; Orson Welles' Masterpiece Is No Longer Controversial but Remains Influential," *Los Angeles Times*, February 11, 1999.

13. Doherty, *Pre-Code Hollywood*.

14. Thomson, *New Biographical Dictionary of Film*; Sherrill and Swisher, "Curtain Call."

15. S. King, "The Oscar Archives: Your Name Here; When Bette Wasn't on the List for 'Of Human Bondage,' the Short Life of the Write-In Began," *Los Angeles Times*, November 18, 2009.

16. C. Colbert, acceptance speech, February 27, 1935, Academy Awards Acceptance Speech Database, http://aaspeechesdb.oscars.org.

17. Mann, *Behind the Screen*; Sherrill and Swisher, "Curtain Call."

18. Dick, *Claudette Colbert*.

BETTE DAVIS

1. J. Fonda, *My Life So Far* (New York: Random House, 2005); M. Pramaggiore and R. Wallis, *Film: A Critical Introduction*, 2nd ed. (Boston: Pearson, 2008); B. Hadleigh, *Hollywood Babble On: Stars Gossip about Other Stars* (New York: Perigee, 1995).

2. W. Frye, "The Devil in Miss Davis," *Vanity Fair*, April 16, 2010.

3. *Screen* 49, no. 1 (2008): 67–76.

4. *American Movie Classics Magazine*, July 1996.

5. J. Basinger, *A Woman's View: How Hollywood Spoke to Women 1930–1960* (London: Chatto and Windus, 1993).

6. D. Thomson, *Bette Davis* (New York: Faber and Faber, 2009).

7. C. Champlin, "Indomitable Bette Davis: Triumphant as 80 Approaches," *Los Angeles Times*, March 3, 1988; D. Thomson, *The New Biographical Dictionary of Film* (New York: Knopf, 2010).

8. S. King, "The Oscar Archives: Your Name Here; When Bette Wasn't on the List for 'Of Human Bondage,' the Short Life of the Write-In Began," *Los Angeles Times*, November 18, 2009.

9. J. Neigher, "Oscar Visions: Actress-Designer Collaborations Have a Dazzling Back Story—Before Kidman and Galliano, There Was Dietrich and Dior," *Los Angeles Times*, February 28, 2010.

10. King, "Oscar Archives."

11. LaSalle, *Complicated Women*.

12. E. Binggeli, "Burbanking Bigger and Bette the Bitch," *African American Review* 40, no. 3 (2006): 475–492.

13. Neigher, "Oscar Visions."

14. *American Movie Classics Magazine*, November 1996; E. Widner, "Tattle," *Philadelphia Daily News*, March 29, 1993.

15. Thomson, *Bette Davis*.

16. Neigher, "Oscar Visions."

17. Thomson, *Bette Davis*.

18. J. Fontaine, *No Bed of Roses: An Autobiography* (New York: Berkley, 1978); D. Thomson, *The Whole Equation: A History of Hollywood* (New York: Knopf, 2005).

19. D. Spoto, *High Society: The Life of Grace Kelly* (New York: Three Rivers, 2010).

20. Thomson, *Whole Equation*; Thomson, *Bette Davis*.

21. T. Balio, *Grand Design: Hollywood as a Modern Business Enterprise, 1930–1939* (Berkeley: University of California Press, 1993).

22. *American Movie Classics Magazine*, July 1996.

23. *New York Times*, March 11, 1938.

24. S. O'Brien, *George Brent—Ireland's Gift to Hollywood and Its Leading Ladies* (Albany, GA: BearManor Media, 2016).

25. S. James, "Why My Mother Wants Me Dead," *Newsweek*, March 5, 2002.

26. J. Vermilye, *The Films of the Thirties* (Secaucus, NJ: Citadel, 1982).

27. W. Frye "Devil in Miss Davis."

28. Thomson, *Bette Davis*.

29. E. Sikov, "Bette Davis's House in Beverly Hills, California," *Architectural Digest*, September 6, 2016.

LUISE RAINER

1. R. D. McFadden, "Luise Rainer Dies at 104: Won Best Actress Oscars for Two Years Running," *New York Times*, December 31, 2014.

2. V. Wilson, *A Life of Barbara Stanwyck: Steel-True 1907–1940* (New York: Simon and Schuster, 2013).

3. M. Brenner, "The Last Goddess," *Vanity Fair*, April 1998.

4. Brenner.

5. Brenner.

6. B. F. Dick, *Claudette Colbert: She Walked in Beauty* (Jackson: University Press of Mississippi, 2008); A Kirscvh, "The System," *New Yorker*, April 6, 2015.

7. Brenner, "Last Goddess."

8. C. Champlin, "For Luise Rainer, Possibly a Return to Hollywood," *Los Angeles Times*, August 15, 1989.

9. S. King, "Best Face Forward: At 100, Oscar Winner and Rule Breaker Luise Rainer Is Still a Commanding Presence," *Los Angeles Times*, May 1, 2010.

10. T. Sims, "Exhibit Recalls Nazi Propaganda of '30s," *Los Angeles Times*, September 5, 1988.

11. S. King, "Luise Rainer's 100 Years of Fortitude: Oscar Winner Was Feisty, Memorable," *Los Angeles Times*, December 30, 2014.

12. Brenner, "Last Goddess."

13. Brenner.

14. Wilson, *Life of Barbara Stanwyck*.

15. J. Fontaine, *No Bed of Roses: An Autobiography* (New York: Berkley, 1978); King, "Best Face Forward."

16. Dick, *Claudette Colbert*.

17. R. Nakamura, "Olivia de Havilland Recalls Feud with 'Dragon Lady' Sister Joan Fontaine," *The Wrap*, July 1, 2016, https://www.thewrap.com/olivia-de-havilland-recalls-feud-with-sister-joan-fontaine/.

18. Wilson, *Life of Barbara Stanwyck*.

19. King, "Luise Rainer's 100 Years."

20. S. King, "New Life for Old Winners: Classic Films That Won Oscars for Best Picture Are Out on Disc, a Chance to See How Academy Votes Have Stood the Test of Time," *Los Angeles Times*, February 27, 2004.

21. King, "Luise Rainer's 100 Years."

22. Brenner, "Last Goddess."

23. D. Friend, "Academy Bashes, 1929 to Now: How Did an Intimate Dinner for 300 Turn into Hollywood's Most Exclusive Extravaganza? An Excerpt from the Book *Oscar Night* Looks Back across the Glittering Arc of 75 Enchanted Evenings," *Vanity Fair*, October 10, 2006.

24. T. Balio, *Grand Design: Hollywood As a Modern Business Enterprise, 1930–1939* (Berkeley: University of California Press, 1993).

25. *The Good Earth*, dir. S. Franklin (1937).

26. R. Ryon, "Season Finale in Brentwood," *Los Angeles Times*, May 4, 1997.

27. Wilson, *Life of Barbara Stanwyck*.

28. S. King, "Hollywood's Decades of Chinese Lessons: A New Documentary Explores Asians in U.S. Film, from the Days of Charlie Chan to Ang Lee's Oscar," *Los Angeles Times*, May 26, 2008.

29. Brenner, "Last Goddess."

30. M. Brenner, *Great Dames: What I Learned from Older Women* (New York: Broadway Books, 2001).

31. Wilson, *Life of Barbara Stanwyck*.

32. Brenner, "Last Goddess"; King, "Luise Rainer's 100 Years."

33. King, "Luise Rainer's 100 Years."

34. D. Thomson, *The New Biographical Dictionary of Film* (New York: Knopf, 2010).

VIVIEN LEIGH

1. M. LaSalle, *Complicated Women: Sex and Power in Pre-Code Hollywood* (New York: Thomas Dunne Books, 2000); A. Tapert, *The Power of Glamour* (New York: Crown, 1998).

2. J. Wester Anderson, *Forever Young: The Life, Loves, and Enduring Faith of a Hollywood Legend* (Allen, TX: Thomas More, 2000).

3. D. Thomson, *The New Biographical Dictionary of Film* (New York: Knopf, 2010).

4. *Gone with the Wind*, dir. V. Fleming (1939).

5. B. Cosgrave, *Made for Each Other: Fashion and the Academy Awards* (New York: Bloomsbury, 2008); *The Making of a Legend: Gone with the Wind*, dir. D. Hinton (1988).

6. History Channel, "Women in the Civil War," accessed March 24, 2019, http://www.history.com/topics/american-civil-war/women-in-the-civil-war.

7. J. Vermilye, *The Films of the Thirties* (Secaucus, NJ: Citadel, 1982).

8. V. Leigh, acceptance speech, February 29, 1940, Academy Awards Acceptance Speech Database, http://aaspeechesdb.oscars.org.

9. V. Wilson, *A Life of Barbara Stanwyck: Steel-True 1907–1940* (New York: Simon and Schuster, 2013).

10. Thomson, *New Biographical Dictionary of Film*; S. Morley, "The British Are Going: Hollywood," *The Times*, March 25, 1993.

11. R. B. Palmer, "Tennessee Williams and 1950s Hollywood: The View from Here and Abroad," *Southern Quarterly* 48, no. 4 (2011): 108–125, 138.

12. Palmer.

13. N. Treanor, "The Personal Is Political: Feminism's Second Wave," in *The Feminist Movement*, ed. N. Treanor (San Diego: Greenhaven, 2002).

14. H. Vickers, *Vivien Leigh* (Boston: Little, Brown, 1988).

GINGER ROGERS

1. D. Richards, *Ginger Rogers: Salute to a Star* (London: Clifton Books, 1969).

2. Richards, *Ginger Rogers*.

3. R. Lord, "The Hollywood School for Girls at Woman's Club of Hollywood," *Discover Hollywood*, Fall 2017.

4. H. Dickens, *The Films of Ginger Rogers* (Secaucus, NJ: Citadel, 1975).

5. A. Eichler, "Ginger Rogers, Katie Couric, 1991 TV Interview," YouTube, October 27, 2015, https://www.youtube.com/watch?v=BLdBaONT5cw.

6. J. Basinger, *A Woman's View: How Hollywood Spoke to Women 1930–1960* (London: Chatto and Windus, 1993); T. J. Gordon, "Film in the Second Degree: Cabaret and the Dark Side of Laughter," *Proceedings of the American Philosophical Society* 152, no. 4 (2008): 440–465.

7. J. Vermilye, *The Films of the Thirties* (Secaucus, NJ: Citadel, 1982).

8. Richards, *Ginger Rogers*.

9. Richards.

10. D. Thomson, *The New Biographical Dictionary of Film* (New York: Knopf, 2010).

11. H. Mandelbaum and E. Myers, *Screen Deco* (New York: St. Martin's, 1985); A. Macaulay, "They Seem to Find the Happiness They Seek," *New York Times*, August 16, 2009.

12. Vermilye, *Films of the Thirties*.

13. Richards, *Ginger Rogers*.

14. K. Longworth, *Seduction: Sex, Lies, and Stardom in Howard Hughes's Hollywood* (New York: Custom House, 2019).

15. K. Milestone and A. Meyer, *Gender and Popular Culture* (Cambridge, UK: Polity, 2011).

16. Milestone and Meyer.

17. Longworth, *Seduction*; Milestone and Meyer, *Gender and Popular Culture*; Basinger, *Woman's View*.

18. L. Jacobs, "The Lipstick Jungle," *Vanity Fair*, March 2004; S. King, "Vows, Spouse Optional: When It Comes to Raising Children, Television and the Movies Have Loosened The Ties That Bind—or Lost Them Altogether," *Los Angeles Times*, April 15, 2003.

19. K. Collins, "Courting Oscar through the Years," *Variety*, November 24–30, 2003.

20. M. Wiley and D. Bona, *Inside Oscar: The Unofficial History of the Academy Awards* (New York: Ballantine Books, 1986).

21. M. Oliver, "Movie Great Ginger Rogers Dies at 83: Hollywood; The Oscar-Winning Actress Was Best Known for the 10 Films She Glided Through with Fred Astaire," *Los Angeles Times*, April 26, 1995.

22. G. Rogers, acceptance speech, February 27, 1941, Academy Awards Acceptance Speech Database, http://aaspeechesdb.oscars.org.

23. Oliver, "Movie Great Ginger Rogers."

24. *Tender Comrade*, dir. E. Dmytryk (1943).

25. J. Michaelson, "The Blacklist Legacy: A New Generation in Hollywood Takes Political Sides Again, but Remembers the Red Witchhunt," *Los Angeles Times*, October 18, 1987.

26. Oliver, "Movie Great Ginger Rogers."

JOAN FONTAINE

1. J. Fontaine, *No Bed of Roses: An Autobiography* (New York: Berkley, 1978).

2. Fontaine.

3. J. Fontaine, acceptance speech, February 26, 1942, Academy Awards Acceptance Speech Database, http://aaspeechesdb.oscars.org.

4. W. Stadiem, "Olivia de Havilland and the Most Notorious Sibling Rivalry in Hollywood," *Los Angeles Examiner*, May 25, 1947.

5. E. Amburn, *Olivia de Havilland and the Golden Age of Hollywood* (Lanham, MD: Lyons, 2018).

6. Stadiem, "Olivia de Havilland."

7. D. Spoto, *Spellbound by Beauty: Alfred Hitchcock and His Leading Ladies* (New York: Harmony Books, 2008).

8. BAMPFA, "Letter from an Unknown Woman," accessed March 24, 2019, https://bampfa.org/event/letter-unknown-woman-0.

9. Spoto, *Spellbound by Beauty*.

10. Spoto.

11. Spoto.

12. G. Speck, "Joan Fontaine," *Interview*, February 1987.

13. TCM, "Joan Fontaine," accessed March 24, 2019, http://www.tcm.com/tcmdb/person/63647|83603/Joan-Fontaine/.

14. "Feuds Star Wars," *Los Angeles Times*, January 4, 1987.

GREER GARSON

1. A. Kirsch, "The System: Two New Histories Show How the Nazi Concentration Camps Worked," *New Yorker*, March 30, 2015.

2. S. Kozloff, "Wyler's Wars," *Film History* 20, no. 4 (2008): 456–473.

3. F. MacDonald, "Mrs. Miniver: The Film That Goebbels Feared," BBC, February 9, 2015, http://www.bbc.com/culture/story/20150209-the-film-that-goebbels-feared; 24fpsfan, "TCM Tribute to Greer Garson," YouTube, March 13, 2013, https://www.youtube.com/watch?v=1FF9PeaPMu0.

4. *Mrs. Miniver*, dir. W. Wyler (1942).

5. M. Troyan, *A Rose for Mrs. Miniver: The Life of Greer Garson* (Lexington: University Press of Kentucky, 1999).

6. J. Basinger, *The Star Machine* (New York: Knopf, 2007); J. Fontaine, *No Bed of Roses: An Autobiography* (New York: Berkley, 1978); V. Wilson, *A Life of Barbara Stanwyck: Steel-True 1907–1940* (New York: Simon and Schuster, 2013).

7. 24fpsfan, "TCM Tribute."

8. Wilson, *Life of Barbara Stanwyck*.

9. Troyan, *Rose for Mrs. Miniver*.

10. Troyan.

11. M. Wiley and D. Bona, *Inside Oscar: The Unofficial History of the Academy Awards* (New York: Ballantine Books, 1986).

12. 24fpsfan, "TCM Tribute."

13. Troyan, *Rose for Mrs. Miniver*; J. Wester Anderson, *Forever Young: The Life, Loves, and Enduring Faith of a Hollywood Legend* (Allen, TX: Thomas More, 2000).

JENNIFER JONES

1. E. Readicker-Henderson, "Lourdes: A Pilgrimage to France's Holy Waters," *AFAR*, August–September 2014.

2. Readicker-Henderson.

3. Readicker-Henderson.

4. E. Z. Epstein, *Portrait of Jennifer: A Biography of Jennifer Jones* (New York: Simon and Schuster, 1995).

5. American Academy of Dramatic Arts, "History & Heritage," accessed March 24, 2019, https://www.aada.edu/about/history-and -heritage/.

6. *The Making of a Legend: Gone with the Wind*, dir. D. Hinton (1988).

7. *The Song of Bernadette*, dir. H. King (1943).

8. G. Fuller, "Julie Christie . . . a Sort of Fabrication," Interview, March 1997.

9. C. Luther, "Jennifer Jones, 1919–2009: 'Sure-Fire' Star of Dramas On Screen and Off," *Los Angeles Times*, December 18, 2009.

10. M. Wiley and D. Bona, *Inside Oscar: The Unofficial History of the Academy Awards* (New York: Ballantine Books, 1986).

11. D. Spoto, *High Society: The Life of Grace Kelly* (New York: Three Rivers, 2010).

12. G. Lambert, *Norma Shearer: A Life* (New York: Knopf, 1990).

13. H. Hayes with K. Hatch, *My Life in Three Acts* (San Diego: Harcourt Brace Jovanovich, 1990).

14. P. A. DeMaio, *Garden of Dreams: The Life of Simone Signoret* (Jackson: University Press of Mississippi, 2014).

15. R. Martinez, "Joan Fontaine Interview (1991) Part 3/3," YouTube, February 4, 2014, https://www.youtube.com/watch?v=NThsSUBpCM8.

16. DeMaio, *Garden of Dreams*.

17. *American Movie Classics Magazine*, March 1998.

18. B. Hadleigh, *Hollywood Babble On: Stars Gossip about Other Stars* (New York: Perigee, 1995).

19. J. Stein, *West of Eden: An American Place* (New York: Random House, 2016).

20. *Song of Bernadette*.

INGRID BERGMAN

1. A. Hall and G. Zoega, "Values and Labor Force Participation in the Nordic Countries," *Economics* 8, no. 41 (2014): 1–44.

2. D. Thomson, *Ingrid Bergman* (New York: Faber and Faber, 2009).

3. J. McGasko, "Ingrid Bergman at 100: When a Star Fell from Heaven," Biography, August 27, 2015, http://www.biography.com/news/ingrid -bergman-100th-anniversary-biography-facts.

4. McGasko, *Ingrid Bergman*.

5. I. Bergman and A. Burgess, *Ingrid Bergman: My Life* (New York: Dell, 1980).

6. L. Tolhurst, *Cured: A Tale of Two Imaginary Boys* (Boston: Da Capo, 2016).

7. Thomson, *Ingrid Bergman*.

8. M. Wiley and D. Bona, *Inside Oscar: The Unofficial History of the Academy Awards* (New York: Ballantine Books, 1986).

9. Bergman and Burgess, *Ingrid Bergman*.

10. E. Buscombe, "Swede Sensation," in *1000 Films to Change Your Life*, ed. S. Cropper (London: Time Out Guides, 2006).

11. J. Kobler, "Tempest on the Tiber," *Life*, February 13, 1950.

12. P. A. DeMaio, *Garden of Dreams: The Life of Simone Signoret* (Jackson: University Press of Mississippi, 2014).

13. Bergman and Burgess, *Ingrid Bergman*.

14. Thomson, *Ingrid Bergman*; Merv Griffin-Show, "Ingrid Bergman Interview (Merv Griffin Show 1980)," YouTube, April 20, 2012, http://www .youtube.com/watch?v=0SkrM5k6-HQ&fea ture=related; "Imagine: Ingrid Bergman—in Her Own Words, Review: An Insight into a Beloved Star Who Never Learned to Love Herself," *Daily Telegraph*, March 26, 2018.

15. *Hello!*, December 11, 2007.

16. H. Hayes with K. Hatch, *My Life in Three Acts* (San Diego: Harcourt Brace Jovanovich, 1990).

17. Thomson, *Ingrid Bergman*.

18. Wiley and Bona, *Inside Oscar*.

19. Thomson, *Ingrid Bergman*.

JOAN CRAWFORD

1. H. John, "Putting a Modern Face on Oscar Classics: Outfits That Turned Heads in Days Past Get a Glamorous Revival," *Los Angeles Times*, March 23, 2003.

2. M. Wiley and D. Bona, *Inside Oscar: The Unofficial History of the Academy Awards* (New York: Ballantine Books, 1986).

3. K. Collins, "Courting Oscar through the Years," *Variety*, November 23, 2003.

4. A. Quirke, "Consumed by Passions," *Sunday Times*, February 20, 2011; D. Chan, "Oscar 1944 and 1945," *Malay Mail*, August 29, 2002.

5. D. Thomson, *Nicole Kidman* (New York: Knopf, 2006); D. Denby, "Escape Artist," *New Yorker*, January 3, 2011; P. Fitzgerald, *Joan Crawford: The Ultimate Movie Star* (2002); Denby.

6. D. Spoto, *Possessed: The Life of Joan Crawford* (New York: William Morrow, 2010); M. LaSalle, *Complicated Women: Sex and Power in Pre-Code Hollywood* (New York: Thomas Dunne Books, 2000); Spoto; J. Fontaine, *No Bed of Roses: An Autobiography* (New York: Berkley, 1978).

7. R. Bennett, "Muzzle the Bitches, Urges Victoria's Secret Model," *The Times*, September 2, 2013; A. Dowling, "'Feud': A Look at Joan Crawford's Many (Many) Leading Men," *Hollywood Reporter*, March 10, 2017.

8. J. Basinger, *The Star Machine* (New York: Knopf, 2007).

9. D. Spoto, *High Society: The Life of Grace Kelly* (New York: Three Rivers, 2010); M. Cousins, *The Story of Film: An Odyssey* (London: Pavilion Books, 2011).

10. C. Paglia, *Sex, Art, and American Culture: Essays* (New York: Vintage Books, 1992); C. Champlin, "An Appreciation: Grace Befitting a True Screen Goddess," *Los Angeles Times*, August 14, 2000.

11. Basinger, *Star Machine*.

12. Spoto, *Possessed*.

13. J. Keller, "It's the Thought That Counts," *Chicago Tribune*, March 3, 2010.

14. M. LaSalle, *Complicated Women: Sex and Power in Pre-Code Hollywood* (New York: St. Martin's Griffin, 2000); V. Wilson, *A Life of Barbara Stanwyck: Steel-True 1907–1940* (New York: Simon and Schuster, 2013).

15. Wilson, *Life of Barbara Stanwyck*.

16. D. Bona, "Oscars 99: A Sneak Peek; Not All Their Works Pure Gold," *Los Angeles Times*, March 14, 1999; Thomson, *Nicole Kidman*.

17. T. Balio, *Grand Design: Hollywood as a Modern Business Enterprise, 1930–1939* (Berkeley: University of California Press, 1993).

18. J. Basinger, *A Woman's View: How Hollywood Spoke to Women, 1930–1960* (London: Chatto and Windus, 1993).

19. L. Williams, *Feminist Film Theory: Mildred Pierce and the Second World War* (London: Verso, 1988).

20. W. Winston Dixon, *American Cinema of the 1940s: Themes and Variations* (New Brunswick, NJ: Rutgers University Press, 2006).

21. J. Hyams, "Who's Got a Date with Oscar?," *Los Angeles Times*, April 3, 1960.

22. Basinger, *Star Machine*.

23. E. Levy, "Women Move into the Lead: For the First Time since the Days of Bette Davis and Joan Crawford, Actresses in Hollywood Are Carrying Movies on Their Own Terms," *Los*

Angeles Times, January 11, 2004; *Spine Tingler! The William Castle Story*, dir. J. Schwarz (2007).

24. R. J. Corber, *Cold War Femme: Lesbianism, National Identity, and Hollywood Cinema* (Durham, NC: Duke University Press, 2011); J. Miller, "Fact-Checking *Feud*: Bette Davis's Thorny Relationship with Her Daughter B.D.," *Vanity Fair*, March 19, 2017

25. E. Helmore, "'I Wouldn't Sit on Her Toilet . . .': Screen Revival of Davis and Crawford Feud Sparks Sexism Debate," *The Observer*, February 19, 2017.

26. H. Harrod, "The True Story behind *Feud*: What Really Happened When Bette Met Joan?," *The Telegraph*, December 16, 2017.

OLIVIA DE HAVILLAND

1. G. Speck, "Olivia de Havilland," *Interview*, February 1987.

2. R. Matzen, *Errol & Olivia: Ego & Obsession in Golden Era Hollywood* (Boulder, CO: Paladin, 2010).

3. "A Life in Quotes: Olivia de Havilland," *Reader's Digest*, accessed April 20, 2019, https://www.readersdigest.co.uk/culture/celebrities/a-life-in-quotes-olivia-de-havilland.

4. L. Smith, "Olivia de Havilland: Hollywood Grande Dame to Celebrate 100th Birthday," CNN.com, June 3, 2016, http://www.cnn.com/2016/06/30/entertainment/cnnphotos-tbt-olivia-de-havilland-100th-birthday/.

5. K. Thomas, "Broadway Glows in Lights of Memory," *Los Angeles Times*, July 2, 2004; T. J. Stipanowich, "She Took on the Studio System," *Los Angeles Times*, July 1, 2016; T. Balio, *Grand Design: Hollywood As a Modern Business Enterprise, 1930–1939* (Berkeley: University of California Press, 1993), 258.

6. Stipanowich, "She Took on the Studio System."

7. R. Martinez, "Joan Fontaine Interview (1989) Part 1/2," YouTube, February 13, 2014, https://www.youtube.com/watch?v=J2heLmQmlTw.

8. *Parade*, September 7, 1986.

9. Balio, *Grand Design*.

10. Balio; Stipanowich, "She Took on the Studio System."

11. J. Basinger, *The Star Machine* (New York: Knopf, 2007); D. Thomson, *The Whole Equation: A History of Hollywood* (New York: Knopf, 2005).

12. Thomson, *Whole Equation*.

13. M. Schwartz, "The Last Star: An Evening with Olivia de Havilland," *Entertainment Weekly*, January 29, 2015.

14. P. H. Brown and J. Pinkston, "59th Academy Awards: Garbo Didn't, Cher Did, Kim Slimmed Oscar Headliners Create a Collection of Footnotes," *Los Angeles Times*, March 29, 1987.

15. Schwartz, "Last Star."

16. Schwartz.

17. Thomson, *Whole Equation*.

18. "Olivia de Havilland Sues FX over Feud: Bette and Joan," BBC.com, July 1, 2017, http://www.bbc.com/news/world-us-canada-40468051; Thomson, *Whole Equation*.

19. D. Thomson, *The New Biographical Dictionary of Film* (New York: Knopf, 2010).

20. T. Schatz, *Boom and Bust: American Cinema in the 1940s* (Berkeley: University of California Press, 1997); S. King, "'Mermaid' Turns 20 Swimmingly," *Los Angeles Times*, May 21, 2009.

21. J. DeBoer, "What about Happy Endings?," *Northwest Florida Daily News*, August 6, 1993.

22. Speck, "Olivia de Havilland."

23. Speck; P. Wuntch, "Robert Osborne: The Oscar Expert: Votes Often Hinge on What the Academy Loves, He Says," *Dallas Morning News*, March 21, 1999.

24. Speck, "Olivia de Havilland."

25. M. Wiley and D. Bona, *Inside Oscar: The Unofficial History of the Academy Awards* (New York: Ballantine Books, 1986).

26. D. Rader, "Rewards and Regrets: Olivia de Havilland Talks about Montgomery Clift, Errol Flynn, and Herself," *Arizona Daily Star*, September 7, 1986.

27. *The Heiress*, dir. W. Wyler (1949).

28. Rader, "Rewards and Regrets."

29. P. Pacheco, "Q&A: Olivia de Havilland: More than Melanie," *Los Angeles Times*, June 17, 1998.

30. "Timelessly Elegant at 100: Gone with the Wind's Olivia de Havilland Celebrates Milestone Birthday and Finally Breaks Silence on Golden Age of Hollywood's Most Infamous Sibling Rivalry," *Daily Mail*, July 1, 2016, http://www.dailymail.co.uk/tvshowbiz/article-3670080/AP-Interview-De-Havilland-breaks-silence-sibling-feud.html.

LORETTA YOUNG

1. J. Basinger, *The Star Machine* (New York: Knopf, 2007).

2. J. Wester Anderson, *Forever Young: The Life, Loves, and Enduring Faith of a Hollywood Legend* (Allen, TX: Thomas More, 2000).

3. T. Balio, *Grand Design: Hollywood as a Modern Business Enterprise, 1930–1939* (Berkeley: University of California Press, 1993); N. Tartaglione, "Olivia and Oscar: Olivia de Havilland Views Her Hollywood Heyday from Her Parisian Perch," *Los Angeles Times*, March 23, 2003.

4. D. Spoto, *High Society: The Life of Grace Kelly* (New York: Three Rivers, 2010).

5. M. R. Desjardins, *Recycled Stars: Female Film Stardom in the Age of Television and Video* (Durham, NC: Duke University Press, 2015).

6. Wester Anderson, *Forever Young*.

7. Wester Anderson.

8. Basinger, *Star Machine*; *American Movie Classics Magazine*, January 1995.

9. S. Simon, "Loretta Young Dies: Elegant Film, TV Star," *Los Angeles Times*, August 13, 2000.

10. Simon; A. H. Petersen, "Clark Gable Accused of Raping Co-Star," BuzzFeed, July 12, 2015, https://www.buzzfeednews.com/article/annehelenpetersen/loretta-young; Wester Anderson, *Forever Young*; Simon; Wester Anderson.

11. Basinger, *Star Machine*.

12. Basinger; Simon, "Loretta Young Dies."

13. S. Dodge, "'Meryl, If You Do It Everyone Else Will': Best Actress Winner Frances McDormand Has All Female Nominees Stand in Solidarity as She Delivers Powerful Speech about Diversity," *Daily Mail*, March 5, 2018, http://www.dailymail.co.uk/tvshowbiz/article-5462525/Frances-McDormand-wins-Best-Actress-Oscars.html; Petersen, "Clark Gable Accused."

14. G. Eells, *Hedda and Louella* (New York: G. P. Putnam's Sons, 1972).

15. K. Hunt, "The Fixers Who Buried Old Hollywood's Biggest Scandals," Atlas Obscura, March 17, 2017, http://www.atlasobscura.com/articles/old-hollywood-fixers.

16. C. Becker, *It's the Pictures That Got Small: Hollywood Film Stars on 1950s Television* (Middletown, CT: Wesleyan University Press, 2009); L. Williams, "Loretta Young, Glamorous Leading Lady of Film and Television, Dies at 87," *New York Times*, August 13, 2000.

17. T. McGonigle, "Book Review: Brecht's Wartime Stay in Finland: Brecht at Night," *Los Angeles Times*, August 9, 2009.

18. Wester Anderson, *Forever Young*.

19. Eells, *Hedda and Louella*.

20. M. Barson and D. Heller, *Red Scared! The Commie Menace in Propaganda and Popular Culture* (San Francisco: Chronicle Books, 2001).

21. Simon, "Loretta Young Dies."

22. H. John, "Putting a Modern Face on Oscar Classics: Outfits That Turned Heads in Days Past Get a Glamorous Revival," *Los Angeles Times*, March 23, 2003.

23. L. Young, acceptance speech, March 20, 1948, Academy Awards Acceptance Speech Database, http://aaspeechesdb.oscars.org.

24. Basinger, *Star Machine*.

25. Simon, "Loretta Young Dies"; Basinger, *Star Machine*; *Movie Collector's World*, September 15, 2000.

JANE WYMAN

1. L. J. Quirk, *Jane Wyman: The Actress and the Woman* (New York: Dembner Books, 1986).

2. R. Severo and M. Fox, "Jane Wyman, 90, Star of Film and TV, Is Dead," *New York Times*, September 11, 2007.

3. J. Meroney, "Rehearsals for a Lead Role: Ronald Reagan Was a Liberal, an Actor, a Labor Chief—but Some Unscripted Plot Twists Forged a New Character," *Washington Post*, February 4, 2001.

4. K. Kelley, *Nancy Reagan: The Unauthorized Biography* (New York: Simon and Schuster, 1991).

5. S. Herhold, "Reagan Played Informant Role for FBI In '40s," *Chicago Tribune*, August 26, 1985; S. Rosenfeld, "Hoover, Reagan, and Spying at

Berkeley," *Chronicle of Higher Education*, August 13, 2012.

6. P. A. DeMaio, *Garden of Dreams: The Life of Simone Signoret* (Jackson: University Press of Mississippi, 2014).

7. "Profile: Early Life and Career of Ronald Reagan," NPR, June 5, 2004.

8. AP, "Report on Reagan-F.B.I. Ties," *New York Times*, August 26, 1985.

9. W. Winston Dixon, *American Cinema of the 1940s: Themes and Variations* (New Brunswick, NJ: Rutgers University Press, 2006).

10. PJ Neely, "TCM Disability In Film Johnny Belinda," YouTube, November 13, 2012, https://www.youtube.com/watch?v=e8s2tGTOw8g.

11. M. Wiley and D. Bona, *Inside Oscar: The Unofficial History of the Academy Awards* (New York: Ballantine Books, 1986).

12. J. D'Emilio, "Gay Politics and Community in San Francisco since World War II, in *Hidden from History: Reclaiming the Gay and Lesbian Past*, ed. M. Duberman, M. Vicinus, and G. Chauncey (New York: Meridian, 1989).

13. A. McCarthy, "Jane Wyman, Ronald Reagan's First Wife, Dies at 93," Politico, September 10, 2007, http://www.politico.com/blogs/anne schroeder/0907/Jane_Wyman_Ronald_Reagans _first_wife_died_at_93.html.

JUDY HOLLIDAY

1. L. E. Davis, "The Spy Who Came In from the Closet," *Gay & Lesbian Review Worldwide* 19, no. 5 (2012): 18–20.

2. G. Swanson, *Swanson on Swanson* (New York: Random House, 1980).

3. W. Sargeant, "Judy Holliday," *Life*, April 2, 1951.

4. G. Lambert, *On Cukor* (New York: Rizzoli, 2000); R. Von Busack, "Holliday Jaunt," MetroActive, August 6–13, 1998, http://www.metroactive.com/papers/metro/08.06.98/judyholliday-9831.html.

5. K. Rowe, *The Unruly Woman: Gender and Genres of Laughter* (Austin: University of Texas Press, 1995).

6. B. Hadleigh, *Hollywood Babble On: Stars Gossip about Other Stars* (New York: Perigee, 1995).

7. L. Lacey, "Who Controls Hollywood?," *Globe and Mail*, July 18, 2014; V. Brook, "Chameleon Man and Unruly Woman: Dustin Hoffman and Barbra Streisand," *Shofar* 33, no. 1 (2014): 30–56, 145.

8. Lacey, "Who Controls Hollywood?"; D. Berrin, "The New Jewess: A Rising Generation of Actresses Overturns Old Tropes," *Jewish Journal*, August 10, 2011, http://www.jewishjournal.com /hollywood/article/jewishness_is_helping_not _hindering_todays_actresses_20110810/.

9. Berrin, "New Jewess."

10. P. Lev. *The Fifties: Transforming the Screen (1950–1959)* (Berkeley: University of California Press, 2003).

11. D. Thomson, *The New Biographical Dictionary of Film* (New York: Knopf, 2010).

12. *Oliver Stone's Untold History of the United States*, dir. O. Stone (2012).

13. M. Pramaggiore and T. Wallis, *Film: A Critical Introduction*, 2nd ed. (Boston: Pearson, 2008).

14. P. Roffman and J. Purdy, "HUAC and the End of an Era," in *Hollywood's America: Twentieth-Century America through Film*, ed. S. Mintz and R. W. Roberts (Hoboken, NJ: Wiley-Blackwell, 2010).

15. L. Grant, *I Said Yes to Everything: A Memoir* (New York: Blue Rider, 2014).

16. C. R. Vigue, "Unfriendly Witnesses: Gender, Theater, and Film in the McCarthy Era," *Theatre Journal* 62, no. 1 (2010): 133–134.

17. Davis, "Spy Who Came In"; L. Ceplair and C. Trumbo, "Battling the Motion Picture Blacklist," *Cineaste* 39 (Fall 2014): 46–50, 61.

18. N. Croce, *The History of Film* (New York: Rosen Education Service, 2015).

19. Sargeant, "Judy Holliday."

SHIRLEY BOOTH

1. J. Ryan, "Shirley Booth: Is She Really That Nice?," *Cumberland Times*, September 16, 1962.

2. "'Real Stars' Shun Phony Hollywood Lights and Makeup," *Hutchinson News*, February 4, 1968; D. C. Tucker, *Shirley Booth: A Biography and Career Record* (Jefferson, NC: McFarland, 2008).

3. Tucker, *Shirley Booth*.

4. C. McNulty, "Theater Review: In 'Sheba,' Despair Eclipses a Marriage; S. Epatha Merkerson Gains Strength as the Play Moves Along at the Kirk Douglas Theatre," *Los Angeles Times*, June 26, 2007; T. Teachout, "Come Back, William Inge," *Commentary* 127 (April 2009): 71–74.

5. Teachout, "Come Back."

6. McNulty, "Theater Review"; Teachout, "Come Back"; R. B. Palmer, "Tennessee Williams and 1950s Hollywood: The View from Here and Abroad," *Southern Quarterly* 48, no. 4 (2011): 108–125, 138.

7. Teachout, "Come Back."

8. B. Atkinson, "At the Theatre," *New York Times*, February 16, 1950.

9. R. Kempley, H. Hinson, and T. Shales, "New on Tape," *Washington Post*, June 6, 1991.

10. D. Sullivan, "In Search of Inge's Little Sheba," *Los Angeles Times*, April 12, 1987.

11. McNulty, "Theater Review."

12. Tucker, *Shirley Booth*.

13. *Come Back, Little Sheba*, dir. D. Mann (1952); R. Osborne, "Oscar Hopefuls Enjoy Their Face Time: 'Sheba' Returns," *Hollywood Reporter*, January 22, 2008.

14. *Come Back, Little Sheba*.

15. Tucker, *Shirley Booth*.

16. Tucker; Osborne, "Oscar Hopefuls."

17. Tucker, *Shirley Booth*.

18. J. Wester Anderson, *Forever Young: The Life, Loves, and Enduring Faith of a Hollywood Legend* (Allen, TX: Thomas More, 2000).

19. D. Spoto, *High Society: The Life of Grace Kelly* (New York: Three Rivers, 2010).

20. *Los Angeles Herald & Express*, December 25, 1952.

21. Tucker, *Shirley Booth*.

22. Tucker.

23. S. Booth, acceptance speech, March 19, 1953, Academy Awards Acceptance Speech Database, http://aaspeechesdb.oscars.org/.

24. M. Wiley and D. Bona, *Inside Oscar: The Unofficial History of the Academy Awards* (New York: Ballantine Books, 1986).

25. Tucker, *Shirley Booth*.

26. R. Osborne, "'Acquaintance' Will Be Renewed after 66 Years," *Hollywood Reporter*, May 29, 2007.

AUDREY HEPBURN

1. L. Dotti et al., *Audrey in Rome* (New York: Harper Design, 2011).

2. A. Pukas, "My Fair Lady: Why Does Audrey Hepburn Still Enchant Us More than 20 Years after Her Death?," *Express*, December 4, 2014.

3. E. Erwin and J. Z. Diamond, *The Audrey Hepburn Treasures: Pictures and Mementos from a Life of Style and Purpose* (New York: Atria Books, 2006).

4. Pukas, "My Fair Lady."

5. A. Fernandez, "Audrey Hepburn's Secret Shame about Her Mother's Nazi Sympathies: New Book Reveals," *People*, April 3, 2019; "Wall Street's Wild Ride: Fred Thompson Drops out of Presidential Race; Authorities Continue Searching for Marine on the," *Finance Wire*, January 22, 2008; Fernandez, "Audrey Hepburn's Secret Shame."

6. L. Garner, "Fair Lady Audrey Hepburn Has Always Identified with Anne Frank, Whose Diary Mirrors Her Own Wartime Childhood in Holland: Lesley Garner Meets the Legendary Actress as She Prepares for This Week's UNICEF Gala Performance," *Sunday Telegraph*, May 26, 1991.

7. S. Harris, "Audrey Hepburn, Actress and Humanitarian, Dies: In Retirement, the Oscar and Tony Winner Campaigned Tirelessly against Hunger. She Was 63," *Los Angeles Times*, January 21, 1993.

8. D. Spoto, *High Society: The Life of Grace Kelly* (New York: Three Rivers, 2010).

9. 41187Dexter, "Audrey Hepburn Interview—Part 2," YouTube, November 22, 2011, http://www.youtube.com/watch?v=VhCajQ0_zBg.

10. Pukas, "My Fair Lady."

11. D. Thomson, *The New Biographical Dictionary of Film* (New York: Knopf, 2010).

12. Spoto, *High Society*.

13. A. Hepburn, acceptance speech, March 25, 1954, Academy Awards Acceptance Speech Database, http://aaspeechesdb.oscars.org.

14. Erwin and Diamond, *Audrey Hepburn Treasures*.

15. P. C. Keogh, "The Classic Style of Audrey Hepburn," *InStyle*, May 1999.

16. Inception Media Group, "Audrey Hepburn: The Magic of Audrey—UNICEF," YouTube, February 16, 2012, https://www.youtube.com/watch?v=1SvddNIIRaw.

17. Harris, "Audrey Hepburn."

18. "Audrey Hepburn, UNICEF Envoy to Somalia," interview transcript, *MacNeil/Lehrer NewsHour*, November 5, 1992, available at http://www.ahepburn.com/interview5.html.

19. A. M. Cal and L. A. Mallette, "Celebrity and the United Nations: Leadership and Referent Power of Global Film Ambassadors," *International Journal of Arts & Sciences* 8, no. 5 (2015): 415–428.

20. A. McFerran, "Susan Sarandon the Crusader," *Sunday Herald-Sun*, April 1, 2001.

GRACE KELLY

1. K. Pilley, "Amazing Grace Land: Bride Is a Film Star, Groom a Non-Pro," *Mail on Sunday*, July 8, 2007.

2. V. Thorpe, "Grace Kelly: Screen Goddess, Princess and an Enduring Source of Scandal: Her Life Was One of Glamour, Privilege and Ultimately Tragedy. Now a New Film about Her Marriage into Royalty, Starring Nicole Kidman, Has Stirred Fresh Controversy," *The Observer*, May 11, 2014.

3. J.-T. Dahlburg, "Prince Rainier III, 81; Ruler Transformed Monaco, Made Grace Kelly His Princess," *Los Angeles Times*, April 7, 2005.

4. *Hello!*, July 5, 2011; Dahlburg, "Prince Rainier III."

5. P. H. Verlhac and Y. B. Dherbier, *Grace Kelly: A Life in Pictures* (Oxford, UK: Pavilion, 2007).

6. D. Spoto, *High Society: The Life of Grace Kelly* (New York: Three Rivers, 2010).

7. Verlhac and Dherbier, *Grace Kelly*.

8. P. B. Flint, "Sanford Meisner, a Mentor Who Guided Actors and Directors toward Truth, Dies at 91," *New York Times*, February 4, 1997.

9. *Hello!*, July 5, 2011.

10. Spoto, *High Society*.

11. Spoto.

12. R. Bell-Metereau, "1953: Movies and Our Secret Lives," in *American Cinema of the 1950s: Themes and Variations*, ed. M. Pomerance (New Brunswick, NJ: Rutgers University Press, 2005); Spoto, *High Society*.

13. Spoto, *High Society*.

14. *The Country Girl*, dir. G. Seaton (1954).

15. Spoto, *High Society*.

16. A. Radnor, "Sex and Star Power at the Oscars," *The Times*, February 23, 2013.

17. G. Kelly, acceptance speech, March 30, 1955, Academy Awards Acceptance Speech Database, http://aaspeechesdb.oscars.org.

18. Spoto, *High Society*.

19. D. Thomson, *The New Biographical Dictionary of Film* (New York: Knopf, 2010).

20. Verlhac and Dherbier, *Grace Kelly*.

21. Dahlburg, "Prince Rainier III."

22. "Princess Grace's Fatal Crash: Her Daughter's Account," *Chicago Tribune*, October 23, 1989.

ANNA MAGNANI

1. D. Fasulo, B. Goff, and D. Holford, *History Alive! World Connections* (Mountain View, CA: TCI, 2013).

2. P. J. Taylor, "Stardom, Italian Style," *Journal of Film and Video* 62, no. 3 (2010): 65–67.

3. R. Brisbin, "Censorship, Ratings, and Rights: Political Order and Sexual Portrayals in American Movies," *Studies in American Political Development* 16, no. 1 (2002): 1–27; J. Stone, "Ecstasy and the Rise of Sex in the Cinema," *Vancouver Sun*, December 8, 2003.

4. R. B. Palmer, "Tennessee Williams and 1950s Hollywood: The View from Here and Abroad," *Southern Quarterly* 48, no. 4 (2011): 108–125, 138.

5. C. Wilder, "The Roman Seasons of Tennessee Williams," *New York Times*, May 15, 2016.

6. S. Harvey, program notes, Pacific Film Archive, December 1988.

7. D. Thomson, *Ingrid Bergman* (New York: Faber and Faber, 2009).

8. Palmer, "Tennessee Williams."

9. C. Chase, "Anna Magnani: Miracle Worker," *Film Comment* 29, no. 6 (1993): 42–47.

10. R. Rea, "Tennessee Williams's *The Rose Tattoo*: Sicilian Migration and the Mississippi Gulf Coast," *Southern Literary Journal* 46, no. 2 (2014): 140–154, 224; T. Vallance, "Hal Kanter," *The Independent*, November 12, 2011.

11. J. Kobler, "Tempest on the Tiber," *Life*, February 13, 1950; R. Thomas, "Italian Actress Anna Magnani, 60, Remains 'She-Wolf' of Rome," *Florence Morning News*, November 17, 1968.

12. *LA Weekly*, February 10, 1989.

13. N. Croce, *The History of Film* (New York: Rosen Education Service, 2015).

14. Rea, "Tennessee Williams's *The Rose Tattoo*."

15. J. Bacon, "The Oscar Derby Is on Again," *Long Beach Independent Press Telegram*, February 24, 1957; Harvey, program notes; Kobler, "Tempest on the Tiber."

16. Kobler, "Tempest on the Tiber."

17. D. Thomson, *The New Biographical Dictionary of Film* (New York: Knopf, 2010).

18. Kobler, "Tempest on the Tiber."

19. Palmer, "Tennessee Williams."

20. Kobler, "Tempest on the Tiber."

21. *LA Weekly*, February 10, 1989.

22. P. Carrano, *La Magnani: Il romanzo di una vita* (Milan: Rizzoli Editore, 1982).

23. Thomson, *Ingrid Bergman*; Chase, "Anna Magnani"; Thomson, *Ingrid Bergman*.

JOANNE WOODWARD

1. *More*, March–April 2000.

2. R. Pogrebin, "An Evening of American Classics," *New York Times*, December 1, 2002; N. Finke, "A Star? Forget It: No Entourage, No Name-Dropping, No Special Treatment—but Joanne Woodward's Artful Performances Have a Certain Glow," *Los Angeles Times*, November 18, 1990.

3. Finke, "Star?"

4. "Ticket Offer for BFI's 'Birth of the Method' Season," *Daily Telegraph*, November 8, 2014.

5. Finke, "Star?"

6. "Ticket Offer."

7. Finke, "Star?"; S. Spacek with M. Vollers, *My Extraordinary Ordinary Life* (New York: Hyperion, 2012).

8. D. C. Tucker, *Shirley Booth: A Biography and Career Record* (Jefferson, NC: McFarland, 2008).

9. S. Levy, *Paul Newman: A Life* (New York: Harmony Books, 2009); D. Lim, "He Starred behind the Camera Too: Paul Newman Made His Directorial Debut in 1968 with the Rarely Seen 'Rachel, Rachel,' Now Out on DVD," *Los Angeles Times*, February 15, 2009.

10. *Hollywood Reporter*, August 21, 1957.

11. Levy, *Paul Newman*.

12. Levy.

13. *Hollywood Reporter*, August 21, 1957.

14. *Hollywood Reporter*, August 21, 1957; J. Bawden, "Oscar Hindsight," *Toronto Star*, May 30,1992.

15. *Hollywood Reporter*, August 21, 1957.

16. S. Barrie-Anthony, "The Last Mystery of Vidal: A Writer Steeped in History and Remembrance Makes His Stand in a City of Reinvention," *Los Angeles Times*, April 2, 2006.

17. Levy, *Paul Newman*.

18. C. Crane with C. Jahr, *Detour: A Hollywood Story* (New York: Arbor House, 1988).

19. J. Neigher, "Oscar Visions: Actress-Designer Collaborations Have a Dazzling Back Story—Before Kidman and Galliano, There Was Dietrich and Dior," *Los Angeles Times*, February 28, 2010; Finke, "Star?"

20. Levy, *Paul Newman*.

21. J. Woodward, acceptance speech, March 26, 1958, Academy Awards Acceptance Speech Database, http://aaspeechesdb.oscars.org.

22. Levy, *Paul Newman*; R. McQuillan, "Secret of Oscar Winning: Pssst! Want to Win an Academy Award? Then Appeal to the Tastes of Studio Executives, Explains Rebecca McQuillan," *The Herald*, March 21, 2003.

23. Levy, *Paul Newman*.

24. Finke, "Star?"

25. J. Stuart, "Wandering Spirit of Jessica Lange: Movies: For the Versatile Actress, 'the Interesting Characters Are the Ones Who Are Not Holding On Quite as Tight' to Life," *Los Angeles Times*, June 19, 1998.

26. *More*, March–April 2000.

27. *More*, March–April 2000.

28. C. Chocano, "An Appreciation: An Anti-Hero of Alarming Beauty," *Los Angeles Times*, September 28, 2008.

29. C. FitzGibbon, "Beatle Film to Restore the Empire," *Life*, August 7, 1964; J. Verniere, "Appreciation," *Boston Herald*, September 28, 2008; *More*, March–April 2000.

30. "Hollywood's Hardest Performances," BBC News, February 6, 2001, http://news.bbc.co.uk/2/hi/entertainment/1156190.stm.

31. D. Thomson, *The New Biographical Dictionary of Film* (New York: Knopf, 2010).

SUSAN HAYWARD

1. A. Camus, *Neither Victims nor Executioners* (Eugene, OR: Wipf and Stock, 1946).

2. D. Bingham, "'I Do Want to Live!': Female Voices, Male Discourse, and Hollywood Biopics," *Cinema Journal* 38, no. 3 (1999): 3–26; P. French, "Review: Screen: Film of the Week: Pride and Prejudice: Todd Haynes's Powerful Study of Racial and Sexual Bigotry in Fifties America Is Heartbreaking and Uncannily Accurate," *The Observer*, March 9, 2003.

3. McGraw-Hill Education, *United States History and Geography* (Columbus, OH: McGraw-Hill Education, 2014).

4. Bingham, "I Do Want to Live!"

5. Bingham.

6. W. Wanger and J. Hyams, *My Life with Cleopatra: The Making of a Hollywood Classic* (New York: Vintage Books, 2013).

7. Bingham, "I Do Want to Live!"

8. Bingham.

9. A. Leve, "Sense and Sensitivity," *Sunday Times*, April 2, 2006.

10. C. McNulty, "An Endless Story: Charles Busch's Bid to Create an Evening of Madcap Entertainment Is Long on the Former and Short on the Latter," *Los Angeles Times*, September 24, 2008.

11. S. Higashi, "1952: Movies and the Paradox of Female Stardom," in *American Cinema of the 1950s: Themes and Variations*, ed. M. Pomerance (New Brunswick, NJ: Rutgers University Press, 2005).

12. *Variety*, October 28, 1958.

13. *Variety*, October 28, 1958; *Motion Picture Daily*, October 28, 1958.

14. Bingham, "I Do Want to Live!"; L. Mulvey, "Visual Pleasure and Narrative Cinema," *Screen* 16, no. 3 (Autumn 1975): 6–18.

15. *I Want to Live!*, dir. R. Wise (1958).

16. M. Wiley and D. Bona, *Inside Oscar: The Unofficial History of the Academy Awards* (New York: Ballantine Books, 1986).

17. Wiley and Bona.

18. Bingham, "I Do Want to Live!"

19. S. Hayward, acceptance speech, April 6, 1959, Academy Awards Acceptance Speech Database, http://aaspeechesdb.oscars.org.

20. R. Osborne, "Robert Osborne on Susan Hayward," TCM, accessed March 24, 2019, http://www.tcm.com/this-month/article/1118123%7C1118124/Robert-Osborne-on-Susan-Hayward.html; Wiley and Bona, *Inside Oscar*.

21. E. Levy, *Oscar Fever: The History and Politics of the Academy Awards* (New York: Continuum, 2001).

22. S. King, "How They've Managed to Stop the Show: Oscars: Almost Every Year, the Ceremonies Are Marked by a Memorable Appearance by Someone. Here Are Some of the Showstoppers through the Years," *Los Angeles Times*, March 18, 2000.

SIMONE SIGNORET

1. P. A. DeMaio, *Garden of Dreams: The Life of Simone Signoret* (Jackson: University Press of Mississippi, 2014).

2. DeMaio.

3. DeMaio.

4. J. Fonda, *My Life So Far* (New York: Random House, 2005).

5. DeMaio, *Garden of Dreams*.

6. S. Hayward, *Simone Signoret: The Star as Cultural Sign* (New York: Continuum, 2004).

7. DeMaio, *Garden of Dreams*.

8. Hayward, *Simone Signoret*.

9. DeMaio, *Garden of Dreams*.

10. L. Winer, "One More Bad Reminder That Bad Isn't New," *Newsday*, February 9, 1996; C. Easton, *No Intermissions: The Life of Agnes de Mille* (Boston: Little, Brown, 1996).

11. Hayward, *Simone Signoret*.

12. S. Signoret, acceptance speech, April 4, 1960, Academy Awards Acceptance Speech Database, http://aaspeechesdb.oscars.org.

13. DeMaio, *Garden of Dreams*.

14. J. Hoberman, "'Room at the Top': An Affair to Remember," *New York Times*, March 6, 2019.

15. Hayward, *Simone Signoret*.

ELIZABETH TAYLOR

1. R. Mead, "Legend of the Fall," *Allure*, July 2011.

2. P. French, "Elizabeth Taylor, 1932–2011: A Great British Beauty and an Enduring Icon of Hollywood's Golden Age: Our Critic Philip French Remembers the Child Star Turned Oscar-Winning Actress, Who Was as Celebrated as Much for Her Tempestuous Relationships as Her Movies," *The Observer*, March 27, 2011.

3. L. Lacey, "The Baubled Brilliance of a Screen Queen," *Globe and Mail*, March 24, 2011; T. Huntington, "All That Glitters," *Historic Traveler* 5 (March 1999): 32.

4. J. Molony, "Judy Garland: The Diva, the Drugs and the Damage," *Sunday Independent*, May 31, 2015.

5. Molony; D. Spoto, *A Passion for Life: The Biography of Elizabeth Taylor* (New York: HarperCollins, 1995).

6. D. Werts, "TV's Tykes Remember: Acting Wasn't Just Child's Play," *Newsday*, September 4, 2000.

7. Spoto, *Passion for Life*.

8. E. Woo, "Elizabeth Taylor, 1932–2011: Icon of Glamour, On and Off Screen; The Film Star's Oscar-Winning Acting Talent Often Took a Back Seat to the Drama of Her Personal Life," *Los Angeles Times*, March 24, 2011.

9. W. J. Mann, *How to Be a Movie Star: Elizabeth Taylor in Hollywood* (New York: Houghton Mifflin Harcourt, 2009).

10. A. Collins, "Films on TV: Andrew Collins' Choice of Television Films," *The Observer*, May 21, 2000.

11. C. Paglia, "Small Talk: One Feminist's Idea of Heaven," *Interview*, February 2007.

12. Paglia; L. Mulvey, "Visual Pleasure and Narrative Cinema," *Screen* 16, no. 3 (1975): 6–18.

13. A. Jacobs, "Something to Wear under That Fur?," *New York Times*, December 12, 2013.

14. C. Paglia, "So Bold, Bad and Beautiful," *Sunday Times*, March 27, 2011.

15. J. Christopher, "Cracked Icon," in *1000 Films to Change Your Life*, ed. S. Cropper (London: Time Out Guides, 2006).

16. M. Wiley and D. Bona, *Inside Oscar: The Unofficial History of the Academy Awards* (New York: Ballantine Books, 1986).

17. E. Taylor, acceptance speech, April 17, 1961, Academy Awards Acceptance Speech Database, http://aaspeechesdb.oscars.org.

18. Wiley and Bona, *Inside Oscar*.

19. *Newsweek*, July 4, 1966.

20. P. Monaco, *The Sixties: 1960–1969* (Berkeley: University of California Press, 2001).

21. T. Teeman, "George Segal, Oscar-Nominated Star of 'Who's Afraid of Virginia Woolf?': On Edward Albee's Legacy," *Daily Beast*, September 17, 2016.

22. G. Jones, *I'll Never Write My Memoirs* (New York: Gallery Books, 2015); R. Brownstein, "The NJ 20: The Most Politically Effective Celebrities of All Time," *National Journal*, April 28, 2011.

23. D. Firestone, "The Unlikely Heroine in the War on AIDS," *Newsday*, June 12, 1987; Brownstein, "NJ 20"; GLAAD, "Elizabeth Taylor at the GLAAD Media Awards," YouTube, March 25, 2011, https://www.youtube.com/watch?v=ElSCFzpYWrc.

24. Firestone, "Unlikely Heroine."

25. S. Edwards, "Elizabeth Taylor Ran an Underground AIDS Pharmaceutical Ring to Provide Drugs to Patients," Jezebel, December 1, 2015, http://jezebel.com/elizabeth-taylor-ran-an-underground-aids-pharmaceutical-1745602507.

26. E. Taylor, acceptance speech, March 29, 1993, Academy Awards Acceptance Speech Database, http://aaspeechesdb.oscars.org.

SOPHIA LOREN

1. "Accepting the Award," *People Weekly*, April 9, 2001.

2. C. North, "'Two Women' Premieres," *Contra Costa Times*, June 11, 2015.

3. S. Levy, *Dolce Vita Confidential: Fellini, Loren, Pucci, Paparazzi, and the Swinging High Life of 1950s Rome* (New York: Norton, 2016).

4. S. Loren, *Yesterday, Today, Tomorrow: My Life* (New York: Atria Books, 2015).

5. E. Levy, *Oscar Fever: The History and Politics of the Academy Awards* (New York: Continuum, 2001).

6. E. Levy; Loren, *Yesterday, Today, Tomorrow*.

7. *Epoca*, April 1962.

8. E. Levy, *Oscar Fever*.

9. S. Kashner, "Sophia's Choices," *Vanity Fair*, March 2012; D. Wigg, "Sophia from Home: Earlier This Month, Sophia Loren Posed for the 2007 Pirelli Calendar Proving She Has Lost None of Her Allure at the Age of 71," *Daily Mail*, July 15, 2006.

10. Wigg, "Sophia from Home"; Kashner, "Sophia's Choices"; Wigg.

11. *Biography*, July 2001; Kashner, "Sophia's Choices."

12. Loren, *Yesterday, Today, Tomorrow*.

13. Loren.

14. Wigg, "Sophia from Home."

15. Kashner, "Sophia's Choices."

16. "Moved Diva Loren Sheds Tears of Joy," *Townsville Bulletin*, June 24, 2005.

17. Kashner, "Sophia's Choices."

18. F. Sanello, "Loren Finds Similarities in 'Fortunate' Role," *Chicago Tribune*, April 3, 1988; G. Jones, *I'll Never Write My Memoirs* (New York: Gallery Books, 2015).

19. Kashner, "Sophia's Choices"; "Sophia: Living and Loving," *Times Leader*, June 9, 1979.

20. S. Levy, *Dolce Vita Confidential*.

21. K. Mikhail, "Italian Style: Lights, Camera, Action . . . : From the Neorealism of Rossellini and the Sumptuousness of Fellini to Sergio Leone's Spaghetti Westerns, Italian Cinema Brings Sensuality to the Screen," *The Observer*, September 30, 2001; S. Levy, *Paul Newman: A Life* (New York: Harmony Books, 2009).

22. S. Hughes, "Helen Mirren: 'Do I Feel Beautiful? I Hate That Word,'" *The Guardian*, September 26, 2015, https://www.theguardian.com/culture/2015/sep/26/helen-mirren-interview-sally-hughes.

23. D. McLellan, "The Nation: Carlo Ponti, 1912–2007: Prolific Producer with 'New Vision,'" *Los Angeles Times*, January 11, 2007; D. Jewel, C. Nolan, S. C. Goulding, S. Delaney, and E. Heyn, "House Mother," *People Weekly*, February 2, 1999.

24. S. King, "Series Takes Loren Back to Where It All Started," *Los Angeles Times*, June 4, 2008; D. Chase, "Anna Magnani: Miracle Worker," *Film Comment* 29, no. 6 (1993): 42–47.

25. R. Thomas, "Italian Actress Anna Magnani, 60, Remains 'She-Wolf' of Rome," *Florence Morning News*, November 17, 1968.

26. D. Hunt, "'La Bamba' Set for January Release; 'Mr. Right,' 'Malone' Out This Week," *Los Angeles Times*, November 6, 1987; S. Levy, *Dolce Vita Confidential*; S. Walker, "Ciao, Bella! Women Made Movie History; Summer Film Series Celebrates the Best of Italian Cinema and the Role

Actresses Play in Its Success," *Toronto Star*, July 10, 2009; B. Crowther, "Sophia Loren in Old Form," *New York Times*, May 9, 1961.

27. G. Rowe, "'Two Women' Never Takes Off," *Contra Costa Times*, June 15, 2015; V. Canby and J. Maslin, *The New York Times Guide to the Best 1,000 Movies Ever Made: An Indispensable Collection of Original Reviews of Box-Office Hits and Misses* (New York: St. Martin's Griffin, 2004).

28. Kashner, "Sophia's Choices."

29. "Accepting the Award."

ANNE BANCROFT

1. T. Robey, "A Crying Shame," *Sunday Telegraph*, February 22, 2015.

2. G. Kilday, "Oscar Needs to Be Less Corporate, More Crass, Chaotic and Controversial," *Hollywood Reporter*, February 16, 2009.

3. "Accepting the Award . . . ," *People*, April 9, 2001.

4. "Accepting the Award."

5. B. Baxter, "Obituary: Anne Bancroft: Oscar-Winning Actor Who Starred in 'The Miracle Worker' and 'The Graduate,'" *The Guardian*, June 9, 2005.

6. M. J. Bandler, "Offstage Bancroft Irrepressible Performer Stands by Her Roles," *Chicago Tribune*, April 4, 1993.

7. A. Kerr, "Anne Bancroft Oscar Winner and Legendary Star of 'The Graduate,'" *The Herald*, June 9, 2005.

8. "Profile: Anne Bancroft, Oscar, Tony and Emmy Winner Who Died Monday," *Morning Edition*, NPR, June 8, 2005.

9. A. Longsdorf, "Unlocking the Mrs. Robinson Within: She Never Cared Much for Her Role in 'The Graduate,' but Anne Bancroft Draws on That Side of Herself Again for 'Up at the Villa,'" *The Record*, May 2, 2000.

10. Baxter, "Obituary."

11. "A Stylish Performer: Obituary Anne Bancroft," *Financial Times*, June 9, 2005; Bandler, "Offstage Bancroft."

12. "Stylish Performer"; M. Cieply, "Will the Academy's Weinstein Meeting Be Haunted by Darryl Zanuck's Ghost?," *Deadline Hollywood*, October 13, 2017, http://deadline.com/2017/10/will-academy-weinstein-meeting-be-haunted-by-zanuck-ghost-1202188246/.

13. Longsdorf, "Unlocking the Mrs. Robinson Within."

14. Baxter, "Obituary"; R. Berkvist, "Anne Bancroft, Stage and Film Star in Voracious and Vulnerable Roles, Dies at 73," *New York Times*, June 8, 2005.

15. Longsdorf, "Unlocking the Mrs. Robinson Within."

16. M. Johnson, "Bancroft Versatile, Glorious: Actress Showed Tremendous Range on Stage, Screen; Appreciation," *Hartford Courant*, June 9, 2005; L. Grant, *I Said Yes to Everything: A Memoir* (New York: Blue Rider, 2014).

17. Longsdorf, "Unlocking the Mrs. Robinson Within."

18. S. M. Shearer, *Patricia Neal: An Unquiet Life* (Lexington: University Press of Kentucky, 2006).

19. "Profile."

20. D. Cook, *A History of Narrative Film*, 4th ed. (New York: Norton, 2004).

21. Shearer, *Patricia Neal*; "Longer Life for Screen Sirens," *Dominion Post*, July 19, 2014.

22. D. Kehr, "Arthur Penn, 88, Director of 'Bonnie and Clyde' in '67," *International Herald Tribune*, September 30, 2010.

23. N. Southern, "End of the Road Rides Again: Revival of a Sixties Anti-Establishment Classic," *Cineaste* 37 (2012): 4–9, 57.

24. Baxter, "Obituary."

25. Kerr, "Anne Bancroft"; C. Chocano, "An Appreciation: She Tried to Seduce Us, and Did," *Los Angeles Times*, June 10, 2005.

26. Bandler, "Offstage Bancroft."

27. S. Wloszczyna, "Here's to You, Anne Bancroft: Her Seductive Skills Lit the Stage, Screen," *USA Today*, June 8, 2005.

PATRICIA NEAL

1. S. M. Shearer, *Patricia Neal: An Unquiet Life* (Lexington: University Press of Kentucky, 2006).

2. Shearer.

3. B. Farrell, "The Gallant Fight for Pat Neal's Life," *Life*, October 22, 1965; P. Neal, *As I Am: An Autobiography* (New York: Simon and Schuster, 1988).

4. Farrell, "Gallant Fight."

5. D. McLellan, "Patricia Neal, 1926–2010: Actress Triumphed amid Tragedies," *Los Angeles Times*, August 10, 2010.

6. M. Dryden, "The Tragedies and Triumphs of Patricia Neal: 'As I Am' by Patricia Neal with Richard DeNeut," *Los Angeles Times*, April 17, 1988.

7. E. Canning Blackwell, "Reel Life," *Northwestern Magazine*, Winter 2012, http://www.northwestern.edu/magazine/winter2012/feature/reel-life_print.html; McLellan, "Patricia Neal."

8. McLellan, "Patricia Neal"; Shearer, *Patricia Neal*.

9. Canning Blackwell, "Reel Life."

10. Shearer, *Patricia Neal*.

11. G. Pearce, "'I Had to Escape Hollywood's Madding Crowd!': Julie Christie on Swapping Glamour for Sheep," *Express*, February 28, 2015, http://www.express.co.uk/entertainment/films/561026/Julie-Christie-reveals-left-Hollywood-stardom-tend-sheep-farm-in-Wales-Madding-Crowd-fame; J. Van Meter, "Star Power: The Producer," *Vogue*, March 1, 2005.

12. D. Spoto, *High Society: The Life of Grace Kelly* (New York: Three Rivers, 2010).

13. Shearer, *Patricia Neal*.

14. J. Wester Anderson, *Forever Young: The Life, Loves and Enduring Faith of a Hollywood Legend* (Allen, TX: Thomas More, 2000); J. Portman, "A Hollywood Survivor: Actress Patricia

Neal, 73, Has Endured Scandal and Personal Tragedy," *The Gazette*, January 10, 2000.

15. S. Sutherland, "Good-Guy Cooper Slept Around," *Ottawa Citizen*, September 12, 1998.

16. Sutherland.

17. McLellan, "Patricia Neal."

18. Shearer, *Patricia Neal*.

19. "Oscar-Winning Actor Who Returned to Films Following Strokes," *Irish Times*, August 14, 2010.

20. Shearer, *Patricia Neal*; McLellan, "Patricia Neal."

21. C. Day, "Paul Newman Played Texas Heel in '63 'Hud,'" *Austin American Statesman*, November 12, 1989; *Listener*, June 20, 1963.

22. Shearer, *Patricia Neal*.

23. *Hud*, dir. M. Ritt (1963).

24. Neal, *As I Am*.

25. Shearer, *Patricia Neal*.

JULIE ANDREWS

1. L. Grossman, "The Confessions of Mary Poppins," *Time*, April 7, 2008; A. Kerr, "Always So Good and Proper: She Tried to Change Her Image, but Julie Andrews Will Always Be Miss Goody Two-Shoes," *The Herald*, September 25, 2000.

2. P. Pacheco, "Mary Poppins Gets Gnarly: Julie Andrews Swaps Her Cheery Cloak—or Is It a Straitjacket?—for the Bittersweet World of Stephen Sondheim," *Los Angeles Times*, March 14, 1993; M. Thornton, "The Nun with a Switchblade," *Daily Mail*, March 24, 2008.

3. Pacheco, "Mary Poppins Gets Gnarly."

4. Thornton, "Nun with a Switchblade."

5. Kerr, "Always So Good."

6. Thornton, "Nun with a Switchblade"; R. Stirling, *Julie Andrews: An Intimate Biography* (New York: St. Martin's, 2008).

7. M. DeBord, "Andrews Unearths Her 'Deeper Level': The Memoir, She Says, Helped Her Understand Her Own Early, and at Times Dark, Years," *Los Angeles Times*, April 25, 2008; Pacheco, "Mary Poppins Gets Gnarly."

8. Pacheco, "Mary Poppins Gets Gnarly."

9. Academy of Achievement, "Dame Julie Andrews," accessed March 24, 2019, https://www.achievement.org/achiever/julie-andrews/.

10. M. Beck, "From Defeat, Rejection to Success: 'Self-Efficacy' Is Key to Conquering Odds; A List of Famous Flops," *Wall Street Journal*, April 29, 2008.

11. Stirling, *Julie Andrews*.

12. S. King, "Caregivers on Screen," *Los Angeles Times*, August 15, 2003.

13. D. Chan, "Oscar Best Actress Debuts," *Malay Mail*, May 13, 2004.

14. V. Heffernan, "Poppins on the Loose: Lock Up Your Children," *New York Times*, December 24, 2004; King, "Caregivers on Screen."

15. A. Gopnik, "Magic Kingdoms," *New Yorker*, December 9, 2002; B. Dowell, "Lost Song Reveals

a Mean Mary Poppins," *Sunday Times*, January 30, 2005.

16. A. McLeer, "Practical Perfection? The Nanny Negotiates Gender, Class, and Family Contradictions in 1960s Popular Culture," *NWSA Journal* 14, no. 2 (2002): 80–101.

17. J. Fryer, "A Spoonful of Spite," *Daily Mail*, April 26, 2012; C. Flanagan, "Becoming Mary Poppins: Life and Letters," *New Yorker*, December 19, 2005.

18. Stirling, *Julie Andrews*.

19. R. Harrison, acceptance speech, April 5, 1965, Academy Awards Acceptance Speech Database, http://aaspeechesdb.oscars.org.

20. J. Andrews, acceptance speech, April 5, 1965, Academy Awards Acceptance Speech Database, http://aaspeechesdb.oscars.org.

21. B. Bawer, "The Other Sixties," *Wilson Quarterly* 28, no. 2 (2004): 64–84.

22. B. Thomas, "Rolling the Credits on Cinema's Extraordinary First Century: Movies: They Make Us Giggle, Sob, Even Swoon. And It All Began with a Sneeze. Or Was It a Kiss?," *Los Angeles Times*, April 18, 1999.

23. J. Stuart, "Happy Days May Be Back for Film Musicals: It's Been Years since Hollywood Tried to Tap Broadway for Inspiration—and Succeeded. 'Evita' Has Made the Genre Seem Possible Again," *Los Angeles Times*, December 24, 1996.

24. Pacheco, "Mary Poppins Gets Gnarly"; J. Stein, *West of Eden: An American Place* (New York: Random House, 2016).

25. W. Friedkin, *The Friedkin Connection* (New York: HarperCollins, 2013).

26. I. Lacher, "The Sunday Conversation: Having a Loverly Time," *Los Angeles Times*, April 17, 2011.

27. Pacheco, "Mary Poppins Gets Gnarly."

28. G. Rollings, "The Secret Dark Side to the Classic 'Mary Poppins,'" *New York Post*, December 25, 2018, https://nypost.com/2018/12/25/the-secret-dark-side-to-the-classic-mary-poppins/; J. Farber, "The Sound of Failure: How the Big Three Movie Musicals of 1964–65 Led to Death of the Genre," *New York Daily News*, January 12, 2014.

29. Pacheco, "Mary Poppins Gets Gnarly."

JULIE CHRISTIE

1. K. Milestone and A. Meyer, *Gender and Popular Culture* (Cambridge, UK: Polity, 2011); D. Staunton, "Rebellion of the Swinging Sixties Evident in Positive Aspects of Brexit," *Irish Times*, October 14, 2016.

2. Milestone and Meyer, *Gender and Popular Culture*.

3. M. Oliver, "Movie Great Ginger Rogers Dies at 83: Hollywood; The Oscar-Winning Actress Was Best Known for the 10 Films She Glided Through with Fred Astaire," *Los Angeles Times*, April 26, 1995.

4. S. Lawrence, "Edwardian Ghosts in a Lost Paradise," *Daily Telegraph*, June 14, 2014.

5. F. P. Whitington, "Christie: The Sixties' Siren Queen of British Film," *Irish Independent*, May 2, 2015.

6. *Look*, March 8, 1966; R. Brooks, "Travel Eastern India: Remnants of Things Past; Richard Brooks Is Struck by the Bustle of Calcutta and Echoes of the Raj in the Mountainous North-East," *The Guardian*, April 9, 1995.

7. *Look*, March 8, 1966.

8. C. Champlin, "A Soul of Discretion: Julie Christie Is Fine with the Fame Game. After All, the Actress, Back on the Screen in 'Afterglow,' Has Played It Well for 30 Years. Celebrity, Now That's Another Matter," *Los Angeles Times*, December 14, 1997.

9. Whitington, "Christie."

10. *Look*, March 8, 1966.

11. N. James, "Dirk Bogarde: A Class Act," *Sight and Sound* 21 (2011): 40–44; A. H. Weiler, "Critics Vote 'Darling' the Best Film of 1965," *New York Times*, December 28, 1965.

12. B.C., "Screen: 'Darling' Is Selfish, Fickle and Ambitious," *New York Times*, August 4, 1965.

13. B. Miles, "An Eye on the Scene: Barry Miles Remembers 1960s Groovy London," *Taschen*, Summer 2012.

14. V. Russo, *The Celluloid Closet: Homosexuality in the Movies*, rev. ed. (New York: Harper and Row, 1987); C. Hickman, "Exile from Happiness," *New Statesman*, October 4, 2004.

15. *Photoplay*, May 1966.

16. T. Ewbank and S. Hildred, *Julie Christie: The Biography* (London: Andre Deutsch, 2009).

17. Ewbank and Hildred.

18. T. Barrell, "50 Makers & Shakers 1962–2012," *Sunday Times*, February 5, 2012; J. Stuart, "Oscars '98: Back to Their Future; This Year's Oscars Could Be Called the Comeback Derby, What with the Careers of Five Veterans Being Rejuvenated by Nominations," *Los Angeles Times*, March 22, 1998.

19. J. Basinger, *The Star Machine* (New York: Knopf, 2007).

20. Ewbank and Hildred, *Julie Christie*.

21. J. Christie, acceptance speech, April 18, 1966, Academy Awards Acceptance Speech Database, http://aaspeechesdb.oscars.org.

22. D. Hutchings, "Julie, Darling," *InStyle*, April 2003.

23. P. French, "Screen Legends: No 31: Julie Christie 1940–," *The Observer*, September 28, 2008; J. Neigher, "Oscar Visions: Actress-Designer Collaborations Have a Dazzling Back Story—Before Kidman and Galliano, There Was Dietrich and Dior," *Los Angeles Times*, February 28, 2010.

24. Neigher, "Oscar Visions."

25. Ewbank and Hildred, *Julie Christie*; "Contender Countdown: 6. Toward 'Away,'" *Los Angeles Times*, January 30, 2008.

26. R. Verkaik, "'I Feared Bush Would Unleash a Wave of Sadism—and he Did,'" *The Independent*, February 21, 2009.

27. Whitington, "Christie."

28. H. Italie, "Julie Christie's Trip of Fools," *Toronto Star*, January 7, 1991.

BARBRA STREISAND

1. M. Wiley and D. Bona, *Inside Oscar: The Unofficial History of the Academy Awards* (New York: Ballantine Books, 1986).

2. J. Fonda, presentation of the Oscar for Best Director, April 14, 1969, Academy Awards Acceptance Speech Database, http://aaspeechesdb.oscars.org.

3. I. Bergman, presentation of the Oscar for Best Actress, April 14, 1969, Academy Awards Acceptance Speech Database, http://aaspeechesdb.oscars.org.

4. A. Rossi, *Barbra: A Retrospective* (New York: Sterling, 2012).

5. B. Streisand, acceptance speech, April 14, 1969, Academy Awards Acceptance Speech Database, http://aaspeechesdb.oscars.org.

6. Rossi, *Barbra*.

7. T. Howard Reich, Barbra Today: Adored by Millions, Jeered by Hecklers and Lambasted by Those Who Tire of Her Political Soliloquies, Barbra Streisand Takes Time Out from a Rare Tour to Give an Even Rarer Interview to the Tribune," *Chicago Tribune*, November 5, 2006; Rossi, *Barbra*.

8. H. de Vries, "Streisand, the Storyteller: The Perfectionist Actress-Director Remembers All the Details, Except for the Good Times," *Los Angeles Times*, December 8, 1991.

9. De Vries.

10. M. Bostridge, "Oh, Barbra: You Either Love Her or Loathe Her—There's No Sitting on the Fence with Barbra Streisand, Says Mark Bostridge. Now, after an Eight-Year Break, She's Back on the Big Screen. Should We Cheer Her Return? Or Run for Cover?," *Independent on Sunday*, January 16, 2005.

11. Bostridge.

12. Rossi, *Barbra*; Lisa Vreeland, *Diana Vreeland: The Eye Has to Travel* (New York: Henry N. Abrams, 2011); J. Michaelson, "The Way I Was," *Forward*, October 12, 2012.

13. Bostridge, "Oh, Barbra"; M. Abernethy, "Decoding Gay Icons: The Appeal of Judy, Babs and Madge Is More than High Camp and Melodrama," *Chicago Sun-Times*, December 17, 2006; Bostridge.

14. M. Dargis and A. O. Scott, "Dystopia, Apocalypse, Culture War: 2018 or 1968?," *New York Times*, May 17, 2018.

15. *Barbra* 2, no. 3 (1982).

16. *Barbra* 2, no. 3 (1982).

17. P. Monaco, *The Sixties: 1960–1969* (Berkeley: University of California Press, 2001).

18. G. Lambert, *Norma Shearer: A Life* (New York: Knopf, 1990).

19. J. McClurg, "Streisand Biography Hits All the High Notes," *USA Today*, March 27, 2006; V. Wilson, *A Life of Barbara Stanwyck: Steel-True 1907–1940* (New York: Simon and Schuster, 2013).

20. McClurg, "Streisand Biography."

21. "Barbra's Coupe Ter Weÿden Dutch interview," April 2, 1984, YouTube, April 1, 2014.

22. *Barbra* 2, no. 3 (1982).

23. N. Gabler, *Barbra Streisand: Redefining Beauty, Femininity, and Power* (New Haven, CT: Yale University Press, 2016).

24. Rossi, *Barbra*.

25. M. Dargis, "Lights, Camera, Taking Action," *New York Times*, January 25, 2015.

26. S. Prince, *A New Pot of Gold: Hollywood under the Electronic Rainbow, 1980–1989* (Berkeley: University of California Press, 2000); *New York Times*, January 21, 2015; M. Haskell, *From Reverence to Rape: The Treatment of Women in the Movies* (Chicago: University of Chicago Press, 1987).

27. De Vries, "Streisand"; Prince, *New Pot of Gold*.

28. BARBRAJC, "Barbra Streisand & Barbara Walters Interview Part 3," YouTube, July 10, 2010, http://www.youtube.com/watch?v=hpd4w9tC2J8&feature=related.

MAGGIE SMITH

1. E. Cowing, "La Creme de la Creme," *Scotland on Sunday*, January 2, 2011.

2. *The Prime of Miss Jean Brodie*, dir. R. Neame (1969).

3. "'Downton Abbey' Fame Spotlights Maggie Smith," interview by S. Kroft, *60 Minutes*, aired February 17, 2013, on CBS.

4. M. Coveney, *Maggie Smith: A Bright Particular Star* (London: Victor Gollancz, 1992).

5. G. Pearce, "'I Had to Escape Hollywood's Madding Crowd!': Julie Christie on Swapping Glamour for Sheep," *Express*, March 10, 2015.

6. Coveney, *Maggie Smith*.

7. S. King, "The Highs and Lows of Being Blanche," *Los Angeles Times*, October 29, 1995.

8. "'Downton Abbey' Fame"; Claire O'Boyle, "Dustin Hoffman on How He's Changing His Life," *The Mirror*, January 8, 2013.

9. M. London, "There Is Nothing like This Dame," *New York Times*, March 18, 1990.

10. E. Grice, "Maggie Smith: Age Cannot Wither Her," *Daily Telegraph*, November 8, 2014.

11. London, "There Is Nothing like This Dame."

12. "The Vulture's Top 100 Actresses," *The Times*, December 23, 2000.

13. D. Thomson, *The New Biographical Dictionary of Film* (New York: Knopf, 2010).

14. "Maggie 'Stunned' at News of Oscar Award," *Los Angeles Times*, April 10 1970.

15. "Maggie 'Stunned.'"

16. "Maggie 'Stunned.'"

17. M. Coveney, "I'm Very Scared of Being Back on Stage: Next Week, Maggie Smith Returns to the West End in an Edward Albee Play That Hasn't Been Revived Since Its Disastrous Broadway Premiere," *Evening Standard*, March 2, 2007.

18. Coveney, *Maggie Smith*.

19. "'Downton Abbey' Fame."

20. J. Clark, "A Forceful Character: Maggie Smith Again Plays a Class-Conscious Snob. But Her Decades of Work Have Taken Her beyond Type," *Los Angeles Times*, December 24. 2001.

GLENDA JACKSON

1. I. Woodward, *Glenda Jackson: A Study in Fire and Ice* (New York: St. Martin's, 1985).

2. Woodward.

3. B. Bugle, "Glenda Jackson Launches Tirade against Thatcher in Tribute Debate," YouTube, April 10, 2013, http://www.youtube.com/watch?v=XDtClJYJBj8.

4. B. Brantley, "Glenda Jackson on Quitting Parliament, Playing Lear and Returning to Broadway," *New York Times*, February 23, 2018.

5. C. Grimshaw, "Glenda Jackson 1976," YouTube, October 12, 2011, http://www.youtube.com/watch?v=UG5Pupbvp98&feature=related.

6. H. Davies, "1966 I Was There . . . (and I Remember It All)," *Daily Mail*, May 20, 2006.

7. H. Als, "Heretics," *New Yorker*, November 10, 2008, 90.

8. "Charles Marowitz—Obituary," *The Telegraph*, May 8, 2014.

9. D. Thomson, *The New Biographical Dictionary of Film* (New York: Knopf, 2010).

10. G. Phillips, "Ken Russell's Two Lawrence Films: The Rainbow and Women in Love," *Literature/Film Quarterly* 25, no. 1 (1997): 68–73.

11. W. Friedkin, *The Friedkin Connection* (New York: HarperCollins, 2013).

12. D. Cook, *A History of Narrative Film*, 4th ed. (New York: Norton, 2004).

13. A. Hornaday, "British Director Stirred Controversy," *Washington Post*, December 1, 2011.

14. "Accepting the Award," *People Weekly*, April 9, 2001; M. Johnson, "Glenda Jackson Learns New Role—Politician," *Los Angeles Times*, April 30 1990.

15. S. Morley, "The British Are Going: Hollywood," *The Times*, March 25, 1993.

16. M. London, "There Is Nothing like This Dame," *New York Times*, March 18, 1990.

17. Woodward, *Glenda Jackson*.

18. Grimshaw, "Glenda Jackson 1976."

19. Brantley, "Glenda Jackson on Quitting Parliament."

20. *A Touch of Class*, dir. M. Frank (1973).

21. L. Barber, "Shrewish Princess as an Election Manifesto: Glenda Jackson's Biography Is Little Better than a Spoilt Vote," *The Observer*, September 12, 1999.

22. M. Coveney, "The Play That Began a Stage Revolution," *The Independent*, October 4, 2011.

23. "The Wild Bunch," *Sight and Sound* 19 (September 2009): 22–36.

24. R. Berkvist, "Anne Bancroft Plumbed Depths of Dramatic Roles," *National Post*, June 8, 2005.

25. J. Riley, "From Glam to Nam," *Backstage*, June 15, 2004.

26. Johnson, "Glenda Jackson."

27. "Blair Aide Apologizes for Remark about Scientist: The Prime Ministers Spokesman Likened David Kelly, Who Killed Himself, to Walter Mitty," *Los Angeles Times*, August 6, 2003.

28. M. Trueman, "Glenda Jackson Hopes to Scale Mount Lear in Her Stage Return," *New York Times*, November 2, 2016.

JANE FONDA

1. C. Shoard, "Jane Fonda: 'Plastic Surgery Bought Me a Decade,'" *The Guardian*, May 21, 2015.

2. S. Bronner, "Jane Fonda: 'We Have to Shame the Studios for Being So Gender-Biased,'" *Huffington Post*, December 6, 2017, http://www.huffingtonpost.com/2015/01/26/jane-fonda-gender-bias_n_6551138.html.

3. J. Fonda, *My Life so Far* (New York: Random House, 2005).

4. Bronner, "Jane Fonda."

5. Program notes, *Paranoia Films of the '70s*, film festival, March 2005, Los Angeles County Art Museum, Los Angeles, CA.

6. TCM, "Gordon Willis," accessed March 24, 2019, http://www.tcm.com/tcmdb/person/207093%7C62919/Gordon-Willis/.

7. R. Schickel, "New Heights for a Fallen Fonda," *Life*, July 30, 1971.

8. M. LaSalle, *Complicated Women: Sex and Power in Pre-Code Hollywood* (New York: Thomas Dunne Books, 2000).

9. "More Iconic Moments," *Variety*, February 25, 2014.

10. M. Wiley and D. Bona, *Inside Oscar: The Unofficial History of the Academy Awards* (New York: Ballantine Books, 1986).

11. *And the Oscar Goes To . . .*, dir. R. Epstein (2014).

12. J. Hoberman, "G.I. Jane," *Village Voice*, May 1, 2001.

13. J. Richey, "Jane Fonda Interview 1972 (Part 1 of 5)," YouTube, June 9, 2009, https://www.youtube.com/watch?v=RHFWzcwkfS4.

14. Hoberman, "G.I. Jane."

15. R. D. McFadden, "Tom Hayden, Civil Rights and Peace Activist Turned Lawmaker, Dies at 76," *New York Times*, October 25, 2016.

16. Wiley and Bona, *Inside Oscar*.

17. J. Fonda, acceptance speech, April 9, 1979, Academy Awards Acceptance Speech Database, http://aaspeechesdb.oscars.org.

18. World Entertainment News Network, "Jane Fonda: Working Out Is Empowering," KCBY, March 4, 2017, https://kcby.com/news/entertainment/jane-fonda-working-out-is-empowering.

19. Women's Media Center, home page, accessed March 24, 2019, http://www.womensmediacenter.com.

20. "Jane Fonda Spat on by Vietnam Vet," WND, April 20, 2005, http://www.wnd.com/2005/04/29945/#csy9elVMJY7g6S7S.99.

LIZA MINNELLI

1. M. Feeney, "A Year We Couldn't Refuse," *Boston Globe*, July 22, 2012.

2. LACMA, "New Objectivity: Modern German Art in the Weimar Republic, 1919–1933," October 4, 2015, http://www.lacma.org/art/exhibition/new-objectivity-modern-german-art-weimar-republic.

3. M. Wiley and D. Bona, *Inside Oscar: The Unofficial History of the Academy Awards* (New York: Ballantine Books, 1986).

4. D. Bona, "A Long, Strange History for Your Consideration: Miramax and DreamWorks Are Going All Out on Their Oscar Campaigns, but They Are Hardly the First to Do So," *Los Angeles Times*, March 19, 2000.

5. Jessica Willis, "10 Best Oscar Dresses Ever," howstuffworks, accessed March 24, 2019, https://lifestyle.howstuffworks.com/style/fashion/trends-looks/10-best-oscar-dresses6.htm.

6. L. Minnelli, acceptance speech, March 27, 1973, Academy Awards Acceptance Speech Database, http://aaspeechesdb.oscars.org.

7. W. Leigh, *Liza: Born a Star* (New York: Signet, 1993).

8. G. Varga, "The Life of Liza: Minnelli Revisits Her Hollywood Childhood with a Quieter, More Intimate Album," *San Diego Union-Tribune*, August 22, 2010.

9. D. Hinckley, "A 'Private' Look Back by Liza," *New York Daily News*, December 11, 2010; "Show Business: Liza—Fire, Air, and a Touch of Anguis," *Time*, February 28, 1972.

10. "Show Business: Liza."

11. D. Thomson, *The New Biographical Dictionary of Film* (New York: Knopf, 2010).

12. C. McNulty, "Here's Liza to a T: Ms. Minnelli Can Be Erratic, but at the Hollywood Bowl, Her Fans Lift Her Up," *Los Angeles Times*, August 31, 2009.

13. E. Lipsky-Karasz, "Liza's New York," *Harper's Bazaar*, March 2011.

14. "Show Business: Liza."

15. TCM, "Liza Minnelli," accessed March 24, 2019, http://www.tcm.turner.com/tcmdb/person/132579|99835/Liza-Minnelli/; *Hollywood Reporter*, February 24, 2012.

16. D. Benedict, "Win When You're Singing: David Benedict Explains How Cabaret Hooked People Who Hate Musicals," *The Observer*, June 16, 2002.

17. M. O'Brien, "Wilkommen, Bienvenue, Welcome!," *Independent on Sunday*, June 16, 2002.

18. G. Carter et al., *Vanity Fair Portraits: Photographs 1913–2008* (Washington, DC: National Portrait Gallery, 2008), 12; D. A. Cook, *Lost Illusions: American Cinema in the Shadow of Watergate and Vietnam, 1970–1979* (Berkeley: University of California Press, 2000).

19. *Interview*, May 1972.

20. T. J. Gordon, "Film in the Second Degree: Cabaret and the Dark Side of Laughter," *Proceedings of the American Philosophical Society* 152, no. 4 (2008): 440–465; J. Hoberman, "Fascist Rants and the Hollywood Response," *New York Times*, March 6, 2016.

21. J. Van Meter, "Looking for the Rainbow," *Vanity Fair*, March 2002.

22. L. Barber, "Secrets and Liza," *The Guardian*, May 4, 2008, http://www.theguardian.com/music/2008/may/04/popandrock.

23. G. Jones, *I'll Never Write My Memoirs* (New York: Gallery Books, 2015).

24. S. Kashner, "Capote's Swan Dive," *Vanity Fair*, November 2012.

25. Jonathan, "Looking for the Rainbow."

26. Barber, "Secrets and Liza."

ELLEN BURSTYN

1. *McCall's*, August 1975.

2. E. Levey, "The Choice of Acting as a Profession," in *Art and Society: Readings in the Sociology of the Arts*, ed. A. W. Foster and J. Blau (New York: SUNY Press, 1989).

3. E. Burstyn, *Lessons in Becoming Myself* (New York: Riverhead, 2007).

4. "Ellen Burstyn Believes in Perseverance," *Los Angeles Herald-Examiner*, May 25, 1975.

5. M. Haskell, *From Reverence to Rape: The Treatment of Women in the Movies* (Chicago: University of Chicago Press, 1987); K. Thomas, "Review: Mix of Turbulence, Change Produces a Diamond Decade," *Los Angeles Times*, May 30, 2003; L. Lacey, "Who Controls Hollywood?," *Globe and Mail*, July 18, 2014.

6. "The Vulture's Top 100 Actresses," *The Times*, December 23, 2000; Thomas, "Review."

7. Haskell, *From Reverence to Rape*.

8. "Friday Review: In the 70s, Scorsese and Altman Both Directed What They Thought Were 'Women's Films.' Sorry, Guys . . . ," *The Guardian*, October 8, 2004.

9. Haskell, *From Reverence to Rape*.

10. J. Basinger, *The Star Machine* (New York: Knopf, 2007).

11. M. McNamara, "The Actresses: Casting Call for the Heirs Apparent; Picturing the Ranks of America's On-screen Royalty 10 Years Hence Has Many Wondering: Who'll Fill the Bill?," *Los Angeles Times*, February 18, 2007.

12. D. Hutchings, "After Seven Oscar Snubs, Geraldine Page May Trip Off to Bountiful at Last," *People*, March 24, 1986.

13. W. Friedkin, *The Friedkin Connection: A Memoir* (New York: Harper, 2013).

14. "Friday Review."

15. Burstyn, *Lessons in Becoming Myself*.

16. Burstyn.

17. J. Willis, *1960s Counterculture: Documents Decoded* (Goleta, CA: ABC-CLIO, 2015).

18. "Friday Review."

19. P. Shearer, "Lumière, Lots of Glitter, But . . . ," *Jump Cut: A Review of Contemporary Media* 16 (1977): 5.

20. *Alice Doesn't Live Here Anymore*, dir. M. Scorsese (1974).

21. S. Macaulay, "Let Your Hair Down and Go On and . . . Cry," *The Times*, September 26, 2002.

22. Macaulay.

23. *More*, July–August 2002.

LOUISE FLETCHER

1. L. Kong, "Social Themes as Reflected in Film: Scholarship, Criticism, and Theory," *Choice* 47, no. 11 (2010): 2047–2058; "Longer Life for Screen Sirens," *Dominion Post*, July 19, 2014.

2. P. French, "Screen Legends: No. 31: Julie Christie 1940–," *The Observer*, September 28, 2008.

3. "Friday Review: In the 70s, Scorsese and Altman Both Directed What They Thought Were 'Women's Films.' Sorry, Guys . . . ," *The Guardian*, October 8, 2004.

4. E. Levy, "Women Move into the Lead: For the First Time since the Days of Bette Davis and Joan Crawford, Actresses in Hollywood Are Carrying Movies on Their Own Terms," *Los Angeles Times*, January 11, 2004.

5. S. Wulf, "25 Years Ago," *Entertainment Weekly*, February 23, 2001.

6. Wulf.

7. D. Liebenson, "How Richard Nixon Inspired the Most Iconic Movie Villain of the 70s," *Vanity Fair*, November 2015.

8. L. Menand, "Acid Redux; Books," *New Yorker*, June 26, 2006; W. Brock, "Alliance Delivers a Taut, Electric 'Cuckoo's Nest': Talented Actors, Moving Moments in Fine Production," *Atlanta Journal-Constitution*, September 12, 2015.

9. K. Webb, "The 10 Best Movies of the 1970s," *Cheat Sheet*, June 12, 2017, https://www.cheat sheet.com/entertainment/the-10-best-movies-of -the-1970s.html/.

10. B. Weinraub, "Oscar's Glory Is Fleeing. Ask One Who Knows," *New York Times*, March 27, 1995; A. Harmetz, "The Nurse Who Rules the 'Cuckoo's Nest,'" *New York Times*, November 30, 1975.

11. J. Walsh, "Woody Allen, Hannibal Lecter & Me," *Independent on Sunday*, February 26, 2012.

12. "One Flew Over the Cuckoo's Nest: 10 Things You Didn't Know about the Film," *The Telegraph*, February 28, 2014; Harmetz, "Nurse Who Rules."

13. L. Fletcher, acceptance speech, March 29, 1976, Academy Awards Acceptance Speech Database, http://aaspeechesdb.oscars.org.

14. B. Weinraub, "Oscar's Glory Is Fleeing. Ask One Who Knows," *New York Times*, March 27, 1995.

15. N. Robertson, "The Fletchers: Family That Heard the Silent Thanks," *New York Times*, April 5, 1976.

16. Harmetz, "Nurse Who Rules."

17. T. Walker, "When the Cuckoo Called," *Belfast Telegraph*, January 30, 2016.

18. E. Kaye, "Louise Fletcher in Search of Herself," *Ladies Home Journal*, July 1977.

19. Walker, "When the Cuckoo Called."

20. "Nonfiction Reviews," *Publishers Weekly* 262, no. 36 (2015).

21. Weinraub, "Oscar's Glory."

22. Red Carpet Report on Mingle Media TV, "Louise Fletcher at the 2011 International Press Academy Satellite Awards Red Carpet," YouTube, December 19, 2011, http://www.youtube.com /watch?v=rBRij5_5oDU.

23. "Nurse Ratched Actress 'Cannot Bear to Watch Film,'" *Irish Examiner*, October 4, 2012, http://www.irishexaminer.com/breakingnews /entertainment/nurse-ratchet-actress-cannot -bear-to-watch-film-569289.html; R. W. Welkos, "After the Afterglow: Once the Parties Are Over and the Statuette Is on the Mantle, Many Oscar Winners Struggle to Recapture the Magic," *Los Angeles Times*, November 7, 2007.

FAYE DUNAWAY

1. F. Dunaway with B. Sharkey, *Looking for Gatsby: My Life* (New York: Simon and Schuster, 1995).

2. Dunaway with Sharkey; F. Lovece, "It Had to Be Comedy: Oscar-Winner Faye Dunaway Has Played So Many Cool, Complicated Women, She Jumped at the Chance to Do a TV Sitcom That Might Just Melt Her Icy Image," *Newsday*, October 6, 1993.

3. P. O'Haire, "Oh Faye! She Worked with H'Wood Superstuds—Now Dunaway Sets the Record Straight," *New York Daily News*, November 26, 1995.

4. Lovece, "It Had to Be Comedy."

5. D. Haithman, "Norma Dearest: Faye Dunaway Became a Star Just as 'Old Hollywood' Was Disappearing," *Los Angeles Times*, June 5, 1994.

6. *Network*, dir. S. Lumet (1976).

7. *Network*; V. Dwyer, "A League of Their Own," *Maclean's*, March 29, 1993.

8. *Network*; R. Salem, "Body & Soul: Drop-Dead Glamorous Faye Dunaway Is Calling Her Role of Wanda, the Lush in Barfly, a Gift Sent from God," *Toronto Star*, November 15, 1987.

9. Lovece, "It Had to Be Comedy"; Dunaway with Sharkey, *Looking for Gatsby*; J. Patterson, "Network at 40: The Flawed Satire That Predicted Trump and Cable 'News Porn,'" *The Guardian*, November 23, 2016.

10. Dunaway with Sharkey, *Looking for Gatsby*.

11. E. Clift, "When Women Said 'No,'" *Newsweek*, December 31, 2012; "Tinseltown in 2011," *Hollywood Reporter*, December 13, 2011.

12. Clift, "When Women Said 'No.'"

13. Women's Media Center, "The Status of Women in the U.S. Media 2015," June 4, 2015, https://www.womensmediacenter.com /reports/2015-statistics.

14. S. Fink, "The Evolution of Glamour," *St. Petersburg Times*, February 24, 2007.

15. F. Dunaway, acceptance speech, March 28, 1977, Academy Awards Acceptance Speech Database, http://aaspeechesdb.oscars.org.

16. S. McGinty, "Following in Faye's Footsteps," *The Scotsman*, May 12, 2012; M. Wiley and D. Bona, *Inside Oscar: The Unofficial History of the Academy Awards* (New York: Ballantine Books, 1986).

17. A. M. Nolan, "No! A Network That Puts Ratings Ahead of Morality, Art and News?," *Washington Post*, March 2, 2014.

18. Haithman, "Norma Dearest"; D. Rosenfelt, "Of Oscars and Outrage," *Los Angeles Times*, April 1, 1977.

19. Rosenfelt, "Of Oscars and Outrage."

20. B. Darrach, "A Gauzy Grenade," *People*, July 29, 1974; Dan O Rama, "Bette Davis vs Faye Dunaway," YouTube, February 26, 2017, https:// www.youtube.com/watch?v=XkqFhfMqz9M.

21. D. Thomson, *The New Biographical Dictionary of Film* (New York: Knopf, 2010); "A Place between Bette and Demi," *New York Times*, October 11, 1992.

22. B. Sharkey, "At 51, Actress Dunaway Fights Age Discrimination," *The Gazette*, October 18, 1992.

23. Sharkey.

24. Lovece, "It Had to Be Comedy."

25. M. Dowd, "The Women of Hollywood Speak Out," *New York Times*, November 20, 2015; Bureau of Labor Statistics, "Women at Work," March 2011, http://www.bls.gov/spotlight/2011 /women/; R. Carter, "International Women's Day: Reflecting on Progress Made and Challenges Still Unmet," *Huffington Post*, December 6, 2017, http://www.huffingtonpost.com/former-first-la dy-rosalynn-carter/international-womens -day_b_9405192.html.

26. M. Haskell, *From Reverence to Rape: The Treatment of Women in the Movies* (Chicago: University of Chicago Press, 1987).

27. N. Willis Aronowitz, "The Feminist Pursuit of Good Sex," *New York Times*, February 18, 2018.

28. *Playboy*, December 1976.

DIANE KEATON

1. J. Wolcott, "Splendor in the Grit," *Vanity Fair*, May 11, 2009.

2. "Theatre Producer Lived Life to Full," *Western Morning News*, August 19, 2008; D. N. Dunkle, "Flow It Show It," *Patriot-News*, April 7, 2011.

3. Dunkle, "Flow It."

4. E. Grode, "Steve Curry, Who Was on 'Hair' Poster, 68," *New York Times*, October 7, 2014.

5. "An Elegant Leading Lady and Effortlessly Versatile Actress, Diane Keaton Shot to Fame in

Francis Ford Coppola's The Godfather but Is Probably Best Known for Her Relationship with Woody Allen," *Irish Independent*, November 26, 2011; D. Bates, "My 5-Year Bulimia Nightmare by Diane Keaton Scot Region," *Daily Mail*, November 11, 2011.

6. D. Itzkoff, "Woody and His Sisters," *International Herald Tribune*, July 20, 2013.

7. D. C. Mitchell, *Diane Keaton: Artist and Icon* (Jefferson, NC: McFarland, 2001).

8. CBS, "The Real Annie Hall," YouTube, November 12, 2010, https://www.youtube.com /watch?v=lypTuUrBHlk.

9. *Annie Hall*, dir. W. Allen (1977).

10. M. Gussow, "Woody Allen Fights Anhedonia," *New York Times*, April 20, 1977.

11. M. McNamara, "Book Review: Diane Keaton—in Bits and Pieces," *Los Angeles Times*, November 19, 2011.

12. S. C. Ong, "Like a Woman, like a Man," *Straits Times*, July 12, 2013.

13. S. Bruzzi, "F: Fashion," *Sight and Sound* 6 (1996): 24–26, 28.

14. K. Milestone and A. Meyer, *Gender and Popular Culture* (Cambridge, UK: Polity, 2011).

15. Ong, "Like a Woman."

16. H. Fawcett, "Fashioning the Second Wave: Issues across Generations," *Studies in the Literary Imagination* 39, no. 2 (2006): 95–113, 149.

17. J. Martinson, "Annie Lennox: 'The World Has Become More Sexualized,'" *The Guardian*, March 5, 2012.

18. R. Ray, "PBS: Woody Allen: A Documentary—American Masters, US Television Review," *The Telegraph*, November 24, 2011, http://www .telegraph.co.uk/culture/film/starsandstories /8912118/PBS-Woody-Allen-A-Documentary -American-Masters-US-television-review.html.

19. D. Keaton, Academy Awards Acceptance Speech Database, April 3, 1978, http:// aaspeechesdb.oscars.org.

20. D. Gebhard and R. Winter, *Los Angeles: An Architectural Guide* (Salt Lake City: Gibbs Smith, 1994).

21. D. Keaton, "Heartbreak Hotel: Demolishing Iconic Buildings Not Only Destroys History, It Wastes Resources," *Los Angeles Times*, October 13, 2008.

SALLY FIELD

1. S. Prince, *A New Pot of Gold: Hollywood under the Electronic Rainbow, 1980–1989* (Berkeley: University of California Press, 2000).

2. J. P. Ogilvie, "How Hollywood Keeps Out the Stories of Women and Girls," *LA Weekly*, November 16, 2015.

3. T. Ariano, "Moore Is Far from a Hollywood Fan," *National Post*, February 20, 2003.

4. W. Friedkin, *The Friedkin Connection* (New York: HarperCollins, 2013).

5. Prince, *New Pot of Gold*.

6. M. Dowd, "Waiting for the Green Light," *New York Times Magazine*, November 22, 2015.

7. V. Dwyer, "A League of Their Own," *Maclean's*, March 29, 1993; Prince, *New Pot of Gold*.

8. Prince, *New Pot of Gold*; "Meryl Streep Barnard Graduation: 'You Just Have to Make Your Mother and Father Proud,'" *Huffington Post*, May 18, 2010, http://www.huffingtonpost.com /2010/05/18/meryl-streep-barnard-grad_n_580335 .html.

9. Dowd, "Waiting for the Green Light."

10. J. Allen, "Sally Straight from the Heart," *Good Housekeeping*, March 2009.

11. E. Lipworth, "Why Sally Field Knows Best: Daniel-Day Lewis Calls Her Mother; to Hanks She's Mama. After 50 Years in Hollywood, the Actress Can Teach a Thing or Two to the Best in the Business," *Daily Mail*, May 25, 2013, http:// www.dailymail.co.uk/home/you/article-2329666 /Sally-Field-After-50-years-Hollywood-actress -teach-thing-best-business.html.

12. D. Thomson, *The New Biographical Dictionary of Film* (New York: Knopf, 2010).

13. Allen, "Sally."

14. "Passings: Margaret Field O'Mahoney; Actress Was the Mother of Sally Field," *Los Angeles Times*, November 10, 2011.

15. Allen, "Sally."

16. Lipworth, "Why Sally Field Knows Best."

17. Allen, "Sally."

18. D. Denby, "Good Ol' Girl Meets David Dubinsky," *New York*, March 12, 1979; G. Hatza, *Reading (PA) Eagle*, September 1, 2014.

19. B. Weber, "Irving Ravetch, 89, Screenwriter of 'Hud,'" *New York Times*, September 21, 2010.

20. *American Movie Classics Magazine*, July 1999.

21. *American Movie Classics Magazine*, July 1999; Hatza, *Reading (PA) Eagle*.

22. *American Movie Classics Magazine*, July 1999.

23. *American Movie Classics Magazine*, July 1999.

24. S. Field, acceptance speech, April 14, 1980, Academy Awards Acceptance Speech Database, http://aaspeechesdb.oscars.org.

25. S. Field, acceptance speech, March 25, 1985, Academy Awards Acceptance Speech Database, http://aaspeechesdb.oscars.org.

26. Lipworth, "Why Sally Field Knows Best."

27. N. Broverman, "Watch: Sally Field's Amazing Speech about Her Gay Son," *Advocate*, October 7, 2012, http://www.advocate.com/arts -entertainment/entertainment-news/2012/10 /07/watch-sally-fields-amazing-hrc-speech-about -her-gay.

SISSY SPACEK

1. D. Hoffman, presentation of the Oscar for Best Actress, March 31, 1981, Academy Awards Acceptance Speech Database, http:// aaspeechesdb.oscars.org.

2. A. Hoffman-Han, "Blood, Freckles, and Tears: Sissy Spacek's Surface Subversions and New Hollywood's Abject Feminism," in *Star Bodies and the Erotics of Suffering*, ed. R. Bell-Metereau and C. Glenn (Detroit: Wayne State University Press, 2015).

3. S. Prince, *A New Pot of Gold: Hollywood under the Electronic Rainbow, 1980–1989* (Berkeley: University of California Press, 2000).

4. K. Wallace, "Adventures in Feministory: Loretta Lynn," *Bitch*, March 22, 2010, https://www .bitchmedia.org/post/adventures-in-feministory -loretta-lynn.

5. S. Spacek with M. Vollers, *My Extraordinary Ordinary Life* (New York: Hyperion, 2012); S. Zacharek, "Loretta's Early Years, Tough as Ever," *New York Times*, May 4, 2003.

6. Spacek with Vollers, *My Extraordinary Ordinary Life*.

7. L. Rosen, "High on 'Low': Sissy Spacek Was Astonished First by the 'Get Low' Script, Then by Costar Robert Duvall and Director Aaron Schneider's Passion," *Los Angeles Times*, July 31, 2010.

8. Rosen; B. Thomas, "For Sissy Spacek, L.A. Is Simply a Winter Respite," *Los Angeles Times*, January 16, 1991.

9. N. Mills, "Strong-Woman Roles Are Most Appealing to Spacek," *Los Angeles Times*, January 3, 1986.

10. Thomas, "For Sissy Spacek."

11. Spacek with Vollers, *My Extraordinary Ordinary Life*; A. Witchel, "After Paying the Price, Reaping the Joy," *New York Times*, March 16, 1997; Spacek with Vollers.

12. R. Collin, "Sissy Spacek Interview: 'The 70s Were Magical,'" *The Telegraph*, April 12, 2015, http://www.telegraph.co.uk/culture/tvandra dio/11526260/sissy-spacek-interview-netflix-blood line.html.

13. Marc Schultz, "Eye on the Stars: Big Week for Celeb Memoirs," *Publishers Weekly*, April 27, 2012, https://www.publishersweekly.com/pw /by-topic/industry-news/tip-sheet/article/51725 -pw-tip-sheet-eye-on-the-stars.html.

14. J. Jurgensen, "The Well-Adjusted Actress," *Wall Street Journal*, April 25, 2012, http://www.wsj .com/articles/SB10001424052702303459004577 363973600426572.

15. Thomas, "For Sissy Spacek."

16. Spacek with Vollers.

17. B. Dart, "Agency Hopes to Match Up Celebrities with Causes," *Palm Beach Post*, August 10, 1997; F. Fiore, "Casting Celebrities to Make Them a Hit on Political Stage: Capital: Cause Celebre Matches the Famous with Issues. Politicians and Hollywood See Benefits, but There Are Pitfalls," *Los Angeles Times*, December 21, 1997.

18. Zacharek, "Loretta's Early Years."

19. M. Blowen, "At Times, Spacek Feels like Sum of Her Roles," *Boston Globe*, April 20, 1986.

MERYL STREEP

1. O. Gettell, "Oscar Senti-Meter," *Los Angeles Times*, March 5, 2012.

2. N. Sperling, "'Iron' Onscreen, like 'a Kid' Off: Meryl Streep Is Surprised at How Giddy She

Feels after Scoring Third Oscar," *Los Angeles Times*, February 27, 2012.

3. Sperling, "'Iron' Onscreen."

4. M. Streep, acceptance speech, February 26, 2012, Academy Awards Acceptance Speech Database, http://aaspeechesdb.oscars.org.

5. S. Zeitchik, "Trying to 'Iron' Out a Big Shocker of a Win: Just How Did Meryl Streep Best Viola Davis as Lead Actress? Sometimes Real Life Wins Out over Fiction," *Los Angeles Times*, February 28, 2012.

6. J. Basinger, *The Star Machine* (New York: Knopf, 2007).

7. A. O. Scott, "The Irrepressible Meryl Streep," *International Herald Tribune*, February 20, 2010; S. Prince, *A New Pot of Gold: Hollywood under the Electronic Rainbow, 1980–1989* (Berkeley: University of California Press, 2000).

8. C. Firth, presentation of the Oscar for Best Actress, February 26, 2012, Academy Awards Acceptance Speech Database, http://aaspeechesdb.oscars.org.

9. "Short Takes: Streep Awes Co-Star MacLaine," *Los Angeles Times*, October 16, 1990.

10. D. Lim, "A Second Look: Under the Guise of Ingenuity," *Los Angeles Times*, December 10, 2006; D. Thomson, *The New Biographical Dictionary of Film* (New York: Knopf, 2010); L. De Moraes, "On 'Today,' All the Savannah Smiles You Can Take," *Washington Post*, July 10, 2012.

11. E. Baskin, "A Pronounced Trend: Today's Films Demand That More and More Actors Speak in Authentic Accents. Enter the Dialect Coach," *Los Angeles Times*, June 4, 2000.

12. G. Pevere, "Sweet Pain of Martyrdom: While Sacrifice Is a Weakness in Action Movies, in Women's Melodramas, It's the Very Stuff of Heroism," *Toronto Star*, October 23, 1999.

13. L. Ortquist-Ahrens, "A New History of German Cinema," *Film & History* 45, no. 1 (2015): 87–88.

14. Ortquist-Ahrens; *Screen International*, January 6, 2009.

15. Ortquist-Ahrens, "New History."

16. W. Benz, *The Holocaust: A German Historian Examines the Genocide* (New York: Columbia University Press, 2000); CNN, *The Seventies*, 2015, http://www.cnn.com/shows/the-seventies.

17. "Meryl Streep Biography"; M. Streep, acceptance speech, April 11, 1983, Academy Awards Acceptance Speech Database, http://aaspeechesdb.oscars.org.

18. "Meryl and Hillary, the Best of Friends Edition 3," *Daily Mail*, December 3, 2012.

19. R. Tichler and B. J. Kaplan, *Actors at Work* (New York: Faber and Faber, 2007).

20. "Meryl Streep Biography."

21. R. W. Welkos, "Can They Give the Big Boys a Run for Their Money? Actresses Were Once Towering On-Screen Presences, Often Eclipsing Their Male Co-stars. But Lately Hollywood Has Been Mainly a Man's World," *Los Angeles Times*, January 16, 2000.

22. G. Siskel, "It's the Streep Mystique: Once She's into a Character What She Does Goes Way beyond Acting," *Chicago Tribune*, September 2, 1990.

23. C. Shoard, "Jane Fonda: 'Plastic Surgery Bought Me a Decade,'" *The Guardian*, May 21, 2015.

24. J. R. Gregory, "Margaret Thatcher, 87, the 'Iron Lady,'" *International Herald Tribune*, April 9, 2013.

25. A. O. Scott, "Polarizing Leader Fades into the Twilight," *New York Times*, December 30, 2011.

26. "Meryl Streep: The Fresh Air Interview," NPR, February 6, 2012, https://www.npr.org/2012/02/06/146362798/meryl-streep-the-fresh-air-interview.

27. "Off Message," *Sunday Business Post*, April 21, 2013; J. Hanvey, "The Divided Kingdom," *America*, May 20, 2013.

28. Barnet Bugle, "Glenda Jackson Launches Tirade against Thatcher in Tribute Debate," YouTube, April 10, 2013, http://www.youtube.com/watch?v=XDtClJYJBj8.

29. L. Barraclough, "Donald Trump Lashes Back at Meryl Streep, Calls Her an 'Overrated' Actress," *Variety*, January 9, 2017, http://variety.com/2017/film/awards/donald-trump-calls-meryl-streep-overrated-actress-1201955800/.

30. R. Abramowitz, "It Only Gets Better: At an Age When Many Starts Lose Their Sparkle, Meryl Streep Is Gaining New Box Office Punch," *Los Angeles Times*, September 12, 2009.

SHIRLEY MACLAINE

1. D. Zak and A. Argetsinger, "The Oscars Always Get It Wrong. Here Are the Real Best Pictures of the Past 42 Years," *Washington Post*, February 27, 2018, https://www.washingtonpost.com/news/arts-and-entertainment/wp/2018/02/27/the-oscars-always-get-it-wrong-here-are-the-real-best-pictures-of-the-past-42-years/.

2. TV Land, "AFI Life Achievement Award Telecast," June 7, 2012.

3. S. MacLaine, Best Actress acceptance speech, April 9, 1984, Academy Awards Acceptance Speech Database, http://aaspeechesdb.oscars.org.

4. J. Carr, "MacLaine Lives Life on Her Own Terms; Movies: The Actress Says Her Role in 'Evening Star' More Than Hit Close to Home," *Los Angeles Times*, January 1, 1997.

5. Carr; T. Pristin, "Tapping the Untapped Market: Women-Oriented Films Find a Growing Audience," *Los Angeles Times*, August 24, 1992.

6. K. Thomas, "TV Review: 'Celluloid Closet' Depicts History of Gays on Screen," *Los Angeles Times*, January 30, 1996.

7. D. Hunt, "Movies for Mothers: 'Psycho,' Anyone?," *Los Angeles Times*, May 5, 1995.

8. S. MacLaine, *I'm Over All That: And Other Confessions* (New York: Atria Books, 2011).

9. *Hello!*, March 5, 2012.

10. MacLaine, *I'm Over All That*.

11. K. Thomas, "Movie Review: Broadway Glows in Lights of Memory," *Los Angeles Times*, July 2, 2004.

12. C. Iley, "The Secrets of a Happy Marriage, by Shirley MacLaine," *The Times*, April 16, 2011.

13. K. De Witt, "At Home with Shirley MacLaine: A Free Spirit of a Certain Age," *New York Times*, March 17, 1994.

14. G. Kilday, "Shirley MacLaine's Oscar Memories: She's Won Once and Lost Five Times. She's Teared Up, Fought with One of Her Dates and Made an Entrance Onstage by Stepping out of a Spaceship. 'And I Always Had a Great Sense of Humor about It,' She Insists," *Hollywood Reporter*, March 2, 2012; R. Bletchly, "I've Had UFOs Hovering over My Hot Tub . . . and I Believe Aliens Told Reagan to Quit Acting for Politics," *Daily Mirror*, September 19, 2012; R. La Ferla, "The Past Lives of Shirley MacLaine," *New York Times*, March 28, 2017.

15. Bletchly, "I've Had UFOs"; R. Williams, "When the Rat Pack Ruled Supreme: Fifty Years Ago Frank Sinatra and His Buddies Helped Catapult JFK into the White House," *The Guardian*, October 8, 2010.

16. Bletchly, "I've Had UFOs."

17. T. Stanley, "It's a Big Part and It's Serious," *Daily Telegraph*, February 13, 2014.

18. Library of Congress "Hope for America: Performers, Politics and Pop Culture," accessed March 25, 2019, https://www.loc.gov/exhibits/hope-for-america/the-embrace-of-arts-and-politics.html.

19. MacLaine, *I'm Over All That*.

20. Stanley, "It's a Big Part."

21. Carr, "MacLaine Lives Life."

22. Carr.

23. S. MacLaine, acceptance speech, April 9, 1984, Academy Awards Acceptance Speech Database, http://aaspeechesdb.oscars.org.

24. MacLaine, *I'm Over All That*.

25. MacLaine.

26. E. Howe, "Quick Takes: MacLaine Accepts Award," *Los Angeles Times*, June 9, 2012.

GERALDINE PAGE

1. C. Taylor, "Family and Friends Bid Farewell to Geraldine Page," *Los Angeles Times*, June 18, 1987.

2. M. L. Fulton, "Oscar Winner Geraldine Page Dead at 62: Stardom Reached in Her Own Way," *Los Angeles Times*, June 15, 1987.

3. G. Rogoff, *Vanishing Acts: Theater since the Sixties* (New Haven, CT: Yale University Press, 2000); C. McNulty, "Theater Review: In True 'Page' Spirit," *Los Angeles Times*, March 9, 2015.

4. McNulty, "Theater Review"; Taylor, "Family and Friends Bid Farewell."

5. J. Patterson, "Walking on Water: After Years of Small-Scale Acclaim, Melissa Leo Is Now in Serious Demand," *The Guardian*, March 6, 2009; "Golden Age of Geraldine Page," *Life*, January 26, 1962.

6. "Golden Age of Geraldine Page."

7. C. Champlin, "Bountiful Career of a True Actress," *Los Angeles Times*, June 16, 1987.

8. M. Forsberg, "Geraldine Page Revels in a Film Odyssey," *New York Times*, December 22, 1985.

9. E. Kolbert, "Geraldine Page, 62, Dies: A Star of Stage and Film," *New York Times*, June 15, 1987.

10. "Ticket Offer for BFI's 'Birth of the Method' Season," *Daily Telegraph*, November 8, 2014; McNulty, "Theater Review."

11. Forsberg, "Geraldine Page Revels."

12. Forsberg.

13. D. Thomson, *The New Biographical Dictionary of Film* (New York: Knopf, 2010).

14. S. Prince, *A New Pot of Gold: Hollywood under the Electronic Rainbow, 1980–1989* (Berkeley: University of California Press, 2000).

15. C. McNulty, "An Appreciation: Champion of Gentle Hearts; Playwright Horton Foote Wrote with Depth and Affection for Small-Town Life," *Los Angeles Times*, March 5, 2009.

16. *Commonweal*, May 28, 1986; C. Champlin, "Page Gives a 'Bountiful' Performance," *Los Angeles Times*, January 4, 1986.

17. *Hollywood Reporter*, December 5, 1985; McNulty, "Theater Review."

18. Forsberg, "Geraldine Page Revels."

19. *The Trip to Bountiful*, dir. P. Masterson (1985).

20. S. Rea, "Geraldine Page: Will She Take a Trip to Oscar Bountiful? After Seven Losses, She's the Favorite to Win a Statue Tonight," *Philadelphia Inquirer*, March 24, 1986.

21. *Los Angeles Herald-Examiner*, June 16, 1987.

22. Rea, "Geraldine Page."

23. F. M. Abraham, presenting Best Actress Award, March 24, 1986, Academy Awards Acceptance Speech Database, http://aaspeechesdb.oscars.org.

24. S. Spacek with M. Vollers, *My Extraordinary Ordinary Life* (New York: Hyperion, 2012).

25. M. Fleming, K. Freifeld, and J. A. Revson, "Inside New York," *Newsday*, June 18, 1987.

26. M. Life, "Homemade," *Texas Monthly*, February 2003.

27. Rogoff, *Vanishing Acts*.

28. C. Taylor, "Bountiful Quality of Page's Acting Career," *Los Angeles Times*, January 7, 1986.

MARLEE MATLIN

1. M. Matlin with B. Sharkey, *I'll Scream Later* (New York: Gallery Books, 2010).

2. "Oscar Winner to Speak on Inclusion, Diversity," *University Wire*, November 14, 2013.

3. D. Kehr, "Oscars for Matlin, Newman, 'Platoon,'" *Chicago Tribune*, March 31, 1987.

4. M. Matlin, acceptance speech, March 30, 1987, Academy Awards Acceptance Speech Database, http://aaspeechesdb.oscars.org.

5. Matlin with Sharkey, *I'll Scream Later*.

6. "Oscar Potshots: The Sound and Fury," *Los Angeles Times*, March 29, 1987; D. Starr Seibel, "How *Dancing with the Stars*' Marlee Matlin Dances without Music," *TV Guide*, March 24, 2008.

7. "Oscar Winner to Speak."

8. "Oscar Potshots."

9. "Oscar Winner to Speak."

10. D. Blum, "Breaking the Sound Barrier," *New York*, October 6, 1986.

11. Matlin with Sharkey, *I'll Scream Later*.

12. *Screen Actor*, Spring 1990.

13. Matlin with Sharkey, *I'll Scream Later*.

14. Matlin with Sharkey, *I'll Scream Later*.

15. P. Rosenfield, "59th Academy Awards: Beating the Odds: They Gambled Their Time and Energy, and Didn't Give Up," *Los Angeles Times*, March 29, 1987.

16. Matlin with Sharkey, *I'll Scream Later*; Rosenfield, "59th Academy Awards."

17. D. Hunt, "'Golden Child' Has Glow of a Summer Rental: Double Shot of Whoopi in 'Purple' and 'Flash,'" *Los Angeles Times*, May 15, 1987.

18. M. C. Smith, "Non-talking Roles, When Well-Acted, Speak Loud and Clear," *Los Angeles Times*, December 23, 1993.

19. Hunt, "Golden Child."

20. P. Attanasio, "Children of a Lesser God," *Washington Post*, October 3, 1986; Matlin with Sharkey, *I'll Scream Later*.

21. Matlin with Sharkey, *I'll Scream Later*.

22. S. Bernstein, "Unreasonable Doubts: Marlee Matlin Overcomes Skepticism to Star in Her Own Series," *Los Angeles Times*, September 22, 1991.

23. Matlin with Sharkey, *I'll Scream Later*.

24. Matlin with Sharkey.

CHER

1. P. H. Brown and J. Pinkston, "59th Academy Awards: Garbo Didn't, Cher Did, Kim Slimmed: Oscar Headliners Create a Collection of Footnotes," *Los Angeles Times*, March 29, 1987.

2. Brown and Pinkston.

3. J. Krantz, *Scruples* (New York: Bantam, 1989); Brown and Pinkston, "59th Academy Awards"; J. Neigher, "Oscar Visions: Actress-Designer Collaborations Have a Dazzling Back Story—Before Kidman and Galliano, There Was Dietrich and Dior," *Los Angeles Times*, February 28, 2010.

4. Cher, award presentation speech, March 24, 1986, Academy Awards Acceptance Speech Database, http://aaspeechesdb.oscars.org.

5. L. Saxberg, "Queen of Comebacks: Cher Is a Pro at Reinventing Herself," *Ottawa Citizen*, February 17, 2000.

6. K. Smith, "Forever Cher," *Vanity Fair*, December 2010.

7. B. Moore, "The Diva Master: When It Comes to Dressing Cher, Bob Mackie Has Always Been King," *Los Angeles Times*, May 18, 2008; L.

Bradner, "Mama Monster Sans Makeup and in Full Get-Up," *Los Angeles Times*, December 4, 2011.

8. Smith, "Forever Cher."

9. AwardsShowNetwork, "Cher Confronts Her High School Principal!," YouTube, August 25, 2011, http://www.youtube.com/watch?v=5NdxHyceid4.

10. P. Brownfield, "Sharing Sonny: Cher Turns Spotlight on Former Other Half in a TV Special of Pop and Personal Memories," *Los Angeles Times*, May 20, 1998; B. Ward, "Cher Returns for One Last Comeback: Singer's D2K Tour Stops by Rogers Arena," *Vancouver Sun*, June 26, 2014.

11. W. Friedkin, *The Friedkin Connection* (New York: HarperCollins, 2013).

12. B. Ward, "Totally Tacky Totally Cher: As Cher Prepares for Her Final Tour after a 40-Year Career, She's Leaving like She Came In. On Top," *Calgary Herald*, June 1, 2002; Saxberg, "Queen of Comebacks."

13. G. Hirshey, "The Seventies," *Rolling Stone*, November 13, 1997.

14. L. Hirschberg, "Cher Goes Solo," *Globe and Mail*, March 31, 1984.

15. Hirshey, "Seventies."

16. H. de Vries, "The Cher Conundrum: The Oscar Winner/Pop Diva/Exercise Goddess Talks about Acting, Relationships, Being Fortysomething and Other Serious Stuff," *Los Angeles Times*, November 3, 1991.

17. F. Bruni, "The Diva Who Turns Back Time," *New York Times*, November 19, 2010.

18. Metro-Goldwyn-Mayer, *Moonstruck* studio production kit, 1987; M. J. Citron, "'An Honest Contrivance': Opera and Desire in 'Moonstruck,'" *Music & Letters* 89, no. 1 (2008): 56–63, 65–83; M. Zimmerman, "The Men's Health Movie Awards," *Men's Health* 20 (2005): 100–103.

19. "Picks the 20 Most Romantic DVDs, *Us Weekly* 659 (2007): 53–53, 56.

20. J. Nash Johnson, "In the Groove: Older Women Enjoy the Rejuvenating Power of Liaisons with Younger Men," *Calgary Herald*, September 17, 1998.

21. D. Caulfield, "The Best Years of Our Lives," *Los Angeles Times*, April 11, 1988.

22. D. Bass, "Oscar Gowns: The Good, the Bad, and the Ugh," *St. Louis Post-Dispatch*, March 6, 2010, http://www.stltoday.com/lifestyles/article_1c0f48df-88da-57b0-a702-a939f5023dde.html.

23. *Village Voice*, January 5, 1988.

24. S. Collins, "Oscar Nod Not Always a Big Boost for Career; Movies: Sure, It Helped John Travolta, but Ask Sally Kirkland What It Did for Her," *Los Angeles Times*, February 13, 1996.

25. Cher, acceptance speech, April 11, 1988, Academy Awards Acceptance Speech Database, http://aaspeechesdb.oscars.org.

26. De Vries, "Cher Conundrum."

JODIE FOSTER

1. K. R. Karlyn, "'Too Close for Comfort': 'American Beauty' and the Incest Motif," *Cinema Journal* 44, no. 1 (2004): 69–93.

2. M. Daum, "Jodie Foster Comes Out—as Human," *Chicago Tribune*, January 18, 2013.

3. "Obsessed: The Scariest Stalker Experiences," *The Telegraph*, August 13, 2013.

4. T. M. Phelps, "How Reagan's Would-Be Assassin Could Go Free: A Well-Behaved John Hinckley May Soon Leave Mental Hospital," *Los Angeles Times*, May 12, 2015.

5. Phelps; "Editorial: Death of James Brady a Loss to Cause and the Nation," *Oakland Tribune*, August 4, 2014.

6. J. Portman, "How Fame Eats Up Child Stars: Bieber, Lohan Are Cautionary Tales amid Successes of Foster, Howard," *Ottawa Citizen*, February 15, 2014.

7. J. Bindel, "Comment: I Was Wrong about ISOYG: The Rape Horror I Spit on Your Grave Is in Fact Less Exploitative than Sugary Fantasies about Justice," *The Guardian*, January 19, 2011.

8. C. Goodwin, "Has Hollywood Gone Too Far?," *The Times*, March 10, 1996.

9. J. Ostrow, "Mayhem for Profit: TV's Assault on Women," *Denver Post*, November 20, 2005.

10. Bindel, "Comment."

11. Ostrow, "Mayhem for Profit."

12. D. Denby, *New York*, October 31, 1988.

13. J. Foster, acceptance speech, March 29, 1989, Academy Awards Acceptance Speech Database, http://aaspeechesdb.oscars.org.

14. M. Wiley and D. Bona, *Inside Oscar: The Unofficial History of the Academy Awards* (New York: Ballantine Books, 1986).

15. P. Plagens, "Violence in Our Culture," *Newsweek*, April 31, 1991.

16. G. Braxton, "The Fear Factor: Warning: The Following Story Contains Graphic and Good-Taste-Defying Descriptions of Bone Snapping, Limb Hacking, Fingernail Pulling and Body Zapping. Read On at Your Own Risk," *Los Angeles Times*, January 29, 2006.

17. Thomas O'Connor, "Triumph over Tradition: Oscar Opens Its Mind to Embrace Eerie 'Lambs,'" *Orange County Register*, March 31, 1992.

18. O'Connor.

19. M. Daum, "Foster—Human after All," *Los Angeles Times*, January 17, 2013.

20. S. Timmons, *The Trouble with Harry Hay: Founder of the Modern Gay Movement* (Boston: Alyson, 1990); *70th Golden Globe Awards*, aired January 13, 2013, on NBC.

21. Daum, "Foster"; *70th Golden Globe Awards*.

22. A. A. Squire Strongheart, "A Time of Lesbian Chic," *St. Louis Post-Dispatch*, January 6, 1994.

23. "Life in a Bubble," *Waterloo (ON) Region Record*, January 19, 2013.

24. P. Kennedy, *Jodie Foster: A Life on Screen* (London: Macmillan, 1995).

JESSICA TANDY

1. C. McNulty, "Role Reversal: Advantage, Men; Women Once Wore Acting Chops on Their Sleeves. Now It's Down to Face Value," *Los Angeles Times*, March 5, 2006.

2. "Shirley MacLaine: Hollywood 'Ignores Older Viewers,'" BBC, August 28, 2012, http://www.bbc.co.uk/news/entertainment-arts-19395987.

3. S. Prince, *A New Pot of Gold: Hollywood under the Electronic Rainbow, 1980–1989* (Berkeley: University of California Press, 2000).

4. B. F. Dick, *Claudette Colbert: She Walked in Beauty* (Jackson: University Press of Mississippi, 2008); *Spine Tingler! The William Castle Story*, dir. J. Schwarz (2007).

5. *New Yorker*, April 16, 1990.

6. I. Scarbrough, "'Driving Miss Daisy' Opens to Large Crowds," *TCA Regional News*, September 15, 2015.

7. D. Chan, "Oscar Race Relations," *Malay Mail*, April 1, 2004; B. Steelman, "Race-Based Initiative: UNCW Series Looks at the History of Race and Film in the South," *Star-News*, September 30, 2004.

8. "How 'Driving Miss Daisy' Became One of the Most Scorned Best Picture Winners Ever," Yahoo Movies, December 12, 2014, https://www.yahoo.com/entertainment/how-driving-miss-daisy-became-one-of-the-most-105004366092.html.

9. S. MacLaine, *I'm Over All That: And Other Confessions* (New York: Atria Books, 2011).

10. C. Taylor, "Women in Film Tribute Set for Gish and Davis," *Los Angeles Times*, October 16, 1987.

11. J. Tandy, acceptance speech, March 26, 1990, Academy Awards Acceptance Speech Database, http://aaspeechesdb.oscars.org.

12. "Jessica Tandy, Star of Stage, Screen and TV, Dies at 85; Theater: The Original Blanche DuBois Went On to Win an Oscar for 'Driving Miss Daisy.' She Succumbs to Cancer," *Los Angeles Times*, September 12, 1994.

13. "Jessica Tandy, Star of Stage."

14. J. Simon and R. Koenig, "Jessica Tandy: The Original Blanche DuBois Starts in *The Glass Menagerie*," *New York*, September 19, 1983.

15. "Jessica Tandy, Star of Stage."

16. S. King, "The Highs and Lows of Being Blanche," *Los Angeles Times*, October 29, 1995.

17. D. Thomson, *The New Biographical Dictionary of Film* (New York: Knopf, 2010).

18. J. Mathews, "Calendar Goes to the Oscars Analysis: It's a Long Road for 'Miss Daisy' but Don't Be Surprised If Jessica Tandy, Morgan Freeman and the Film Are All Winners on Monday Night," *Los Angeles Times*, March 25, 1990.

19. Tandy, acceptance speech, March 26, 1990.

20. "Longer Life for Screen Sirens," *Dominion Post*, July 19, 2014.

KATHY BATES

1. K. Blakeley, "Women in Horror Films," *Forbes*, August 26, 2010.

2. *Mirabella*, December 1991.

3. D. Clarke, "Hollywood Head Mistress," *Irish Times*, July 10, 2015.

4. D. C. Mitchell, *Diane Keaton: Artist and Icon* (Jefferson, NC: McFarland, 2001); J. Rosen, "New York in the '70s: The Grit Wasn't So Splendid," *Slate*, June 12, 2009.

5. Clarke, "Hollywood Head Mistress."

6. J. Arkatov, "'Frankie's' Kathy Bates Gets Intimate,: *Los Angeles Times*, December 5, 1988; J. Cagle, "Woman of 'Misery,'" *Entertainment Weekly*, January 11, 1991.

7. Arkatov, "'Frankie's' Kathy Bates."

8. "Women's Impact Report: Class Actors," *Daily Variety*, September 23, 2011.

9. Clarke, "Hollywood Head Mistress."

10. "Women's Impact Report."

11. Arkatov, "'Frankie's' Kathy Bates."

12. *Village Voice*, December 4, 1990.

13. P. Rainer, "Movie Review: 'Misery' a la King and Reiner," *Los Angeles Times*, November 30, 1990.

14. *Village Voice*, December 4, 1990.

15. Clarke, "Hollywood Head Mistress."

16. *Village Voice*, December 4, 1990.

17. *Today Show*, aired October 11, 2015, on NBC.

18. S. Macaulay, "Worth the Weight," *The Times*, January 23, 2003.

19. K. Bates, acceptance speech, March 25, 1991, Academy Awards Acceptance Speech Database, http://aaspeechesdb.oscars.org.

20. Macaulay, "Worth the Weight."

21. Clarke, "Hollywood Head Mistress."

22. D. Kehr, "A Weighty Issue: Sizing Up the Role of Fat People in the Movies," *Chicago Tribune*, February 24, 1991.

23. Macaulay, "Worth the Weight."

24. A. Wolfe, "Kathy Bates Bestrides *Bad Santa 2* and the American Turdscape," *LA Weekly*, November 21, 2016.

25. B. Brownstein, "Misery Has Company: In Montreal to Shoot Bad Santa 2, Kathy Bates Reflects on a Career That Has Included a Remarkable Variety of Roles," *Montreal Gazette*, February 20, 2016.

EMMA THOMPSON

1. E. Guthmann, "A Classy 'Howards End': James Ivory's Film Adaptation Is Subtle Story of Friendship and Forgiveness," *San Francisco Chronicle*, April 17, 1992.

2. *More*, February 2006.

3. J. Stuart, "Emma Thompson, Sensibly: The Levelheaded Actress Turns Screenwriter with Her Adaptation of Jane Austen's 'Sense and Sensibility' (and Please, Let's Have No Mention of You-Know-Who.)," *Los Angeles Times*, December 10, 1995.

4. J. Millman, "Oscars' 'Year of the Woman' Rings Hollow; Comment; The Hurray-for-Women Theme Proved Most Ironic When the Woman of the Hour Turned Out to Be a Man," *Globe and Mail*, March 31, 1993.

5. Chrystala67, "65th Academy Awards—Best Director Award (Clint Eastwood)," YouTube, March 18, 2009, https://www.youtube.com /watch?v=fAdvAZbZJm4.

6. E. Dutka, "Dressed for Success: For Hollywood's Long-Suffering Leading Actresses (Remember 'Year of the Woman'?), There's a New Optimism about Their Ability to Open and Carry a Movie. But the Big Bucks Still Go to the Boys," *Los Angeles Times*, December 17, 1995; Millman, "Oscars' 'Year of the Woman.'"

7. J. Noveck, "Will Women See a Break in Hollywood's 'Celluloid Ceiling'?," *Concord Monitor*, February 23, 2016; E. Thompson, acceptance speech, 1993, Academy Awards Acceptance Speech Database, http://aaspeechesdb.oscars. org.

8. R. Traister, "Jane Fonda: The Original Movie Star Activist Has Played Every Female Archetype," *Elle*, October 17, 2008.

9. Guthmann, "A Classy 'Howards End'"; R. Corliss and D. Cray, "Doing It Right the Hard Way," *Time*, March 16, 1992; R. Alleva, "The Dead & the Living—Madame Bovary Directed by Claude Chabrol / Howard's End Directed by James Ivory," *Commonweal*, February 28, 1992.

10. "Books of the Times," *New York Times*, March 9, 1982.

11. P. Galanes, "Ruth Bader Ginsburg and Gloria Steinem on the Unending Fight for Women's Rights," *New York Times*, November 14, 2015.

12. T. Pristin, "Emma Thompson's Sense and Sensibility Movies: The Star of 'Howards End' Is Doing Something about the Lack of Roles for Women by Writing a Screenplay of Jane Austen's Novel," *Los Angeles Times*, April 14, 1992.

13. R. E. Long, *James Ivory in Conversation: How Merchant Ivory Makes Its Movies* (Berkeley: University of California Press, 2006).

14. Pristin, "Emma Thompson's Sense and Sensibility Movies."

15. "Girl Power," *New Indian Express*, October 14, 2014.

16. E. Brockes, "Frankly, My Dear: Emma Thompson Couldn't Give a Damn about Fame, or Getting Older; She Just Wants to Save the Planet, and Be a Good Parent in the Meantime," *The Guardian*, September 13, 2014.

17. Pristin, "Emma Thompson's Sense and Sensibility Movies."

18. Stuart, "Emma Thompson"; "Emma and Elena, Exposing the Sex Trade," NPR, October 31, 2009, http://www.npr.org/templates/story/story .php?storyId=114328601.

19. Brockes, "Frankly, My Dear"; P. Case, "Angry Farmer Sprays Slurry at Emma Thompson," *Farmers Weekly* 165, no. 13 (2016): 10.

20. T. Hicks, "Meryl Streep Rips Walt Disney, Praises Emma Thompson," *Oakland Tribune*, January 9, 2014.

21. "Girl Power"; "Walden's World: How Emma Thompson Impressed Hollywood," *Daily Telegraph*, March 5, 2019.

22. S. Waldron, "Standing Tall: Feminists Can Wear Heels If They Want," *Irish Times*, January 17, 2014.

HOLLY HUNTER

1. Walkoffame, "Holly Hunter Honored with Hollywood Walk of Fame Star," YouTube, June 8, 2011, http://www.youtube.com/watch?v=68e8w XGNoYs.

2. H. De Vires, "Holly Hunter Lets Her Hair Up," *Los Angeles*, November 14, 1993.

3. *Beverly Hills Magazine*, November 17, 1993.

4. J. Bihlmeyer, "The (Un)speakable Femininity in Mainstream Movies: Jane Campion's The Piano," *Cinema Journal* 44, no. 2 (2005): 68–88.

5. "Praise Jack, Shoot 'The Piano'—The Piano Directed by Jane," *National Review*, December 27, 1993; *Beverly Hills Magazine*, November 17, 1993.

6. J. P. Ogilvie, "How Hollywood Keeps Out the Stories of Women and Girls," *LA Weekly*, November 16, 2015; J. R. Dapkus, "Sloughing Off the Burdens: Ada's and Isabel's Parallel/Antithetical Quests for Self-Actualization in Jane Campion's Film *The Piano* and Henry James's Novel *The Portrait of a Lady*," *Literature/Film Quarterly* 25, no. 3 (1997): 177–187.

7. *Beverly Hills Magazine*, November 17, 1993.

8. Dapkus, "Sloughing Off the Burdens."

9. *The Piano*, dir. J. Campion (1993).

10. R. Weaver, "Forever Jane," *Pittsburgh Tribune-Review*, March 12, 2013.

11. D. Thomson, *The New Biographical Dictionary of Film* (New York: Knopf, 2010); *Beverly Hills Magazine*, November 17, 1993.

12. M. C. Smith, "Non-talking Roles, When Well-Acted, Speak Loud and Clear," *Los Angeles Times*, December 23, 1993; *Beverly Hills Magazine*, November 17, 1993.

13. *Beverly Hills Magazine*, November 17, 1993.

14. K. Turan, "Calendar's Big Oscars Issue: Oskar's Race Is All but Over," *Los Angeles Times*, March 20, 1994.

15. H. Hunter, acceptance speech, March 21, 1994, Academy Awards Acceptance Speech Database, http://aaspeechesdb.oscars.org.

16. *V*, March 30, 2008.

JESSICA LANGE

1. KatawebTV, "Meryl Streep: 'Troppo brutta per King Kong' | 'Too Ugly for King Kong,'"

YouTube, December 16, 2008, http://www .youtube.com/watch?v=MihpVBrtGLM.

2. K. Turan, "Telluride Marks Its Silver Anniversary; Movies: In Its 25th Year, the Festival Celebrates the Past and Looks to Future Changes. Meryl Streep Is among Those Honored," *Los Angeles Times*, September 7, 1998; J. Stuart, "Wandering Spirit of Jessica Lange; Movies: For the Versatile Actress, 'The Interesting Characters Are the Ones Who Are Not Holding On Quite as Tight' to Life," *Los Angeles Times*, June 19, 1998.

3. A. Leve, "Sense and Sensitivity," *Sunday Times*, April 2, 2006.

4. K. McKenna, "Steeled Magnolia: It Seems as If Jessica Lange Is a Supermarket Shelf of Emotions. And That Doesn't Even Count What She Manages to Do on the Screen," *Los Angeles Times*, March 19, 1995.

5. McKenna.

6. McKenna.

7. Stuart, "Wandering Spirit."

8. McKenna, "Steeled Magnolia."

9. G. Trebay, "Drawn to His Shining Light," *New York Times*, August 30, 2012; "Drawn to Art of Antonio Lopez," *Los Angeles Times*, October 5, 1995.

10. R. Padiha, *Antonio Lopez: Fashion, Art, Sex, and Disco* (New York: Rizzoli, 2012).

11. G. Jones, *I'll Never Write My Memoirs* (New York: Gallery Books, 2015).

12. *Greater Paris Magazine*, Winter 2009.

13. Jones, *I'll Never Write My Memoirs*.

14. R. Preston and S. Writer, "A Kind of Sanity: In Buddhism, Jessica Lange Says She Has Found a Spiritual Approach Devoid of the Extremist Leanings of Other Religions," *Star Tribune*, November 4, 2001; "The Vulture's Top 100 Actresses," *The Times*, December 23, 2000; Trebay, "Drawn to His Shining Light."

15. Stuart, "Wandering Spirit."

16. "Vulture's Top 100 Actresses"; Leve, "Sense and Sensitivity."

17. *Variety*, September 12, 1994.

18. *LA Weekly*, September 16–22, 1994.

19. E. Dutka, "We, the Oscar Jury: Three Drama Coaches Bluntly Assess the Acting Nominees. (Hint: Grand Gestures and Phoning It In Don't Cut It.)," *Los Angeles Times*, March 26, 1995.

20. S. Spacek with M. Vollers, *My Extraordinary Ordinary Life* (New York: Hyperion, 2012).

21. J. Lange, acceptance speech, March 27, 1995, Academy Awards Acceptance Speech Database, http://aaspeechesdb.oscars.org.

22. R. W. Welkos, "The Golden Globes Finally Get Some Respect; Awards: A Wide Range of Movie and TV Stars Fire Up the 52nd Annual Event, Which Is Often Seen as a Precursor to the Oscars," *Los Angeles Times*, January 23, 1995.

23. J. Lange, acceptance speech.

24. S. King, "Calendar Goes to the Oscars: So You Think You Know Movies? Try This . . . Put Your Cinematic Memories to the Test," *Los Angeles Times*, March 25, 1990; Leve, "Sense and Sensitivity."

25. *AARP*, March–April 2004.

26. S. King, "Jessica Lange's Inner Stillness: The Actress Shares Another Side of Herself: She's in Print with a Coffee-Table Collection of Still Photographs," *Los Angeles Times*, December 2, 2008.

SUSAN SARANDON

1. A. McFerran, "Susan Sarandon the Crusader," *Sunday Herald*, April 1, 2001.

2. E. Nussbaum, "Vixen of Pong," *New York*, September 13, 2010.

3. G. Fuller, "Susan Sarandon: The Bigger-Picture Revolution," *Interview*, October 1994.

4. D. Clarke, "Hollywood Is More Upset about People Getting Fat and Old than about Politics," *Irish Times*, June 25, 2016.

5. D. Itzkoff, "She's No One's Idea of a Grandma," *New York Times*, June 29, 2014; Clarke, "Hollywood."

6. C. Morgan, "'It Was Really Disgusting': Susan Sarandon Reveals She Was Exploited on the Casting Couch as a Young Actress," *Daily Mail*, October 13, 2012, http://www.dailymail.co.uk/tvshowbiz/article-2217415/It-really-disgusting-Susan-Sarandon-reveals-exploited-casting-couch-young-actress.html.

7. J. McClurg, "Streisand Biography Hits All the High Notes," *USA Today*, March 27, 2006.

8. "Gwyneth Paltrow 'Afraid Casting Couch Still Exists in Hollywood,'" *Hindustan Times*, September 21, 2010; J. Kantor and R. Abrams, "Gwyneth Paltrow, Angelina Jolie and Others Say Weinstein Harassed Them," *New York Times*, October 10, 2017, https://www.nytimes.com/2017/10/10/us/gwyneth-paltrow-angelina-jolie-harvey-weinstein.html.

9. J. Christie and A. Harris, "Sydney Confidential," *Daily Telegraph*, October 16, 2012.

10. Itzkoff, "She's No One's Idea."

11. Nussbaum, "Vixen of Pong."

12. R. Abcarian, "Susan Sarandon's Got a Pretty Wonderful Life: Just Don't Ask Her to Dish about Tim Robbins," *Los Angeles Times*, October 24, 1999; R. Rauzi, "Oscar Officials Slam Presenters' Political Plugs," *Los Angeles Times*, March 31, 1993.

13. Abcarian, "Susan Sarandon's Got."

14. 1stAmendmentCenter, "Susan Sarandon—'Speaking Freely,'" YouTube, January 8, 2013, http://www.youtube.com/watch?v=5Ls7NJKGzYo.

15. J. Stuart, "Emma Thompson, Sensibly: The Levelheaded Actress Turns Screenwriter with Her Adaptation of Jane Austen's 'Sense and Sensibility.' (And Please, Let's Have No Mention of You-Know-Who.)," *Los Angeles Times*, December 10, 1995.

16. Abcarian, "Susan Sarandon's Got."

17. M. Miller, "No Place for Politics at Oscars: Producer Upset over Speeches by Gere, Robbins, Sarandon," *San Francisco Chronicle*, April 1, 1993.

18. J. Anderson, "The Movies Seldom Combine Real Life with Death Penalty Situations: Dramatic Tension and Pathos, Not the Justice of State-Sponsored Executions, Are the Stuff of Most Films on the Subject," *Los Angeles Times*, March 17, 2003.

19. T. Rafferty, "Dead Man Walking," *New Yorker*, January 8, 1996.

20. E. Levy, "Dead Man Walking," *Variety*, December 1995.

21. *Dead Man Walking*, dir. T. Robbins (1995).

22. Anderson, "Movies Seldom Combine."

23. S. Sarandon, acceptance speech, March 25, 1996, Academy Awards Acceptance Speech Database, http://aaspeechesdb.oscars.org.

24. *The Independent*, November 3, 2016; *Weekly Press*, October 17, 2002.

25. T. Hicks, "Susan Sarandon Says She Was Victim of Sexual Assault," *Oakland Tribune*, October 15, 2012.

26. "The Latest: Stranded Migrants Chant 'Open the Borders!,'" *University Wire*, December 18, 2015.

27. A. Leve, "Still Angry after All These Years," *The Guardian*, May 31, 2003, http://www.theguardian.com/film/2003/jun/01/features.review1.

28. Clarke, "Hollywood."

FRANCES MCDORMAND

1. V. Heffernan, *Magic and Loss: The Internet as Art* (New York: Simon and Schuster, 2016).

2. Margaret Herrick Library, Academy of Motion Picture Arts and Sciences, "Society of Independent Motion Picture Producers v. United Detroit Theatres Corp. Case Proceedings," accessed March 25, 2019, http://collections.oscars.org/link/bio/82.

3. C. King, "Stage Entranced," *The Times*, May 2, 1998.

4. F. McDormand, acceptance speech, March 24, 1997, Academy Awards Acceptance Speech Database, http://aaspeechesdb.oscars.org.

5. J. Kisner, "Frances McDormand's Difficult Women," *New York Times*, October 3, 2017.

6. D. Gritten, "Staying in Character: Actress Frances McDormand's Post-Oscar Year Hasn't Been Like Most People's. But That's the Way She Likes It," *Los Angeles Times*, July 19, 1998.

7. L. Smith, "A Real Pro, and So Full of 'Grace': Holly Hunter Is All Over Her Complex TV Character, and She Also Plays Many Roles behind the Scenes," *Los Angeles Times*, July 13, 2008.

8. "Coen Brothers to Jointly Head Cannes Jury," *Hindustan Times*, January 22, 2015.

9. M. Wakim, "Kathy Bates Has One of the Most Interesting Careers in Hollywood," *Los Angeles Magazine*, December 8, 2016.

10. "The Vulture's Top 100 Actresses," *The Times*, December 23, 2000.

11. *Fargo*, dir. J. Coen and E. Coen (1996); D. Thomson, *The New Biographical Dictionary of Film* (New York: Knopf, 2010).

12. S. Riley, "Film Critics Fail to Underscore Fargo's Gruesome Violence," *Ottawa Citizen*, January 13, 1997.

13. "Dark Wit and Tight Editing Are the Hallmarks of a Coen Brothers Movie: Their Great Ensemble Casts—Which Have Become More Star-Studded with Each Foray—Also Help," *The Star*, January 8, 2009.

14. R. Lyman, "Marge's Other Job, You Betcha," *New York Times*, October 31, 1997.

15. Gritten, "Staying in Character."

16. C. Crowe, "Frances McDormand," *Interview*, October 2000.

17. The Hollywood Reporter, "Cannes: Frances McDormand on Women's Struggles in Cinema at Women in Motion Panel (Video)," YouTube, May 22, 2015, https://www.youtube.com/watch?v=kbz6IbVEXu4.

18. Kisner, "Frances McDormand's Difficult Women"; W. Morris, "Does 'Three Billboards' Say Anything about America? Well . . . ," *New York Times*, January 21, 2018.

19. Morris, "Does 'Three Billboards.'"

20. S. Dodge, "'Meryl, If You Do It Everyone Else Will': Best Actress Winner Frances McDormand Has All Female Nominees Stand in Solidarity as She Delivers Powerful Speech about Diversity," *Daily Mail*, March 5, 2018, http://www.dailymail.co.uk/tvshowbiz/article-5462525/Frances-McDormand-wins-Best-Actress-Oscars.html; E. Leight, "Man Arrested for Stealing Frances McDormand's Best Actress Oscar," *Rolling Stone*, March 5, 2018, https://www.rollingstone.com/movies/news/man-arrested-for-stealing-frances-mcdormands-oscar-w517475.

21. S. Liao, "Frances McDormand Champions 'Inclusion Riders' during Her Best Actress Speech," *The Verge*, March 5, 2018, https://www.theverge.com/2018/3/5/17079744/frances-mcdormand-wins-best-actress-inclusion-rider-oscars-2018.

22. F. McDormand, acceptance speech, March 4, 2018, Academy Awards Acceptance Speech Database, http://aaspeechesdb.oscars.org.

23. Dodge, "Meryl."

24. C. Puig, "The 69th Academy Award Nominations; Analysis: The Indies Fat Tuesday; Domination Renews Debate of Prestige vs. Bottom Line," *Los Angeles Times*, February 12, 1997; C. McNulty, "Lost Connections in 'Macbeth': Different Acting Styles, Lack of Chemistry Mar Berkeley Repertory Theatre Production," *Los Angeles Times*, February 29, 2016.

25. D. Clarke, "Hollywood Head Mistress," *Irish Times*, July 10, 2015.

26. B. Weinraub, "Oscar Gets Set for the Big Night of the Little Independent Film: For the First Time in Academy Award History, Only One Studio Film Has Been Nominated as Best Picture," *Vancouver Sun*, March 24, 1997.

HELEN HUNT

1. G. Pearce, "The Trying Game," *Sunday Times*, December 10, 2000; A. Wallace, "Talk about Connected: Four Films with Four Heavyweight Actors. Sounds like Clout, but to Helen Hunt, It's about Bonds—to Her Characters, to the World," *Los Angeles Times*, September 10, 2000.

2. Wallace, "Talk about Connected."

3. D. Hutchings, "Mad about Manhattan," *InStyle*, November 2000.

4. Hutchings.

5. M. Dowd, "Waiting for the Green Light," *New York Times Magazine*, November 22, 2015.

6. J. P. Ogilvie, "How Hollywood Keeps Out the Stories of Women and Girls," *LA Weekly*, November 16, 2015; R. W. Welkos, "Can They Give the Big Boys a Run for Their Money? Actresses Were Once Towering On-Screen Presences, Often Eclipsing Their Male Co-Stars. But Lately Hollywood Has Been Mainly a Man's World," *Los Angeles Times*, January 16, 2000.

7. M. J. Bandler, "Offstage Bancroft Irrepressible Performer Stands by Her Roles," *Chicago Tribune*, April 4, 1993.

8. D. Alberge, "Glenda Jackson Laments Continuing Lack of Key Acting Roles for Women," *The Observer*, September 12, 2015.

9. F. Cronin, "Dame Helen Mirren: Women Should Chase Male Roles," BBC, April 15, 2016, http://www.bbc.com/news/entertainment-arts-35997213.

10. Welkos, "Can They Give the Big Boys"; "Isabella Rossellini: Don't Call Me Beautiful," *Brampton Guardian*, July 9, 2016.

11. "A+E Notes," *Chicago Tribune*, April 6, 2016.

12. P. Galanes, "Love and All That Comes with It," *New York Times*, May 25, 2014.

13. B. Lowry, "Why She's Keeping a Day Job; Television: Oscar Winner Helen Hunt's Sticking to Sitcom Reflects State of Female Roles in Film," *Los Angeles Times*, April 1, 1998.

14. A. Gates, "Any Oscars with That, Hon?," *National Post*, February 17, 2005; A. Gates, "Sunny Side Up, and an Oscar on the Side," *New York Times*, February 16, 2005.

15. L. Stone, "As Good as It Gets," *Village Voice*, December 30, 1997; S. Mitchell, "As Funny as It Gets? Jack Nicholson and James L. Brooks Have Different Ways of Working on the Edge, Which Makes Their Collaborations So Special," *Los Angeles Times*, December 25, 1997.

16. *As Good as It Gets*, dir. J. L. Brooks (1997).

17. Pearce, "Trying Game."

18. G. Siskel, "The Oscar Hunt," *TV Guide*, March 21, 1998; E. Mitchell, "Leading Men Getting Older and Older," *Greensboro News Record*, July 3, 1998.

19. C. Goodwin, "The Jowl and the Pussycat," *Sunday Times*, June 27, 1999; C. Reed, "Over the Hill in Hollywood," *Globe and Mail*, December 16, 2002; N. Angier, "In the Movies, Women Age Faster," *New York Times*, December 9, 2001; R. Natale, "A Closer Look at Older Men, Younger Women; Commentary: May–December Romances in Cinema Are Not Abating Because Audiences Buy into the Double Standard. (Oh, and, Of Course, There's the Vanity Issue.)," *Los Angeles Times*, June 19, 1998.

20. Angier, "In the Movies."

21. R. Guzman, "'The Intern' Review: Robert De Niro, Anne Hathaway in Pleasant Fluff," *Newsday*, September 24, 2015, http://www.newsday.com/entertainment/movies/the-intern-review-robert-de-niro-anne-hathaway-in-pleasant-fluff-1.10882685; M. McCarty, "Commentary: Hollywood Rules Out Romance for Women Past 40," *Dayton Daily News*, June 17, 1998.

22. Reed, "Over the Hill."

23. Goodwin, "Jowl and the Pussycat."

24. "Swept Away," *People Weekly*, April 6, 1998; Siskel, "Oscar Hunt."

25. Pearce, "Trying Game."

26. Lowry, "Why She's Keeping a Day Job."

27. M. Gray, "Talk of 'Town' Is Full of Raves: Latest 'Town' Is a Moving Play," *Los Angeles Times*, January 8, 2012.

28. Ogilvie, "How Hollywood."

GWYNETH PALTROW

1. R. W. Welkos, "Spotlight Dims, Not Memories," *Los Angeles Times*, March 21, 2003.

2. *Hello!*, February 19, 2008.

3. M. Matlin with B. Sharkey, *I'll Scream Later* (New York: Gallery Books, 2010).

4. E. Snead, "In the Pink on the Red Carpet: New Designers Make Splash in Fashion Pond," *USA Today*, March 22, 1999; *New York Post*, January 12, 2013.

5. H. Gensler, "Plenty of Discrimination to Go Around in Hollywood," *Philadelphia Daily News*, January 26, 2016.

6. R. Martinez, "Joan Fontaine Interview (1991) Part 1/3," YouTube, February 4, 2014, https://www.youtube.com/watch?v=OvIpps3hrFQ.

7. V. Friedman, "The Red Carpet Is Its Own Economy," *New York Times*, January 7, 2018.

8. J. Portman, "Oscar's Changing Face Causes Unhappiness in Movie Industry," *Standard-Freeholder*, March 21, 1999.

9. S. Snow, "Morning Report: Arts and Entertainment Reports from the Times, News Services and the Nation's Press," *Los Angeles Times*, March 25, 1999.

10. G. Paltrow, acceptance speech, March 21, 1999, Academy Awards Acceptance Speech Database, http://aaspeechesdb.oscars.org.

11. S. Linfield, "Camera Lucida; Women: Photographs by Annie Leibovitz; Essay by Susan Sontag; On Beauty and Being Just by Elaine Scarry," *Los Angeles Times*, December 19, 1999.

12. J. Painter, "Still Learning: Jessica Lange Tackles Shakespeare for the First Time in Julie Taymor's Screen Adaptation, Titus," BackStage, February 20, 2001, http://www.backstage.com/news/still-learning-jessica-lange-tackles-shakespeare-for-the-first-time-in-julie-taymors-screen-adaptation-titus/.

13. V. Friedman, "The Goop Effect," *New York Times*, November 16, 2014.

14. W. Sargeant, "Judy Holliday: *Born Yesterday*'s Not So Dumb Blonde Prefers Slacks to Mink, Likes Proust, Hates Hollywood, Hopes Someday to Play Ophelia," *Life*, April 2, 1951.

15. A. Mullany, "Gwyneth Paltrow Goes to Market," *Fast Company*, September 2015; T. Brodesser-Akner, "The Big Business of Being Gwyneth Paltrow," *New York Times*, July 29, 2018.

16. Mullany, "Gwyneth Paltrow."

17. M. Freedman, "The Web Has Gone Snark Raving Mad," *Sun Herald*, June 21, 2009.

18. Mullany, "Gwyneth Paltrow."

19. Mullany, "Gwyneth Paltrow."

HILARY SWANK

1. L. Bennetts, "The Lady's on a Roll," *Vanity Fair*, August 2006.

2. N. Mills, "Hilary: I Like a Challenge; Swank Tries the French Revolution," *New York Daily News*, November 27, 2001.

3. Bennetts, "Lady's on a Roll."

4. *Elle*, November 2010; Bennetts, "Lady's on a Roll."

5. F. Durham, "Down and Out: Days Left Behind," *Sunday Mercury*, May 7, 2000.

6. Bennetts, "Lady's on a Roll."

7. R. Welkos, "A Role Worth Fighting For: With 'Million Dollar Baby,' Hilary Swank Returns to the Kind of Part That Generates Oscar Talk," *Los Angeles Times*, December 13, 2004; Bennetts, "Lady's on a Roll."

8. Bennetts, "Lady's on a Roll."

9. *Elle*, November 2010.

10. C. Holmlund, "1999: Movies and Millennial Masculinity," in *American Cinema of the 1990s: Themes and Variations*, ed. C. Holmlund (New Brunswick, NJ: Rutgers University Press, 2008).

11. C. Allen, "Man, She Feels like a Woman," *The Times*, April 6, 2000.

12. N. Floyd, "Altered Image," *The Scotsman*, April 1, 2000; S. Eckhardt, "Hilary Swank on Why Hollywood Still Favors Men and Her 60-Eggs-a-Day Diet for 'Million Dollar Baby,'" *Hollywood Reporter*, November 16, 2014, http://www.hollywoodreporter.com/news/hilary-swank-why-hollywood-still-749463?facebook_20141116.

13. Floyd, "Altered Image."

14. Allen, "Man, She Feels."

15. *Elle*, November 2010.

16. Floyd, "Altered Image."

17. Allen, "Man, She Feels"; Hetrick-Martin Institute, home page, accessed March 25, 2019, https://hmi.org/.

18. Eckhardt, "Hilary Swank."

19. S. Abramovitch, "Killer Films' Daring Survival Instinct," *Hollywood Reporter*, October 2, 2015; J. Olson, *The Queer Movie Poster Book* (San Francisco: Chronicle Books, 2004).

20. R. W. Welkos, "Building the Buzz for Oscar: For Actors, Directors and the Studio Publicity Machines, It's High Season on a Campaign Trail That Grows More Crowded and Competitive Each Year," *Los Angeles Times*, January 30, 2001.

21. Welkos.

22. H. Swank, acceptance speech, March 26, 2000, Academy Awards Acceptance Speech Database, http://aaspeechesdb.oscars.org.

23. J. Frey, "From a Role to the Polls: Actress Hilary Swank Is Newly Enfranchised as an Advocate of Voting," *Washington Post*, February 13, 2004.

24. Welkos, "Role Worth Fighting For."

25. J. Mottram, "Hilary: 'When You Leap, Sometimes You Fly . . . and Other Times You Fall," *Belfast Telegraph*, November 22, 2014; Eckhardt, "Hilary Swank on Why Hollywood."

26. Welkos, "Role Worth Fighting For."

27. "Million Dollar Question," *Oakland Tribune*, February 26, 2005; *Elle*, November 2010; S. Waxman, "Groups Criticize 'Baby' for Message on Suicide," *New York Times*, January 31, 2005.

28. S. Timberg, "The Oscars: Swank-Bening Rematch Ends Same as First Time," *Los Angeles Times*, February 28, 2005.

29. H. Swank, acceptance speech, March 27, 2005, Academy Awards Acceptance Speech Database, http://aaspeechesdb.oscars.org.

JULIA ROBERTS

1. D. Thomson, "Road Map to Enrichment: Need a Primer, or an Advanced Studies Course, in Music and Movies? Read On," *Washington Post*, January 1, 2006; A. Thompson, "Stars Find B.O. Sweet Spot," *Variety*, June 2008.

2. Thompson, "Stars Find B.O. Sweet Spot."

3. R. Abramowitz, "It's a Joy and Triumph in this Arena: Academy Award Affirms Roberts' Role as a Force in Hollywood," *Los Angeles Times*, March 26, 2001.

4. R. Ascher-Walsh, "Lucky Star," *Hollywood Reporter*, October 12–14, 2007.

5. J. Roberts, "Motherhood Means I Have No Time for a Pedicure but I'm So Happy That I Don't Care," *Mail on Sunday*, August 1, 2010.

6. Ascher-Walsh, "Lucky Star."

7. R. W. Welkos, "Can They Give the Big Boys a Run for Their Money? Actresses Were Once Towering On-Screen Presences, Often Eclipsing Their Male Co-Stars. But Lately Hollywood Has Been Mainly a Man's World," *Los Angeles Times*, January 16, 2000.

8. Abramowitz, "It's a Joy."

9. T. O'Neil, "Hey, They Can't Have It All: The Academy Has an Uneasy Time with Box-Office Names. Often It Overlooks Them. Sometimes It Plays Catch-Up, Honoring Lesser Roles Later," *Los Angeles Times*, March 25, 2001.

10. Abramowitz, "It's a Joy."

11. J. Roberts, acceptance speech, March 25, 2001, Academy Awards Acceptance Speech Database, http://aaspeechesdb.oscars.org.

12. H. McGill, "The Rise and Fall of Star Power," *Sight and Sound*, February 2010.

13. "The Gossip and the Glory," *Vanity Fair*, July 2012; N. Finke, "Jodie Foster Hates New Era of Social Media," *Deadline Hollywood*, August 16, 2012, http://www.deadline.com/2012/08 /jodie-foster-hates-new-era-of-social-media/.

14. H. Ryan, "Cameras Are Always on Standby at LAX: Paparazzi Regulars Have Their Routines and Blame Outsiders for the Latest Incident," *Los Angeles Times*, September 27, 2010.

15. L. Dotti et al., *Audrey in Rome* (New York: Harper Design, 2011).

16. J. Gay, "A World Apart," *Vogue*, August 2015.

17. C. Champlin, "A Soul of Discretion: Julie Christie Is Fine with the Fame Game. After All, the Actress, Back on the Screen in 'Afterglow,' Has Played It Well for 30 Years. Celebrity, Now That's Another Matter," *Los Angeles Times*, December 14, 1997.

18. B. Alexander, "Halle Berry Goes Full Throttle in Her New Thriller 'Kidnap,'" *USA Today*, August 22, 2016.

19. McGill, "Rise and Fall."

20. "Fading Stars: The Film Business," *Economist*, February 27, 2016; S. Waxman, "How Orlando Lost His Bloom," *Globe and Mail*, December 31, 2005; "Fading Stars."

21. "Fading Stars."

22. "From Coast to Toast," *Vanity Fair*, August 2013.

HALLE BERRY

1. H. Berry, acceptance speech, March 24, 2002, Academy Awards Acceptance Speech Database, http://aaspeechesdb.oscars.org.

2. M. Diawara, "Black American Cinema: The New Realism," in *Black American Cinema*, ed. M. Diawara (London: Routledge, 1993); M. Avins, "The Dandridge Drama" *Los Angeles Times*, August 21, 1999, https://www.latimes.com/archives/la-xpm -1999-aug-21-ca-2172-story.html.

3. G. Jordan and L. Casiano Jr., "Newport Beach Council Backs 'John Wayne Day,'" *Orange County Register*, June 2, 2016.

4. D. Thomson, *The New Biographical Dictionary of Film* (New York: Knopf, 2010).

5. S. Vaughn, "Ronald Reagan and the Struggle for Black Dignity in Cinema, 1937–1953," *Journal of African American History* 87 (2002): 83–97.

6. S. Poitier, *The Measure of a Man: A Memoir* (London: Pocket Books, 2000).

7. *Monster's Ball*, dir. M. Forster (2001).

8. J. Van Meter, "Fashion: Solid Gold," *Vogue*, December 1, 2002.

9. G. Susman, "Angela Bassett Slams Halle Berry's Oscar Role," *Entertainment Weekly*, June 24, 2002.

10. Reelz, "Hollywood Uncensored: Halle Berry Interview," accessed April 1, 2014, http:// www.reelz.com/trailer-clips/52944/hollywood -uncensored-halle-berry-interview/.

11. L. Gordon, "Frederick's Uplifting Museum Is Dismantled: When the Store Moved to a New Location, There Was No Longer Any Room for Madonna's Bustier, Tom Hanks' Boxers or Natalie Wood's Bra," *Los Angeles Times*, December 19, 2006; R. Johnson, "Oscars 2012: Despite Halle and Denzel, Gold Mostly Eludes Nonwhites," *Los Angeles Times*, February 24, 2012.

12. J. Guerrero, "Sarah Jessica Parker, Halle Berry, Tom Cruise 2002 Barbara Walters," YouTube, August 9, 2017, https://www.youtube .com/watch?v=wvBoGnioVhM.

13. "Hollywood Films 'Do Not Reflect Diversity' in US," BBC News, August 5, 2014, http:// www.bbc.com/news/entertainment-arts-28656531.

14. B. K. Thorp, "What's Valued in a Black Performance?," *New York Times*, February 21, 2016.

15. J. Noveck, "Will Women See a Break in Hollywood's 'Celluloid Ceiling'?," *Concord Monitor*, February 23, 2016.

16. I. Wilkerson, "C Rock," *Essence*, March 2016.

17. L. Munoz, "Famous Firsts: They've Made History; Denzel Washington's and Halle Berry's Wins Are an Unprecedented Oscar Moment for Black Actors," *Los Angeles Times*, March 25, 2002.

NICOLE KIDMAN

1. D. Thomson, *The Whole Equation: A History of Hollywood* (New York: Knopf, 2005).

2. C. Landesman, "Three Go Mad for an Oscar," *Sunday Times*, February 16, 2003.

3. C. Kaltenbach, "Winning Transformations in Films: Many Actors Have Drastically Altered Their Appearances to Better Perform a Role. And Some Have Won Oscars for the Effort," *Los Angeles Times*, February 4, 2003; *Sunday Times*, February 16, 2003.

4. M. Caro, "Nicole Kidman Explains Her Disappearing Act in 'The Hours,'" *Los Angeles Times*, January 3, 2003.

5. Caro.

6. S. King, "Award-Winning Year Rolls On for Kidman: The American Cinematheque Honors the Actress—Who Won Her First Oscar in March for 'The Hours'—for Career Achievement," *Los Angeles Times*, November 17, 2003.

7. Landesman, "Three Go Mad."

8. M. Caro, "Nicole Kidman's Crash Course in Virginia Woolf," *Chicago Tribune*, January 2, 2003.

9. D. Thomson, *Nicole Kidman* (New York: Vintage, 2008).

10. Landesman, "Three Go Mad"; J. Hiscock, "Nicole Kidman as Never Seen Before: The Actress, Unrecognisable in the Role of Virginia Woolf, Tells John Hiscock about the Making of Her Latest Film, The Hours," *Daily Telegraph*,

November 2, 2002; *The Hours*, dir. S. Daldry (2002).

11. Thomson, *Nicole Kidman*.

12. T. Keneally, "Nicole Kidman, from Down Under to 'Far and Away,'" *New York Times*, May 24, 1992.

13. Thomson, *Nicole Kidman*; Keneally, "Nicole Kidman."

14. Keneally, "Nicole Kidman."

15. K. Smith, "The Lady Is Yar," *Vanity Fair*, October 2007; Thomson, *Nicole Kidman*.

16. Smith, "Lady Is Yar"; King, "Award-Winning Year."

17. J. Gay, "A World Apart," *Vogue*, August 2015.

18. *Los Angeles Times*, October 9, 2015.

19. Thomson, *Nicole Kidman*.

20. A. Singh, "Oscar Winners in Plea for an End to Conflict," *Coventry Evening Telegraph*, March 24, 2003.

21. D. Washington, award presentation speech, 2003, Academy Awards Acceptance Speech Database, http://aaspeechesdb.oscars.org.

22. Thomson, *Whole Equation*.

23. N. Kidman, acceptance speech, March 23, 2003, Academy Awards Acceptance Speech Database, http://aaspeechesdb.oscars.org.

24. "Nicole Kidman: Divorcing Tom Cruise Was the Best Thing to Happen to My Career," *The Telegraph*, October 9, 2015.

25. Thomson, *Nicole Kidman*.

CHARLIZE THERON

1. *New York*, December 22, 2003.

2. M. Pramaggiore and T. Wallis, *Film: A Critical Introduction*, 2nd ed. (Boston: Pearson, 2008).

3. D. Thomson, *The New Biographical Dictionary of Film* (New York: Knopf, 2010).

4. T. Doherty, "Aileen Wuornos Superstar," *Cineaste*, Summer 2004; M. Goodridge, "Monster," *Screen Daily*, December 21, 2003.

5. Goodridge, "Monster."

6. Doherty, "Aileen Wuornos."

7. M. Dargis, "Life and Death Issues: A Moving Documentary Revisits the Nightmarish Existence That Spawned and Shaped Notorious Serial Killer Aileen Wuornos," *Los Angeles Times*, January 9, 2004.

8. M. Dargis, "A Battered Soul Turned Brutal: Charlize Theron Makes a Startling Physical Transition as Murderer Aileen Wuornos, but 'Monster' Lacks Depth," *Los Angeles Times*, December 26, 2003.

9. R. Moore, "Theron Has Always Wanted a Killer Role: The Actress Happily De-glamorizes Herself on the Set of 'Monster' to Play a Serial Murderer: 'I Had to Look Right,'" *Los Angeles Times*, March 16, 2003.

10. A. Manzano, "Monster: The Retelling of the Aileen Wuornos Story," *Off Our Backs* 34 (2004): 60–61.

11. Doherty, "Aileen Wuornos."

12. "Kay Loughrey: Speaker and Registered Dietitian Nutritionist Kay Loughrey Offers a Holistic Approach to Weight Loss for Survivors of Sexual Assault," *Women's Health Weekly*, April 6, 2017.

13. Moore, "Theron"; J. Gay, "Breaking Away," *Vogue*, December 2011.

14. A. Bhattacharji, "Charlize Theron: Hollywood's Humble Heroine," *Wall Street Journal*, March 28, 2016.

15. "South African President Lauds Theron," *Los Angeles Times*, March 2, 2004.

16. Thomson, *New Biographical Dictionary*.

17. L. Hirschberg, "Charlize Angel," *New York Times*, February 24, 2008.

18. Bhattacharji, "Charlize Theron."

19. Bhattacharji.

20. K. Turan, "The Naked Truth about 'Showgirls,'" *Los Angeles Times*, September 22, 1995.

21. Bhattacharji, "Charlize Theron."

22. D. De Burca, "Celebs Who Said No to a Cover-Up," *Daily Mirror*, September 18, 2012.

23. S. Ontiveros, "Hewitt's Disrobing Act Could Land Her in Trash Heap," *Chicago Sun-Times*, February 17, 2006.

24. R. Gay, "Comment: It's Different for Girls: A Leak of Naked Celebrity Photos Is a Reminder That Privacy Is a Privilege Often Denied to Women," *The Guardian*, September 2, 2014; R. Gay, "The Great 2014 Celebrity Nude Photos Leak Is Only the Beginning," *The Guardian*, September 30, 2014.

25. "Jennifer Lawrence: Stolen Nude Photographs Were 'Sex Crime,'" *The Telegraph*, October 7, 2014.

26. Goodridge, "Monster."

27. Thomson, *New Biographical Dictionary*; S. King, "'Monster' Package Missing Key Voices," *Los Angeles Times*, June 3, 2004.

28. E. Snead, "She Raises the Barre: With Her Ballet Past (and the Help of Some Designers), Charlize Theron Moves Gracefully in the Award Dance," *Los Angeles Times*, December 5, 2007.

29. C. Theron, acceptance speech, February 29, 2004, Academy Awards Acceptance Speech Database, http://aaspeechesdb.oscars.org.

30. "South African President."

31. Gay, "Breaking Away."

REESE WITHERSPOON

1. "A 'Beautiful' and Historic Oscar Night," *Seattle Post-Intelligencer*, March 25, 2002; C. Kaltenbach, "Winning Acceptance: Oscar Nods for 'Brokeback,' 'Capote' May Represent a Cultural Watershed—Films Seen as Good Because They're Good, Not Because Their Characters Are Gay or Straight," *The Sun*, February 1, 2006.

2. P. Bast, "Who Deserves Oscar's Gold? Arts Editor Must Walk the Line from Brokeback Mountain to Junebug, Transamerica, Crash, and Hustle and Flow," *The Record*, March 4, 2006.

3. T. Cox, "Telecast Had Neither Hustle nor Flow," *Daily Herald*, March 6, 2006.

4. R. Witherspoon, acceptance speech, March 5, 2006, Academy Awards Acceptance Speech Database, http://aaspeechesdb.oscars.org.

5. "Saddle Up for the Cowboy Oscars: Mathew Scott Tips Ang Lee's Film to Win at Least Two Major Gongs," *South China Morning Post*, March 5, 2006; T. McCarthy, "Biopic on Legendary Singer Aims to Cash In," *Variety*, September 2005.

6. "Pet Sounds: Biopics That Make All the Right Noises," *Irish Independent*, July 11, 2015.

7. Bast, "Who Deserves Oscar's Gold?"; L. Brown, *Reese Witherspoon: The Biography* (New York: Da Capo, 2007).

8. K. Milestone and A. Meyer, *Gender and Popular Culture* (Cambridge, UK: Polity, 2011).

9. *Walk the Line*, dir. J. Mangold (2005).

10. McCarthy, "Biopic."

11. 20th Century-Fox, *Walk the Line* studio production kit, 2005; Brown, *Reese Witherspoon*.

12. A. Edmond, "The Reinvention of Reese," *Marie Claire*, October 2011.

13. Brown, *Reese Witherspoon*.

14. S. Cheng, "Acting on Dual Intentions: Being Able to Play Both Heroines and Villains Is Reese Witherspoon's Forte. And No Wonder: Beneath Her Southern Charm Is a Hint of a Rebel," *Los Angeles Times*, April 11, 1999.

15. P. A. DeMaio, *Garden of Dreams: The Life of Simone Signoret* (Jackson: University Press of Mississippi, 2014).

16. K. Fallon, "Is Reese Witherspoon's Drunken Arrest the Best Thing to Happen to Her Career?," *Daily Beast*, May 3, 2013.

17. D. Freydkin and A. Mandell, "For Reese Witherspoon, Arrest Is a 'PR Nightmare,'" *Gannett News Service*, April 22, 2013; Fallon, "Is Reese Witherspoon's Drunken Arrest."

18. Fallon, "Is Reese Witherspoon's Drunken Arrest."

19. S. MacLaine, *I'm Over All That: And Other Confessions* (New York: Atria Books, 2011).

20. "Emma Thompson Attacks Young Actors Who 'Can't Act' and Only Get Cast Due to Social Media Following," *The Telegraph*, May 6, 2016; C. McNulty, "Role Reversal: Advantage, Men; Women Once Wore Acting Chops on Their Sleeves. Now It's Down to Face Value," *Los Angeles Times*, March 5, 2006.

21. J. Basinger, *The Star Machine* (New York: Knopf, 2007).

HELEN MIRREN

1. "As the National Youth Theatre Marks Its 60th Anniversary, Can You Identify Today's Stars Who Cut Their Teeth There?," *Daily Mail*, September 16, 2016.

2. "This Sexist 1975 Helen Mirren Interview Proves She's Always Been a Queen," *Hindustan Times*, August 31, 2016.

3. beretsheri0001, "Helen Mirren—The Sexist Parkinson's Interview 1/2," YouTube, March 22, 2008, http://www.youtube.com/watch?v=gmlP_cFOoAM.

4. N. Johnson, "Great Dame," *Courier-Mail*, July 19, 2014.

5. L Gray, "We Are Still Sexy, Say Older Women Stars . . . and Film Fans Agree," *The Telegraph*, March 28, 2011.

6. "In Her Own Words: Helen Mirren," *Daily Mail*, January 2, 2016.

7. H. Mirren, acceptance speech, February 25, 2007, Academy Awards Acceptance Speech Database, http://aaspeechesdb.oscars.org.

8. B. Longino, "Crowning Achievement: Praised for Portrayal of Elizabeth I, Mirren Now Captures Current Queen," *Atlanta Journal-Constitution*, October 26, 2006.

9. B. Kantrowitz, "The Royal Treatment: In 'The Queen,' Helen Mirren Is Sublime as Princess Di's Distant Mother-in-Law," *Newsweek*, October 2, 2006; "Christmas and New Year Film Guide—Our Festive Favourites," *Western Daily Press*, December 19, 2015.

10. "Mirren May Get Palace Invite," *Nanaimo Daily News*, February 28, 2007; Longino, "Crowning Achievement."

11. O. Jones, "Her Majesty," *People*, October 16, 2006; Longino, "Crowning Achievement."

12. "Helen Mirren Reveals Her Admiration of Queen Elizabeth," *Brampton Guardian*, March 30, 2015.

13. Johnson, "Great Dame."

14. Johnson; S. Schama, "Helen Mirren Talks to Simon Schama," *Financial Times*, February 26, 2011.

15. Johnson, "Great Dame."

16. Johnson.

17. Schama, "Helen Mirren."

18. P. Goldstein, "Soldiering On: In an Age in Which Everyone Is Spilling Their Guts, Two Films Resurrect an Old Virtue: Dignified Reserve in Tough Times," *Los Angeles Times*, October 31, 2006.

19. A. Deevoy, "Dame of Thrones," *Mail on Sunday*, March 29, 2015.

20. K. Palacios, "Dame Helen Mirren Gets Saucy on SNL," *Hollywood News*, April 10, 2011, https://www.hollywoodnews.com/2011/04/10/dame-helen-mirren-gets-saucy-on-snl/.

21. K. Sullivan, "Bubbly and Small Talk with Her Majesty," *Washington Post*, March 29, 2007.

MARION COTILLARD

1. S. Zeitchik, "Silence Isn't Golden: 'Blind's' Bullock Campaigned. 'Julia's' Streep Was Silent," *Los Angeles Times*, March 3, 2010.

2. J. Kelly, "Fantastic Voyage," *InStyle*, July 2009; "Black and Red, Oh My," *Los Angeles Times*, February 25, 2008.

3. C. Chocano, "Sparrow in Flight: Marion Cotillard Astonishes as Edith Piaf in 'La Vie en Rose,'" *Los Angeles Times*, January 8, 2008.

4. M. Cotillard, acceptance speech, February 24, 2008, Academy Awards Acceptance Speech Database, http://aaspeechesdb.oscars.org; M. Olsen, "Cotillard Is on Top of the World," *Los Angeles Times*, February 25, 2008.

5. J. Horn, "Borders Fall as the Academy Reaches around the Globe," *Los Angeles Times*, January 24, 2007.

6. M. Magnier, "Outsourcing the Bad Guy: Despite India's Increasingly Global Outlook, the Nation's Film Industry Has Plenty of Roles for 'the Evil Foreigner,'" *Los Angeles Times*, May 25, 2012.

7. S. Zeitchik, "Global Flair: One's French (Marion Cotillard), One's Spanish (Penelope Cruz). Both Flourish in Hollywood and Internationally," *Los Angeles Times*, May 12, 2011.

8. K. Hohenadel, "Roles off the Usual Tongue: The Allure of the Foreign Brings English-Speaking Actors and French Directors Together in French Films," *Los Angeles Times*, August 10, 2003.

9. Zeitchik, "Global Flair."

10. Zeitchik.

11. L. Hirschberg, "Maid Marion," *New York Times*, December 2, 2007; D. Ansen and D. Gordon, "There Will Be Oscars," *Newsweek*, January 28, 2008; S. Bowers with L. Friedberg, *Full Service: My Adventures in Hollywood and the Secret Sex Lives of the Stars* (New York: Grove, 2012).

12. L. Smith, "Costner Gets Candid about 'Mr. Brooks,'" *Variety*, June 4, 2007; G. Fuller, "In Full Bloom," *Vanity Fair*, May 2007.

13. R. Alleva, "'Behind the Music': *Once* and *La Vie en Rose*," *Commonweal*, July 13, 2007.

KATE WINSLET

1. R. Abramowitz, "Worth the Wait in Gold: Directors Praise Six-Time Nominee Winslet's Near Obsession with Her Craft. She Is Free and Focused, Says Husband Sam Mendes," *Los Angeles Times*, February 23, 2009.

2. K. Winslet, acceptance speech, February 22, 2009, Academy Awards Acceptance Speech Database, http://aaspeechesdb.oscars.org.

3. L. Brown, "Kate Winslet Looks Ahead," *Harper's Bazaar*, August 2009; S. King, "Genuine Emotion, but Few Surprises," *Los Angeles Times*, February 23, 2009.

4. Brown, "Kate Winslet."

5. S. Zeitchik, "Double Trouble: Actors with Dual Roles in Oscar Races Face a Nice Problem, but It's a Problem," *Los Angeles Times*, October 26, 2011; C. Grant, "A Quick Ticket Back to the '50s," *Daily Townsman*, February 23, 2016.

6. "Kate Winslet," *Extras*, aired August 2005, on BBC.

7. P. Vallely, "The Golden Girl," *The Independent*, January 17, 2009.

8. P. Travers, "The Reader," *Rolling Stone*, December 25, 2008.

9. R. Alleva, "Summer Intern," *Commonweal*, February 13, 2009.

10. R. Abramowitz and J. Horn, "'Reader's' Happier Ending: The Film Had a Turbulent Time Coming to the Screen, but It Pays Off with Five Nominations, Including for Best Picture," *Los Angeles Times*, January 23, 2009.

11. T. Perrotta, "On Kate Winslet," *New York Times*, February 8, 2009.

12. Abramowitz, "Worth the Wait"; J. Woods, "Kate Winslet: Actress's Golden Globes Success Has Put the Win into Winslet," *The Telegraph*, January 12, 2009.

13. D. Colman, "The Winslet Way," *InStyle*, February 2009.

14. Brown, "Kate Winslet."

15. "Kate Winslet," NNDB, accessed March 25, 2019, http://www.nndb.com/people/582/000023513/; K. Smith, "Isn't She Deneuvely?," *Vanity Fair*, November 3, 2008.

16. Brown, "Kate Winslet."

17. K. Smith, "Forever Cher," *Vanity Fair*, November 2010.

18. M. Kalfus, "Jane Fonda Is 74, and That's Not a Typo," *Orange County Register*, June 25, 2012, https://www.ocregister.com/2012/06/25/jane-fonda-is-74-and-thats-not-a-typo-2/.

19. K. Haynes, "12 Stars Who Refuse to Have Plastic Surgery," Purple Clover, April 12, 2018, https://purpleclover.littlethings.com/entertainment/3543-12-stars-say-no-to-plastic-surgery/.

20. C. Iley, "More, More, Moore," *Weekend Australian Magazine*, August 9, 2008.

21. J. Allen, "Sally Straight from the Heart," *Good Housekeeping*, March 2009.

22. *Ladies' Home Journal*, May 2008.

23. Colman, "Winslet Way."

24. L. Day and C. Kugler, *Her Next Chapter: How Mother-Daughter Book Clubs Can Help Girls Navigate Malicious Media, Risky Relationships, Girl Gossip, and So Much More* (Chicago: Chicago Review Press, 2014).

25. K. Winslet, "It's the Oscar Girl Next Door: Part III," *Sunday Times*, December 30, 2012.

26. Abramowitz, "Worth the Wait"; N. Mills, "Child's Play," *Herald Sun*, November 27, 2004.

27. Winslet, "Oscar Girl."

28. P. Vallely, "The Golden Girl," *The Independent*, January 17, 2009.

29. Abramowitz, "Worth the Wait."

30. Brown, "Kate Winslet."

SANDRA BULLOCK

1. M. Shnayerson, "The Girl Can't Help It: At 42, Sandra Bullock Is Full of Surprises," *Vanity Fair*, July 2006.

2. J. Powell, "Sandra Bullock's Great Escape," *Good Housekeeping*, May 2000.

3. J. Bartolomeo, "Sandra's Dream Wedding!," *Us Weekly* 546 (2005): 46–51; G. Piccalo, "A Real Possibility: Sandra Bullock Doesn't Aim for Critical Acclaim, but Now, with 'The Blind Side,' an Oscar Is . . . ," *Los Angeles Times*, December 16, 2009.

4. C. Lee, "It's Rookies versus the Veterans: Sidibe and Mulligan Are in the Race with Streep, Mirren—and Dark Horse Bullock," *Los Angeles Times*, February 3, 2010.

5. B. Sharkey, "Send in Bullock: In 'The Blind Side,' the Actress Scores a Role She Was Meant to Play," *Los Angeles Times*, November 20, 2009; G. Burris, "Race and Class in The Blind Side," *CineAction* 92 (Summer 2013): 24–32.

6. A. Deacon, "'The Blind Side' and Putting Caring into Action," *Christian Science Monitor*, February 5, 2010; C. Kelly, "Stop the Blitz," *Texas Monthly*, 2010.

7. "Big Screen Insight into the Blind Side," *Hills Shire Times*, February 16, 2010.

8. Burris, Race and Class."

9. Kelly, "Stop the Blitz."

10. A. O. Scott, "Two Films, Two Routes from Poverty," *New York Times*, November 22, 2009.

11. Burris, "Race and Class."

12. Shnayerson, "Girl Can't Help It"; S. Lopez, "Getting a 'Crash' Course on Race," *Los Angeles Times*, March 12, 2006.

13. P. Goldstein, "A Game Changer: In the Oscar-Nominated Sports Documentary 'Undefeated,' Issues of Race Come into Play," *Los Angeles Times*, February 23, 2012.

14. Burris, "Race and Class."

15. J. Crowe, "Text Messages from Press Row," *Los Angeles Times*, March 12, 2010.

16. Entirely Sandra, "Sandra Bullock Interview in Barbara Walters Special 2010," YouTube, June 5, 2011, https://www.youtube.com/watch?v=E499RlpyOEk.

17. S. Zeitchik, "Silence Isn't Golden: 'Blind's' Bullock Campaigned. 'Julia's' Streep Was Silent," *Los Angeles Times*, March 3, 2010; R. Thomas, "Consider This: How Film-Makers Court the Oscar Voters," BBC News, February 19, 2013, https://www.bbc.com/news/entertainment-arts-21412228.

18. S. Bullock, acceptance speech, March 7, 2010, Academy Awards Acceptance Speech Database, http://aaspeechesdb.oscars.org.

19. M. Tauber, "Betrayed: Sandra's Marriage in Crisis," *People*, April 5, 2010.

20. D. Spoto, *High Society: The Life of Grace Kelly* (New York: Three Rivers, 2010).

NATALIE PORTMAN

1. D. C. Chmielewski and R. Johnson, "Viewers Get Chance to Call the Shots," *Los Angeles Times*, February 28, 2011.

2. R. Keegan, "Water for Ms. Portman! Off in the Wings, the Stars Giggle, Eat Snacks and Get Last-Second Advice. It's the One Spot Where They Can Be Spontaneous," *Los Angeles Times*, February 28, 2011.

3. T. Roston, "Turning into an Unhinged 'Swan': A ballerina Role Challenges Natalie Portman Emotionally And Physically," *Los Angeles Times*, October 31, 2010.

4. A. Kaufman, "Ruffled Feathers: 'Black Swan' Puts Natalie Portman and Mila Kunis' Friendship to the Test," *Los Angeles Times*, November 28, 2010.

5. S. Maslin Nir, "To Some Dancers, 'Black Swan' Is a Cautionary Tale," *New York Times*, January 7, 2011.

6. R. Abramowitz, "The Skinny on Hollywood: Bony Bodies May Be Ridiculed in the Media, but the Pressure to Look Thin Is Fiercer than Ever. It's Enough to Make an Actress Wonder: Will I Ever Eat in This Town Again?," *Los Angeles Times*, August 19, 2007.

7. L. Brown, "Becoming Jane," *Harper's Bazaar*, September 2011.

8. Abramowitz, "Skinny on Hollywood."

9. R. Abramowitz, "Females in Tinseltown Are under Immense Pressure to Be Thin. The Paparazzi Used to Hang Around Hotel Rooms Trying to Snap the Latest Scandal. Now, They're Staking Out Pizza Joints," *Edmonton Journal*, August 2, 2007.

10. A. Agresti and D. Holloway, "How I Was Discovered," *Us Weekly* 719 (2008).

11. J. Riley, "Dancing Queen," *Back Stage* 52, no. 5 (2011): 8–9.

12. A. Trope, "Little Mary: Formidable Philanthropist," in *Mary Pickford: Queen of the Movies*, ed. C. Schmidt (Lexington: University Press of Kentucky, 2012).

13. E. Nyren, "Natalie Portman's Step-by-Step Guide on How to Topple the Patriarchy," *Variety*, October 12, 2018.

14. S. Holden, "An Allegorical Plea for Harmony in the Middle East in 'Free Zone,'" *New York Times*, April 7, 2006.

15. blankfist, "Natalie Portman Talks to Columbia University about Terrorism," VideoSift, July 2008, https://videosift.com/video/Natalie-Portman-Talks-to-Columbia-University-About-Terrorism.

16. R. Gay, "The Great 2014 Celebrity Nude Photos Leak Is Only the Beginning," *The Guardian*, September 30, 2014, http://www.theguardian.com/commentisfree/2014/sep/01/celebrity-naked-photo-leak-2014-nude-women.

JENNIFER LAWRENCE

1. "2nd Annual! Awards Season Awards," *Hollywood Reporter*, March 1, 2013.

2. "Hollywood's Rebel Belle," *Vanity Fair*, July 2012; "2nd Annual! Awards Season Awards"; M. Ryzik, "Jennifer Lawrence's Choice Words," *New York Times*, January 22, 2013.

3. "Owning It," *Vogue*, September 2013; "Star Quality," *Vogue*, September 2013.

4. S. Grossbart and J. O'Neill, "I'm Just Like a . . . ," *Us Weekly*, September 2, 2013.

5. A. Kaufman, "Before the Big Show: The View from the Red Carpet: Meet 'n' Greets, the 'Les Miz' Cast, Loose Lips and More," *Los Angeles Times*, February 25, 2013.

6. J. Lawrence, acceptance speech, February 24, 2013, Academy Awards Acceptance Speech Database, http://aaspeechesdb.oscars.org.

7. "Star Quality."

8. CNN, "Raw: Jennifer Lawrence Backstage after 2013 Oscar Win," YouTube, February 25, 2013, http://www.youtube.com/watch?v=CLKZb1wLmAY.

9. G. Serpe, "Jennifer Lawrence Flips Off Oscar Press Room after Best Actress Win," E! Online, February 25, 2013, https://www.eonline.com/news/391627/jennifer-lawrence-flips-off-oscar-press-room-after-best-actress-win.

10. "Star Quality."

11. M. Ryzik, "Jennifer Lawrence, with Sass Unfiltered," *New York Times*, November 9, 2012; "Star Quality."

12. Ryzik, "Jennifer Lawrence."

13. R. Setoodeh, "Jennifer Lawrence: Comedy's New Queen," *Newsweek*, November 11, 2012.

14. Ryzik, "Jennifer Lawrence."

15. P. McCormick, "Human Conditions," *U.S. Catholic*, April 2013.

16. McCormick.

17. "Star Quality"; Grossbart and O'Neill, "I'm Just Like a . . ."

18. "Star Quality."

19. "Hollywood's Rebel Belle"; Grossbart and O'Neill, "I'm Just Like a . . ."

20. J. P. Ogilvie, "How Hollywood Keeps Out the Stories of Women and Girls," *LA Weekly*, November 16, 2015.

21. S. Wloszczyna, "The Big O: The Cry for Equal Pay, the Need for Equal Screen Time, & the Death of the Mani-Cam," IndieWire, February 23, 2015, https://www.indiewire.com/2015/02/the-big-o-the-cry-for-equal-pay-the-need-for-equal-screen-time-the-death-of-the-mani-cam-204476/.

22. R. Setoodeh, "Sandra Bullock on Hollywood Sexism, Pay Disparity and 'the Worst Experience' of Her Career," *Variety*, November 10, 2015, https://variety.com/2015/film/news/sandra-bullock-sexism-pay-gap-1201637694/; E. Nyren, "Emma Stone Says Her Male Co-Stars Took Salary Cuts So She Could Receive Equal Pay," July 7, 2017, *Variety*, https://variety.com/2017/film/news/emma-stone-male-co-stars-took-salary-cuts-1202489493/; V. Wilkins, "Sandra Bullock Addresses Gender Pay Gap, Says 'It's a Bigger Issue than Money,'" ABC News, November 12, 2015, https://abcnews.go.com/Entertainment/sandra-bullock-addresses-gender-pay-gap-bigger-issue/story?id=35154131.

23. "They Said What?," *Western Mail*, November 12, 2015.

24. Setoodeh, "My Dinner."

CATE BLANCHETT

1. "Highlights of the AAP World Wire at 14:00 March 3," *AAP General News Wire*, March 3, 2014.

2. B. Shapiro, "Comfy in Any Costume," *New York Times*, March 2, 2014.

3. "Highlights."

4. M. Orth, "10 Undeniable Facts about the Woody Allen Sexual-Abuse Allegation," *Vanity Fair*, February 7, 2014, https://www.vanityfair.com/news/2014/02/woody-allen-sex-abuse-10-facts.

5. M. Ryzik, "Desperate Times Call for Her," *New York Times*, February 13, 2014.

6. A. Quinn, "Film Review: Blue Jasmine—Blanchett Delivers Astounding Performance as Fallen Park Avenue Princess," *The Independent*, September 27, 2013, https://www.independent.co.uk/arts-entertainment/films/reviews/film-review-blue-jasmine-cate-blanchett-delivers-astounding-performance-as-fallen-park-avenue-8842086.html; "Cate Blanchett: Equality for Women Being Lost," Sky News, September 17, 2013, https://news.sky.com/story/cate-blanchett-equality-for-women-being-lost-10434059.

7. G. Whipp, "In Full Bloom: 'Blue Jasmine' Fulfilled Cate Blanchett's Long-Held Goal of Working in a Woody Allen–Directed Film," *Los Angeles Times*, November 7, 2013.

8. C. Blanchett, acceptance speech, March 2, 2014, Academy Awards Acceptance Speech Database, http://aaspeechesdb.oscars.org.

9. L. Shaw, "Oscars: Cate Blanchett Rips Hollywood for Treating Women as a 'Niche' Audience," The Wrap, March 2, 2014, http://www.thewrap.com/oscars-cate-blanchett-puts-hollywood-notice-continued-sexism/.

10. Blanchett, acceptance speech.

11. R. K. Carrie, "Statistics Show Current Hollywood Movies Are Too Male, Too Pale," *Las Vegas Review-Journal*, May 19, 1991.

12. M. Cousins, *The Story of Film: An Odyssey* (London: Pavillion Books, 2011); *Miss Representation*, dir. J. Siebel Newsom (2011).

13. S. Prince, *A New Pot of Gold: Hollywood under the Electronic Rainbow, 1980–1989* (Berkeley: University of California Press, 2000); M. Lauzen, "Gender Inertia in Hollywood," Women's Media Center, January 30, 2014, http://www.womensmediacenter.com/feature/entry/gender-inertia-in-hollywood.

14. Lauzen, "Gender Inertia."

15. B. Longmire, "Jane Fonda Oozes Glamour as She Attends 42nd Chaplin Award Gala in Chic Embroidered Suit," *The Express*, April 28, 2015.

16. B. Lee, "Quentin Tarantino–Produced Film Posts Casting Call for 'Whores,'" *The Guardian*, June 7, 2016, https://www.theguardian.com/film/2016/jun/07/quentin-tarantino-film-posts-casting-call-for-whores-on-facebook.

17. "Cate Blanchett."

18. G. Steinem, "Why Our Revolution Has Just Begun," *Ms. Blog*, February 27, 2014, http://msmagazine.com/blog/2014/02/27/gloria-steinem-why-our-revolution-has-just-begun/.

19. R. Gay, "The Great 2014 Celebrity Nude Photo Leak Is Only the Beginning," *The Guardian*, September 30, 2014, http://www.theguardian.com/commentisfree/2014/sep/01/celebrity-naked-photo-leak-2014-nude-women; Steinem, "Why Our Revolution."

20. Steinem, "Why Our Revolution."

21. A. Vincent, "Bechdel Test Films Triumph at the Box Office," *The Telegraph*, January 7, 2014, http://www.telegraph.co.uk/culture/film/film-news/10555209/Bechdel-Test-films-triumph-at-the-box-office.html.

JULIANNE MOORE

1. S. Wloszczyna, "The Big O: The Cry for Equal Pay, the Need for Equal Screen Time, & the Death of the Mani-Cam," IndieWire, February 23, 2015, https://www.indiewire.com/2015/02/the-big-o-the-cry-for-equal-pay-the-need-for-equal-screen-time-the-death-of-the-mani-cam-204476/.

2. C. Buckley, "Female Celebrities Define the Agenda," *New York Times*, January 7, 2018.

3. R. Setoodeh, "Tearing Up the Rules," *Variety*, November 10, 2015.

4. J. Moore, acceptance speech, February 22, 2015, Academy Awards Acceptance Speech Database, http://aaspeechesdb.oscars.org.

5. R. Gilbey, "Richard Glatzer Obituary," *The Guardian*, March 15, 2015.

6. L.P. "Reviews," *Townsville Bulletin*, March 7, 2015; Gilbey, "Richard Glatzer Obituary."

7. A. Stephens, "Starstruck: Review," *Sunday Age*, February 23, 2003.

8. J. Lahr, "The Sphinx Next Door," *New Yorker*, September 21, 2015.

9. Lahr.

10. Lahr.

11. G. Macnab, "The Erotic Scenes That Make 50 Shades Darker Look Vanilla," *The Independent*, February 9, 2017, https://www.independent.co.uk/arts-entertainment/films/features/50-shades-darker-jamie-dornan-last-tango-in-paris-basic-instinct-nine-and-a-half-weeks-nymphomaniac-a7571741.html; M. Turner, "Naked Ambition: Why Tinseltown's Most Talented Actresses Are Willing to Take It Off," *New York Post*, February 6, 2000.

12. "Hefner Wants 'Nude' Winslet for Playboy," *Asian News International*, February 24, 2009.

13. Turner, "Naked Ambition."

14. Lahr, "Sphinx Next Door."

15. Turner, "Naked Ambition."

16. Lahr, "Sphinx Next Door."

BRIE LARSON

1. J. Rottenberg, "A Year That's Making Them Think," *Los Angeles Times*, February 25, 2016.

2. K. Taylor, "The Birth of a Scandal," *Globe and Mail*, August 20, 2016.

3. "'Spotlight' Grabbed Critics' Attention at Festivals," *Buffalo News*, February 29, 2016.

4. A. Mason, "#SoWhite," *Livingston County Daily Press & Argus*, February 19, 2016.

5. "Halle Berry Says Lack of Diversity Is 'Heartbreaking,'" *Telegram & Gazette*, February 4, 2016.

6. "People in the News," *Dayton Daily News*, February 7, 2016.

7. B. Child, "Barack Obama on Oscars Diversity: Are We Giving Everyone a Fair Shot?," *The Guardian*, January 28, 2016, https://www.theguardian.com/film/2016/jan/28/barack-obama-speaks-oscars-diversity-academy-awards-2016.

8. Taylor, "Birth of a Scandal."

9. "I Felt like I Was Hallucinating . . . It Was Like . . . ," *New York Post*, February 9, 2016.

10. "Oscar Winners in Full: Watch Leonardo DiCaprio's Best Actor Speech," *Yorkshire Post*, February 29, 2016.

11. A. D'Alessandro, J. Utichi, and A. N'Duka, "Backstage at the Oscars," *Deadline Hollywood*, February 28, 2016, http://deadline.com/2016/02/oscars-backstage-reactions-2016-academy-award-winners-1201710650/.

12. E. Retter, "I Haven't Seen My Dad for 10 Years . . . I Don't Think He Ever Wanted to Be a Parent," *Daily Mirror*, March 2, 2016.

13. K. Smith, "Brie Spirit," *Vanity Fair*, May 2017.

14. Retter, "I Haven't Seen My Dad."

15. Smith, "Brie Spirit."

16. J. Basinger, *The Star Machine* (New York: Knopf, 2007).

17. M. Roth, "Brie Larson Is in a (Probably Magical) Group Text with Emma Stone and J-Law," MTV News, April 25, 2017, http://www.mtv.com/news/3006231/brie-larson-group-text-emma-stone-jennifer-lawrence/.

18. M. Halberg, "Casey Affleck and Joaquin Phoenix Don't Want to Be Roommates Anymore," *New York Observer*, March 9, 2017.

19. "Larson Speaks on Affleck Win," *News Mail Bundaberg*, March 13, 2017.

20. N. Gordon, "Brie Larson, Judd Apatow and More Speak Out after Harney Weinstein Sexual Harassment Allegations," *Elle*, June 10, 2017, http://www.elleuk.com/life-and-culture/culture/news/a39151/celebrity-reactions-harvey-weinstein-sexual-harassment/.

EMMA STONE

1. B. Martin, "A New Direction," GQ, August 2017.

2. Martin; Z. Baron, "The New Rules for Making It in Hollywood," GQ, July 24, 2017, https://www.gq.com/story/new-rules-for-making-it-in-hollywood.

3. R. Carroll, "Hollywood's Acting Workshops Are Really 'Exploitative' Auditions, Insiders Say," *The Guardian*, April 1, 2016, https://www.theguardian.com/media/2016/apr/01/hollywood-acting-workshops-pay-for-play-casting.

4. S. Hughes, "Helen Mirren: 'Do I Feel Beautiful? I Hate That Word,'" *The Guardian*, September 28, 2015.

5. C. Shoard, "Maggie Smith: I Couldn't Make It as a Young Actor Today as They Have to 'Strip Off Every Second,'" *The Guardian*, March 3, 2017, https://www.theguardian.com/film/2017/mar/03

/maggie-smith-i-couldnt-make-it-as-a-young-actor-they-have-to-strip-off.

6. "Jane Fonda Reveals Rape and Child Abuse," BBC News, March 3, 2017, http://www.bbc.com/news/entertainment-arts-39151842.

7. "Brie Larson: 'Don't Judge a Woman on Her Looks,'" You, News24, March 6, 2017, https://www.news24.com/You/Archive/brie-larson-dont-judge-a-woman-on-her-looks-20170728.

8. B. Harris, "Emma Stone Wins Best-Actress Oscar for 'La La Land,'" AP Worldstream, February 27, 2017.

9. K. Lengel, "Emma Stone Talks about Phoenix Roots on CBS," Arizona Republic, February 16, 2017; N. Clarke, "How Emma Stone Plotted Her Path to Hollywood to Combat Her Crippling Anxiety Attacks," Daily Mail, January 16, 2017.

10. "Emma Stone Felt Trapped by Anxiety," Brampton Guardian, April 28, 2017.

11. Clarke, "How Emma Stone Plotted."

12. "La La Land," Shenzhen Daily, February 17, 2017; G. Macnab, "La La Land Review: Ryan Gosling and Emma Stone's Performances Hit Some Very High Notes," The Independent, August 31, 2016.

13. "Their City of Stars," Orlando Sentinel, February 26, 2017; Clarke, "How Emma Stone Plotted."

14. Macnab, "Best of the Rest"; "La La Land: Here's to the Good Old," Mint, January 6, 2017.

15. K. Frey, "Emma Stone Wears a Showstopping Sparkly Gold Gown to Oscars," People, February 26, 2017, http://people.com/style/oscars-2017-emma-stone-red-carpet-dress/.

16. E. Stone, acceptance speech, February 26, 2017, Academy Awards Acceptance Speech Database, http://aaspeechesdb.oscars.org.

17. "Faye Dunaway Feels 'Very Guilty' about Mistake at Oscars," Shenzhen Daily, April 26, 2017.

18. M. Puente, A. Mandell, and B. Alexander, "Here's How the Worst Flub in Oscar History Went Down," Tallahassee Democrat, February 28, 2017.

19. P. Larsen, "Emma Stone, Barry Jenkins Talk 'Moonlight' Mix-Up at Oscars Backstage," Daily News, February 27, 2017, https://www.dailynews.com/2017/02/27/emma-stone-barry-jenkins-talk-moonlight-mix-up-at-oscars-backstage/.

20. E. Yahr and E. Izadi, "Oscar Mixup a La La Land Fiasco," Southland Times, March 1, 2017.

21. K. Elkins, "Emma Stone Is the World's Highest Paid Actress—but Her Male Co-Stars Still Take Pay Cuts So She Can Have Parity," CNBC, September 30, 2017, https://www.cnbc.com/2017/09/29/emma-stone-says-her-male-co-stars-take-salary-cuts-so-she-can-get-equal-pay.html.

INDEX

ABOUT THE AUTHOR

Stephen Tapert earned his M.A. from the University of Chicago. He worked for eight years at the Academy of Motion Picture Arts and Sciences, where, as a museum researcher, he provided foundational work for the Academy Museum of Motion Pictures. He subsequently curated an exhibition on the Best Actress Oscar winners at the Museo Nazionale del Cinema in Turin, Italy, and at the Deutsche Kinemathek in Berlin, Germany. He currently teaches film studies at the New York Film Academy in Los Angeles.